What the Artists Are Say[ing about]
Billboard₍ᵣ₎'s American Rock 'n' R[oll in Review]

"Jay Warner has done it again. His *Billboard's American Rock 'n' Roll in Review* stands aside his *The Billboard Book of American Singing Groups* as another valuable source of musical information and history. Jay is most certainly our state of the art archivist."

—Tim Hauser, The Manhattan Transfer

"Since Jay's book is packed with so much information, you'll probably be able to write your own!"

—Bruce Johnston, The Beach Boys

"Jay Warner brings it all back to me. . . . It's not just a nostalgia trip but social (and business) history of an era, an era I'm indebted to."

—Paul Anka

"In 1957 Buddy Holly told me rock 'n' roll would only last a year. Rock 'n' roll is now in its fifth decade. I'm sure Buddy would be amazed and entertained, as I am, by Jay Warner's enlightening study of the rich pedigree of this music that has so profoundly affected us all."

—David Somerville, The Diamonds

"Ya know something, I don't even want to know about this stuff anymore, my brain cells are already overloaded with information and yet, it was *darn* near impossible to put this book down."

—Dean Torrence, Jan and Dean

"Jay Warner has done it again. *Billboard's American Rock 'n' Roll in Review* is a unique perspective of some of my favorite artists. Reading the original reviews is like going back in time and space. I am very proud to be included in this collection."

—Lesley Gore

"Absolutely the most thorough, accurate and insightful rock history ever assembled. Readers will learn startling facts about their favorite rock stars . . . things they would never have imagined!"

—Joe Butler, Lovin' Spoonful

"I find it so informative and well-researched. Many have written history books on various R & B and rock 'n' roll groups but none as thorough."

—Carl Gardner, The Coasters

"After 39 years in this business, I finally found a way to sound like an insider. I read Jay's books."

—Bob Gaudio, The Four Seasons

"Terrific reading for the serious collector or weekend rocker! Loaded with excellent artifactual information. I knew those reviews would come back to haunt me! It reminded me that I'm still waiting for my Philippine royalties."

—Bobby Vee

"Back then, we thought everything we did would only last for ten weeks. Jay's book will keep the legends alive, well into the 21st century."

—Phil Margo, The Tokens

"*Billboard's American Rock 'n' Roll in Review* is much more than another stroll down memory lane. It allows you to reach out and touch the lives of those who made musical history. Jay Warner's research (as usual) is on the money, but what's particularly interesting is how he punctuates the facts with such fascinating trivia."

—Zeke Carey, The Flamingos

"Jay Warner did not write this book capriciously! Unlike many other books of this genre, he did his homework and his writing is accurate and fun."

—Florence LaRue, The 5th Dimension

"I just had to write and tell you how much I enjoyed reading *Billboard's American Rock 'n' Roll in Review*. It is informative, entertaining and a great idea. A must for my library."

—Tommy Roe

"I read Jay's book on vocal groups and truly enjoyed every page. So here he comes again with another one to really enjoy. It's an encyclopedia of what's going on."

—Otis Williams, The Temptations

"I found it to be very informative, fun and exciting. It was great going back down memory lane."

—Ron Isley, The Isley Brothers

"Once again, Jay Warner has gone where no writer has gone before . . . into the depths of rock 'n' roll history to bring us the most truthful and complete information ever to be put in print about these true rock 'n' roll legends."

—Jerry Gross, The Dovells

"Informative and thorough, as well as being entertaining . . . most of all, pertinent information readers may never be able to get from other sources."

—Tommy James

"This book certainly gives a worldwide view of rock 'n' roll and a veritable plethora of facts."

—Russ Giguere, The Association

"The book is a tremendous volume of previously unavailable information and insights, which will be an invaluable tool for present and future historians as well as being an interesting read for fans of authentic rock 'n' roll music!"

—Frankie Ford

"What a fun book for anyone who is a real fan of rock 'n' roll and interested in knowing all they can about their favorite artists."

—Ray Stevens

"Often as we were living it, we missed some facts about our own music. I am as fascinated with the other artists' stories as I am with my own. At last, some new information!"

—Jiggs Sirico, The Angels

"Your effort to accurately document and preserve an original American art form such as rhythm & blues and rock 'n' roll is necessary, and important."

—Johnny Rivers

"I loved seeing my chart numbers and reading all the old reviews."

—Sam Moore, Sam & Dave

"I flashed back to when I was a new, young recording artist who would race to his manager's office every Monday to read the [*Billboard*] reviews. Not only of our records but of all the new releases by our contemporaries. Would it be a Spotlight Pick? *Billboard's American Rock 'n' Roll in Review* is a great trip back in time for me and a must for anyone who loved the artists and music of the era."

—Jimmy Beaumont, The Skyliners

Billboard'S AMERICAN ROCK 'N' ROLL IN REVIEW

Billboard's AMERICAN ROCK 'N' ROLL IN REVIEW

JAY WARNER

SCHIRMER BOOKS
An Imprint of Simon & Schuster Macmillan
New York

Prentice Hall International
London   Mexico City   New Delhi   Singapore   Sydney   Toronto

Music reviews © 1948–1994 by Billboard Magazine/BPI Communications. Billboard ® and various charts are registered trademarks and trademarks of Billboard Magazine/BPI Communications.

Schirmer Books
An Imprint of Simon & Schuster Macmillan
1633 Broadway
New York, NY 10019

Library of Congress Catalog Card Number: 96-9851

Printed in the United States of America

Printing Number
1 2 3 4 5 6 7 8 9 10

Library of Congress Cataloging-in-Publication Data

Warner, Jay.
  Billboard's American rock & roll in review / Jay Warner.
    p. cm.
  Includes index.
  ISBN 0-02-872695-2
  1. Rock music—United States—Bio-bibliography. 2. Rock musicians—United States. 3. Rock music—United States—Discography. I. Billboard (Cincinnati, Ohio : 1963) II. Title.
ML106.U3W18   1997
781.66'092'273—dc20   96-9851
                                                    CIP
                                                         MN

This paper meets the requirements of ANSI/NISO Z39.48–1992 (Permanence of Paper).

I wish to dedicate this book to
my two biggest believers
My mom and dad,

RAY LILLIAN WAX BLACKSTEIN
and
ROBERT WAYNE WARNER

May your Spirit, Faith and Love
forever guide me and
may G-d always Bless You

Contents

Foreword

I've been in love with rock 'n' roll since I was a boy growing up in Greensboro, North Carolina. It's provided the soundtrack for every important moment of my life, and our love affair continues to this day (with the full knowledge and consent of my wife, Julie). Now I find that someone shares my infatuation: Jay Warner. *Billboard's American Rock 'n' Roll in Review* is like a diary of his ongoing romance with the music and the people who created it. He writes about each group, artist, and song with the unbridled enthusiasm of a true fan, yet the information he presents reflects the meticulous research of a scholar.

Having hosted the *Weekly Top-40 Countdown* for more than a decade, I thought I had uncovered every bit of artist trivia known to man. But Jay has managed to come up with information even I didn't know. For example, "U.S. Bonds" changed his name to "Gary U.S. Bonds" at the request of the U.S. Treasury Department. Who knew? That's the kind of behind-the-scenes information that makes this book such a terrific read. Anyone who loves rock will not only enjoy Jay's refreshing presentation of known facts, but will also find surprising revelations about famous and not-so-famous performers. More than once I got the feeling that Jay must have been hiding in the dressing room closet taking notes! Of course the most entertaining anecdotes are meaningless unless they are supported by facts, and once again Jay comes through. Names, places, dates, reviews . . . it's all there.

As with Jay's first publication, *The Billboard Book of American Singing Groups, 1940–1990,* this book was inspired by his love for the subject (the guy has a 25,000-plus record collection) and his search for a definitive source on rock 'n' roll. Although this uniquely American art form has dominated world music for nearly half a century, there were surprisingly few comprehensive tomes on the subject. Jay's unique career as a singer-turned-publisher and radio personality placed him in the ideal position to author such a book. His innumerable contacts in the music industry supplied him with the kind of first-hand information most authors can only fantasize about. Whenever a question arose, Jay was usually able to pick up the phone and go right to the source. His efforts have paid off with a book that will find a place on the bookshelf of every devotee of rock 'n' roll, whether a casual fan or a dedicated scholar.

Contemporary music changes with the speed of a stealth bomber, and that's what makes it so exciting. But it's important that we have a chronicle of how and where it all started. To paraphrase an old saying, How can you know where you're going if you don't know where you've been? With *Billboard's American Rock 'n' Roll in Review,* Jay Warner has provided a musical road map, and I, for one, am very grateful!

Rick Dees

Preface

On a warm, quiet Spring day in Los Angeles (quiet meaning no earthquakes, riots, fires, or mudslides), having recovered from the writer's cramp and computer double vision of my last book, I determined to find a new approach to writing another (hopefully) entertaining history of music. Ever on the prowl for unique ways to interpret the musical past, I didn't realize I had already tested the waters in my last work, *The Billboard Book of American Singing Groups,* in which I occasionally used a *Billboard* review to emphasize and define certain recordings.

When *Singing Groups* was published in late 1992, letters began to pour in (one of the things authors live for besides the royalty checks) with overwhelmingly positive responses. It wasn't until this Spring day, while reading some of those letters, that I realized how many people had enjoyed the use of those reviews as adding a "you-are-there" dimension to the stories. The reviews in *Billboard* (a magazine that is respected as the *Wall Street Journal* of the music industry for over a hundred years), however, are different than typical reviews in two essential ways. First, unlike critics whose partial purpose is to impress the public with their cacophony of catch phrases and college-bred linguistics, *Billboard* music reviews have always been anonymous, assuring the reader that the essence of the review is the music, not the reviewer. Second, *Billboard* reviews are always intended to reach the music industry's disc jockeys, record companies, record distributors, stores, juke-box operators (hence, the repeated references to "coin"), producers, artists, and publishers, and are largely unavailable to the public.

Because *Billboard* is a trade publication as opposed to an entertainment magazine, its main focus is to factually inform. However, that in no way minimizes its importance. Without trying, these reviews have, over the decades, evolved into very entertaining slices of recording life. What a store ordered or a deejay played that reached the public was often based on those two- to four-sentence synopses of a recording artist's work. The reviews have become historic headstones and summaries of the recordings that were born, charted, and died, yet live on in our memories.

No one knew Elvis Presley in 1954, Jerry Lee Lewis in 1956, Chubby Checker in 1959, or Diana Ross and The Supremes in 1962. Yet, the anonymous reviewer evaluated their earliest recordings along with hundreds of others each week to come up with the most likely future successes, without the advantage of hindsight that we enjoy. It is easy to read this book and laugh at how *Billboard*'s brain trusts could give a now-legendary "In the Still of the Night" (by The Five Satins in 1956) a two-star rating, or The Elegants' multimillion-seller "Little Star" a review rating without even a comment. Remember, they were there on the spot, having to make impromptu decisions, and, more often than not, their decisions were on the money.

Over ten thousand reviews were evaluated for this work and over three thousand used in the stories of rock 'n' roll's founders and first- and second-generation stars. These profiles include the reviewers' professional insights into the type of music the artists were creating, often following an artist's musical changes through later reviews. Many a song's tempo, feel, and origin (whether a cover recording; derivative of a film, TV show, or reissue; or who the artist and/or recording seemed to be influenced by) was packed together in those cleverly worded, short yet succinct studies.

You may notice that some hit songs were never reviewed by *Billboard.* Sometimes, an artist would have a hit right out of the box, and so the record would go unreviewed. Sometimes, a record would be listed without comment and simply given a rating; other times, it would be unrated and unreviewed, and in some cases the record company would slip up and forget to send them a review copy at all. In the early days, *Billboard* made an attempt to review fairly widely; but as record companies increased the number of releases that hit the market, obviously it became impossible to review everything. In the following, I will describe briefly the rules that *Billboard* used to determine what and how it reviewed records. I will also mention from time to time in the text when a noteworthy release went unreviewed. When both an "A" and "B" side were reviewed, the date of the review and chart numbers, if any, follow the "B" side.

Because of space limitations, every review relating to an artist's career cannot be included. The author has made painstaking efforts to include an interesting mix of as many of the most important and most intriguing reviews of hits and misses in each artist's recording life as possible.

Obviously, many stars' lives have been written about in great depth, but, thanks to these reviews, and the inclusion of interesting trivia from personal interviews of many of the stars herein (especially relating to their musical influences and who they musically influenced), I'm hopeful that this work will add a new insight and scope to our rock 'n' roll heritage.

Acknowledgments

I wish to express my sincerest appreciation to the legendary recording artists who took the time to personally provide me with first-hand information and insights into their historic past. May their musical contributions never be forgotten. Phyllis "Jiggs" Allbut Sirico (The Angels), Paul Anka, Carmine Appice (Vanilla Fudge), Frankie Avalon, Chuck Barksdale (The Dells), Jay Black (Jay and The Americans), Gary U.S. Bonds, Joe Butler (The Lovin' Spoonful), Freddy Cannon, Zeke Carey (The Flamingos), Earl Carroll (The Cadillacs), Les Cauchi (The Brooklyn Bridge), Felix Cavaliere (The Rascals), Lou Christie, Gretchen Christopher (The Fleetwoods), Doug Clifford (Creedence Clearwater Revival), Bobby Colomby (Blood, Sweat and Tears), Carol Connors (The Teddy Bears), Herb Cox (The Cleftones), Joey D'Ambrose (Bill Haley and The Comets), Joey Dee (The Starliters), Lenny Dell (The Dimensions), Bob Duncan (The Diamonds), Cleve Duncan (The Penguins), Warren Entner (The Grass Roots), Fabian, Chuck Fassert (The Regents), Eddie Floyd (The Falcons), Bobby Freeman, Carl Gardner (The Coasters), Bob Gaudio (The Four Seasons), Russ Giguere (The Association), Lesley Gore, Johnny Grande (Bill Haley and The Comets), Jerry Gross (The Dovells), Ron Isley (The Isley Brothers), Fred Johnson (The Marcels), Jimmy Keyes (The Chords), Ben E. King (The Drifters), Bubba Knight and Gladys Knight (Gladys Knight and The Pips), Florence LaRue (The 5th Dimension), Brenda Lee, Marshall Leib (The Teddy Bears), David Lerchey (The Dell-Vikings), Bobby Lewis, Ed Lewis (The Olympics), Mark Lindsey (The Raiders), Ronnie Lipinsky (The Regents), Little Eva Boyd Harris, Little Richard, Marshall Lytle (Bill Haley and The Comets), Walt Maddox (The Marcels), Phil Margo and Mitch Margo (The Tokens), Bill Medley (The Righteous Brothers), Bob Miranda (The Happenings), Sam Moore (Sam & Dave), Ron Mundy (The Marcels), Dick Petersen (The Kingsmen), John Phillips (The Mamas and The Papas), Vito Picone (The Elegants), Bill Pinkney (The Drifters), Gene Pitney, Bill Reed (The Diamonds), Herb Reed (The Platters), Martha Reeves (Martha and The Vandellas), Dick Richards (Bill Haley and The Comets), Sylvia Robinson (Mickey and Sylvia), Tommy Roe, Mitch Ryder, Nick Santa Maria (The Capris), Jay Siegel (The Tokens), Arlene Smith (The Chantels), David Somerville (The Diamonds), Ray Stevens, Joe Terry (Danny and The Juniors), Russ Titleman (Spectors' Three), Dean Torrence (Jan and Dean), Ike Turner (Ike and Tina Turner), Frankie Valli (The Four Seasons), Bobby Vee, Mark Volman (The Turtles), Billy Ward (The Dominoes), Laura Webb (The Bobbettes), Rudy West (The Five Keys), Maurice Williams (The Zodiacs), Billy Williamson (Bill Haley and The Comets), and Harold Winley (The Clovers).

Additionally, I wish to thank those artists' associates (managers, agents, producers, publicists), industry individuals and organizations, record collectors, and dealers for helping to separate the facts from the myths. This edition could not have reached its degree of proficiency without your help. Bob Abrams (Ray Charles), Bob Alcivar, Kevin Allyn, Connie Alvarez (Ritchie Valens), John Apostle, Cinnamon Atchley (Sonny Bono), Sam Atchley, Jim Austin (Billy Ward), Dan Bourgoise (Del Shannon), Nathaniel Brewster (Sony Records), Maria Byers (Dionne Warwick), Susan Cassidy, Bob Celli (Bobby Vee), Alan Clarke (Tommy Roe), David Cohen (The Righteous Brothers), Frank Cullen (Sonny Bono), Charlie Davis (Chubby Checker), Jin Dawson Millie Della Villi (Dell-Vikings), Walter DeVenne Jr., J. T. Doggett (The Dominoes), Carole Ross Durborow (Tommy James), Richard Duryea, Al Embry (Jerry Lee Lewis), Dee Erwin, Beatrice Fakhrian (Ike Turner), Henry Farig (The Spaniels), Donn Fileti (Relic Records), Bob Fischer, Dick Fox (Bobby Rydell), Veta Gardner (The Coasters), Zack Glickman (Dion), Joe Grant (Dionne Warwick), Eddie Gries (Relic Records), Peter Gryndesia, Lorna Guess (Carole King), Joe Haertel (Little Eva), Jack Haley (Bill Haley and The Comets), Reggie Hall (Fats Domino), Milton Hardaway (Stevie Wonder), Steve Harris (The Doors), Fannie Harrison (Wilbert Harrison), Ken Held, Terry Hinte (Fantasy Records), Dave Hoffman (Bobby Vee), Bill Hollingshead (Jan and Dean), Bones Howe (The Association), Joe Isgro (Raging Bull Records), Ronnie Italiano, Dave Jackson (Bill Haley), Karen Jacobson (James Brown), Fred Kaplan, Susan Kaplan (Watson and Guptill Publications), David Kapralick (Sly Stone), Wendy Kay, Ken Keene (Frankie Ford), Kathryn Korniloff (Johnny Rivers), Morty Kraft (Warwick Records), George Lavatelli (Relic Record Shop), Judy Lee (Joey Dee), Sherrie Levy (Neil Diamond), Margo Lewis (The Falcons), Floyd Lieberman, Ace Liebowitz (Martha Reeves), Deborah Lindsey (Paul Revere and The Raiders), Donna Malyszko (RCA Records), Ernie Martinelli (The Five Satins), Andy McKaie (MCA Records), Sarah McMillan (Roy Orbison), Stan Perkins (Carl Perkins), Silvio Pietroluongo (*Billboard* Research), Joope Plaage (BMG Music, Holland), Raymond Quick (The Dell-Vikings), Joe Rock (The Skyliners), David Rosner (Neil Diamond), Chuck Rubin, Nick Saunders (The Five Keys), Joel Scherzer, Robby Scherzer, Sid Seidenberg, Bill Sobel (Little Richard), Buck Spur (The Platters), Dr. John Stalberg, Erik Sterling (The 5th Dimension), Ron Strassner (The Four Tops), Bob Tucker, Chris Tuthill (Eddie Floyd), Hy Weiss (Old Town Records), Shirley Welsh (Ray Stevens), John Wilson, Howard Wolf, and Allison Zenato (Neil Diamond).

Also, my appreciation is boundless for Schirmer Books' "editors supreme," Jonathan Wiener, Richard Carlin, Paul Boger, and Lucia Read, as well as *Billboard*'s Georgina Challis and Ken Schlager, the group that had the foresight and belief (with cajoling) in this book's attributes to let me creatively run amok.

A special thanks to my research "dream team," Joie Miller-Shadis, Peter Shadis, and Dean Landon.

Last, my everlasting love and appreciation to my wife, Jackie, for her encouragement, patience, ever-constant smile, and unique ability to turn nearly every one of my crises into a positive experience.

The History of *Billboard*'s Reviews

Billboard was founded in 1894 and even before it started printing popularity charts in 1940, it was reviewing records. In fact, the first review was of Jimmy Dorsey on April 24, 1937. As rock 'n' roll changed through the 1950s, 1960s, and early 1970s, *Billboard* reviews changed their style, size, and ratings system during those years. The following listing and descriptions show how the reviews and their guidelines evolved.

In 1950, *Billboard* offered ratings based on a numerical system, with 90–100 designated "Tops," 80–89 "Excellent," 70–79 "Good," 40–69 "Satisfactory," and 0–39 "Poor." These were further placed in four categories, labeled "Overall," "Disk jockey," "Retailer," and "Operator." These numbers were derived from "nine key categories."

Billboard stated:

> Each category is assigned a maximum number of points within which new releases are rated. The best possible rating is 100. Maximums are subject to change depending on results of a survey of the music trade now being conducted. N.S. indicates a record is not suitable for approval within the market.

The categories were given as:

> song caliber, 15; interpretation, 15; arrangement, 15; "name" value, 15; record quality (surface, etc.), 5; music publisher's air performance potential, 10; exploitation (record advertisements, promotion film, legit and other "plug" acts), 10; manufacturer's distribution power, 10; manufacturer's promotion efficiency, 5.

This rating system was in place through 1951.

In 1952, the four-number system was replaced by a single number. In *Billboard*'s words:

> A continuing study of the pop charts has shown that most records achieve comparable popularity in all three areas [i.e., among jockeys, dealers, and operators]. Because of this, only the overall rating will be listed in future reviews. Whenever the music staff of Billboard believes that a particular record warrants special attention by either jockeys, dealers or operators, this information will be included in the review copy.

Also by 1952, the nine categories of evaluation were reduced to six: "vocal and/or instrumental interpretation, 25; overall exploitation potential, 20; song caliber, 20; artist's name value, 15; manufacturer's distribution power, 10; arrangement, 10."

By 1954, the ratings numbers were now categorized as: "90–100, tops; 80–89, excellent; 70–79, good; 60–69, satisfactory; 50–59, limited; 0–49, poor."

In 1958, a system of stars replaced the rating numbers:

SPOTLIGHT: Strongest sales potential of *all* records reviewed this week:

* * * * Very Strong Sales Potential

* * *   Good Sales Potential

* *   Moderate Sales Potential

*   Limited Sales Potential

In 1961, four stars' "Very Strong Sales" became "Stronger Sales Potential;" three stars' "Good" became "Moderate Sales Potential;" and two- and one-star ratings were eliminated. A more detailed statement of *Billboard*'s reviewing and rating policy illuminated how past practices had been modified:

SPOTLIGHT WINNERS are judged to have the strongest sales potential of all singles reviewed during the week and are picked to hit the top 50 of the Hot 100 chart.

FOUR-STAR singles are those with strong sales potential. All Spotlight and Four-Star records have been heard and evaluated by the full Reviewing Panel, and descriptive reviews are published for these.

THREE-STAR records, having moderate sales potential, are listed thereafter; these frequently will be of interest for disc jockey programming. Other records, with limited sales potential, are listed following the Three-Star records.

SPECIAL MERIT SPOTLIGHTS, in the opinion of the Reviewing Panel, have outstanding merit and deserve exposure.

As noted, three-star records (and below) were now listed without comments: Only name of act, song, A- and B-side, label, and number were given.

By 1963, only "Pop Spotlight" and "Special Merit Programming Singles" were reviewed with comments. "Four-Star Singles" remained but were now limited to listings of artists, A- and B-side, ASCAP or BMI affiliation, time, label, and number without comment. By 1964, "Spotlight" releases (records expected to reach the top 50) were the only reviews with comments.

In 1965, the reviews were slightly expanded. Two categories of "Spotlights," records expected to reach the top 20 or top 60, respectively, were reviewed. In 1967, "Special Merit Spotlight" also got a brief commentary review.

For a period during 1972, a radio report feature replaced the reviews. This was the dark ages of *Billboard* reviews. No comments, just "New Radio Action" and "*Billboard* Picks Singles" with radio station call letters indicating initial radio action. Luckily, the ill-conceived radio report didn't last through the year, and "Pop Picks" releases again began to be reviewed with comments.

In 1973, reviews were now called "Top Singles Picks." "Also Recommended" were records without comments. Later that year, "First Time Around Picks" were added, offering reviews with comments on new acts.

By 1983, "First Time Around" became "New and Noteworthy" and "Top Single Reviews" became simply, "Single Reviews."

JOHNNY ACE

Real Name: John Marshall Alexander, Jr.
Birthdate: 6/29/29
Birthplace: Memphis, TN
Died: 12/24/54
Influences: B. B. King, Bobby Bland
Influenced: Simon and Garfunkel, Elvis Presley

As well known for the way he died as for the way he lived, Johnny Ace was one of the superior balladeers of the 1950s.

The Memphis high school dropout spent a few of his teen years in the Navy. Upon his discharge in 1947, he began playing music on his mother's newly acquired piano. By 1949, his proficiency on the keys led to a spot in The Beale Streeters, a band that at various times included Bobby "Blue" Bland, Earl Forrest, and B. B. King. In 1951, local radio station WDIA was scouting for a studio piano player and Johnny got the job. He also acquired a new name, Johnny Ace, taken from a group he admired, The Four Aces.

His first break came a year later at a recording session for Bobby Bland. Bland could not handle the intricacies of a tune, so David Mattis (owner of Duke Records and an executive at WDIA) asked Ace to sing "My Song." It was his first released recording, reaching #1 on *Billboard*'s chart in August of 1952.

1953 started off with two more ballads.

Cross My Heart 86
Johnny Ace's first warbling since the smash hit "My Song" is another powerful slicing. The warbler turns in a sincere and moving rendition of a pretty slow-tempo ballad, over the attractive ork arrangement. Side is potent and should be a real coin-grabber for the young warbler. (1/17/53) (#3 R&B)

The Clock 84
Looks like a real smash. It's another heart ballad, sung by the warbler in his own meaningful style, over a moody ork backing. Tune is melodic, and the clock ticks gimmicks should help it too. A solid coin-grabber. (6/27/53) (#1 R&B)

In 1952, Ace moonlighted for the rival Flair label, resulting in one release.

Midnight Hours Journey 74
This doesn't sound like the Johnny Ace now on Duke Records, but it may have been made a while ago. Under any circumstances, it is an effective performance and it should pull spins and loot on the basis of the name, if for no other reason. (9/19/53)

Ace's first "up side" was "Yes Baby" ("a powerful rendition on this jump effort"), but it was obvious the public only wanted his mellow moods as "Saving My Love for You" became his fourth Top-5 R&B hit in a row.

Saving My Love for You 86
Johnny Ace has had three hits in a row; with this new disk, he should stretch his string to four, and this one could be his biggest to date. It's another touching ballad, and the boy sings out his heart on it over a great beat by the combo. A real coin-grabber this. (12/19/53) (#2 R&B)

1954 continued with two more hits.

Please Forgive Me.
Johnny Ace should do it again with this fine new release and keep his lengthy string of hits unbroken. "Forgive Me" is a tuneful ballad which he sings with soul; the flip ["You've Been Gone So Long"] is a bouncy item and is handled brightly. Potent wax for operators and dealers. (5/22/54) (#6 R&B)

Never Let Me Go.
Johnny Ace sings this new ballad with his usual sincerity and the record has a chance for the big time. (9/18/54) (# 9 R&B)

Johnny's career was in high gear when he performed on Christmas Eve at The Civic

Auditorium in Houston with B. B. King and Willie Mae "Big Mama" Thornton. *Cashbox* magazine had just named him "Most Programmed Artist of 1954," but before the sun came up on Ace and his award, he was dead. Apparently, he accidentally shot himself while participating in a round of Russian Roulette, with his own gun. Twenty-one days later his name began a trip to rock 'n' roll immortality with the release of "Pledging My Love."

> The recent death of Ace gave added impetus to what would probably have been heavy first week sales in any case. It is spiraling upwards at dazzling speed, and is almost as popular with pop customers as with r&b. (1/15/55) (#17 Pop, #1 R&B)

His last charter was his next single, "Anymore."

> This is the first Ace record issued since the top artist's recent death. It's a potent ballad similar in mood to his last, long-enduring smash, "Pledging My Love," and it could be the one his tremendous following has been waiting for. (7/16/55) (#7 R&B)

Duke kept the commemoratives coming.

I'm Crazy Baby/So Lonely.
> The late great Johnny Ace lives on [on these] two fine sides cut shortly before his death. On top is an exciting, emotion-packed love ballad. The flip contains some wonderful blues sound in the typical Johnny Ace style. These are two classy efforts with loads of commercial appeal. (1/21/56)

Don't You Know.
> Another blues job . . . comes out of the can, and tho the loyal fraternity may want the disk, it's not up to previous top efforts. (8/18/56)

In 1958, Duke revised "Pledging."

★ ★ ★ *The original Johnny Ace recording gets an updated, souped-up backing to go with the vocal. (12/1/58)*

The original "Pledging" was reissued in 1960, along with "Anymore" with a reworked backing track.

Pledging My Love.
★ ★ ★ ★ *The original of the great tune. It's been recently released with Johnny Tillotson on Cadence among other new versions. Naturally, Ace's original should come in for its worthy share of the spins and sales.*

Anymore.
★ ★ ★ *The late great Johnny Ace has another ballad effort here. The background has been built up a bit to bring the side up to date. The fans of the chanter will want this. (5/2/60)*

Interestingly, when Elvis Presley (an admirer of Ace's style) died some 23 years later, the B-side of his then-current single was "Pledging My Love." In 1981, Paul Simon wrote the tribute "The Late, Great Johnny Ace."

THE ANGELS

Linda Jansen: Lead vocalist
Born: Hillside, NJ
Phyllis "Jiggs" Allbut
Born: 9/24/42, Orange, NJ
Barbara Allbut
Born: 9/24/40, Orange, NJ
Peggy Santiglia
Born: 5/4/44, Bellview, NJ
Influences: McGuire Sisters, Everly Brothers, Chantels, Hilltoppers, Andrews Sisters
Influenced: Linda Ronstadt

The "girl group" era was at its peak during the four-year chart life of The Angels. They were the first white female group in rock 'n' roll history to have a #1 record.

They started as a quartet in Orange, New Jersey. Calling themselves the Starlets, the group included sisters Jiggs and Barbara Allbut, Linda Malzone, and Bernadette Dahlia. After some shuffling, Linda Jensen joined. They recorded a satisfying version of the oldie, "P.S. I Love You" (Astro) as their debut disk.

★ ★   *A ballad, in dreamy tempo. Chicks do a nice vocal chore. (4/25/60)*

With the failure of "P.S." they embarked on a career as studio background singers.

By the end of 1960, each member put a name in a hat to choose a new name. The paper read The Blue Angels, which was then shortened to the Angels. During 1961, the trio of the Allbuts and Jansen scraped together enough money to demo a song they believed in, the former Roger Williams' hit "Till." Taking the acetate to New York's Caprice Records, the girls not only found themselves with a contract, they wound up with a hit, as "Till" and its shimmering string arrangement by Hutch Davie reached #14. The Angels' harmonies were so high that "Till"'s flip, "A Moment Ago," played at 33⅓ RPM (instead of 45 RPM) sounds like an R&B male group! The B-side of their followup, "Cry, Baby, Cry," was their second chart single in a row (#38 Pop).

 The lead singer contributes a feelingful reading on ["Cry"], an appealing ballad.

After that 45, Linda quit, replaced by former Delicates' member Peggy Santiglia on lead. Peggy had also appeared in the Broadway production of "Do Re Mi," but her addition coincided with the group hitting a chart slump.

In 1963, the girls met producers Jerry Goldstein, Bobby Feldman, and Rich Gottehrer. They began doing demos for the producers, and Jiggs began dating Goldstein while the guys created a song, tailor-made for The Angels.

Bought out of their Caprice deal by Goldstein et al., the trio was brought to Mercury's Smash affiliate. The result was their biggest and best-known hit, "My Boyfriend's Back."

The girls who scored a few seasons back with "Till" can make it a repeat chart performance with their bow on Smash. It's a handclappin' Mashed Potatoes-styled delighter tagged "My Boyfriend's Back" that can bust wide open. (8/3/63)

By August 31, it was #1 Pop and amazingly, the now tough-sounding gals registered #2 R&B.

They followed up with "I Adore Him," which, despite *Billboard*'s enthusiasm, did not fare as well on the charts.

 The earthy sound the group scored with is as effective on this new one as on "My Boyfriend's Back." The beat is there and some fine guitar effects too. (10/12/63) (#25 Pop)

The arrival of the Beatles on the U.S. charts put a dent in the popularity of all American groups. The Angels were among the first to respond to this onslaught with the charming novelty, "Little Beatle Boy."

 The gals sing of their British boyfriends in soft, dulcet tones, quite a bit different from other Beatle-oriented disks. (3/7/64)

In between touring the United States and Europe, The Angels were constantly busy doing studio backups for a wide variety of acts, from Jackie Wilson's "Higher and Higher" and Bobby Lewis "Tossin' & Turnin' Again" to sides by Frankie Valli, Lesley Gore, Neil Diamond, Frank Sinatra, Ben E. King, Sal Mineo, and footballer turned singer, Rosie Grier. Their biggest supporting role was on Lou Christie's #1 "Lightning Strikes" in 1966. While all that was happening, Peggy cowrote The Four Seasons hit "Beggin'."

In 1967, the group signed with RCA, but six singles saw little radio daylight. In the late 1960s, Peggy joined The Serendipity Singers, whereas Jiggs did commercials for The Money Store with New York Yankee legend, Phil Rizzuto, and Barbara retired. No matter what they worked on individually, Jiggs and Peggy continued performing on the oldies revival circuit through the 1990s. In 1974, they recorded their final 45 for Polydor, "Papa's Side of the Bed." By the 1990s, Jiggs Allbut Sirico and Peggy Santiglia Davison were still active on their well-traveled performance road as The Angels.

PAUL **A**NKA

Birthdate: 7/30/41
Birthplace: Ottawa, Canada

One of rock 'n' roll's first teen idols, Paul Anka segued into superstar status for three decades by being as exciting a writer and performer as he was a recording artist.

During a summer vacation in Los Angeles while visiting his uncle, the 14-year-old Anka was perusing records at Wallich's Music City when he came upon a favorite, The Cadets' "Stranded in the Jungle." Noting the label (Modern Records), he traveled to the company's office, original song ("Bleu Wile Deveest Fontaine") in hand. With no appointment and no introduction, he wrangled an audition with Modern/RPM heads, the Bihari brothers. They were impressed enough to record him on the condition he do one of their songs, "I Confess." Anka jumped at the chance and wound up singing lead with his favorites, The Cadets, in the background.

> *Youthful sounding warbler is quite impressive on this r&r-style ballad, sounding like a slightly older Frankie Lymon. Bears watching. (9/22/56)*

Paul returned to Ottawa as "I Confess" failed. It did not deter him, however, as he took every opportunity to meet stars coming into town. He offered a new song that he had written, "Diana," to every act that came to town, but they all (including Frankie Lymon, The Platters, and The Diamonds) turned the song down. In March 1957, he even worked his way backstage to Fats Domino's dressing room, only to be shown the door by Domino's manager, Irvin Feld (who ironically would later manage Anka). A month later, Paul collected enough soup can labels to win a contest sponsored by Campbell's Soup. The prize was a trip to New York at Easter time. Anka's friends, The Canadian group The Rover Boys, were staying at The President Hotel, so young Paul stayed with them (sleeping in their bathtub).

Opening the New York phone book to the first record company name (ABC Paramount), Anka stormed their offices the next day. Don Costa, head of A&R, liked the 15-year-old and his song "Diana."

> *A smart, 16-year-old Canadian newcomer piles thru with a mighty rockabilly debut. Disk has a beat, classy arrangement, great sound, and most of all, mighty chanting by the youngster. An exciting talent find who can easily make it on this initial disk. (6/10/57)*

The song (#1 Pop *and* R&B!), inspired by his infatuation for an older girl he met in Sunday school (Diana Ayoub) went on to sell more than 10 million copies over the decades.

By 1958 Paul was a teen heartthrob with numerous hits. He issued a duet with Micki Marlo, "What You've Done to Me" (a "Cajun-type country number," 8/12/57), followed by his next solo hit, "You Are My Destiny" (#7 Pop, #14 R&B).

> *This is Anka's strongest since "Diana." It's a dramatic production with strings, but the best still comes thru. Anka cleffed the tune. (12/23/57)*

"Verboten" was the first song he wrote for a film soundtrack ("the title waltz from a coming flick . . . his vocal is given lush ork backing;" 6/23/58), followed by his first "*Billboard* Pick," "Just Young" ("a teen-slanted lyric that could hit the mark for big coin;" 9/8/58) (#80 Pop). The hokey "Teen Commandments," a trio recording cut with George Hamilton IV and Johnny Nash, followed (#29 Pop).

> *The three lads give out with a series of rules that will help teens live moral and healthy lives. The song is delivered against good ork backing by Don Costa. Side is fine jockey chatter platter, and it could also do well saleswise. (11/3/58)*

By the age of 17, Anka had toured half of Europe as well as Japan and Australia and turned himself into an idol of millions. His chart renaissance came in 1959, starting with "Lonely Boy."

> *Anka should click again with this powerful two-sider. Top side is a pounding rockaballad that is shouted in fine,*

dual-track style. Flip ["Your Love"] is a haunting ballad on which he is lushly backed by Don Costa's ork and chorus. Both should click. (5/11/59) (#1 Pop, #6 R&B)

He also made his first appearance on the silver screen in *Girl's Town* with Mamie van Doren.

By 1960, the 19-year-old had become the youngest performer to star at the world famous Copacabana night club. The year also began with the hit "Puppy Love," a song he wrote for his girlfriend Annette Funicello, followed by more hits.

Anka sells the attractive rockaballad strongly. He gets lush support from a fem chorus and the ork. Side should be another big one for him. (1/8/60) (#2 Pop)

Something Happened/My Home Town.

Two potent sides that should take off in short order. "Something Happened" is a pretty ballad with beat. "My Home Town" is a ballad with Latin traces. He's strongly backed on both. (4/25/60) (B-side, #8 Pop)

I Love You in the Same Old Way/Hello Young Lovers.

Two interesting switches for the successful chanter. Top side is a rip-roaring rocker of a tune of his own cleffing. Flip is done somewhat in the recent style of Bobby Darin with a hip-styled smart backing. Anka is at home with both and both could go. (7/25/60) (A-side, #40 Pop; B-side, #23 Pop)

Summer's Gone.

An emotional rockaballad with timely teen-appeal lyrics. (9/12/60) (#11 Pop)

In 1961, Paul expanded his activities in film, both acting in and writing the title song for *The Longest Day,* while continuing to prolifically write and record several Top-20 hits, including "Tonight, My Love, Tonight," issued as a B-side to "I'm Just a Fool Anyway," but his first major hit of the year.

Here are two of Paul Anka's best sides in recent months. First is a bright new tune, and Anka is backed by a swinging

arrangement. Second side is based on a classical melody, and lad sells it well. (2/27/61) (#13 Pop)

"Dance On Little Girl" ("an infectious Latin rocker;" 5/22/61) followed. (#10 Pop)

Anka moved to RCA in 1962 as his teen-idol image diminished but his pop-star status grew. His first RCA release was an international hit, "Love Me Warm and Tender" b/w "I'd Like to Know."

Anka's first RCA Victor singles release spotlights two potent sides. "Love Me Warm and Tender" is an emotional, Latin-flavored ballad with a moving reading by the star. The flip is a lovely ballad with sweeping strings, piano and vocal chorus adding to the side's effectiveness. (2/17/62) (#12 Pop)

Although not one of his biggest American hits, "Eso Beso" ("That Kiss") had such international appeal that it turned up on a dozen foreign charts.

Anka steps into the bossa nova groove with a torrid pop effort in the rhythm. It's a swinger that should score with the teens and features a strong production for chorus and ork that builds and builds. (10/20/62) (#17 Pop)

By 1963, Anka was peppering his releases with "oldies" and memories of "oldies," including a reworking of his first hit, "Remember Diana."

Paul conjures up his first hit with this tribute to Diana. It's a driving item with a shouting vocal. Definitely in the same hit class as the original. (4/6/63) (#39 Pop)

As the 1960s came to a close, he reduced touring and settled in Las Vegas, becoming a regular performer there. He had a couple of minor hits in 1969.

In the Still of the Night.

★ *Anka returned to the disk scene with solid sales impact with "Goodnight My Love," which came close to the Top Twenty. This powerful follow-up, a smooth updating of the Five Satins' hit of the fifties, will take him right up to the top this time out. (3/8/69) (#64 Pop)*

Sincerely.

★ *The smash hit of the mid-fifties by both the Moonglows and the McGuire Sisters is revived by Anka in a sensitive treatment that should keep him riding high on both the Hot 100 and Easy Listening Charts. (#80 Pop)*

In 1974, his new association with United Artists records brought Paul his first #1 hit in 15 years, "You're Having My Baby," a duet with Odia Coates.

The words say it's really knocking out the guy with joy that his baby loves him enough to have his baby. Anka really sells it for all its worth, even adopting a countryish Mac Davis style of diction, rather than his usual crisp interpretation. Commandingly catchy package could easily cross over to a Hot 100 monster. (6/29/74)

This was followed by two more hits, another duet with Odia Coates on "One Man Woman/One Woman Man" and 1975's solo "I Don't Like to Sleep Alone." He then returned to RCA for his last significant hit, the David Wolfert-produced "This Is Love."

This romantic ballad [was] featured in Anka's recent t.v. special. A simple instrumental backup keeps the focus on the lyrics. (10/7/78) (#35 Pop)

Anka recorded the theme song for the film *No Way Out* in 1987, a duet with Julia Migenes; the mysterious "familiar" vocal was provided by Michael McDonald.

This track from the forthcoming film and Migenes's solo outing is a charming pop ballad duet that features a very familiar and "brotherly" third vocal accompaniment. (8/22/87)

The multitalented Anka has written over 400 songs recorded by artists like Buddy Holly ("It Doesn't Matter Anymore"), Tom Jones ("She's a Lady"), and Frank Sinatra ("My Way"), not to mention the "played to death" theme from Johnny Carson's "Tonight" show. Anka continues to perform on the oldies and Vegas circuit.

THE ASSOCIATION

Russ Giguere: Lead vocals, percussion
Born: 10/18/43, Portsmouth, NH
Jim Yester: Guitar
Born: 11/24/39, Birmingham, AL
Jules Alexander: Guitar
Born: 9/25/43, Chattanooga, TN
Terry Kirkman: Winds
Born: 12/12/41, Salinas, KS
Brian Cole: Bass
Born: 9/18/42, Tacoma, WA
Ted Bluechel, Jr.: Drum
Born: 12/2/42, San Pedro, CA
Influences: Hi-Lo's, Modern Folk Quartet
Influenced: Doobie Brothers

One of the finest vocal harmony bands of the 1960s, The Association was formed in 1965 by Terry Kirkman (a former member of Frank Zappa's Mothers of Invention) and Jules Alexander. The soft-rock sextet signed with a small Pasadena, California, label, Davon records. Their first single, "One Too Many Mornings," received enough radio attention that the only slightly larger Valiant label purchased Davon, although the song didn't chart.

Bob Dylan's folk-rock material serves as a hot Valiant debut for a group loaded with today's pop market appeal. Strong rock dance beat in support. (12/4/65)

Their first hit was their second single, the unique soft-voiced/ instrumentally hard-edged, "Along Comes Mary" (#7 Pop) followed by the "instant standard," "Cherish" from their first LP, *Along Comes The Association.*

Smooth folk-flavored ballad serves as a strong follow-up to their initial hit, "Along Comes Mary." (8/20/66) (#1 Pop)

Their next two singles, "Pandora's Golden Heebie Jeebies" and "Looking Glass," didn't have the "Cherish" magic, but deejays "flipped" the latter, and "No Fun at All," a hauntingly beautiful rhythm ballad, became a fan favorite.

The band's "golden year" was 1967. Warner Brothers acquired Valiant and issued "Windy."

The "Cherish" group has a top of the chart contender in this pulsating mover loaded with discotheque appeal and a groovy lyric reading. (5/20/67) (#1 Pop)

In June, the group was the opening act at the now-legendary Monterey Pop Festival. Alexander left, replaced by tenor/guitarist Larry Ramos of The New Christy Minstrels. The Addrisi Brothers' "classic," "Never My Love," followed, and, by the end of 1967, The Association had been named "the #1 Group of the Year" by the trade-oriented *Bill Gavin Radio-Record Report,* displacing the previous three-time winners, The Beatles.

They started 1968 with what is considered their finest vocal performance, "Everything that Touches You."

Long awaited follow-up to "Never My Love" is another compelling ballad with a driving dance beat in strong support. Chalk up another top 10 winner for the smooth group. (1/20/68)

"Time for Livin'" (a "swinger, a good change of pace," 5/4/68) (#39 Pop) followed, and then "Six Man Band."

Here's the easy beat funky rocker to put the group right back in the Top 20. (8/10/68) (#47 Pop)

In January of 1969, Alexander returned from a sabbatical in India just in time to work with the now-septet on the music for the Paramount film, *Goodbye, Columbus.*

Fast-paced rhythm number, title tune from the forthcoming film has the feel and flavor of an "Up, Up and Away." The catchy Jim Yester . . . material will prove a sales topper for their "Six Man Band."

However, it was their last Warner charter, as the group found the harder sound of the times difficult to compete with. They took a more rock-oriented approach in subsequent singles but to no avail, despite many favorable predictions in *Billboard.* By 1970, Giguere left the group and was replaced by Richard Thompson (not to be confused with Richard Thompson of Farpoint Convention fame).

Yes, I Will.

Driving rock item has all the ingredients to go to a high spot on the Hot 100 and bring them back once again. Their strongest entry in some time. (7/5/69)

Just About the Same.

Change of pace and sound for the group, this infectious rhythm item with good lyric line will put them back up the Hot 100 with sales impact. Strong entry—their most commercial in some time. (2/14/70)

P. F. Sloan.

The infectious Jim Webb rhythm ballad gets a smooth vocal treatment by the Association, and it should prove the one to bring them back to the best selling charts. (3/13/71)

The group moved to Mums records in 1973 and RCA in 1975, before having their last Top-100 single in 1981, "Dreamer" original group (minus Cole who died on August 2, 1972 from drugs) began working the pop/rock revival circuit through the 1990s. After 15 millon sales of nine albums and 24 singles, and close to 800 concert appearances, The Association have established their niche in rock 'n' roll history.

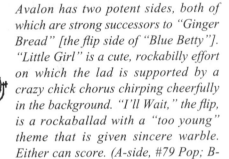

FRANKIE AVALON

Real Name: Francis Thomas Avallone
Birthdate: 9/18/39
Birthplace: Philadelphia, PA
Influences: Harry James, Frank Sinatra
Influenced: Joey Lawrence

One of the most successful teen idols of the 1950s, Frankie Avalon actually started not as a singer but as a trumpet-playing child prodigy.

By 1954, the 15-year-old was a TV celebrity, having performed on Jackie Gleason's and Paul Whiteman's shows, and recorded for RCA's "X" label (the misinformed reviewer gave Avalon's age as 11).

Trumpet Serenade . . . .**.68**

> *A listenable trumpet solo on the evergreen aided by The Texter Singers. Good for jock programming. (3/6/54)*

In 1957 Frankie formed his own band, Rocco and The Saints (with future teen star Bobby Rydell), and soon met songwriters/producers Bob Marcucci and Peter De Angelis. That same year Avalon and company landed a performance spot in the film *Disc Jockey Jamboree,* with Frankie singing "Teacher's Pet." It became his second single on Marcucci's Chancellor label. Neither it nor "Cupid," his first single, received much notice, but the third, "Dede Dinah," aided by Frankie's performance on Philadelphia's "American Bandstand" TV show (hosted by Dick Clark), made him a household teen name.

> *Smart selling by Avalon on this cute rocker makes it an appealing item. The lyric utilizes the titles of several other currently popular tunes with girls' names. "Ooh La La," the flip, is a medium-beat rockabilly with a slight Latin flavor. (12/23/57) (#7 Pop)*

Several charters followed, ranging from country and western and calypso to rockabilly grooves.

Blue Betty/Ginger Bread.

> *"Blue Betty" is a rocker which the artist belts against Dominoish ork support. It's a strong side that should also cop R&B buys. "Ginger Bread" is in a rock-a-calypso vein, and Avalon is helped by a chorus on this side. A likely dual market click. (6/23/58) (B-side, #9 Pop)*

What Little Girl/I'll Wait for You.

> *Avalon has two potent sides, both of which are strong successors to "Ginger Bread" [the flip side of "Blue Betty"]. "Little Girl" is a cute, rockabilly effort on which the lad is supported by a crazy chick chorus chirping cheerfully in the background. "I'll Wait," the flip, is a rockaballad with a "too young" theme that is given sincere warble. Either can score. (A-side, #79 Pop; B-side, #15 Pop)*

By 1959, the teen idol was a top star breaking through with five Top-10 singles, including the number one: "Venus" ("a bit of a switch for [Avalon]. The lovely beguine is warbled stylishly over excellent ork backing;" 2/2/59). Its success inspired another Spanish-tinged number, "Bobby Sox to Stockings," b/w "A Boy Without a Girl," both hits.

> *Avalon has two hot contenders. "Bobby Sox" is a clever topical beguine, done in an arrangement similar to Venus. "A Boy" is a pretty rockaballad that should also be a chart side. (5/18/59) (A-side, #8 Pop; B-side, #10 Pop)*

"Why?" ("a charming ballad on which he registers strongly;" 11/9/59) followed. Amazingly, five of his first 11 hits were also R&B charters. (#1 Pop)

Although 1960 brought Avalon seven more hot 45s (three were two-sided charters) none reached the Top 20. "Don't Throw Away All Those Teardrops" was his highest charter of the year.

> *"Don't Throw" is a countryish waltz that is smoothly handled over good backing. (2/29/60) (#22 Pop)*

Avalon then intuitively sidestepped into an acting career with a part in John Wayne's *The Alamo.*

Other flicks (and records) followed, including the theme song for *Voyage to the Bottom of the Sea.*

★★★★ *Here's the title tune to the new Avalon flick, upcoming shortly. It's done to a lush ork background with plenty of surf sound effects. Side has merit and it could move. (6/26/61)*

Although the hits stopped with 1962's "A Miracle," a new niche opened in 1963 when ex-Mouseketeer Annette Funicello and Frankie began a string of "sun and surf" films (beginning with *Beach Party*) that forever emblazoned the "safe to be your future son-in-law" stereotype on the crooner.

Married.

 A lively, upbeat rocker done with a fancy arrangement for ork and chorus. Good lyric is the clincher. It should go. (9/4/61)

You Are Mine.

 Dealers in areas where this new side has been exposed say it's the strongest [in] months for the chanter. . . . He's in top vocal form on a fine ballad and it adds up to a big reading. It has what it takes. Watch it. (3/17/62) (#26 Pop)

In 1964, Avalon signed with United Artists for four singles, but light fare wasn't working anymore, even when the subject was about going topless ("New Fangled, Jingle Jangle Swimming Suit from Paris").

Frankie's strongest entry in quite some time. Novelty ditty could be the one topless rendition to make it. (7/25/64)

Singles for Reprise, Amos, and Metromedia went nowhere, and, by the 1970s, Frankie settled into resort performances. He then made one more chart challenge with a disco rendition of "Venus" in 1976. In 1978, he cameoed in the movie *Grease,* and by 1985 was touring extensively with former idols, Fabian and Bobby Rydell. Coming full circle, the "Cowabonga Kid" teamed once again with Annette for the Paramount flick, *Back to the Beach,* in 1987.

LAVERN BAKER

Real Name: Delores LaVern Baker
Birthdate: 11/11/29
Birthplace: Chicago, IL
Influences: Ella Fitzgerald, Dinah Washington, Billie Holiday, Varetta Dillard
Influenced: Johnny Ray, Tina Turner, Jackie Wilson, Mary Wells, Bobby Lewis, Little Eva

One of America's first successful female rock 'n' rollers, LaVern Baker began singing gospel music at her Baptist Church choir in Chicago when she was just 12 years old. By 1946, she was performing in local clubs, and by the late 1940s had acquired the strange but apparently complimentary nickname of "Little Miss Sharecropper."

Nat "King" Cole saw her perform at Chicago's Club Delisa and gave Baker her first taste of touring. Although her staple was the blues (she taught a young Johnny Ray how to wail while working at Detroit's Flame Show Bar), during the late 1940s LaVern was basically a nightclub singer doing pop and comedy material. Her early blues singles for RCA (as Little Miss Sharecropper in 1949), Columbia (as Bea Baker, 1951), Okeh (uncredited with Maurice King, 1951), National (again as Little Miss Sharecropper, 1951), and King (again uncredited with Todd Rhodes) garnered little action. By 1953, LaVern landed at Atlantic Records.

Soul on Fire **70**
Blues-singing thrush does a fine job on a most attractive blues ballad opus while the ork backs her with a strong beat and driving cymbal. Good wax, this. (8/29/53)

It was followed by "I Can't Hold Out Any Longer" ("Building quickly, she achieves a wild climax that impresses. Girl could get attention with this one;" 6/5/54). Both were well-accepted portents of things to come.

"Tweedlee Dee" became Atlantic's first Pop Top-20 hit, but would have done better if Georgia

Gibbs hadn't immediately issued a copycat version that reached #2. Angered by the Gibbs imitation, Baker petitioned her congressman, requesting that the copyright law be changed to penalize note-for-note infringements, but to no avail.

Tweedlee Dee **90**

> *Miss Baker, who still remains undiscovered by the mass of people, won't remain that way long if she keeps turning out disks like this one. Material, cute as can be, is in a samba tempo. She sings up a storm for her best disk yet. Could break through, too. (11/20/54) (#14 Pop, #4 R&B)*

Before leaving for a January 1957 Australian tour with Bill Haley and Joe Turner, LaVern (who was still smoldering over the pilfering popster) went to the sarcastic extreme of sending a note to Gibbs saying: "Dear Georgia, Inasmuch as I'll be flying over quite a stretch of blue water on my forthcoming tour, I am concerned about making the trip safely. My thoughts naturally turn to you at this time, and I am enclosing an insurance policy on my life in the amount of $125,000. This should be at least partial compensation for you if I should be killed or injured, and thereby deprive you of the opportunity of copying my songs and arrangements in the future. Tweedlee Dee and Tra La La, LaVern Baker."

Her next single, "Bop Ting-a-Ling" rushed up the charts while she headlined Alan Freed's first rock 'n' roll Jubilee during Easter 1955 at the Paramount Theatre.

> *The solid set of sales reports returned from almost all parts of the country on this disk indicate that retailers and operators must be expecting a repeat performance of "Tweedle[e] Dee." Operators generally and Southern retailers have been particularly keen about "Bop-Ting-a-Ling," while the pop quality of the flip ["That's All I Need"] has given that side strong appeal in the North. (4/23/55) (A-side, #3 R&B; B-side #9 R&B)*

A trio of hits followed, and soon LaVern was earning upward of $10,000 a week at performances.

Play It Fair.

> *One of the few consistent female hit-makers in this field, LaVern Baker is showing familiar power with her latest. (10/22/55) (#2 R&B)*

I Can't Love You Enough/Still.

> *Not many of this summer('s) releases can match the quick take-off that this disk has seen. Many cities have had the record only 10 days, but report that it is establishing itself with no delay. Eastern cities like Boston, New York, Philadelphia and Baltimore account for much of the disk's success to its unusual pop acceptance. (9/8/56) (#22 Pop, #7 R&B)*

Jim Dandy/Tra La La.

> *The thrush is following up "Still" with another solid seller. This is hitting on both sides with a slight edge this week on "Jim Dandy." Sales are well distributed over both Northern and Southern markets, showing good national acceptance. (11/24/56) (A-side, #17 Pop; #1 R&B; B-side, #94 Pop)*

With the follow-up release of "Jim Dandy Got Married" ("Another sassy rhythm opus, somewhat reminiscent of the folk standard 'John Henry'"; 4/22/57), Baker was assuredly the "Queen of Novelty Rock 'n' Roll."

Films followed as LaVern performed "Tra La La" in Alan Freed's *Rock, Rock, Rock* and "Humpty Dumpty Heart" in *Mr. Rock 'n' Roll.*

> *Gay, bouncy tune . . . is a strong effort. Usual exuberant delivery by Miss Baker should click both pop and r&b. (7/29/57)*

The years 1958 through 1960 saw a variety of gospel/blues singles chart along with her biggest pop hit, "I Cried a Tear," which varied greatly from her previous efforts.

I Cried a Tear/Dix-a-Billy.

> *The thrush has two powerful sides. "I Cried a Tear" is a country-styled waltz that is sung with feeling. Mild rock backing is effective. "Dix-a-Billy," the flip, is a vocal version of a Dixieland*

tune that should also attract. (11/10/58) (#6 Pop; #2 R&B)

I Waited Too Long/You're Teasing Me.

The thrush could have successful follow-ups to her smash "I Cried a Tear" with either of these fine offerings. "I Waited" is a gospelish tune that is sung most pleasantly. Flip, "You're Teasing Me," is a rocker with a Latinish flavor. (3/30/59) (#33 Pop; #5 R&B)

Shake a Hand.

The thrush revives "Shake a Hand," the old Faye Adams click, with a hit sound. It has gospel overtones and her delivery is first rate. (1/17/60) (#13 R&B)

In 1960, she dueted with Ben E. King, formerly with the Drifters, on "Help-Each-Other-Romance" ("essential blending . . . on solid rhythm item with catchy tempo. Spinnable." 7/11/60). In 1961, Baker paired with legendary Raven's bass Jimmy Ricks for "You're the Boss" while both headlined at the Apollo Theatre.

> *The blending of vocal styles by LaVern and Jimmy Ricks is wild on this new record as the duo sings about who's the boss, on the swinging top side. Flip is the oldie ["I'll Never Be Free"], all dolled up in a bright new arrangement. Sock sides from a strong duo. (1/9/61)*

A new production team in 1961 (Leiber and Stoller) gave Little Miss Sharecropper one of her perennial favorite rockers, "Saved."

This should be a smash dual-market hit for the canary. "Saved" is a driving gospel item with sock lyric, an exciting beat, and a solid showmanly vocal. (4/3/61) (#37 Pop; #17 R&B)

Baker's hit-making days ended in 1962 with a cover of the traditional blues song, "See See Rider."

★ ★ ★ ★ *The old blues-standard is handed a wild, swinging, middle tempo reading. The tune is handled in a modern groove with smart backing that should get the teen-agers dancing. (#34 Pop; #9 R&B)*

Her last charter was in early 1966 in a duet with New Brunswick label mate Jackie Wilson ("Think Twice"). Another oddity from the time was the novelty release, "Batman to the Rescue."

> *In the same groove as her "Jim Dandy" hits, this swingin' Lincoln Chase rocker should put Miss Baker's name back on the chart. (7/30/66)*

By the late 1960s Baker was performing in Viet Nam and then in 1969 moved to The Philippines where she became a nonstop performer for the Marines and (would you believe!) Entertainment Director at the Subic Bay Military Base. LaVern was finally lured back to the states in 1989 for Atlantic's 40th anniversary bash at Madison Square Garden, her first stage show in New York in 21 years. It convinced her to come home permanently. In 1990, LaVern recorded "Slow Rolling Mama" for the film *Dick Tracy* and spent nine months in the Broadway musical *Black and Blue*, replacing old friend and Atlantic rocker Ruth Brown.

HANK BALLARD AND THE MIDNIGHTERS

Henry Ballard: Lead vocals
Born: 11/18/36, Detroit, MI
Henry Booth: Lead vocals, 1950–1953
Born: c. 1930s, Detroit, MI
Charles Sutton
Born: c. 1930s, Detroit, MI
Sonny Woods
Born: c. 1930s, Detroit, MI
Lawson Smith
Born: c. 1930s, Detroit, MI
Influences: Clyde McPhatter, Drifters, Orioles, Gene Autry
Influenced: Beatles, James Brown, Allman Brothers, Buddy Holly, Gladys Knight and The Pips, Temptations

One of the genre's "rockingest" pioneer groups, The Midnighters changed from a quartet of blissful balladeers into the raunchiest of rock 'n' rollers.

Formed in Detroit in 1950, they originally named themselves The Royals. Two local lads who reportedly sang with Woods and Smith (before Sutton and Booth joined) were Levi Stubbs (later the lead singer of The Four Tops) and the now-legendary Jackie Wilson. A 1952 amateur contest at the Paradise Theatre was the start of their career, as King/Federal talent scout Johnny Otis spotted them and had them signed.

Their first Federal 45 was an Otis-penned ballad, "Every Beat of My Heart," that would go on to be Gladys Knight and The Pips first hit nine years later. Wynonnie Harris guested on the record as co-lead singer.

Every Beat of My Heart 68–68–68–68
> *This is a little disappointing . . . judged by this effort, the Royals are more effective with a tempo that has a strong beat. (4/12/52)*

The reviewer preferred the top side, "All Night Long," which was an uptempo number. History would show that the group was better suited to faster paced material.

After five slow singles with sluggish sales, The Royals became The Five Royales for touring. A quick court injunction by the "real" Five Royales (who currently had a hit) sent The Royals back to square one. Smith joined the army in 1953, replaced by a 16-year-old Ford assembly plant worker, Hank Ballard. Ballads now took a back seat to Hank's gospel/country and western-influenced rockers. Their first tune with Hank was "Get It."

Get It 72
> *Group sells itself all the way on this hunk of blues material. (6/20/53) (#6 R&B)*

Their next single (and 10th overall), "Work with Me, Annie," was so big it ended The Royals' career. The for-the-time risqué lyrics joined with a powerful performance to make a solid hit.

Work with Me, Annie 83
> *This group has been coming up fast in the past year, and this is one of their best records to date. Everything is sub-*

ordinated to beat here, and the singers handle it solidly. A strong side. (2/17/54) (#22 Pop, #1 R&B)

The recording launched the "Annie" series of records, and started the trend of "answer records," most with the same melody and different lyrics. Revised (and sanitized) covers of Ballard's raunchy lyrics abounded, such as "The Wallflower" ("Roll with Me Henry") by Etta James and "Dance with Me Henry" by Georgia Gibbs.

Now known as The Midnighters, the group's second hit was "Sexy Ways," another risqué (for the time) number.

> *With "Work with Me, Annie" still at the top of the r.&b. retail chart, this group's most recent release moved out slowly in the first three weeks of release, but is now breaking rapidly. Areas where the record was reported having most strength included Philadelphia, Buffalo, Cincinnati, Atlanta and St. Louis. Volume was good in Detroit, Nashville, and Durham also. (6/26/54) (#2 R&B)*

The group reworked the Annie theme in 1954 with "Annie Had a Baby."

> *This follow-up to "Work with Me, Annie," could make it three hits in a row for the group . . . the record is already rocking in its first week, with Buffalo, Philadelphia, Cincinnati, Cleveland, Pittsburgh, Durham and Atlanta reporting that the disk is moving fast across the counter and on jukes. (8/28/54) (#23 Pop, #1 R&B)*

"Annie's Aunt Fannie" was the next in the series. The year 1955 brought the even more suggestive "Switchie Witchie Titchie."

> *Because of the off-color lyrics, this disk has been bucking considerable deejay resistance. All this notwithstanding, it is shaping up as one of the group's strongest since the "Annie" series. Among the territories where the record is now strong are Baltimore, Buffalo, Cincinnati, Detroit, Atlanta, Durham and St. Louis. (4/30/55)*

The last in the series also came in 1955, "Henry's Got Flat Feet" ("this spoof of a big hit record is now beginning to click in a number of widely scattered territories;" 6/11/55) (#14 R&B). They had one more R&B hit, "It's Love Baby," later that year, although cover versions cut into their business.

By late 1955, the well went dry, even though the group pounded out some fine sides, including "Rock and Roll Wedding." They continued to struggle through 1959.

The group wraps up [a] hard drivin' rhythm [tune] in [a] happy, uninhibited vocal reading, with infectious phrasing and a solid beat . . . a particularly sock item. (11/19/55)

Sweet Mama, Do Right 79
The boys knock off this blues with lots of heart and style, and the side has a good funky sound.

Let Me Hold Your Hand 82
A good commercial ballad, with the lead pleading feelingly. Beat and backing are very effective, and should go over in a big way with Midnighters' fans.

In 1957 Sutton left and Smith returned, with Woods leaving in 1958 and replaced by Norm Thrasher. Dropped by Federal in 1958, Hank went label hunting with a demo he'd written called "The Twist" (actually a revised version of the 1955 Drifters hit "What Cha Gonna Do"). Vee-Jay records turned thumbs down, but King then wisely picked up the group's option. "The Twist" became Ballards' B-side for the ballad "Teardrops on Your Letter." Only Hank was credited as artist in the review, even though the Midnighters were prominent on the label and vocals. *Billboard* gave both A- and B-sides two stars, with only a brief description devoted to the record that would spawn a thousand shaking hips: "A new dance style is sung about by the boys as they describe how to do the 'twist'" (1/5/59).

After a cover of Wilbert Harrison's "Kansas City" and "The Coffee Grind" faded from the charts, Hank and company finally had the crossover hit they were looking for: "Finger Poppin' Time."

Lively rocker is handled with verve by Ballard with a bright assist from the Midnighters. Danceable side can appeal in pop and r&b marts. (4/18/60) (#7 Pop; #2 R&B)

Strangely, while "Finger Poppin'" was charging up the Top 100, a blatant soundalike of "The Twist" by ex-chicken plucker Ernest Evans (now known as Chubby Checker) stormed the hit list, giving new life to The Midnighters' reissued version. Hank himself said that when he first heard Checker's cloning on his car radio, he thought it was his recording. Hank's label retaliated by reissuing "Teardrops on Your Letter" and "The Twist," still as the B-side.

Fervent vocalizing by Hank Ballard backed solidly by the group on "Teardrops." There's a sock, rockin' blues shouting on the driving novelty "The Twist." Both sides could grab coins. (6/27/60) (A-side, #87 Pop, #4 R&B; B-side, #28 Pop, #16 R&B)

Ballard's favorite single, "Let's Go, Let's Go, Let's Go" ("more swinging wax . . . has a free-swinging rhythm;" 9/12/60) (#6 Pop; #1 R&B) came hot on the heels of "The Twist" and "Finger Poppin' Time," making The Midnighters the first act in history to have three simultaneous singles in the Top 40.

Hank knew a good thing when he saw it and, like the "Annie" series, churned out a slew of fairly big dance sides.

The Hoochi Coochi Coo.

Ballard and his combo turn in a danceable rhythm-novelty with a great r&r beat. Watch it. (11/28/60) (#23 Pop, #3 R&B)

The Continental Walk.

This . . . catchy ditty is a gospel-styled, exciting vocal with a pounding beat. (3/27/61) (#33 Pop, #12 R&B)

The Switch-a-Roo/The Float.

A bouncy blues with a sock dance tempo is accorded solid ork and vocal treatment by Ballard and the boys. Flip is another danceable side with effective novelty sound gimmicks. (6/12/61)

(A-side, #26 Pop, #3 R&B; B-side, #92 Pop, # 10 R&B)

Keep on Dancing.

The kids will keep on dancing to Hank Ballard with these two strong sides. He handles the dance side with his usual enthusiasm and sells the bright "Nothing But Good" in exciting fashion. And the backing rocks. (8/7/61)

Do You Know How to Twist.

The pioneer of the Twist comes through with a rhythmic new twist item that has a good sound and a warm vocal. . . . Could be strong. (1/20/62) (#87 Pop)

"It's Twistin' Time," which was actually "Finger Poppin' Time" with "Twist" lyrics, finally exhausted the Twist series.

After 13 pop charters and 58 singles, the group disbanded in the mid-1960s, and Hank joined up with one of the many artists he influenced, James Brown, as part of the latter's revue. By the mid-1990s, Hank and a new contingent of Midnighters were still rockin' on the tour circuit. Ballard and company's contribution is especially impressive when you consider that their music created a dance "fad" that for the first time brought parents onto the dance floor with their kids, thus legitimizing rock 'n' roll.

THE BEACH BOYS

Mike Love: Lead vocals
Born: 3/15/41, Los Angeles
Brian Wilson: Lead Vocals, bass
Born: 6/20/42, Hawthorne, CA
Dennis Wilson: Vocals, drums
Born: 12/4/44, Hawthorne, CA (died 12/28/83)
Carl Wilson: Vocals, guitar
Born: 12/21/46, Hawthorne, CA
Al Jardine: Vocals, guitar
Born: 9/3/42, Lima, OH
Influences: Four Freshmen, Chuck Berry, George Gershwin, Bill Haley and The Comets
Influenced: Bangles, Captain and Tennille, Jan and Dean, Beatles, Wilson-Phillips, Danny and The Juniors, Happenings, Ronny and The Daytonas, G.T.O.s

Using Chuck Berry rhythms and Four Freshmen harmonies, The Beach Boys parlayed songs about surfin', cars, and girls into one of America's longest-running success stories.

Formed in Hawthorne, California, in 1961, the three Wilson brothers, cousin Mike Love, and friend Al Jardine were consecutively called Kenny and The Cadets, Carl and The Passions, and The Pendletons (after their Pendleton shirts). Their surf song style surfaced when Dennis (the only one who really surfed) suggested the subject matter to Brian, who then wrote "Surfin'" and "Surfin' Safari" with Mike. Their demos earned them a record deal with Candix records, but not before promotion master Russ Regan renamed them The Beach Boys.

In December 1961, "Surfin'" was issued and amazingly went to #75 nationally. By May of 1962, Candix folded and the Wilson boys' dad, Murry, went label shopping with a new demo done by Brian, Dennis, and Val Puluto (of The Jaguars). Capitol liked "Surfin' Safari," and the February demo became the June master, with the rest of The Beach Boys overdubbing harmony parts. At the same time, Al Jardine decided to enroll in college, and new member David Marks replaced him.

★ ★ ★ ★ *The beach scene gets a rolling, rocking treatment on this side by the boys. Tune swings along neatly on lead singer's talent and support of the rest of the group. (6/9/62) (#14 Pop)*

The flip side, "409," was not reviewed, although it was given three stars, and was also a chart success. The car lovers and surf lovers heard more of the same with "Surfin' U.S.A."

The boys scored with their last "Surfin'" side and this one will go right up after it. The side has strong beat and can be expected to blast off in LA. (3/9/63) (#3 Pop)

By 1963, Al returned and replaced David. The boys went from singers to stars as their *Surfin' U.S.A.* LP reached #2 and two more almost simultaneously issued singles ("Surfer Girl" and "Little

Deuce Coupe") hit the Top 10. These were quickly followed by "Be True to Your School" (with the Honeys, featuring Brian's future wife Marilyn Rovell and her sisters, providing a rah-rah-rah/sis-boom-bah backing vocal).

Be True to Your School/In My Room.

Two new big sides for the Beach Boys. The first is a swinger that ties in neatly with the teen lyric idea and the teen surf sound. The second is a bit of a departure for the boys, a soft folk-type ballad that could serve well. (10/19/63) (A-side, #6 Pop; B-side, #23 Pop)

The classic "Fun, Fun, Fun" came next.

A strong tune in the drag-surf groove all about a chick with a groovy rig. (2/8/64) (#5 Pop)

The group's first #1 was "I Get Around," topping the Hot 100 on July 4, 1964. The flip, "Don't Worry Baby" has been called "one of the greatest singles ever" by no less than Mick Jagger.

"Baby" is medium tempo with boys sounding like 4 Seasons. Could go all the way. Flip has surfin' sound punctuated by hand-clapping and chanting by the group. (5/16/64) (#24 Pop)

More double-sided classics followed, including "When I Grow Up to Be a Man" (with its unique harpsichord accompaniment) (#9 Pop) and "Dance, Dance, Dance."

A smash entry. Expected outdoor sound featuring a tremendous rock-surfin' beat and groovy lyrics. Boys have never sounded better. (10/31/64) (#8 Pop)

In December 1964, Brian suffered a nervous breakdown from overwork (he was responsible for not only composing the group's songs but also for producing all of their recordings), and was replaced on tour by a young unknown studio guitarist named Glen Campbell. A more permanent replacement was found in Bruce Johnston, who would tour with the group and eventually become a "full member" on records as well. The group also began remaking oldies, a trend that would help ensure their longevity.

Do You Wanna Dance/Please Let Me Wonder.

Bobby Freeman's former hit serves as a hot followup to the Beach Boys' "Dance Dance Dance." Flip is an interesting and well done change of pace ballad. (2/20/65) (A-side, #12 Pop; B-side, #52 Pop)

Their second #1, "Help Me Rhonda" ("an intriguing off-beat rouser . . . can't miss;" 4/10/65) came from a revitalized Brian's pen, followed by an equally arresting song with the most instantly identifiable keyboard introduction of the decade, "California Girls."

Hot follow-up to their "Help Me Rhonda" is this Brian Wilson rhythm number from the new "Summer Days, Summer Nights" LP. (7/17/65) (#3 Pop)

By 1966, the group was crafting doo wop oldies (The Regents' "Barbara Ann," with lead vocals contributed by Dean Torrence of Jan and Dean, from their unrehearsed *Party* LP, #2), folk rock ("Sloop John B," #3), and originals ("Wouldn't It Be Nice" and the gorgeous "God Only Knows," which Paul McCartney has called the greatest love song ever written) with incredible success.

Sloop John B.

Fine up-beat rhythm revival of the Kingston Trio hit with exciting production will quickly equal their "Barbara Ann" smash. (3/22/66) (#3 Pop)

Wouldn't It Be Nice/God Only Knows.

Two hot follow-ups to their "Sloop John B" smash, with a swinging surf sound rocker backed by an easy-go ballad. Either could go all the way. (7/16/66) (A-side, #8 Pop; B-side, #39 Pop)

The Beach Boys' next single was the epic rock symphony, "Good Vibrations," a major international hit and trendsetter of the times. The song was unique at the time, because it took so long to record (and cost so much money). It also featured an unusual electronic instrument, the theremin, which supplies the famous oscillating "whoo-whoo" sound in the instrumental background.

Good Vibrations.

Penned by Brian Wilson and Mike Love, group has a sure-fire hit in this off-beat and intriguing rhythm number. Should hit hard and fast. (10/22/66) (#1 Pop)

The group then toured England and was voted "The World's Best Group" in the *New Music Express* Poll, unseating The Beatles. Ten months passed before Capitol tried to equal the success of "Vibrations" when they issued the complex "Heroes and Villains" on the group's own short-lived Brother Records.

Clever off-beat rock material with an arrangement that encompasses barbershop harmony and jazz! (7/29/67) (#12 Pop)

By late 1967, the Beach Boys returned to straight-ahead rock 'n' roll originals like "Wild Honey" ("an easy rocker with a steady and solid dance beat"; 10/21/67) and "Darlin'" (a "raucous rocker"; 12/16/67), "Friends" (4/13/68), and the nostalgic "Do It Again."

Much in the vein of the earlier Beach hits, this smooth rocker with a summertime smash sound should fast prove one of their biggest hits. (7/13/68) (#20 Pop)

These were followed by a few oldies like "Bluebirds Over the Mountains" (11/23/68) and The Ronettes' "I Can Hear Music."

With an arrangement that builds into a production with traces of their "Good Vibrations," the group should spiral to the top with this powerful rhythm number, a past hit for the Ronettes. Culled from their hit LP, "20/20" by popular demand. (3/1/69) (#24 Pop)

Their last charter for Capitol, written by Murry Wilson, was entitled "Breakaway" ("Performed in their unique, smooth rock style, this one will hit hard and fast"; 6/21/69) (#63 Pop).

In 1970 the boys signed with Reprise and reestablished their Brother label, but through 1975 none of their 22 releases reached the Top 50. Capitol was doing better with reissues like "Surfin' U.S.A." (#36). Brian Wilson worked spo-

radically with the group, although he spent most of the 1970s recovering from his ongoing psychological and drug problems.

The Beach Boys hit the comeback trail with the tried-and-true oldies formula (and Brian back in the producing and performing fold) on "Rock and Roll Music" (1976). In 1974, the quintet sang back up for Chicago's "Wishing You Were Here." Producer James Guercio returned the favor in 1977 when The Beach Boys debuted on his Caribou label with a disco revision of their 1967 cut "Here Comes the Night" (from the *Wild Honey* LP). They stayed with Caribou for six years, turning out timeless rock 'n' roll like "Come Go with Me" (1981) (#18 Pop) and "Getcha Back."

A summer snapshot from 1963; the harmonies, the high school lyrics, quasi-Spector production. Highly resonant. (5/25/85) (#26 Pop)

Capitol jumped on the "Stars on 45" craze in 1981 and issued a similarly styled Beach Boys medley that reached #12. In the mid- and late 1980s, the group collaborated with various other oldies acts, including "East Meets West" with the Four Seasons (1984), "Happy Endings" (Little Richard, 1987), and "Don't Worry Baby" (The Everly Brothers, 1988). The group made a surprise comeback in 1988, with their fourth #1 single (their first #1 in 22 years, and their first that did not include Brian Wilson), the classic "Kokomo" from the film *Cocktail*.

The Beach Boys were inducted into the Rock and Roll Hall of Fame in 1988 and are still rockin' in the 1990s. Meanwhile, Brian Wilson has recorded as a solo artist, as well as working with producer Don Was, who is said to be trying to engineer a reunion with the rest of the group.

CHUCK BERRY

Real Name: Charles Edward Anderson Berry
Birthdate: 10/18/26
Birthplace: St. Louis, MO
Influences: Charlie Christian, Carl Hogan (Tympany Five),
Fats Domino
Influenced: Beach Boys, Rolling Stones, Beatles, Jimi
Hendrix, E.L.O., Paul Anka, Freddy Cannon,
Creedence Clearwater Revival, Paul Revere and The
Raiders, Lovin' Spoonful, Buddy Holly, Monkees,
Buffalo Springfield, Tommy Roe, Steppenwolf,
Ritchie Valens, many more

A true pioneer of rock 'n' roll, nobody this side of Elvis made you move to a record like Chuck Berry. His early musical influences were blues and jazz, but when he translated his influences through his guitar, songs, and voice, it came out R&B with a touch of rockabilly, the chemistry of rock 'n' roll.

Chuck formed a trio with Johnnie Johnson (piano) and Ebby Harding (drums) in 1952 while he was still a teenager. By day, Berry worked on the assembly line at General Motors before learning cosmetology and becoming a hairdresser in his mid-twenties. Before long, The Chuck Berry Trio was a hot item among black audiences. Chuck set off for Chicago in search of a musical career with two songs, the traditional blues "Wee Hours" and the country folksong "Ida Red." He met Muddy Waters at a club, and asked to play along. Waters was so impressed he sent Chuck to Leonard Chess of Chess records. The youngster played his two songs, and when "Ida Red" was reportedly changed by Chess to "Maybellene," Berry's career was off and running.

> *Berry socks across an amusing novelty with ace showmanship and expressive good humor. The tune has a catchy rhythm and a solid, driving beat. Fine jockey and juke wax. (7/30/55) (A-side, #5 Pop, #1 R&B; B-side, #10 R&B)*

In November 1955, he was named "Most Promising R&B Artist" in *Billboard*'s annual deejay poll.

With a million seller his first time out, Chuck had a lot to live up to, but his unique ability to recognize relatable teen concepts and turn them into rock 'n' roll lyrics made him legendary. "Thirty Days" was his follow-up hit.

> *In very much the same way that "Maybellene" made a quick sweep of the country, so "Thirty Days" is coming forward with great speed and should be on the national charts shortly. (10/22/55) (#2 R&B)*

His next song, "No Money Down," caused some controversy for radio programmers because of its mention of specific brands of automobiles.

> *Despite the fact that "No Money Down" is getting little air play due to its references to Cadillac and Ford cars, the word about it has spread and is as hot a novelty as has been seen in some time. . . . "No Money Down" is the preferred side, but the reverse ["Down Bound Train"] is also faring well since it is getting more radio exposure. (2/4/56) (#8 R&B)*

The two-sided hit, "Brown-Eyed Handsome Man" ("a novelty blues with a solid beat and a touch of Calypso in the backing") (#5 R&B) and "Too Much Monkey Business" ("more of a pure blues with novelty appeal in the lyrics"; 9/8/56) (#4 R&B) was his next charter. "Roll Over Beethoven" followed, cracking the pop charts as well as the usual R&B. By the end of 1956, Berry appeared in the film *Rock, Rock, Rock*, singing "You Can't Catch Me."

> *Over a lickity-split guitar backing, Berry gives the amusing lyrics a very appealing reading. It's a catchy tune that the teen-agers will dig the most. (12/1/56)*

Chuck churned out more outstanding fodder for the teens, starting 1957 off with "School Days."

> *Berry has another sensational jumpin' story novelty that packs the same sort of appeal as did his previous smashes. Look for this one to go pop also. It can't miss. (3/16/57) (#3 Pop, #1 R&B)*

It was followed by the all-time classic, "Rock and Roll Music."

> *Top side is high-voltage go at a blues rocker. Sock styling by Berry with good backing makes side a strong loot type. (10/7/57) (#8 Pop, #6 R&B)*

In September, he appeared in Alan Freed's *Mr. Rock and Roll,* and was becoming as legendary a stage performer as a recording artist, often appearing on 100 stages in 100 days. During one show at the Brooklyn Paramount theater, Chuck invented his now-famous bent-knee slither across the stage, known as the "duck walk," that drove audiences wild.

He started 1958 with another soon-to-be series of classics.

Sweet Little Sixteen/Reelin' and Rockin'.

> *Two strong sides by Berry. It's a toss as to which will take command. Both are vigorously presented rockers with rhythmic guitar backing. Berry is cleffer of both. Naturals for r.&b. coin also. (2/3/58) (#2 Pop, #1 R&B)*

Johnny B. Goode/Around & Around.

> *Berry figures to keep his hit string going with these two powerful sides. "Johnny" is a rocker sold in smash style. "Around" is a cute stop-and-go effort that should also be in there. Strong r.&b. potential also. (4/7/58) (#8 Pop, #2 R&B)*

Carol.

> *A spirited blues rocker reading by the Chess master. Has a lot of sound and beat and the kids should dig it. Strong pop and r.&b. potential. (8/11/58) (#18 Pop, #9 R&B)*

Sweet Little Rock and Roller/Joe Joe Gun.

> *Berry has two hot sides to follow up "Carol." Top tune is similar to "Sweet Little Sixteen." Berry handles the rocker-blues in his form. Flip . . . is a novelty rocker about a cat who lives in the jungle and has encounters with various beasts. Strong r.&b. prospects also. (#47 Pop, #13 R&B)*

Merry Christmas, Baby/Run, Rudolph, Run.

> *Berry has two interesting sides that will pull in plenty of coin. Top side is a slow blues that is read against really fine guitar and piano. It's an off-beat treatment that can click. "Run, Rudolph," the flip, is a rousing rock and roll efort about one of Santa's reindeer. (12/1/58) (A-side, #69 Pop; B-side, #71 Pop)*

Berry had an acting part in 1959's *Go, Johnny, Go!,* which birthed "Little Queenie," issued as the B-side to "Almost Grown" (on which Berry is backed by the Moonglows).

> *These are Berry's strongest efforts in a while, and both can coast in. Berry sells each with strong know how and they should also reap heavy coin in r.&b. marts. "Almost Grown" is a rocker blues. "Queenie" is a lot more of a gutbucket groove. (3/9/59) (A-side, #32 Pop, #3 R&B; B-side, #80 Pop)*

The classic "Back in the U.S.A." ("a pounding rocker blues, and Berry belts the tune with rhythmic zest"; 6/1/59) b/w "Memphis, Tennessee" ("fine guitar backs the vocal") followed. (#37 Pop, #16 R&B)

Sadly, by mid-1959, Chuck was mired in a legal hassle over the claim of a 14-year-old girl that he had transported her across state lines for "immoral purposes." The case was thrown out when testimony revealed the girl was a prostitute when he met her, and she willingly came to St. Louis to work as a hatcheck girl in his club. Only after he fired her did she go to the police. Still prosecutors weren't giving up on bringing down a star, and a second seemingly racially motivated trial brought Berry two years in jail in 1962.

By 1964 music had changed and Chuck was seeing his own 1950s hits coming back at him and the world via his British fans who were now teen idols like The Rolling Stones (their first single was Berry's "Come On," #21 U.K.), The Beatles ("Roll Over Beethoven"), The Animals ("Memphis"), and The Yardbirds ("Too Much Monkey Business") just to name a few. His American fans weren't ignoring his legacy either as The Beach Boys thinly disguised "Sweet Little 16" as "Surfin' U.S.A."

Still, Chuck managed a comeback on the pop

charts with such stalwarts as "Nadine/Is It You?," "No Particular Place to Go" ("Sounds just right for summer"; 5/16/64) (#10 Pop), "Little Marie" (#54 Pop), "You Never Can Tell" (#14 Pop), and "Promised Land."

A true blue Berry rocker with plenty of get up and go. Rinky piano and wailing Berry electric guitar fills all in neatly. (12/5/64) (#41 Pop)

In 1966 Chuck signed with Mercury for a reported $50,000 advance, but the late 1960s were not his time on record. Berry continued to tour through the early 1970s, scoring a novelty hit in 1972 with the slightly off-color "My Ding-a-Ling." In 1978 Chuck played himself in the film about deejay Alan Freed, *American Hot Wax*. In one of the most bizarre months a rocker's career could have, Berry went from the high of playing at The White House for President Carter (on June 7th) to being jailed for four months on July 10th for income tax evasion.

In 1986, Rolling Stones' guitarist Keith Richards organized Chuck's 60th birthday party performance, which became the basis for the documentary, *Hail, Hail, Rock and Roll*. That same year, Berry was inducted into the Rock and Roll Hall of Fame. A noted songwriter and recording artist once summed up the St. Louis dynamo's contribution to rock music by saying, "If you tried to give rock and roll another name, you might call it Chuck Berry!" The writer was John Lennon.

THE BOBBETTES

Reather Dixon: Lead vocals
Born: 5/1/44, New York City
Emma Pought
Born: 4/28/42, New York City
Janice Pought
Born: 1/11/44, New York City (died 1980)
Laura Webb
Born: 11/8/41, New York City
Helen Gathers
Born: 3/18/43, New York City

Influences: Five Keys, Clyde McPhatter and The Drifters, Sam Cooke, Charts, Cookies, Coasters, Lee Andrews and The Hearts
Influenced: Shirelles, Marvelettes

The Bobbettes were the first female group in the rock era to have a Top-10 pop hit and a number one R&B record.

They started as an octet whose ages ranged from nine to 11. The Harlem teens (and preteens) formed in the glee club of P.S. #109 in 1955. Dubbing themselves with the exotic moniker, The Harlem Queens, they shrunk to a quintet over a two-year period of amateur shows. Manager James Daily signed the group in 1956, and his first official act was to can their nom de plume for a more sanitized "bobbysoxer" teen image; hence, The Bobbettes!

Daily had the girls sign with Atlantic in 1957, and their first four recorded songs were (uncharacteristically for the time) written by the teens themselves, including their first 45, "Mr. Lee." The smash hit was written about their teacher at P.S. #109, but the original lyric had to be toned down, because the quintet really despised the strict educator.

The lead, with excellent assistance, sounds like she really misses Mr. Lee on this contagious rocker. The alto voice here is also something to hear. (6/10/57) (#6 Pop, #1 R&B)

Several singles through 1957, 1958, and 1959 fared poorly, although they were chart quality, especially The Chantels-meet-Marvin-and-Johnny-styled, "You Are My Sweetheart."

Speedy.
An even better side than their hit "Mr. Lee." The tune is a subdued rocker. (11/11/57)

Rock and Ree-ah-Zole 79
Here's a side that's packed with plenty teen-age lingo. Has a cute, boppy, hic-cupy feeling in the first wax for the gals in a spell. Could go with the teen element. (4/7/58)

You Are My Sweetheart.
★★ *The girls sing this sly effort pleasantly over a riff backing. (6/8/59)*

Between package tours (as many as 16 acts all on the road together touring in buses), the group did some background session work for one of their idols, Clyde McPhatter, in addition to Ivory Joe Hunter. As the only girl group on many of these tours, the five teens were often taken under the wings of such veterans as LaVern Baker and Ruth Brown, who taught them what to wear on stage and how to do their makeup. When the girls issued "Oh My Papa" in 1960, the original hit artist, Eddie Fisher, came into the studio to coach them.

Oh My Papa.

★ ★ ★   *The hit of some years back gets a reading which has a well-marked rhythm, violin licks and a fresh-sounding vocal. (1/11/60)*

In 1960 The Bobbettes left Atlantic and signed with producer George Goldner's Triple X label. Their first release more honestly emoted how they felt about Mr. Lee.

I Shot Mr. Lee.

★ ★ ★   *A sort of follow-up to "Mr. Lee" hit these gals enjoyed a couple of years back . . . There's a good bit of vocal drive here. Gals sound a bit more grown-up on this outing. Could pick up spins. (6/20/60) (#52 Pop)*

Atlantic's own release (recorded 2/19/59) created a rare "cover battle" between two versions of the same song by the same act.

★ ★ ★ ★ *Here's a version of the breaking hit which Atlantic made several years ago, when the chicks were still on the label. They have a younger sound here. The other version has a strong head start but this can get action, despite obvious chances for a lot of confusion. (7/11/60)*

The Bobbettes' only two-sided pop charter followed.

Have Mercy Mercy Baby/Dance with Me Georgie.

 First side features some exciting and energetic vocal work by the lead canary with plenty of drive. Flip is another version of the old folk tune,

"Work with Me, Annie." Either can score. (9/19/60) (A-side, #66 Pop; B-side, #95 Pop)*

Goldner had the group record for several of his labels, with stops at Triple X, End, and Gone. Through 1961 and 1962, The Bobbettes moved to King and Jubilee. Although their sound matured and skills improved, those sides received little attention.

Over There (Stands My Baby).

★ ★ ★ ★ *Some fine lead singing as well as cohesive work from the rest of the girls. Infectious beat and combo playing add to the side. (7/7/62)*

Just before their first release on Diamond in 1965, the girls sang backup for Johnny Thunder's hit "Loop De Loop" (#4) (without label credit). It was their last chart hit. Helen Gathers left as the Diamond sides were being issued, leaving The Bobbettes a foursome.

Love Is Blind.

   Slow, hard-driving rock blues . . . Rich, wailing vocal performance and solid dance backing has a winning sound throughout. (9/18/65)

In 1966, they recorded "Love That Bomb" for the film *Dr. Strangelove,* and moved to RCA for an out-of-character though effective recording of "It's All Over."

It's All Over.

   The girls really groove with the rocking Rolling Stones' material. Strong performance that should prove a hot chart entry. (10/22/66)

The quartet moved through the remaining 1960s, 1970s, and 1980s to the beat of the oldies revival scene, touring England and the United States into the 1990s.

GARY U.S. BONDS

Real Name: Gary Anderson
Birthdate: 6/6/39
Birthplace: Jacksonville, FL
Influences: Jackie Wilson, Clyde McPhatter, Sam Cooke
Influenced: Bruce Springsteen, Steve Perry, Bob Seger,
    Huey Lewis, Robert John

Probably the most patriotic name in rock 'n' roll, Gary never even heard his new stage moniker until his record was climbing the charts.

As a boy, Gary Anderson sang in church and high school. After moving to Norfolk, Virginia, with his parents, he sang with a local quintet, The Turks, from 1954 until 1959. He was discovered by Frank Guida, owner of Frankie's Birdland, a record emporium with a tiny recording studio in the back. Frank and shoe salesman Joe Royster had written a country song, "New Orleans," and felt Anderson would be perfect for it. Between Gary's song rearrangement, his strong, shouting style, and the tin-can sound of Guida's rinky-dink studio, "New Orleans" emerged quite differently than it started.

Before issuing it, Frank got the idea to change Gary's name to the mysterious "U.S. Bonds" from the next door delicatessen. Its walls were plastered with "Buy U.S. Savings Bonds" signs, and it sounded more commercial than Anderson. He just never bothered to let Gary know his new name. *Billboard* mistakenly thought the name referred to a group, rather than an individual.

A new group and a new effort that could step right out. The tune is a breezy, rhythmic rocker and moves along in a swingin' fashion. An impressive debut. (9/19/60) (#6 Pop, #5 R&B)

It was followed in early 1961 by "Not Me," that did not chart.

A wild driving rocker is sung with emotional intensity here by U.S. Bonds and

it should be a strong follow-up to his recent hit. (2/20/61)

Another Guida act, The Church Street Five, had an instrumental out in mid-1961 called "A Night with Daddy G," which had stiffed on the charts. One evening, when the group and Bonds were hanging out in the studio, Daddy "G" (Frank Guida) himself asked Gary to write a lyric for the tune. Ten minutes later, the spontaneous, raucous, all-time party record, "Quarter to Three" was created, and Guida threw on the tape recorder as the almost impromptu jam began (#1 Pop).

Bonds's next release was the first to be credited to "Gary U.S. Bonds," reportedly at the request of The U.S. Treasury Department (apparently not wanting the public thinking they were moonlighting in the record business). Fans became confused as many thought U.S. Bonds was a group. But the hits kept coming.

School Is Out/One Million Tears.

Bonds wraps up "School Is Out," a wild rocker, in his usual exciting, vital warbling style. He also chants with feeling on the flip, a moving rockaballad. Both sides are good, with "School Is Out" a bit stronger. (7/17/61) (#5 Pop, #12 R&B)

Bonds's next single was a predictable followup, "School Is In."

This should be another smash for Bonds. The chanter is in solid form on a novelty rocker with an infectious beat. Side has appeal in r.&b. as well as pop markets. (10/9/61) (#28 Pop)

His last 1961 single was the two-sided "Havin' So Much Fun" and "Dear Lady Twist," with the B-side charting.

Bonds wraps up "Havin' So Much Fun" in a frantic rocking vocal and ork treatment. Flip spotlights more exuberant vocalizing on a happy, bouncy Twist-tempo tune. Both sides are potent. (12/4/61) (#9 Pop, #5 R&B)

The success of this twist song led to a followup, 1962's "Twist, Twist Senora" (#9 Pop). His first film appearance yielded his next hit.

Seven Day Weekend.

Bonds is back with a sharp rhythm side in "Seven Day Weekend" from the pic, "It's Trad-Dad." It swings with a solid beat and a swinging vocal as well. Flip ["Getting a Groove"] has that "Quarter to Three" party feeling with hand-clapping and vocal chorus effects. Strong teen wax. (6/16/62) (#27 Pop)

"Copy Cat" was his last hit of the 1960s.

Another winner from Bonds who gives his typical exciting performance on this driving rocker that builds from the opening chord. Femme group adds the swing of the side. (8/16/62) (#92 Pop)

Bonds might have had another hit in 1963, but Gary rejected "If You Wanna Be Happy," the song Norfolk vocalist Jimmy Soul turned into #1 gold. His last 1962 single, "I Dig This Station," an attempt to gain deejay airplay by mentioning various noteworthy AM jockeys, went nowhere.

Bonds consistently played clubs and "oldies" shows through the 1960s and 1970s. On one such night in 1978, he let a youngster on stage to jam with him on "Quarter to Three." The "kid" was Bruce Springsteen, already a budding superstar, although Gary had never heard of him. Springsteen, a big fan of Gary's as a child (he regularly played "Quarter to Three" in his shows), spent the next two years working on his own album *The River,* and, upon its completion, began coproducing Gary's comeback LP, *Dedication.* He wrote Bonds's first hit since 1962, "This Little Girl."

> *Bonds should return to the charts after an 18-year absence with this exhilarating, exuberant rocker coproduced by The Boss and Steve Van Zan[d]t. It's piano boogie rock 'n' roll at its most exciting. (4/18/81) (#11 Pop)*

A duet with Springsteen on Moon Mullican's "Jole Blon" followed (#65 Pop). A second LP with The Boss followed, *On the Line,* featuring a remake of The Box Tops' "Soul Deep" and the Springsteen-penned "Out of Work."

In 1984, Gary recorded an album for Phoenix, *Standing in the Line of Fire,* and continues to work, mostly on the East Coast.

JAMES BROWN

Birthdate: 5/3/33

Birthplace: Macon, GA

Influences: Louis Jordan, Roy Brown, Hank Ballard and The Midnighters

Influenced: Michael Jackson, Prince, Rolling Stones, Jimi Hendrix, Hammer, Ohio Players, Kool & The Gang, Sly Stone, Mitch Ryder, Donald Byrd, George Clinton, many others

Known as "The Hardest Working Man in Show Business," James Brown is a legendary performer who melded gospel-influenced shouting with R&B subjects to create the "soul" sound.

Growing up on gospel and blues in Augusta, Georgia, he shined shoes, picked cotton, and danced in the streets for coins all before he was 16. A three-year stay at a juvenile detention center taught him the folly of armed robbery, and music became his life when he began touring with gospel groups and learned to play organ and drums. In the early 1950s he met Bobby Byrd in the Augusta Baptist Church Choir. They formed The Swanees gospel group with Johnny Terry, Sylvester Keels, and Floyd Scott. By 1954, The Swanees became The Famous Flames, pouring forth uptempo blues tinged with gospel.

In 1955 Brown and company cut a demo at WIBB in Macon. That demo of a song called "Please, Please, Please" became their first record, after being spotted during a performance by Ralph Bass of Federal Records.

Please, Please, Please 75
> *A dynamic religious fervor runs through the pleading solo here. Brown and the Famous Flames group let off plenty of steam. (3/3/56) (#105 Pop, #5 R&B)*

Several singles followed in 1956 and 1957, garnering the group only regional successes. Then, in 1958, they crossed into the Pop Top 50 for the first time, while James had his first of 17 #1 R&B hits.

Tell Me What I Did Wrong 75
A nicely shouted, upbeat blues by Brown. He gives it a spirited reading, again in a traditional framework. This side swings. (10/13/58) (#48 Pop)

By now, Brown was breaking box office records in black venues with the hottest road show in America—The James Brown Revue—featuring his own emcee, opening acts, his own house band, The J.B.s, and The Famous Flames, who were also accomplished musicians. At one point in 1960 The J.B.s became Nat Kendrick and The Swans who hit with "Mashed Potatoes."

I Know It's True.
★ ★ ★ ★ *Brown sings with great passion and soul on a slow blues. Twin horn accompaniment sounds nice. Side has a real gospel feel, and it can get excitement in traditional areas. (1/11/60) (#15 R&B)*

Think/You've Got the Power.

Brown gives "Think," the big hit of a few seasons ago, a bright shouting approach that is likely to account for heavy pop and r.&b. buys. "You've Got the Power" is a pounding ballad with beat that also comes in for a listenable vocal. (4/4/60) (A-side, #33 Pop, #7 R&B; B-side, #86 Pop, #14 R&B)

I Don't Mind/Love Don't Love Nobody.

The first is a virtuoso blues performance in slow insinuating tempo. The second is a swinger with Brown's lead in a wild, high-pitched delivery. (5/1/61) (#47 Pop, #14 R&B)

Baby, You're Right/Never Never Let You Go.
Two standout efforts by Brown, who has been consistently on the charts of late. Both are shouts, with a lot of gospel feeling. The top side is the slower paced of the two. Either or both could step out. (7/31/61) (#49 Pop, #2 R&B)

"Mr. Dynamite" (as James was called) began recording so often that Federal was issuing (and reissuing) a single every two to three months, and would continue to do so for the next ten years. By 1963, Brown was filling super-sized concert halls and was pulling in $12,500 a night, an unheard-of payday for that era. (Around this time, a young guitarist named Jimi Hendrix was working for Brown.)

James finally crashed the Pop Top 20 in 1963 by combining a more-commercialized ballad arrangement with 11 strings and nine voices on an old standard with his intense vocals for "Prisoner of Love" (#18), followed by another standard, "These Foolish Things" (#55). His orchestral era was short-lived as he jumped back into his rockin' ways. He broke through big time in 1965 with the classics, "Papa's Got a Brand New Bag (Part 1)" (a Grammy Winner) and "I Got You (I Feel Good)," while losing seven pounds a night during his high-energy shows.

I Got You (I Feel Good).
Rocking blues wailer that will hit hard and fast. (11/16/65) (#3 Pop, #1 R&B)

1966 opened with another big hit, "It's a Man's Man's Man's World."
The wailer has a top of the chart disk in this slow blues shouter that will quickly hit both pop and r&b markets. (4/23/66) (#8 Pop, #1 R&B)

By late 1966, Brown was in search of a hit, turning out everything from Christmas carols and oldies to show tunes, recutting Nat "King" Cole's "A Christmas Song" for the 1966 holiday season, followed by a remake of the traditional blues stomper "Kansas City," and even George Gershwin's "I Loves You Porgy," produced by Brown himself.
The Gershwin standard is treated to an unusual interpretation loaded with soul and electricity and headed for the top of the r&b chart with much appeal for the pop field as well. (6/10/67)

Brown returned to form with a series of funky hits.

Cold Sweat.
More solid soul rhythm sounds from Brown . . . Hot entry for both pop and r&b charts. Dynamic performance of strong material. (7/8/67) (#7 Pop, #1 R&B)

By the start of 1968, Brown had already amassed 36 pop hits and 40 R&B charters and was getting funkier with each new release.

I Got the Feelin'.

More blockbuster material from Brown with a wailing performance to match. Disk moves from start to finish . . . one of Brown's top outings. (3/9/68) (#6 Pop, #1 R&B)

Licking Stick.

Brown comes on strong again with a driving rhythm item headed straight for the top. (5/18/68) (#14 Pop, #2 R&B)

After Martin Luther King's assassination, Brown made a national TV appeal for calm. The effect of the highly revered soulster's appearance resulted in an official commendation from Vice President Humphrey. Brown took his role as a black spokesman seriously with his seventh hit of 1968, "Say It Loud—I'm Black and I'm Proud (Part 1)."

Brown socks the message home with a steady and solid beat and should prove a hot sales winner for both pop and r&b markets. (8/31/68) (#10 Pop, #1 R&B)

In 1969, he turned out more hot dance records and was voted "#1 male R&B vocalist" by *Cashbox* Magazine. Best known is the single "Give It Up or Turn It Loose."

Pulsating rhythm entry from Brown, loaded with discotheque appeal that should prove a hot chart item for the soulful wailer. Backing beat moves from start to finish. (1/18/69) (#15 Pop, #1 R&B)

Brown finished up 1969 with a dance novelty that inspired a follow-up hit.

Mother Popcorn (You Got to Have a Mother for Me).

The popular discotheque winner proves powerful material for Brown and his dynamic style. Strong entry loaded with sales potential pop and r&b. (6/7/69) (#11 Pop, #1 R&B)

Let a Man Come In and Do the Popcorn.

The popcorn king comes up with more potent funky dance material with a top vocal workout that should be riding

high on the charts. (10/4/69) (#21 Pop, #2 R&B)

By 1970 The Famous Flames broke up, and Brown reorganized The J.B.s, adding Bootsy Collins, Fred Wesley, and Alfred Ellis. In 1971 James formed his own label, People Records, and hit with "Escapism" and "Hot Pants." A year later, he had moved to Polydor, hitting with "Talking Loud and Saying Nothing" (#27 Pop, #1 R&B).

During 1973, Brown made the unusual move of cutting two versions of the same song, "Think." The first version garnered this review:

There's the standard scream, the solid, standard down to home rhythm and James offers within this setting advice to think about good things, bad things, "outasight things"—things which are inexplicably tied into man-woman relationships. (4/21/73) (#77 Pop, #15 R&B)

Just a few weeks later, the second version with different lyrics was issued, to somewhat lesser success. Vickie Anderson sang with Brown on the second recording (#80 Pop, #37 R&B).

Within two years, the newly christened "Godfather of Soul" was experiencing tax problems, the death of his son, and the end of his second marriage. His recordings between 1975 and 1984, although as hot as ever, were being overlooked as teens became ironically drawn to acts he influenced, such as Kool and The Gang and The Ohio Players. Only one charted Top-10 R&B in that 10-year span ("Get Up Offa That Thing," 1976).

In 1980, Brown appeared as a singing and dancing preacher (some say parodying himself) in the classic film, *The Blues Brothers*. He returned with a vengeance in 1985 with a huge pop hit, "Living in America" (#14 Pop) from the *Rocky IV* soundtrack. Brown was among the first artists inducted into the Rock and Roll Hall of Fame in 1986, and continued to make exciting, soulfully intense recordings into the 1990s.

BUFFALO SPRINGFIELD

Stephen Stills: Vocals, guitar
Born: 1/3/45, Dallas, TX
Neil Young: Vocals, guitar
Born: 11/12/45, Toronto, Canada
Richie Furay: Vocals, guitar
Born: 5/9/44, Dayton, OH
Dewey Martin: Drums
Born: 9/30/42, Chesterville, Ontario, Canada
Bruce Palmer: Bass
Born: 1946, Liverpool, Canada
Influences: Lovin' Spoonful, Jefferson Airplane, John Lee
   Hooker, Pete Seeger, Vanilla Fudge, Jimi Hendrix,
   Eric Clapton, Phil Spector, Gene Pitney, Bob Dylan,
   Chuck Berry, Rick Nelson, Roy Orbison

Even though their lifespan was less than two stormy years, and their yield was only nine singles and three albums, Buffalo Springfield was an important incubator for numerous folk-rock stars.

Stephen Stills, a political science major at the University of Florida, found folk music more to his liking. He ventured to New York in the early 1960s where he joined The Au Go Go Singers, which also included Richie Furay.

While touring, the group found themselves in Canada performing alongside Neil Young and The Squires. Young later joined The Mynah Birds, which included Bruce Palmer and a hot guitarist/lead singer named James Johnson, later known as Rick James.

Stills and Furay migrated to Los Angeles in 1966, and folk-rock folklore has it that, while stuck in a traffic jam, Stills looked across at a hearse being driven by none other than Young with Palmer as a passenger. With the addition of ex-Dillards drummer Dewey Martin, the group named themselves, The Herd. Within months, they became the house band at L.A.'s famed Whiskey Au Go Go and signed with Charles Greene and Brian Stone, managers of Sonny and Cher. The result was a record deal with Atlantic's Atco affiliate. They remained The Herd until one member saw a steamroller bearing the brand name, Buffalo Springfield.

The promotional "buzz" on the group was so great that they were able to perform as a featured act at The Hollywood Bowl on July 25, 1966 before their first record was issued. Their initial singles, "Nowadays, Clancy Can't Even Sing" and "Burned" received little radio response outside of L.A., but the third, a Stills song called "For What It's Worth (Stop, Hey What's That Sound)," led vocally by Furay, became a protest anthem.

> *Based upon what's happening today in the teen-age world of protest from coast to coast, producer Charlie Greene and Brian Stone have a top of the chart contender here. Strong, slow beat, message lyric and top performance should hit hard and strong. (12/31/66) (#7 Pop)*

Before they could enjoy the rewards of their hit, Palmer was deported to Canada because of a visa infringement. He was replaced by Jim Fielder (later of Blood, Sweat & Tears). Rifts developed between Young and Stills, resulting in Young leaving and returning several times. By September 1967, their engineer, Jim Messina, was a member of the group, playing bass.

The group issued a series of singles in 1967, but none had the chart impact of their initial hit.

Bluebird.
> *The West Coast group offers an intriguing folk-rock item that should prove to be a sales giant. (7/1/67) (#58 Pop)*

Rock 'n' Roll Woman.
> *With even more sales and programming potential than their recent "Bluebird" hit, the group should quickly surpass the former disk on the Hot 100. (9/16/67) (#44 Pop)*

Expecting to Fly.
> *Easy-beat, folk-flavored Neil Young ballad, culled from their LP by popular demand, is well performed by the group. (12/16/67) (#98 Pop)*

1968 brought forth two more singles, neither of which showed much action.

Uno Mundo.
> *Raucous rocker, well performed, is a catchy discotheque winner. (4/20/68)*

On the Way Home.
> *Driving easy-beat rocker with much play and sales potential. (9/28/68) (#82 Pop)*

In May 1968, after a final Los Angeles show, the band disbanded. Furay and Messina formed Poco, and Messina later became half of the hit duo, Loggins and Messina. Young attained star status as a solo act. Stills formed the first so-called super-group, Crosby, Stills and Nash, which also included Neil Young in 1970, 1971, and again in 1988.

Dewey Martin tried keeping the Buffalo Springfield name alive by recruiting three new members, but they never recorded and soon separated. Dewey needn't have bothered, as fans have kept the name and their music alive longer than anyone imagined.

B THE JOHNNY URNETTE TRIO

Johnny Burnette: Guitar, vocals
Born: 3/25/34, Memphis, TN (died 8/1/64)
Dorsey Burnette: Bass, vocals
Born: 12/28/32, Memphis, TN (died 8/19/79)
Paul Burlison: Guitar
Born: 2/4/29, Brownsville, TN
Influences: Elvis Presley

Rockabilly artists Johnny and Dorsey Burnette were compared with Elvis Presley in their early days.

The Burnettes were born in Memphis, went to high school with Presley, and even worked at Crown Electric Company in 1954, the same place Elvis worked. Brought up on country music and The Grand Ole Opry shows, the two formed a country band in the early 1950s playing dances and clubs throughout Mississippi, Arkansas, and Louisiana.

In 1953, Johnny and Dorsey joined with neighbor and fellow Crown Electric employee, Paul Burlison, forming The Johnny Burnette Trio (sometimes called The Johnny Burnette Rock and Roll Trio). Paul played guitar with a buzzsaw style, and was a former sideman for Howlin' Wolf. They cut their first record, "Your Undecided" in late 1953 for the tiny Von label of Mississippi. Not long after, their friend Elvis recorded his first single and appeared as a guest artist on one of Burnette's shows. When Presley became a hit with Sun Records, the trio auditioned for Sun owner Sam Phillips, who turned them down, concluding they sounded too much like "The King."

In March 1956, after seeing Elvis on TV, the trio took off for New York. Johnny worked in a factory and Dorsey and Paul became electricians while they pursued auditions. After three winning weeks on Ted Mack's Amateur Hour, Coral Records signed the trio, although their debut was reviewed only as Johnny Burnette.

You're Undecided/Tear It Up.
> *Burnette shapes up as an impressive country talent in the popular country rock and roll vein. On the basis of a tremendous primitive quality, the lad rates plenty of exposure, both on disks and in other entertainment medium. (5/26/56)*

"Tear It Up," originally issued as the B-side, is generally considered the classic today (recorded by The Yardbirds, mid-1960s). Two more singles followed.

Oh Baby Blue 74
> *Burnette gives a spirited tune the old Presley approach with a frantic delivery and a strong band. (8/4/56)*

The Train Kept a-Rollin' 84
> *Lively, uninhibited warbling in the Presley groove by Burnette, with solid guitar backing. . . . Could go both pop and c.&w. (10/13/56)*

"Train" became the first single with a fuzz tone guitar sound when, during a performance, Paul's Fender Deluxe amp fell down, loosening a tube and creating the unique sound. When they went into record, Paul just loosened the tube again! (It was also a 1960s hit for the Yardbirds.)

In November, Dorsey quit live performances and signed with Abbott Records as a solo act.

Let's Fall in Love **69**
> *Presley-type vocal on an attractive up-tempo ballad with a steady beat. (11/24/56)*

At a Distance **73**
> *A weeper, slow-paced in tempo. Burnette sings it with a lot of heart. Builds as it goes along. (2/23/57)*

Dorsey was replaced by Tommy Austin, and the trio soon found themselves performing in an Alan Freed film classic.

Lonesome Train **78**
> *A rockabilly style blues that was featured in the pic, "Rock, Rock, Rock." Burnette, with help from echo chamber and a down home guitar backing, gets a good marketable sound. Demand is still good for this. (1/5/57)*

With little success, Burlison returned to Memphis and started a construction business while John and Dorsey moved to Los Angeles in September 1957, concentrating on writing and recording. Johnny began recording as a solo act.

Eager Beaver Baby **75**
> *Burnette sells a fast-moving rock and roller with verve and breathless vitality. The Presley-styled warbler hasn't made it yet but this side could pull a sizable amount of jockey play even if counter action is slow. (5/20/57)*

If You Want It Enough **73**
> *An interesting rockabilly performance, exaggerated to the point where some of the grunts and groans sound like a native Hawaiian chanter. Side has the best chance of a moderately interest coupling. (12/16/57)*

Within a year, the brothers had four hits with Rick Nelson, "Waitin' in School," "It's Late," "Believe What You Say," and "Just a Little Too Much" (written by Johnny alone). Dorsey signed with Imperial, still searching for the elusive hit, which

he finally achieved with "(There Was a) Tall Oak Tree," a song Nelson had rejected.

You Come as a Miracle.
★ ★ ★   *Expressive reading by Burnette on effective rockaballad. With choral backing. Merits spins. (3/9/59)*

Misery.
★ ★ ★   *Burnette sings of the heartache he undergoes with a fickle chick. Good blues pairing by the chanter. (9/7/59)*

(There Was a) Tall Oak Tree.
★ ★ ★   *Light, bright rocker receives a happy reading by Burnette over a solid rhythm backing. This could get some action. (1/11/60) (#23 Pop)*

Hey Little One.

> *Burnette has strong followup to his hit, "Tall Oak Tree," in an emotion-packed reading. (5/2/60) (#48 Pop)*

Johnny meanwhile joined Freedom, which was later folded into Liberty Records.

I'll Never Love Again.
★ ★ ★   *Soft warbling by Burnette on a pretty rockaballad. Light chorus and rhythm accompany. Side rates spins. (7/20/59)*

Don't Do It.
★ ★ ★   *Countryish rocker gets a peppy outing from Burnette with a bright chorus and ork assist. This, too, can move. (3/21/60)*

The brothers reunited briefly in 1960.

Blues Stay Away From Me.
★ ★ ★   *The Burnettes chant in a dual-shouting style an interesting country-based blues in the train tradition. This side has interest. (4/18/60)*

Johnny, meanwhile, started to score some hits.

Cincinnati Fireball/Dreamin'.

> *Burnette's showmanly vocalizing is aptly showcased on . . . an infectious r.&r. ditty with a catchy beat. Flip is pleasant theme with attractive reading by the lad. One to watch. (5/30/60) (B-side, #11 Pop)*

I Beg Your Pardon/You're Sixteen.

Here's a nicely contrasting coupling for Burnette. Top side is a pretty ballad with good lyrics while the flip also features solid chanting of an up-tempo effort. (10/17/60) (B-side, #8 Pop)

Little Boy Sad.

Johnny Burnette will have three smashes in a row with this new disk. He sings the rhythm tune with real feeling over a substantial ork and chorus backing. (1/23/61) (#17 Pop)

God, Country and My Baby.

Burnette, a hot man on the charts recently, has a good cover of the martial, patriotic styled love ballad, of the boy who's leaving for duty in Germany. It can cash in as a timely item, well performed. (10/2/61) (#18 Pop)

In 1961, Dorsey moved to Dot and a more country style; a year later, he was recording for Reprise, whereas Johnny journeyed to Chancellor.

Johnny Burnette:
Clown Shoes.

An impassioned performance of a story of a broken love affair . . . ably supported by the chorus and ork arrangement. A first-rate side for the market. (2/10/62) (#35 Pop [U.K.])

Damn the Defiant.

★ ★ ★ ★ *Bright march novelty about the British ship the H.M.S. Defiant and its World War II exploits. It has a rather confusing lyric though, which hurts its chances. Burnette sings it with spark. (8/18/62)*

Party Girl.

Young Burnette . . . [gives] an impassioned reading of a surging ballad about a fickle lass. Country-styled tune with a wild pop backing has a chance for sales. Watch it. (10/20/62)

Dorsey Burnette:
Feminine Touch.

★ ★ ★ *Unusual material, based on the Biblical story of how woman was made.*

Burnette sings this to lush backing which always carries a strong rhythm figure. Watch it. (9/25/61)

Dyin' Ember.

★ ★ ★ ★ *The boy is reminiscing on this weeper. He sells the lyric with proper pathos while strings and voices fill the background. Latin beat adds character, too. (12/11/61)*

Castle in the Sky.

★ ★ ★ ★ *Lovely ballad here is handled with good feeling by the lad. Arrangement is tastefully done, featuring strings and vocal chorus.*

In 1964, Johnny formed his own label, but after one release ("Bigger Man") he drowned in a boating accident in Clear Lake, California.

After nine years off the charts, Dorsey hit with "The Greatest Love" in 1969. In 1972, he joined Capitol, beginning a streak of 14 country hits, including "I Let Another Good One Get Away" (#42 Pop), "In the Spring" (#21 Pop), and "Darling, Don't Come Back."

Burnette has had some near misses, and now he has a genuine hit on his hands. With help from the Sound Company, he has handled a Larry Muhoberac arrangement with skill. It's his best ever. (7/28/73) (#26 Pop)

In 1973, after a 20-year career, Dorsey was ironically voted "Most Promising Newcomer" by The Academy of Country Music. His last country hit was "Here I Go Again" (#77 Pop) on Elektra in 1979. That same year, Dorsey, aged 46, passed away of a heart attack at his Woodland Hills, California home.

Both Burnette brothers' legacy have continued through their sons, Rocky (Johnny's) and Billy (Dorsey's); Billy even played lead guitar for a while with Fleetwood Mac.

THE BYRDS

James "Roger" McGuinn: Vocals, guitar
Born: 7/13/42, Chicago, IL
Gene Clark: Vocals, percussion
Born: 11/17/41, Tipton, MO
David Crosby: Vocals, guitar
Born: 8/14/41, Los Angeles
Chris Hillman: Vocals, bass
Born: 12/4/42, Los Angeles
Mike Clarke: Drums
Born: 6/3/43, New York City
Influences: Beatles, Limeliters, Bob Dylan, Chad Mitchell Trio, New Christy Minstrels
Influenced: Eagles, Fleetwood Mac, Tom Petty, Crosby, Stills and Nash

One of the early exponents of folk-rock and the founding fathers of country-rock, the Byrds have enjoyed enduring popularity since their original hits of the 1960s.

The group came together in 1964 as a result of the meeting of Jim McGuinn, David Crosby, and Gene Clark at L.A.'s Troubadour on a hootenanny night. McGuinn (whose parents authored the best-selling book, *Parents Can't Win*) had already apprenticed with The Chad Mitchell Trio for two years, worked with The Limeliters, was Bobby Darin's lead guitarist, and wrote arrangements for Judy Collins. Crosby was a member of Les Baxter's Balladeers, whereas Clark had been with The New Christy Minstrels. Chris Hillman, who was a cowboy in northern California cattle country during his teens, led a folk-country group, The Hillmen. The only nonfolk influenced member was jazz drummer Mike Clarke.

First called The Jet Set and soon after The Beefeaters, the group recorded one single for Elektra, "Please Let Me Love You." When it failed, the band recorded an LP's worth of demos, including four songs by Bob Dylan.

They now became The Byrds (as with The Jet Set, McGuinn was enamored with planes, flight, and music that would fly) and through the efforts of erstwhile A&R director Jim Dickson garnered a showcase for Columbia A&R executive, Terry Melcher (son of Doris Day and former member of the surf group, The Rip Chords). The band was signed in September 1964, and while they prepared their first LP, a friend of Dickson's came to see the group, Bob Dylan. He was impressed enough to offer them a song of his, "Mr. Tambourine Man." The Byrds' recording was the start of the "electric folk-rock" band sound and it climbed to #1 by June 26, 1965. Interestingly, the song had already been recorded by Dylan but not yet released.

Unlike many acts whose electrifying performances were part and parcel of their talent from the start, The Byrds' first shows (at Ciro's on the Sunset Strip in Hollywood, March 1965) were an embarrassment. Frayed nerves, unreliable equipment, and less-than-enthusiastic fans earned them dubious reviews. The group had found a comfortable recording niche, however, and their second single, "All I Really Want to Do" kept the momentum going.

Another hot pop folk-flavored Bob Dylan tune is offered by the dynamic group. (6/26/65) (#46 Pop)

Their next single, a cover of Pete Seeger's adaptation of a Biblical text called "Turn, Turn, Turn," became The Byrds' biggest success.

Performed with respect and taste and a solid dance beat backing. A Winner! (10/16/65) (#1 Pop)

Unfortunately, it was also their last Top-10 hit. Although their singles were no longer chart toppers, the group's first few LPs all went Top 30.

The group turned to a more psychedelic sound on the classic "Eight Miles High."

Big beat rhythm rocker with soft lyric ballad vocal and off-beat instrumental backing could be another "Turn, Turn, Turn." (4/2/66) (#14 Pop)

5 D (Fifth Dimension).
Hot on the heels of "Eight Miles High" comes this off-beat lyric rocker with chart-topping potential. (7/2/66) (#44 Pop)

This was followed by two novelties.

Mr. Spaceman.
> *Off-beat rhythm material with clever lyrics from the pen of Jim McGuinn. Novelty has the ingredients of a top-of-the-chart item. (9/10/66) (#36 Pop)*

So You Want to Be a Rock 'n' Roll Star.
> *Powerful rocker with teen-oriented lyric about becoming rock star and the outcome of that stardom. Could prove a giant. (1/14/67) (#29 Pop)*

The latter was inspired by the overnight success of the Monkees.

In mid-1967, The Byrds returned to their roots, folk, and Dylan, including Bob's "My Back Pages."

> *Group returns to the sound of their earlier hits, and this plaintive folk rocker should match their success. (3/8/67) (#30 Pop)*

You Ain't Going Nowhere.
> *Bob Dylan material and the group's first session cut in Nashville offers a strong sales item for both pop and country charts, infectious rhythm material and good lyric line, well performed. (4/13/68) (#74 Pop)*

By this time, the band made a variety of changes, with Crosby leaving over creative differences. Gene Clark could no longer deal with his fear of flying, and Mike Clarke also left. New members Gram Parsons (guitar, vocals) and Kevin Kelly (drums) added a decidedly country element. Jim McGuinn at this time changed his name to Roger McGuinn.

Although relatively unsuccessful, their late 1960s singles and LPs became influential in the 1970s country rock boom. Parsons left the group to form The Flying Burrito Brothers along with Chris Hillman; they were replaced by Skip Battin and Clarence White. The group enjoyed some success thanks to the inclusion of McGuinn's countryish "Ballad of Easy Rider" in the famous hippie motorcycle film starring Dennis Hopper and Peter Fonda. Minor hits followed.

Jesus Is Just Alright.
> *Group made a Hot 100 comeback with their recent "Ballad of Easy Rider"*

> *and this potent folk rocker . . . should bring them even higher on the chart. The Terry Melcher production work is first rate. (1/10/70) (#97 Pop)*

Chestnut Mare.
> *The rock ballad will put them back in the Hot 100 rapidly. (11/7/70) (#19 Pop [U.K.])*

From 1968 to 1973, several performing personalities were part of the Byrds, including John Hartman, Skip Battin (of Skip and Flip "It Was I" fame), and Daryl Dragon (later of the Captain and Tennille). In 1973, the original band reformed for a reunion album, and then disbanded. Crosby went on to form the supergroup Crosby, Stills and Nash, Hillman formed The Flying Burrito Brothers with Gram Parsons, and then played in Stephen Stills's Manassas and with the short-lived supergroup, Souther, Hillman, and Furay. Gene Clark also was a "Burrito" and a member of Firefall; he performed as a solo artist into the early 1990s, when he died of natural causes at age 46. McGuinn segued between solo early Byrd style LPs and occasional reunions with Hillman and Clark. During 1975, he was featured in Bob Dylan's "Rolling Thunder Revue," and in 1977 formed a new band, Thunderbyrd. Through the 1990s, he has performed in smaller concerts and colleges as a solo. A boxed set of Byrds recordings issued in 1992 brought yet another reunion, this time of McGuinn, Hillman, and David Crosby, who recorded a few tracks to end the set.

THE CADILLACS

Earl Carroll: Lead vocals
Born: 11/2/37, New York City
Robert Phillips: Vocals
Born: 1935
John "Gus" Willingham: Vocals
Born: 1937
James "Papa" Clark: Vocals
Born: 1937
Laverne Drake: Vocals
Born: 1938

Influences: Five Keys, Five Crowns
Influenced: Frankie Lymon and The Teenagers,
    Temptations, Skyliners, Marcels, Monotones,
    Capris, many others

The first successful rock 'n' roll group to stress choreography, The Cadillacs were one of the 1950s' most exciting visual acts.

Led by Earl Carroll, the quintet of New York City (7th Avenue and 131st Street) youths cut their vocal eye teeth on R&B at Saint Mark's Church's Friday night "Battle of the Groups" starting in 1953. They were known as The Carnations, because each member wore one in his lapel. An introduction by Five Crowns member Lover Patterson to Esther Navarro resulted in the song-writing secretary changing their name to The Cadillacs.

Within four weeks, Esther had the first of the so-called "Car Groups" signed to Josie records, and their first single "Gloria" hit the market (July 1954). Although only a regional seller, the song became the yardstick by which thousands of singing groups would measure their harmonic abilities in practices, auditions, and recordings for the next 20 years.

Excellent singles like "Wishing Well," "No Chance," and "Down the Road" solidified their local base but still couldn't bring them national attention. They began to polish their performing skills, matching their zany personalities to ever-more-intricate dance routines in small clubs. On a fateful night in the spring of 1955, the Quintet sat down front at The Apollo Theater to hear an Atlantic group, The Regals, wailing, "Got the Water Boiling." Anyone having heard that "jump" classic will know where the melody came from for The Caddy's next 45, the classic "Speedoo." Written lyrically by Navarro or Carroll (whose nickname was "Speedy"), depending upon which story of doo wop folklore you believe, "Speedoo"'s national prominence was so great that Speedy changed his nickname to "Speedoo." The song was reviewed twice in *Billboard,* once on its release, and after it started to race up the charts.

> *Aptly titled, this rollicking ditty comes on like a blockbuster and gives the ever more popular group one of their best possibilities yet to hit the big money. (10/29/55) (#17 Pop, #3 R&B)*

> *This record has been a "sleeper" that has taken on major proportions the past two weeks. It has been stirring as much action in pop markets as in the r&b. In fact, it placed on the Detroit and Cleveland pop territorial charts this week. It is also a good seller in New York, Atlanta, Durham, St. Louis and Chicago. (12/10/55)*

Three more masterful singles followed in 1956. J. R. Baily replaced Drake as "Zoom," "Woe Is Me" ("A good rhythm side . . . with an insistent toe-tickling beat"; 6/9/56), and "The Girl I Love" continued their East Coast popularity.

By Christmas time, the group parlayed their dance steps into full routines courtesy of dance master Cholly Atkins (who went on to teach most of the Motown acts their steps). The Cadillacs' Christmas single, "Rudolph, The Red-Nosed Reindeer," became their second R&B hit as the group debuted their now polished skills at Alan Freed's Academy of Music Holiday show.

> *This novelty has a lot of appeal apart from its holiday theme, and as a result it has started to sell well ahead of most Christmas records. As well established as it is now, it is clear that this will be one of the records that is going to be programmed and sold most of this season. The trade should be forewarned. (12/8/56) (#11 R&B)*

For a short period in 1957, The Caddys split into two entities and, in a rare development, both recorded for Josie. The "New" Cadillacs were Baily, Bobby Spencer, Champ Rollow, and Bill Lindsey. The "Original" Cadillacs (as the label and reviews read) were Carroll, Phillips, Earl Wade, and Charlie Brooks.

Cadillacs:
Sugar Sugar 83

> *A high-flying chunk of rhythm wax. There's a great beat and the lead and backup boys give it a strong outing. This can stir action. Watch it. (2/16/57)*

Cadillacs:
My Girl Friend 78
> *Up-tempo tune with fast-paced hand-clapping gets a vigorous workout . . .*

Performance is better than material, but it has a chance. (6/3/57)

Original Cadillacs:
Buzz Buzz Buzz 70
Cover of the number launched by the Hollywood Flames. . . . Group lacks its old vitality and polish here. (12/2/57)

The acts soon merged (Carroll, Wade, Baily, Phillips, and Spencer) as neither was succeeding nationally. The resulting next single was "Speedoo Is Back" ("A swinging, driving rocker with cute lyrics and a good vocal by the boys. It has a chance for coin"; 4/14/58), an inevitable attempt to cash in on their original hit that didn't chart.

When it failed, the group took a page out of The Coasters' book, cutting the novelty "Peek-a-Boo" ("the same, infectious quality as 'Yakety Yak' . . . [a] catchy novelty [that] could mean big coin"; 10/27/58) (#28 Pop, #20 R&B). More Coasters' "Copy Cat" 45s followed, "Copy Cat" (2/23/59) and "Cool It Fool" ("sparkling group work on the teen-appeal lyrics. Honking tenors and danceable rhythm help give [it] the hit sound"; 4/20/59).

1960 started with some promising sides, although no chart makers, and ended with the act signed to a larger label, Mercury. Mercury paid to get The Cadillacs, but by now three-fifths of the group were from The Solitaires. By 1961, the "Revolving Door Car Company" issued their last chart single with a lineup including one Cadillac, two Penguins, one Miracle, one Solitaire, The Ray Charles Singers, and Doc Severinsen on trumpet. Speedoo then packed his Cadillac and drove over to sing with The Coasters.

Through various changes (at one point in 1964, four ex-Solitaires recorded as The Cadillacs on "Fool"), Earl Carroll (who rejoined in 1979) has maintained a well-oiled Cadillac machine that still personifies their rock 'n' roll tradition.

FREDDY CANNON

Real name: Frederick Picariello
Birthdate: 12/4/39
Birthplace: Lynn, MA
Influences: Chuck Berry, Big Joe Turner, Buddy and Ella Johnson
Influenced: Matchbox (British Group)

With a contagious beat, boundless enthusiasm, and a trademark primal scream—"Woo"—Freddy Cannon made an exciting and endearing contribution to early 1960s' rock 'n' roll.

In 1956, as a 16-year-old guitarist, he played on The G-Clefs' hit "Ka-Ding-Dong" (#24). Shortly thereafter, he became the lead singer of a local vocal group, The Spindrifts, whose 45 "Cha Cha Do" on Hot is a collector's treasure today.

In the late 1950s, Picariello formed a band named Freddy Karow and The Hurricanes. Among his early compositions was a song he cowrote with his mother titled "Rock & Roll Baby." He played a demo of it for Boston deejay Jack McDermott who sent it to Swan Records' owner Frank Slay. Slay gave the tune to producer Bob Crewe, who renamed it "Tallahassee Lassie." The tune wasn't the only thing renamed. Swan co-owner Bernie Benick christened the teenager Freddy Cannon. He immediately quit his job as a truck driver and soon became known as "Boom-Boom," inspired by the pounding drum sound on his record as well as his new last name.

Cannon makes his debut with a pounding rocker that should place him on the charts in short order. The side really moves, and the lad handles the tune with spirit. (5/4/59) (#6 Pop, #13 R&B)

Freddy was an immediate hit in England, although hometown lad Tommy Steele's version of Cannon's song narrowly beat out the original, reaching #16 on the charts. Cannon's updating of "Chattanooga Shoe-Shine Boy" and other old Southern-style standards kept his star on the rise.

Way Down Yonder in New Orleans.

Gets a driving new treatment with lots of colorful ork effects to back the solid warble. (11/2/59) (#3 Pop, #14 R&B)

Chattanooga Shoe-Shine Boy.

Cannon revives "Shoe-Shine Boy" in his familiar dynamic way over a rhythmic ork assist. (1/25/60) (#34 Pop)

Cannon's only two-sided charter came in 1960 with two originals, "Jump Over" and "The Urge."

Freddy Cannon has two hot bids to keep his hit string alive. "Jump Over" is a rousing rocker that is handled with zest. "The Urge" is a pounding blues. (4/11/60) (#28 Pop, #60 R&B)

When his first LP, "The Explosive Freddy Cannon," reached #1 in Britain, he set off on a U.K. tour. His label Swan kept cranking out oldies (e.g., "Muskrat Ramble") revisited, although, as in the case of "My Blue Heaven," the flip received all the action.

My Blue Heaven/Humdinger.

Cannon is in great form with a pairing that adds up to something old and something new. The first standard is done rock style for effective results. Flip features more lively work on a driving beat tone. Both have a chance. (9/19/60) (B-side, #59 Pop)

Buzz Buzz a-Diddle-It/Opportunity.

[Buzz] is a swinging novelty-rhythm item with effective banjo work on the backing. Flip, similar in mood and tempo to Lloyd Price's "Personality" hit, has a fine rocking beat. (4/3/61) (#51 Pop)

Walk to the Moon/Transition Sister.

Freddie Cannon, who improves with each outing, handles these two bright sides in engaging style. Top side, a catchy blues ballad, is sung with style and the second, another fine novelty, receives a potent vocal, too. Arrangements are in the teen groove. (7/3/61) (#35 Pop)

1962 started with the support of Danny and The Juniors on "Twistin' All Night Long" (#68) but it wasn't a hit. Then Cannon hammered American radio with the pulsating "Palisades Park," written by future "Gong Show" host Chuck Barris.

★ ★ ★ ★ *Showmanly multitrack vocal by Cannon on exuberant r.&r. ditty with bright beat. Teen appeal side. (4/21/62) (#3 Pop, #15 R&B)*

In 1963, he had a feature performance in the British film *Just for Fun.* Meanwhile, his U.S. releases, such as "What's Gonna Happen when Summer's Gone" and "If You Were a Rock and Roll Record" settled into the middle of the charts. By 1964, Cannon fired his first volley under the Warner Brothers logo, "Abigail Beecher." It put him back in the Top 20.

His best effort in some months. It's a wild, tearing swinger that has humor and drive. Abigail is a real Beecher. (1/18/64) (#16 Pop)

Action.

From the TV series "Where the Action Is" this wailing rouser has the hot possibilities of Cannon's past hit "Palisades Park." (7/17/65) (#13 Pop)

"The Dedication Song" was also a hit during the mid-1960s. Although record success eluded him after 1966, he remained a top celebrity in England. His late 1960s' recordings of exuberant versions of past hits like "Rock Around the Clock" and "Sea Cruise" kept him going.

By the 1970s, Freddy was employed in promotion at Buddah records, but the energy never left him. In 1981, with the support of The Belmonts, he crafted the bubbly and appropriately titled, "Let's Put the Fun Back in Rock & Roll," his last hit. As of 1995, Cannon was still zealously performing on the oldies circuit.

THE **C**HANTELS

Arlene Smith: Lead vocals
Born: 10/4/41, Bronx, NY
Jackie Landry: Second alto
Born: 1940, Bronx, NY
Lois Harris: First tenor
Born: 1940, Bronx, NY
Sonia Goring: Second tenor
Born: 1940, Bronx, NY
Rene Minus: Alto/bass
Born: 1943, Bronx, NY
Influences: Frankie Lyman, Dinah Washington, Ruth Brown, Jerry Vale, Patti Page
Influenced: Crystals, Marvelettes, Orlons, Shirelles, Royalettes, Kathy Jean, Supremes, Ronettes

Considered by many to be the best female singing group of all time, The Chantels brought a choir-like harmony to rock 'n' roll.

Arlene Smith and her classmates were all pre-teens when they began rehearsing Gregorian chants at choir practice. By the time they reached Saint Anthony of Padua School, the 14- to 17-year-olds were seasoned harmonizers. Their performing experience came at Saint Augustine's Church talent shows with recording acts such as The Crows and The Sequins. The girls' greatest asset was Arlene, with her vibrant voice and terrific writing ability.

In 1957, the group named itself after a rival school, Saint Francis de Chantelle. Their trip to stardom started when they ran into Richard Barrett, lead singer of The Valentines, and, most importantly, End Records' A&R man. They wowed him with an impromptu a cappella performance right in front of the Broadway Theatre. Barrett was mesmerized but wondered how this angelic sounding five-girl choir would do singing rock 'n' roll.

By the summer of 1957, The Chantels' first single, "He's Gone"/"The Plea," (both written by Arlene) was issued on End. It eventually reached #71 on the pop charts. The group's next 45 was

their ticket to immortality, as *Billboard*'s reviewer enthusiastically summed up Smith's latest writing effort.

Maybe.

> *Organized confusion reins on this side. There's a powerfully belted lead, dedicated backing by the rest of the group and pounding church-like piano chords. This one has to be watched— and it has to be heard to be believed. A dangerous reading. (12/2/57) (#15 Pop, #2 R&B)*

Barrett was so excited by the group's sound and success that he quit his own group to devote more time to The Chantels. Their next review proved his decision was a good one.

Every Night/Whoever You Are.

> *The girls have two potent follow-ups to their current hit "Maybe." Both are rockaballads delivered with a danceable beat. The lead fem is given good group support with fine ork backing. (3/3/58) (#39 Pop, #16 R&B)*

The Chantels' unique sound and exquisite harmonies so captivated the public that End felt compelled to issue the first-ever EP by a female rock 'n' roll group. Of that four-song EP, "I Love You So" and "How Could You" became their fourth disk and "Sure of Love" and "Prayee" their fifth.

How Could You Call It Off?

> *The wailing chicks have strong bids with either of these two sides to keep their hit string going. "I Love You So" is a ballad-with-beat that is presented with fervent style by the lead fem with good support. "How Could You" is taken at a slower clip, but the girls register equally well. (5/2/58) (#42 Pop, #14 R&B)*

Congratulations.

> *The gals have strong contender with their latest effort. The lead fem offers an emotional warble with fine group and ork support. Excellent pop and r.&b. potential. (8/4/58)*

Prayee.

> ★★★★ *The girls hand this listenable ballad a churchy sound as they sing of love and*

prayer. It has a celestial quality, and the lead voice sells it with fervor.

Sure of Love.

★ ★ ★ *On this side the strong voiced lead comes through with another solid reading, backed well by the rest of the chicks. The backing is strong with piano featured. (11/3/58)*

Although successful, changes were in store for the group. Arlene opted for a solo career and Lois left for college. So, late in 1959, Barrett himself took over lead vocals on two superb Chantels singles. But by now the End/Gone complex was more interested in the careers of male groups like The Imperials and The Flamingos. Still, in September 1958, End released one of the first LPs of the rock age to feature a female act.

In 1960, Barrett produced a Chantels soundalike group named The Veneers, but their 45 went unnoticed. Undaunted, he paired Veneers' lead Annette Smith (no relation to Arlene) with Sonia, Jackie, and Rene and brought the revamped fem quartet to Carlton Records. In the ongoing game of record-business revenge roulette, End took The Veneers' recording and released it as by The Chantels; it became an instant collectable, but Carlton's "Look in My Eyes" kept The Chantels recording and touring with some success.

Look in My Eyes.

★ ★ ★ ★ *The gals perform with colorful vocal touches on a pleasant ballad. They are well backed by a big arrangement consisting of strings and chorus. (7/3/61) (#14 Pop, #6 R&B)*

Well I Told You.

The Chantels have a solid follow-up to their current hit with this bright item, which is almost an answer to "Hit the Road, Jack." They sell it well and the unidentified male vocal adds style. (11/6/61) (#29)

Summertime.

★ ★ ★ ★ *The Gershwin standard is treated to a tasteful performance by the girls over moody ork support. (2/24/63)*

Their last chart single, "Eternally" (#77 Pop) produced by Barrett, was released in 1963 by Luther Dixon's Ludix label. Stops at 20th (1965),

Verve (1966), and RCA (1970) did not prove successful and the girls retired in 1970. Arlene, meanwhile, joined forces with then-prodigy Phil Spector for one single, a cover of The Clovers' "Love, Love, Love" (Big Top, 1961). In 1973, by then a Juilliard School of Music graduate, Arlene started a new Chantels with Pauline Moore and Barbara Murray. To this day, when not working as a Bronx school teacher, she and her Chantels still perform at oldies shows. The other original Chantels all married and stayed in the New York area.

RAY CHARLES

Real Name: Ray Charles Robinson
Birthdate: 9/23/30
Birthplace: Albany, GA
Influences: Nat "King" Cole, Muddy Waters, Charles Brown
Influenced: Rascals, Righteous Brothers, Tom Jones, Paul Revere and The Raiders, Johnny Rivers, Ray Stevens, Joe Cocker, Maurice Williams, Joey Dee, many more

Ray Charles is one of the best-known, most consistent hit makers in any style of popular music.

Ray Charles is known simply but eloquently as "The Genius." That accolade is even more profound when you consider that the singer, composer, arranger, and pianist has been blind (owing to untreated glaucoma) since age six. Although he played classical music at Saint Augustine's School for the Blind in Orlando, Florida, from 1937 to 1945, his preference was boogie woogie and pop. By the time both of his parents died (within a five-year span), the 16-year-old Ray Charles Robinson was playing with Joe Anderson's and Henry Washington's bands in Jacksonville.

Having studied composing and arranging (by Braille) in addition to trumpet, clarinet, alto sax, and organ, 17-year-old Ray was ready to seek out new musical styles.

He asked a friend to point out the farthest place from Florida on a map and, with $600 in savings, R. C. moved to Seattle, Washington, and began playing piano at the Rockin' Chair Club.

In 1947, he formed a Nat "King" Cole-styled act, The Maxson Trio, performing blues and jazz. The combination of his Southern gospel, blues, and pop upbringing blended with jazz gave him a style that attracted Downbeat Records, who signed him in 1949. To avoid confusion with noted fighter "Sugar" Ray Robinson, he dropped his last name as his first single, "Confessin' Blues," became a hit (#2 R&B).

Though most fans are familiar with Ray's Atlantic releases, he had almost 40 singles on Swingtime (formerly Downbeat) between 1949 and 1952.

All to Myself 72–72–71–72
Charles, in the Nat Cole-Chas Brown school, does a good job with a mournful lonesome blues, with quiet, effective trio backing. (6/30/51)

Kissa Me Baby 77–78–76–77
Charles teams with another male singer in a shout reading of a typical rocker. The ork and the chanters' spirit are formidable, but the material is just average. (2/16/52) (#8 R&B)

His first parlay into a more bluesy influenced style was 1952's "Hey Now."

Hey Now 76
Using a blues shouting style, Charles comes up with rocker in the vein of the Rubber Legs Williams item of a few years back called "That's the Blues."

Baby, Won't You Please.
Again Charles comes up with a fine reading on an oldie in which he sounds so very much like Nat Cole. Trouble is, Nat Cole is still around and kicking up a storm of his own. (9/20/52)

In 1952, Atlantic bought Ray's contract from Swingtime for $2,500 and issued the single "Roll with My Baby."

Charles goes to town on a rollicking rhythm opus for a spirited effort. Platter should do right fine on the coin boxes. (10/18/52)

His first Atlantic hit was "It Should Have Been Me" (#5 R&B, April 1954) followed by "Don't You Know."

This disk has been climbing at a steady, slow pace and made the charts this week. It has maintained steady strength in Boston, New York, Philadelphia, Cleveland, Detroit and Chicago, and is particularly strong down South. (8/21/54) (#10 R&B)

Having now formed his own band, Ray began merging his secular lyrics with gospel tunes, so that "This Little Light of Mine" became "This Little Girl of Mine" and "How Jesus Died" became "Lonely Avenue." 1955 was a banner year, opening with the two-sided smash, "I've Got a Woman" (#1 R&B) b/w "Come Back."

"Woman" is one of the most infectious blues sides to come out on any label since the summer. It has a rocking, driving beat and a sensational vocal by the chanter. "Come Back" is a slow, meaningful ballad, and it also features a wonderful vocal. Both sides are outstanding. (1/1/55) (B-side, #4 R&B)

Another two-sided hit followed, "A Fool for You"/"This Little Girl of Mine."

Records like this don't come along often. Charles, who wields an incredible spell over his live audiences, gets much of that commanding quality across on these almost gospel-styled blues disks of his. "Fool" is the potent slow blues side, while "Girl" is the uptempo romp. In both, Charles['s] feeling and his great musicianship emanate from every bar of the vocal and arrangement. Look for double-barreled action with this one. (6/4/55) (A-side, #1 R&B; B-side, #9 R&B)

A third two-sided smash ended the year, "Greenbacks"/"Blackjack."

1956 opened with another #1 R&B song, "Drown in My Own Tears" ("another powerhouse blues weeper," 2/18/56), followed by "Hallelujah, I Love Her So" (#5 R&B) in May and "Lonely Avenue" in September.

Lonely Avenue.

> *Some uncommon and extremely classy slow blues material in a minor strain. It couples Charles's inimitable spiritual and blues moods into a potential smash. (9/15/56) (#6 R&B)*

1957 brought his first pop crossover hit, "Swanee River Rock" ("a snappy adaptation of the Stephen Foster cleffing with smart, staccato choral backing"; 8/9/57) (#34 Pop, #14 R&B). After eight years of recording and 17 R&B hits, Ray finally had a Pop Top-10 million seller in 1959 with the now legendary "What'd I Say."

> *Fine rhumba blues effort by Charles. He shouts it out in persuasive style, and he backs his vocal with some great piano work and good ork support. (6/15/59) (#6 Pop, #1 R&B)*

Also in 1959 came Ray's first country cover of Hank Snow's "I'm Movin' On," a bold move for an R&B act.

> *He reads "I'm Movin' On" the Hank Snow hit of a few seasons ago in his usual, gospel-flavored manner with a fem chorus in strong support. (10/19/59) (#40 Pop, #11 R&B)*

A few more releases (including instrumentals like "Sweet 16 Bars" [#13 R&B]) and Ray moved to ABC Paramount when Atlantic couldn't match their unheard-of offer for him to own his own recordings. His first ABC single was "Sticks and Stones" followed by the immortal "Georgia On My Mind."

> *Ray Charles packs a powerful emotional wallop . . . with violins and chorus giving backing a big sound. (8/29/60) (#1 Pop, #3 R&B)*

Charles won four Grammy Awards in 1961, including "Best Male Vocal Performance" and "Best Performance by a Pop Singles Artist" (for "Georgia"), "Best Male Vocal Album Performance" for *The Genius of Ray Charles* (his first chart LP) on Atlantic, and "Best R&B Performance" for "Let the Good Times Roll" ("Charles hands this great blues a reading to match. Good band backing"; 12/28/59) (#78 Pop). Even

his instrumentals were golden, such as "One Mint Julep" ("The old R&B hit is handed a strong performance . . . Sparkling instrumental wax"). (2/27/61) (#8 Pop, #8 R&B) *Billboard* missed its mark in 1961 when it relegated "Hit the Road Jack" to an unreviewed B-side (8/28/61) (#1 Pop, #1 R&B). It became another million seller. 1961 ended with another smash, "Unchain My Heart" backed with the bluesy "On the Other Hand Baby."

> *Charles could have another two-sided smash with this waxing. "Unchain My Heart" is an exuberant, out-going rocker. Flip spotlights a tender reading by Charles on a moving blues. (11/20/61) (A-side, #9 Pop, #1 R&B; B-side, #72 Pop, #10 R&B)*

In 1962 Ray astounded fans and critics alike with his next directional change, tackling country music, but it was done so tastefully that his next single, "I Can't Stop Lovin' You" became his biggest record ever and another Grammy winner ("Best R&B Recording").

> *From Charles's current smash album of country songs come this fine coupling. First up is Don Gibson's familiar ballad while the flip ["Born to Lose"] is also an effective ballad treatment. Both can go but the first has the edge. (4/28/62) (#1 Pop, #1 R&B)*

This was followed by more singles from his album *New Sounds in Country and Western Music.* His country-pop dominance continued through 1965 with another Grammy winner for Best R&B Vocal Solo, "Crying Time."

> *The top Buck Owens country ballad is beautifully revived here much in the vein of Charles's "I Can't Stop Loving You." Top arrangement and performance. (11/20/65) (#6 Pop, #5 R&B)*

However, Charles had not forsaken his funky roots as his many mid-1960s hits testified, including "Let's Go Get Stoned."

> *Easy-go blues wailer gets an emotional reading from Charles for a strong R&B and pop market entry. (5/21/66) (#31 Pop, #1 R&B)*

In 1967–1968 Charles decided to create his own Beatles period.

Yesterday.

> *The Beatles' poignant ballad is revived in a gospel oriented sytle that should send it soaring right to the top of the Hot 100. Charles's emotional reading is hard to beat and could prove to be one of his all time greats. (11/4/67) (#25 Pop, #9 R&B)*

Eleanor Rigby.

> *A winning Charles reading . . . aimed for a high spot on the Hot 100. (6/1/68) (#35 Pop, #30 R&B)*

By 1971 Ray had spent 25 years in the business and ABC joined with Atlantic in issuing a Salute to Ray Charles LP of his hits on each label. Ray's performance of "Shake a Tail Feather" in the film *The Blues Brothers* (1980) was the catalyst for his many appearances on series TV as an actor ("St. Elsewhere," "Moonlighting").

The Genius moved to Columbia in 1983 and began a series of duets with country stars George Jones, Mickey Gilley, and Hank Williams. Ray's last R&B charter was 1979's "Just Because"; his last pop hit was "I'll Be Good to You" with Chaka Khan in 1989. In 1986 he received a special Kennedy Center award medallion from President Reagan for his achievements. Ray recorded numerous duets through the 1980s, primarily with country singers. One of the more interesting duets was cut with Billy Joel, who wrote a song especially for them to record, "Baby Grand."

> *Ever-facile composer's latest genre piece is tongue-in-cheek but letter-perfect as the two piano men warm up to those ol' melancholy blues. (3/21/87) (#75 Pop)*

To this day Ray performs worldwide.

CHUBBY CHECKER

Real Name: Ernest Evans
Birthdate: 10/3/41
Birthplace: Philadelphia, PA
Influences: Eddy Arnold, Fats Domino
Influenced: Michael Jackson

The man who made "The Twist" a household term, Chubby Checker narrowed the generation gap, bringing parents and kids onto the same dance floor.

The Philadelphia youngster started his career in the most humble of surroundings, entertaining customers by doing singing imitations at his job as a chicken plucker in a poultry market. In 1958, his boss Henry Colt arranged an audition with Cameo/Parkway owner Kal Mann.

When local TV personality Dick Clark and his wife Bobbie asked Mann to create a novelty record as a verbal Christmas card, Evans received the singing assignment. The Clarks were delighted with the results and Bobbie commented how much the rotund Evans reminded her of a young Fats Domino. Hence, Parkway's newest artist became Chubby Checker.

Six months later, Mann decided to release Chubby's recording, now called "The Class," as the B-side of "School Days, Oh School Days." *Billboard,* however, picked up on the novelty side and it became a surprise hit.

The Class.

> *Checker has a real hot side about a teacher conducting a class. As the tale unfolds, he imitates Fats Domino, the Coasters, Elvis Presley and the Chipmunks. Great novelty side. (5/11/59) (#38 Pop)*

More novelties, including "Dancing Dinosaur," followed but they couldn't get to the head of "The Class."

Samson and Delilah.

★ ★ ★ ★ *Wild drive receives a shoutin' reading by Chubby over soft ork backing. This has a shoutin' chance. (12/7/59)*

Meanwhile, Clark was getting tremendous response to a year-old Hank Ballard side called "The Twist" on his "American Bandstand" show. He asked both Freddy Cannon and Danny and the Juniors if they'd record it but both turned him down. Chubby didn't. Supported by The Dreamlovers, he recorded the song in less than 40 minutes.

★ ★ ★ ★ *A blues and it's a shouter too. The Twist is a dance and Checker tells all about it. Good rhythm side with a sound that could catch on. (6/27/60) (#1 Pop, #2 R&B)*

Checker's single was on its way to dance history and sold millions. His next 45 was his first two-sided smash. Parkway didn't miss a trick, even having Chubby guest on another version of the twist.

Whole Lotta Shakin' Goin' On/The Hucklebuck.

Chubby Checker comes through with two more wild readings in "Twist" style here and he should rack up lots of sales with both sides. Both tunes were hits a while back. (10/3/60) (A-side, #42 Pop; B-side, #14 Pop, #15 R&B)

The Little Sisters:
The Twist.

★ ★ ★ ★ *Electronic high-pitched fem voices—a la the Chipmunks—chant vivaciously on the recent hit. Watch it. Chubby Checker contributes brief vocal seg. (11/21/60)*

The New York Safety Council reported that out of one week's 54 cases of back problems reported, 49 were due to the Twist. Parkway continued issuing Checker dance sides, including another million seller, "Pony Time."

Pony Time.

 Checker has a sock cover of a catchy bluesy item with a fine teen-styled terp beat. (1/16/61) (#1 Pop, #1 R&B)

Good Good Lovin'/Dance the Mess Around.

 Another gasser of a coupling for the wild chanter. On top is a reprise of an old hit for James Brown and the Famous Flames, while the flip is another rip-roaring rocker, also out by Bobby Freeman. Both these sides should be watched. (4/10/61) (A-side, #43 Pop; B-side, #24 Pop)

The Jet/The Ray Charles-ton.

 These two items are the big ones on Chubby Checker's new compact double 33 single (four tunes on a seven-inch 33 disk) which lists as $1.49. Checker could have a smash with these wild dance sides even though they are only available on the small 33. (5/22/61)

One year after "The Twist," Checker hit with "Let's Twist Again," not only his third golden 45 but a Grammy winner for "Best Rock & Roll Record of 1961."

Let's Twist Again/Everything's Gonna Be All Right.

Chubby Checker is back and the teens should be dancing again, to both sides. "Let's Twist Again" is a rocker in his usual "Pony Time" style, and sung enthusiastically; flip is a slower, moderate paced ballad, handled with feeling. (6/12/61) (#8 Pop, #26 R&B)

"The Fly" followed ("... a wild blues with a sock swinging dance beat"; 9/18/61). (#7 Pop, #11 R&B)

In late 1961, Chubby made his film debut in the appropriately titled *Twist Around the Clock*, costarring Dion. At the same time a strange phenomena occurred. Adults started dancing to "The Twist" just as their kids were a year before. The light went on at Parkway. Checker's recording became the only non-Christmas record to top the pop charts on two separate releases.

 Parkway has re-released Checker's old hit to cash in on the new "Twist" dance fad. Checker recently sung the tune on Ed Sullivan's TV show, which should also help sales. A rocking performance which could make the charts again. (11/6/61) (#1 Pop, #4 R&B)

By early 1962, "The Twist Master" issued a couple of duets, first with Bobby Rydell and then with an uncredited Dee Dee Sharp.

 Jingle Bell Rock/Jingle Bells Imitations.

Here's a sock coupling (from the new Rydell-Checker album) which should move out fast. "Jingle Bell Rock," the old Bobby Helms hit, is wrapped up in a solid duo vocal. Flip features show-manly imitations of other disk stars. Watch both sides. (12/4/61) (#92 Pop)

Slow Twistin'/La Paloma.

 Here's Chubby again, with another powerful coupling. First up is a breezy rockin' twister, with an unbilled femme companion who is good. Flip is the old Latin-based tune, given a smart Twist treatment. (2/24/62) (#3 Pop, #3 R&B)

By mid-1962, "Mister Twister" redirected his dance posture to the "Limbo Rock" and with "Popeye the Hitch Hiker" on the flip, they were his last Top-10 singles. The dance charters kept coming with everything from "The Birdland" to "The Monkey."

Dancin' Party.

 Chubby turns away from the Twist for a smart, hand-clapping side that spots an enthusiastic vocal from the chanter over a rocking teen-slanted dance beat. (6/16/62) (#12 Pop)

Let's Limbo Some More.

 The Mann-Appell team writes another hit. Chubby's on the limbo kick with the sequel to his last hit. It's a smash that's got solid singing and danceable support. (2/9/63) (#20 Pop, #16 R&B)

Birdland.

 Chubby Checker is back with a new dance called "Birdland" and he tells the teen how to dance it with his usual enthusiasm. (5/11/63) (#12 Pop, #18 R&B)

Do the Freddie.

New dance on the scene and Checker's got it! Exciting number done is his familiar style. (3/20/65) (#40 Pop)

Cu Ma La Be Stay.

Exciting new dance from South America and more dance instruction from master Checker. (7/31/65)

Karate Monkey.

Combining the popular sport with the equally popular dance serves as a powerhouse chart contender for Checker. (12/3/66)

In 1969, Checker signed with Buddah and charted with the Beatles cover, "Back in the U.S.S.R." (#82 Pop). Through the 1970s and 1980s Chubby became a regular on the club and rock revival circuit and charted with "Running" (#91, MCA). Then, in 1988, everything came full circle for "King Twister" in a duet with the Fat Boys, as a whole new generation made "high tech twistin'" fashionable.

The Twist.

A hefty combination of the Rotund Ones and guest Chubby Checker delivers a pop/rap interpretation of the classic pound for pound. (6/11/88) (#16 Pop, #40 R&B)

THE CHIFFONS

Judy Craig: Lead vocals
Born: 8/6/46, Bronx, NY
Barbara Lee
Born: 5/16/47, Bronx, NY
Sylvia Peterson
Born: 9/30/46, Bronx, NY
Patricia Bennett
Born: 4/7/47, Bronx, NY
Influences: Shirelles

A fine female foursome, The Chiffons were the first vocal group in history to have a #1 hit produced by another vocal group.

The original trio of 13- and 14-year-olds (Judy, Barbara, and Pat) began practicing at James Monroe High School and soon met local song-smith Ronnie Mack. They literally picked their name out of a hat, as The Angels did. By the summer of 1960, they had recorded their version of a new Shirelles single, "Tonight's the Night." The surprising chart single did little for their career as two more 45s, "Never, Never!" on Wildcat and "Doctor of Hearts" on Reprise, went unnoticed.

Tonight's the Night.

★ ★ ★ ★ *The girls come through with a smart, slick reading of swinging ballad that has a bright sound. Very similar to the Shirelles' record of the tune that is already happening. (8/29/60) (#76 Pop)*

Mack, hawking his songs, came upon Bright Tunes Productions, aka The Tokens of "The Lion Sleeps Tonight" fame. They liked one of his demos, "He's So Fine," but wanted a group to record it. Afraid of losing the opportunity, Mack claimed he knew a great group, then went back to the Bronx to find one. His discovery was The Chiffons. To bolster the harmonies, he added Sylvia who had previously sung with Little Jimmy and The Tops ("Puppy Love"), another Mack creation. The Tokens then produced it (as well as playing the instruments on the session) and brought it to their first-refusal partner, Capitol Records. When Capitol passed on the song, it was released on Laurie.

This all-girl group has a great sound and they show off their bright style with a flourish on this rhythmic waxing. It has a beat and it moves. (2/9/63) (#1 Pop, #1 R&B)

The million seller by the female Chiffons as produced by the male Tokens became an industry first. The excitement of their success was tempered by the death of mentor/writer Ronnie Mack from Hodgkins disease soon after he was awarded a gold record while hospitalized.

When The Chiffons' next single, "Lucky Me," failed, The Tokens took no chances. The Chiffons' next single, "My Block," was issued under the name The Four Pennies. Their next single was again issued under The Chiffons' name. Coincidentally, both were reviewed the same day.

My Block.

Here's a new girl group with a lot of style. They do a ditty with musical significance in an arrangement that's reminiscent of some of the hit sides by The Drifters. The whole concept is mighty smart and the side could happen. (5/25/63) (#67 Pop)

One Fine Day.

The gals sell their teen-slanted rocker with feeling, showing off their fine harmonies and their fresh sound. It swings. (5/25/63) (#5 Pop, #6 R&B)

The group continued on the hit trail but abandoned The Four Pennies alter ego after their second record ("When the Boy's Happy") stalled at #95 Pop. 1964 found the girls opening for The Rolling Stones on the British group's first U.S. tour. However, during this period, they only charted once, with "Sailor Boy" ("soft romantic ballad hauntingly sung by group"; 7/4/64) (#81 Pop).

The British invasion put a halt to hits through 1964 and 1965. They stormed back in 1966 with "Sweet Talkin' Guy" (#10 Pop). It was cowritten by a young producer/writer named Doug Morris, later a top executive at Atlantic, Warner Brothers, and MCA Music. Laurie kept releasing Chiffons singles but light pop wasn't competing with psychedelic rock, soul, and the British in the late 1960s. The girls recorded one-shots for B. T. Puppy ("Secret Love") and Buddah ("So Much in Love").

Meanwhile, George Harrison was found guilty of subconscious plagiarism for his first solo single, "My Sweet Lord," which just happened to contain the melody of "He's So Fine." In a bit of belated tit-for-tat, The Chiffons came back to Laurie in 1975 for a new single, "My Sweet Lord," but it never charted. Their last hit was a reissue of "Sweet Talkin' Guy" in England, which stunned everyone by going to #4 in 1972. At the time, the girls were not even on an American label.

The Chiffons continued performing through the 1970s and 1980s. Although Barbara died in 1994, Judy, Pat, Sylvia, and Connie Haynes continue to carry on The Chiffons' tradition.

THE **C**HORDS

Carl Feaster: Lead vocals
Born: 1930s, Bronx, NY (died 1/23/81)
Jimmy Keyes: First tenor
Born: 5/22/30, Bronx, NY
Floyd McRae: Second tenor
Born: Bronx, NY
Claude Feaster: Baritone
Born: Bronx, NY
Ricky Edwards: Bass
Born: Bronx, NY
Influences: Ravens, Orioles, Four Freshmen,
     Modernaires, Ink Spots, Mills Brothers, Bing Crosby,
     Dick Haymes
Influenced: Diamonds, Fleetwoods

The Chords, a relatively obscure vocal act, carved their niche in rock 'n' roll history by becoming the first R&B group to reach the Pop Top 10.

The quintet formed in 1951 and included Carl and Claude Feaster (Tunetoppers), Jimmy Keyes (Four Notes), Floyd McRae (Keynotes), and Ricky Edwards (a previous group called The Chords). Not your typical R&B group, they never sang on street corners and were primarily practitioners of jazz and pop with a touch of R&B thrown in. By 1954, they became known as The Chords and amassed some original tunes for auditions. They first performed for Red Robin Records owner Bobby Robinson, but The Chords' timing was unlucky. Bobby listened to their song, "Sh-Boom," while lying in bed sick and impatiently turned them away.

Soon after, the quintet was heard singing their way through the turnstiles of a Manhattan subway by Joe Glaser of Associated Booking. He and his partner, Oscar Cohen, brought The Chords to Atlantic's Jerry Wexler who was looking for a group to do an R&B version of Patti Page's "Cross Over the Bridge." The Chords fit the bill and were allowed to have "Sh-Boom" issued as the B-side on Atlantic's Cat affiliate.

A rhythm version of the tune currently high on the pop charts. This beautifully harmonized reading . . . with its solid beat and happy spirit has good potential for both the pop and r.&b. markets.

The playful bounce and tasty, restrained styling of this material will also appeal to customers in both pop and r.&b. markets. The group achieves a distinctive "sound" and with it builds to an exciting climax. (4/24/54) (B-side, #5 Pop, #2 R&B)

When the record started breaking in California, Atlantic was exhilarated. When they found out "Sh-Boom" was the side making the noise, they were stunned. The record was selling so fast that Cat enlisted the aid of a competitor, Mercury Records, to help with distribution. The March 15, 1954 recording hit the Top 5 by the summertime.

Sh-Boom.
A "sleeper" that is beginning to break through. This week the disk appears on both the New York and Philadelphia territorial charts. Boston, Upstate New York, Cleveland, St. Louis and Los Angeles reports are also good. Flip is "Cross Over the Bridge." (5/22/54)

"Zippity Zum" was released while "Sh-Boom" was still climbing. Unfortunately, it might have been issued too soon and fizzled.

The Chords are sizzling in both the r.&b. and the pop fields right now with "Sh-Boom" and this new cutting should keep them just as hot. It has the feel and the flavor of "Sh-Boom" plus some new cute gimmix. Should grab plays, loot and sales. (9/11/54)

The highlight of their performing career came on the "Colgate Comedy Hour" TV show when they sang backup for New York Giants superstar outfielder Willie Mays on "Say Hey Willie."

By late 1954, the Chords' luck changed for the worse. They became The Chordcats owing to a lawsuit by the earlier named Chords group that recorded on Gem. They issued "Hold Me Baby," a soundalike for their earlier hit, under the new name to little success.

Hold Me Baby 77
> *The Chords . . . are now known as the Chordcats. If the name is unfamiliar, their material won't be, being little more than a re-write of their first hit. It swings and has a beat and their fans will want it. (12/18/54)*

Hoping for better luck, they changed their name again. This time they became The Sh-Booms in 1955, but to no avail.

In 1957, Carl and company (McRae and Edwards were replaced by now with Arthur Dix and Joe Dias) joined Vik records for one release, a reworking of the standard "I Don't Want to Set the World on Fire." The group then disbanded, but the original Chords came together in 1960 and signed with Atlantic for one last valiant effort, a version of the Rodgers and Hart standard, "Blue Moon."

> *The boys . . . turn out this standard and manage to make it sound much like "Sh-Boom" in their arrangement.*

In 1961, Atlantic reissued The Chords/Sh-Booms first single, trying once more to recapture the glory.

> ★ ★ ★ ★ *This is a reissue of the big hit of five or six years ago. Sound is not so good but disk could get new action in the current market. (11/20/61)*

Although their career was short, "Sh-Boom" was destined to be one of the earliest signs of the birth of rock 'n' roll.

LOU CHRISTIE

Real Name: Lugee Sacco
Birthdate: 2/19/43
Birthplace: Glen Willard, PA
Influences: Skyliners, Diablos, Crows, Flamingos, Hank Williams, Jacks, Four Lads, Peggy Lee

Influenced: Paul Simon, Bee Gees, Madonna, John Lennon, Robert John

Another of the falsetto fellowship of the 1960s (including Del Shannon and Frankie Valli), Christie was the only one who benefited by having a clairvoyant writing partner, a lady who, it is said, had the power to predict which of their collaborations would be hits.

Lugee Sacco's first foray into singing was with his sister Amy in the group, The Crewnecks. He attended Moon Township High School studying music and vocal technique. At 15, Christie met Twyla Herbert, a 30-year-old, red-haired mystic, during an audition in his hometown church's basement. Herbert needed a lead singer for her group, The Classics. Christie made the grade.

In 1959, they recorded "Close Your Eyes" with an introduction out of "Whispering Bells." The Classics' recording sounded like the Fleetwoods on a Dell-Vikings track but the local Starr label couldn't promote the 45. Their 1961 single, "The Jury," as Lugee and The Lions fared just as badly.

> ★ ★ ★ *The boy is guilty only of loving the girl on this new rockaballad side. Courtroom motif gets backing by a young vocal group as the boy sings in high-pitched voice. (4/17/61)*

Christie and Herbert's first collaboration to be recorded came in 1962. "The Gypsy Cried" became Christie's solo debut on Pittsburgh's C&C label. While he was considering a stage name, the record company picked one for him. When "Gypsy" started moving, the name Lou Christie was on the label (much to his chagrin). Within months, Roulette licensed the 45 for distribution and Christie had his first hit. The follow up, "Two Faces Have I" (also by Christie and Herbert) did even better (#6) but subsequent Roulette singles failed.

The Gypsy Cried.
> ★ ★ ★ ★ *Some mighty tantalizing high note work from the lad on this ballad with a beat. He is backed by a chorus of chicks and strong rhythm combo. (10/20/62) (#24 Pop)*

By 1964, Christie was on Colpix. During a Dick Clark Caravan of Stars tour, the singer became enamored with the young lead of a new group, The Supremes. But his infatuation with Diana Ross was cut short. Three days after the tour ended, Christie was ordered into the Army reserve at Fort Knox.

Guitars and Bongos.

Lou's switch to Colpix may well bring him a hit right off. Plenty of sound excitement on this side. High pitched chorus and driving beat. (8/1/64)

Have I Sinned.

Highly distinctive sound and arrangement. High registar vocal coupled with great dance beat and effective teen lyrics. The little gals should go out of their skulls with this offering. (10/31/64)

Upon his six-month discharge, Christie linked with Bob Marcucci for management (Bob handled Fabian and Frankie Avalon). Marcucci signed his newest client with MGM. But when the record company heard his latest collaboration with Herbert, they despised it so much that its final resting place became the garbage can. Pressured by Marcucci, MGM relented and issued "Lightnin' Strikes," Lou's biggest hit and only #1 record. Past labels then jumped on the Christie bandwagon.

Outside the Gates of Heaven.

With the excitement and high pitched vocal work of "Lightnin' Strikes" this one has the hit potential of all the Christie records currently in release. (2/26/66) (#95 Pop)

His next release caused more commotion than his #1 hit, being banned by stations across the country. Christie had used the term "making out." To quiet the controversy, Christie changed the lyric, rerecorded, and "Rhapsody in the Rain" became another hit.

Exciting production and excellent Christie vocal boost this as fast as his million seller, "Lightnin' Strikes." (3/12/66) (#16 Pop)

If Herbert was truly a clairvoyant, she must have known their next single, "Painter," would fail (#81 Pop). By 1967, Christie had moved to Columbia.

Shake Hands and Walk Away Cryin'.

Marking his move to Columbia, Christie has a sure-fire winner in this exciting rocker in the "Lightnin' Strikes" bag. His highpitched vocal dance beat and clever arrangements should spiral Christie back to the Hot 100 once again. (3/18/67) (#95 Pop)

In 1969, he bounced to Buddah and recorded his comeback on a Tony Romeo song.

I'm Gonna Make You Mine.

Here's just the potent bubble gum item Christie needs to spiral him back up the hot 100 chart. His most commerical entry in a long while. (7/5/69) (#10 Pop)

Christie's last chart single, "Beyond the Blue Horizon," came in 1974.

Beyond the Blue Horizon.

This is strictly from left field, but it will grow on you quickly. The old "soap opera" special is back with a sensual arrangement and Christie, now strongly into country, brings something new to the song. (12/22/73) (#80 Pop)

From the 1970s until the present day, Christie has been a regular on the oldies tour circuit. He still issues an occasional single like the medley of "Since I Don't Have You" and "It's Only Make Believe" in duet with Lesley Gore.

Medley: "Since I Don't Have You"; "It's Only Make Believe." Nostalgic pairing of '60s stars will have you reminiscing about your junior prom—or your parents' junior prom. (7/5/86)

THE CLEFTONES

Herb Cox: Lead vocals
Born: 5/6/39, Jamaica, NY
Charlie James: First tenor
Born: 2/3/39, Jamaica, NY
Berman Patterson: Second tenor
Born: 1/18/38, Jamaica, NY
William McClain: Baritone
Born: 2/19/38, Jamaica, NY
Warren Corbin: Bass
Born: 9/12/38, Jamaica, NY
Influences: Moonglows, Penguins, Cardinals, Swallows
Influenced: Excellents

The only rock 'n' roll group to form because of an election campaign, The Cleftones were a unique sounding, solid harmony quintet that haunted the halls of Jamaica High School in Queens, NY, in 1955. It was there that Cox, James, Patterson, McClain, and Corbin became campus heroes when they sang campaign slogans for the school elections.

The quintet was an outgrowth of two groups, The Clefs with Cox, Corbin, and Patterson and The Silvertones' members, James and McClain. By late 1955, The Cleftones had auditioned and been turned down by Old Town, Apollo, and Baton records but latched onto entrepreneur George Goldner, whose first Gee release was their "You Baby You." "You Baby You" sold over 150,000 singles.

> *The Cleftones chant this lively ditty with plenty of beat and nice harmony. (12/24/55) (#78 Pop)*

The Cleftones (who loved ballad style groups yet sang mostly uptempo originals) soon came up with another fine rocker destined to sell over a million copies over the decades (and 750,000 singles the first year alone). The song was "Little Girl

of Mine." 1956 continued with other high quality, upbeat 45s written by Cox, Patterson, or both.

Little Girl of Mine.
> *Sparked by a quick take-off in New York, Philadelphia, Baltimore and other Eastern cities this disk has now started to make a clean sweep of the country. Retailers and one-stops in Detroit, St. Louis, Nashville, Cleveland, Buffalo and other markets indicate that it is now one of their stronger sellers. (4/14/56) (#57 Pop, #8 R&B)*

Can't We Be Sweethearts?
> *A strong follow-up to "Little Girl of Mine." The youngsters have another tricky-beat rhythm-ballad right in the current teen-age taste groove. (6/23/56)*

Happy Memories/String Around My Heart.
> *Another strong double-header from the group that created "Can't We Be Sweethearts?" and "Little Girl of Mine." The top-listed is a spiritedly harmonized opus with a fine, swingy beat. The flip is an artfully styled ballad in which the Cleftones invest considerable emotion. Either side could bring in the teen-age crowds. (10/13/56)*

By the end of 1956, The Cleftones had performed a record 12 times at the famed Apollo Theater in New York City and appeared in nine Alan Freed shows. The "Cleffies" (friend and fan Little Richard called them, "my little Cleffies") turned out some classic rock 'n' roll sides in 1957 and 1958, including "See You Next Year," "Lover Boy," and "Beginners at Love" but Gee was not promoting their records as before.

Why You Do Me Like You Do.
> *Despite the plaintive note in the lyrics, this is a cheerful beat-ballad with a real sparkle. The group hits a swingy pace for a delightful effect. (2/2/57)*

See You Next Year.
> *Teens may go for this pretty rhythm ballad. Expressive rendition by the lead with breathy support. Fair chances. (7/1/57)*

Hey Baby.

Smartly-produced side has a cheerful group vocal with bright guitar and brass band support. Side can attract in both pop and r.&b. markets. (8/9/57)

Lover Boy.

Blues with an unusual lyric. The group's chanting is backed by smartly-arranged instrumentation featuring precise, insistent beat.

Beginners at Love.

Teen-slanted ballad with conventional triplet figure by the piano. Lead chanter does a good job, putting a lot of heart into his effort. (1/20/58)

By the middle of 1958, the group signed with Roulette Records but weak material like "Mish Mash Baby" (written by famed deejay Murray The K's mother) didn't help their chances. The Cleftones had reinvented their sound by the late 1950s as McClain and Patterson left while Gene Pearson (lead singer of The Rivileers) and Patricia Span took their place. A&R man Henry Glover, who brought the quintet to Roulette, convinced the act that old standards could be their ticket up the charts. He was right. When "Heart and Soul" took off, Roulette issued "Little Boy of Mine," one of the group's old hits as done by a teen female aggregation. Interestingly, singing along with the Delicates (who included Peggy Santiglia, later of The Angels) were none other than The Cleftones. More reworked standards followed and, although the quality was good, the promotion wasn't.

Heart and Soul.

This was a hit group a few seasons back and this rendition could bring them back into the action. It's the standard tune and it's done in the rocking, teen-slanted fashion with a swinging beat. This could happen. (4/17/61) (#18 Pop, #10 R&B)

'Deed I Do/For Sentimental Reasons.

The group has had a powerful revival with their disking of "Heart and Soul" and either of these two new offerings of oldies could click in the same manner. Both are done with style and a sound.

Watch them. (7/24/61) (B-side, #60 Pop)

Lover Come Back to Me.

★ ★ ★ ★ *The group has had hits before and they could do it again with their interesting rock arrangement of the standard. Good lead vocal is coupled with a solid backing with harmonica. Watch it. (10/27/62) (#95 Pop)*

By 1963, Pearson left for The Drifters. In 1964, smack dab in the middle of the Beatles' invasion, the #1 record in Pittsburgh was a 6-year-old reissue of "Lover Boy."

Their last single was 1990's "My Angel Lover" on Classic Artists. The group never broke up and still performs at clubs and oldies shows. In fact, in 1991, 36 years after they started, the Cleftones made their first tour of Europe. Herb Cox recently stated, "You know, we're performing more now than we did in the '60s!"

THE CLOVERS

John "Buddy" Bailey: Lead vocals
Born: 12/27/31, Washington, DC
Mathew McQuater: Second tenor
Born: 1924, Washington, DC
Harold Lucas: Baritone
Born: 8/27/32, Washington, DC
Harold Winley: Bass
Born: 5/13/33, Washington, DC
Influences: Ink Spots, Orioles, Ravens, Mills Brothers, Cats and Fiddle, Four Tunes, Dinah Washington, Billy Eckstine
Influenced: Flamingos, Five Satins, Cadillacs, Penguins, Dell-Vikings, Skyliners, Crests

The Clovers were the most successful R&B singing group of the 1950s and one of the first to be considered rock 'n' roll artists.

The brainchild of Harold "Hal" Lucas, the D.C. quartet was founded at Armstrong High School in 1946. Lucas, feeling he could use all the luck he could get, named the teens The Four Clovers and, by 1949, just The Clovers. Record store owner Lou Krefetz became their manager and brought them to New York's tiny Rainbow label, where their first Ink Spots-influenced single, "Yes Sir, That's My Baby," was issued. The Rainbow label was so small that they shared storefront space with Sonny's Deli.

Yes Sir, That's My Baby 65–66–63–65
Oldie is sung in a slow tempo on what sounds like an attempt to be different. It is, but not enough. (12/2/50)

Krefetz then moved his fledgling vocalizers to the larger Atlantic Records. Ahmet Ertegun, president of Atlantic (and the son of the former Turkish ambassador to the United States, who started the label with a $10,000 investment from a family dentist in 1949), began writing R&B songs for The Clovers. Among his songs were their debut Atlantic 45, "Don't You Know I Love You" (#14 R&B). Ertegun, writing under the name Nugetre (Ertegun spelled backward), wrote eight A- or B-sides out of the group's first nine singles. The deception was meant to avoid embarrassing his aristocratic family. After spending 21 weeks in the Top 10, The Clovers followed with a series of Ertegun-penned R&B classics.

Fool, Fool, Fool 85–85–85–85
The Clovers, riding high at the moment, should maintain their disk popularity with this well-sung, well-arranged blues. Hard-hitting performance of a clever blues idea. (10/6/51) (#1 R&B)

One Mint Julep 83–83–81–85
The Clovers come thru with a great reading of a swinging novelty item with good lyrics. The combo supports them with a good beat. A strong juke entry.

Middle of the Night 80–80–79–81
A rocking novelty is given a solid go by the vocal group, sparked by the vocal lead. The ork backs the group with gusto. (3/15/52) (A-side, #2 R&B; B-side, #3 R&B)

Wonder Where My Baby's Gone . . . .
84–84–8[sic]–84
The Clovers have a solid waxing here, one that should be a healthy follow-up to their smash "One Mint Julep." It's a blues weeper and the boys give it a

warm, heart-felt reading over an exciting ork backing.

Ting-a-ling 81–81–80–82
An attractive, fast-tempo novelty item, with a fine beat receives a rousing reading from the Clovers. Ditty explains why the girls make the guys' hearts go ting-a-ling. This side too could catch loot. (7/5/52) (A-side, #7 R&B; B-side, #1 R&B)

Hey Miss Fannie .85
The Clovers probably have another winner here, with this bright, infectious novelty item. The boys tell it in powerful style, backed forcefully by the rhythm group.

I Played the Fool .75
An appealing blues ballad receives a good reading from the Clovers, who sing it most attractively with class support from the combo. (10/18/52) (A-side, #2 R&B; B-side, #3 R&B)

The Moonglows' 1954 "Real Gone Mama" and The Paragons' 1957 hit "Hey Little School Girl" had their roots in "Hey Miss Fannie."

Lead Buddy Bailey soon entered the Army and was replaced by ex-Dominoes member Charlie White by the time "Crawlin'" charted. White's first lead was on "Good Lovin'."

Crawlin' 87
The Clovers, now the hottest group in the r.&b. field, have another solid entry here and one that could be another smash hit, their sixth in a row. It's a bright bouncy effort and the boys hand it a sock vocal in their own powerful style. A really potent wax entry for the market, and a coin-grabber. (2/28/53) (#3 R&B)

Good Lovin' 85
The group figures to break through again with a socking blues for another big side. It's strong all the way. Looks like the seventh hit in a row for the Clovers. (7/4/53) (#2 R&B)

Comin' On 79
A new ballad is handled with skill by the group, backed with a slow, pulsat-

ing beat by a combo. Side is in a different vein than the flip, but it still should pull its share of play and coin. (11/7/53) (B-side, #9 R&B)

In 1954, White joined The Playboys and former Atlantic soloist Billy Mitchell became the lead on "Your Cash Ain't Nothin' but Trash." By late 1954, Bailey returned, Mitchell was relegated to second lead, and the group had settled in as a top touring attraction with other Atlantic acts like Ruth Brown and The Drifters. The classic ballad "Blue Velvet" followed and became their first record to chart but not reach the Top 10. 1956 began with the group's sixth and last two-sided hit.

Blue Velvet.

The Clovers pull a style-switch on the lovely oldie . . . and warble it with a lush, smooth vocal touch that should pull spins from jocks and jukes. (2/5/55) (#14 R&B)

Nip Sip.

Relaxed and swingy, with a cute lyric and solid vocal performance. (8/27/55) (#10 R&B)

Devil or Angel/Hey, Doll Baby.

The group offers an impressive reading of "Devil or Angel," a poignant ballad with effective lyrics. "Hey, Doll Baby" is a swingy vocal treatment of a bouncy novelty with an infectious beat. Both sides should pull plenty of play. (1/14/56) (A-side, #3 R&B; B-side, #8 R&B)

In mid-year, after seven seasons and 16 singles, The Clovers finally reached the pop charts with "Love, Love, Love." Having finally crossed pop, they began losing their R&B base. Consequently, none of the quartet's next six releases charted.

Love, Love, Love.

The Clovers have a red-hot side here, which should take off big. It's a swing disk, with a catchy and cute melody arrangement that has considerable pop feeling. Plenty of play in store by this one in this field; and also pop-wise. (5/26/56) (#30 Pop, #4 R&B)

With their Atlantic deal over by 1958, Krefetz formed Poplar Records and drafted The Clovers. A move to United Artists in 1959 didn't help, until

Leiber and Stoller, the producers of The Coasters' hits, joined forces to create "Love Potion #9."

 A cute and clever novelty about a gent who visits a gypsy to get a magic potion to help out with his wooing. (8/3/59) (#23 Pop, #23 R&B)

1961 saw the emergence of two Clovers acts, Bailey's and Winley's group (Winley) and Lucas's quartet known as Tippie and The Clovers. Finding chart action hard to come by, in 1965 Bailey rejoined Lucas along with Jimmy Taylor and Robert Russell for "Poor Baby" (Port), produced by former Atlantic co-owner, Herb Abramson.

Lucas and a new Clovers recorded for Josie in 1968 and the group's last 45 surfaced on Ripete records in 1991. Ironically, The Clovers' last single ("Don't Play That Song," a hit for Ben E. King in 1962) was written by none other than Ahmet Ertegun.

THE COASTERS

Carl Gardner: Lead vocals
Born: 4/29/28, Tyler, TX
Leon Hughes: Tenor
Born: 1938, Los Angeles, CA
Billy Guy: Baritone
Born: 6/20/36, Ittasca, TX
Bobby Nunn: Bass
Born: 6/25, Los Angeles, CA (died 11/5/86)
Influences: Ink Spots, Billy Eckstine, T. Bone Walker
Influenced: Cadillacs, Olympics, Cadets, Stevie Wonder, Ray Stevens, Bobbettes

If rock 'n' roll's early life was nourished by a diet of love songs and novelty tunes, one of the acts that practically force fed baby rock were the novelty kings, The Coasters.

The quartet from Los Angeles was an outgrowth of a seasoned R&B group formed in 1947 named The Robins. The Robins consisted of Bobby Nunn, Ty Tyrell, and twins Billy and Roy Richard. They were originally named The Four

Bluebirds. A slew of singles released in 1950 were recorded with backing by legendary producer Johnny Otis's quintet.

The Robins:
If I Didn't Love You So **83–83–83–83**
> *Quartet slide smoothly thru a slow ballad, with note-bending lead voice getting strong harmonic support. (1/14/50) (#10 R&B)*

There Ain't No Use Beggin' **76–77–75–77**
> *A ballad with a catch figure is handled Ink Spot style with a lead voice carrying the tune, giving way to a "honey chile" recitation. (4/1/50)*

I'm Living O.K. **52–52–51–55**
> *Sub-par effort . . . in this attempt at a rhythm novelty with small combo jump backing. (6/24/50)*

The raunchy rockers had already been on eight labels, with 20 singles to their credit, by 1954, when the black quartet met two Jewish songwriter/producers named Jerry Leiber and Mike Stoller. Later that year, they added Carl Gardner and Grady Chapman, making the act a sextet. Leiber and Stoller transformed the R&B veterans into spokesmen for humorous vignettes of ghetto life with sides like "Riot in Cell Block #9."

> *A new group, a new label, a song with a bright set of lyrics and a good performance . . . make this add up to a strong new release. Clever and catchy. (6/5/54)*

Four more outrageous Robins records, like "Framed," were issued until they found the catalyst, "Smokey Joe's Cafe."

> *A fine piece of material, this ditty tells the story of an interrupted flirtation at Smokey Joe's. Plenty of beat and fine chanting. One to watch. (10/15/55) (#79 Pop, #10 R&B)*

That 45 made Mike and Jerry two of the first contracted independent producers in rock 'n' roll. Atlantic Records' Atco affiliate signed the duo to produce Robins disks, while acquiring "Smokey Joe."

Problems arose when most of the members refused to pact with the new East Coast company.

Nunn and Gardner were paired with Billy Guy, Leon Hughes, and guitarist Adolph Jacobs, forming The Robins' Atco replacements, The Coasters. The Coasters name emanated from their residence as West Coasters. But that didn't last long as writers and artists alike moved to New York. Meanwhile, the remaining Robins, with H. B. Barnum added (Dootones), moved to Whippet and became a pop act with little success as The Coasters began 1956.

Down in Mexico.
> *Here's a new and definitely swinging crew and they deliver a couple of highly commendable sides. "Down in Mexico" is a fetching ditty which is very close to "Smokey Joe's Cafe." This group carries the lead and bass singer from the Robins unit which recorded the "Smoke" side. (2/25/56) (#8 R&B)*

One Kiss Led to Another.
> *The Coasters have racked good sales with their two previous disks, and this clever novelty could be their biggest yet. Humor and slick styling set it apart. (7/28/56) (#73 Pop, #11 R&B)*

1957 started The Coasters on their way to the Rock and Roll Hall of Fame. Leiber and Stoller grafted the style they created for The Robins onto The Coasters and broadened its appeal with songs about teen trials and traumas, like "Young Blood" (written with Doc Pomus) and "Searchin'." The group's novelty rock 'n' roll was really a thinly veiled and sometimes primitive sounding blues styling.

Young Blood.
> *The group has a swingy attractive side in "Young Blood" which is bound to pull considerable jockey attention. The rhythm-ballad has powerful lyric appeal for teen-agers and standout trick-voicing effects. Flip is "Searchin'." (3/23/57) (A-side, #8 Pop, #2 R&B; B-side, #3 Pop, #1 R&B for 13 weeks!)*

My Baby Comes to Me/Idol with the Golden Head.
> *The group comes on strong with their selling of "Baby." With "Young Blood" and "Searchin'" still going*

well, their similar approach here can make for a smash follow-up. "Idol" is interesting material with unusual lyrics and is presented at an attractive medium-tempo pace. Both sides appear winners. (8/26/57) (B-side, #64 Pop)

In 1957, Nunn and Hughes left, replaced by Cornel Gunter (Flairs and Platters) and Will "Dub" Jones (Cadets). Then came the immortal "Yakety Yak." With two million sellers to their credit ("Searchin'" and "Yakety Yak"), The Coasters next issued the teen national anthem, "Charlie Brown."

Yakety Yak.

The group has a salable sound on this rocker novelty. The lyrics are amusing and the harmonies are attractive. This could also collect pop coin. Flip is a rhythmic revival of "Zing! Went the Strings of My Heart." (5/5/58) (#1 Pop, #1 R&B)

Charlie Brown.

★ ★ ★ ★ *The Coasters turn in an attractive reading concerning the problems of Charlie Brown on this rocking side. Could get coins. Watch it. Good teen lyrics. (1/19/59) (#2 Pop, #2 R&B)*

The next subjects to feel Mike and Jerry's rapier wit were Westerns, weeds, and poverty.

Along Came Jones/That Is Rock & Roll.

 Usual hit approach by the Coasters on hilarious tunes afford them with a likely two-sider. "Jones" is a parody of Westerns with Jones coming to the rescue whenever the damsel is in distress. Flip is a ditty about the birth of rock and roll. (5/4/59) (#9 Pop, #1 R&B)

Poison Ivy.

 The Coasters are a likely bet to click again. "Ivy" is an interesting bit of material that compares a gal to the well-known weed. (8/10/59) (#7 Pop, #1 R&B)

Run Red Run/What About Us.

 The group figures to continue its hit spree with this great coupling. Top side is a wild poker game and features crazy piano backing by Mike Stoller. Flip is a

complaint about a friend who has everything. (11/23/59) (A-side, #36 Pop, #29 R&B; B-side, #47 Pop, #17 R&B)

The first sides not by Leiber and Stoller, "Besame Mucho" and "Wake Me, Shake Me," proved less potent for the public, although both were *Billboard* Picks.

By 1961, Gunter left and ex-Cadillac lead, Earl "Speedoo" Carroll, joined the crew for some more noteworthy satire.

Wait a Minute.

 The boys wrap up "Wait a Minute" (a solid novelty co-cleffed by Bobby Darin in the "Alley-Oop" groove) in a top-notch vocal. (1/9/61) (#37 Pop)

Little Egypt/Keep on Rolling.

 The boys come through with two sensational performances here. Top side is an item about a fabled belly dancer that really rocks. Hard-hitting blues in the train groove makes the flip potent, too. Both sides are in the best Leiber-Stoller tradition. (4/10/61) (#23 Pop, #16 R&B)

Girls, Girls, Girls (Parts 1 and 2).

 The boys have their sharpest effort in quite a spell. Cute material, written by Leiber and Stoller, is done in straight shuffle tempo on side 1, with a double time, rocking beat spotlighted on the flip. Side 2 could have an edge but both are strong. (7/24/61) (#96 Pop)

The Coasters, finding tough going during the mid-1960s' British invasion, resorted to cutting oldies remakes, like "Lovey Dovey" (Clovers) and "Money Honey" (Drifters), as their Atco days drew to a close. During 1967 and 1968, the foursome was on Columbia's Date label but to no avail. Ironically, one of their releases was a Leiber and Stoller song recently popularized by the Monkees, "D. W. Washburn."

The Monkees just made this infectious Leiber-Stoller rhythm material a hit and now the smooth blended Coasters add a touch of blues to it which should bring it through for the top sales all over again. (7/20/68)

In 1971, they returned to the charts for the first time in seven years when King Records bought some old Date masters by Leiber and Stoller and released The Coasters' version of "Love Potion #9" (#76 Pop, #23 R&B).

By the 1980s, Gunter, Nunn, Guy, Hughes, and Gardner each had their own Coasters group performing in nostalgia shows coast to coast. Gunter was gunned down in Las Vegas in 1989 and Nunn died of a heart attack in 1986. They and the other Coasters left behind a legacy of 19 hit records and their status as rock 'n' roll pioneers.

EDDIE COCHRAN

Full Name: Edward Ray Cochran
Birthdate: 10/3/38
Birthplace: Oklahoma City, OK
Died: 4/17/60 (age 21)
Influence: Elvis Presley
Influenced: George Harrison, Rod Stewart, The Who, Rolling Stones, Jimi Hendrix, Bobby Vee

An important influence on early American and British rock 'n' roll, Eddie Cochran started as a country and western singer/musician.

By age 15, he was an accomplished, self-taught guitar player. When his family moved from Minnesota to Bell Gardens, California in 1953, he joined a local band. In 1955, Eddie teamed up with Hank Cochran (no relation) and formed the country duo, The Cochran Brothers. Soon after, Eddie met songwriter Jerry Capehart, who was searching for an act as the vehicle for his songs. That led to the Cochrans' first single, "Tired and Lonely" (Ekko). When it failed, the "brothers" split up. Hank went on to be a country music star. Eddie's new direction wasn't long in coming. After seeing Elvis Presley perform, Eddie Cochran knew his future would be rock 'n' roll.

In 1956, Cochran and Capehart moved to Nashville and signed with American Music Publishing. There Eddie had his first solo single, "Skinny Jim," for American's Crest label. When the cowritten effort stalled, Capehart, using it as a

demo, traveled to Los Angeles and interested Liberty Records' Si Waronker in Cochran.

Meanwhile, 20th Century-Fox was searching for singers to appear in *The Girl Can't Help It,* a comedy starring Jayne Mansfield. Liberty Records offered their roster and Fox picked Nino Tempo, Julie London, and Cochran, who sang "Twenty Flight Rock."

Cochran's first Liberty 45 and first hit was a Johnny Dee (John D. Loudermilk) song, "Sittin' in the Balcony." Capehart's next writing effort, "Mean When I'm Mad," was a disappointment. Meanwhile, Cochran managed another film appearance, this time in *Untamed Youth,* starring another sex symbol, Mamie Van Doren.

Sittin' in the Balcony.
This one has plenty of teen-age appeal and could move out with the right exposure. Cochran warbles with sock showmanship—a la Presley. (3/2/57) (#18 Pop, #7 R&B)

One Kiss.
An appealing moderate-beat tune with rockin' chorus backing and teen-bait lyrics . . . should pull plenty of play. (5/13/57)

Cradle Baby **83**
She may be young, but she's just right for him. Good enough rocker for teen tastes, pop and country.

Twenty Flight Rock **81**
From the flick "The Girl Can't Help It." Cochran rocks this rockabilly in Presley fashion. Good job all around. Can do okay. (12/2/57)

Several singles followed in 1957 and 1958, but none had the impact of "Sittin' in the Balcony." Halfway through 1958, Cochran and Capehart penned the tune that would become a rock 'n' roll anthem, "Summertime Blues." Most of Cochran's L.A. sessions featured black musicians and their tight rockin' sound. That sound, coupled with Cochran's Elvis-styled rockabilly/blues vocals, was irresistible.

Summertime Blues.
Lad who had a hit a while back with "Sittin' in the Balcony" may have another one here with this driving

effort. He sings the infectious tune brightly. It could happen. (7/21/58) (#8 Pop, #11 R&B)

C'Mon Everybody.

> *Uptempo blues receives a bright, breezy reading by the lad over pounding combo support. Side has a lot of drive and could grab coin. (10/27/58) (#35 Pop)*

Cochran appeared in his third film, Alan Freed's *Go, Johnny, Go!* in early 1959. His next single, "Teen-Age Heaven," came out only a week after the death of Buddy Holly, Ritchie Valens, and the Big Bopper. Ironically, Cochran might have been on that same plane, as he was booked for Holly and company's Winter Dance Party. Only a last-minute schedule change for Freed's film kept him from the tour. He confided to friends that, after the crash, he felt he was living on borrowed time. Soon after, Cochran had his last U.S. chart single, "Something Else," written by his girlfriend Sharon Sheeley.

Teen-Age Heaven.

> *Cochran should coast to a high position on the charts with this strong side. It's a smart, new adaptation of "Home on the Range" with clever lyrics done in rockabilly fashion. It appears a sure winner. (2/23/59) (#99 Pop)*

Somethin' Else.

> *Cochran should bounce back onto the charts with these strong efforts. "Somethin' Else" is a moving rocker that is given a rhythmic chant. "Boll Weevil" is a rockabilly adaptation of the traditional folk tune. (7/27/59) (#58 Pop)*

Cochran, who seemed to be more popular in England than America, joined a tour of Europe from Italy to England in January 1960 with friend Gene Vincent and British hearthrob, Billy Fury. His new single was a hit in Britain but never charted stateside.

Hallelujah, I Love Her So/Little Angel.

> *Cochran belts "Hallelujah," the Great Ray Charles tune over a gospelish arrangement that includes strings. It's a standout side, and a likely winner. "Little Angel" is also on the spiritual*

order, and it's also afforded a smart warble. (11/16/59) (#22 Pop [U.K.])

Cochran's performances were electrifying, and one of the mesmerized masses who attended nearly every U.K. show was a youngster named George Harrison. The tour ended in March but was so successful that Cochran and Vincent were asked back for additional dates, starting two weeks later. The last date added to the tour was in Bristol on Easter Sunday eve. When the show was over, rather than board a late train, Cochran, Vincent, and Sheeley took a chauffeured limousine to London. A tire blew out on the road near Chippenham Wilts and the car careened into a lamppost. All were injured but recovered, except Cochran. He was dead, having been thrown from the car, suffering fatal head injuries.

His next British release was his only #1, "Three Steps From Heaven." Back home, his first posthumous release (and follow ups) went unnoticed.

Sweetie Pie.

> ★ ★ ★ ★ *Strong rockabilly vocal by the late Eddie Cochran on a fast-moving r.&r. rhythm item. (8/22/60) (A-side, #38 Pop [U.K.]; B-side, #41 Pop [U.K.])*

In England, his last of 11 hits was the same as his first, "Summertime Blues," only ten years apart (1958–1968). English fans established The Eddie Cochran Memorial Society, while in the United States his music finally received its due years after his death, in 1987, when he was inducted into the Rock and Roll Hall of Fame.

SAM COOKE

Birthdate: 1/22/35 (some publications claim 1/2/31)
Birthplace: Clarksdale, MS
Died: 12/11/64
Influence: Rebert H. Harris
Influenced: Rod Stewart, Marvin Gaye, Isley Brothers, Stevie Wonder, Sam & Dave, Otis Redding, Five Satins, Al Green, Bob Marley, Bobbettes, Olympics, Gary U.S. Bonds, Jimmy Cliff, many more

Well-remembered as a premier performer and recording artist whose smooth gospel style developed into a superior pop sound, Sam Cooke was also a consummate song writer.

One of eight children of Baptist minister, Reverend Charles S. Cooke, Sam first sang with The Singing Children, which consisted of himself, one of his brothers, and two sisters. He later sang with The Highway QCs, The Pilgrim Travelers, and, by 1950, The Soul Stirrers, replacing legendary lead singer Rebert (R. H.) Harris. He toured and recorded with The Stirrers for over five years, when Specialty Records A&R man, "Bumps" Blackwell recorded Sam as Dale Cook on "Lovable," a revision of The Soul Stirrers' "Wonderful."

Lovable 66
Cook is a new artist on the label, and he makes a personable debut. Of interest are the church touches he injects into his style. The material is the only weak ingredient here.

Forever 65
Cook's styling of this ballad also shows talent and imagination, but he struggles against pale material and weak backing. (3/9/57)

When Specialty and the group got wind of Sam's secular sojourn, he was quickly fired. Blackwell, obviously believing more in Sam's future as a pop artist than his own future at Specialty, moved to L.A.'s Keen Records and brought Sam with him in 1957.

His third release (initially reviewed as a B-side) was "You Send Me," written by his brother L. C. Cooke. It became his first and only #1 pop record, selling over two and a half million singles.

Summertime 73
The great Gershwin standard gets an uncommonly interesting reading here. Cooke's vocal is full of heart. He's backed up by a chorus and an instrumental backing with attractive melodic figures.

You Send Me 72
[Cooke] displays good technical equipment and style in his vocal. Material is tasteful. (8/9/57) (#1 Pop, #1 R&B)

Specialty had earlier feared Sam's pop pursuits would hurt their heavy gospel image. They jumped on the Cooke bandwagon two months later with a year-old recording, "Forever"/"I'll Come Running Back to You." Meanwhile, Sam continued to turn out pop ballads on Keen.

Cooke figures to score again with these two solid sides. "Forever" is a pretty ballad taken at a leisurely rhythm clip with chorus support much in the manner of his current smash, "You Send Me." Flip, "I'll Come," is similarly styled. Both are powerful entries. (11/25/57) (A-side, #60 Pop; B-side, #18 Pop, #1 R&B)

Love Song from 'Houseboat' 84
Pretty tune from the flick . . . is handed a potent piping from Sam Cooke what could turn into a big one for the chanter. Tune and strong chanter add up to a coin-catcher. (7/14/58) (#22 Pop, #4 R&B)

Blue Moon 81
Warmly tender reading of the great standard. Strong contender.

Love You Most of All 77
Pleasant warbling tint of folk-flavored ditty. (10/27/58)

On November 10, 1958, Sam and Lou Rawls, then a vocalist with The Pilgrim Travelers (Sam's backing group), were injured in an Arkansas car crash but both fully recovered.

1959 ushered in the first of Sam's dance and novelty hits, "Everybody Likes to Cha Cha Cha," another B-side pick. His next hit, "Only Sixteen," was a writer collaboration with Herb Alpert and Lou Adler under the outrageous pseudonym, Barbara Campbell. He then took his second shot at "Summertime." Sam's last charter for Keen, "There I've Said It Again," followed. One of Cooke's lesser known but highly charged dance records was his last Keen release, "No One Can Ever Take Your Place."

Little Things You Do/Everybody Likes to Cha Cha Cha.

Cooke has two powerful sides that can attract buys a-plenty. "Little Things" is a celestial-type rockaballad that is

given an emotional belt with soft chorus and ork helping all the way. Flip, "Everybody," is a cha cha with a cute story about a gal who can't do the Latin dance. Both are also hot r.&b. contenders. (2/2/59) (B-side, #31 Pop, #2 R&B)

Only Sixteen/Let's Go Steady Again.

Cooke treats both songs in easygoing attractive style. "Only Sixteen" is a rockaballad with a teen-slanted lyric that can create interest. "Let's Go Steady" is a lush ballad on which he is given chorus backing. Either can figure. (5/25/59) (#28 Pop, #13 R&B)

Summertime, Parts 1 and 2.

Cooke reads the Gershwin song in two different styles. Side one spotlights a ballad with beat approach. Side two, is a bit swifter and with an interesting rhythmic variation. This could be the side to take command. Both are strong, however. (8/10/59)

In January 1960, a $100,000 guarantee lured him to RCA where his first 45 was "Teenage Sonata." Keen countered with one more wonderful effort, "Wonderful World." RCA, however, had Sam in his prime and nothing could stop his rise with such songs as "Chain Gang."

Wonderful World.

★ ★ ★ ★ Moderate rocker gets a smooth belt from Sam Cooke in his usual, salable style. Worth watching. (4/4/60) (#12 Pop, #2 R&B)

Chain Gang.

Cooke has been hot with "Wonderful World" on his former label, and the new Victor coupling can move him right up again. "Chain Gang" is a smart, rhythmic side that can go. (8/1/60) (#2 Pop, #2 R&B)

In late 1960, Cooke became one of the first pop/rock artists to own a record label when he formed SAR Records, a company that eventually included recordings by his brother L. C., The Valentinos (The Womack Brothers), and Jackie Ross. Cooke's chart renaissance continued with a slew of singles.

Cupid/Farewell My Darling.

Two fine warbling stints here by the smooth-voiced Sam Cooke and both could happen. "Cupid" is a tenderly told story of love, and the flip has a Western flavor. (5/22/61) (#17 Pop, #20 R&B)

Twistin' the Night Away.

Cooke has a solid effort, well keyed to the Twist rhythm, but clever in the song styling and arrangement as well. He sings with a neat touch here and the side can go. Flip is "One More Time." (1/20/62) (#9 Pop, #1 R&B)

Having a Party.

Sam has another swinger in his "Twistin' the Night Away" groove here that's bound to get the kids dancing. The side features same spirited vocal style in front of strings, punching ork and chorus. The other side is "Bring It on Home to Me." (5/19/62) (A-side, #17 Pop, #4 R&B; B-side, #13 Pop, #2 R&B)

In November 1962, Cooke made his only foreign tour when he headlined with Little Richard in England. Meanwhile, the hits continued.

Baby, Baby, Baby.

A swinging side featuring Cooke in a moving vocal over a driving beat by the ork. Chorus adds to the backup. Flip is "Send Me Some Lovin'." (1/12/63) (A-side, #66 Pop; B-side, #13 Pop, #2 R&B)

Another Saturday Night/Love Will Find A Way.

Sam Cooke should stay way up on the charts with both of these strong sides. "Saturday Night" is a limbo-ish effort with a bit of that "Chain Gang" feel. (4/13/63) (#10 Pop, #1 R&B)

Frankie & Johnnie.

There have been a lot of versions of Frankie & Johnnie but few with the feeling and fervor of this swinging arrangement by Sam Cooke. His vocal is groovy and the disk builds all the way, winding up in fiery fashion. (7/20/63) (#14 Pop, #4 R&B)

Little Red Rooster.

A definite blues feel with a provocative lyric that swings in a middle tempo groove. (10/19/63) (#11 Pop, #7 R&B)

On September 16, 1964, Cooke performed with The Everly Brothers and The Righteous Brothers on the first episode of ABC-TV's "Shindig." On December 10, 1964, Sam Cooke was shot in a Los Angeles motel and died the next day. The circumstances of his death are shrouded in mystery. At the time, the manager of a hot-sheets motel accused him of brutally attacking her. She claimed to have shot him in self-defense. The police investigation was scanty, and many fans continue to wonder what really happened to Cooke. His funeral services in Chicago drew almost 200,000 fans.

Sam's first posthumous release was the thought-provoking original, "A Change Is Gonna Come" (#31 Pop), along with the dance offering, "Shake" (#7 Pop). Cooke's last hit was "Let's Go Steady Again" (originally the flip of "Only Sixteen").

It's Got the Whole World Shakin'.
Right on the heels of the late singer's smash, "Shake," comes an equally hot original piece of swinging material. (4/3/65) (#41 Pop, #15 R&B)

When a Boy Falls in Love.
Change of pace from his "It's Got the Whole World Shakin'" is this plaintive ballad written by and soulfully performed by the late Cooke. (5/29/65) (#52 Pop)

In 1986 Sam Cooke was inducted into the Rock and Roll Hall of Fame.

CREEDENCE CLEARWATER REVIVAL

John Fogarty: Lead vocals
Born: 5/28/45, El Cerrito, CA
Tom Fogarty: Guitar
Born: 11/9/41, El Cerrito, CA (died 9/6/90)
Stu Cook: Keyboards
Born: 4/25/45, Oakland, CA
Doug Clifford: Drums
Born: 4/24/45, Palo Alto, CA
Influences: Elvis Presley, Carl Perkins, Chuck Berry, Jerry Lee Lewis, Otis Williams and The Charms, Hank Williams, Muddy Waters, Howlin' Wolf, Buck Owens, Jimmy Reed, Johnny Cash
Influenced: Bruce Springsteen, Lynyrd Skynyrd, Brian Jones, Bill Wyman, Garth Brooks, Travis Tritt

The creators of "swamp rock" (modern-day rockabilly), Creedence made a career of finishing number two on the charts.

The band came together at Portola Junior High School in El Cerrito as a trio of John Fogarty, Clifford, and Cook in 1959. Soon after, John's brother Tom joined and the band started playing San Francisco area clubs under the name, The Blue Velvets. When they signed with the Berkeley-based Fantasy label, the company envisioned their future as British-beat stylists. In keeping with that image, Fantasy issued the group's first single, "Don't Tell Us No Lies," in November 1964, under the name, The Golliwogs. It bombed along with several other efforts on Fantasy's Scorpio affiliate.

In January 1966, John Fogarty and Clifford were drafted into the Army, serving until July 1967. The band then underwent a musical and image change. The direction became hard-edged rockabilly/blues and their name became Creedence (name of a friend) Clearwater (after a beer commercial they saw) Revival (as in hope of a group resurgence).

When a local radio station played the demo of "Suzie Q" the song received a strong reaction.

Suzie Q.

> *Group should get immediate progressive rock airplay and quickly prove hot on Top 40 with this bluesy revival of the early Dale Hawkins rock hit. (8/31/68) (#11 Pop)*

Fantasy revived the band's career with a recording of it. "I Put a Spell on You," the old Screamin' Jay Hawkins hit followed in late 1968 but from then on, the John Fogerty writing machine took over. He wrote "Proud Mary" on the morning of his Army discharge. It became the first of five #2 hits (#1 was Tommy Roe's "Dizzy") and their first million seller.

Proud Mary.

> *The "Suzie Q" group has another winner to equal the sales of that Top 10 item. A powerhouse follow-up to their "I Put a Spell on You," this driving blues item with a strong beat will [hit] hard and fast. (1/14/69) (#2 Pop)*

The group's next single, "Bad Moon Rising," was the first of seven, two-sided hits in-a-row (#1 this time was "Love Theme from Romeo and Juliet" by Henry Mancini).

Bad Moon Rising.

> *Loaded with rhythm and drive, the two side can't miss going right to the top. Equally powerful for top play and sales is the easy-beat "Lodi" with much of the feel of the recent smash. (4/26/69) (A-side, #2 Pop; B-side, #52 Pop)*

In August 1969, CCR starred at the legendary Woodstock concert but few today remember that appearance because they refused to allow their performance to be used in the film or album. "Green River," their third million seller (#1 was "Sugar, Sugar" by The Archies), led to more two-sided hits including, "Fortunate Son"/"Down on the Corner," "Who'll Stop the Rain"/"Travelin' Band" (#1 was Simon and Garfunkel's "Bridge Over Troubled Water"), "Up Around the Bend"/"Run Through the Jungle," and "Lookin' Out My Back Door"/"Long As I Can See the Light" (#1 was "Ain't No Mountain High Enough" by Diana Ross).

Fortunate Son/Down on the Corner.

> *With their "Green River" smash still riding high on the "Hot 100" chart, the powerful group makes still another bid for top honors. . . . the first with the feel and flavor of the recent winner, the flip has got infectious calypso beat. (10/18/69) (A-side, #14 Pop; B-side, #3 Pop)*

Who'll Stop the Rain/Travelin' Band.

> *The first side has the beat and feel of their hits, while the flip is a wild blues shouter that could take over! (1/24/70) (A-side, #2 Pop; B-side, #2 Pop)*

Lookin' Out My Back Door.

> *A clever rhythm item . . . headed for the top. (8/1/70) (A-side, #2 Pop; B-side, #20 Pop)*

In 1971, Tom Fogarty opted for a solo career and the band carried on as a trio. Unlike a preponderance of 1960s' and 1970s' rockers, the Creedence members lived relatively private lives among their families when not touring. However, that didn't keep dissension from arising when it came to creative equality. The magical mix couldn't be maintained and the remaining trio disbanded in October 1972. Four years after separating, they still could chart with "I Heard It Through the Grapevine" (#43 Pop).

The group reunited twice in the 1980s, once for Tom's wedding in 1980 and at CCR's 1983 school reunion in El Cerrito. John created a nonexistent group (playing all instruments) called The Blue Ridge Rangers and had a hit with the Hank Williams oldie, "Jambalaya" in addition to The Charms' doowopper, "Hearts of Stone." He then retired from the business and moved his family to Oregon. He returned in 1985 with the LP, *Center Field,* and the smash, "The Old Man Down the Road" and the title track.

Meanwhile, Clifford and Cook recorded with Doug Sahm on the *Groovers Paradise* LP (1974) and with the Don Henderson Band (1976). Clifford also did an album for Fantasy, *Cosmo* (which was his nickname), and a single, "Latin Train" (1973). Tom recorded several Fantasy albums and eventually sold real estate in Hawaii. He died in 1990.

Creedence Clearwater Revival was inducted into the Rock and Roll Hall of Fame in 1993.

THE CRESTS (THE BROOKLYN BRIDGE)

Johnny Mastrangelo (Maestro): Lead vocals
Born: 5/7/39, New York City
J. T. Carter
Born: 1939, New York City
Harold Torres
Born: 1940, New York City
Talmadge Gough
Born: 1940, New York City
Patricia Van Dross
Born: 1942, New York City
Influences: Five Keys, Harptones, Clovers, Penguins, Orioles, Flamingos, Moonglows, Spaniels, Mills Brothers, Ames Brothers, Johnny Ray
Influenced: Manhattan Transfer, Joey Dee, Criterions

The first of two talented groups tied together by the sumptuous and stratospheric vocals of Johnny Maestro, The Crests reflected New York's Lower East Side melting pot.

In 1955, P.S. #160 Junior High School students Van Dross, Torres, and Gough formed a group, soon adding Delancey Street's Jay (J. T.) Carter. By the time they added Mulberry Street's Johnny Mastrangelo in 1956, the mix included two black males (Tal and J. T.), one black female (Pat), one Puerto Rican (Harold), and one Italian (Johnny).

On one of their many trips thru the subway system, a woman, impressed with The Crests' vocalizing, handed them a card that read, "Al Browne and Orch." Browne was the famous arranger for The Heartbeats. Upon hearing Johnny's powerful pipes and the smooth sound of the quintet, Al recorded them in June 1957 for the tiny Joyce label, which was situated in the back-room of a record store. Mastrangelo was renamed Maestro and the group earned $17.50 each for their hit, "My Juanita"/"Sweetest One."

Group packs plenty of feeling and emotional impact into moving ballad with a solid beat. Spinnable wax. (10/7/57) (#86 Pop)

The Crests' next single, the haunting "No One to Love," failed, and Pat's mom pulled her out of the act. Mama Van Dross felt touring with four male teens was not a good idea for her daughter. Pat's younger brother loved listening to the group and, by the 1980s, Luther Vandross would have his own hit career.

In 1958, publisher George Paxton's Coed Records became their new home. Although the Crests' debut, "Pretty Little Angel," made no great impression, their next effort, "Beside You," was issued. Both Dick Clark and Alan Freed took a liking to its flip side and "16 Candles" (originally titled "21 Candles") was off and running. Soon after, the quartet appeared at their first major concert, Freed's 1958 Christmas show with Buddy Holly, Ritchie Valens, and The Big Bopper. All three died in a plane crash less than six weeks later.

16 Candles.
★ ★ ★ *Lyrics state that the light of 16 candles on a birthday cake are not as bright as the light in his chick's eyes. Tune is a weeper sort. Side has lots of teen bait. (11/10/58) (#2 Pop, #4 R&B)*

1959 was good to The Crests—all four of their singles, "Six Nights a Week," "Flower of Love," "The Angels Listened In," and "A Year Ago Tonight," charted.

Six Nights a Week/I Do.

The Crests, who are still up there with "16 Candles," have a strong sequel disk. "Six Nights" is an attractive ballad that is powerfully sold. "I Do" is a ballad with beat that is accorded a warm reading. (3/9/59) (#28 Pop, #17 R&B)

The Angels Listened In.

A smooth rockaballad that is given a stylish and salable approach. (7/27/59) (#22 Pop, #14 R&B)

A Year Ago Tonight/Paper Crown.

The Group can keep their hit string alive via these powerful offerings. "A Year Ago Tonight" spotlights the crew on a fine reading of a ballad with beat. "Paper Crown" is a rockaballad that is nicely handled by the lead with excellent group and ork assistance. (11/9/59) (#42 Pop)

In 1960, the quartet started strong but faded as Coed decided Johnny's future was as a soloist. "Trouble in Paradise" was the first record to read, "Johnny Maestro and the Crests."

Step by Step.

A contagious, medium-beat tune that tells of various steps that lead to romance. (1/8/60) (#14 Pop)

Trouble in Paradise.

A light, melodic rocker. Potential dual-market sales prospects. (5/30/60) (#20 Pop)

Journey of Love/If My Heart Could Write a Letter.

The boys have been consistent chart makers and the pairing also has what it takes. Top side is the story of love's evolution from teen crush to the wedding day. Smart idea well handled with fem vocal support. Flip is a good ballad with Latin rock rhythm. (7/22/60) (#81 Pop)

Remember (In the Still of the Night)/Good Golly Miss Molly.

The boys have been hot for a good spell and they have two more winners here. Top side is a ballad with a strong lead performance, while the flip is a listenable up-dating of the Little Richard hit. Watch both. (12/19/60)

In 1961, Maestro broke away for a solo career, beginning with "Model Girl," a minor hit.

Model Girl.

Johnny Maestro, former lead of the Crests, bows as a soloist with a fine performance on a bright song with strong backing. This could go. Flip is "We've Got to Tell Them." (1/23/61) (#20 Pop)

The Crests were now led by James Ancrom but he did not have Maestro's magic. "Little Miracle" was not what its name promised, even though it was a *Billboard* pick. Similarly, Maestro's magic also seemed muted without The Crests. Signing to United Artists, he was saddled with inferior material like "Fifty Million Heartbeats."

Maestro could return to the winner's circle on his debut outing for the label. [He] comes through with a fine reading of a bright hunk of material sparked by a strong arrangement. (7/21/62)

Mired in a dispute with Coed over ownership of their name, The Crests joined Selma records, then Trans World in 1962, but their chart run was over. Maestro, reassessing the changing record scene, resurfaced when he joined the revised Del-Satins (Les Cauchi, Mike Gregorio, and Fred Ferrara) in 1968. The group then performed at a Farmingdale, Long Island, talent show that also featured a seven-piece jazz-oriented band, led by Tom Sullivan, named The Rhythm Method. By morning, the two small groups had joined into one very big group. One of their friends even noted, sarcastically, that the eleven member musical mob "had about as much chance for success as they'd have at selling the Brooklyn Bridge." Voila, a name was born!

Their doo wop vocals and jazzy horn style earned them a regular spot at New York's most popular disco, The Cheetah, where they were spotted by a Buddah Records executive. Although not as successful as trendsetting groups like Blood, Sweat and Tears or Chicago, The Brooklyn Bridge preceded both and were the first of the horn-dominated rock bands that would have such a large influence on 1970s music. Their first single was "The Little Red Boat By the River," which deejays promptly scuttled. Their second 45, "Worst That Could Happen," was the best that could happen to Maestro and company.

Worst That Could Happen.

Written by Jim Webb and produced by Wes Farrell, this group should jump on the chart with impact and establish themselves as hot disk sellers. Strong sound with exceptional lead vocalist. Watch this one move fast. (11/23/68) (#3 Pop)

"Blessed Is the Rain"/"Welcome Me Love" followed and was the Bridge's only two-sided charter (A-side, #45 Pop; B-side, #48 Pop). Their other 1969 singles, such as "Your Husband—My Wife" (#46 Pop), "You'll Never Walk Alone" (#51 Pop), and "Free as the Wind" were just as powerful but lacked Buddah's total commitment.

The group appeared in the 1970 film *Hair*. They came away with a harder sound while covering other artists' recent songs. Among their recordings during this period were, "Down By the River," "Day Is Done," "Nights in White Satin" (their version was a single two years before The Moody Blues' 1968 album cut became a hit), and "Wednesday in Your Garden."

Down By the River.

> *Penned by Neil Young of the Crosby, Stills, Nash and Young group, this powerful rock ballad should prove the one to bring the solid sounding group back to the Hot 100 in a hurry. Good material and performance. (5/30/70) (#91 Pop)*

Nights in White Satin.

> *The Justin Haywood rock ballad proved a minor success for The Moody Blues a while back. The Brooklyn Bridge, with a driving, raucous reading, should prove an important Hot 100 item. Top vocal workout and heavy production work. (12/26/70)*

The group left Buddah in 1972. They performed on the oldies circuit continually thru the 1990s. In June of 1987, Maestro and the original Crests reunited for a show in Peekskill, New York. J. T. Carter's new Crests are still performing to this day.

THE CROWS

Daniel "Sonny" Norton: Lead vocals
Born: 1932, New York City
Bill Davis: Tenor
Born: New York City
Harold Major: Tenor
Born: New York City
Jerry Wittick: Tenor
Born: New York City
Gerald Hamilton: Bass
Born: New York City
Influences: Flamingos, Ravens, Cardinals, Five Keys
Influenced: Gene Pitney, Lou Christie

The Crows, a solid R&B group of the early 1950s known mostly by collectors, garnered their place in history thanks to an angry disk jockey's girlfriend. Her spontaneous outburst made The Crows the act with the first rock 'n' roll hit record.

Products of the New York sidewalks (142 Street and Lenox Avenue), Sonny Norton and company were fans of the era's bird groups (Ravens, Flamingos, etc.) and decided they should be a bird group too, hence, The Crows. In 1952, they were spotted by agent Cliff Martinez at an Apollo Theater amateur night contest. The quintet temporarily lost its name when their first recording was released under the name The Four Notes. The recording featured the group supporting vocalist/trumpeter Frank "Fat Man" Mathews on the Jubilee ("I Can't Get Started with You") label. After the record's demise, Wittick enlisted in the Army and was replaced by Mark Jackson.

The next year, Martinez's connection with Rama Records mogul George Goldner led to the group's next 45, another backup assignment, this time with the Viola Watkins single, "Seven Lonely Days." Now, however, they were billed as The Crows. Interestingly, according to *Billboard*'s review, the top side was selling country and pop. Surprisingly, there was not any reference to Viola Watkins in the review.

No Help Wanted 74
> *Tune has already hit in both the country and pop fields. This cutting has a good bouncy beat and is well handled by the group. Something could stir here.*

Seven Lonely Days 68
> *R.&B. coverage of the pop hit. The Crows put a lot of zip into it. Gimmick comes at the end with the group breaking into tears. (5/9/53)*

Goldner encouraged Davis to write and the result was a song he spent all of six minutes on in his sister's house. The song was "Gee" and, in April 1953, it was recorded at Beltone studios. "Gee" was released in June, becoming the first "Crows only" single. Initially, the flip gained most of the attention in the East (*Cashbox* had it at #10 in Philadelphia), but by the summer it was relatively dead.

Gee 76
> *The boys have a bright rocker here, and they hand it a lively reading backed solidly by the combo. Side has enough action to pull spins and coins. With the right material, this group could move thru with a big one.*

I Love You So 75
> *A typical r.&b. ballad is performed in strong style here by the boys, with a good lead sparking the disk and the boys keeping the beat in the background. Should get spins. (6/27/53) (#14 Pop, #2 R&B)*

Their next platter came in July, the instant collectable, "Heartbreaker." That, seemingly, was the end of The Crows.

Three thousand miles away, in January of 1954, Los Angeles disk jockey, Dick "Huggy Boy" Hugg, was a nighttime fixture, playing hot R&B disks over the air from the window of Dolphins of Hollywood record store. "Gee" was also a fixture there, only in Hugg's garbage can. His girlfriend liked the song and resurrected it from the trash every time he dumped it. One fateful evening they argued and she departed abruptly. "Huggy Boy," in a panic, searched out The Crows discard and began playing "Gee" repeatedly. She

called, pleading with him to stop for fear of his losing his job. "I'm not taking it off until you come back here" he responded.

By February 1954, 50,000 copies were sold in Los Angeles alone and, by the spring, it was a national pop and R&B hit, two months before Bill Haley's "Rock Around the Clock" and four months before "Sh-Boom's" chart run. Unbeknownst to The Crows as they toured the West Coast and Mexico, courtesy of "Gee," their hit was being called something new, rock 'n' roll!

Their next single, "Baby"/"Untrue," disappeared almost as quickly as it came, even though both sides were exceptional singles. "Mambo Shevitz" (a satire of the Manischevitz wine commercial) and "I Really Really Love You" also were given short shrift on radio, as was their backing of Lorraine Ellis's "Perfidia," via Goldner's new label, reportedly named after their hit, "Gee." All four came out in only two months and were obviously allowed little chance to succeed.

The Crows' last 45, a rockin' version of Earl Burnett's hit, "Sweet Sue," had the same fate. By late 1954, the group's recording career was over. Hamilton passed on in the 1960s and Sonny died in 1972, but their legacy as the first successful link between R&B and rock 'n' roll will never die.

THE CRYSTALS

Delores "La La" Brooks: Lead vocals
Born: 1946, Brooklyn, NY
Dee Dee Kennibrew (Delores Henry)
Born: 1945, Brooklyn, NY
Merna Girard
Born: 1944, Brooklyn, NY
Mary Thomas
Born: 1943, Brooklyn, NY
Patricia Wright
Born: 1943, Brooklyn, NY
Barbara Alston
Born: 1943, Brooklyn, NY
Influences: Bobbettes, Chantels, Shirelles

The brainchild of a Brooklyn big-band member, The Crystals were the first act on Phil Spector and Lester Sill's legendary Philles label.

In 1960, musician-turned-manager Benny Wells formed his female quintet (starting with his 17-year-old niece, Barbara Alston) and rehearsed them at P.S. #73 on MacDougal Street in Brooklyn. Since Benny didn't write, he enlisted the aid of Leroy Bates, a local songsmith hopeful. In 1961, the group acquired its name courtesy of Bates's baby daughter, Crystal. Wells then met Hill and Range Publishing Company professionals, Bill Giant and Bernie Baum, who allowed the girls to rehearse in their office. It was there in March 1961, that the quintet met Spector, while practicing Bates's "There's No Other." Spector changed the girls' uptempo version into a ballad and on the night of their high school prom, the ever-unpredictable Spector called them in to record. It was so unexpected, that three of the teens, Mary, Merna, and Barbara arrived in their prom dresses.

The two sides they recorded were released almost four months later, with the A-side listed as "Oh Yeah, Maybe Baby"; however, it was the B-side "There's No Other (Like My Baby)" that proved to be a hit. The Chantels-styled ballad captivated teen buyers. Their second single featured six Crystals. Sixteen-year-old La La Brooks was to replace pregnant Merna, but Merna held on long enough and cut two more sides. Once again, the A-side was not what the public picked.

Oh Yeah, Maybe Baby/There's No Other (Like My Baby).

Here's a wild sounding new girl vocal group with much of the excitement of the Shirelles. On top, they tie into a swingin' rocker with great backing. Flip is a strong rockaballad reading with an equal chance. Watch both. (10/30/61) (B-side, #20 Pop, #5 R&B)

What's a Nice Way to Turn Seventeen?/Uptown.

The gals have two unusual sides here and they sell both with emotional impact and sincerity. "What's a Nice Way to Turn Seventeen" is a tender teen-appeal ballad with good lyrics and nice performance by lead chirper. Flip is a saga-type ditty about a guy who gets kicked around downtown, but is a

king when he returns at night to his gal uptown. Dual market wax with appeal for both pop and r.&b. buyers. (3/3/62) (#13 Pop, #18 R&B)

The Crystals' next single was too hot a topic for the times as the Carole King–Gerry Goffin miniepic told of a guy hitting his girl. It was based on a story told to the writers by their babysitter, Eva Boyd, who had been struck by her boyfriend. While "He Hit Me (And It Felt Like a Kiss)" was being banned and then withdrawn by Philles, Eva was charging up the charts as Little Eva on "The Loco-Motion."

Much thought went into the lyrics . . . The [song] is a serious ballad with a telling message. (7/21/62)

The next two Crystals records were not exactly by The Crystals. The Crystals recorded them but Spector, constantly overdubbing, adding and subtracting voices, wound up with Darlene Love singing lead with The Blossoms. Nonetheless, "He's a Rebel" is a classic rock production.

He's a Rebel.

The group has a winning sound on this new ballad. They handle it with much feeling over a martial-styled big ork background that builds. Watch this one. (8/25/62) (#1 Pop, #2 R&B)

He's Sure the Boy I Love.

The Crystals, just off their big hit "He's a Rebel," have come up with another sock performance of a mighty strong hunk of rock material. They sell the driving tune with savvy, over rousing ork backing. (12/22/62) (#11 Pop, #18 R&B)

In the next episode of "lets switch-a-singer," La La temporarily became the lead of The Blossoms on "Da Doo Ron Ron" while Darlene Love began her solo sojourn.

Da Doo Ron Ron.

The Crystals show again what they can do with a solid piece of material, coming through here in first-rate fashion on an infectious rocker. (4/13/63) (#3 Pop, #5 R&B)

The record that most assuredly ushered in the age of Spector's "wall of sound," "Then He Kissed Me," was happily an all-Crystals affair as Philles was now occupied with the separate career of Darlene.

Here's a mighty powerful performance of a first-rate piece of teen material penned and produced by Phil Spector, with the Crystals backed by a big, splashy ork that sounds like the New York Philharmonic. Should be one of their biggest. (8/3/63) (#6 Pop, #8 R&B)

Little Boy.

The big, rolling, almost overwhelming sound, backs the girls again on this powerful side arranged by Jack Nitzsche. Side builds to a wild frenzy. It's chart-destined. (1/18/64) (#92 Pop)

To close out 1963, The Crystals contributed three sides for Phil's now-legendary Christmas album. 1964 started with more "power pop," but Philles was preoccupied with its new find, The Ronettes, and The Crystals' singles were promotionally shunted aside. Seeing the decline, Pat left, replaced by Francis Collins, a member of The Crystals' February 1964 British tour. Realizing their situation, the girls moved to United Artists but Paul Tannen's productions didn't have the Philles panache. Neither "My Place" or their last single, "I Got a Man," stirred any interest.

The group disbanded by 1967 but reformed with Dee Dee, La La, Mary, and Barbara in 1971. By 1973, all but Dee Dee were gone. She has kept their spirit alive with new Crystals, Darlene Davis and Marilyn Byers, through the 1970s and 1980s. A 1986 LP of Crystals oldies rerecorded by La La, Dee Dee, Darlene, and Gretchen Prendett were the last recordings made by the group. Darlene Love, the unintentional lead, continued to record and is today recognized as one of the great rock 'n' roll voices of the 1960s.

Darlene Love:
He's Sure the Boy I Love.

Vocalist captures the essence of her days of old on this galloping, all-grown-up remake. (8/20/88)

DANNY AND THE JUNIORS

Danny Rapp: Lead vocals
Born: 5/10/41, Philadelphia, PA (died 4/8/83)
David White: First tenor
Born: 9/40, Philadelphia, PA
Frank Maffei: Second tenor
Born: 11/40, Philadelphia, PA
Joe Terry (Terranova): Baritone
Born: 1/30/41, Philadelphia, PA
Influences: Frankie Lymon and The Teenagers, Four Lads, Four Freshmen, Ravens, Schoolboys, Louis Prima and Keely Smith
Influenced: Beach Boys, Dovells, Sha Na Na, Eddie Rabbitt, Oak Ridge Boys, Jan and Dean

One of the first white vocal groups to transpose black music into rock 'n' roll, Danny Rapp and his friends became The Juvenairs in 1955.

Danny, Dave, Frank, and Joe were all Bertram High School students in Philadelphia who began practicing in a car. When they found out where record producer John Madara lived, The Juvenairs began singing under his window until he offered assistance. It came in the form of an introduction to Singular Records' owner, Artie Singer. The Philly foursome played Singer two originals, "Sometimes" and a dance tune, "Do the Bop." Artie liked the music but not their name, transforming them into Danny and The Juniors.

He took the song to Dick Clark, then hosting "American Bandstand" out of Philadelphia. Clark felt the bop was a dying dance and suggested a name change to "At the Hop." Singer recorded the sides and issued them in November 1957, but they went nowhere. However, on December 2, when Little Anthony and the Imperials couldn't make their "American Bandstand" appearance, Clark rushed Danny and company onto the show. One performance of "At the Hop" and the switchboard lit up like a Christmas tree. A week later the record was bought by ABC-Paramount and charted on *Billboard*'s Top 100. Danny and The Juniors became the first white doo wop group with a #1 Pop hit. The two-and-a-half million seller was on top for seven weeks, and remained in the Top 100 for over five months. Further emphasizing the official unification of black and white music, "Hop" also reached #1 on the R&B charts, and became one of the white vocal group genre's first international hits.

At the Hop.

> *Platter was purchased from Singular Records. The medium-paced rockabilly blues is a very danceable item with a strong vocal by the group that can attract plenty of teen coin. Flip, "Sometimes" is a ballad with rhythm backing that is also well-treated. (11/11/57)*

"Hop"'s success motivated an answer record, "After the Hop," emanating from a former member of the original Drifters, Bill Pinkney and his group, The Turks.

Danny and The Juniors scored big with their follow up, "Rock and Roll Is Here to Stay," which became the teen national anthem. However, the rest of 1958 was an uphill battle in search of another hit.

Rock and Roll Is Here to Stay.

> *"Rock and Roll" is a rocker that is very similar in melody and delivery to the group's current smash. (2/3/58) (#19 Pop, #16 R&B)*

Dottie/In the Meantime.

> *"Dottie" is a happy rocker tribute to a girl friend that is solidly rendered by the crew. "Meantime" is a rockaballad that is also chanted in winning style. Both tunes are changes of pace from their previous clicks, but the new sound can catch on. (5/12/58) (#39 Pop)*

The quartet was so entrenched in people's minds as an up-tempo act that the fine ballad "Thief" was overlooked.

Thief 74

> *Rockaballad is presented in listenable approach by the young group. Teens could go for this. (9/1/58)*

Their only remaining distinction on ABC was the 1959 single, "Somehow I Can't Forget," which history will note was the first stereo 45 RPM record. The group's last for ABC, "Playing Hard to Get," followed.

White then left to be a record producer, replaced by Billy Carlucci. The Juniors joined Swan Records for one fair-sized hit, "Twistin' U.S.A.," and a few lesser ones.

Twistin' U.S.A.

> *Here's a sort of follow-up to the current hit, "The Twist," which is much in the style of the group's original hit, "At the Hop." Arrangement and performance are fine and the lyric is timely. (7/22/60) (#27 Pop)*

Pony Express.

> ★ ★ ★ ★ *A rocker marks the comeback of the group, silent for a spell. The boys turn in the reading with a good bit of verve. The lads here have some of the blues feeling. A listenable side. (2/6/61) (#60 Pop)*

Back to the Hop.

> ★ ★ ★ ★ *The boys had a smash a few years back with "At the Hop" and here's a sort of reprise of the original hit with much the same rhythm and figures. A lot of beat and sound here and it could click. (9/4/61) (#80 Pop)*

In 1962, another ride on the twist bandwagon featured an interesting guest vocalist. Trying to stay visible, they jumped on the limbo craze for their last charter.

Twistin' All Night Long.

> ★ ★ ★ ★ *Rock and roll version of "She'll Be Comin' 'Round the Mountain" with Freddy Cannon as guest artist and timely lyrics. Should pull play. (11/27/61) (#68 Pop)*

Oo-la-la-limbo.

> *Here's a happy, shouting version of the limbo rhythm that is attracting a lot of attention from both adult and teen dance buffs. The boys sing the song with vigor, sparked by solid ork backing that builds. (12/1/62) (#99 Pop)*

Danny and The Juniors broke up in 1964, but reformed in 1968 on Capitol with a new version of "Rock and Roll Is Here to Stay."

Meanwhile, Dave achieved production success with Chubby Checker's "The Fly" and Len Barry's "1, 2, 3," while Frank became an optometrist. Lead singer Danny Rapp worked as an assistant manager in a toy factory and died of an apparent suicide at age 41.

Through the 1990s, Danny and The Juniors featuring Joe Terry (as they are now called) are enthusiastically maintaining their rock 'n' roll tradition.

BOBBY DARIN

Real Name: Walden Robert Cassotto
Birthdate: 5/14/36
Birthplace: Bronx, NY
Died: 12/20/73
Influences: Elvis Presley, Fats Domino, Little Richard, Ray Charles, Five Keys, Frank Sinatra, Peggy Lee
Influenced: Del Shannon, Bobby Rydell

Bobby Darin was considered a consummate entertainer, but he began his career in search of a style. His early records alternated between folk, pop, rock, and blues, but their common denominator was failure.

Darin was born into poverty in the Bronx and was raised by his grandmother. He learned guitar, piano, and drums while writing his own songs in the 1950s. After a year of studying drama at Hunter College, he dropped out, giving the entertainment business his undivided attention. He then changed his name from Cassotto to Darin (which he selected from the phone book).

Bobby placed a few songs at Aldon Music, where publishing honcho Don Kirshner introduced him to manager George Scheck. George, who also handled Connie Francis, arranged a Decca deal for Darin and his short-lived group, The Jaybirds. In March 1956, Bobby had his first single, "Timber"/"Rock Island Line," and debut TV appearance on Tommy Dorsey's show.

Among his early noncharters were "Blue-Eyed Mermaid"/"Silly Willie" and "Help Me"/"Dealer in Dreams."

Timber 73
Young Singer scores well on a folkish opus with a "Ghost Riders" beat. Spirit and song savvy in evidence.

Rock Island Line 68
Lonnie Donegan has a big head of steam already, but this version could still get plays. New artist shows solid promise. (3/31/56)

Silly Willie 74
Young singer comes up with a fast and furious bit of nonsense . . . Jaybirds group gets in the spirit of things with fancy backing sounds. Excitement could kick off juke spins. (5/26/56)

Dealer in Dreams 69
Darin styles in a way that is reminiscent of Johnnie Ray. Projects strong emotion in a vigorous outgoing way. Deserves exposure. (2/23/57)

After four misses (*Billboard* didn't even bother to review his last Decca single, "Hear Them Bells"), Kirshner's influence (and belief) garnered Darin a roster spot on Atlantic's new Atco label. His first three singles again went nowhere.

Million Dollar Baby/Talk to Me Something.
The former Decca artist can break big with either side of this strong debut disk on Atco. The top is a hefty, rocking commercial reading of a great standard, while the flip finds the chanter showing equally well on a slow rhythm ballad. Styling has a spiritual touch. (6/17/57)

Pretty Baby 84
Uptempo blues. Darin rocks right along with this one. Vocal performance is country-oriented in the style that's fashionable with pop right now.

Don't Call My Name 80
A rock and roller, Darin sings this side in Fats Domino style, with prominent guitar backing. Tenorman comes in midway to good effect. A chorus adds a big sound. (11/18/57)

Then, as can only happen in rock 'n' roll folklore, Darin wrote a song in 12 minutes about taking a bath (from an idea put forth by deejay Murray the K's mother). Label head Ahmet Ertegun produced it, and the result was "Splish Splash." Prior to "Splash," Darin was suffering doubts as to his future with Atco so he recorded two sides, "Early in the Morning"/"Now We're One," for Brunswick as The Ding Dongs. However, Atco stopped the illegal single and, in retaliation, Brunswick had both sides rerecorded and issued by Buddy Holly. Meanwhile, Darin issued two more rock classics under his own name, and soon he had three million sellers.

Splish Splash/Judy, Don't Be Moody.

These are the artist's two strongest sides recently. "Splish Splash" is a blues with a novelty lyric that is belted in a bright rock and roll tempo. Flip, "Judy," is also a rhythm side that is sung with a listenable chorus and ork assistance. Also strong r.&b. prospects. (6/2/58) (#3 Pop, #1 R&B)

Queen of the Hop/Lost Love.

★ *Darin has two fine sides that should score. Top side is a rocker that makes use of other song titles in the lyrics. The artist handles it in hit fashion. Flip, "Lost Love," is a class go on a calypso-oriented tune. Either can make it. (9/15/58) (#9 Pop, #6 R&B)*

Dream Lover/Bullmoose.

 Darin has two potent sides that should keep him on the charts. "Dream Lover" is a medium rhythm side that is chanted strongly over fine ork support. "Bullmoose" is a rocker and Darin presents it with drive. (4/6/59) (#2 Pop, #4 R&B)

During that time, Bobby began a romance with Connie Francis, but her father ended it by chasing Darin from the set of the Jackie Gleason Show at gun point. The stage was now set for Darin to find his superstar style, that of a young Sinatra, and the vehicle was the Brecht-Weill song, "Mack the Knife." Originally, Darin was against its release but luckily his label didn't agree. His fourth gold single, it won Bobby two Grammy Awards, "Best Male Vocal Performance

of 1959" and "Best New Artist." Following the disk's success, Decca tried to steal some of Atco's thunder with the re-release of "Hear Them Bells"/"The Greatest Builder."

Mack the Knife.

 Side is a bit of a switch for the singer. Tune is from his current L.P. He sings the "Three-Penny Opera" song smartly over complementary ork background. This can be another big one for him. Flip is "Was There a Call for Me?" (8/10/59) (#1 Pop, #6 R&B)

Darin's swing style standards ushered in his fifth gold 45.

Beyond the Sea/That's the Way Love Is.

 Both sides are from the singer's LP, "That's All." They are strong follow-ups to his big "Mack the Knife," and either could register just as strongly saleswise. They're done along similar lines to his current click. (1/17/60) (#6 Pop, #15 R&B)

Clementine.

 Darin swings thru another fine rendition of an oldie that should mean another click. He shows a fine performance, and the side should take off quickly. Flip is "Tall Story." (3/14/60) (#21 Pop)

Won't You Come Home Bill Bailey.

Another winning side for Bobby Darin, featuring a great vocal by the lad over smart backing by the Bobby Scott Trio. Flip side is "I'll Be There." (5/16/60) (A-side, #19 Pop; B-side, #79 Pop)

In 1960, Bobby married actress Sandra Dee, who he had just costarred with in his film debut, *Come September.* Showing his piano prowess (on "Beachcomber") and crooning a Christmas single ("Christmas Auld Lang Syne"/"Child of God") augmented his continuing trip through the oldies songbook.

Beachcomber/Autumn Blues.

 Bobby Darin is exposed for the first time as a pianist in a pair of non-vocal titles. He plays interesting boogie work on the top against solid, string backing by Shorty Rogers. Flip is equally good

in a similar vein. Both have a feeling of the Rose-Previn "Like Young" hit. (8/15/60) (#100 Pop)

Artificial Flowers/Someone to Love.

Darin comes thru with a sock reading of "Artificial Flowers" effective nostalgic item from Maurice Evans's forthcoming Broadway musical, "Tenderloin." Backing is in Darin's hard-driving, swingin' "Mack the Knife" tradition. Flip returns artist to his old rock and roll groove on a catchy rocker. (9/12/60) (A-side, #20 Pop; B-side, #45 Pop)

Lazy River/Oee-Ee-Train.

A sock couple of sides by the chanter. On top is the great Hoagy Carmichael tune done in Darin's highly stylized, night club fashion. Flip is a rockin' bluesy item, penned by the chanter. This also has a big chance. (1/30/61) (#14 Pop)

Irresistible You/Multiplication.

Darin has a solid follow-up to his recent hit "You Must Have Been a Beautiful Baby." "Irresistible You," a blues oriented tune, in a swingin' rocker groove. The flip, penned by Darin for his movie "Come September," is a clever rocker with a bright, happy beat. (12/4/61) (A-side, #15 Pop; B-side, # 30 Pop)

Bobby then took on rock ("What'd I Say") and country ("Things") for the start of 1962. "Things" became his sixth million seller and his last hit before signing with Capitol. During Darin's country phase, his guitarist for club dates was Roger McGuinn (then known as Jim) in his pre-Byrds apprenticeship.

Things.

A stylish reading, almost in the country groove, by Bobby Darin, of a bright ditty that he penned himself. Arrangement is sharp and fem chorus is hip. This could be another hit for Bobby. Flip is "Jailer Bring Me Water." (6/23/62) (#3 Pop)

If a Man Answers/A True, True Love.

Two powerful sides by Bobby in his new label affiliation. The lad sings tunes associated with his forthcoming pic, "If a Man Answers" and is writer of both sides. The top side is a medium tempo swinger which should appeal to the teeners. Second is the love theme from the pic and is sung with feeling by Bobby against strings and chorus. (9/15/62) (#32 Pop)

Now You've Gone/You're the Reason I'm Livin'.

Two solid pieces of material for Darin here. The artist, who fits into so many different grooves, swings into the bluegrass sound on the first weeper with violins and chorus in support. The second has a definitive Ray Charles touch with swinging strings and chorus backing the vocalist's poignant reading of the weeper. (1/5/63) (B-side, #3 Pop, #9 R&B)

In between records, Bobby was making marked strides in his acting career with an Oscar nomination for "Captain Newman, M.D.," and a costarring role with Steve McQueen in "Hell Is for Heroes." His records, however, were only reaching the lower rungs of the charts. In 1966, he returned to Atlantic and established himself in another new direction, folk-rock.

If I Were a Carpenter.

The versatile Darin has done it again. In the folk-rock bag, he excels here with an intriguing composition written by Tim Hardin. Watch this one, could be a giant. (9/10/66) (#8 Pop)

Lovin' You.

Composed by John Sebastian with the feel of "Daydream" and an old-timey arrangement, this rhythm number with top Darin vocal work has the earmarks of a No. 1 item. (1/7/67) (#32 Pop)

The Lady Came from Baltimore.

Back in the "Carpenter" bag with Tim Hardin material. . . . Moving story line and fine Koppelman-Rubin production work in strong support. (3/25/67) (#62 Pop)

Divorced in 1967 and shaken by the death of Robert Kennedy, Darin maintained a year-long, low-profile existence, living in a mobile home in Big Sur. After his self-exile, he formed Direction Records and issued five singles of the folk/protest variety, but only one charted.

Long Line Rider.

> *Darin's initial outing on his own label, distributed by Bell, should hit hard and fast and take him right [to] the top. The original rhythm ballad has a compelling lyric line, and should prove as big as his "If I Were a Carpenter." (11/30/68) (#79 Pop)*

In 1971, Darin moved from the frying pan (Direction) to the fire (Motown), a label that rarely *saw* a white act, let alone knew what to do with one. Still, Bobby was an accomplished performer with a wide following. In 1972, that popularity earned him a summer replacement show on NBC, and a January through April 1973 run of "The Bobby Darin Show."

By 1973, the multitalented 37-year-old was experiencing heart problems, which had plagued him since contracting rheumatic fever as a child. On December 20, he died in Cedars Sinai Medical Center in Los Angeles of heart failure.

In 1990 that gifted talent was inducted into the Rock and Roll Hall of Fame.

JOEY DEE AND THE STARLITERS

Joseph DiNicola (Joey Dee): Lead vocals
Born: 6/11/40, Passaic, NJ
David Brigati: Saxophone
Born: 1940
Larry Vernieri: Saxophone
Born: 1940
Carlton Latimer: Keyboards
Born: 1939
Willie Davis: Drums
Born: 1940

Influences: Ray Charles, Jackie Wilson, Isley Brothers, Jimmy Reed, Crests
Influenced: Rascals

If Chubby Checker was the king of the Twist era, Joey Dee was the crown prince. The New Jersey youth, one of nine brothers and sisters, was a singer and saxophone player by the time he formed The Starliters in 1958. They built such a strong reputation at local clubs and parties (owing to their set based on current dance crazes), that by mid-1960, Dee and company became The Peppermint Lounge's house band. The high society club on New York's West 45th Street was fast becoming the "in" spot.

The Starliters weren't performing very long before Scepter Records gave them an opportunity. The backup group on their debut disk, "Face of an Angel," was none other than label mates, The Shirelles.

Face of an Angel.

★★★ *Dee handles this ballad quite nicely against string and chorus backing. The chanter exhibits quite a vocal range in this reading. Chorus has an interesting fill between lines of the chorus, which might cause some confusion as to what they're saying.*

Shimmy Baby.

★★★ *A shimmy, twisting blues by Dee and his vocal supporting group. Good pounding passages here by the piano and the singers. Side is worth a hearing. (10/24/60)*

By 1961, "The Twist" was the teenage rage, and when adults started twisting at the Peppermint Lounge, the fad really took off internationally. The group incorporated go-go dancers at that time; Dee's dancing dolls were a young trio known as The Darling Sisters (they were later known as The Ronettes). During their tenure with Dee, they backed his recording of "Down by the Riverside" (Roulette, 1964).

Meanwhile, the media attention Joey and the band received due to their Twist set earned them a deal with Roulette Records. The Starliters' first single was cowritten by Dee and A&R director Henry Glover, "Peppermint Twist," named after the night spot. Their million seller threw their careers into high gear, and in February 1962, Joey et al. were featured in the film *Hey, Let's Twist*, which also spawned a 45 of the same name.

Peppermint Twist (Parts 1 and 2).

★ ★ ★ ★ *Joey Dee, now playing at the Peppermint Lounge in New York has made a wild disking here with his group and it could turn into a good seller. It features Dee singing the slight lyrics while the rhythm pounds away in Twist fashion. Good side. (10/30/61) (#1 Pop, #8 R&B)*

Hey, Let's Twist.

 From the flick of the same name comes this bright, swinging Twist side by Joey Dee and his combo. It's in the vein of the "Peppermint Twist" and it rocks. Solid sales item here. (1/27/62) (#20 Pop)

The frantic pace continued with a cover of the Isley Brothers' "Shout." By October, Dee and the guys appeared in another film, *Two Tickets to Paris*. Roulette kept issuing singles that alternated (at least in the *Billboard* reviews) between being credited to Joey Dee and Joey Dee and The Starliters.

Shout (Parts 1 and 2).

 From Joey Dee's current album, "Hey, Let's Twist," comes this rocking, pounding upbeat version of the Isley Brothers' hit of a couple seasons back. Either side has the excitement to go. (3/17/62) (#6 Pop)

Everytime (I Think About You) (Parts 1 and 2).

 The swinging Twist man has a frantic coupling here that the dancers will dig all the way. Tune is from the new Dee flick, "Two Tickets to Paris," and it features a strong vocal by the lad with wild background sounds and a compelling Twist beat. (6/9/62)

What Kind of Love Is This/Wing Ding.

 Two wild ones from the Peppermint Lounge man. The first is a romper that the lad sells in strong style of pulsing backing. The tune is from the lad's forthcoming flick "Two Tickets to Paris." The flip is an instrumental that should get lots of calls. It's got a lot

going for it rhythmically in the Latin-rock-Twist vein. Two sides that really rate. (7/28/62) (#18 Pop)

Trying to widen his appeal, Dee changed directions in late 1962 with "I Lost My Baby"/"Keep Your Mind on What You're Doing" but instead, it precipitated the group's slide. Their last charter, "Hot Pastrami with Mashed Potatoes," was back in the dance groove. Joey's last Top-100 outing was "Dance, Dance, Dance" (#89) in the summer of 1963.

Hot Pastrami with Mashed Potatoes (Parts 1 and 2).

This wild, driving, swinger, featuring some exciting organ work and Dee's vocal shouting could climb the charts quickly. Side 1 is the stronger of the two, with an infectious beat adding to the organ and vocal work. (4/20/63) (#36 Pop)

In 1964 Dee opened his own club in New York, Joey Dee's Starliter, and built a new group including Felix Cavaliere (keyboards), Eddie Brigati (percussion and brother of former Starliter, David), and Gene Cornish (guitar). By early 1965, the three Starliters joined with drummer Dino Danelli to form The Young Rascals. At the same time, Dee sold his club and returned to the tour circuit with yet another Starliters, featuring a young guitarist named Jimi Hendrix.

Dee has maintained an active career through the decades of the rock 'n' roll revival, and in the 1990s still does oldies shows, with his son Joey, Jr. at the keyboard.

THE DELLS

Johnny Funches: Lead vocals
Born: Harvey, IL
Marvin Junior: Lead and baritone
Born: 1/31/36, Harvey, IL
Verne Allison: Tenor
Born: 6/22/36, Harvey, IL
Mickey McGill: Baritone
Born: 2/17/37, Harvey, IL
Chuck Barksdale: Bass
Born: 1/11/35, Harvey, IL
Influences: Moonglows, Billy Ward and The Dominoes, Jackie Wilson
Influenced: Olympics

Many acts have been famous for 40 years or more, but few have actually been together recording and performing for that period of time. The Dells have and, except for one member change, the group of 1953 is the same as the quintet of 1995.

The Thornton Township High School teens were led by Johnny "Junior" Funches from their inception in 1953. Picking a name out of a textbook, Mickey first called them The El Rays (The Kings). In 1954, armed with two original songs, "Darling I Know" and "Christine," they traveled to Chicago and signed with Checker Records. After the songs were released and failed, label owner Leonard Chess told Marvin, the lead vocalist on "Christine," that he should give up singing and go drive a cab!

Darling I Know 76
The El Rays come thru with an unusual reading of a new ballad selling out-of-the-orinary sounds over a fair beat by the ork. Wax could get some attention due to the nature of the performance.

Christine 63
A Clovers-styled effort . . . on a swinging rocker. Only trouble is that the El Rays are not the Clovers. But the disk could get some spins. (5/22/54)

Realizing they were rough and not ready, they enlisted the aid of an area group for help with their harmony. They couldn't have chosen better, as the helpers were The Moonglows. Now fully confident, they crossed the street from Checker in early 1955 to prove their worth to Vee-Jay Records' Vivian Carter. She signed The El Rays but opted for a name change. The group picked one of five names dropped in a hat, and, from then on, they were The Dells. The group's first single, in April 1955, "Tell the World" did little, as did the group's follow up, "Dreams of Contentment."

Dreams of Contentment 74
A slow, pulsing beat supports a dreamy rendition of a tender ballad. Lead singer, with a wide-ranging tremolo, is effective. (3/3/56)

Johnny and Marvin then wrote "Oh, What a Night" after a fun-filled evening featuring The Dells, some female companions, and a lot of chicken. It would become the song most closely associated with the group.

Oh, What a Night 77
The group sings with strong feeling on a leisurely paced ballad, highlighted by the lead singer's outstanding solo work. (9/15/56) (#4 R&B)

Classic Dells '45s like "Why Do You Have to Go?" followed but none had "Nights'" strength.

Why Do You Have to Go? 80
The Dells invest a sweetly sad ballad with considerable emotional impact. Good performance by lead singer. (3/9/57)

Q-Bop She-Bop 74
A wild, jungle-like mixture of sound in minor key. Solo man wails with group in a constantly moving tricky backing. Has a sound which could generate some action. (8/5/57)

Time Makes You Change.
The flashy, swinging group figures to have another [hit] here. This has powerful rock and roll chanting of above average material. A lot of action likely here. Watch it. (11/4/57)

In 1958, their careers and lives were jeopardized in a car accident, and the group did not perform for two years. Funches left in 1959, replaced by Flamingos' veteran, Johnny Carter, who was working as a plastering contractor when he joined The Dells. By 1960, Vee-Jay was reissuing their singles, including their original hit, "Oh, What a Night."

Oh, What a Night.

The group turns in a spirited, semi-shouted reading on a medium paced ballad effort. Satisfying wax . . . released previously. (2/1/60)

In 1962, the label made a deal with the Chess/Checker/Argo complex, and The Dells were now singing for them. After four singles with Argo and no hits (although "The [Bossa Nova] Bird" reached #97 Pop, their first pop charter), they returned to Vee-Jay and had their first R&B hit in nine years, the first version of "Stay In My Corner" (#23). As Vee-Jay collapsed, the quintet found themselves back at Chess's Cadet affiliate in 1966. Their single of "O-O, I Love You" (#61 Pop, #22 R&B) started The Dells' renaissance period and the flip, "There Is" (#20 Pop, #11 R&B), brought them face to face with the soul era.

Wear It on Your Face.

Hot on the heels of their smash "There Is," group wails this blues rocker with all the ingredients to fast top the sales of the mentioned hit. (4/6/68) (#44 Pop, #27 R&B)

The Dells then made a six-minute revision of "Stay in My Corner" followed by a slew of soul gems.

Stay in My Corner.

Fast follow-up to "Wear It on Your Face" is this bluesy ballad performed in a top emotional and soulful performance. Should prove a big one. (6/22/68) (#10 Pop, #1 R&B)

Always Together.

Group went right up there to No. 10 on the Hot 100 with "Stay in My Corner" and this smooth blues ballad has all the drive to match the sales of the recent smash. (10/5/68) (#18 Pop, #3 R&B)

Does Anybody Know I'm Here.

Group went right up there with "Always Together" and "Stay in My Corner," and this soulful ballad beauty will send them back to the Top 20 once again in short order. Top vocal workout and arrangement by Charles Stepney. (12/21/68) (#38 Pop, #15 R&B)

I Can Sing a Rainbow/Love Is Blue.

Strong medley with potent performance offers much for play and sales in both pop and r.&b. markets. (5/10/69) (#22 Pop, #5 R&B)

In 1969, The Dells remade "Oh, What a Night" into a soul ballad with more of a Moonglows style than a Dells sound and it became their biggest hit.

Oh, What a Night.

This brand new recording of original hit of the '50's has the ingredients to go to the top once again, and proves a potent follow-up to their "Can Sing a Rainbow"/"Love Is Blue" smash. (8/2/69) (#10 Pop, #1 R&B)

By the late 1960s, The Dells were not only a star attraction, they were the most popular background singers around, having sung on hundreds of other artists' recordings (without credit), including Jerry Butler, Wade Flemons, Etta James, and Barbara Lewis's #1 hit, "Hello Stranger." Through the 1970s, the group mixed their own originals with past hits like "Long, Lonely Nights" (#74 Pop, #27 R&B) and "Glory of Love" (#92 Pop, #30 R&B).

Oh, What a Day.

Hot off their their "Sittin' on the Dock of the Bay" chart rider, the soul group comes on strong with a smooth rock ballad that should bring them back to the top, and repeat the success of their "Oh, What a Night" hit. (1/10/70) (#43 Pop, #10 R&B)

A Whiter Shade of Pale.

The Procol Harum hit of the past is currently attracting attention via the R. B. Greaves version, and with this soul-

ful treatment by the Dells, it should prove a big sales and programming item once again. (12/5/70)

The Love We Had (Stays on My Mind).

Group's first for the year is a heavy blues ballad that has it to put them right back on the Hot 100 and soul charts with sales impact. (7/17/71) (#30 Pop, #8 R&B)

In 1973, The "Heroes of Harvey" had their first million seller, "Give Your Baby a Standing Ovation" (#34 Pop, #3 R&B). By the 1970s, R&B records were going gold without much pop help and "Ovation" was a perfect example.

I Miss You.

Just an all-around fine record by respected veteran group which has never quite attained the adulation it deserves. An infectiously ominous instrumental chart and husky-throated baritone lead vocal combine for direct emotional plaint. (11/10/73) (#60 Pop, #8 R&B)

Learning to Love You Is Easy (It's So Hard Trying to Get Over You).

After almost two decades together the group still ranks as one of the super groups of soul. Usual superb mix of lead and backup vocals and usual fine production of Don Davis. With strings, horns and five voices there's lots going on here in this disco-flavored tune, but it all fits together perfectly. (8/31/74) (#18 R&B)

The group created an unusual LP in 1975 when they combined voices with The Dramatics, featuring the single "Love Is Missing from Our Lives" (#46 R&B). Also in 1975, the quintet moved to Mercury after 27 R&B hits with Cadet. Later moves to ABC, 20th, and Private I brought them into the 1980s, where their last charter was 1984's "Love On." The Dells were still soulfully satisfying the public as of the mid-1990s.

THE DELL-VIKINGS

Corinthian "Kripp" Johnson: Lead vocals
Born: 5/15/33, Cambridge, MA (died 6/22/90)
Norman Wright: Lead vocals, first tenor
Born: 10/21/37, Philadelphia, PA
Donald "Gus" Backus: Second tenor
Born: 1938, Southampton, LI
David Lerchey: Baritone
Born: 2/3/37, New Albany, IN
Clarence Quick: Bass
Born: 2/2/37, Brooklyn, NY (died 5/5/83)
Influences: Platters, Moonglows, Flamingos, Drifters, Spaniels, Clovers, Penguins, Dominoes
Influenced: Marcels, Imaginations

America's first racially mixed, hitmaking rock 'n' roll vocal group, The Dell-Vikings, are best remembered for the doo wop classic, "Come Go with Me."

The group was established thanks to the U.S. Air Force. Stationed at Pittsburgh's airport in 1956, Clarence Quick fashioned his group at the N.C.O. club with "Kripp" Johnson, Sam Patterson, Bernard Robertson, and Don Jackson. Quick originally played basketball in Brooklyn with The Vikings, and borrowed the name, adding The Del for the quartet's purposes. Contrary to popular belief, the original members were all black. However, soon after forming, Sam and Bernard were shipped to Germany and in came Norman Wright and the first white member, Dave Lerchey. Producer Joe Averback noticed the quintet at a local talent show and the result was nine a cappella recordings in Averback's basement. By November 1956, he had added some instrumentation to several songs, including Quick's original "Come Go with Me," and issued it on his own Fee Bee label. It became the first Top-10 hit by a mixed act.

Come Go with Me.

On the Fee Bee label, this waxing started taking off two weeks ago. Now Dot has the master and will undoubtedly break it out in numerous new areas. This is a relaxed, well sold rhythm-ballad that has most of the commercial elements neccesary for a big teenage click. Flip is "How Can I Find True Love?" a more traditionally styled ballad. Tho, it too, has moments of appeal, it is a little too pretentious to make much impact. (2/9/57) (#4 Pop, #2 R&B)

Little Billy Boy/What Made Maggie Run.

The group comes off its "Come Go with Me," bought-master smash to register very heavily with two coin-worthy sides. On top is a powerful cover of a tune originally on the Paris label. On the flip is another cover which sports a novelty angle and a strong rhythm emphasis. Either can go. (5/6/57)

After their second release, Don was sent to a German base, and the quintet's second white vocalist, Donald Backus, joined, just in time for the "Whispering Bells" single. New manager, Al Berman, broke the Fee Bee/Dot contract by taking all the under-legal-age members of the group to Mercury (Wright, Quick, Backus, Lerchey, and Quick's friend Bill Blakely), releasing "Cool Shake." Undeterred, Kripp added Eddie Everette, Art Budd, Chuck Jackson, and returning Don Jackson (no relation) for his new "Dot" Dell-Vikings, issuing "Whispering Bells"/"Don't Be a Fool." Both records were on the charts at the same time, confusing deejays as to who was who. The arbitrary use of various spellings of the group's name didn't help.

Whispering Bells.

Uptempo rhythm side, the group chants it to a rollicking beat with the sound of bells integrated in the arrangement. Bright sound.

Don't Be a Fool.

A ballad on this side for a change of pace. Pace is slow but swingy not quite the impact of the flip. (6/17/57) (#9 Pop, #5 R&B)

Cool Shake.

The first on the label by the hot group stands a good chance of taking off. It's a fast, rollicking blues with several catchy phrases that should go over big with the teens. Flip, "Jitterbug Mary," is a rhythm side in the novelty vein that should also be right in there. (6/17/57) (#12 Pop, #9 R&B)

Dell-Vikings and Kripp Johnson: I'm Spinning/When I Come Home.

Bright, cheerful effort by the hot group on a cute Latin-beat tune. . . . Fine vocal stint by Johnson is backed with usual sock mastery by the Vikings. Flip . . . is a slow ballad with rhythm backing that can also be in there. (8/9/57)

The Dell Vikings:

(Note: Mercury called them The Del-Vikings but *Billboard* wrote Dell-Vikings on some Mercury reviews.)

Come Along with Me.

Fine group performance on a tune quite similar to their first hit, "Come Go with Me." Sock selling here should attract. (9/23/57)

In December 1957, Mercury came into legal possession of the group's name and the "Dot" Dell-Vikings disbanded. Sides later released by that group came out under the name The Versatiles or Chuck Jackson (who was still three years away from solo success with "I Don't Want to Cry" and "Any Day Now"). Kripp then joined his Mercury friends, whereas Gus was sent to (you guessed it) Germany.

The Voodoo Man 78

Good rhythmic wax by the group. Okay chirping sound by the boys, tho side isn't their strongest.(2/17/58)

Johnson took over lead for their last two Mercury singles, "You Cheated"/"Pretty Little Things Called Girls" and "Flat Tire"/"How Could You." The interesting aspect of "You Cheated" was that The Dell-Vikings, a mixed aggregation from Pittsburgh, had covered a black group from Los Angeles (The Shields) who had copied a white group from Texas (The Slades).

You Cheated 80

> *Rockaballad is given a bluesy flavor in this smooth reading . . . Rates spins.(7/21/58)*

Flat Tire.

★ ★ ★   *Story song about a car that gets a flat tire is performed neatly by the Del Vikings, as the boys tell about their troubles with their gal and their car. Good side here. (11/17/58)*

By 1960, the quintet was free from the Air Force and free of Mercury, signing a one-shot deal with Alpine, and then enjoyed a seven-single run with ABC. Although their recordings were praiseworthy, they never charted again.

Pistol Packin' Mama.

> *The Del Vikings wrap up the old novelty hit in a sock reading with a zestful r&r beat. Strong dual market side. (10/24/60)*

Bring Back Your Heart.

★ ★ ★ ★   *Lead singer gets out neatly on this fine Latin-tinged ballad. He does a moving job on the tune while the group fills in appropriately.*

I'll Never Stop Crying.

★ ★ ★   *The tune is a slow ballad with an effective lead job. Incidental comments from the bass a la the Ink Spots, add interest. (4/3/61)*

I Hear Bells.

★ ★ ★ ★   *A swingin' side in the earlier rock and roll style. The boys turn out an exuberent reading of the tune, assisted by chimes and bass voice breaks. (9/18/61)*

Face the Music.

★ ★ ★ ★   *Here's a tune with a feeling of some of the arrangements of the Drifters, with their trick rhythm backings. The lead adds a wailing quality to the performance. Could catch spins. (11/27/61)*

The Big Silence.

> *The boys may have their first hit in some time with this showmanly side. The plaintive rockaballad is sung with*

> *considerable feeling and sales savvy by the lead warbler, who also contributes a sock narration bit. Watch it. (3/3/62)*

Kilimanjaro.

> *Here's another potent teen item. The side combines an infectious "Skoklan" type rhythm with some sharp singing by the lead and the group. The disk has a sound that's built to attract the high school crowd. (6/23/62)*

The act split up in the mid-1960s, but reformed in 1970 with Johnson, Quick, Lerchey, Wright, and Blakely. They recorded a new version of "Come Go with Me" (Scepter) in 1972. Performing everywhere, from New York's Radio City Music Hall and London's Palladium to the Far East, The Dell-Vikings were once again two acts by 1979. Johnson's group with Wright, Lerchey, and newcomers John Byas and Ritzy Lee competed with Quick's collaborators including Blakely and rookies Herb McQueen, Louis Valdez, and Arthur Martinez. Johnson died in 1990 at the age of 57, leaving Quick's group to carry on The Dell-Vikings legacy, even though Clarence himself had passed on in 1983. Their last single was a brilliant two-sided probe of the past, "Rock and Roll Remembered"/"My Heart" in 1991.

NEIL DIAMOND

Birthdate: 1/24/41
Birthplace: Brooklyn, NY
Influences: Everly Brothers, Pete Seeger, Les Paul, Weavers, Elvis Presley, Bo Diddley, Ritchie Valens, Burl Ives, Tex Ritter
Influenced: Melissa Etheridge, Billy Ray Cyrus, Urge Overkill

One of rock's most intense performers, Neil Diamond brings dramatic flair to even the simplest of songs.

Neil's singing desire goes back to 1951 when, at age 10, he harmonized with a Brooklyn-based streetcorner group, with the odd name of The Memphis Backstreet Boys. By the age of 13, he had formed a folk group called The Roadrunners.

In 1955, during a winter holiday at Surprise Lake Camp, a performance by folk legend Pete Seeger lured him into the new world of songwriting.

As the new decade dawned, Neil and friend Jack Parker formed the duo Neil and Jack and recorded two Everly Brothers styled 45s for Duel records. Both "What Will I Do" (1960) and "I'm Afraid" (1961) became instant obscurities. Meanwhile, the Erasmus High School grad entered NYU as a premed student on (of all things) a fencing scholarship, but his heart was in his songs and he spent all his free time writing, singing, and chasing an elusive staff writing gig. In 1961, Neil was hired by Roosevelt Music, earning $25 a week and college abruptly ended. By 1963, Diamond managed to obtain a record deal with Columbia, producing one single, but it was short-lived.

Clown Town.

Here's an impressive new chanter with strong touches of both Neil Sedaka and Bobby Vee. The tune is a bright one, done with a solid arrangement and handled with good dual track effects. Definitely worth watching. Flip is "At Night." (7/13/63)

His songwriting finally bore fruit in 1965, when Jay and The Americans broke the Top 20 with his "Sunday and Me." Persevering, Neil landed a new record deal with the Atlantic-distributed Bang label after being seen performing by Brill Building mavens, Jeff Barry and Ellie Greenwich, at a Greenwich Village coffeehouse. His first big hit as a performer came with "Cherry, Cherry."

Solitary Man.

Diamond debuts on Bang with his own material as he sings this ballad of a loner looking for love. Aimed at the teen market, the disk has a solid dance beat and excellent production backing. (4/16/66) (#55 Pop)

Cherry, Cherry.

Dance-beat disk of the week. Exciting production features bass piano backing and choral support of Diamond's vocal work. (7/30/66) (#8 Pop)

Through 1966, Neil had three hits as a vocalist and four as a writer, when the Monkees' "I'm a Believer" reached #1, selling almost four million

singles worldwide. He then hit The Monkees button again in 1967 with "A Little Bit Me, a Little Bit You," another million seller. His own 45s weren't doing badly either.

You Got to Me.

Penned by Diamond, and given a powerful vocal workout, this infectious rhythm number is destined for the top of the Hot 100. Fine Jeff Barry and Ellie Greenwich production. (1/21/67) (#18 Pop)

Girl, You'll Be a Woman Soon.

The hot composer-performer has another sure-fire chart topper to fast replace his "You Got to Me." Easy rhythm backs a soulful reading of compelling lyric. One of Diamond's best efforts. (3/25/67) (#10 Pop)

Kentucky Woman.

Folk rocker proves one of Diamond's most potent entries that should fast top the sales of the successful "Thank the Lord for the Nighttime." Strong material. (10/7/67) (#22 Pop)

His first nonoriginal single was a remake of Gary U.S. Bonds's "New Orleans," but when it only reached #51, Diamond went back to his own pen with "Red Red Wine"/"Red Rubber Ball." Neil then bolted Bang for MCA's new Uni label when the former refused to issue his new song, "Shilo." Diamond finally had his first million seller as an artist with "Sweet Caroline," and Bang, not to be outdone, belatedly but successfully released "Shilo."

Red Red Wine/Red Rubber Ball.

Two strong sales entries from Diamond. First is a compelling, original folk-flavored ballad while the flip is a good contrast in pace as he updates the Cyrkle's past hit with a strong dance beat. (3/16/68) (#62 Pop)

Brother Love's Travelling Salvation Show.

This powerful piece of rhythm material with a potent lyric line will prove one of Diamond's biggest hits ever. Infectious and stirring is his performance of the rousing material. (2/15/69) (#22 Pop)

Sweet Caroline.

> *Hard hitting love ballad should bring Diamond back to the charts to exceed his "Brother Love's Travelling Salvation Show" smash. Exceptional production and vocal workout. (6/14/69) (#4 Pop)*

Shilo.

> *Riding high on the Uni label, Bang comes up with one of Diamond's former top performances that offers much for sales and chart action. (1/17/70) (#24 Pop)*

As another decade turned, Neil went from star to superstar. "Cracklin' Rosie" became his first #1.

Soolaimon.

> *Diamond is right back in his hot selling bag of "Sweet Caroline" and "Holly Holy" with this clever piece of rhythm material delivered in a powerful vocal workout and arrangement. (4/11/70) (#30 Pop)*

Cracklin' Rosie.

> *Diamond comes up with a clever rhythm item that has to hit with all the potent sales of another "Sweet Caroline" or "Holly Holy." (8/15/70)*

He Ain't Heavy . . . He's My Brother.

★ *The Bobby Scott-Bob Russell number, a smash for the Hollies six months ago, is given the unique Diamond treatment which will prove a smash all over again. Top Lee Holdridge arrangement, production by Tom Catalano and exceptional vocal work. (10/31/70) (#20 Pop)*

His fourth gold smash, the autobiographical "I Am, I Said," is said to have been Diamond's most difficult creation.

Once again Bang browsed through their vaults and with a little additional sweetening came up with Neil's six-year-old original "I'm a Believer," while Uni kept pace and then some.

I Am, I Said.

> *Diamond's first for the year is another piece of dynamite material with a lyric line that tells quite a story. The driving*

ballad with exceptional performance will follow in the footsteps of his last two Top 10 winners. (3/20/71) (#4 Pop)

I'm a Believer.

★ *Diamond's potent swinger (No. 1 hit in 1967 for the Monkees) is updated here with the addition of strings, gospel style piano and strong vocal group. Whole new sound to the oldie headed for the Top 10! (6/12/71) (#51 Pop)*

Stones.

> *Diamond does it again! In what will prove to be a sales monster, this exceptional ballad material with a performance to match can't miss. (10/30/71) (#14 Pop)*

In 1972, a year before his Uni contract expiration, Diamond signed with Columbia for the then-unheard-of guarantee of $5 million! Columbia certainly got its money's worth.

The soundtrack from the film *Jonathan Livingston Seagull*, which included "Longfellow Serenade," earned Neil a Grammy for Best Film Soundtrack LP.

Longfellow Serenade.

> *Soft rocker . . . has already jumped on the charts, and this return to the type of material that has propelled him to the top so many times should do the same again. Ideal for virtually all types of radio formats, with the distinctive Diamond vocal and writing styles as standout as always. (10/5/74) (#5 Pop)*

I've Been This Way Before.

> *Diamond has been knocked in the past for doing formula type songs, but the man has come up with a distinctive style and, when one is a major success, there is no need to change. Actually, this cut is stronger lyrically than recent product, the vocals are more versatile and the arrangement, moving from soft to mid tempo to booming, symphonic sound is interesting. (1/25/75) (#34 Pop)*

If You Know What I Mean.

> *First single in many months for Diamond is a powerful ballad with*

good words, stronger, more emotional vocals than the artist has shown in recent years and excellent, building, lush production from Robbie Robertson. (6/12/76) (#11 Pop)

Desiree.

This is one of the strongest outings from this gifted composer/singer in some time. An infectious back beat sets the pace all the way through as Diamond weaves his tale of a first love on this high tempo ballad. Producer [Bob] Gaudio adds strings and horns throughout to give sweeping orchestral depth. (12/3/77) (#16 Pop)

Unbeknownst to most, Diamond collapsed on a San Francisco stage in the late 1970s and was diagnosed as having a career- and life-threatening tumor on his spinal cord. Fortunately, surgery proved successful and he fully resumed his career.

In 1978, both Diamond and Barbra Streisand recorded versions of "You Don't Bring Me Flowers," coincidentally, in the same key. After a Louisville, Kentucky deejay edited the versions together, the phone response was so great that Columbia brought Four Seasons producer Bob Gaudio into the studio to record the duo on "Flowers." The result was "stereo superstars" at their best. Diamond and Streisand performed "Flowers" on the Grammy Awards in February 1979 and collected two Grammy nominations.

You Don't Bring Me Flowers.

The first teaming of superstars Streisand and Diamond is highlighted by piano and violin orchestration. The lush interplay of vocals brings commanding depth and appeal to the ballad, which first appeared on Diamond's "I'm Glad You're Here with Me Tonight" album. (10/21/78) (#1 Pop)

September Morn.

Diamond serves up one of his traditional midtempo ballads that boasts several lyrical hooks. While his voice is the record's predominant strength, the tasty keyboard work gives the track an extra sparkle. (12/22/79) (#17 Pop)

Again working with Gaudio, Diamond wrote and sang the soundtrack for the film *The Jazz Singer* while starring opposite Laurence Olivier in the Al Jolson remake. Although the film was not a critical success, it produced more hit singles for the singer. Diamond continued to produce lesser hits through the 1980s.

Love on the Rocks.

From the "Jazz Singer" film and soundtrack, this is a beautiful ballad featuring Diamond's patented smokey vocals. Strings add an epic feel to the disk. (11/1/80) (#2 Pop)

America.

The third release from "The Jazz Singer" soundtrack is nothing less than Diamond's best single in years. It marries the bristling dynamics of rock with Diamond's long-standing vocal and narrative skill. And it's an excellent change of pace after a pair of back-to-back top 10 ballads. (4/25/81) (#8 Pop)

Heartlight.

Diamond's latest was cowritten and coproduced with Carole Bayer Sager and Burt Bacharach, with Bacharach also arranging and conducting the track. It's a pretty, romantic ballad with a light lifting melody line. (1/4/82) (#5 Pop)

I'm Alive.

Gruff and sentimental as ever, Diamond follows the top five "Heartlight" with a paean to dogged optimism. Handclaps and familiar chord changes recall the good old days of his earliest pop hits. (1/15/83) (#35 Pop)

This Time.

Diamond's soon-to-be-high media profile with a forthcoming HBO special and tour can only help Diamond regain his chart hold. Elegant ballad release marks the artist's first studio album in two years. (12/24/88)

Having already sold over 100 million albums and singles, in February 1984, Neil Diamond was honored by his peers and inducted into the Songwriters Hall of Fame.

THE DIAMONDS

David Somerville: Lead vocals
Born: 10/2/33, Toronto, Canada
Ted Kowalski: Tenor
Born: 5/16/31, Toronto, Canada
Phil Leavitt: Baritone
Born: 7/9/35, Toronto, Canada
Bill Reed: Bass
Born: 1/11/36, Toronto, Canada
Influences: Chords, Willows, G-Clefs, Golden Gate
    Quartet, Crew Cuts, Four Lads, Four Aces
Influenced: Carole King, Four Seasons

The best of the mid-1950s' white rock 'n' roll cover groups, The Diamonds often competed on the black charts (seven times, in fact) against the same acts and songs that they copied.

The group was forged into a quartet at the University of Toronto in 1954; soon after, Ted came up with their name. During their 1955 summer vacation, the vocalists auditioned in New York for Coral Records courtesy of their new manager, Nat Goodman. A single, "Black Denim Trousers and Motorcycle Boots," was the result, but it was overwhelmed by The Cheers' original and the group dejectedly returned home. They rekindled their confidence by traipsing to Cleveland where deejay Bill Randall had previously helped another Toronto quartet, The Crew Cuts, gain success with Mercury. When the foursome auditioned for Mercury with spirituals, the label's brain trust signed them to the rock 'n' roll division (another name for "the white imitators of R&B singles" department) instead of the pop division. Going up against one of the first R&B records to beat out a white imitator, The Diamonds competitive version of "Why Do Fools Fall in Love" became their debut hit, and encouraged Mercury to copy every black track they could find, including such tunes as "Church Bells May Ring," "Every Night About This Time"/"Love, Love, Love" and "Ka-Ding-Dong."

Why Do Fools Fall in Love 74
A nice cover side with the lead singer showcased well by the arrangement. Could share the loot if the number continues to climb via the Teen-Agers' original.

You Baby, You 73
This side moves right along with a lively beat and good chanting. (2/11/56) (#12 Pop)

Church Bells May Ring.
Combination here of a hot tune (The Willows' version is now moving well in r.&b. circles) and a hot group makes this a potent entry. Features great bell sounds with some solid strength in the vocal department. A solid loot-puller. (3/24/56) (#14 Pop)

Every Night About This Time/Love, Love, Love.
The group is riding high on the charts right now and their new disk is another two-sided hit. "Every Night About This Time" is a strong cover of the Sophomore's Dawn disk, with an outstanding contribution by the lead singer. The flip is a bouncy, persuasive vocal performance of the current r.&b. Clovers' click. (8/18/56) (B-side, #30 Pop, #14 R&B)

Ka-Ding-Dong.
A sock rendition of this opus which is coming up on the r.&b. charts via the G-Clefs recording. A natural for the rock and roll crowd. (6/9/56)

A Thousand Miles Away 80
Cover of the current Heartbeats' hit. The Diamonds offer an attractive styling of the ballad, but it comes a little too late to get maximum exposure. Some pop stores may stock this in preference to the Heartbeats, however. (12/22/56)

When a ballad was slipped in and failed ("A Thousand Miles Away"), they went back to the uptempo format via a record Goodman found sitting on the desk of Mercury's orchestra leader, David Carroll. He rehearsed The Diamonds all night on the R&B song "Little Darlin'," and by the session, the group was so giddy, they began exaggerating the bass and falsetto portions of the song. It turned out to be one of music history's delights. Incredibly, The Diamonds' version outdistanced The Gladiolas' effort on the R&B charts as the original reached #11. The Diamonds' "Darlin'" sold over four million singles worldwide.

Little Darlin'/Faithful and True.

This is about as fine a coupling as this group has had and they've been up in the chips before. Pacing is highly commercial with a bright and slightly wild rhythm side (a cover of the Gladiolas' r.&b. original) on top, coupled with a melodic and tenderly handled ballad. The kids will flip for both of these and either can go all the way. A sharp r.&b. entry as well. (2/23/57) (#2 Pop, #2 R&B)

By then, no one was spared the group's versatile cloning and such artists as Buddy Holly ("Words of Love") were next in line for The Diamonds treatment.

Words of Love.

Strong . . . entry should pile plays in both the pop and r.&b. markets. "Words" is an unusual rhythm item, featuring an infectious rock and roll tempo and excellent lead. (6/3/57) (#13 Pop, #12 R&B)

The Stroll.

This is the best in several tries by the "Little Darlin'" crew. Their expert chanting on this medium-beat rockablues makes it a good bet to score in all marts. (12/9/57) (#4 Pop, #5 R&B)

They became "the kings of covers" when, in September 1957, the quartet went to the extreme of recording not one, but both sides of The Rays' current 45, "Silhouettes" (#10 Pop vs The Rays' #3) and "Daddy Cool." By early 1958, Ted and Bill left and were replaced by John Felton and Evan Fisher. From that time on, the group recorded mostly originals with notable exceptions by Chuck Willis, The Solitaires' "Walkin' Along," and their last charter, a quality remake

(not a cover) of The Danleers' 1958 hit "One Summer Night."

High Sign.

Rockabilly tune with fine group vocals and good ork support. Contender in all markets. (3/17/58) (#37 Pop)

Happy Years.

★ *A very strong piece of material deals with the happy years at school. Has a nice Western flavor and the boys give it a good lyrical reading. A most timely item that can step up quickly.*

Kathy-O.

★ *The attractive pic ballad is warbled nicely by the group with good results. Side has also been cut by juvenile actress Patty McCormack on Dot but this could share the loot. (6/9/58) (A-side, #73 Pop; B-side, #16 Pop)*

Walking Along 80

Driving rocker gets a strong, cheerful reading from the group. Highly danceable. Strong potential. (9/29/58) (#29 Pop)

From the Bottom of My Heart/She Say Oom Dooby Doom.

Either side can keep the hit string alive for the crew. "From the Bottom" is a Chuck Willis tune that is sold with vigor. Backing is wild, and the side really moves. Flip, "She Say," is a cute tune with nonsense lyrics that should also place well. (1/5/59) (#18 Pop)

A Mother's Love.

David Somerville is featured lead on "A Mother's Love, " a charming rockaballad that is read with a strong group assist. Side is a bit of a switch for the group, but they register strongly. (3/30/59)

Batman, Wolfman, Frankenstein, Dracula/Walkin' the Stroll.

"Batman" is a cute novelty that tells of a chick who cuddles in the movies only when there is a horror film showing. The boys read it nicely over good ork support. "Walkin' the Stroll" is a

danceable blues item sung well in stroll tempo. Both can happen. (11/16/59)

One Summer Night.

★ ★ ★ ★ *The side, a rockaballad, was a big one in the r.&b. world some years ago. It's handled with moving affection by the lead here with the rest of the boys adding appropriate figures. (6/20/61) (#22 Pop)*

In 1961, Felton was promoted to lead when Somerville became a folk singer known as David Troy. He then joined The Four Preps until 1969. He and Preps leader Bruce Belland sang as a duo thereafter. In 1974, 13 years after their last appearance, the original foursome came together for an oldies show in New York City; they reunited again 13 years later in 1995 at the Greek Theater in Los Angeles. In 1978, Bob Duncan became lead, reformed the group, and led them to a country charter, "Just a Little Bit" in 1987 (#63). Membership changed so often that as of 1994, 27 different vocalists had called The Diamonds home. Ted later became an engineer, Bill went into record promotion in Florida, and David joined a new Four Preps in 1990.

Although purists consider what they (and other groups like them) did to be the homogenizing of R&B originals, there's no doubt that within the confines of their musical direction, The Diamonds raised the "cover record" to an art form, albeit a dying one.

BO DIDDLEY

Real Name: Otha Ellas Bates McDaniel
Birthdate: 12/30/28
Birthplace: McComb, MS
Influence: John Lee Hooker
Influenced: The Who, Bruce Springsteen, Rolling Stones, Yardbirds, Doors, Neil Diamond, Ronnie Hawkins, Ritchie Valens

Bo Diddley's legendary influence as a musician and writer during rock's infancy contrasts sharply with his actual recording success, which yielded only five pop hits (nothing higher than #20) and 11 R&B chart titles.

Although he was born Otha Ellas Bates, his mother's cousin Gussie McDaniel adopted him at infancy, and they moved to Chicago in 1934. Surprisingly, considering his larger-than-life image, Bo's first instrument was not the guitar but the violin as taught by Professor O. W. Frederick at the Ebenezer Baptist Church. Bo also played trombone in the church band. He was self-taught on guitar by age ten and played on street corners for change with a washboard player and second guitarist, calling themselves The Hipsters.

When not in Foster Vocational School (where he learned to build guitars and violins), Bo was training as a boxer. Constantly being taunted by schoolmates because he was a "country boy" caused Bo to take up sparring. "When I got to be 14, 15 years old, I started boxing and started crackin' heads . . . the Bo Diddley thing started back then, I think it was a girl that started that mess, 'Man you're a Bo Diddley!' something like that, and I could never figure out what the hell that meant."

Working at unskilled labor in the daytime, by 1951 Bo was playing at the 708 Club on Chicago's south side. The band became The Langley Avenue Jive Cats, because Bo lived at 4746 Langley. In 1955 he auditioned for Vee-Jay, and label owner Ewart Abner threw him out saying, "What is that shit?" Bo replied, "I don't know, I just play it." He then auditioned for Chess Records' Leonard Chess. Leonard was interested in his vocalizing and intrigued by Bo's "bomp, bomp, bomp-bomp bomp" guitar style that Diddley called, "the muted sound," a style he learned on violin and transferred to guitar (today the style is called "funk").

The only time in rock history that an artist's name became the title of his first single helped make "Bo Diddley" an instant hit. With nonstop airplay from the likes of Alan Freed, Bo had a two-sided smash. Dressed in black, wearing horn-rimmed glasses and playing a rectangular, low-slung electric guitar (which he invented), the 200-pound Diddley was an awesome sight to behold and his "you can't stand still" rhythm was infectious.

I'm a Man/Bo Diddley.

> *This unusual record has been blazing an impressive trail since release three weeks ago. Territories that have been reporting strong action include St. Louis, Atlanta, Durham, Nashville, Chicago, Cleveland and Buffalo. Both sides are doing well, with an edge on "I'm a Man" this week. A previous Billboard "Spotlight" pick. (4/23/55) (B-side, #1 R&B)*

A Moonglows-backed hit followed.

Diddley Daddy 80

> *After the sensational success of "Bo Diddley," this follow-up has a ready-made market. This has much of the flavor of the original, including the off-beat arrangement that perked up all ears. The singer gives a lively, characteristic performance.*

She's Fine, She's Mine 77

> *While this is a traditional blues in form, the unusual, almost exotic, arrangement with its hypnotic beat combined with Bo Diddley's anguished vocal takes this far out of the range of the ordinary. Both sides undoubtedly will see vigorous action. (6/11/55) (#11 R&B)*

Bo played "Bo Diddley" on Ed Sullivan's TV show on November 20, 1955, a day after "Pretty Thing" was reviewed in *Billboard*. Mesmerizing rhythmic rockers like "Diddy Wah Diddy" and "Who Do You Love" followed. Though neither charted, they would serve as part of the reason for his longevity via recordings by the next-decade's artists. Bo's trademark guitar style was also heard on such rockers as Chuck Berry's 1958 hit "Sweet Little Rock and Roller."

Pretty Thing.

> *Another sock disk . . . It packs the same kind of wild, rhythmic wallop that put his "Bo Diddley" platter up on the charts. A showmanly performance makes the exuberantly paced platter one to watch. (11/19/55) (#4 R&B)*

Hey Bo-Diddley.

> *Bo-Diddley hasn't had a big one for some time now, but this disk could turn the sales tide. It's styled in the Usual Bo-Diddley rhythm groove, with a strong, insistent beat and a show-wise wrap-up of amusing auotbiographical lyrics by the artist. (4/6/57)*

In 1959, Bo's hit, "I'm Sorry" (#17 R&B) backed by The Carnations of "Long Tall Girl" fame, was followed by his first pop charter, "Crackin' Up" and his biggest pop hit, "Say Man."

Crackin' Up.

★★★ *Blues with a touch of rhumba and calypso feeling, and a lyric which tells a story. Bo Diddley is in good voice here, and will get plenty of play.*

The Great Grandfather.

★★★ *A terrific folk blues, with a lyric telling of life during pioneer days. Bo Diddley sings this in slow tempo, and he builds all the time. (5/25/59) (#62 Pop, #14 R&B)*

The Clock Strikes Twelve.

★★★ *Blues instrumental is given a fine ork treatment. Good side for pop and r.&b. jocks.*

Say Man.

★★★ *Bo Diddley handles this tune about a gossipy friend over sock backing with a Latinish touch. Amusing lyrics at times. (8/24/59) (B-side, #20 Pop, #3 R&B)*

Say Man, Back Again/She's Alright.

> *"Say Man, Back Again" could prove a hot follow-up to "Say Man." It's a similarly close side, and Bo Diddley's sly rendition could generate the same appeal. "She's Alright" is a wild, revival-styled item that should also figure. (11/9/59) (#23 R&B)*

In September 1963 Diddley did his first British tour, performing with The Rolling Stones and The Everly Brothers. Although Bo's hits stopped by 1962, it became apparent in the mid-1960s that British bands in particular had learned their lessons well from the Chicago innovator.

Acts like The Yardbirds, Rolling Stones, and Animals all recorded Diddley tunes and professed his influence on them. American acts (The Doors, Ronnie Hawkins, Quicksilver Messenger Service) also revived Diddley's style and songs.

In 1967, Bo had his last charter, "Oh Baby" (#17 R&B, #88 Pop) and continued to tour extensively (sometimes backed by Elephant's Memory). In 1969, he was part of promoter Richard Nader's first 1950s' rock 'n' roll revival show. He performed on Nader shows through the 1970s, and in 1973 appeared in the film, "Let the Good Times Roll" with Bill Haley, Little Richard, and Fats Domino. Enjoying his effect on younger acts and audiences, he opened for The Clash on their first U.S. tour in 1979. He made a cameo appearance in the Eddie Murphy film "Trading Places" in 1982, and in 1987 he was inducted into the Rock and Roll Hall of Fame.

DION AND THE BELMONTS

Dion DiMucci: Lead vocals
Born: 7/18/39, Bronx, NY
Angelo D'Aleo: First tenor
Born: 2/3/40, Bronx, NY
Fred Milano: Second tenor
Born: 8/22/39, Bronx, NY
Carlo Mastrangelo: Bass
Born: 10/5/38, Bronx, NY
Influences: Hank Williams, Penguins, Nutmegs, Robert Johnson, Mississippi John Hurt
Influenced: Bruce Springsteen, Billy Joel, Paul Simon, Tokens, Robert Plant, Jan and Dean, Lou Reed, Capris, Dave Edmunds, Excellents, Concords

One of the finest vocal groups of all time, The Belmonts gave history a rock 'n' roll original, Dion.

Although The Belmonts, Angelo, Carlo, and Freddy (the latter two of the street gang, The Imperial Hoods), knew Dion (of the similarly tough Fordham Daggers) and were all from the same neighborhood and school, the Bronx teens recorded separately at first, yet on the same label. Dion auditioned for Mohawk Records courtesy of neighboring songwriter, Phil Noto, who knew the owners. DiMucci's first single was done by adding his voice to an already existing track, "The Chosen Few," including a poppish vocal group, the Timberlanes, whom he never met. Dion and the Timberlanes:

The Chosen Few 80
Moving performance by Dion and the group on an unusual ballad, which combines a rock and roll beat with a churchy feeling. Watch this one. If label gets exposure, it could move out.

Out in Colorado 74
Lively rendition of a happy tune with a vigorous tempo and an attractive Western flavor. However, flip is stronger side. (6/24/57)

Dion then introduced The Belmonts (named after the Bronx's Belmont Avenue) to Mohawk. They recorded "Teenage Clementine" without Dion before joining forces as Dion and The Belmonts on "We Went Away" in late 1957. Their superb harmony was a mixture of Dion's country and blues influence, Freddy's love of doo wop, and Carlo's inclination toward jazz all brought together around Angelo's perfect pitch. The group practiced everywhere, from the Sixth Avenue subway to a chicken coop on a roof.

In the Spring of 1958, Dion and The Belmonts signed with Laurie records and were an instant hit with "I Wonder Why" backed by "Teen Angel." Their unusual blend earned the foursome performances at a variety of traditionally black venues, and that same year they became the first white group to sing at the legendary Apollo Theater in Harlem.

I Wonder Why.
The group has a frantic sound on this up-tempo ballad. There are already good reports on the side in several areas. Flip, "Teen Angel," is a rocka-ballad. (5/5/58) (#22 Pop)

No One Knows/I Can't Go On (Rosalie).
Top side is a slow ballad that gets an emotional reading by the lead with good group backing. "I Can't," the flip, is a frantic, blues side handled with

gusto by the lads. Both sides are given solid ork backing and appear strong contenders. (7/28/58) (#19 Pop, #12 R&B)

Don't Pity Me.

A moving rockaballad on which the lead is nicely backed. (11/24/58) (#40 Pop)

In January 1959 the quartet nearly became a sad footnote in rock history. While on "The Winter Dance Party" tour, Dion was asked by Buddy Holly if he cared to take a small plane to the next performance since their bus had, once again, broken down. The price was $35, a large amount for Dion, who remembered it being the exact amount needed for the rent on his parents' apartment. He declined and, the next day, February 3, 1959, the world heard of the death of Buddy Holly, Ritchie Valens, and The Big Bopper in a plane crash.

The Belmonts' first single in 1959, issued a month later, became their biggest hit to date, even though it was considered the B-side by *Billboard*.

I've Cried Before/A Teen-ager in Love.

Two salable sides, "I've Cried" is an interesting weeper ballad. Fine backing helps sell the strong side. "Teen-ager in Love" is a clever, teen-slanted tune on which the group scores equally well. (3/30/59) (B-side, #5 Pop)

Laurie then decided The Belmonts should be balladeers. Although initially successful, the decision would soon cause the group's demise.

Every Little Thing I Do/A Lover's Prayer.

Dion and the Belmonts are strong bets to score again with these two potent efforts. "Lover's Prayer" is a rocking waltz that is well-sung. "Every Little Thing I Do" is a rhythmic ballad. (8/31/59) (A-side, #48 Pop; B-side, #73 Pop)

Where or When/That's My Desire.

Strong up-dated readings of the two oldies. Both are given attractive mild rock treatments, and the disk should be another two-sider for them. (12/14/59) (A-side, #3 Pop, #19 R&B)

In the Still of the Night.

The boys have a strong follow-up to their current "Where or When" in the great Cole Porter standard. It's handled in relaxed, unison vocal style. (6/20/60) (#38 Pop)

Dion began recording on his own. However, he wanted to rock more, but instead was fed a diet of syrupy mid-tempo singles.

Little Miss Blue/Lonely Teenager.

The artist works for the first time without his usual group . . . and he has a pair of salable efforts. The top side is a pleasing tune with good lyrics and it's done with heart by Dion and a fem group. Flip is a wistful workout by the chanter, again with fem group support. Either can make it. (9/26/60) (A-side, #96 Pop; B-side, #12 Pop)

Havin' Fun.

Dion can do it again with these sock sides. "Havin' Fun" is in the style of his current hit "Lonely Teenager." (1/23/61) (#42 Pop)

The Belmonts, content as balladeers, cut one more with "We Belong Together"/"Such a Long Day."

Singing without their former lead . . . the boys wrap up a pleasant rockaballad . . . in their usual emotional r.&r. style. Flip, a breezy rhythm tune, is also handed a solid reading by group. Both sides have dual market potential. (1/16/61)

They then began rocking, including uncredited backups on Gerry Granahan's "Dance, Girl Dance," the Rob-Roys' 1957 classic. In late summer 1961, The Belmonts formed Sabrina records and their first 45 became the trio's biggest charter sans Dion, another Rob-Roys rocker, "Tell Me Why" (#18). More terrific harmony-driven singles followed. Their last 1960s' Top-100 single was "Anne Marie" (unreviewed in *Billboard*). By 1964, new lead Frank Lyndon had replaced Carlo, and The Belmonts moved to United Artists. The Belmonts:

Searching for a New Love.

The boys are in showmanly form on this happy rocker. They . . . could chalk up another winner with this one. Flip is "Don't Get Around Much Anymore." (8/14/61) (B-side, #57 Pop)

I Confess.

★ ★ ★ ★ *Here's a hot rockaballad from the hit-making group. The tune is a slow, nostalgic melody that's sung with emotion by the lead with strong support from the rest of the group and a stirring string section. (3/17/62)*

Come on Little Angels.

Teen buyers should find this a sock item. It's got a strong dance beat, pounding rhythm and much excitement from the group. (6/16/62) (#28 Pop)

Diddle-Dee-Dum (What Happens When Your Love Has Gone)/Farewell.

The group's two sides here show heartbreak at two different tempi. The first is a rocker that has an anguished vocal by the lead, ably abetted by the rest of the boys. The second is a strong, moody rockaballad sung in tight harmony against simple, triplet backing. Either or both here. (10/27/62) (#53 Pop)

Dion's first single with The Del-Satins backing (though uncredited), "Runaround Sue," ironically issued as the B-side, was the beginning of self-penned rockers that established him as the musical messenger of relatable teen tales. "Sue"'s success brought immediate "answer records" and spinoffs including Ginger Davis's "I'm No Run Around" ("a sock answer record . . . the thrush hands it a solid reading over good support from the ork"; 10/31/61) and Linda Laurie's "Stay-at-Home Sue" ("Sue explains why she hasn't been a stay-at-home. Gal sells it with verve and sparkle"; 11/31/61).

Runaway Girl/Runaround Sue.

Dion wraps up "Runaway Girl"—a pretty ballad—in a plaintive, tender vocal treatment, reminiscent of his earlier hits. "Runaround Sue" is a swinging rocker with hand-clapping beat.

Both sides are strong. (9/4/61) (B-side, #1 Pop, #4 R&B)

Dion's street-language magic continued through 1963, when he signed with major label Columbia.

The Majestic/The Wanderer.

Here's a solid follow-up in Dion's current hit "Runaround Sue." The catchy rocker (about a new dance) has the same infectious rhythm pattern. The flip is a hard-driving rocker with solid teen appeal. Dion is in top form on both sides. (11/20/61) (A-side, #36 Pop; B-side, #2 Pop)

Lovers Who Wander/(I Was) Born to Cry.

Here's another waxing that could be a smash for Dion. It features a catchy tempo reminiscent of the singer's hit "Runaround Sue" and a sock performance by the lad. Flip is a driving rocker with exciting vocal and pounding ork backing. (4/14/62) (A-side, #3 Pop, #16 R&B; B-side, #42 Pop)

After five straight hits with Dion, the Del-Satins had an East Coast hit with "Teardrops Follow Me."

Teardrops Follow Me.

★ ★ ★ ★ *The group has a quick-stepping rocker here that swings on a driving vocal from the lead singer. The side is simply arranged with combo support. (6/16/62)*

Meanwhile, Dion continued to produce hits on his own.

Little Diane.

Dion has another hard-hitting effort as a follow-up to his "Lovers Who Wander" smash. The side has an intense, pounding sound. The backing adds to the excitement with strong effort from the vocal group and novel kazoo sound. (6/30/62) (#8 Pop)

Love Came to Me.

This may well be a big one for Dion. First side is a bright rocker handed a swinging reading by the singer while the boys hand-clap behind him. (10/27/62) (#10 Pop, #24 R&B)

Ruby Baby.

Dion makes his debut on the Columbia label with . . . a shouting, pounding blues that shows off a down home vocal by the chanter with a strong beat. (1/12/63) (#2 Pop, #5 R&B)

Sandy.

This side is out of the can from the chanter's old label but it's still a hot one with the driving beat and solid vocalizing that has made a number of hits for Dion in the past. Rocker has a real sound. (2/23/63) (#21 Pop)

Dion Di Mucci:
You're Mine/Donna the Prima Donna.

Dion is now known by his full name Dion Di Mucci, but he's still the same exciting singer. Here he is with a powerful piece of material on the top side that shows off his emotional style and some driving backing. Flip is a first-rate hand clapper that mounts in excitement and has that rocking Dion beat. Solid sales are in store. (8/31/63) (B-side, #6 Pop, #17 R&B)

By 1965, his future seemed to be in folk-rock with such titles as "Spoonful" and "Tomorrow Won't Bring the Rain." Dion rejoined the Belmonts for an exceptional reunion LP in 1966, but their time together was short-lived. They did release one single, "Berimbau," which *Billboard* described as a "groovy rocker that will bring them back into the chart spotlight" (11/5/66), although the record failed to make it. By 1968 The Belmonts were on Dot, still turning out impressive, although dated, recordings. Dion found himself back at Laurie in 1968 with his first Top-10 hit in five years. He followed this with an acoustic-folk reading of (believe it or not) Jimi Hendrix's hard-rock hit, "Purple Haze."

Abraham, Martin and John.

Dion marks his return to the Laurie label with one of his best performances of all time. Folk-flavored message ballad material is important and exceptionally well handled. (9/28/68) (#4 Pop)

Purple Haze.

He made a fantastic return to the disk scene with "Abraham, Martin and John," and he has another winner in this compelling revival of the Jimi Hendrix hit of the past. Strong entry. (1/11/69) (#63 Pop)

On June 2, 1972, The Belmonts and Dion performed together at New York's Madison Square Garden for the first time since the 1959 Winter Dance Party, a concert that formed the basis for a wonderful live LP. Dion created some of his most interesting music in the 1970s, working with Phil Spector and Cashmen and West productions, but *Billboard* only reviewed them as Top-60 contenders without comment. Sides included "Make the Woman Love Me," "Born to Be with You," and "Midtown American Main Street Gang."

In 1981, with Freddy Cannon doing a guest lead, The Belmonts charted for the first time in 18 years with "Let's Put the Fun Back in Rock and Roll" (#81). In 1989, after a few barely noticed Christian albums, Dion returned to rock with his first Top-100 single in 19 years, "And the Night Stood Still." That same year Dion was inducted into the Rock and Roll Hall of Fame.

And the Night Stood Still.

Recommended. Subtle, well-produced rock/pop offering lifted from the living legend's "Yo Frankie" project finds the singer in excellent form and could be the track to win radio's heart. (7/15/89) (#75 Pop)

Both The Belmonts and the man who invented the rock 'n' roll attitude, Dion, are still performing in the 1990s.

FATS DOMINO

Real Name: Antoine Domino

Birthdate: 2/26/28

Birthplace: New Orleans, LA

Influences: Fats Waller, Amos Milburn, Dave Bartholomew, Little Willie Littlefield, Albert Ammons

Influenced: Beatles, Mick Jagger, Chubby Checker, Bobby Darin, Lovin' Spoonful, Righteous Brothers, Johnny Rivers, Lloyd Price, Ray Stevens, Bobby Vee, Teddy Bears, Maurice Williams, Frankie Ford, many more

One of the first and most popular 1950s' rock 'n' roll stars, Fats Domino's recordings outsold every pioneer rocker except Elvis during the decade, with over 65 million in sales.

The French-speaking 10-year-old began learning piano from his brother-in-law, New Orleans musician Harrison Varrett. By the time he was in his teens, Domino was accomplished at ragtime, blues, and boogie woogie piano techniques. He quit school to play honky tonk at night while working days at a bed spring factory, where an accident nearly cost him a finger. His performances (for $3 a week) at The Hideaway Club earned him the nickname "Fats" as bestowed by bandleader Bill Diamond. The short (5'5") and stout (220+ pounds) Domino was discovered there by Imperial Records scout/bandleader Dave Bartholemew in 1949.

His first single was a rewrite of "Junkers Blues" by Dave and himself appropriately titled, "The Fat Man." Its #6 ranking was the start of Fats's phenomenal career, and by 1953 was a million seller. "Little Bee" and others followed, including "Every Night About This Time" and "Rockin' Chair."

"Fats" Domino and His Sextet:

Little Bee 84–84–83–85
Warbler has a highly effective delivery; combo plays with fine beat; material is novel and persuasive—a standup side in all respects.

Boogie Woogie Baby 72–72–70–74
Jump boogie with short vocal bits swings hard. (4/29/50)

Domino's debut #1 R&B single and his first pop hit, "Goin' Home"/"Reeling and Rocking," came in 1952. He and Dave continued to write together and a slew of R&B successes ensued.

Goin' Home 75–76–73–76
Minor blues is sung well by Domino and the ork comes thru with a big beat. A good job.

Reeling and Rocking 72–72–70–74
Fats Domino sings the blues about his gal with feeling. The ork supports him strongly thruout. Item should get plays. (4/26/52) (#30 Pop, #1 R&B)

Please Don't Leave Me 82
Domino could have a winner in this ultra-simple blues. The big beat and boogie-ish piano add to the sales appeal.

The Girl I Love 75
The chanter sounds fine on a bluesy ballad with a routine lyric. (7/18/53) (#3 R&B)

You Said You Love Me 84
Domino has a potential big one . . . There's melancholy warmth in the singer's voice that is hard to resist. Solid beat by ork adds to strength of disk. Watch this one.

Rose Mary 80
Tempo picks up on this side with Domino turning in another fine performance. Again the ork provides a compelling rhythmical backing. Two potent sides. (9/19/53) (B-side, #10 R&B)

You Done Me Wrong.
Once again Domino comes up with a solid hunk of wax. This is a pulsating tune, short on vocal but long on beat. It should grab a lot of action. Flip is "Hey Little Schoolgirl." (2/27/54) (#10 R&B)

In both 1955 and 1956 Domino was named "America's Favorite R&B Artist" by *Billboard*'s annual deejay poll. Domino was a dynamo when it came to recording, and his piano performances are heard on records by numerous artists, including Joe Turner and Lloyd Price. On January 28, 1955, Domino joined The Top 10 R&B Show including The Moonglows, Joe Turner, and The Clovers for a 42-city tour. Fats's initial Pop Top-10 smash came shortly after the tour.

Ain't [That] a Shame/La-La.

The great blues singer socks over two showmanly sides with a personable rendition of the blues rocker "Ain't [That] a Shame" and an amusing interpretation of the novelty "La-La." Both sides are wrapped up in Domino's inimitable style and a pounding ork beat. (4/23/55) (#10 Pop, #1 R&B)

By 1956, the year of the rock 'n' roll explosion, Fats had already had seventeen R&B hits, and "Ain't That a Shame" soon made the white teenagers aware of him. It was also a year when hits like "I'm in Love Again" and "Blue Monday" would later be looked back on as standards.

Poor Me.

Domino belts out a lusty rhythm novelty with great good humor and his usual superb vocal showmanship. The disk has much of the infectious lyric quality and brisk pacing that made Domino's "Ain't That a Shame" waxing a best seller. This one should prove an equal success with deejays, jukes and across the counter. Flip is "I Can't Go On." (11/5/55) (A-side, #1 R&B; B-side, #6 R&B)

I'm In Love Again/My Blue Heaven.

Domino is still the most consistent hitmaker on the r.&b. scene. Markets sampled thruout the country indicated he has another seller here that is speedily working its way to the charts. "I'm in Love Again" is the preferred side to most Southern markets, while north of the Mason-Dixon Line, Domino's unusual styling of a familiar ballad has shown greatest strength. A previous Billboard "Spotlight" pick. (4/14/56) (A-side, #21 Pop, #5 R&B; B-side, #3 Pop, #1 R&B)

When My Dreamboat Comes Home.

[Domino] warbles the attractive standard with sock vitality, great good humor, and a strong, infectious beat. Domino's personable blues style is spotlighted on the flip "So-Long." (7/14/56) (A-side, #14 Pop, #2 R&B; B-side, #3 Pop, #1 R&B)

Blueberry Hill/Honey Chile.

Domino, an artist who hits both the pop and r.&b. charts and holds his position there for a long time, should hit again with this two-sided entry. He warbles the attractive standard, "Blueberry" with his usual vitality while the flip is an upbeat blues shout. Both sides have the familiar infectious beat. (9/22/56) (A-side, #2 Pop, #1 R&B; B-side, #2 R&B)

What's the Reason I'm Not Pleasing You/Blue Monday.

Fats Domino, who has long been king in r.&b. realms and more recently has dominated the pop scene with an equally strong grip, offers another dealer bonanza in this fine disk. The ASCAP tune is an oldie on which Domino puts his characteristic stomp, giving it a whimsy and beat it's never known before. "Blue Monday" is an imaginative original with memorable lyrics and firm rhythm. On either side, pop and r.&b. dealers alike can clean up. (12/15/56) (A-side, #50 Pop, #12 R&B; B-side, #5 Pop, #1 R&B)

By the end of 1956, Domino appeared in the film *Shake, Rattle and Rock* and starred in the 1956 teen film classic, *The Girl Can't Help It*. Two more motion picture showcases in 1957 and '58, respectively (*Jamboree* and *The Big Beat*) helped fuel Fats's 45 and LP sales.

I'm Walkin'/I'm in the Mood for Love.

Both sides can make it in r.&b. and pop as well. "Walkin'" is a driving sensational rhythm side. Flip is an individualized treatment of the great standard, taken at a slower pace than the previous Domino revivals, but with that same basic, built-in beat. Stock up! (2/23/57) (#4 Pop, #1 R&B)

Valley of Tears/It's You I Love.

"Valley of Tears" is a poignant slow blues with a moving church feeling, while the flip is a charming Creole-flavored theme with a lively pace. Domino's sock showmanship and vitality spark each side. (4/29/57) (A-side, #6 Pop, #2 R&B; B-side, #22 Pop)

Coquette/Whole Lotta Loving.

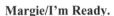
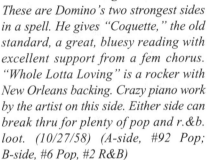

These are Domino's two strongest sides in a spell. He gives "Coquette," the old standard, a great, bluesy reading with excellent support from a fem chorus. "Whole Lotta Loving" is a rocker with New Orleans backing. Crazy piano work by the artist on this side. Either side can break thru for plenty of pop and r.&b. loot. (10/27/58) (A-side, #92 Pop; B-side, #6 Pop, #2 R&B)

Margie/I'm Ready.

Domino rocks his way thru the oldie with a hit sound. His New Orleans approach is heard to good advantage on the great side. "I'm Ready," the flip is a driving rocker blues, and Domino also give this a lusty belt. Both sides should coast in. (4/27/59) (B-side, #16 Pop, #7 R&B)

I'm Gonna Be a Wheel Someday/I Want to Take You Home.

Domino should click again with this potent two-sider. It's hard to choose a top side. Both are given the artist's easy-going hit vocal treatment, and both appear to be likely clicks. (7/13/59) (A-side, #17 Pop, #22 R&B; B-side, #8 Pop, #1 R&B)

The 1960s started with Domino's 23rd million seller, "Don't Come Knockin'"/"Walking to New Orleans," and his last. Still, the New Orleans rocker continued to hit the Top 40 regularly for another three years.

Don't Come Knockin'/Walking to New Orleans.

The great Fats is back again with his inimitable vocal style and the interest-

ing added fillip of jaunty string backing. Top side is a neat rocker, with the flip an excellent walkin' rhythm job. Either can step. (6/13/60) (A-side, #21 Pop, #28 R&B; B-side, #6 Pop, #2 R&B)

My Girl Josephine/Natural Born Lover.

This is one of the great Fats Domino records. The top side, which will probably have the most appeal, is a rhythmic rocker with Fats singing solidly. The other side, also a strong one, features strings and shows off another, outstanding Domino vocal. (10/17/60) (A-side, #14 Pop, #7 R&B; B-side, #38 Pop, #28 R&B)

Let the Four Winds Blow/Good Hearted Man.

Fats Domino continues his happy way on both of these very satisfying sides. Topper is a swinging uptempo effort handled brightly by the pianist. Flip is a tender ballad, sung with soul by Domino. (7/10/61) (#15 Pop, #2 R&B)

You Win Again/Ida Jane.

The great Hank Williams oldie, "You Win Again" is warbled by Domino with feeling and a fine r.&b. beat for a solid blend of country and r.&b. rhythm. "Ida Jane," an infectious rock and roll ditty, is chanted with good humor and showmanship. (2/17/62) (A-side, #22 Pop; B-side, #90 Pop)

In April 1963, after 59 Top-100 entries and 58 R&B hits, Domino moved to ABC-Paramount. Curiously, although he had 18 Top-20 pop hits, he never had a #1 in America, but he did have nine R&B #1s. His ABC sides brought Fats his last R&B hits, although he occasionally took the country roads for a few 1960s singles ("You Win Again" and "Red Sails").

There Goes (My Heart Again)/Can't Go on Without You.

Two outstanding sides. Topper is a rocker, featuring a solid vocal from Fats with a gals' group behind him. Side II shows the fine style of Fats with a ballad. Both could make it. (5/11/63) (#59 Pop)

Red Sails in the Sunset.

The great Domino style in full sail on this standard. Fat sings it in his inimitable fashion against walking shuffle beat with which he's identified. (9/7/63) (#35 Pop)

In 1965, Fats left ABC for Mercury.

I Left My Heart in San Francisco.

Marking his Mercury Records debut the distinctive stylist comes on strong backed by effective strings and chorus. Should spiral Domino back up the charts. (7/24/65)

Although he had been performing for 18 years and had 21 hits in England, it wasn't until 1967 that Fats finally performed there, debuting at London's Seville Theatre. 1968 saw Fats on the Reprise roster. His last Top-100 single was "Lady Madonna," which had been purposely written in Domino's style by Paul McCartney for The Beatles six months earlier.

Lady Madonna.

Fats with the Beatles material has all the ingredients for a left field sales winner. He never sounded better and there's a big chart potential here. Watch this one! (8/10/68) (#100 Pop)

Through the 1970s, Domino continued to showcase his inimitable style in clubs and theaters on an average of eight months each year. In the 1980s and 1990s he regularly played Las Vegas and occasionally recorded. He was elected to the Rock and Roll Hall of Fame in 1986 and the Grammy Hall of Fame in 1987, receiving their Lifetime Achievement Award that same year. Domino still lives in New Orleans with his wife and eight children.

THE DOVELLS

Leonard Borisoff (Len Barry): Lead vocals
Born: 12/6/42, Philadelphia, PA
Jerry Gross (Jerry Summers): First tenor
Born: 12/29/42, Philadelphia, PA
Mike Freda (Mike Dennis): Second tenor
Born: 6/3/43, Philadelphia, PA
Jim Meeley (Danny Brooks): Bass
Born: 4/l/42, Philadelphia, PA
Arnie Silver (Arnie Satin): Baritone
Born: 5/11/43, Philadelphia, PA
Influences: Frankie Lymon and The Teenagers, Danny and The Juniors
Influenced: Dee Dee Sharp, Beatles, Miami Steve Van Zandt, Rolling Stones

The dominant dance exponents of the early 1960s, The Dovells dedicated eight of their 20 singles to the medium in a 13-year career.

Originally known as The Brooktones of Overbrook High School in Philadelphia, the teens all used aliases in their recording careers. An attorney they knew arranged an audition with Cameo/Parkway label heads Kal Mann and Bernie Lowe, and the group's first single was the Len Barry tune, "No, No, No."

No, No, No.

★ ★ ★   *A rocker with drums, chimes and other instruments contributing a busy quality.*

Letters of Love.

★   *A rockaballad in slow tempo. (3/20/61)*

The second 45 was to be the Teenagers' 1957 ballad "Out in the Cold Again." But, as first tenor Jerry Gross explained, "that all changed when Parkway promo man Billy Harper brought them the news of a wild new dance called the Stomp he saw teens doing in Bristol, Pennsylvania's Goodwill fire hall." Billy put on The Students' (1958) record, "Every Day of the Week" and that's what they were dancing to. Mann and A & R exec Dave Appell said, "We should write a song called, 'The Bristol Stomp'" and they did, overnight. Even so, *Billboard* reviewed "Out in the Cold" as the A-side but the flip hit instead. A deluge of dance singles ensued.

Out in the Cold Again.

★ ★ ★ ★ *The oldie is a slow-tempo performance, with a vocal gimmick at the end of phrases.*

Bristol Stomp.

★ ★ ★ ★ *A rocking performance pitching a dance. Plenty of rollicking rhythm here. (8/21/61) (B-side, #2 Pop, #7 R&B)*

Do the Continental.

The Dovells follow up their big hit "Bristol Stomp" with more of the same. A bright novelty aimed at the teen set and the lads sell it with spirit. (1/6/62) (#37 Pop)

Bristol Twistin' Annie.

The group has done well with danceable sides . . . and here's another bright sounding effort, done to a breezy twist tempo. Good sound and beat here and it should move. (4/28/62) (#27 Pop, #28 R&B)

Hully Gully Baby/Your Last Chance.

Two strong items for the lads calculated as follow-ups to their current hit: "Bristol Twistin' Annie." The first fits both Hully Gully and Twist dance steps and is a sure thing for teeners. The second should score with the kids, too. It moves along at a fast clip with strong vocal by the lead singer. (7/28/62) (#25 Pop)

The Jitterbug.

The Dovells continue their parade of teen dances with this rousing, bouncy side that could bring back the 1940 craze. (11/10/62) (#82 Pop)

Their first big performance was at Detroit's Fox Theater in late 1961 with Ray Charles and Fabian. During a break, the group slipped out to the back alley where three young girls were practicing their own brand of harmony. Jerry felt compelled to inspire the trio and said, "Keep pluggin' man, you girls are gonna make it, you're good." His encouragement was an understatement: The girls went on to become The Supremes!

During 1962, The Dovells appeared in the film *Don't Knock the Twist*, with Gene Chandler and Chubby Checker (they sang backup for him on the hit "Let's Twist Again"). By early 1963, the group was slowly losing its grip on the charts until another B-side took off, "You Can't Sit Down" (unreviewed by *Billboard*).

Wildwood Days.

A real bright rocker that's given a swinging performance by the lads over equally driving support from chorus and combo. It could be a really big one for the group. Flip is "You Can't Sit Down." (4/6/63) (B-side, #3 Pop, #10 R&B)

Betty in Bermuda/Dance the Froog.

Two more smash sides. . . . Side 1 is a wild and woolly effort that's done in a hot cookin' groove, with wailing mouth organ and thumping beat. On Side II the lads come through with a fine version of an exciting dance side. Both are hot. (8/17/63)

By late 1963, the dance craze was dying, and The Dovells had their last Top-100 single, "Stop Monkeyin' Aroun'."

Stop Monkeyin' Aroun'.

The monkey theme comes in for another working-over in reverse this time. Side has humor and swing and should go all the way. (10/26/63) (#94 Pop)

Still, the act was in tune with what was happening. They heard a British record they believed was a "smash" and covered it, only to discover that Parkway wasn't interested in releasing it. Swan records, however, did issue the English 45 by four "moptops" from Liverpool, and for The Dovells it was, oh! what might have been. The Dovells' version of "She Loves You" has still never been released.

The group became a trio in 1964 when Len went solo for a few fine chart entries, starting with "Lip Sync" (#84) and his biggest hit, "1, 2, 3" (#2; listed, but unreviewed), both in 1965.

Like a Baby.

Just as "1–2–3" starts to slip down the Hot 100 Chart, this powerful rocker with driving beat will fast replace the initial hit. *(12/18/65) (#27 Pop)*

Somewhere.

An exciting Barry vocal on the "West Side Story" song in a solid dance beat version. (3/12/66) (#26 Pop)

The Dovells continued with excellent 45s, such as "What in the World" and "Be My Girl" and then moved to Swan in 1965 for "Happy" with backup vocals by a pre-Three Dog Night member, Danny Hutton. Although their singles were missing the chart mark, the group continued touring.

In 1968, with the addition of Jean Hillery, Jerry and Mike recorded one single under the name of The Magistrates. They wrote the song while traveling on the New Jersey Turnpike.
The Magistrates:

Here Come the Judge.

Clever novelty based on the popular phrase introduced on the Rowan and Martin "Laugh In" TV show is given a rousing workout by a groovey new group. (5/18/68) (#54 Pop)

Their last single, a revival of Chuck Berry's "Roll Over Beethoven," came two years later. The Dovells never broke up, as Jerry and Mike, with various band members, have kept the group performing through the 1990s. Of the other original Dovells, Arnie went on to manage a Lincoln/Mercury dealership in Atlantic City, Len became a bartender, and Jim died in the 1970s.

THE DRIFTERS (1953–1958)

Clyde McPhatter: Lead vocals
Born: 11/15/33, Durham, NC (died 6/13/72)
Bill Pinkney: Tenor
Born: 8/15/25, Dalzell, SC
Andrew Thrasher: Second tenor
Born: Wetumpka, AL
Gerhart Thrasher: Baritone

Willie Ferbie: Bass
Influences: Ravens, Mills Brothers, Golden Gate Quartet, Orioles, Deep River Boys, Dixie Hummingbirds, Swan Silvertones, Swanee Quartet
Influenced: Jackie Wilson, Gene Pitney, Ray Stevens, Hank Ballard and The Midnighters, Isley Brothers, Dell-Vikings, Diablos, El Doradoes, Silhouettes, Bobbettes, Penguins, Marcels, Gary U.S. Bonds, Lee Andrews and The Hearts, many more

One of only a handful of pioneer R&B acts who became legendary rock 'n' roll stars, The Drifters accomplished that in part because they were not one, but two different groups.

The "historic" Drifters came into being in 1953 when the lead singer of Billy Ward's Dominoes, Clyde McPhatter, decided to form his own act and signed with Atlantic Records. His first attempt was short-lived as he recruited members of his former gospel group, The Mount Lebanon Singers, including David Baughn, William Anderson, David Baldwin, and James Johnson. Their name was chosen out of a hat, and was Baldwin's pick from a book of his dad's about birds. When their session turned out to be subpar, Clyde restructured with Bill Pinkney (Jerusalem Stars), Andrew and Gerhart Thrasher (Thrasher Wonders), and Willie Ferbie. Their first single became their debut hit. Without going pop, it became a million seller.
Clyde McPhatter:

Money Honey 82
The ork sets a real infectious beat behind the high piping of McPhatter for a powerful slicing for the market. This could pull well over the air and thru jukes, in addition to retailer loot.

The Way I Fell 80
McPhatter's voice soars to stratospheric heights as he tackles this romantic ballad. An outstanding effort that's also due for plenty of action. This is McPhatter's first waxing for the label since leaving the Dominoes. (9/19/53) (#1 R&B)

The perils of touring didn't evade the group just because they were stars. While driving through Fredricksburg, Virginia, they were arrested at gunpoint and jailed because they looked like a gang that had robbed a loan company.

The Drifters' November 12, 1953 recording of

"Such a Night" proved the quintet's popularity, and even the flip, "Lucille," charted. However, the B-side was left over from The Mount Lebanon Singers' session and so, except for Clyde, the single featured two different Drifters groups.

Clyde McPhatter and The Drifters:
Such a Night 85
Clyde McPhatter turns in a sock reading here of a swinging new effort, selling the tune with lots of feeling and emotion backed solidly by the Drifters. This could be another smash for McPhatter on the heels of his current "Money Honey."

Lucille 83
The warbler himself penned this slow-tempo opus, which he sings here with his usual passion, over fine help from the Drifters. The chanter could pull a lot of spins and plays on this one via his vocal, and he might have a two-sided hit. (1/30/54) (#7 R&B)

On May 7, 1954, Clyde was called by Uncle Sam just before the release of "Honey Love," another million seller. With McPhatter stationed in relatively nearby Buffalo, New York, the group kept recording hits.

> *"Honey Love" is a calypso-type opus that could start a new trend in the market. Infectious beat, clever lyrics and a spicy delivery add up to a powerhouse package. (5/27/54) (#1 R&B)*

Someday You'll Want Me to Want You/Bip Bam.
> *Clyde McPhatter and the Drifters, whose "Honey Love" is still a big seller, have come thru with another potent outing. "Someday" is the standard, sung effectively by Clyde over good help by the boys, and the flip is a lively novelty effort. Both have a chance for the big-time, sales-wise and box-wise. (10/2/54) (B-side, #7 R&B)*

In the winter of 1954, The Drifters had the most popular vocal group Christmas record ever, a recording of the most-recorded Christmas song ever, "White Christmas." Their first of 1955, although known mostly to R&B collectors today, was one of rock 'n' roll's most influential songs; "Whatcha Gonna Do" became the basis for "The Twist."

White Christmas.
> *This version of the Berlin favorite is one that should grab a lot of sales in the field for the next seven weeks. It features Clyde McPhatter and Bill Pinckney [sic] plus the boys. A real holiday item. Flip is the standard "The Bells of St. Mary." (11/13/54) (#80 Pop, #2 R&B)*

Whatcha Gonna Do.
> *Plenty of rocking rhythm and honking horns behind this spirited reading of McPhatter's. Disk has movement and pace, and merits plenty of deejay and box exposure. (3/5/55) (B-side, #2 R&B)*

In July 1955, Clyde decided to go solo, and his last Drifters' single, "Everyone's Laughing"/ "Hot Ziggity," was wholly ignored by Atlantic, resulting in its failure. In confusion, *Billboard* first reviewed it as by Clyde, not The Drifters, then reviewed it again, a month later, as "McPhatter's first solo disking without his old cohorts, The Clovers [sic]."

With new lead Johnny Moore (Hornets, States), who was found singing in a men's room, The Drifters continued their assault on the charts with tunes including "Adorable," a cover of The Colts' original recording on the small Vita label. It wasn't unusual for a name group to take advantage of its clout (and better label) to cover another group's song and drive it off the charts.

> *Since the appearance of the original Vita disk, excitement on this tune has mounted. The Colts started off with a bang in Los Angeles and later began making noise in New York, Philadelphia, Baltimore and Buffalo. The Drifters' record started later, but in areas where the Vita disk had not been distributed—and in many where it had—it showed very good sales, too. While the Colts are already on the national retail chart, the Drifters are not far behind. (10/29/55) (A-side, #1 R&B; B-side, #5 R&B)*

Ruby Baby.

The high lead takes over on this pounding 16-bar blues theme taken at a good rock tempo. . . . It's an infectious item. (4/7/56) (B-side, #10 R&B)

Soldier of Fortune.

The popular vocal group tries with a ballad here, similar in idiom to such hits as "The Great Pretender" and "Magic Touch." Potent, deeply-felt performance hands this potential in the pop field as well. (7/28/56) (#11 R&B)

By mid-1956 Bill and Andrew were fired by manager George Treadwell. (Bill asked for a raise and Andrew defended him.) Charlie Hughes (Du Droppers lead and another men's room discovery) and Bill Evans (Ravens) took their places. In 1957, Moore and Hughes left and back came Pinkney with lead Bobby Hendricks (Flyers). Numerous changes in 1958 left the group as a shadow of its former self. The last so-called "original" Drifters were Hendricks, Thrasher, Evans, and Jimmy Millender.

Moonlight Bay 79

★ *The fine standard is handed a bright and fetching reading . . . over a most enjoyable, nostalgic backing by the multi-horned ork. Watch this one.*

Drip Drop 78

★ *Listenable rock and roller receives a strong performance . . . again over a strong ork backing. Side has a sound and could catch loot. (5/19/58) (A-side, #72; B-side, #58)*

Meanwhile, starting in 1955, McPhatter became a star, dueting with Ruth Brown and as a solo on Atlantic, MGM, Amy, and Deram. Clyde McPhatter and Ruth Brown:

Love Has Joined Us Together.

Two top personalities in the field team up on a moving ballad of mutual devotion with a distinctive prayer-meeting flavor. Figures to get maximum initial attention from the spin set, then should carry thru well on its own. Flip is a good shouter called "I Gotta Have You." (10/15/55) (#8 R&B)

Seven Days.

Another strong McPhatter platter enters the race for the gravy and this could break fast. There's a great chorus and full ork sound, and most of all, McPhatter is his same great chanting self. A stong production that shapes up as an all-level entry. Flip is "I'm Not Worthy of You," a well-delivered weepy styled ballad. (12/17/55) (#44 Pop, #2 R&B)

Treasure of Love/When You're Sincere.

Here's another great two-sided disk by the velvet-voiced McPhatter. The warbler sings with poignancy and feeling on "Treasure of Love," an attractive ballad, while the flip—another pretty ballad—is also handed a smooth, listenable vocal treatment. McPhatter is backed by a pop vocal group and a big band, and the disk should move in pop as well as r.&b. (4/28/56) (#16 Pop, #1 R&B)

Without Love.

Here's a beautifully syled weeper-ballad that offers the singer one of his most powerful vehicles to date. Its churchly sound and emotional build-up are memorable features of a disk that has unusually great r.&b. and pop commerical potential. (12/1/56) (#19 Pop, #4 R&B)

Come What May.

A . . . swinging uptempo side strongly presented . . . with excellent ork backing. It can also go in r.&b. markets. (4/7/58) (#43 Pop, #3 R&B)

A Lover's Question 77

Medium-beat ballad is told with chorus and good ork support. Strong warble by the artist on the attractive side. (9/15/58) (#6 Pop, #1 R&B)

In 1959, McPhatter moved to MGM from Atlantic, and then a year later to Mercury.

I Told Myself a Lie/The Masquerade Is Over.

Top side is a classy reading of a new rockaballad with good ork support, while the flip spots a listenable go on the evergreen. Both can score. (3/23/59) (#70 Pop)

Ta Ta/I Ain't Givin' Up Nothin'.

A terrific debut for the chanter on his new label. The top side has the wonderful, old-time McPhatter feeling in the rockin' vein. Ditto the flip, a cute tune by Clyde Otis and Brook Benton. Watch both, they can go all the way. (7/4/60) (#23 Pop, #7 R&B)

His biggest pop hit came in early 1962 with "Lover Please."

Lover Please.

★ ★ ★ ★ *A snappy rhythm number with a hand-clapping beat. McPhatter shouts on the message in fine style. Good dance number, with upward modulations that help it build. (2/10/62) (#7 Pop)*

Little Bitty Pretty One/Next to Me.

First side is an expansive reading of the old rock and roll smash. Pretty ballad gets a feelingful reading on the flip. (6/2/62) (#25 Pop)

Deep in the Heart of Harlem.

McPhatter comes through with a highly emotional reading of a slow, dramaballad fraught with social significance. Side can be expected to get wide r.&b. play then zoom popward. (12/7/63) (#90 Pop, #90 R&B)

From 1955 through 1965 he had 16 R&B Top 100s and 21 Pop charters. Because of his unique and distinctive sound he became one of the most influential vocalists in rock history. Clyde McPhatter died in 1972, scarcely aware of his effect on music history.

THE DRIFTERS (1959–1979)

Benjamin Earl Nelson (Ben E. King): Lead vocals
Born: 9/23/38, Henderson, NC
Charlie Thomas: Tenor
Born: 4/7/37, New York City
Dock Green: Baritone
Born: 10/8/34, New York City
Elsberry Hobbs: Bass
Born: 1/17/36, New York City
Influences: Five Keys, Orioles, Ravens, Harptones, Spaniels, Five Blind Boys of Mississippi, Dixie Hummingbirds
Influenced: John Lennon, Billy Joel, Jay and The Americans, Tony Orlando and Dawn, O'Jays, Corsairs, Simply Red

As successful as The Original Drifters had been, The New Drifters were even more so. Of the 36 pop hits under the Drifters' name, 31 were attributed to the new entourage.

In June 1958, the original quartet played one of their many nights at the Apollo Theater. Manager George Treadwell had a contract with the venue for two shows a year for ten years by The Drifters, any Drifters! Treadwell's idea to replace them gained momentum when they hadn't had a hit in a year. On the same bill that night was a group called The Five Crowns.

The Five Crowns:
You Came to Me 78

Some outstanding solo work by the lead singer distinguishes this group vocal of an appealing weeper. Should get considerable jockey and juke play. (3/19/55)

The Crowns:
Kiss and Make Up 76

Group sounds good in a rhythmic, meshuga styled pleaser with a slightly Latinish beat. Side has potential if pushed. (3/10/58)

The Crowns were the show openers, thanks to their first and only recently issued single. Treadwell was so impressed with the young, exuberant Crowns that he went backstage, hired them as The Drifters, walked across the stage, and fired his old quartet. Thomas, Green, and Hobbs were all former Five Crowns alumni, and Benjamin Nelson was a Holidays and Millionaires member.

After touring for ten months, the new aggregation settled down to record Benjamin's new song, which he wrote about the same time he took the name of his uncle Jimmy King and became Ben E. King. His song was titled, "There Goes My Baby." The record almost missed seeing the light of day since Atlantic's A&R whiz, Jerry Wexler, supposedly hated it, and producers Leiber and Stoller and label head Ahmet Ertegun just weren't sure. With their first 45, The New Drifters had a greater success than any of the original group's 13 releases.

There Goes My Baby.

★ ★   *The Drifters turn in a good reading of a ballad with strings filling out the background, while the boys moan along behind. (5/4/59) (#2 Pop, #1 R&B)*

(If You Cry) True Love, True Love/Dance with Me.

The crew has two hot sides to follow their big "There Goes My Baby." "True Love" is a ballad that gets a strong vocal over an interesting arrangement. "Dance with Me" has a Latinish tinge, and the vocal here is also first-rate. (9/28/59) (A-side, #33 Pop, #59 R&B)

This Magic Moment.

The lead voice offers a feelingful vocal on "Magic Moment," a rockaballad, and he gets fine group support. (1/8/60) (#16 Pop, #4 R&B)

Lonely Winds.

The Drifters show off their fine vocal form again here, featuring a warm lead vocal by Ben E. King. (5/9/60) (#54 Pop, #9 R&B)

In the Spring of 1960, Ben recorded his last sides with The Drifters, including "I Count the Tears" and "Save the Last Dance for Me." By the time "Save" was a hit, Ben was not even a Drifter.

Save the Last Dance for Me/Nobody but Me.

The Drifters should continue their hit string with this new recording. Both tunes are attractive ballads and Ben E. King handles the lead on both with spirit. (7/22/60) (#1 Pop, #1 R&B)

The group was now an international success but the membership's revolving door was as active as with the old group.

By 1961, the quartet was Rudy Lewis (Clara Ward Singers), lead; Thomas, tenor; Green, baritone; and Tommy Evans (of the 1957 version), bass. With all the changes however, The Drifters were still magical.

Some Kind of Wonderful.

The boys warble an effective, easygoing medium-beat ballad . . . with good lead performance and lofty femme chorus. (3/13/61) (#32 Pop, #6 R&B)

Please [Stay].

[A] melodic ballad. The lead sells it strongly and the backing by the boys and the group is fine too. (5/29/61) (#14 Pop, #13 R&B)

Loneliness or Happiness/Sweets for My Sweet.

Sock sides. Topper is a moving rockaballad sung smartly by the lead. Flip is a driving, gospel-flavored blues. (8/21/61) (B-side, #16 Pop, #10 R&B)

Room Full of Tears.

★ ★ ★ ★ *Effective warbling by lead singer and group on an attractive r.&r. item. (11/20/61) (#72 Pop)*

When My Little Girl Is Smiling.

A potent hunk of material, well sung by the group. The lead explains that his girl's smile gets her anything she wants. Most attractive backing too. Watch this one. (1/27/62) (#28 Pop)

Sometimes I Wonder.

★ ★ ★ ★ *The Drifters have a powerful piece of ballad material here that is gospel oriented and they sell it with feeling over strong support from the ork. This has a chance for the big time. Watch it. (6/30/62)*

Up on the Roof.

Sparked by a fresh and appealing arrangement, the Drifters turn in a warm performance on an interesting new piece of material with some sophisticated, philosophic touches. (9/29/62) (#5 Pop, #4 R&B)

The last original Crowns/Drifters member, Dock Green, left soon after, replaced by Gene Pearson (Rivileers, Cleftones).

The all-pro writing team of Leiber, Stoller, Barry Mann, and Cynthia Weil collaborated on the next Drifters biggie in which fledgling producer Phil Spector played guitar, "On Broadway."

On Broadway.

Here's another side much in the "Up on the Roof" hit groove. Lead sings its clever, social awareness message with a good feel which arrangement and production are topnotch. (3/9/63) (#9 Pop, #7 R&B)

Saturday Night at the Movies.

Combination of several of their past hits effectively blended to make a great smash entry. Good lyrics, top performances and infectious Latin instrumentation. (11/7/64) (#18 Pop)

In February 1964, the long-overshadowed Rudy Lewis died and was replaced by Johnny Moore (of the original group) as The Drifters kept on rolling. The foursome was now Moore, Pearson, Thomas, and Evans. Translated, it meant the quartet was actually made up of members of The Hornets, Cleftones, Five Crowns, and Ravens.

Progressing to pop-soul, The Drifters had their last Top-10 hit with "Under the Boardwalk" (#4) but kept charting through 1966.

Memories Are Made of This.

Exciting revival of the Dean Martin goldie with top Drifters vocal backed by Mariachi brass, aimed right at today's pop market. (3/12/66) (#48 Pop)

By the mid-1960s, several Drifters groups were performing, including acts led by Bill Pinkney and Charlie Hughes. The Drifters last single for Atlantic, "A Rose by Any Other Name (Is Still a Rose)," signaled their recording demise in America.

The Drifters make a strong bid for airplay and sales with this infectious rhythm ballad that has much of the feel of their "Save the Last Dance for Me" hit of the past. (2/20/71)

In 1972, the release of a seven-year-old single in England, "Come On Over to My Place" amazingly reached #9, and Johnny Moore et al. found a home for years to come on Bell records of Britain. As for Ben E. King, the magical first voice of The New Drifters, his career as a solo artist took off with the megahit "Stand by Me."

First Taste of Love/Spanish Harlem.

Top side is in the vein of "Save the Last Dance for Me," while the flip is an intriguing Latinish tune. (11/21/60) (A-side, #53 Pop; B-side, #10 Pop, #15 R&B)

Stand by Me.

A winning performance by Ben E. King of an emotional rockaballad with a churchy feel makes this look like another hit for the former lead of the Drifters. (4/24/61) (#4 Pop, #1 R&B)

Don't Play That Song (You Lied).

★ ★ ★ ★ *The chanter begs frantically that a certain song not be played because it brings back unhappy memories. A smart song by the well-known writer, Nugetre, and it's done stylishly with a femme chorus. Watch this one. (4/7/62) (#11 Pop, #2 R&B)*

What Now My Love.

The Gilbert Becaud ballad gets a warm, wide production treatment from Ben and supporting players. The sound is huge with strings and voices adding to the building effect of the dramatic tune. (1/18/64)

King's career languished for about a decade; then he made a surprising comeback in 1975.

Supernatural Thing, Part 1.

King returns . . . with a mid tempo, infectious cut that efectively repeats the title as a hook throughout. King has lost none of his skill as a stylist, and this should be a disco as well as radio and sales hit. (1/11/75) (#5 Pop, #1 R&B)

King was inducted into the Rock and Roll Hall of Fame in 1987; that same year, he recut the old Drifters hit on which he originally sang lead, "Save the Last Dance for Me." The Drifters themselves hit the Hall of Fame in 1988. King continues to perform today on the oldies and supper-club circuits.

BOB DYLAN

Real Name: Robert Allen Zimmerman

Birthdate: 5/24/41

Birthplace: Duluth, MN

Influences: Woody Guthrie, Buddy Holly, Little Richard, Hank Williams, Sonny Terry

Influenced: Byrds, Peter, Paul and Mary, Turtles, Manfred Mann, The Band, Dire Straits, David Bowie, Rolling Stones, Beatles, Elvis Costello, Sly Stone, Buffalo Springfield, Blood, Sweat and Tears, many more

The most influential singer/songwriter of the 1960s, Bob Dylan was a superstar who only registered four Top-10 hits, yet his importance transcends his singles successes. A folk protester, he was also a rock 'n' roll trendsetter and a country-rock pioneer who had more hits via other interpretations of his songs than by himself.

Born Robert Allen Zimmerman of a middle-class Jewish family who moved to the small mining town of Hibbing, Minnesota, young Bob learned guitar at age 12. He formed The Golden Chords while in high school, stating in his yearbook that he was leaving "to follow Little Richard." Instead, he began playing coffeehouses near the University of Minnesota in 1959 as Bob Dylan, naming himself after a favorite poet, Dylan Thomas. By January 1961, he moved to New York to become a singer or songwriter. His early attempt at joining the establishment ended in failure when he pursued a $50 weekly songwriting job at Hill and Range Publishing, but was rejected.

April 11, 1961, saw his first performance in the Greenwich Village club Gerde's Folk City as the opening act for blues great, John Lee Hooker. On April 24, Bob made $50 playing harmonica on the Harry Belafonte album, *Midnight Special*. In September, his harmonica performance on a Carolyn Hester album caught the attention of Columbia Records producer, John Hammond. It coincided with a favorable *New York Times* review of his Gerde's showcase, and Dylan was signed to Columbia.

His first folk LP (*Bob Dylan*) in March 1963 and his debut single, "Mixed Up Confession," did little, but his second LP, *The Freewheelin' Bob Dylan* (#22, May 1963), established him as one of the emerging singer/writers of the protest movement. Dylan's own version of "Blowin' in the Wind" never charted, but Peter, Paul and Mary's cover reached #2, followed by another Dylan cover, "Don't Think Twice" (#9). Dylan's *Times They Are A-Changin'* album (#20) continued his folk-protest formula, and the title song became a hit in England (#9) before he ever had a charter in the colonies.

In early 1965, Dylan made the unexpected leap to rock 'n' roll with the LP *Bringing It All Back Home,* which contained his first hit, "Subterranean Homesick Blues" (#39). Issuing only his fourth U.S. 45 from four albums, Dylan's folk-rock development reached the masses with, "Like a Rolling Stone." At the unheard-of length of six minutes, "Rolling Stone" was Bob's first million seller.

Like a Rolling Stone.

As off-beat as his "Subterranean Homesick Blues" with the same hit potential! Original composition has a stronger, far out lyric aimed at the teen market with dance beat to boot. (7/17/65) (#2 Pop)

Meanwhile, the world's rock community jumped on Bob's bandwagon choosing his creations for their own career covers, including The Byrds ("Mr. Tambourine Man"), The Turtles ("It Ain't Me Babe"), Cher ("All I Really Wanna Do"), and Joan Baez ("It's All Over Now, Baby Blue"). Dylan too had found the mainstream. Folk fans were livid over the change, and he was booed on stage at 1965's Newport Folk Festival. Still, Dylan's songs were being analyzed in greater depth and quoted more often than any rock star before him.

Positively 4th Street.

> On the heels of his ebbing "Like a Rolling Stone" comes more power-house off-beat, commercial Dylan material aimed at the top of the charts. (9/18/65) (#7 Pop)

Can You Please Crawl Out Your Window.

> More strong folk-rock Dylan material which will have no trouble finding its way up the singles chart. Strong material and performance. (12/18/65) (#58 Pop)

Rainy Day Women Nos. 12 & 35.

> Off-beat Dylan tune with old-blues sound and shuffle rhythm is a solid bet to put the folk rocker back on top of the charts. (4/2/66) (#2 Pop)

On July 29, 1966, the musical guru's world almost ended when a motorcycle accident near his Woodstock, New York, home left him with a broken neck. His return was slow but his records kept coming.

I Want You.

> Unique, easy-go lyric balad with solid dance beat backing should quickly replace his hit, "Rain Day Woman Nos. 12 and 35." (6/25/66) (#20 Pop)

Just Like a Woman.

> Dylan's in top form with this much recorded bluesy ballad aimed right at the top of the chart. (9/3/66) (#33 Pop)

Most Likely You Go Your Way and I'll Go Mine/Leopardskin Pill-Box Hat.

> Two powerful off-beat Dylan entries culled from his Blonde on Blonde album. Both rhythm sides offer strong dance beats and compelling Dylan lyrics loaded with teen sales appeal. (5/6/67) (#66 Pop)

Dylan's Blonde on Blonde LP (#9) and his Greatest Hits collection (#10) both went gold, his fourth and fifth gold albums. A rock 'n' roll "lion" at the time of his accident, Dylan came out of seclusion as a countrified rock "lamb" with a softer voice, no thoughts of protest, and songs of starkly visual love like "Lay, Lady, Lay." "Lay"

was written for the film *Midnight Cowboy* but was not finished in time.

Lay, Lady, Lay.

> Infectious and appealing folk number with a country flavor culled from his hit LP Nashville Skyline should quickly bring Dylan back to a high spot on the Hot 100. Exceptional performance. (7/12/69) (#7 Pop)

In June 1970, Dylan received an honorary doctorate in music from Princeton University. Bob joined George Harrison for the Concert for Bangladesh at New York's Madison Square Garden in July 1971, about the same time as "Watch the River Flow" took off. Dylan spent most of 1972 writing the soundtrack for, and starring in the Sam Peckinpah film *Pat Garrett and Billy the Kid*, which featured his classic song, "Knockin' on Heaven's Door."

Knockin' on Heaven's Door.

> An infectious repeat of the main theme by Dylan and some support voices creates an ear warming effect. The song is, of course, from the film "Pat Garrett and Billy the Kid" and is the best piece of music from the film. Dylan's voice sounds gentle and controlled and the guitar work in the background is simple and properly stated. (8/25/73) (#12 Pop)

Dylan's contract with Columbia ended, leading him to David Geffen's Asylum label, along with his old backup group, The Band. Together they cut one studio and one live album for Geffen.

On a Night Like This.

> A spunky tune about reminiscences and things that sure feel right, with harmonica playing contributing to his vocal work. The band plays happy. Dylan's voice sounds a bit strained but he carries the song along. (2/9/74) (#44 Pop)

Bob Dylan/The Band:
Most Likely You Go Your Way (and I'll Go Mine).

> From Dylan's live LP, this cut from the old Blonde on Blonde album is the most exciting thing he's done single

wise in some time. Uptempo material with the fine Band behind him (who may do well on the flip with their "Stage Fright") the single showcases the distinctive Dylan vocals and should wend its way to the top of the charts rapidly. (7/27/74) (#66 Pop)

A year later, Dylan patched up his Columbia differences and returned with the excellent, confessional album, *Blood on the Tracks,* with its lead-off single, "Tangled Up in Blue."

Dylan comes up with the most powerful and at the same time commercial single he's had in years. The haunting, rough Dylan vocals many of us remember from the early days so well are featured here, along with a strong acoustic background. Should re-establish artist as a Top 40 threat. (3/8/75) (#31)

By 1979, Dylan was lured into the world of the born-again Christians by Debby Boone and his music over the next few years reflected it, as only "Gotta Serve Somebody" charted (#24). In 1982, he was elected to the Songwriters Hall of Fame. By 1983, he renounced Christianity and returned to the Jewish faith. He also returned to rock 'n' roll. "Sweetheart" was his last Top-100 hit.

Sweetheart Like You.

From the "Infidels" LP that many acclaim as his finest in years; intensity and breadth of imagery no less arresting than in the legendary old days. (12/17/83) (#55 Pop)

In 1985, Dylan performed on a variety of charitable recordings and shows, including *We Are the World*, *Live Aid*, and *Farm Aid* (the latter festival was inspired by an off-the-cuff remark Dylan made at the *Live Aid* concert, stating that musicians should do something to help Americans at home).

Dylan joined a group of superstars masquerading as The Traveling Wilburys in 1988, the same year he was inducted into the Rock and Roll Hall of Fame.

Traveling Wilburys:
Handle with Care.

The participants on this project aren't "new" by any imagination stretch, but

"noteworthy" is a given. George Harrison, Bob Dylan, Tom Petty, Roy Orbison, and Jeff Lynne pool their many talents to produce what is worthy of a spin by merit of its contributors alone. Rootsy rock piece sounds like it could have fit nicely on the ex-Beatle's recent "Cloud Nine" project. Warm, burlesque feel. (10/29/88) (#45 Pop)

In 1991, he received the Grammy's Lifetime Achievement Award. Dylan continues to tour tirelessly, playing over 100 shows a year, while also writing new material.

Isaac Donald Everly
Born: 2/1/37, Brownie, KY
Philip Everly
Born: 1/19/39, Chicago, IL
Influences: Elvis Presley, Hank Williams (Don), Lefty Frizell (Phil)
Influenced: Beatles, Animals, Simon and Garfunkel, Neil Diamond, Bobby Vee, Angels, Grass Roots, Teddy Bears, Tommy James, Fabian, Dave Edmunds, many more

The Everly Brothers blend velvet, high harmonies, clean, innovative country style, and a rhythmic rock beat to earn themselves a place as rock 'n' roll superstars.

The duo came from a performing family, their parents, Ike and Margaret Everly, were well known Midwestern country singers during the 1930s through the 1950s. The brothers' first performance (Don was eight, Phil, six) was on KMA radio in Shenandoah, Iowa, and was followed by summer tours with Ike and Margaret. They began writing songs in high school, and Don's first success happened in 1954 when Kitty Wells had a country hit with, "Thou Shalt Not Steal." The money from "Steal" enabled the teens to relocate in Nashville and pursue their careers.

In November 1955, they recorded four sides

for Columbia, including the duo's first single, "The Sun Keeps Shining."

The Sun Keeps Shining 67
> *This bright, optimistic ditty gives the brothers good opportunities for close harmony warbling. A pleasant, not overly weighty side.*

Keep a-Loving Me 65
> *Another smooth harmony job to an easy-going danceable beat. (11/55)*

A recording of their "Here We Are Again," by Anita Carter, helped pay the bills as Columbia's deal ended unsuccessfully. Through their dad's contact with Nashville producer/guitarist Chet Atkins, they met publisher Wesley Rose, who signed them and brought the twosome to Cadence Records' president, Archie Bleyer. Archie, having passed on a previous Everly demo, signed them with the proviso that they record a song he liked. The song had been turned down by 30 artists but that didn't faze Don and Phil who recorded it for $128, money they desperately needed for food. The tune was, "Bye, Bye Love."

> *Cadence's first fling in the c.&w. market netted the label a pair of outstanding artists in The Everly Brothers. The Tennessee teen-agers have a distinctive, appealing sound and could click big in the pop as well as the c.&w. field. "Bye Bye Love" is a plaintive Boudleaux Bryant blues with an unusual rhythm pattern. The flip ["I Wonder If I Care as Much"], penned by the brothers, is an effectively mournful blues. (4/20/57) (#2 Pop)*

In less than a month, the brothers were performing at the Grand Ole Opry as "Bye, Bye" became their first million seller. Their broad appeal was apparent when the single reached #1 Country and #5 R&B. The boys became so hot that four of their next six A- and B-sides charted.

Wake Up, Little Susie/Maybe Tomorrow.
> *The brothers still have a hit going with "Bye Bye Love." Their sock selling here on a rocker type with cute lyrics seems a strong bet to repeat. Flip, "Maybe Tomorrow," is a country ballad, cleffed by the brothers, and pre-*

sented with attractive hill harmonies. Platter can click in all markets. (9/2/57) (#1 Pop)

This Little Girl of Mine/Should We Tell Him.
> *A strong contender with . . . two choice sides from their EP and LP. "Little Girl" is an agreeable rockabilly performance on the old Ray Charles tune. Flip, "Should We Tell Him," is also a rockabilly tune, and it's delivered with the same sock approach. Either can score in all fields. (1/20/58) (#26 Pop)*

All I Have to Do Is Dream/Claudette.
> *A change of pace for the duo. The sound is different but effective and both are good bets to go all the way. "Dream" is a country ballad with a Latinish beat. "Claudette," the flip, is an untempo ballad that is read just as strongly. (4/7/58) (A-side, #1 Pop; B-side, #30 Pop)*

Bird Dog/Devoted to You.
> *Hard to pick a top side on this latest platter . . . Both appear excellent bets to score. "Bird Dog" is a swingy, upbeat blues about a cat who's being warned to stay away from other guys' girls. "Devoted" is a slow ballad much along the lines of their current click. "All I Have to Do Is Dream." Strong potential in all markets. (7/28/58) (A-side, #1; B-side, #10 Pop)*

Problems/Love of My Life.

> *Another likely two-sided click with . . . great warbling on these fine sides. "Problems" is a rockabilly, done with a "Bo Diddley" rhythm. "Love" is a warm reading of a Latin-tinged medium-beater. Both tunes are by the Bryants. Top potential. (10/27/58) (A-side, #2 Pop; B-side, #40 Pop)*

With nine hits by the end of 1958, it's small wonder The Everlys were headlining tours, including Alan Freed's Christmas show at New York's Loews State Theater with Chuck Berry and Jackie Wilson. The duo was becoming an institution in England and upon their first trip in January 1959, received the New Musical Express's "World's #1 Vocal Group Award."

Take a Message to Mary/Poor Jenny.

Two great sides that should show strongly. "Message" is an intriguing tale about a gent who turns bad when he loses his love. "Jenny" is a spirited, countryish rocker. Both are hot efforts. (3/23/59) (A-side, #16 Pop; B-side, #22 Pop)

Oh, What a Feeling/'Till I Kissed You.

Another likely two-sided smash . . . It's hard to put a side on top. "Feeling" is the ballad side. "'Till I Kissed You" is a medium-beater. Vocal on each is highly salable. (8/3/59) (B-side, #4 Pop)

Since You Broke My Heart/Let It Be Me.

Double-barreled waxing here, and either side could be the big one. "Heart" is a haunting item, penned by Don Everly that the duo handles smartly. "Let It Be Me" is a pop ballad that shows off the boys in a new light. Watch them both. (12/28/59) (B-side, #7 Pop)

In February 1960, the brothers inked a ten-year, million-dollar record agreement with Warner Brothers. They recorded eight sides in Nashville but none were considered hits so Don and Phil wrote one more song, "Cathy's Clown." It became their premier piece of plastic, topping the charts for five weeks and selling three million 45s.

Cathy's Clown/Always It's You.

"Cathy's Clown" is an attractive, teen-slanted item with a catchy rhythmic figure in the backing. "Always It's You" is a lovely, countryish ballad. (4/4/60) (A-side, #1 Pop; B-side, #56 Pop)

Cadence, meanwhile, issued a very credible competing single, "When Will I Be Loved"/"Be-Bop a-Lula." Both companies went at it until Cadence exhausted its supply of unreleased songs.

When Will I Be Loved/Be-Bop a-Lula.

The boys are extremely hot right now and this coupling . . . can step right out, too. First is a good ballad penned by Phil Everly that gets a creamy harmony styling while the flip is a rock reading

of the old hit by Gene Vincent. (5/23/60) (A-side, #8 Pop; B-side, #74 Pop)

Lucille/So Sad.

Either side could go . . . "Lucille"— Little Richard's Old Hit—spotlights a strong reading by the boys, with a sharp Fancey bass blues figure on the intro. Flip is a plaintive ballad, penned by Don Everly, with effective guitar backing and tender warbling stint by the brothers. (7/22/60) (A-side, #21 Pop; B-side, #7 Pop)

In January 1961, The Everlys moved to Hollywood. Don then decided to start his own Calliope label and recorded instrumentally as Adrian Kimberly ("Pomp and Circumstance," #34) in 1961. Meanwhile, the duo continued to cut for Warners.

Ebony Eyes/Walk Right Back.

The Everly Brothers could have their biggest hit to date with "Ebony Eyes," a tragedy song with recitation about a girl who dies in a plane wreck. The flip is an appealing weeper sparked by a clever arrangement. (1/23/61) (A-side, #8 Pop; B-side, #7 Pop)

Stick with Me Baby/Temptation.

An ingratiating Latin rhythm marks this fine vocal effort by the boys on the first side. Tune was penned by Mel Tillis. The boys lend a wild rocker interpretation to the standard on the flip. (5/22/61) (A-side, #41 Pop; B-side, #82 Pop)

Don't Blame Me/Muskrat.

The boys contribute a soulful vocal on "Don't Blame Me," the dreamy oldie. Flip is a catchy full-flavored ditty, featuring showmanly warbling by the brothers. This is the first record in the label's new "plus two oldies" series, wherein edited segments of an artists' old hits are included as a bonus. The Everlys' hits "Walk Right Back" and "Lucille" are featured here. (9/4/61) (A-side, #20 Pop; B-side, #82 Pop)

Crying in the Rain.

The boys register strongly on "Crying in the Rain," a heartfelt weeper sung with a strong rhythmic accent. Should do very well. (1/6/62) (#6 Pop)

That's Old-Fashioned/How Can I Meet Her?

High styled singing by the Everlys plus distinctive arrangements make these new sides strong contenders. Top side has a fine beat and tells a good story of teen romances; flip is a good rocker spotlighting harmonica licks in the arrangement. Good wax. (5/5/62) (A-side, #9 Pop; B-side, #75 Pop)

In October 1962, Don collapsed during a rehearsal at London's Prince of Wales Theatre and was rushed home for treatment. Phil finished the tour with guitarist Joey Page handling Don's part. Having recovered, Don rejoined Phil in January 1963. In September 1964, they appeared on the debut episode of ABC TV's, "Shindig" singing "Gone, Gone, Gone."

Gone, Gone, Gone.

And that they are! Fantastic beat coupled with outstanding performance. Anglo-American grooving should shoot this disk right in to Top 50. (10/10/64) (#31 Pop)

By 1965, the brothers had entered a brief oldies phase with recordings like "That'll Be the Day" and "Love Is Strange." Although less popular in the United States, they remained major draws in England, where they recorded an album during 1966 in London titled, *Two Yanks in England,* with backing by The Hollies, John Paul Jones, and Jimmy Page (both later of Led Zeppelin).

By the late 1960s, their record sales had waned; the pair's last 1960s Top-100 45 was "Bowling Green," an early country-rock-styled recording.

Bowling Green.

The most commercial entry from the duo in some time. Soft folk-rock ballad should once again put the million sellers back on the charts. Interesting Al Capp dance arrangement and Dick

Glasser production. (4/22/67) (#40 Pop)

In 1970, the duo hosted "The Everly Brothers Show," a TV summer replacement for Johnny Cash. A month after signing with RCA in June 1973, Don and Phil performed at The John Wayne Theater in Knotts Berry Farm. Tension that had been building surfaced as Phil smashed his guitar and left the theater, leaving Don to announce the duo's demise. Actually, they'd planned to separate more than two weeks earlier.

In June 1983, ten years later, the estranged brothers hugged and made up. In mid-1984, Phil and Don signed with Mercury and had their first Top-100 entry in 17 years, and their last, "On the Wings of a Nightingale," produced by Dave Edmunds and written by Paul McCartney. The Rock and Roll Hall of Fame swung open its doors to The Everlys in 1986 while the duo continue to create.

Real Name: Fabiano Forte
Birthdate: 2/6/43
Birthplace: Philadelphia, PA
Influences: Elvis Presley, Everly Brothers, Lee Andrews and The Hearts

Often maligned by music critics, Fabian, nonetheless, was the apple in millions of teens' eyes during the late 1950s.

Most accounts of Fabian's discovery were condensed to a distorted degree, stating in effect that he accepted an offer to record at the same time his father was being taken away in an ambulance after suffering a heart attack. Actually, 14-year-old Fabian sat on his front steps as his policeman father was being lifted into an ambulance. His mother had left him there so he could oversee his two younger brothers while she went to the hospital. At that moment, Chancellor Records president, Bob Marcucci, drove up. He had a friend who lived next door and thought it was the friend's pregnant wife being taken away. Marcucci then got out, introduced himself, and, noticing Fabian's youthful good looks, ignored the tribulations of the moment and asked, "Are you interested in being in the singing business?" Fabian, caught up in his anguish and Bob's bad timing fervently exclaimed, "Go to Hell!"

Marcucci persisted over the next few months as Fabian continued to refuse. When his family's finances suffered from his dad's incapacity, the teen finally relented. The money from disability and his own $6-a-week delivery job couldn't cover the bills, and so Fabian became, initially, a reluctant rock 'n' roller. *Billboard* added to the confusion of his discovery by noting (probably due to a bogus press release) that Frankie Avalon discovered him in the review of his first single, "I'm in Love." Neither this nor his second single charted.

I'm in Love 73

Artist who is a discovery of Frankie Avalon makes his disk debut in fair teen-slanted style. It's a rhythm tune and there is a wild sounding girl group in the backing. (6/16/58)

Lilly Lou.

Okay rockabilly effort by Fabian who gets support from the Four Dates group. Moderate potential. (9/15/58)

Marcucci then commissioned hot songwriters Doc Pomus and Mort Shuman to create a hit song to fit Fabian's image; the result was "I'm a Man." Fabian followed with another Pomus/Shuman, Elvis styled rockaballad, "Turn Me Loose."

I'm a Man.

★★ *Uninhibited reading on fast-moving shoutin'-blues. (12/1/58). (#31 Pop)*

Turn Me Loose/Stop Thief!

Two rockin' sides that should prove salable items. "Turn Me Loose" is a pounding, danceable ditty that is vigourously chanted. "Stop Thief!" is a rockabilly that is also read energetically. (3/9/59) (#9 Pop)

Now a full-fledged teen idol, his fifth single, "Tiger"/"Mighty Cold (to a Warm, Warm Heart)", became Fabian's only million seller (and even charted #15 R&B). His next two singles were dual-sided hits.

Tiger/Mighty Cold (to a Warm, Warm Heart).

Fabian belts these rocker-blues with his usual hit sound. Both sides are given energetic vocals. He should have a two-sider with these danceable items. (6/8/59) (#3 Pop)

Got the Feeling/Come On and Get Me.

Two strong contenders to follow "Tiger." "Feeling" is a driving rocker sort. "Come On and Get Me" is a medium-beat rocker. Vocals on both are highly saleable. (8/24/59) (A-side, #54 Pop; B-side, #29 Pop)

With six hits in the Top 40 by age 16, teen heartthrob Fabian made his film debut in November of 1959, costarring with Stuart Whitman in *Hound Dog Man*.

Hound Dog Man/Friendly World.

Two hot ones . . . from his coming flick. "Hound Dog Man," a rocker, is the title tune, and "Friendly World" is a pretty tune with inspirational values. (10/26/59) (A-side, #9 Pop; B-side, #12 Pop)

1960 saw Fabian's career direction take a decided turn toward acting as he starred in *High Time* with Bing Crosby as well as *North to Alaska* with John Wayne. That year also saw his last two charters.

String Along/About This Thing Called Love.

"String Along" is a countryish rocker, delivered strongly. "About This Thing Called Love" is a rocker with a Latin flavor. Both appear hit bound. (1/8/60) (A-side, #39 Pop; B-side, #31 Pop)

Kissin' and Twistin'.

★★★★ *A wild rocker by the chanter with a crazy fem chorus heard in support. Smartly enough, it brings in the twist idea and it figures as a side to be watched.*

Long Before.

★★★★ *Another rocker which details the fact that love was a hit long before rock and roll, the twist, the stroll, etc. A cute idea and it has a strong chance to go. (10/10/60) (#91 Pop)*

Another half-dozen Chancellor singles emerged but it was becoming evident that Fabian's heart was in film.

You're Only Young Once.

★ ★ ★ ★ *From the flick "Love in a Goldfish Bowl" comes this attractive ballad which is sung brightly by Fabian over an uptempo arrangement. Worth exposure. (5/22/61)*

Kansas City.

★ ★ ★ ★ *The Wilbert Harrison hit of three years ago is in swinging groove by Fabian. Combo cooks along nicely in the background, and vocal support by the chorus adds to the atmosphere of the side.*

Tongue-Tied.

★ ★ ★ ★ *Boy is back somewhat, in his "Tiger" groove in this rockin' blues item. Strong guitar work and vocal chorus beef up the side. Both are from Fabian's latest LP,* Rockin' Hot. *(10/2/61)*

Fabian with the Fabulous Four: Wild Party.

★ ★ ★ ★ *Solid rocker is sung with verve . . . Strong teen-appeal lyric and frantic beat. Could put lad back on charts. (10/23/61)*

Fabian joined Dot in 1962 for what would become his last single, "She's Stayin' Inside with Me"/"Break Down and Cry."

> *A bright reading of a happy rhythm tune that could win teen attraction. This could grab sales—watch it. (11/3/62)*

He continued to do films (making over 30) and TV appearances through the 1960s, 1970s, and 1980s while performing in nostalgia shows, including, "Fabian's Good Time Rock 'n' Roll Revue." Even in the 1990s, he's still an entertaining "Tiger" for millions of teens turned baby boomers.

THE FALCONS

Eddie Floyd: Lead vocals (1956–1959)
Born: 6/25/37, Montgomery, AL
Wilson Pickett: Lead vocals (1961–1963)
Born: 3/18/41, Prattville, AL
Joe Stubbs: Lead vocals (1959–1961)
Born: 1930s, Detroit, MI
Bob Menardo: First tenor
Born: 1930s
Tom Shetler: Baritone
Born: 1930s
Willie Schofield: Bass
Born: 1937
Influences: Hank Ballard and The Midnighters, Frankie Lymon and The Teenagers
Influenced: Tyrone Davis, Esquires, Clarence Carter

One of the first integrated vocal groups, The Falcons made an early connection between rock, R&B, and soul music.

Detroit jewelry store employees Eddie Floyd and Bob Menardo formed a quintet with Tom Shetler, Arnett Robinson, and Willie Schofield. Arnett came up with the name, not realizing there had already been four Falcons groups since 1952 on Regent, Savoy, Flip, and Cash. Menardo and Shetler were the white members and the group originally sang modern harmony with a touch of R&B and gospel.

Eddie's uncle Robert West became their manager and arranged the quintet's first record deal with Mercury in 1956. By the time they recorded, their sound was rock 'n' roll. With nothing to show for their first 45, "This Day"/"Baby, That's It," The Falcons moved to Falcon records and two more outstanding sides.

Now That It's Over .75
> *Fancy tenor lead intones a plaintive rockaballad. A good enough job, but interest lags midway.*

My Only Love 73
> *The rhythm side. Good group wails it against choppy, Latin tinged beats. Interesting, somewhat "different" sound here. (12/2/57)*

Soon after, Shetler, Robinson, and Menardo left, replaced by new lead Joe Stubbs (brother of Four Tops lead, Levi Stubbs), Bonnie "Mack" Rice, and Lance Finnie. The Falcons were now an all black affair. Having no luck when he loaned out the group, West decided to put them on his own Flick label in 1959 for what would become their career maker. The raw, funky, shuffle style made "You're So Fine" one of rock's first crossover soul singles and became The Falcons' biggest Top-100 hit.

You're So Fine (A-side).
★ ★ ★ ★ *The group comes thru with the authentic church sound on this pulsating effort, sung with feeling by the strong lead with help from the group. It could grab coins. It was originally issued on the Flick label.*

Goddess of Angels (B-side).
★ ★ *A celestial type ballad is sung tenderly by the high voiced lead. (3/16/59) (#17 Pop, #2 R&B)*

West kept issuing tracks on Flick and licensing the soulsters to Chess and United Artists so you rarely knew where their next single was coming from.

You're Mine/Country Shack.

> *Fine readings on two bright tunes. "You're Mine" is an infectious rocker-type. "Country Shack" is also an up side and the verveful vocal should attract coin a-plenty. (8/17/59)*

Just for Your Love (A-side).
★ ★ ★ ★ *A solid reading . . . of a driving ditty with sock beat and an insinuating rhythm. A first-rate side that could break loose.*

This Heart of Mine (B-side).
★ ★ ★ ★ *A tender ballad [sung] with much feeling over a strong rhythm backing. The lead singer has a standout style and the group work is good. Watch this. (11/16/59)*

You Must Know I Love You.
★ ★ ★ *The Falcons sing this rocker with enthusiasm over bright support. It moves and could pick up coins, if exposed. (3/7/60)*

The Teacher.
★ ★ ★ ★ *A good, low-down blues with a dramatic lead job. Side gets the big fiddle treatment in back of the vocal. Chorus is also heard. This side could move out. (6/6/60) (#18 R&B)*

Wonderful Love.
★ ★ ★ ★ *Moving performance by lead singer on emotional rockaballad with dual market potential. (9/12/60)*

Working Man's Song (A-side).
★ ★ ★ ★ *The boys have a strong sound here on a solid rhythm job. Good beat and a fine lead performance. There's a lot going on here.*

Pow! You're in Love (B-side).
★ ★ ★ *Sam Cooke is the writer of this tune which has a folkish blues quality. Boys do it well but flip has an edge. (2/6/61)*

The Falcons' flight path continued to have departures and arrivals, as Stubbs left to sing with The Contours and was replaced by a 19-year-old Alabaman named Wilson Pickett.

It was a year before their next release, which was on another of Uncle West's labels, and although its *Billboard* reviewer made no comment, save awarding it three stars, "I Found a Love" became The Falcons' biggest R&B hit (#75 Pop, #6 R&B).

West then lent the group again, this time to Atlantic, for three underexposed singles. When Schofield joined Uncle Sam in 1963, the group disbanded. West, determined to beat his horse into the ground, found a local group, The Fabulous Playboys, featuring Sonny Monroe, renamed them

The Falcons, and charted once more with "Standing on Guard"/"I Can't Help It."

Already getting some chart activity, this medium-paced rocker should go to the top of the r&b charts in short order. (10/29/66) (#107 Pop, #29 R&B)

Aside from their group achievements, The Falcons were a spawning ground for solo talent. Bonnie "Mack" Rice became "Sir" Mack Rice, hitting with "Mustang Sally" (#15 R&B) in 1965. Eddie Floyd had 13 Top-100 and 18 R&B hits, including the legendary, "Knock on Wood" (#28 Pop, #1 R&B, 1966), and Wilson Pickett became the "Franchise" Falcon with 40 Pop and 49 R&B winners like "Funky Broadway" (#8 Pop, #1 R&B, 1967) and "In the Midnight Hour" (#21 Pop, #1 R&B, 1965).

THE 5TH DIMENSION

Marilyn McCoo: Lead vocals
Born: 9/20/43, Jersey City, NJ
Florence LaRue
Born: 2/4/44, Plainfield, NJ
Billy Davis, Jr.
Born: 6/26/40, St. Louis, MO
Lamont McLemore
Born: 9/17/40, St. Louis, MO
Ron Townson
Born: 1/20/41, St. Louis, MO
Influences: Four Tops, Temptations, Ella Fitzgerald, Mamas and The Papas, Lena Horne, Sammy Davis, Jr., Nat "King" Cole
Influenced: Boyz II Men, Earth, Wind and Fire, Friends of Distinction

Among the classiest vocal groups of the 1960s, The 5th Dimension were also one of the most consistent hit makers, racking up 30 Top-100 singles in just seven years.

Lamont was a professional photographer when he met 20-year-old Marilyn McCoo, who had just

been named Miss Bronze America 1963. They formed a short-lived group (The Hi-Fi's) with Floyd Butler and Harry Elston; soon after, the latter twosome founded the Friends of Distinction. Lamont then added his cousin, Billy Davis, formerly of the St. Louis R&B group, The Emeralds. The Emeralds:

That's The Way It's Got to Be.
★★   *Emotional sing on a rockaballad. (5/25/59)*

Ron and Marilyn next added school teacher Florence LaRue to the group; she had been Miss Bronze America 1962 and the lady who crowned Marilyn in 1963. They named themselves the Versatiles and joined up with ex-Motown executive Marc Gordon for management. He brought the quintet to Johnny Rivers and his new Soul City label, distributed by Liberty.

Their first single ("I'll Be Loving You Forever") was issued under a new name, The 5th Dimension, and was barely given a chance, when their second single, "Go Where You Wanna Go," came out a month later, which was a Top-20 pop hit. The group's early sound was that of a black Mamas and Papas.

Go Where You Wanna Go.
Powerhouse rocker penned by Papa John Phillips and top production by Johnny Rivers and Marc Gordon has all the ingredients of a fast smash. The dynamic quintet has excitement that should hit the teen market with impact. (12/31/66) (#16 Pop)

Another Day, Another Heartache.
Moving Sloan-Barrie folk-rock number with much of the feel of their initial winner . . . should put the group rapidly back up, the top half of the chart. (4/22/67) (#45 Pop)

In May 1967, while working on their first album, producer Rivers decided to close down for the weekend so he could go to the San Remo Song Festival. That fateful weekend, session pianist Jimmy Webb took in a fair and saw a hot air balloon ascend, inspiring him to write, "Up-Up and Away." The million seller went on to win five Grammys, including Best Song of the Year and Record of the Year.

The title tune of the group's hit LP should make it three in a row on the Hot 100. Infectious beat and groovy vocal workout should carry this even higher than their initial hit "Go Where You Wanna Go." (5/27/67) (#7 Pop)

Their style now fully developed, The 5th next scored in a big way with Laura Nyro's classic "Stoned Soul Picnic" in 1968.

Paper Cup.
The "Up, Up and Away" gang has a sure-fire winner in this long-awaited follow up. Easy beat rhythm item has all the sales potential of their past hits. (10/28/67) (#34 Pop)

Stoned Soul Picnic.
A groovy piece of rhythm material, penned by Laura Nyro. Will rapidly surpass the sale of their recent success. (5/18/68) (#3 Pop, # 2 R&B)

Sweet Blindness.
Following up their "Stoned Soul Picnic" smash, the inventive group gives this exceptional Laura Nyro rhythm material a powerhouse vocal workout. This'll go straight to the top of the Hot 100. (9/14/68) (#13 Pop, #45 R&B)

The group's biggest hit happened because Billy lost his wallet in a New York City cab. A good samaritan returned it and was rewarded with a night at The 5th's local performance. He turned out to be the producer of the Broadway play, *Hair*, and reciprocated by inviting the whole group to see the show. Producer "Bones" Howe created a medley from the show's opening number, "Aquarius," with another segment, "Let the Sunshine In," to create the group's biggest single. A worldwide hit, the two-million seller spent six weeks at #1.

Aquarius/Let the Sunshine In (the Flesh Failures).
A coupling from the musical smash "Hair" serves as strong material for the group. The rhythm items are given their most commercial outing to date and should prove a top chart item. (3/1/69) (#1 Pop, #6 R&B)

In 1969, wedding bells were everywhere as Marc married Florence and Billy wedded Marilyn, so their next single was no surprise.

Wedding Bell Blues.
Group should make it three Top 20 hits in a row with this exciting treatment of the Laura Nyro classic, recently released by Lesley Gore. First rate performance and material makes this a potent follow up to their "Workin' on a Groovy Thing" hit. (9/20/69) (#1 Pop, #23 R&B)

By 1970 "Bones" had taken The 5th to Bell Records for a new string of hits. They began with the social commentary of "The Declaration," but soon retreated to the potent pop for which they were famous. They returned to the Top 10 with their #2 smash, "One Less Bell to Answer."

The Declaration/Medley: A Change Is Gonna Come & People Gotta Be Free.
The exceptional group offers a change of pace . . . Culled from their in-person performance, it has a timely and vital message. Flip is equally timely and has equal sales and chart potency. Top performances. (2/14/70) (#64 Pop)

Puppet Man.
Neil Sedaka-Howie Greenfield rhythm material and a potent Dimension vocal workout spells Top 10 entry. (4/11/70) (#24 Pop)

One Less Bell to Answer.
This compelling Bacharach-David material . . . features Marilyn on solo. Featured recently on their "It Takes a Thief" TV show guest shot. (10/10/70) (#2 Pop)

Love's Lines, Angles and Rhymes.
Group climbed back into the Top 10 with "One Less Bell to Answer" and this strong, driving ballad offers the same sales and chart potency. (2/13/71) (#19 Pop, #28 R&B)

Never My Love.
The group turns in a strong delivery of the Association's past smash. Powerful solo work by Marilyn McCoo Davis with much of that "One Less Bell to

Answer" potential. (9/4/71) (#12 Pop, #45 R&B)

In 1972, the quintet performed at the White House for President Nixon, but the group's hit-making days were drawing to a close as "Ashes to Ashes" became the act's last Top-60 charter.

Ashes to Ashes.

> *Solid ensemble vocal work encompassing rich harmonies . . . The melody is beautifully played by the orchestra; the 5th lilts along with the beat of a prominent conga. This medium tempoed swinger rides nicely. (7/21/73) (#52 Pop, #54 R&B)*

By 1975, Billy and Marilyn became a duo, while Danny Beard and Margorie Barnes joined The 5th; both entities signed with ABC. The group's last hit was "Love Hangover" (#80, 1976), but they remain a top club and Las Vegas attraction to this day.

Marilyn and Billy went on to duo success with, "You Don't Have to Be a Star" (#1, 1976) and "Your Love." They also cohosted a TV variety show in 1977 that led to her role as host of "Solid Gold." She went solo in 1983, and, in 1995, she took over the part of Julie in the Broadway revival of *Show Boat.*

THE FIVE KEYS

Rudy West: Lead vocals (ballads)
Born: 7/25/32, Newport News, VA
Bernie West: Bass
Born: 2/4/30, Newport News, VA
Maryland Pierce: Lead vocals (uptempo)
Born: 1933, Newport News, VA
Ripley Ingram: Tenor
Born: 1930, Newport News, VA
Raphael Ingram: Baritone
Born: 1931, Newport News, VA
Influence: Orioles

Influenced: Bobby Darin, Cadillacs, Crests, Flamingos, Harptones, Solitaires, Marcels, Bobbettes, Five Crowns, Ben E. King's Drifters, Five Sharps, many more

A key link between the 1940s' gospel and pop groups and the 1950s' R&B and rock 'n' roll acts, The Five Keys waxed some of the finest harmony ever recorded.

Originally named The Sentimental Four, the Newport News teens were two sets of brothers, Rudy and Bernie West and Raphael and Ripley Ingram. They assembled in 1949, singing gospel music, and by 1951 were sophisticated secular singers taking on all comers as New York's Apollo Theater Amateur Night contest winners.

They were signed in February 1952 to Aladdin Records, but Raphael was Army-bound before they could record. His replacements, Maryland Pierce (Avalons) and Dickie Smith, more than made up for his absence. Now calling themselves The Five Keys, they boasted three of the era's finest lead singers, comprising Pierce's incredible blues energy, Smith's soulful style, and Rudy's crystal clear ballad tenor.

The group's first single, "With a Broken Heart"/"Too Late," came in April 1951. It opened the door for their standard-to-be and biggest R&B hit, "Glory of Love" (#1, four weeks). A million-seller, "Glory" kept them working the chitlin' circuit while equally great singles were issued and underpromoted by Aladdin.

With a Broken Heart 83–83–82–84
> *Group gets a load of feeling into a pretty slow ballad; lead tenor shows an expressive style, rest of group puts down neat harmony. (5/5/51)*

Old MacDonald 70–72–68–69
> *The familiar folk ditty is handed a rocking reading from the group with a few lyric modernizations adding spice to the proceedings.*

It's Christmas Time 70–72–68–69
> *A pleasant new seasonal ballad is given a warmly blended reading. (12/8/51)*

Red Sails in the Sunset (A-side) .78–80–76–78
> *The Five Keys give the old fave a mighty strong reading. This one could do well.*

Be Anything (But Be Mine) (B-side) 72–75–70–71

> *The Five Keys, using a style somewhat similar to the Ink Spots, do an adequate job. (4/12/52)*

In 1953 the Army once again stepped in, as Rudy and Dickie were captured by Uncle Sam's siren song. Ramon Loper and Ulysses Hicks then joined The Keys.

I'm So High 74

> *Relaxed chanting marks this item, which should prove of some attraction to jazz buyers, as well as strictly r.&b. trade. The lead voice of the Five Keys is backed by a rhythmic vocal arrangement. (9/26/53)*

Oh Babe 74

> *The Five Keys, who have been without a hit for a long time, have a listenable slicing here, one that could get some action, even tho it is not nearly as frantic as their past sides. The boys sing it well, and the ork punches out the rhythm.*

My Saddest Hour 74

> *The boys get a bit wild here as they sing this new ballad with all the stops pulled out. It has a lot to it; and it, too, should pull spins. (12/12/53)*

Some Day, Sweetheart 79

> *The pop evergreen is sold with taste here . . . sparked by some fine tenor lead work. With the action on pop-styled ballads in the field this one has a chance for coins. It is one of the best cuttings by the group in a while. (3/27/54)*

The quintet moved to RCA's Groove label in 1954 for one release, "I'll Follow You" but when their manager, Sol Richfield, gained a better deal with Capitol, RCA pulled "I'll Follow You," making it one of the rarest R&B 45s in history.

Capitol's pop capabilities helped the smoothly rocking Keys breach the Top 100 for the first time on their now-legendary "Ling Ting Tong," which was issued as the B-side.

Ling, Ting, Tong.

> *The title is right here. This is a r.&b. platter about a hip Chinese warbler. The boys sing of the troubles of Ling Ting Tong on this cute, new platter, selling it neatly. (10/16/54) (#28 Pop, #5 R&B)*

Unfortunately, Hicks died after the first Capitol session. Rudy returned just in time to be a part of their most popular period.

Close Your Eyes/Doggone It, You Did It.

> *The top side is a powerful new ballad, and the flip is a wild swinging effort. Both feature sock performances, and both are coin-grabbers. (1/29/55) (#5 R&B)*

The Verdict.

> *This appears to be their strongest entry yet. The material is powerful, and so is the way the boys sock it over. It's difficult to see how this side can possibly miss. It's all there from the first beat. (5/14/55) (#13 R&B)*

Don't You Know I Love You?/I Wish I'd Never Learned to Read.

> *The Keys have been clicking consistently of late, and both sides are capable of continuing the streak. "Don't You Know" is a brisk-beat plaint by Singleton and McCoy, while the flip is a weeper occasioned by receipt of a "Dear John" letter. (7/16/55)*

Gee Whittakers!/'Cause You're My Lover.

> *The group wraps up a bright novelty "Gee Whittakers!" in a bouncy, solidly commercial vocal treatment and a happy-beat. The lyrics spotlight a series of teen-age slang phrases, and the side could easily go pop too. The flip . . . is a suavely styled, slow-tempo ballad with a memorable melody and an excellent performance by the lead singer. (11/5/55) (A-side, #14 R&B; B-side, #12 R&B)*

In mid-1956, another B-side earned the group its second and last million seller and biggest pop disk, "Out of Sight, Out of Mind." It was their last

R&B and pop charter as well, though many beautiful and competitive singles followed.

Out of Sight, Out of Mind.

> *Lead singer does a sincere job with the despairing theme of this Ivory Joe Hunter ballad. Balance of group is augmented by a chorus in the backing. Has a strong appeal. (8/25/56) (#23 Pop, #12 R&B)*

Wisdom of a Fool.

> *Group stands a good chance to make it in both pop and r.&b. markets with this one. Tune is a slow ballad with a philosophical message, intoned with great feeling and solid harmony. (11/24/56) (#35 Pop)*

In 1958 Rudy retired, replaced on lead by Dickie Threat, and in 1959 the quintet signed with the King label.

I Took Your Love for a Toy.

★ ★ ★ *A warm reading of a very pretty ballad that should get some air time and could pull some coins. (7/31/59)*

Dancing Senorita.

★ ★ ★ ★ *A samba-rocker blues by the boys. The side has touches of the Coasters in the material and the chanting. An interesting song about the lady from Barcelona, and the boys give her a fine sound. Definitely worth watching. (10/26/59)*

Rudy came out of retirement to record and did some fine solo work also on King.
Rudy West:

Just to Be with You.

★ ★ ★ *West's chanting of this ballad is relaxed and sensitive. There's a chorus and a tasteful arrangement. (10/26/59)*

As Sure as I Live.

★ ★ ★ ★ *A first-rate reading of a solid rockaballad. West has a McPhatter touch here, and the backing has a warm flavor. Good wax. (11/16/59)*

In 1962, West, West, and Smith, along with John Boyd and Willie Friday, redid "Out of Sight."

Out of Sight.

★ ★ ★ ★ *This pretty Ivory Joe Hunter-Clyde Otis tune receives a smooth and tender performance from the Keys backed by a chorus and ork arrangement. Worth spins. (9/1/62)*

New members continued to back Rudy on occasional performances through the 1970s and 1980s. During the 1970s, Ramon Loper became a New York shoe salesman, Bernie West worked in a Virginia shipyard, and Rudy joined the Hampton, Virginia, post office. The last single recording under The Five Keys name was "I Want You for Xmas" (Classic Artists, 1989). Thanks to a wave of nostalgia-minded audiences, most of the original Five Keys (with Rudy singing lead) are still performing in the United States and England, usually in tandem with The Cleftones.

THE FIVE SATINS

Fred Parris: Lead vocals
Born: 3/26/36, New Haven, CT
Lou Peebles: Tenor
Born: 1937, New Haven, CT
Stanley Dortch: Tenor
Born: 1930s, New Haven, CT
Ed Martin: Baritone
Born: 1930s, New Haven, CT
Jim Freeman: Bass
Born: 1940, New Haven, CT
Influences: Clovers, Dominoes, Four Freshmen, Five Crowns, Jackie Wilson, Sam Cooke, Velvets, Five Royales, Joe Williams
Influenced: Paul Anka, Dimensions, Fleetwoods

Thoughts of The Five Satins conjure up memories of kids holding hands, moonlight strolls, soda shops, and teenage love in the 1950s. Such imagery and nostalgia is the result of their revered classic, "In the Still of the Night," considered by many to be the most beloved rock 'n' roll oldie of all time.

The Five Satins' story started in 1955 when

lead singer Fred Parris (formerly of The Scarlets on Red Robin) fashioned his New Haven quintet and christened them The Five Satins. Parris's passion for things red led to the name, as it did with his former group. The Satins met teenage record producers Marty Kugell and Tom Zachariah who owned a two-track tape recorder. A session was arranged at the local VFW post. When the musicians didn't show, the group recorded "All Mine" and "Rose Mary" a cappella. Kugell and Zachariah then issued it on their own Standord label and, although it received little attention, that fine ballad is acknowledged as the first rock 'n' roll a cappella single. Peebles and Dortch then left the group, and Al Denby (Scarlets) joined. Note that at the time there were only Four Satins.

It was those same Four Satins that recorded in St. Bernadette's church in East Haven on a December night in 1955. One of the two songs they put on tape (this time the musicians did show up) was written by Parris while he was on guard duty in the Army at about 3:00 AM. He was stationed at an army base in Philadelphia and commuted back and forth on leave. The song was, of course, "In the Still of the Night" and Standord released it as the B-side of "The Jones Girl," another praiseworthy Parris composition. As airplay developed, New York's Ember label took notice and bought the masters. The record so typifies the rock 'n' roll era that most fans assume it was a #1 hit. Even without that status, it has sold millions in its 40-year career. More smooth Satins singles ensued.

The Jones Girl 69
> Enthusiastic vocal treatment of a bouncy rhythm opus with a strong solid beat.

I'll Remember (In the Still of the Night) . . .67
> The Satins chant with warm expressiveness on a smoothly paced ballad with dramatic lyrics. (6/9/56) (B-side, #24 Pop, #3 R&B)

Wonderful Girl.
> This group came out of nowhere to score with "In the Still of the Night." The "sound" and smart pacing here proves that this was no flash-in-the-pan success. This relaxed ballad has the same elements of performance and production to bring the house down again. (10/27/56)

Parris was then stationed in Japan, and Ember brought in lead Bill Baker (Chestnuts) for what would become another Satins standard.

To the Aisle.
> The group is very attractive on pretty ballad. Rhythm backing includes a wailing alto. Side could be a repeat of their hit, "In the Still of the Night." (6/10/57) (#25 Pop, #5 R&B)

Our Anniversary.
> Side gets an unusual treatment with a bassoon featured prominently thruout. Excellent warbling by the lead with good group support could easily repeal success of "To the Aisle." (10/14/57)

In 1958, Parris returned and created still another Scarlets with Richie Freeman and Wes Forbes (both former Starlarks), Peebles (Satins), and Sylvester Hopkins (Scarlets). When the remaining Satins split up, Baker returned to The Chestnuts, and The Scarlets became yet another contingent of Satins. Trying to capitalize on Parris's success, Event Records issued old Scarlets' Red Robin sides ("Dear One"), whereas Bill Baker and the Chestnuts covered The Five Satins' "Wonderful Girl" in May 1959.

Fred Parris and The Scarlets:
She's Gone 71
> Parris sells this ballad effort nicely, helped by the boys and the band. (2/24/58)

The Satins:
A Night to Remember 77
> The reconstituted Satins group—the originals are now out of the armed forces—offer an emotional reading of the ballad. Good performance that could go. (7/21/58)

The Scarlets:
Dear One 74
> The r.&b. hit of a few seasons ago is handed a smart rockaballad reading by the crew with pounding piano triplets prominent in support. It can attract in pop and r.&b. markets. (10/27/58)

Bill Baker and The Chestnuts:
Wonderful Girl.

★ ★ *A slow, click click rhythm rockabal-*
lad, which gets flute spots in the back-
ing, plus a chorus. Fair prospects.
(5/18/59)

In 1959, Ember loaned Parris, et al., for one release to First records ("When Your Love Comes Along"), while continually issuing solid, but over-looked gems.

When Your Love Comes Along.

★ ★ *Fervent wailing by lead singer and*
group on an okay rockaballad. (6/1/59)

Shadows.

 A spirited reading of a ballad with
beat. Fervent sound by the lead is nice-
ly backed by the group and band. It's
their best in a while. (10/5/59) (#87
Pop, #27 R&B)

I'll Be Seeing You.

 The group backs the lead singer
strongly in this feelingful presentation
of the standard. They wrap it up with
hit sound, and the attractive side can
score. (3/28/60) (#79 Pop)

By 1960, the Satins were on Cub.

Your Memory.

★ ★ ★ ★ *Lead singer warbles with fervent show-*
manship on strong r.&b. theme. (6/13/60)

The Time.

★ ★ ★ ★ *A very listenable reading of a good*
rockaballad here, over interesting
string support. Lead vocal is strong
enough to make this record get some
action. (10/3/60)

These Foolish Things.

★ ★ ★ ★ *A pulsing reading of the great stan-*
dard. Arrangement features chorus and
fiddles. Nice sound. (10/31/60)

Trying every formula imaginable for a hit, they changed their name to The Wildwoods and then The New Yorkers.

The New Yorkers:
Miss Fine.

 A rhythmic little rocker is handed a
swinging go . . . over bright percussion
backing. (4/10/61)

Meanwhile, "In the Still" charted twice more (#81, 1960 and #99, 1961) because of constant air-play. Throughout the 1960s, Parris and company made numerous singles for Chancellor, Warner Brothers, and Roulette, including a rerecording of "In the Still of the Night" under the name of Fred Parris and The Restless Hearts. The oldies revival that took hold in 1969 carried The Five Satins through the 1970s, 1980s, and 1990s as one of the genre's prime examples of the 1950s' sound. In 1982 their recording of "Memories of Days Gone By" (Elektra) became their first chart single (#71) in 21 years.

THE FLAMINGOS

"Sollie" Sylvester McElroy: Lead vocals (1953–1954)
Born: 7/16/33, Gulfport, MS (died 1/15/95)
Nate Nelson: Lead vocals (1955–1965)
Born: 4/10/32, Chicago, IL (died 6/1/84)
John Carter: First tenor
Born: 6/2/33, Chicago, IL
Ezekiel "Zeke" Carey: Second tenor
Born: 1/24/33, Baltimore, MD
Paul Wilson: Baritone
Born: 1/6/35, Chicago, IL (died 5/6/88)
Jacob Carey: Bass
Born: 9/9/23, Baltimore, MD
Influences: Five Keys, Orioles, Ravens, Dominoes, Four
    Freshmen, Clovers
Influenced: Miracles, Rascals, Gladys Knight and The
    Pips, Little Anthony and The Imperials, Temptations,
    Skyliners, Jackson Five, Dell-Vikings, Supremes,
    Heartbeats, Spinners, Jesters, Monotones, Gene
    Pitney, Lou Christie, Bobby Freeman, Crows, Crests,
    Capris, Chi-Lites, Del Satins, Shirelles, many more

From the standpoint of sheer vocal harmony magic, The Flamingos were the best singing group in rock 'n' roll history.

The group's rich musical quality owes its uniqueness in part to the Jewish hymns Jake and Zeke Carey sang in the Jewish Church of God in Chicago where they met Johnny Carter and Paul Wilson. The four began harmonizing in 1950 and, with original lead singer Earl Lewis, called themselves The Swallows, El Flamingos, and then, The Five Flamingos. When the group met Sollie McElroy at a party, Earl moved out and joined The Five Echoes (on Sabre records). Booking agent Ralph Leon heard the quintet and became their manager in 1952. Leon then took his finely tuned group to United Records, who passed on the act's intricately clean harmonizing.

In February 1953, Leon arranged a deal with Chance Records, and the first of their gorgeous harmonies were married to disk. The 45, featuring "Someday, Someway," was reviewed as a country & western title! The label read, The Flamingos, but the group remained The Five Flamingos in performance for almost two years.

Someday, Someway (A-side) 77
A happy bounce effort, almost on a spiritual-type kick, is sung with life and spirit by the boys over a hand-clapping background and good ork work. Group is a good one, and the side can grab loot.

If I Can't Have You (B-side) 75
The Flamingos, a new group on the label, turn in another satisfactory side here, sparked by the lead singer on this new ballad. The group backs the lead nicely, and the beat is strong. (3/14/53)

That's My Desire 83
This, of course, is the ditty revived into hit status a few years ago by Frankie Laine. The group comes up with a good reading in ballad style which should get big action. (8/15/53)

Regional success led to numerous bookings with Lionel Hampton and Duke Ellington. It also set the stage for what many historians call the most perfect record of all time, "Golden Teardrops," originally a B-side.

Carried Away . . . . .8[5]
A very powerful side that builds and builds. It's a hand clapper with a solid beat. Group turns in a solid performance. Watch this one: it can be a big winner.

Golden Teardrops .75
Tempo slows way down on this side. Lead carries this one, with the group chiming in behind. (10/3/53)

Their last Chance single was The Flamingos' finest jump side to date ("Jump Children"), and earned the quintet an opportunity to sing it five years later in Alan Freed's film, *Go, Johnny, Go!*

Jump Children 72
A bouncy item with a good scat vocal. Should pull juke play. (11/13/54)

In 1955, Chicago's finest briefly connected with the local Parrott label.

Dream of a Lifetime 78
A mighty attractive new ballad is handed a smooth and listenable performance . . . over a pretty backing. This is a good entry that has a chance for action. (1/5/55)

Their choreography became a model for acts like The Temptations and The Four Tops a decade later. Their instrumental skills made them the first self-contained R&B vocal group.

Later that year, Nate Nelson became the group's lead vocalist, and they moved to Checker Records. Meanwhile, Sollie joined The Moroccos, debuting on their recording of the classic "Over the Rainbow" (performing, in *Billboard*'s words, excellently, in "sock, r.&b. style"; 10/15/55). The Flamingos finally broke the chart ice with, "I'll Be Home." The beautiful and now-classic, "A Kiss From Your Lips" followed and, although *Billboard*'s reviewer thought little of it, the fans loved it.

When.
The boys warble . . . a poignant ballad with appealing warmth and a relaxed charm. (4/30/55)

I'll Be Home.
The boys blend smoothly and sweetly on a pretty ballad with a relaxed, romantic tempo and a standout performance by the lead singer. This one

should grab off plenty of attention from jocks, jukes and cross-counter buyers. (1/14/56) (#5 R&B)

A Kiss from Your Lips 80
Tho the material on both sides is below par for this fine group, the rendition should carry them into the money. This one's a ballad, with an especially tender voice handling the lead thruout. (5/12/56) (#12 R&B)

Their first involvement with an Alan Freed film came on the next single, "The Vow," which was reviewed as the B-side. Freed became such a fan that he put the group and "The Vow" in *Go, Johnny, Go!* even though they didn't have a current hit. Another appearance in a Freed flick quickly followed.

The group intones a slow, fervent recital of devotion with the same mighty fancy wailing by the lead man. Strong appeal here all the way. (10/5/56)

Would I Be Crying 73
From the Alan Freed "Rock, Rock, Rock" pic, this slow pulsing ballad gets a dedicated, but not especially salable, reading . . . Disappointing effort. (12/8/56)

In 1957, Zeke and Johnny were drafted. Nate, Jake, Paul, and Tommy Hunt (Five Echoes) signed with Decca, but Checker, still holding a contract on Nelson, killed Decca's sides through legal maneuvers.

The Ladder of Love 70
A ballad, slow in tempo, and of the tender sort. (7/1/57)

In 1958, Carter joined The Dells and Zeke returned, clearing up the Checker mess and moving the group to George Goldner's End label. Once again, a classic appeared as a B-side ("Lovers Never Say Goodbye") but that one became their first pop hit.

The Love Is You 80
A deeply soulful ballad reading. Lead shows much spirit and the backing moves nicely. This side's worth watching.

Lovers Never Say Goodbye 76
★   *A slow, meaningful ballad is handled with dedication by the group with fem chorus backing. A pleasant side. (10/27/58) (#52 Pop, #25 R&B)*

But Not for Me.

 The group, currently scoring with "Lovers Never Say Goodbye," could have a big one with their smooth, rock-aballad treatment of the Gershwin evergreen. Solid performance is neatly backed. (2/9/59)

Unlike their early originals, The Flamingos were now recording masterful versions of standards.

Goodnight Sweetheart.
★ ★ ★   *The lead gives a sensitive reading of the classic standard. It's pleasant, dreamy wax which could hit paydirt.*

I Only Have Eyes for You.
★ ★ ★   *The boys have an offbeat arrangement of the standard which has a crazy mixed-up start. Parts of the side have a jazz quality, but the r.&r. triplets are still there. (5/11/59) (B-side, #11 Pop, #3 R&B)*

Love Walked In.

 Given a strong interpretation by the lead voice with complimentary group support. (8/17/59) (#88 Pop)

I Was Such a Fool.
★ ★ ★ ★ *The Flamingos sell this pretty ballad with warmth over full-stringed backing. A good side with a sound that can happen. (12/7/59) (#71 Pop)*

Nobody Loves Me Like You.

 A ballad, cleffed by Sam Cooke . . . gets a sock delivery. (2/14/60) (B-side, #30 Pop, #23 R&B)

Mio Amore.

 The boys are at their feelingful best on this disk. "Mio Amore" is a pretty ballad with a melodic Latin flavor. Watch it. (5/27/60) (#74 Pop, #27 R&B)

Your Other Love.

★ ★ ★ ★ *The lead singer does a fine job on this quick-paced ballad that is faintly reminiscent melodically of "Save the Last Dance for Me." Group as a whole sounds fine and accompanying fiddles add a lush swinging background. (11/21/60) (#54 Pop)*

Tommy Hunt left The Flamingos for a solo career in 1961.

Kokomo.

 The r.&r. oldie . . . gets a high-flying reading from the group with a vocal full of showmanship. (1/20/61) (#92 Pop)

In 1965, the group signed with Philips and, in keeping with the times, got funky.

The Boogaloo Party.

The famous group make a powerful second comeback with this hot discotheque entry. Solid beat and vocal work are exceptional. (1/22/66) (#93 Pop, #22 R&B)

Their last charter, "Buffalo Soldier" (#86 Pop, #28 R&B), was in 1970, but the group, with Zeke and Jake still at the helm, continued performing nationally through the 1990s for appreciative fans and the hundreds of stars they'd influenced.

THE FLEETWOODS

Gary Troxel: Lead vocals
Born: 11/28/39, Olympia, WA
Gretchen Christopher
Born: 2/29/40, Olympia, WA
Barbara Ellis
Born: 2/20/40, Olympia, WA
Influences: Five Satins, Penguins, Johnny Mathis, Teddy Bears, Julie London, Chet Baker
Influenced: Carpenters, Bruce Johnston (Beach Boys)

Some of the softest and sweetest sounds of the late 1950s came from the lips of The Fleetwoods.

The trio of talented teens started as a 1958 duo of Olympia High School seniors. Barbara and Gretchen were cheerleaders who named themselves The Saturns and began playing opposite a local band called The Blue Comets. They tried auditioning several girls but when they heard trumpet player/wispy voiced vocalist Gary Troxel, they found their lead singer and quickly changed their name to Two Girls and a Guy.

In the Spring of 1958, the trio made an a cappella tape containing their composition "Come Softly" and traveled to Seattle to meet Dolphin records' owner Bob Reisdorff. He loved the song but not their name, and during a subsequent phone conversation with Barbara, he looked down at his dial and noticed the area's phone prefix, "Fleetwood." The song was then retitled, recorded (which took them six months), and issued to a flurry of acceptance. The single shot from nowhere to #1 in three weeks and remained there for four. Although the song never said, "Come Softly to Me," Reisdorff changed the title, feeling "Come Softly" was too risqué for 1959 radio. Incidentally, there are no drums on the million-selling record. The percussion was the sound of Gary shaking his car keys!

Come Softly to Me.

 The kids have an interesting sound on this catchy, folkish tune. It's of the ballad type and different enough to attract play and coin. There's already some West Coast action. (2/16/59) (#1 Pop, #5 R&B)

Oh, Lord Let It Be/Graduation's Here.

The threesome follow "Come Softly to Me" with two strong contenders. Top side is a ballad that is warmly read. Flip is a contagious tune about high school fun. They could repeat with either of these. (5/4/59) (B-side, #39 Pop)

The trio's next 45 happened because songwriter DeWayne Blackwell had written a tune for The Platters but didn't know how to reach them. Instead, he met Reisdorff and wound up singing "Mr. Blue" for The Fleetwoods in a Seattle hotel room.

You Mean Everything to Me/Mr. Blue.

Attractive sides. "You Mean" is an interesting rockaballad type that they sing softly over smooth ork backing. "Mr. Blue" is also a strong hunk of material, and they present it smartly. Either can make it. (8/17/59) (A-side, #84 Pop; B-side, #1 Pop, #3 R&B)

With two gold singles in three tries, the "Washington Wonders" were bound for a whirlwind of Dick Clark and Ed Sullivan TV show appearances. International touring was out, however, as Gary had joined the Naval Reserve in high school and could have been called up at any time.

Magic Star/Outside My Window.

Two hot sides to follow their big "Mr. Blue." The top tune, penned by Bonnie Guitar, is presented along similar lines to their current hit. Flip is an attractive reading of a gently and plaintive ballad. (1/25/60) (B-side, #28 Pop)

Truly Do/Runaround.

"Truly Do," a melodic ballad is accorded a smooth vocal treatment by the group with pleasant harmonica backing. Flip, a hit for the Chuckles a few years back, is also handled effectively. (5/2/60) (B-side, #23 Pop)

Gary was called up and that same month his label issued "The Last One to Know." In anticipation of Troxel's departure, Dolton (formerly Dolphin) recorded a wealth of Fleetwoods' material and augmented it when Gary visited on leave. Gary returned for good in 1962.

The Last One to Know/Dormilona.

The group sells "The Last One to Know," a tender ballad with moving sincerity. Flip, an attractive theme, is sung smoothly in Spanish and English. Either side could make it. (9/5/60) (#96 Pop)

Confidential.

★ ★ ★ ★ *A soft, crooning ballad effort by the group. The cat takes a pleasant lead abetted by the chords from the gals. This has a strong chance.*

I Love You So.

★ ★ ★ ★ *The "Mr. Blue" kids have a slow ballad with triplet backing. It's soft and much in the tradition of their earlier hits. Side is worth watching. (11/14/60)*

Tragedy.

Lead singer comes through with a gentle ballad on the lost-love theme. The fine work of the rest of the group in support and excellent ork effects make this a strong item. (4/3/61) (#10 Pop)

(He's) The Great Imposter.

★ ★ ★ *A slightly Latinish rhythm is used behind this harmony vocal job. (8/14/61) (B-side, #30 Pop)*

Although Troxel sang most of the leads, Ellis was up front on their last chart single in 1963, "Goodnight, My Love" (#32). The group disbanded after their recording contract expired and, to their fans' dismay, The Fleetwoods never tried to find another deal. They did perform together in 1971 through 1973 and, later, Troxel and Christopher added Cheryl Huggins when Ellis decided to retire. Gary eventually went to work in a plywood mill in Anacortes, Washington, whereas Barbara Ellis became Barbara Pizzutello and managed a mobile home park in Ontario, California. Gretchen Christopher became Gretchen Matzen, part-time modern dance teacher and occasional solo act in Olympia.

FRANKIE FORD

Real Name: Frank Guzzo
Birthdate: 8/4/39
Birthplace: Gretna, LA
Influences: Fats Domino, Clarence "Frog Man" Henry, Huey "Piano" Smith
Influenced: Mick Jagger, Billy Squires, Robert Plant, Shakin' Stevens, Tommy Boyce

"Come on, Let Me Take You on a Sea Cruise." With that exuberant request, a career, and a classic, were born.

Thanks to a neighbor's enthusiasm over his backyard vocalizing, 8-year-old Frankie Guzzo began taking singing lessons and found himself appearing on "Ted Mack's Amateur Hour." That opportunity allowed him to perform alongside such luminaries as Sophie Tucker and Carmen Miranda. In high school, Frankie sang with The Syncopates and in 1958 he was discovered by Ace Records' owner, Johnny Vincent. Their debut project was, "Cheatin' Woman" in midyear.

Now in need of a name change, Frankie and Johnny started thinking about cars and, since his manager owned a Ford, the decision was made. Frankie fondly reminisces that he's glad he didn't own an Edsel! The newly christened Ford then hit the road to promote his single while Ace's top act, Huey Smith and The Clowns, entered the studio to record Huey's new song, "Sea Cruise." When Frankie returned, the producer put Ford's voice on Smith's track, removing Smith's vocalist, Bobby Marchan. The record gained in stature over the decades as an archetypical rock 'n' roll standard.

Sea Cruise/Roberta.

 Ford, a new artist has two strong debut sides. "Sea Cruise" is a rocking blues on which the artist is backed by a driving, colorful arrangement. "Roberta" is also a blues that gets an authentic shout. They can click for both pop and r.&b. coin. (12/22/58) (#14 Pop, #11 R&B)

His next single didn't fare nearly as well, even though it was recorded in the same manner as "Sea Cruise."

Can't Tell My Heart/Alimony.

 Ford could repeat the success of "Sea Cruise" with either of these hot contenders. "Can't Tell" features Huey (Piano) Smith on piano in support of Ford's emotional reading of the rocka-ballad. "Alimony" is a shouter and it's handled with equal appeal. (6/22/59) (B-side, #97 Pop)

His last two Ace singles paired rockers with old standards as Ford hoped to take his career in a more MOR direction.

I Want to Be Your Man/Time After Time.

 Ford sells both tunes strongly. "I Want to Be Your Man" is a rhythmic item that he delivers over bright brassy support. "Time After Time" also comes in for a rhythmic reading. His interpretation of the tune is different enough to catch interest. (12/21/59) (#75 Pop)

What's Going On (A-side).

★ ★ ★ ★ *A wild rocker is sold with ferver by the chanter over frantic backing by the group. A side that could bring in lots of juke coin.*

Chinatown (B-side).

★ ★ ★ *The well-known oldie is handed a solid go by the chanter over big band backing by the ork in this new slicing. Ford sings it brightly and it could catch coins. (5/30/60)*

In mid-1960, Frankie moved to Imperial Records and covered Joe Jones's recording of "You Talk Too Much," but the original beat him to the money. His last vinyl chart climber was "Seventeen."

You Talk Too Much.

★ ★ ★ ★ *The chanter bows on the label with a first-rate performance of a very attractive hunk of material that has an intriguing beat. Good wax here. (8/15/60) (#87 Pop)*

Seventeen.

★ ★ ★ *The old Boyd Bennett hit is given a solid updating by Ford in front of a swingin' band. He's also helped by a fem group. (3/13/61) (#72 Pop)*

Frankie's career came to a halt when he was drafted in 1962. It was small consolation that his tour of duty involved directing and writing musical stage shows throughout Viet Nam and Korea. The music scene had totally changed by 1965 when Ford returned to New Orleans but he continued working clubs, and by 1971 had bought his own. As of the mid-1990s, he was still performing and occasionally recording.

Whiskey Heaven.

"Sea Cruise" meets "Blueberry Hill" with wonderful results. (4/27/85)

THE FOUR SEASONS

Frankie Valli (Francis Castelluccio): Lead vocals; 5/3/37;
    Newark, NJ
Bob Gaudio: Tenor
Born: 11/17/42, Bronx, NY
Nick Massi
Born: 9/19/35, Newark, NJ
Tommy DeVito
Born: 6/19/36, Belleville, NJ
Influences: Four Freshmen, Jean Valley
Influenced: Happenings, Shangri-Las, Four Evers

Winter, Summer, Spring, and Fall, The Four Seasons had hits in them all. One of the most popular and successful groups of all time, the Seasons were the only act that could go head to head, hit for hit, against The Beatles' mid-1960s onslaught.

Even before there was a group, young Francis Castelluccio recorded for Mercury as Frankie Valley, naming himself after country singer Texas Jean Valley.

Frankie Valley:
Somebody Else Took Her Home 80
> *The label has come up with a new singer with an exciting style and a sound somewhat in the vein of the early Johnnie Ray. He sings the pretty ballad with a lot of life and feeling over a guitar backing. The chanter bears watching and with exposure this record has a chance. (5/29/54)*

The quartet's history started in 1955 when Frankie formed The Variety Trio, who performed a strange mix of rockabilly, pop, and Italian love songs. The group became the Variatones and in 1956, The Four Lovers, with Frankie, Hank Majewski, Tommy, and Nick DeVito. Signed to RCA that spring, the label made the unusual move of releasing two singles on the same day! More

45s followed their first surprise charter, "You're the Apple of My Eye," but success didn't.

The Four Lovers:
Honey Love 81
> *This was a big hit some months back in r.&b., as done by Clyde McPhatter and the Drifters. The satiric style here may give it the edge to revive it for present-day rock and rollers. (5/5/56)*

You're the Apple of My Eye 79
> *A catchy, pop-styled r.&b. item, with satiric overtones. Likely to get good play. (5/5/56) (#62 Pop)*

The group fizzled out in 1957; Frankie still recorded an occasional single (Valley becoming Valli) and even sang back-up on the legendary, "Rock and Roll Is Here to Stay" with Danny and The Juniors.

Meanwhile, another New Jersey group, The Royal Teens, led by writer/keyboardist Bob Gaudio, were having true success with novelty recordings, including "Short Shorts" and "Big Name Button," among others.

The Royal Teens:
Short Shorts.
> *Side is a purchased master from Power Records. The group delivers the rocker with vigor. Teens can go for the funky sound and solid beat. (1/13/58) (#3 Pop)*

Open the Door.

> *The "Short Shorts" crew presents the zany novelty in spiritual fashion. Clever lyrics and crazy backing help make this a strong bet to make it. Teens should go for this. (9/8/58)*

Believe Me.
★ ★
> *Their first ballad effort. Side has a long intro by the group and piano. It's steered to the teen market and could catch spins. (8/24/59) (#26 Pop)*

Gaudio left The Royal Teens after "Believe Me" to concentrate on writing while working in a print factory. His friend Joe Pesci (the now-famous actor) introduced him to Frankie. They regrouped with Bob, Frank, Tommy, and Nick

Massi. That entity recorded one single for Decca in 1959, "Please Take a Chance"/"It May Be Wrong." They then recorded briefly for Capitol in 1960.

The Royal Teens:
The Moon's Not Meant for Lovers Anymore.

★ ★ ★ ★ *A snappy, danceable rockin' effort and the group turns in a winning sound. This could be a second hit for them on the label. (2/1/60)*

By 1960, the group had worked half the lounges in Jersey, but it was a bowling alley (that didn't hire them) that gave them their new name, Union New Jersey's Four Seasons Lanes. The Four Seasons debut disc in January 1962, "Bermuda" (issued on the Gone label) lost to Linda Scott's version, but their next single, originally titled, "Jackie" (after Jacqueline Kennedy), took the world by storm under its released name, "Sherry" on Vee-Jay records. It sold 200,000 copies in one day after the group's "American Bandstand" appearance. Incidentally, the "femme chorus" the reviewer mentioned was actually The Seasons' high harmonies. When "Sherry" hit, Gone reissued "Bermuda."

Sherry.

The Four Seasons, a rocking teen-style group, come through with a wild performance of a rhythmic effort here, supported neatly by a femme chorus and a pounding band beat. For the youthful set. (8/4/62) (#1 Pop, #1 R&B)

Spanish Lace.

★ ★ ★ ★ *Buyers might be interested in this early recording of the "Sherry" winners. The group sings with emphasis against a good beat.*

Bermuda.

★ ★ ★ ★ *The old hit is sung with biting attack . . . Strong backing is sharply accented in a Latin vein. (10/20/62)*

Their second hit came from a line in a John Wayne Western as the heroine dusted herself off and proclaimed, "Big Girls Don't Cry" (#1 Pop, #1 R&B) (unreviewed by *Billboard*). More "monster" hits followed.

While touring England in 1963, The Seasons heard a song by a British group on the radio. When they returned stateside, Gaudio mentioned the song, "Please, Please Me," to Vee-Jay. This resulted in one of The Beatles' first singles coming out in America thanks to their competitors, The Four Seasons. Meanwhile, The Seasons scored a #1 hit with the classic "Walk Like a Man," a *Billboard* pick described as "a swinging novelty that's set in march tempo" (1/19/63) (#1 Pop, #3 R&B).

In 1964, the quartet created some of the 1960s' most memorable hits for new label Philips, like "Dawn" and "Ronnie." Vee-Jay's vaults kept pace as they'd stockpiled Four Seasons smashes to compete with Philips. The success of "Rag Doll" was such that producer Bob Crewe decided to build another entity, The Rag Dolls. And The Seasons rolled along.

Goodnight My Love/Stay.

Two strong sides by the hit-making teens. The group comes in with powerful singing and solid harmony on rock ballad "Goodnight My Love." Flip features another strong interpretation of standard "Stay" spotlighting high-pitched solo work. Side also has fine dance beat. (2/1/64) (B-side, #16 Pop)

Ronnie/Born to Wander.

First is the strongest in high-voiced stompie "Dawn" groove. The flip is good change-of-pace hot pop programming in a folksie groove. (4/4/64) (#6 Pop)

Rag Doll.

Sentimental slow dance ballad. Usual 4 Seasons delivery. Now there's two! (6/13/64) (#1 Pop)

Sincerely.

Dreamy, moaning delivery of old standard in expected 4 Seasons' high-pitched style. (8/15/64) (#75 Pop)

Save It for Me.

Another smasheroo culled from the group's current "Rag Doll" LP. Medium tempo ballad, featuring ethereal organ support. (8/22/64) (#10 Pop)

Big Man in Town.
>   *Usual top commercial high-pitched pathos. Good teen lyric with big sound. (10/31/64) (#20 Pop)*

Girl Come Running.
>   *Powerful production and vocal performances on a good Bob Crewe teen ballad with a driving dance beat in strong support. (6/5/65) (#30 Pop)*

By mid-1965, Nick left, replaced by a former Four Lovers member, Charlie Callelo, and then Joe Long. The group continued to churn out hits, while Valli also embarked on a solo career. As a marketing ploy, Philips issued some Seasons' sides under the name "The Wonder Who?" in 1966–1967.

Let's Hang On.
>   *Hard-driving dance rhythm from the pen of Bob Crewe serves as a powerhouse follow-up to "Girl Come Running." (9/18/65) (#3 Pop)*

Frankie Valli:
(You're Gonna) Hurt Yourself.
>   *Lead singer of the 4 Seasons has a hot sales item with this pulsating rocker from the pen of Bob Crewe and Charlie Callelo. Has the same hit potential as the 4 Seasons group hits. (1/1/66) (#39 Pop)*

Opus 17 (Don't Worry 'Bout Me).
>   *The boys have another smash hit in this Linzer-Randell rocker with excellent vocal and instrumental production. (5/14/66) (#13 Pop)*

The Guess Who—On the Good Ship Lollipop.
>   *Exciting side from the "Mystery" group. Shirley Temple's classic gets a humorous dance beat revival. (6/11/60) (#87 Pop)*

I've Got You Under My Skin.
>   *The creative team of Bob Crewe and the foursome have added a new dimension to the Porter standard and the result has all the earmarks of a No. 1 hit. Fascinating sounds from start to finish. (8/27/66) (#9 Pop)*

Tell It to the Rain.
>   *Powerful blues rocker with a solid dance beat and the wild Frankie Valli sound. (12/3/66) (#10 Pop)*

Beggin'.
>   *The "sound" of Frankie Valli leads the way in this powerful rocker that should ride to the top of the charts. First-rate Bob Crewe production. (3/25/67) (#16 Pop)*

Valli's first big solo hit came with the mid-tempoed ballad, "Can't Take My Eyes Off You." Meanwhile, he continued to lead the Seasons and the mythical "Wonder Who?"

Can't Take My Eyes Off You.
>   *Strong rhythm ballad material from the pen of Bob Crewe and Bob Gaudio with an exceptional Valli vocal combined with an exciting Artie Schroeck arrangement makes for a powerful chart contender. (4/29/67) (#2 Pop)*

C'Mon Marianne.
>   *This exciting, driving rocker with Valli at his best and top Gaudio arrangement should put the group at the No. 1 spot on the Hot 100 in short order. (6/3/67) (#9 Pop)*

Watch the Flowers Grow.
>   *By far one of their most unusual entries, this timely, easy-beat ballad is sure to go right up the chart in the "C'Mon Marianne" selling fashion. (10/21/67) (#30 Pop)*

As the 1960s progressed, the Seasons attempted to update their sound by cutting more contemporary-flavored material, with little success.

Saturday's Father.
>   *Unusual and compelling piece of ballad material penned by Bob Gaudio and Jake Holmes is given an exceptional vocal performance by the consistent chart climbers. (6/15/68)*

Idaho.
>   *A wild departure for the group in this clever and camp take-off on the big*

band sounds of yesterday. The writing of Jake Holmes and Bob Gaudio is right out of a Sonja Henie movie, and the performance is wild. (3/15/69) (#95 Pop)

The Seasons changed labels in 1969, but for just one single, "And That Reminds Me (My Heart Reminds Me)" (#45 Pop). By 1972, Gaudio left the performance side to concentrate on writing and producing. DeVito left, and a series of personnel and label changes did not bode well for the act. In 1974, however, Frankie found new life with a new ballad.

My Eyes Adored You.

Veteran star takes first shot on new label and makes it a good one with this pretty ballad that could easily cross over into the Top 40 market place. Well done all the way around, with Frankie's better than ever vocals working against superb instrumental arrangements. (11/9/74) (#1 Pop)

The hit gave Frankie and Bob the motivation to form a new Seasons with Don Ciccone, Gerry Polci, Lee Shapiro, and John Pavia. They linked with Warner Brothers and sired a whole new generation's worth of excitement with the hits, "Who Loves You" (#3 Pop) and "December, 1963 (Oh, What a Night)" (#1 Pop), both in 1975. It was followed by another minor hit, "Silver Star," in 1976.

December, 1963 (Oh, What a Night).

Following their recent top live effort, the foursome combine the flavor and fun of '60s rock with a disco feel. Strong harmonies throughout as well as good lead vocals. Absolutely superb production from Bob Gaudio. (12/13/75)

Silver Star.

Another infectious rocker with a disco feel that is already a major hit in Britain. Sounds in spots like the early Who, with intricate musical changes and clever vocal arrangements. Another perfect AM single from a group that appears to be back on top to stay. (5/22/76) (#38 Pop)

In 1977, Valli left the group and scored solo a year later with the title tune from the soundtrack of the film *Grease*.

Frankie Valli: Grease.

Finds Valli's vocals in top form supported tastefully by backing harmonies. The infectious hook and catchy melody [keep] the song flowing at an upbeat pace. (5/27/78) (#1 Pop)

In 1984, Bob and Frankie regrouped for The Four Seasons meet The Beach Boys' single, "East Meets West." Frankie and a Four Seasons contingent are still active in the 1990s, and their reworked, rerecording of "December, 1963," amazingly, excited still another generation of buyers when it reached #15 in late 1994.

With 85 million in record sales and 46 chart hits, it's little wonder the group for all seasons was inducted into the Rock and Roll Hall of Fame in 1990.

THE FOUR TOPS

Levi Stubbs: Lead vocals
Born: 6/6/36, Detroit, MI
Abdul "Duke" Fakir
Born: 12/26/35, Detroit, MI
Renaldo "Obie" Benson
Born: 6/14/36, Detroit, MI
Lawrence Payton
Born: 3/2/38, Detroit, MI
Influences: Four Freshmen, Billy Eckstine, Frank Sinatra, Olympics, Four Aces
Influenced: 5th Dimension, Boyz II Men

The Four Tops are one of music's premier soul/rock vocal groups. The same four members have been performing for over 40 years with hits covering three decades.

The childhood friends began singing at a birthday party in 1954 and were so well received they decided to make it an occupation. Levi, Duke, Obie, and Lawrence worked the club circuit in Detroit and by the mid-1950s were singing backup at shows for Della Reese, Billy Eckstine, and Brook Benton. Starting as The Four Aims, when they recorded "Could It Be" for Chess in 1956 they became The Four Tops. Their next recording opportunity came four years later for Columbia.

Ain't That Love.
★★★   *Wild rocker is sung with beat by the boys, sparked by a lead who has a Sam Cooke sound. Side has possibilities. (8/1/60)*

Although that song, along with a follow up for Riverside in 1962 on a jazzy "Pennies from Heaven," failed to chart, they persevered, nonetheless.

The group's jazz influence helped them sign with Motown in 1963, where they became backup singers for The Supremes on their hit "When the Lovelight." Their solo chance came when Motown writers Holland, Dozier, and Holland crafted "Baby, I Need Your Loving" for them. It was the start of a tremendous streak of international hits.

Without the One You Love (Life's Not Worthwhile).
Here's a hot group right in the commercial groove with wailing hot-pop r.&b. song. Tremendous beat and excellent performances. (11/14/64) (#43 Pop)

I Can't Help Myself.
A spirited, fast-paced wailer performed in their unique style. (5/8/65) (#1 Pop, #1 R&B)

Motown was so anxious to keep the streak going that their next single, "It's the Same Old Song," was recorded on a Thursday, pressed on Friday, on the radio Saturday, and in the stores by Monday!

It's the Same Old Song.
Pulsating Detroit sound proves a winner once again in this swinger to replace "I Can't Help Myself." (7/17/65) (#5 Pop, #2 R&B)

Shake Me, Wake Me (When It's Over).
Another strong rocker that will rapidly climb the chart. (2/12/66) (#18 Pop, #5 R&B)

The quartet's most famous hit came in the summer of 1966 with "Reach Out, I'll Be There" (#1 Pop, #1 R&B). It was followed by a series of chartbusters.

Standing in the Shadows of Love.
Hot on the heels of their No. 1 smash, the group comes up with another solid rhythm rocker headed fast for the top. (12/10/66) (#6 Pop; #2 R&B)

Bernadette.
Hard-driving rocker will quickly surpass their successful "Standing in the Shadows of Love" at the top of the Hot 100. Outstanding performance by the group is right in the Motown bag. (3/4/67) (#4 Pop, #3 R&B)

You Keep Running Away.
Solid easy beat rocker that moves from start to finish has all the ingredients for another chart topper for the powerful group. (9/9/67) (#19 Pop, #7 R&B)

When their primary writing force, Holland, Dozier, Holland, left Motown, the foursome began recording mostly oldies.

Walk Away Renee.
The former hit of the Left Banke proves an exciting rock-ballad change of pace for the consistent Top 20 winners. Driving vocal workout and exciting production will hit hard and fast. (1/27/68) (#14 Pop, #15 R&B)

Love (Is the Answer)/It's All in the Game.
Two sided strong item from the Tops. First is a pulsating rhythm ballad while the flip, with equal potential is an updating of the Tommy Edwards ballad hit of the '50s. (4/11/70) (B-side, #24 Pop, #6 R&B)

Still Water (Love).
A solid rhythm item that is sure to prove equally successful. Top programmer and sales item. (8/22/70) (#11 Pop, #4 R&B)

Just Seven Numbers (Can Straighten Out My Life).
The Tops kick off the year with a powerhouse. Funky beat blues ballad is a

natural for the top of the Soul chart as well. *(1/16/71) (#40 Pop, #9 R&B)*

MacArthur Park.
> *A unique blues reading of the Jim Webb classic with much appeal for the Top 40 soul and MOR. (8/21/71) (#38 Pop, #27 R&B)*

In 1971, The Tops and Supremes paired for the *Magnificent Seven* album, which contained a sparkling, soul version of Ike and Tina Turner's, "River Deep, Mountain High" (#14 Pop, #7, R&B), but it was The Tops' last Top-20 hit for Motown. By 1972, Motown moved to Los Angeles and The Four Tops moved their hit-making machine to Dunhill. "Ain't No Woman (Like the One I've Got)" ensued as the quartet's top, non-Motown hit.

Ain't No Woman (Like the One I've Got).
> *Levi Stubbs's lead vocal carries the quartet through a moving arrangement which has pop as well as soul overtones. Nice mellow strings give the tune a soft lilt as the tale of fond affection unravels. (1/27/73) (#4 Pop, #2 R&B)*

Are You Man Enough.
> *Be cautious—"they're out to get you"—that's the Message the Tops offer to their compatriots. Top lyrics and first-rate orchestral production are plusses in this all-out attempt to put people on the spot and aware of "danger." (6/21/73) (#15 Pop, #2 R&B)*

One Chain Don't Make No Prison.
> *With Steve Barri, Lambert & Potter again behind the scenes, the Tops have another custom-tailored single. Melody is a grittier funkier approach to "The Keeper of the Castle" sound. Crossover potential is always strong with this group, should be immediate soul airplay hit. (4/13/74) (#41 Pop, #3 R&B)*

From 1975 through 1978, they recorded for Dunhill's parent, ABC, with, "Seven Lonely Nights" (#71 Pop, #13 R&B) and "Catfish" (#71 Pop, #7 R&B) their best entries. The Tops' debut with Casablanca in 1981 ("When She Was My Girl") was their first R&B #1 since "Reach Out." In 1983, they appeared on Motown's 25th

Anniversary TV extravaganza and then resigned with the label. With little to show for three years' work the second time around, The Tops moved to Arista, starting with a song taken from the 1988 Summer Olympics.

Indestructible.
> *The fearless four return on a new label with a single that showcases their venerable vocal talents in a contemporary pop setting. (7/30/88) (#35 Pop)*

The Four Tops with Aretha Franklin: If Ever a Love There Was.
> *Dream duet of Levi Stubbs and Franklin should make up for ground lost by "Indestructible." (10/15/88)*

In 1990, The Four Tops were named to the Rock and Roll Hall of Fame.

ARETHA FRANKLIN

Birthdate: 3/25/42
Birthplace: Memphis, TN
Influences: Clara Ward, Sam Cooke, Mahalia Jackson, Marion Williams, Isley Brothers, James Cleveland
Influenced: Stevie Wonder, many more

The first lady inducted into the Rock and Roll Hall of Fame (1987), Aretha Franklin has been known for most of her career as "The Queen of Soul."

Aretha was one of three singing daughters (along with Carolyn and Erma) of the famed gospel preacher Reverend C. L. Franklin. As pastor of the New Bethel Church in Detroit, he had all three singing in his choir, but Aretha's four-octave range and gritty intensity made her a standout from the beginning. The Reverend James Cleveland, then living at the Franklin home, encouraged and taught 9-year-old Aretha to sing. Later, touring on the gospel circuit, she learned the fine points from such luminaries as Mahalia Jackson and Clara Ward. When Ward performed "Peace in the Valley" in 1952 at a funeral, ten-year-old Aretha knew what she wanted to do with her life. Her first recordings were in 1956 for the local JVB label and then in 1960 for Checker Records. The noise referenced in the review came from the live performance made at Franklin's church.

Precious Lord.

★ ★ ★ *A performance full of emotion and vocal assurance. Side seems to be marred by extraneous noises in the background, otherwise a gas. (2/1/60)*

While touring in 1960, Sam Cooke suggested she move from gospel to secular, and that took her to New York where on August 1 she recorded four demos, including "Over the Rainbow" and "Today I Sing the Blues." That same month she auditioned for Columbia's John Hammond and "Today" became her debut disk.

Today I Sing the Blues.

★ ★ ★ *A slow rhythm blues chant with the gal backed in okay style by guitar, piano and bass. The artist has talent and should be watched. (9/26/60) (#10 R&B)*

Her singles charted well R&B but barely made it pop, and the Columbia phase of her career could best be defined as Aretha in search of a style. Her New York performing debut was at the Village Vanguard doing mostly standards.

Are You Sure.

 From the musical "The Unsinkable Molly Brown" comes this swinging gospel item which the thrush sings with ferver and feeling over a driving bass. Strong wax. (4/10/61)

Operation Heartbreak.

★ ★ ★ ★ *The gal delivers a slow, triplet-backed ballad with much spirit and style. She works with a chorus and a fine ork backing here. Watch this side.*

Rock-a-Bye Your Baby with a Dixie Melody.

Tune has had many go-arounds, but none like this smart-jazzy version, delivered by the classy thrush. She hands it much spirit and jocks will likely give it attention. (9/11/61) (A-side, #6 R&B; B-side, #37 Pop)

Without the One You Love.

★ ★ ★ ★ *Miss Franklin does a lovely job on this straight ballad. Her hard-hitting vocal style is backed nicely by strings and ork. She's also the writer.*

Don't Cry Baby.

★ ★ ★ ★ *A wonderful gospel lilt in three-quarter time is given to this blues based r.&b. oldie. The side swings in strong fashion, building on trombone and strings. (6/9/62) (B-side, #92 Pop)*

Just for a Thrill/Try a Little Tenderness.

 Here are a pair of the best sides that Aretha has ever cut and that's saying a lot. She shows off some of her best vocal work yet on the two standards, and either or both could turn into her biggest seller to date. Backing is by the Bob Mersey ork. (8/11/62) (B-side, #100 Pop)

Here's Where I Came In (Here's Where I Walk Out).

 An abrupt change of pace for Aretha but a goodie just the same. It's a powerful country-styled ballad sung with a lot of feeling against voices and strings in three-quarter time. Watch it. (5/25/63)

When Franklin's contract ended, she realized her gospel fire had been rained on at Columbia. Her direction was dictated by the musically moribund Mitch Miller. So, in 1967, Aretha linked with Atlantic and producer Jerry Wexler began unleashing her soul power. Number 1 for seven weeks on *Billboard*'s R&B chart, Aretha's first million seller, "I Never Loved a Man (the Way I Loved You)," opened the floodgates, providing a two-sided hit. By 1967's end, *Billboard* had named Franklin "Female Vocalist of the Year."

I Never Loved a Man (the Way I Loved You).

Marking her debut on Atlantic, Miss Franklin offers a powerful blues wailer that will create much excitement in both pop and r.&b. markets. Production by Jerry Wexler is tops. Flip: "Do Right Woman—Do Right

Man." (2/25/67) (A-side, #9 Pop, #1 R&B; B-side, #37 R&B)

Respect.

With her smash hit "I Never Loved a Man" . . . currently riding in the top 10, this driving revival of the Otis Redding hit is destined to follow the same successful groove. Performance is exceptional. (4/22/67) (#1 POP, #1 R&B)

Baby I Love You.

Hot on the heels of "Respect" comes this driving rocker, penned by Ronny Shannon, produced by Jerry Wexler, and brought to life in this electric performance. Should groove right to the top. (7/15/67) (#4 Pop, #1 R&B)

A Natural Woman.

Chalk up four goldies in a row for the exciting Miss Franklin. Another top-notch ballad produced by Jerry Wexler will hit the top fast, with impact. Flip: "Baby, Baby, Baby." (9/23/67) (#8 Pop, #2 R&B)

Chain of Fools.

With the solid beat feel of "Respect," this sure-fire blues mover has all the ingredients of a No. 1 chart topper. (12/2/67) (#2 Pop, #1 R&B)

In February 1968, she won her first of 14 Grammys as Best Female R&B Vocal Performance for "Respect." Soon after, she had her first gold single as a writer, on "Think." Through the year, "Lady Soul" had eight R&B and nine pop hits.

Think.

Make way for another fast million seller for this pulsating swinger with another wild performance. Much of the "Respect" feel here. Flip: "You Send Me." (5/11/68) (#7 Pop, #1 R&B)

The House That Jack Built.

This blockbuster blues outing, loaded with her sensational gospel feel, is Miss Franklin at her swinging best. Flip "I Say a Little Prayer." (8/10/68) (A-side, #6 Pop, #2 R&B; B-side, #10 Pop, #3 R&B)

See Saw.

This blockbuster of a swinger should prove the outing to put her at the No. 1 spot on the Hot 100 and the r&b charts. Much in the sales and excitement sound of "Respect." (11/16/68) (A-side, #14 Pop, #9 R&B; B-side, #31 Pop, #10 R&B)

In 1969, Aretha leaned heavily on oldies done her way to stay hot. Showing a great interest in Beatles' tunes, she included, "Let It Be" on her *This Girl's in Love with You* album before it was issued by the Beatles! Through the early 1970s, she covered everyone from Ben E. King to Elton John.

The Weight/Tracks of My Tears.

Chalk up another chart topper for the soul star. The driving Jaime Robertson blues material brought to the Hot 100 by both Jackie DeShannon and by The Band will prove a sales blockbuster this time around. Flip, a past hit for Smokey Robinson, has much sales potency as well. (2/15/69) (A-side, #19 Pop, #3 R&B; B-side, #71 Pop, #21 R&B)

I Can't See Myself Leaving You/Gentle on My Mind.

Two potent sounds from the soul lady. First is a driving blues ballad much in the successful bag of her initial smash "I Never Loved a Man." Flip is a wild gospel flavored treatment of the Glen Campbell classic. (4/12/69) (A-side, #28 Pop, #3 R&B; B-side, #76 Pop, #50 R&B)

Share Your Love with Me.

Driving, funky beat blues swinger that has all the ingredients to put her right back in the No. 1 spot . . . in short order. One of her finest vocal workouts. (7/19/69) (#13 Pop, #1 R&B)

Eleanor Rigby.

The Beatles classic gets a driving soul interpretation. (11/1/69) (#17 Pop, #5 R&B)

Call Me/Son of a Preacher Man.

First side is an original soul ballad, while the flip is a driving reworking of the recent Dusty Springfield hit. (1/13/70)(#13 Pop, #1 R&B)

**Aretha Franklin with the Dixie Flyers:
Spirit in the Dark.**
>Blockbuster follow-up to "Call Me" is this wild gospel-rock item certain to take her right up to the top. Top vocal workout. (5/16/70) (#23 Pop, #3 R&B)

Don't Play That Song.
>Updating and unique treatment of the past Ben E. King hit is a blockbuster that will spiral her right back into the Top Ten. Potent vocal workout and arrangement. (8/1/70) (#11 Pop, #1 R&B)

You're All I Need to Get By.
>The Nick Ashford-Valerie Simpson ballad, a past smash for Marvin Gaye and Tammi Terrell, gets a wild workout from the soul queen and it's headed for the top, pop and soul. Should prove one of her biggest. (2/13/71) (#19 Pop, #3 R&B)

Paul Simon was inspired by Aretha's gospel style to write "Bridge Over Troubled Water"; although he recorded it first with his partner Art Garfunkel, the Queen managed a Top Pop and R&B hit with the song.

Bridge Over Troubled Water.
>The Paul Simon blockbuster gets a potent workout here that will spiral the soul queen up the pop and soul charts. One of her finest. (4/10/71) (#6 Pop, #1 R&B)

Spanish Harlem.
>Ben E. King's classic hit of the past comes to life all over again with this dynamite updating from the soul queen. (7/24/71) (#2 Pop, #1 R&B)

The remainder of the 1970s were tougher for Franklin, and the hits sparser.

Until You Come Back to Me.
>Ms. Franklin is closer to the pop groove than she has been in some time with this bouncy, beautifully orchestrated tune focusing on her distinctive vocals. Fine segue from relatively slow

material to powerful middle segment. (11/10/73) (#3 Pop, #1 R&B)

Without Love.
>The Queen of Soul comes up with her most commercial entry in some time with this soulful, medium tempo ballad highlighted by her superb styling. Excellent instrumental changes and effective use of backup chorus make song even more exciting. (11/9/74) (#45 Pop, #6 R&B)

One bright spot occurred in 1975, when the Queen of Soul won her eighth Best Female R&B Vocal Performance Grammy in a row, with "Ain't Nothing Like the Real Thing" (#47 Pop, #6 R&B).

>Extremely powerful vocals highlight this moody, blues ballad . . . Melodic, almost supper club string backup, gathers momentum with the vocals as Aretha comes up with her strongest mix of pop, soul and blues in a long while. (8/17/74)

In 1980, she gave a memorable performance as a singing waitress in the film *The Blues Brothers*, belting her 12-year-old hit, "Think." She also made a major decision to jump start her sagging singles' sales by moving to Arista. By the mid-1980s, she was back on the charts with contemporary material.

Freeway of Love.
>Just in time for summer: a light-hearted funk-pop item, muscled into shape by that voice. (6/15/85) (#3 Pop, #1 R&B)

Who's Zoomin' Who.
>Followup to the smash "Freeway of Love" takes a slower, bluesier tempo, maintains the extraordinary vitality. (9/21/85) (#7 Pop, #2 R&B)

In 1986, after 79 Pop charters, Franklin finally had her first TV special for Showtime titled simply, "Aretha."

By the mid-1980s, she made a new career out of dueting with the Eurythmics, George Michael, and Elton John, among others.

Eurythmics and Aretha Franklin:
Sisters Are Doin' It for Themselves.

> *Two varieties of charisma plus a*
> *furious funk production should easily*
> *overcome resistance to the still-unfash-*
> *ionable feminist message. (10/19/85)*
> *(#18 Pop, #66 R&B)*

Aretha Franklin and George Michael:
I Knew You Were Waiting (for Me).

> *Not an obvious pairing, but with her*
> *holding back and him cutting loose, it*
> *makes theatrical sense; hook-rich r&b*
> *tune is (natch) a smash in England.*
> *(2/14/87) (#1 Pop, #5 R&B)*

Aretha Franklin and Whitney Houston:
It Isn't, It Wasn't, It Ain't Never Gonna Be.

> *Vocal performance keeps this together*
> *as Re Re and Whitney hop happily onto*
> *that new jack swing bandwagon—rid-*
> *ing in the front seat, of course.*
> *(6/24/89) (#41 Pop)*

By 1990, Franklin had amassed 25 gold singles and was given the Grammy Legends Award—all for just singing from her soul.

Real Name: Marvin Pentz Gay, Jr.
Birthdate: 4/2/39
Birthplace: Washington, DC
Died: 4/1/84
Influences: Moonglows, Isley Brothers, Bobby Freeman
Influenced: Rascals, Brooklyn Dreams

One of the mainstays of Motown, Marvin Gaye is remembered both for his sensual pop ballads and his songs of social protest.

Like so many other black singers of the 1960s, Gaye's upbringing centered on gospel music. By the age of three, he was soloing at his father's church. He played piano and drums while a member of his high school orchestra.

Long before his individual career took off, Gaye was a part of three noted vocal groups. The first, in 1956, was the Washington, D.C., group, The Rainbows (of "Mary Lee" fame), whose members also included Don Covay and Billy Stewart. By 1957, The Rainbows were gone and The Marquees were formed, featuring former Rainbows James Nolan, Chester Simmons, Gaye, and newcomer Reese Palmer. Discovered by Bo Diddley, they recorded one terrific rocker.

Hey Little School Girl 78

> *Smart group swings on this interesting*
> *rockabilly chant. Has a fine beat, sound*
> *and a message that can get thru. Side*
> *has definite potential. Not same*
> *"Schoolgirl" as the one in the second*
> *row. (12/9/57)*

The other "Schoolgirl" referred to at the end of the review was a hit single by teen popsters Tom and Jerry, later known as Simon and Garfunkel!

In 1958, The Marquees gave an impromptu audition in the alley of Washington's Howard Theater for Moonglows leader, Harvey Fuqua. He later exclaimed, "They sang us in the gutter with our own songs!" Fuqua was bent on Moonglows changes; he made The Marquees (and ex-Dells bass Chuck Barksdale) into The "New" Moonglows, starting with "Twelve Months of the Year," on which Gaye performed a talking introduction. Gaye also sang on the single, "Beatnik," as well as lead on "Mama Loochie." He and the group are also heard singing backup on Chuck Berry's "Almost Grown."

By 1960, The Moonglows were dissolved and, in a burst of energy, Mr. Harvey (as Gaye called him) brought the singer to Detroit, formed Tri Phi Records, and signed a new group, The Spinners, with Gaye playing drums on their sessions. When, later that year, Fuqua signed as an artist to Anna Gordy's Anna Records, Gaye came to the attention of Anna's brother, Berry, and his fledgling Motown label. Gaye's start for Berry Gordy was not as a soloist but as a studio drummer for The Miracles, and as a background singer for The Marvelettes.

His first actual single was "Let Your Conscience Be Your Guide," cut in May 1961, although an unnumbered Tamla promo of "Witchcraft" was issued prior; "Sandman" and "Soldier's Plea" followed, all receiving the same lack of response. Then came the Martha and The Vandellas-backed hit, "Stubborn Kind of Fellow," that kick-started his career. 1963 saw Marvin mania established among teens.

Stubborn Kind of Fellow.

★ ★ ★ ★ *This side has powerful impact thanks to its smart, catchy arrangement. The lad sings with strong style and infectious walking, rock rhythm help to make the side go. Chanting of a fem chorus and general excitement should get it exposure. (8/11/62) (#46 Pop, #8 R&B)*

Hitch Hike.

Gaye broke into the charts with his last disk . . . and this one should prove an apt successor. The lad sings it with a beat and it should get the kids dancing and keep 'em that way. (12/24/62) (#30 Pop, #12 R&B)

One of These Days/Pride and Joy.

Two more sides that should boost "Hitch Hike" Gaye up a few notches through the Top 50. The first is a walking blues ballad with great vocal effort against punching words and chorus. The second side has a great beat with mighty healthy singing from the young fem chorus. (5/4/63) (B-side, #10 Pop, #2 R&B)

Can I Get a Witness.

This swinger is a bit in the blues tradition and should mark Gaye's return to the chart ranks. Chorus of chicks and strong Detroit sound add to the effect. (10/5/63) (#22 Pop, #15 R&B)

You're a Wonderful One.

This is another stomper somewhat in the "Can I Get a Witness" vein. Side pumps along on middle tempo with fine, shouting chorus in support. (3/7/64) (#15 Pop)

Gaye's duet career began with Mary Wells. His solo single "I'll Be Doggone" registered as his first million seller amidst a new batch of hits.

Marvin Gaye and Mary Wells:
Once Upon a Time.

Soft, easy tandem singing against Latinish backing. (4/25/64) (A-side, #19 Pop; B-side, #17 Pop)

How Sweet It Is (to Be Loved By You).

Steady hand-clappin' Detroit beat featuring educated chanting by Gaye backed by high-register chorus. A smash all the way around. (11/14/64) (#6 Pop, #4 R&B)

I'll Be Doggone.

Powerful follow-up to "How Sweet It Is." Gaye's wailing vocal performance is pitted against a driving dance beat backing. (3/13/65) (#8 Pop, #1 R&B)

Marvin Gaye and Kim Weston:
It Takes Two.

Duo comes up with a winning blend in this driving rocker with good lyric content. Has all the ingredients for a hot chart item. (12/17/66) (#14 Pop, #2 R&B)

Gaye's first duet with Tammi Terrell introduced a series of hit recordings for the pair.

Marvin Gaye and Tammi Terrell:
Ain't No Mountain High Enough.

Chalk up another pulsating fast smash for Gaye with his new partner Tammi Terrell. The electricity of the duo combined with the blockbuster rhythm material grooves all the way. (5/6/67)

If I Could Build My Whole World Around You.

Solid rhythm follow up to their smash "Your Precious Love" in this groovy blues item headed right for a choice spot on the Top 10. Powerful vocal performance by the duet. (11/25/67) (A-side, #10 Pop, #2 R&B; B-side, #68 Pop, #27 R&B)

Ain't Nothing Like the Real Thing.

A mover aimed right at the top of the Hot 100. Duo grooves beautifully with the driving, easy-beat rhythm item. (4/6/68) (#8 Pop, #1 R&B)

You're All I Need to Get By.

> *Hot on the heels of their Top 10 smash, "Ain't Nothing Like the Real Thing," the dynamic duo has a blockbuster in this driving rhythm follow-up. Will hit hard and fast. (7/20/68) (#7 Pop, #1 R&B)*

In October 1968, Tammi Terrell collapsed in Gaye's arms while the two were performing at Hampton Sydney College in Virginia, the first sign of a fatal brain tumor. A month later, Motown issued what would become Gaye's biggest hit, "I Heard It Through the Grapevine." Number 1 for seven weeks, Gaye's "Grapevine," which went gold for Gladys Knight and The Pips a year earlier, became Motown's best seller during its first 20 years.

I Heard It Through the Grapevine.

> *His most exciting and commercial entry in a long while should put him rapidly at the top of the charts. The Gladys Knight hit comes off with a different and potent hit sound with a driving beat in strong support. (11/16/68)*

Too Busy Thinking About My Baby.

> *His million seller "I Heard It Through the Grapevine" went right up to No. 1 and this blockbuster swinger has the same potential. It moves from start to finish and Gaye is at his best. (4/12/69) (#4 Pop, #1 R&B)*

That's the Way Love Is.

> *Chalk up another top of the chart winner for Gaye. This swinging ballad with much of the rhythm of "I Heard It Through the Grapevine" will hit hard and fast. (8/16/69) (#7 Pop, #2 R&B)*

On March 16, 1970, Terrell died at the age of 24 of a brain tumor. Gaye was so despondent over her death that he temporarily retired, just as their last single, "The Onion Song," charted. When Gaye re-emerged, he had gained a new awareness and concern about current issues, such as Viet Nam and ecology. Having demanded and received greater writing and producing control from Motown, the results were reflected in his new recordings contained on the classic *What's Going On* album.

What's Going On.

> *It's been a long time between releases for Gaye, but this easy beat rocker has it to put him right up the Hot 100 and Soul charts. (2/6/71) (#2 Pop, #1 R&B)*

Mercy Mercy Me (The Ecology).

> *A super original rhythm number with a strong lyric line and vocal workout. (6/26/71) (#4 Pop, #1 R&B)*

Inner City Blues (Make Me Wanna Holler).

> *Gaye went Top 10 with "Mercy Mercy Me," and this funky beat blues swinger followup offers all the same sales potential. (10/2/71) (#9 Pop, #1 R&B)*

In 1973, he took still another musical turn, creating sexually explicit material, such as "Let's Get It On" and "You Sure Love to Ball." Gaye also continued to cut duets, this time with Diana Ross.

Let's Get It On.

> *This is a male tear-jerker, Marvin asking his baby to let her "love come out" and get on with the business of loving. There is lots of vocal energy emerging from Marvin's pleas as well as supporting voices and a large orchestra which adds to the pleading. (6/30/73) (#1 Pop, #1 R&B)*

Diana Ross and Marvin Gaye: A Special Part of Me.

> *Could two artists whose last singles have been no. one chart records, create a stiff when teaming up for a duet? The answer is NO! This Ross-Gaye duet revives the classic early Motown sound with great energy and verve. Let's have more from the pair. Lot's more! (9/22/73) (#12 Pop, #4 R&B)*

You Sure Love to Ball.

> *You can't be more explicit about the sexual meaning of this tune, complete with a moaning girl at the beginning of the arrangement. Gaye sings the song softly, telling his sexy mama that he's aware of her main desire in life. The tune is fare for adults, but for subteens*

it certainly sounds risqué. (1/19/74) (#50 Pop, #13 R&B)

I Want You.

> *From Gaye's huge LP of the same title, an easy disco cut with interesting over-dubbed vocals featuring the artist duet-ing with himself. Good production, good vocals, good song. Likely to be Gaye's biggest single hit in years. (4/17/76) (#15 Pop, #1 R&B)*

By the late 1970s, despite almost two decades of success, Gaye was heavily in debt, had drug problems, owed the IRS over $2 million, and had gone through two divorces (Anna Gordy Gaye and Janis Hunter Gaye). Still, he bounced back in a huge way when, after severing ties with Motown following his final #1, "Got to Give It Up (Part 1)," he coupled with Columbia. His first release, "Sexual Healing," was a million seller and his first Grammy winner (Best Male Vocal Performance of the Year) after eight nominations. However, his renewed hit status was short-lived.

Sexual Healing.

> *Gaye's first single for CBS boasts a silky rhythm that should push it to the top of the black chart and a frank lyric that may cause problems in terms of pop crossover. The hypnotic vamp is well-suited to Gaye's cool, sensuous style. (9/9/82) (#3 Pop, #1 R&B)*

Little more than a year later, Gaye was shot to death by his minister father after a violent argu-ment. A year later he had his last two chart sin-gles, "Sanctified Lady" and "It's Madness."

It's Madness.

> *Lush string arrangement belies a quiet-ly agonized performance, another dis-turbing but artful glimpse at the man behind the voice. (6/13/85) (#55 R&B)*

In 1987, Marvin Gaye was honored for his music by induction into the Rock and Roll Hall of Fame.

LESLEY GORE

Birthdate: 5/2/46
Birthplace: New York City
Influences: Ella Fitzgerald, Dinah Washington, June Christy, Sarah Vaughan, Chris Connor, Anita O'Day, Mary Wells
Influenced: Paul McCartney

Lesley Gore endeared herself to millions of 1960s' teens as the first of the "tell it like it is" female rock singers.

The daughter of a New York swimsuit manu-facturer, she attended Dwight Preparatory School for Girls in Englewood, New Jersey. While per-forming with a seven-piece jazz ensemble at New York's Prince George Hotel, she was discovered by Mercury Records producer, Quincy Jones. In February 1963, Jones trudged to the teen's Tenafly, New Jersey, home with over 250 song demos. The tune they picked to be her first single, "It's My Party," turned feminine vulnerability into teenage temper tantrums. At that same moment, unbeknown to them, hot producer Phil Spector was also cutting "Party" with The Crystals. When Mercury found out, they rush-released Lesley's version. The April release received little notice from *Billboard*, who gave it four stars but no com-ment. The buying public, however, went wild, making the 17-year-old's 45 a million seller in less than four weeks (#1 Pop, #1 R&B). In 1964, "Party" received a Grammy nomination as Best Rock and Roll Record of the Year.

Her second single, "Judy's Turn to Cry" took on the tone of teen revenge as the reviewer enthused, "platter is a stomping multi track sequel to her initial success. Companion piece, 'Just Let Me Cry' is a 'Song of India' teen rewrite hand-clapper that also stomps along in smash style." It skyrocketed to #5 Pop, #10 R&B.

Passivity had no place in Lesley's lacquers, as "She's a Fool" (#5 Pop, #26 R&B) demonstrated her strong, yet simplistic, attitude toward tough teen emotional situations.

Her pièce de résistance, in late 1963, was the

fiercely defiant, prototype feminist declaration of independence, "You Don't Own Me." Her second gold single would have gone #1 but for The Beatles' "I Want to Hold Your Hand." *Sixteen Magazine*, the American D.J. Poll, and the National Academy of Record Manufacturers (NARM) all voted Lesley "Best Female Vocalist of 1963."

In 1964, she continued her string of hits.

That's the Way Boys Are.

Lesley's latest is a hot entry that has the young gal's voice multi-tracked over impelling beat and chorus. Another topper. (3/21/64) (#12 Pop)

I Don't Wanna Be a Loser.

Fine teen ballad sung with grace and feeling. Lyric packs meaning for young set. (5/16/64) (#37 Pop)

Five singles into her career, the 18-year-old star graduated high school and went on to Sarah Lawrence College while continuing her chart run. In August, Lesley appeared in her first film, "Girls on the Beach." By the end of 1964, *Record World, Music Business,* and *Cashbox* magazines all named Gore the "Year's Best Female Vocalist." Lesley appeared in her second teen film, *Ski Party,* starring Frankie Avalon, while continuing to churn out teen pop.

Hey Now.

Hand-clappin' rock beat featuring dual track chanting. 'Tis very commercial. Flip: "Sometimes I Wish I Was a Boy." (10/10/64) (A-side, #76 Pop; B-side, #86 Pop)

Look of Love.

In the vein of her early hits this one will be a fast chart climber. (12/12/64) (#27 Pop)

Sunshine, Lollipops and Rainbows.

Back on the happy rhythm trail, Lesley comes up with a winner in this summertime rouser. (6/5/65) (#13 Pop)

My Town, My Guy and Me.

With this exciting rhythm number with clever lyric, she tops her "Sunshine, Lollipops and Rainbows" hit! Intriguing backing and powerful vocal make it a fast chart contender. (8/28/65) (#32 Pop)

I Won't Love You Anymore (Sorry).

Hot on the heels of "My Town, My Guy and Me" she has a fast hit sound throughout this exciting rocker composed by her young brother. (11/20/65) (#80 Pop)

(The "young brother" was Michael Gore who, 15 years later, wrote the mega-hit "Fame.")

In February 1966, Leslie appeared on the last episode of NBC's "Hullabaloo" along with Peter and Gordon and Paul Anka. In July, Gore made her TV acting debut on "The Donna Reed Show." She later showed up on the Batman series as Pussycat, Catwoman's aide. Six months later she had her last Top-20 hit "California Nights"; her last Top-100 single followed, the appropriately titled "Brink of Disaster."

Young Love.

Culled from her current LP by popular demand, this well-done revival of the former Sonny James-Tab Hunter hit has strong possibilities for today's pop market. (2/26/66) (#50 Pop)

California Nights.

Production rhythm ballad with groovy dance beat and strong vocal work has the hit ingredients to put Miss Gore back up the Hot 100. Powerful support from the Bob Crewe prduction. (1/7/67) (#16 Pop)

Summer and Sandy.

Hot follow up to "California Nights" is this summertime powerhouse which should have them dancing on the beach in short order and prove another sales winner for the pop favorite. (5/27/67) (#65 Pop)

Brink of Disaster.

Good rock ballad material, right in the teen groove, should prove to be even more successful than her recent "Summer and Sandy" hit. Outstanding production work by Steve Douglas. (9/16/67) (#82 Pop)

By May 1968, Leslie graduated Sarah Lawrence with a B.A. in American and English literature. In 1969, she left Mercury for Bob

Crewe's new label where she dueted with the hit artist Oliver ("Good Morning Starshine") as Billy and Sue.

Why Doesn't Love Make Me Happy.

> *Stylist moves to the Crewe label with a ballad beauty that will bring her back to the charts. Hot 100 and Easy Listening. Fine performance. (1/17/70)*

Billy and Sue:
Come Softly to Me.

> *A super duo who sound strangely like two well-known stars have a potent and fresh revival of the Fleetwoods oldie. This could easily prove a left field summertime smash for producer Bob Crewe. Top Hutch Davie arrangement. (5/2/70)*

Mowest Records was her next stop in 1972, and by 1975 she was appearing on the oldies circuit starting with Richard Nader's Rock and Roll Revival Concert in Madison Square Garden. She then reunited with Quincy Jones for an A&M album, *Love Me by Name*. In 1980, Lesley cowrote two songs, including "Out Here on My Own" (Irene Cara, #19), for the Academy Award winning score of *Fame*.

Lesley is still active, performing in clubs and nostalgia shows as a well-remembered hitmaker.

THE GRASS ROOTS

Rob Grill: Lead vocals/bass guitar
Born: 11/5/44, Los Angeles, CA
Warren Entner: Guitar
Born: 7/7/44, San Francisco, CA
Creed Bratton II: Guitar
Born: 2/8/43, Sacramento, CA
Rick Coonce: Drums
Born: 8/1/47, Los Angeles, CA
Influences: Everly Brothers, Buddy Holly, Beatles, Ray Charles, Mitchell Trio
Influenced: Bangles, Psychedelic Furs

A group born of necessity, The Grass Roots were the brainchild of producer/writers, Steve Barri and P. F. Sloan.

Barri, who was working for Lou Adler's Dunhill label, wanted to create music in a folk-rock direction in the style of The Turtles or The Byrds but without having to spend time searching for the right act. Therefore, in 1966, he and Sloan became The Grass Roots; their debut effort was "Mr. Jones."

Mr. Jones.

> *Bob Dylan material serves as a strong and commercial debut for interesting new group. Ballad performance builds into a frenzy with a high spot on the chart anticipated. (10/2/65)*

Their next 45, "Where Were You When I Needed You," eight months later, put their name on the map. In early 1967, Barri found an L.A. bar band named The Thirteenth Floor and hired them to become The Grass Roots. "Let's Live for Today" was actually a cover of The Rokes (RCA), a band that had the original hit in their native Italy.

Where Were You When I Needed You.

> *Great folk-rock tune from the pens of P. F. Sloan and Steve Barri is given a rousing, big beat treatment by the exciting group. Could go all the way. (5/21/66) (#28 Pop)*

Let's Live for Today.

> *The "Where Were You When I Needed You" group has powerful sales potential with this folk-rock ballad. Lyric content is right up the alley of the teen buying market. If exposed, should prove a smash. (4/29/67) (#8 Pop)*

Sloan and Barri continued singing with the group through their next hit.

Things I Should Have Said.

> *Hot on the heels of "Let's Live for Today," the quartet offers another blockbuster. Sloan-Barri rhythm number loaded with discotheque appeal and appealing lyric line. (7/29/67) (#23 Pop)*

A year later, in 1968, Sloan left, although Barri carried on with the band. In 1969, Bratton left, replaced by Denny Provisor.

Midnight Confessions.

Exciting dance beat, top vocal work and fine Steve Barri production make the group's latest outing one of their most potent in some time. Should prove a hot seller. (6/29/68) (#5 Pop)

Bella Linda.

Following up their "Midnight Confessions," still riding the Hot 100, group has a driving rhythm ballad which has much of the sales potential of their current smash. (11/23/68) (#28 Pop)

The River Is Wide.

This powerhouse production rocker will put them high on the chart. A past hit for the Forum, this revival is a strong commercial one. (4/5/69) (#31 Pop)

I'd Wait a Million Years.

More infectious rock material to this potent follow up to their recent chart winner "River Is Wide." Equal chart and sales potential here. (6/21/69) (#15 Pop)

Heaven Knows.

The consistent chart group really lets loose with a solid rocker that is sure to skyrocket them right back into the spotlight. Good material and an equally good vocal performance. (10/25/69) (#24 Pop)

Baby Hold On.

A rhythm item that should prove an immediate Top 10 winner. Good production and vocal work. (4/25/70) (#35 Pop)

Sooner or Later.

Bubblegum rocker loaded with . . . sales and chart potency. Much of the "My Baby Loves Lovin'" flavor. (5/22/71) (#9 Pop)

Consistent with the group's singles prosperity, Grill and company's most significant album was their *Greatest Hits* compilation in 1971, selling over half a million copies.

In 1972, Virgil Weber (guitar), Joel Larson (drums), and Reed Kailing (guitar) replaced Coonce and Provisor as The Roots headed toward their twilight chart days. "Love Is What You Make It" (#55) was the band's last Dunhill hit in 1973. Two years later they recorded their last Top-100 single, "Mamacita," for Haven Records.

In 1980, Rob Grill, with most of Fleetwood Mac behind him, recorded the ill-fated *Uprooted* album. Grill and company received some unexpected publicity when Interior Secretary James Watt banned The Grass Roots and The Beach Boys from performing on the Washington, D.C. mall, at the annual July 4th celebration that year, stating they appeal "to the wrong element of people." In 1983, Entner became executive producer of the film version of *The Pirates of Penzance*. Different versions of The Grass Roots continued to perform their 21 chart hits for "every element of the people" over the next decade.

BILL HALEY AND THE COMETS

William John Clifton Haley, Jr.: Lead vocals
Born: 7/6/25, Highland Park, MI (died 2/9/81)
Joey D'Ambrose: Saxophone
Born: 3/23/34, Philadelphia, PA
Frannie Beacher: Guitar
Born: 3/29/21, Norristown, PA
Johnny Grande: Piano
Born: 1927, Philadelphia, PA
Dick Richards: Drums
Born: 2/12/24, Lansdown, PA
Billy Williamson: Guitar
Born: 2/9/25, Conshohocken, PA
Marshall Lytle: Bass
Born: 1927, Old Fort, NC
Influences: Hank Williams, Big Joe Turner, Gene Autry, Louis Jordan
Influenced: Elvis Presley, Beatles, Led Zeppelin, Rolling Stones, Dave Clark Five, Jefferson Airplane, Beach Boys

Bill Haley is acknowledged to be the father of rock 'n' roll, not only in America but throughout the world.

Although he started with country and western music, Haley was anything but a Southerner. He was, in fact, raised in Wilmington, Delaware, where the sounds of his mother's piano and father's banjo echoed country tunes.

After high school, the 17-year-old guitar-picking yodeler performed with traveling shows and country bands, such as The Range Drifters and The Down Homers. (Haley earned his job as a singing yodeler with The Down Homers after answering an ad in *Billboard*. They recorded their first 78 in 1946, "Who's Gonna Kiss You When I'm Gone.")

In 1948, Haley became a deejay at Bridgeport, New Jersey's WSNJ. Also that year, young Bill formed The Four Aces of Western Swing and recorded four 78s, including "Too Many Parties, Too Many Pals" (Cowboy Records). In 1949, the self-proclaimed "Ramblin' Yodeler" became a deejay for Chester Pennsylvania's WPWA, performing on his show with The Aces. He recorded, "Loveless Blues," as Johnny Clifton and His String Band.

By 1950, Haley had traded in The Aces for The Saddlemen (Williamson, Lytle, and Grande) and began recording a series of small-label country and western singles (Keystone, Atlantic) that went unnoticed. By the time he had reached Essex Records' affiliate, Holiday Records, in 1951, he described his music as "cowboy jive." His first Holiday single, "Rocket 88," a cover of R&B artist Jackie Brenston's Chess hit, gave Haley his first seller of any kind, registering about 10,000 copies. Other less exposed singles followed.

Bill Haley (The Saddlemen):
Juke Box Cannon Ball 69–72–66–70
Bouncy and lively, this semi-novelty number is sung strongly by Haley. Use of a train whistle is cleverly worked into the arrangement. Might spin well in rural jukes. (2/23/52)

Haley's early sides usually had a faster beat than typical country cuts. The seeds of change were sown by 1952, when another cowboy jive version of an R&B tune, "Rock The Joint," sold over 75,000 disks.

Bill Haley (The Saddlemen):
Rock The Joint 70–72–66–72
Jumpy opus in an odd mixture of c.&w. and r.&b. Nevertheless, Bill Haley and the Saddlemen manage to generate a sense of excitement. Ops might take a listen.

Icy Heart 66–66–66–66
Ballad about spurned love gets typical rustic treatment. May earn spins here and there. (3/25/52)

Bill Haley:
Stop Beatin' Round the Mulberry Bush . . .73
There's a frenetic quality to this exciting, lively rendition of the oldie. Guitars and bass make a driving beat to back Haley's vocal. This wild rendition could create action with exposure, and should pull juke loot.

Real Rock Drive 72
Plenty movement and rhythm to this side, with vocal by Bill Haley. Delivery is relaxed, free swinging. The flip side, however, is the stronger. (1/24/53)

Haley noticed something strange happening. His shows were now attracting teenagers. With the release of 1953's "Crazy Man, Crazy," the sideburns and cowboy boots were gone and The Saddlemen, with drummer Dick Richards aboard, had become The Comets. Actually, WPWA radio program director Bob Johnson had recommended the name "Haley's Comets" and, by Thanks-giving, 1952, all involved concurred. "Crazy" (#12 Pop) showed Bill his new rock 'n' roll transition was viable and his first hit became the first rock 'n' roll single to hit *Billboard*'s pop charts. Their debut review as Haley's Comets was another hit.

Bill Haley with Haley's Comets:
Fractured 84
The Haley combo has come up with another wild driving disking in the same groove as their "Crazy, Man, Crazy." This ditty is sung powerfully by Haley over a crazy backing by the Comets that really goes. This looks like solid juke fare, and it could grab stacks of coins. (8/4/52)

By early 1954, the Comets, helped by song-writer Jimmy Myers (aka Jimmy De Knight), moved to Decca. They recorded a song written by De Knight and postal employee Max C. Freedman titled, "Rock Around the Clock," which had been recorded a year earlier by Haley's friend Sonny Dae (Paschal Vennitti) on Haley's own Arcade label. It's likely Myers' title came from an even earlier Hal Singer recording (Mercury, November 1950). The legendary guitar solo played by Danny Cedrone was lifted note for note from his earlier performance on "Rock The Joint." "Clock" nearly went unrecorded as the band arrived late and were given only a half hour to tape it. Two takes were made but each lacked something: The first drowned out Haley's vocals and the second had the band lost in the background. Producer Milt Gabler's answer was to synchronize the two, making a third master that became the legendary release. Released as the B-side, with the label misidentifying the song as a foxtrot, "Clock" went unnoticed until Myers began a one-man promotional campaign, calling deejays and embarking on a 2,000 mile trek to reignite the overlooked side. His efforts paid off. "Clock" reached #23, although no one had any idea of its future importance.

Thirteen Women 74
> *Ops could make good use of a rhythm and blue-ish item about a guy in a town where he's the only man. The beat is strong and Haley sells the lyrics smart-ly.*

Rock Around the Clock 74
> *Big beat and repetitious blues lyric makes this a good attempt at "cat music" and one which should grab coin in the right locations. (5/15/54)*

Next, Haley lyrically sugar-coated the sexually explicit Joe Turner hit, "Shake, Rattle and Roll," for his first Top-10 smash. Notice that Haley's reviews in the early Decca days refer only to Bill Haley Ork, with no mention of The Comets. Haley, his trademark spit curl and six-piece combo, continued to rock the teens both stateside and abroad.
Bill Haley Ork:

Shake, Rattle and Roll/A.B.C. Boogie.
> *This one is especially recommended for operators, and the pulsating manner in which the ork plays and shouts these tunes could help the disk attract a lot of coins. Pop side is the current r.&b. hit; flip is an infectious boogie. (7/10/54) (#7 Pop)*

Dim, Dim the Lights/Happy Baby.
> *Here are two pounding efforts in the usual Bill Haley manner. "Dim, Dim the Lights" is perhaps a mite slower, but both wild outings are for the kids who want to dance. Boxes should grab coins with these follow-ups to "Shake, Rattle and Roll." (10/30/54) (#11 Pop, #10 R&B)*

Mambo Rock/Birth of the Boogie.
> *The kids who Lindy to Bill Haley will continue to do so. These two new sides have the same rocking blues beat as his previous disks, and the ideas on both are cute. Fine juke wax here. (2/12/55) (A-side, #18 Pop; B-side, #17 Pop)*

In 1955, writer/director Richard Brooks, needing a song for his new film, found it on his daughter's Victrola in the old "Rock Around the Clock," which found its way into his classic *The Blackboard Jungle.* Reissued, "Clock" (actually a revision of an old blues tune, "My Daddy Rocks Me with a Steady Beat"), shot to #1 (#3, R&B) around the world, eventually selling over 22 million copies. In England alone, it charted eight times in 20 years and is still the world's anthem of rock some 40 years later. Haley recorded several successful followups.

Burn That Candle/Rock-a-Beatin' Boogie.
> *This looks like a big walloping two-sider for the Haley crew. Both tunes rock along at a great pace with Haley delivering the usual exciting, hard-driving vocal treatment. All the elements needed for big loot are right here. (1/22/55) (A-side, #9 Pop, #9 R&B; B-side, #23 Pop)*

See You Later, Alligator.
> *Another solid, rockin' rouser. It's a story with a touch of humor . . . Styled in the typical Haley success pattern. (12/31/55) (#6 Pop, #7 R&B)*

In April 1956, the first rock 'n' roll film, named after Haley's big hit, stormed the theaters, starring Alan Freed, The Platters, and of course, Bill Haley and The Comets. In December 1956, Haley et al. hit with another film, *Don't Knock the Rock*, and its title song.

The Saints Rock and Roll/R-O-C-K.

With the tremendous stir being set up by Haley and the crew via their "Rock Around the Clock" flick, it's hard to see this one missing. These are two great rollicking sides, full of wild beats and driving, shouting delivery in the best Haley style. Two very hot pay-off entries. (3/24/56) (A-side, #18 Pop; B-side, #16 Pop, #1 R&B)

Rip It Up/Teenager's Mother.

"Rip It Up," a cover of the Little Richard platter, is a hard-driving, sock rhythm item with spirited warbling and a solid beat. The flip is a fast-moving piece of material with an interesting lyric theme (e.g. "Why condemn rock and roll, Ma, when you used to do the Charleston"). Both sides are bound to pull down plenty of play. (7/28/56) (A-side, #25 Pop; B-side, #68 Pop)

Don't Knock the Rock . . .

[This] is the title of a forthcoming pic in which this tune is featured. It is a lively exciting essay in the vein of so many other Haley rock and roll hits, and this will undoubtedly have the same success in the teen-age market. (12/1/56) (#45 Pop)

In becoming the first rock 'n' roll star to visit England (February 1957), Haley bore the brunt of the British teens' rock-starved adulation and was constantly mobbed. However, his stateside hit-making days were over, although he did manage a few more minor hits.

(You Hit the Wrong Note) Billy Goat 88

Altho this one appears to come from the bottom of the Haley barrel, the strength of the act could carry it thru. Haley has had much better. (5/27/57) (#60 Pop)

Skinny Minnie 76

No relation to the one out on Victor with the Sprouts. It's a swinging item, which the Haley combo sells in "Bony Moronie" style. Listenable wax. (3/3/58) (#22 Pop)

Don't Nobody Move/Lean Jean.

Two great sides that could be successful follow-ups to Haley's hit "Skinny Minnie." "Don't" is a catchy danceable side—a freeze. Flip, "Lean Jean," is a rocker with a driving beat. New sound by the crew can continue to find favor. (7/7/58) (B-side, #67 Pop)

Corrine, Corrina.

★ ★ ★ ★ *The great blues standard gets a solid Haley vocal. The group blows up a good storm in the backing. Watch this one. It could go. (11/17/58)*

Throughout the early 1960s, the band tried covers and a variety of styles, but their time as teen stars was over. In 1960, the band signed with Warner Brothers. Several small label releases followed. A short stay at Decca in 1964 produced "Green Door," but Haley's recordings were sparse by the late 1960s.

I Got a Woman/Charmaine.

Haley has his strongest sides in a while. Both are top efforts that stand a chance to cop heavy loot. He reads, "I Got a Woman," the Ray Charles tune, with plenty of feeling. "Charmaine," the oldie, is also handled with a hit sound. (2/16/59)

Skokiaan.

★ ★ ★ ★ *The tune with South African origins gets an updating by the Comets. It has almost a mariachi flavor. Alto has the lead as in the original hit. Danceable, listenable side. Should be watched. (12/28/59) (#70 Pop)*

Flip, Flop and Fly.

★ ★ ★ ★ *The old Joe Turner hit is given another updating, following several recent versions. Haley pounds out the vocal in his familar style against a bounding backing. Worth spins. (6/19/61)*

Tenor Man.

> *It's been a long time since Bill Haley has had a hit, but it could happen again with this exciting, shouting side. He sells the lyric with gusto backed by a "ya ya" girls' chorus. Watch it. (4/27/63)*

In 1969, the group performed at Richard Nader's first rock 'n' roll revival show in New York and received an incredible eight-minute standing ovation! Haley reappeared on United Artists, releasing one single that was well-reviewed in *Billboard*, if not a chart hit.

That's How I Got to Memphis.

> *With "comebacks" to the disk scene happening all the time in today's market, this one will be no exception. Producer Henry Jerome has a hot sales entry in this powerful Tom T. Hall rhythm ballad. Haley is at his best with the pop-country item. (2/8/69)*

Haley continued on the worldwide nostalgia bandwagon through the 1970s. In 1981, he passed away at his home in Harlingen, Texas, at age 55, broke and forgotten. His last hit, in 1974, was a reissue of the 20-year-old "Rock Around the Clock"; a whole new generation of music fans took it to #39. In 1987, Bill Haley and The Comets were inducted into the Rock and Roll Hall of Fame. The same year, the "Original" Comets came together for a show; they are still performing today. In fact, the 60- and 70-year-old Comets undertook a major European tour in June 1995. Although they sold over 60 million records, Haley and the Comets are better remembered as the men behind the beginning of the rock 'n' roll era.

THE HAPPENINGS

Bob Miranda: Lead vocals/guitar
Born: 4/29/42, Paterson, NJ
Tom Giuliano: Tenor vocals/percussion
Born: 5/11/43, Paterson, NJ
Ralph DiVito: Baritone vocals/guitar
Born: 1941, Paterson, NJ
Dave Libert: Bass vocals/keyboard
Born: 1/20/43, Paterson, NJ
Influences: Four Freshmen, Hi-Lo's, Mel Tormé and The Meltones, Four Seasons, Beach Boys, Frankie Lymon and The Teenagers

The Happenings were a clean-cut vocal group who scored big with their covers of standards in the mid- to late 1960s, despite the fact that the era preferred more psychedelic and soulful sounds. Their ability to master complex jazz and pop harmonies with a doo wop style made for one of the singular sound surprises of the decade.

Bob Miranda, leader of the group, remembered, "My friend Ralph and I knew that all the singers here in Paterson hung out at Saint Leo's church dances. We decided that forming a group would be the way to go." On a fateful night in 1961, the duo entered the men's room of Saint Leo's and found two teen hopefuls (Giuliano and Libert) harmonizing their hearts out. Miranda noted, "We were serious and determined to develop our sound, so we practiced our asses off. Often our rehearsals ended late at night, when the cops showed up to shut us up." The quartet of 17- and 18-year-old recent high school graduates decided to name themselves The Four Graduates.

In 1963, manager Chuck Rubin brought a demo of one of Miranda's originals, "Step into the Future," to Laurie Records' Bob Schwartz. He decided to take a chance with The Grads on a rhythm version of The Ink Spots' 1944 hit, "A Lovely Way to Spend an Evening." During 1964, Laurie/Rust issued one more Four Grads single, "Candy Queen," but to no avail. By then, Miranda was determined to make a living as a songwriter, and brought some demos to Hank

Medress of Bright Tunes Productions, home of the multitalented Tokens (Phil and Mitch Margo, Jay Siegel, and Hank).

The Tokens, producing for Laurie, met The Grads and, after hearing Miranda's tunes, made him a staff writer for $25 a week. Soon after, Miranda met Four Seasons producer Bob Crewe. Crewe was more impressed with Miranda's group than the youngster's songwriting and hired The Grads as backup singers on Mitch Ryder and Eddie Rambeau recordings.

The group was finally signed on their own to The Tokens' B.T. Puppy label. "The Tokens loved us because we emulated them," Bob enthused. In the final days of 1965, the Grads felt a new name should accompany their new recording opportunity. They considered The Chord-a-roys, The Bitter Lemons, and, in the midst of the changing times, The Happenings.

After their February 1966 "Girls on the Go" debut fizzled, the group came up with a song they'd been performing for four years, "See You in September."

See You in September.

Excellent group vocal blend on this revival of the Tempos' hit should repeat in the charts as a vacation time smash. (6/25/66) (#3 Pop)

To keep the momentum going, the quartet rearranged another recent oldie, "Go Away Little Girl."

Go Away Little Girl.

With equal potential of "See You in September," group has a sure-fire winner in this well done revival of Steve Lawrence's hit. (9/24/66) (#12 Pop)

By late 1966, the group broke the oldies formula, opting for an original song, "Goodnight My Love."

Goodnight My Love.

Chalk up another "Go Away Little Girl" winner for the "See You in September" group. Easy dance beat backs smooth vocal workout. (11/26/66) (#51 Pop)

The quartet rifled the Gershwin songbook for their next bit of inspiration. Their double time arrangement of Al Jolson's 1921 hit "My Mammy" was another surprise pop hit.

I Got Rhythm.

With the 4 Seasons proving a smash with their revival of Cole Porter's "I've Got You Under My Skin," the Happenings have strong possibilities with this Gershwin revival. In today's market dance arrangement, the group excels with a powerful vocal workout. (3/25/67) (#3 Pop)

My Mammy.

This raucous revival of the Jolson favorite should prove a smash with today's teen buying market. Loaded with excitement, vitality and dance appeal. (7/8/67) (#13 Pop)

In September, America's favorite revivalists reversed their strategy by slowing down a previous uptempo smash, "Why Do Fools Fall in Love." Covers of "Music, Music, Music" and "Breaking Up Is Hard to Do" followed, but were less successful.

Why Do Fools Fall in Love.

Frankie Lymon hit of the past serves as strong production ballad for the group in their fresh smooth approach to fast follow "My Mammy." Well arranged by Herb Bernstein. (9/9/67) (#41 Pop)

Breaking Up Is Hard to Do.

The Neil Sedaka hit . . . gets a top-notch revival that's in the groove of the group's past hits, and should prove especially successful. (6/29/68) (#67 Pop)

For some inexplicable reason, they abandoned remakes for originals, like "Crazy Rhythm," and, by 1969, had issued their last Puppy single, "That's All I Want from You," which was the first to read Bob Miranda and The Happenings.

The group next moved to Jubilee. Their first single became the group's biggest hit in two years but last Top-100 single.

Where Do I Go/Be In.

A solid rock medley of more hot numbers from B'way's "Hair." Top-notch commerical performance and arrangement. (6/21/69) (#66 Pop)

In 1970, producer Charlie Callelo renamed the group The Honor Society for one ill-fated Jubilee 45 ("Sweet September").

During 1973, The Happenings, now on Musicor, became a rock/reggae act named Sundog ("We're Almost Home"), in hopes of catching a contemporary hit wave. Giuliano and Miranda continued with a four-piece band until 1980, when Giuliano retired. As of the mid-1990s, Giuliano was reportedly in the catering business. DiVito lived in Las Vegas, Libert in Los Angeles, managing rock bands, and Miranda continued The Happenings tradition with a backup group in New Jersey.

With nine Top-100 hits out of 29 singles they left a lasting legacy that anything old, done well, can be new . . . and successful.

WILBERT HARRISON

Birthdate: 1/6/29
Birthplace: Charlotte, NC
Died: 10/26/94
Influences: Frankie Laine, Chuck Willis, Fats Domino

A veritable one-man band, Wilbert Harrison enjoyed one major hit, "Kansas City," that left its mark on the history of rock 'n' roll.

Harrison was one of a reported 23 kids, so it's not surprising that when he strolled out of the house, he marched into another large family, the U.S. Navy.

In 1953, after his service, he won an amateur talent contest in Miami singing "Mule Train." His recording life started with "This Woman of Mine" (Rockin), followed by "Gin and Coconut Milk" (Deluxe). In 1954, Wilbert had a regional hit in Florida when he signed with Savoy, which gained an unusual two notices in *Billboard.*

> *A listenable new singer bows on Savoy Records with an appealing reading of the country hit, "Don't Drop It" . . . Harrison has a warm style and could get action. (9/18/54)*

Don't Drop It 80
> *The label has come up with a fine new singer . . . who has a bright, listenable*

> *style. He does a mighty fine job here with the country hit, selling it in spritely fashion over happy backing. Watch this warbler. (9/25/54)*

His sporadic follow ups did little but his regular performance experiences as a solo made him a proficient, if strange, sight. Harrison wore a brace on his neck with a harmonica on one side and a microphone on the other. He also had a cymbal on one foot and a bass drum on the other, leaving his hands free to play guitar. Gyrating with a rocking motion, he indeed made a lot of music.

Confessin' My Dreams 81
> *Pulsating, insistent chant whose very monotony could be its biggest point of appeal. Definitely a disc to watch. (9/1/56)*

I Know My Baby Loves Me 72
> *Cat has an interesting nasal quality on this Domino inspired styling. Harrison has a little trouble hitting his low notes, but the side has a certain amount of appeal just the same. (8/5/57)*

In 1959, Wilbert landed on the doorstep of Bobby Robinson, owner of Fury Records in New York, pitching a song he'd been performing for five years. When he told Bobby the tune was "Kansas City," Robinson responded that it was an old 1952 Little Willie Littlefield song that didn't do anything. Harrison agreed saying: "I know, but everywhere I go, people like this song!" On a hunch, Robinson cut the tune using guitarist Jim Spruill, who created a rhythmic sound that gave the song a special bounce.

"Kansas City" (originally recorded as "K.C. Lovin'," and written by Leiber and Stoller as one of their first songs) was recorded in 10 minutes and two takes, although the first take was used. Robinson spent $40 all told and pressed 12 test pressings. He then embarked on an 11-city radio station tour, giving copies to deejays in cities from Philadelphia to New Orleans. When he returned in 13 days, his mail was knee deep in orders for "Kansas City," thanks to a deejay in Cleveland who broke it a week before Robinson returned.

Amazingly, competing cover versions were in the marketplace before Robinson could issue his own record. Word spread that he was not going to license it through the big boys so they began cutting their own versions. One deejay went to the extreme of taping the record off the air, teaching it, note for note, to a local white kid named Rocky Olson, and then cutting it and selling it to Chess Records.

Kansas City.
Wilbert Harrison (Fury) 1023
Hank Ballard and The Midnighters (King) 5195
Little Willie Littlefeld (Federal) 12351
Rocky Olson (Chess) 1723
Rockin' Ronald and The Rebels (End) 1043

> *This promises to be a big tune. It has already broken out in several areas. The Fury disk is the original, and the other versions are similar. The song is a finger-snappin' blues with a highly contagious sound. It can be a strong dual-market entry. (3/30/59) (#1 Pop, #1 R&B)*

A week after the review, even Little Richard put a competing version out. But Wilbert's sound won hands down, selling over two million copies. Happy ending? No way. Robinson was immediately sued by Savoy, who claimed they still had a contract with Harrison. Court proceedings kept Harrison from recording, so he went on tour while Fury fought the suit.

By the time things were settled, Harrison's new Fury singles "Cheatin' Baby" and "Goodbye Kansas City" didn't so much as stir a review. Further records also stiffed on the charts.

Little School Girl.

> *Catchy teen appeal ditty is chanted with verve and showmanship. Dual market item for the "Kansas City" man. (10/3/60)*

★★★★ Happy in Love.

> *Interesting blues theme is wrapped up in a solid vocal by Harrison, who had a smash with "Kansas City" sometime back. (4/17/61)*

★★★★ Drafted.

> *Harrison has a blues based topical item here that moves nicely in a medium tempo. The boy isn't going to "Kansas City" on this one, but into the Army.*
> ★ ★ ★ ★ *(11/20/61)*

After ten singles on Fury, Wilbert continued

chasing brass rings through the 1960s on labels like Port, Vest, Seahorn, and Neptune, but to no avail. In 1969, Wilbert finally hit again with his own song, "Let's Work Together" (#32, Sue), which was a revision of "Let's Stick Together," a record he had out on Fury in 1961. Ironically, his last charter was the B-side of his Fury disking of "Let's Stick Together," a rerecording of "My Heart Is Yours."

> *This Harrison revival is already attracting airplay and sales attention in various markets, and it could easily spread nationally and prove a winner on the Hot 100 and Soul charts. (2/27/71) (#98 Pop)*

In 1971, Wilbert toured as an opening act for Creedence Clearwater Revival, still performing as a one-man band. Harrison continued to record for a variety of small labels through the 1990s, he died of a stroke in 1994.

BUDDY HOLLY AND THE CRICKETS

Charles Hardin "Buddy" Holly: Guitar/lead vocals
Born: 9/7/36, Lubbock, TX (died 2/3/59)
Niki Sullivan: Guitar
Born: 1930s, Lubbock, TX
Joe B. Mauldin: Bass
Born: 1930s, Lubbock, TX
Jerry Allison: Drums
Born: 8/31/39, Hillsboro, TX

Influences: Elvis Presley, Hank Williams, Little Richard, Hank Ballard and The Midnighters, Chuck Berry, Mickey and Sylvia

Influenced: Beatles, Bob Dylan, Rolling Stones, Linda Ronstadt, Bobby Vee, Tommy Roe, Hollies, Tom Jones, John Denver, Grass Roots, Waylon Jennings, many more

One of rock's most prized pioneers, Buddy Holly exemplified the country to rockabilly to rock 'n' roll development of the mid-1950s. He was among the first to write for himself and to use overdubbing on his studio vocals. His experimentation with the two guitars-bass-and-drums formula made this the standard format for rock groups.

Buddy began playing piano and violin at four and guitar at seven, winning a local talent show singing "Down the River of Memories" at five. In September 1953, Holley and friend Bob Montgomery formed an act and sang on Lubbock's KDAV radio. Soon they were performing Saturdays as "The Buddy and Bob Show." On October 14, 1955, Holley, Montgomery, drummer Jerry Allison, and bass player Larry Welborn appeared alongside Bill Haley and The Comets at a KDAV-sponsored show where they were noticed by Nashville agent Eddie Crandell. The next night, the Lubbock locals opened at the Cotton Club for a young Elvis Presley. He made such an impression on Holley that the newcomer's country style would soon develop into rock 'n' roll.

Meanwhile, Crandell arranged a Decca deal for Holley only. With Montgomery's blessings, Buddy, Allison, new guitarist Sonny Curtis, and bass player Don Guess headed for Nashville and recorded on January 26, 1956, as Buddy Holley and The Three Tunes. Their first single was "Blue Days, Black Nights," in April 1956. His next 45 came eight months later. Due to a mistake in his Decca contract, Buddy's last name was spelled "Holly," and thus it remained for the rest of his career.

Modern Don Juan 79
This is patterned after the Presley medium tempo rhythm numbers. The material has a simple and appealing riff that is very much in the current teen-age groove. Will be appreciated by many.

You Are My One Desire 70
Holly quavers through this ballad in a way that resembles the styling of Presley's "Love Me Tender." There's a sound here of arresting quality. (12/21/56)

Holly recorded several sides for Decca, including

a country version of "That'll Be the Day," which wasn't issued until his glory days; none were successful.

In September 1956, Buddy and Decca parted company and he formed a new group with Allison, Mauldin, and Sullivan: The Crickets. (He first considered calling them The Beetles!) It's no coincidence that four years later a British band named Johnny and The Moondogs became The Beatles. (The Hollies also named themselves in tribute to Buddy.) After Roulette, Columbia, RCA, and Atlantic turned them down, new producer Norman Petty arranged a deal with Brunswick, ironically a Decca subsidiary.

Their first release was a rerecording of "That'll Be the Day." Owing to contractual arrangements between Petty and Brunswick, Crickets sides came out on Brunswick whereas Holly singles were issued on Coral, even though the same musicians performed on all the singles over the next two years.

The Crickets:
That'll Be the Day 72
Fine vocal by the group on a well-made side that should get play. Tune is a medium beat rockabilly. Performance is better than material.

I'm Lookin' for Somone to Love 72
As with the flip, the material is inferior to the rendition. The up-tempo rockabilly gets bright, vigorous treatment. (6/10/57) (#1 Pop)

Words of Love 84
Soft, low-toned dual track vocal with bright, sharp guitar backing on a Latin-type theme. Good clear sound. Side can do business.

Mailman, Bring Me No More Blues 80
Sock selling effort on a well-phrased, medium beat rockabilly blues. Tune has also been done by Herb Jeffries, but attractive reading here could prove stronger version. (6/24/57)

Following Holly's success on Coral/Brunswick, Decca finally issued the earlier "That'll Be the Day," without indicating that it was an old recording.

Rock Around with Ollie Vee 73
> *Exuberant delivery of a rockabilly rocker with bright tenor and guitar support can attract coin in all markets. Talented artist.*

That'll Be the Day .72
> *Cover of the tune which is big for the Crickets. Holly, who is one of the Crickets, and a co-cleffer of the tune, registers well with an appealing go, but platter may be late to see top loot. (8/19/57)*

Holly and company's next 45 was called "Cindy Lou" but a last-minute change in favor of Allison's girlfriend's name made it the immortal "Peggy Sue." Their second million seller in two tries, the group toured Australia with Paul Anka and Jerry Lee Lewis.

Peggy Sue/Everyday.
> *Holly, one of the Crickets, makes a strong solo bid on "Peggy Sue," a rockabilly item that can cop plenty of pop and c.&w. coin. Flip, "Everyday," is another strong dual-market side with a folkish flavor. Vocal gimmicks by the artist on the medium-beat tune could make a winner. (9/30/57) (#3 Pop)*

The Crickets:
Oh, Boy!
> *The group has a good bet to follow up their hit, "That'll Be the Day," with their strong presentation of this frantic rockabilly. Wild sounds and hollering build a lot of excitement. Flip is an interesting interpretation of an off-beat piece of material called "Not Fade Away." (11/4/57) (#10 Pop)*

The Crickets:
Maybe Baby/Tell Me How.
> *Two likely successes to the group's previous clicks. "Maybe Baby" is rock-abilly, and the crew gives it their usual exuberant delivery. "Tell Me More" is a rock-a-calypso type that is belted with the same appeal. A threat in all markets! (2/3/58) (#17 Pop)*

Rave On/Take Your Time.
> *Holly appears to be back in chart form on "Rave On," a rockabilly item that he belts with hiccupy gusto. "Take Your Time" is a less frantic effort, but it also has the money sound. Also a strong bet for c.&w. coin. (4/21/58) (#37 Pop)*

The Crickets:
Think It Over/Fool's Paradise.
> *Good group vocals on both of these rockabilly efforts make each a strong contender in pop and c.&w. marts. "Think" is a medium-tempo tune that is helped by wild piano support. "Paradise" is a countryish theme that is also given a strong rendition against plucked string backing. (6/2/58) (A-side, #27 Pop; B-side, #58 Pop)*

In June 1958, Holly recorded without The Crickets for the first time, cutting two Bobby Darin-written songs, "Early in the Morning" backed with "Now We're One."

Early in the Morning.
> *A swinging blues, and Holly belts it solidly against a New Orleans beat. (6/30/58) (#32 Pop)*

In July, Holly failed his army physical due to a stomach ulcer. By October, Holly and Petty were at odds and the problems spilled into his relationship with The Crickets. Buddy parted company with them and moved to New York, marrying Maria Elena Santiago, a secretary at a publishing company who he proposed to on their first date.

Short of cash, Holly reluctantly joined The Winter Dance Party tour in January 1959 with Dion and The Belmonts, Ritchie Valens, and The Big Bopper. Buddy's new band featured Tommy Allsup, Charlie Bunch, and a newcomer, Waylon Jennings, on bass. On February 2, after their Surf Ballroom performance in Clear Lake, Iowa, Holly, Jennings, and Allsup decided to take a small plane to Fargo, North Dakota, rather than rumble along in the ever-fragile, underheated bus. Before the flight took off, the lineup changed, when the "Bopper" (J. P. Richardson) fell ill and took Jennings' seat; Allsup and Valens tossed a coin for the last seat, and Valens won. Taking off in a howling snowstorm, the plane crashed minutes into the flight, killing all three stars and the 21-year-old pilot, Roger Peterson.

On February 7, Buddy Holly was buried at Lubbock City Cemetery. Pallbearers included Crickets Allison, Sullivan, and Mauldin along with Curtis, Montgomery, and Phil Everly.

The irony of his next release escaped few. "Anymore" was #1 in England for six weeks, where the martyred singer was even more revered than in America.

It Doesn't Matter Anymore/Raining in My Heart.

Holly switches style in the ballad kick on "It Doesn't Matter Anymore," a tune cleffed by Paul Anka. "Raining" is a ballad by [Felice and Boudleaux Bryant] that is also warmly read. Excellent ork backing on both helps. These could be big sides. (1/19/59) (A-side, #13 Pop; B-side, #88 Pop)

Holly's original demo of "Love's Made a Fool of You," cut for the Everly Brothers, was issued shortly thereafter as a Crickets' B-side, becoming a hit in England.

Rocker with a Latin flavor is given a stylized vocal . . . Tune has a folkie sound, and it's nicely handled. (3/9/59)

The Crickets continued with Lubbock local Earl Sinks and then Sonny Curtis. One of Holly's demos, "Peggy Sue Got Married," with overdubs by the Jack Harum Combo was next. When the song failed under Holly's name, Coral tried it by The Crickets.

Peggy Sue Got Married.

★ ★ ★ ★ *Follow-up to Holly's big hit. Attractive warbling job on catchy rockabilly-styled item.*

Crying, Waiting, Hoping.

★ ★ ★ ★ *The late Buddy Holly sings plaintively on an appealing rockabilly ditty. (8/3/59) (#13 Pop [U.K.])*

By 1962, The Crickets were Allison, Jerry Naylor (lead guitar), and Glenn Hardin (piano). Meanwhile, Decca continued to mine the vaults to issue "new" material by Holly.

Wait Till the Sun Shines Nellie.

★ ★ ★ ★ *Here's the oldie done in a highly distinctive rockabilly style by Holly. He gets a smart backup from his combo and a vocal group. Holly fans should dig this side, not previously released.*

Reminiscing.

★ ★ ★ ★ *Here's one of two previously unreleased sides which find the late Buddy Holly working with the swinging tenor man, King Curtis. The chanter still has a wonderful touch on this medium beater. He displays an interesting fillip of a semi-yodel here. Should get a lot of play. (8/18/62)*

Bo Diddley/True Love Ways.

An exciting version of the old r.&b. hit by the late Buddy Holly that could turn into a sock seller. The flip, a warm ballad, should be a big one in Europe. (3/30/63) (B-side, #25 Pop [U.K.])

In 1978, the bio flick *The Buddy Holly Story*, starring Gary Busey, hit theaters. Holly was inducted into the Rock and Roll Hall of Fame in 1986 but, as the song goes, February 3, 1959 was "the day the music died."

THE ISLEY BROTHERS

Ronald Isley: Lead vocals
Born: 5/21/41, Cincinnati, OH
O'Kelly Isley
Born: 12/25/37, Cincinnati, OH (died 3/31/86)
Rudolph Isley
Born: 4/1/39, Cincinnati, OH

Influences: Billy Ward and The Dominoes, Clyde McPhatter, Nat "King" Cole, Sam Cooke, Frank Sinatra, Jackie Wilson

Influenced: Michael Jackson, Smokey Robinson, Rod Stewart, Beatles, Rolling Stones, Marvin Gaye, Jimi Hendrix, Whitney Houston, Aretha Franklin, Baby Face, Angela Winbush, Joey Dee

The Isleys were the most conspicuous exponents of gospel music in late 1950s' rock 'n' roll.

The three brothers, along with their brother Vernon, toured Ohio and Kentucky accompanied by their mother, Sally. When Vernon died in a bicycle accident, the group stopped performing but, a year later, with their parents' encouragement, they once again began making appearances. In 1957, with $20 and bus tickets, the trio went to New York. They were discovered before they even arrived: A woman on the bus recommended them to a booking agent upon hearing the Isleys' harmonizing.

One of their performances was seen by Teenage Records' Bill Gordon, who recorded them for the first time in a doo wop style.

Angels Cried 79
> With proper exposure this might grab off action nationally. Group sells a plaintive blues-ballad with powerful emotion and sock performance by lead singer Ronald Isley.

The Cow Jumped Over the Moon 70
> Vitality and verveful lead a la Frankie Lyman make this otherwise ordinary blues-novelty a lively bidder for jockey spins. (6/3/57)

A meeting with label legend George Goldner led to singles on his Cindy, Gone, and Mark X diskaries.

This Is the End 72
> Attractive new tune is sung with feeling by one of the Isley Brothers on lead, over simple rockaballad backing. Could get spins. (8/4/58)

The Drag.
★★   *The Isley Brothers sing of The Drag, a new dance that really moves, on this new recording. Tune goes. (12/8/58)*

In 1959, while performing at Washington, D.C.'s Howard Theater, they were noticed by RCA's Howard Bloom. Bloom loved their energetic style and felt a song should be built around a line they improvised in Jackie Wilson's "Lonely Teardrops"; the line was, "You know you make me want to shout." Recorded on July 29, "Shout" epitomized the fusion of gospel and rock 'n' roll. Surprisingly, it never charted R&B but has become a multimillion selling classic. More power-packed and underpromoted singles followed.

Shout (Parts I and II).

> These are two of the most frantic sides to come along in a spell. It's a mixture of gospel and rockabilly, and the trio has a likely smash. Side One is great, but Side Two is even more intense, building in volume, sound and excitement. Watch 'em! (8/31/59) (#47 Pop)

Respectable.

> The boys can have a hit successor to their "Shout." It's a frantic novelty type, and driving combo support helps. (12/7/59)

He's Got the Whole World in His Hands/How Deep Is the Ocean.

> The Isley Brothers could have another "Shout" with either of these fine outings. "He's Got the Whole World" is given a spirited belt. They take attractive, melodic liberties with "How Deep Is the Ocean" and read the tune as a rocker. Both can step out. (3/21/60)

Tell Me Who/Say You Love Me Too.

> The boys are out with their first in a spell and two wild, rocking performances they are. On top, there's much shouting, who-whoing and other vocal gymnastics on display while the flip, tho a bit toned down, also has its exciting touches. Either has a solid chance. (9/19/60)

They fared no better upon moving to Atlantic, even though they were produced by Leiber and Stoller. Meanwhile, RCA reissued "Shout" and it charted again (#94 Pop).

Teach Me How to Shimmy.
★★★★ *A side that's much in the downhome groove of the shimmy. It's done in a slow, exaggerated rhythm, with the lads shouting out the message. This type of strongly r.&b.-slanted side is making it now. Watch this. (1/30/61)*

Shine on Harvest Moon.
★★★★ *Tin Pan Alley might have trouble recognizing this oldie in its 1961 garb. The Brothers give it a slow rocking ride*

with a heavy blues bass line predominating. Effective wail. (5/1/61)

In 1962, producer Bert Berns capitalized on "Shout" and Chubby Checker's "Twist" to create "Twist and Shout" (not reviewed by *Billboard*) followed by "Twistin' with Linda."

Twistin' with Linda.
★ ★ ★ ★ *The "shout" cats have another shouting rhythm twist effort here. Good beat and a wild sound can keep the boys on the charts. (9/8/62) (#54 Pop)*

In 1966, The Isley Brothers recorded some of their finest sides for Tamla/Motown.

This Old Heart of Mine.
Powerhouse comeback of the wailing, cooking trio who should fast find their way up the r.&b. and pop charts. Loaded with excitement. (2/12/66) (#12 Pop, #5 R&B)

I Guess I'll Always Love You.
Another chartbuster for the writing-producing team of Holland and Dozier. With solid Detroit backing, the tune has potential. (7/2/66) (#61 Pop, #31 R&B)

After leaving Tamla, while touring England in 1968, the group was encouraged to start up their T-Neck label again (a one-shot single, "Testify Part 1," in 1964 failed). When their Tamla sides started hitting in Britain, the trio's first try on T-Neck (named after Teaneck, the New Jersey town they lived in) proved the charm.

It's Your Thing.
A blues blockbuster loaded with excitement and a wild vocal workout. Rocker on the new label, part of Buddah, should prove a hot sales item, both r&b and pop. (3/8/69) (#2 Pop, #1 R&B)

I Turned You On.
A driving soul rocker with all the sales power of their million seller "It's Your Thing." The same raucous beat and dance appeal, this will take them right back to the top. (5/24/69) (#23 Pop, #6 R&B)

Although most of the trio's records to date were originals, they now applied their high-octane

gospel touch to other artists' rock and folk songs for a series of R&B and lesser pop hits.

Love the One You're With.
The recent Stephen Stills smash gets a powerful workout by the Isleys that will put it up the soul chart and should prove a big pop hit all over again. (5/29/71) (#18 Pop, #3 R&B)

Spill the Wine.
Group made a powerful return to the . . . chart with "Love the One You're With." Followup reading of Eric Burdon's smash has all that sales and chart potency. (9/18/71) (#49 Pop, #14 R&B)

Lay, Lady, Lay.
The Dylan number is updated in a smooth blues reading loaded with potential for MOR as well as pop and soul. (11/20/71) (#71 Pop, #29 R&B)

In 1973, T-Neck moved from Buddah to Columbia distribution and hit with "That Lady." Between 1974 and 1984, the trio, with support from younger brothers Marvin (bass), Eric (guitar), and cousin Chris Jasper (keyboards), entered the pop lists 12 times and the R&B charts on 27 occasions, including "Fight the Power," "The Pride," "Take Me to Your Place," "I Want to Be with You," and "Don't Say Goodnight," all #1s R&B.

Choosey Lover.
The veteran soulmen whose chart career has spanned nearly three decades were back on top again last month when "Between the Sheets" reached number three on the black chart. Now they continue the tradition with another mellow ballad that features their characteristic lead guitar sound and more X-rated subject matter. (7/2/83) (#6 R&B)

In 1985, Ronald, O'Kelly, and Rudolph mothballed T-Neck and signed with Warner Brothers.

Colder Are My Nights.
Regrouped (after the spinoff of Isley, Jasper, Isley) and on a new label, the Brothers are back in stride with a quietly seductive dance track reminiscent

of their 1983 hit "Between the Sheets."
(11/2/85) (#12 R&B)

On March 31, 1986, O'Kelly died of heart failure, ending the trio's career. Their last R&B Top-5 smash was issued about that time. Ronald joined Rod Stewart for a remake of "This Old Heart of Mine" (#10) in 1990.

Smooth Sailin' Tonight.
> *Plush production teams the brothers with Rene and Angela Winbush, matching her dreamy, sensual material with their sinuous harmonies. (5/9/87)*

The Brothers were inducted into the Rock and Roll Hall of Fame in 1992.

TOMMY JAMES AND THE SHONDELLS

Thomas Jackson: Lead vocals
Born: 4/29/47, Dayton, OH
Eddie Gray: Guitar
Born: 2/27/48, Pittsburgh, PA
Ronnie Rosman: Keyboards
Born: 2/28/45
Mike Vale: Bass
Born: 7/17/49
Pat Lucia: Drum
Born: 2/2/47
Influences: Elvis Presley, Gene Vincent, Buddy Holly, Everly Brothers
Influenced: Billy Idol, Joan Jett

When a Pittsburgh deejay pulled an obscure, three-year-old 45 to play on his show, he had no idea of the journey on which he was sending young Tommy (Jackson) James and The Shondells, a journey that took them through the late 1960s as one of America's most successful singles acts.

Jackson received his first guitar at age nine and, by 1959, he had formed a school group named The Shondells. They played their first

show at the local American Legion Hall in Niles, Michigan, earning $11. In 1963, they recorded "Hanky Panky" (the B-side of The Raindrops' Jubilee single, "That Boy John") for WNIL deejay Jack Douglas's Snap label and, except for some sales in Michigan and Indiana, it slipped into oblivion.

About three years later, KDKA deejay Bob Lovorro began receiving overwhelming teen response to his play of "Hanky Panky," a record he rescued from the dead pile. With 80,000 sales in ten days, it was inevitable that Jackson would be whisked in for radio and TV shows. When his own band refused to move to Pittsburgh, Jackson drafted a local group, The Raconteurs, and made them The Shondells. Meanwhile, Roulette Records of New York picked up the "Hanky Panky" rights, renamed Jackson "Tommy James," and before long the single was a #1 million seller.

The band signed with Roulette in July 1966 and finished the year with "Say I Am (What I Am)" and "It's Only Love."

It's Only Love.
> *Infectious rocker from the group is a top contender for high chart honors. Powerful performance and arrangement cleverly utilizing maracas has that hit sound. (10/29/66) (#31 Pop)*

1967 began with the record many believe was the beginning of bubblegum, "I Think We're Alone Now." More pop pablum ensued.

I Think We're Alone Now.
> *The "Hanky Panky" group has another hot chart contender in this easy rhythm number with good teen slanted lyric. Good vocal workout and top Jimmy Wisner arrangement. (1/28/67) (#4 Pop)*

Mirage.
> *Their "I Think We're Alone Now" is No. 4 on the Hot 100, and this pulsating rocker should fast top the current smash. (4/22/67) (#10 Pop)*

I Like the Way.
> *Powerful easybeat ballad should quickly match the success of the group's current smash "Mirage." (6/24/67) (#25 Pop)*

Gettin' Together.
> *Powerhouse rocker with the feel and flavor of "Gimmie Some Lovin'" in the arrangement, should prove a fast topper for "I Like [the Way]" with even more sales potential. (8/19/67) (#18 Pop)*

By 1968, Tommy and the boys were trying a harder dance music direction with "One Two Three and I Fell/Mony, Mony"; the flip would become a million seller.

> *Top side is a solid beat rocker much in the hot selling vein of the early James hit. Flip is an equally potent number with a strong beat and wild blues wailing. (2/23/68) (#3 Pop)*

In late 1968, Tommy convinced Roulette he should be producing ("Do Something to Me"). Their biggest hit came in early 1969 with the psychedelic single "Crimson and Clover" selling over five million disks. James's personal favorite, "Crystal Blue Persuasion," went gold.

Sweet Cherry Wine.
> *Powerhouse sales appeal in this swinger with infectious beat and lyric line. (3/15/69) (#7 Pop)*

Crystal Blue Persuasion.
> *Change of pace for James, as he comes up with a powerful summer sound that will fast take him right back up to the top . . . Infectious, easy-beat rhythm. (5/31/69) (#2 Pop)*

In May 1970, Tommy James and The Shondells' last charter together was "Come to Me." By June, Tommy had collapsed on an Alabama stage and The Shondells began a new career as Hog Heaven with one minor chart 45, "Happy," in 1971. James, meanwhile, was recuperating from his nonstop schedule and the pressures that led to drug abuse. His hiatus was short-lived. Tommy was back in the studio by August producing "Alive and Kicking" for Roulette on a song he'd written for himself, "Tighter and Tighter" (#7). His first solo single was "Ball and Chain." Interestingly, the B-side of "Church Street," listed in the review as "no info," was "Draggin' the Line." Six months later it was issued as an A-side and became James's biggest solo single.

Ball and Chain.
> *James, sans the Shondells, follows up his "She" with a solid rocker certain to put him way up the Top 100 with heavy sales. (7/18/70) (#57 Pop)*

Church Street Soul Revival.
> *His fifth release for the year is an infectious, funky blues rocker with a gospel feel and a powerful vocal workout. A sure-fire chart topper for the recent "Ball and Chain." (12/5/70) (Flip: no info)*

Draggin' the Line.
> *This is the driving rhythm item James needed to bring him back to the Top 100 with sales impact. Loaded with Top 40 potential, it could go all the way. (5/29/71) (#4 Pop)*

Tommy left Roulette in 1974 and signed with Fantasy, where he finally cut his own version of "Tighter and Tighter" two years later. In 1980, he signed with Millennium and came up with his last Top-20 title, "Three Times in Love." His influence on later rock 'n' rollers was epitomized in 1987 when Tiffany's version of "I Think We're Alone Now" was elbowed from its #1 position by Billy Idol's cover of "Mony, Mony."

With 14 gold singles and 30 million records sold, Tommy James and The Shondells certainly earned their place in the annals of rock 'n' roll history.

JAN AND DEAN

Jan Berry
Born: 4/3/41, Los Angeles, CA
Dean Torrence
Born: 3/10/40, Los Angeles, CA
Influences: Four Freshmen, Hi-Lo's, Dion and The
    Belmonts, Monotones, Nutmegs, Elegants, Danny
    and The Juniors, Four Coins, Four Lads

The sovereigns of surf music, Jan and Dean amassed 26 hit singles in their eight-year recording career. A key factor in the West Coast's 1960s' image of "fun in the sun music," the duo were friends dating back to their Emerson Junior High days where they were both on the football team. In 1957, they fashioned a foursome of friends into the vocal group, The Barons, with locals Sandy Nelson on drums and Beach Boy-to-be Bruce Johnston on piano.

By 1958, the group had become a trio consisting of Jan, Dean, and Arnie Ginsburg, and began making experimental recordings in Jan's garage. One of their first such trials was a song Berry and Ginsburg wrote, "Jennie Lee," about a stripper with whom Arnie was enamored. The recording wound up at Arwin Records of Beverly Hills (owned by actress Doris Day). Due to Dean's absence for a six-month army reserve hitch, only Berry and Ginsburg's names appeared on the 45 and contracts, even though Torrence sang lead on the song.

Jan and Arnie:
Jennie Lee.

    The duo gives the old Civil War ballad an exciting fling. It's done in novelty fashion and could easily click with the kids. (4/28/58) (#8 Pop, #4 R&B)

Jan and Arnie really were sans Dean for "Bonnie Lou," which, like their first hit, was reviewed inexplicably as "an old Civil War ballad." When their next single, "I Love Linda," flopped, Arnie joined the Army and Dean returned.

In 1959, Jan and Dean met Lou Adler and Herb Alpert of Dore Records and covered The Laurels' "Baby Talk," which was issued as the B-side, a song that *Billboard*'s reviewer strangely found "distasteful." Because no one knew Jan and Dean, the first, now rare, pressings of "Baby Talk" read Jan and Arnie.

Jeanne Get Your Hair Done.

★ ★   *Jan and Dean sell this rocker stylishly over a snappy beat. It's a cute side that could get some coin.*

Baby Talk.

★ ★   *The duo turns in fair reading here of a tale of very young love that is rather distasteful. (6/8/59) (#10 Pop, #28 R&B)*

With two Top-10 hits, the garage duo started churning out better quality but less successful sides. They also continued their educations; Jan was an art major at USC and Dean in pre-med at UCLA.

Clementine.

★ ★ ★ ★ *A rock and roll version of the old familiar folk melody. Side modulates upward at various stages. It's got a good sound and beat and could step.*

You're on My Mind.

★ ★ ★ ★ *The lead here has a good high school type sound. Side makes use of a slight echo effect. It could go. (1/4/60) (#65 Pop)*

Gee.

    The old hit of the Crows is sung in the Crows' style here by the boys and the backing is also in the nostalgic old style. Mighty attractive wax. (10/31/60) (#81 Pop)

A new version of "Heart and Soul" by the boys convinced Alpert their musical direction was not for him. While Adler took the twosome to Gene Autry's Challenge label, Herb formed The Tijuana Brass and became the "A" in A&M Records.

Heart and Soul.

★ ★ ★ ★ *A swingin' rocker arrangement of the standard by the duo. Side has some wild touches in the arrangement and* the boys hand in a commercial vocal reading. It has those "Blue Moon" gimmicks. (6/12/61) (#25 Pop)

Convinced their records would do more with a major label, the pair linked with Liberty in 1962 where they recorded such songs as "Sunday Kind of Love" and "My Favorite Dream." But the move was a temporary disappointment.

Sunday Kind of Love.

The appealing oldie is wrapped up in an exuberant reading and a fast-moving rock and roll beat. Watch it. (11/20/61) (#95 Pop)

The boys revived Ray Noble's 1947 #1 "Linda," which was written by Jack Lawrence about his lawyer's daughter, Linda Eastman, now known as Mrs. Paul McCartney.

Jan and Dean's friendship with The Beach Boys (they met in August 1962 while playing a dance together just as the latter were hitting with "Surfin' Safari") led Adler to recommend that the duo join the surfin' society. With the help of a new Brian Wilson song, they did. With The Beach Boys on harmony, "Surf City" became their biggest single and a million seller. Surf songs alternated with car songs through 1963.

Surf City/She's My Summer Girl.

Two more swinging sides by the hot West Coast team. The first is a solid item that changes the pace from "Linda" but is right in line with the surfing scene. The second has a crystal-clear sound and fits in well with summer vacation time. (6/1/63) (#1 Pop, #3 R&B)

Honolulu Lulu.

The "Surf City" lads are still on the surf kick as they explain about a Honolulu lass who can shoot the curls with the best of them. It's a bright and cheery side with a beat that should have the teen set dancing from the Oahu beaches to the New Jersey shore. (8/31/63) (#11 Pop)

Drag City/Schlock Rod (Part 1).

Jan and Dean turn from surf to track for these red hot entries. First is a fast moving roarer with the boys singing

against strong beat. Second is a comedy side that has hip hot rod gags and "Alley Oop" feel. (11/23/63) (#10 Pop)

Dead Man's Curve/New Girl in School.

The first side is another in the string of red hot hits but this tune is quite different from the pack. Tells the story of a frantic race between dragsters resulting in an epic crash. Flip features high-voice singing and the surf-hot rod sound. (2/29/64) (A-side, #8 Pop; B-side, #37 Pop)

Another smash by the twosome was penned by a deejay (Roger Christian) and a medical student (Dan Altfield), as "The Little Old Lady From Pasadena" sped to #3. "Sidewalk Surfin'" was really a revision of The Beach Boys' "Catch a Wave" (the ellipses were in the original review).

Sidewalk Surfin'.
Seems we've heard this tune before. Hit-making duo . . . new lyric line . . . interesting musical effects. Can't miss! (10/24/64) (#25 Pop)

The dragsters were performing at New York Paramount's Labor Day show with Del Shannon and The Animals, when their new single from Fabian's film was issued.

Ride the Wild Surf.
Movie tune and first rate surfin' sound. Flip: "The Anaheim, Azuza, Cucamonga Sewing Circle, Book Review and Timing Association." West Coast inside joke featuring cute lyrics and surfin' sound. (9/12/64) (A-side, #16 Pop; B-side, #77 Pop)

Things started to slow down in 1965. Owing to an argument over the quality of "You Really Know How to Hurt a Guy," Dean left the studio and only Jan is heard on the cut.

You Really Know How to Hurt a Guy.
The hot new expression is developed into a good piece of teen ballad material, well performed and arranged in a slow dance beat. Can't miss! (5/15/65) (#27 Pop)

A technical failure at a Jan and Dean session (in October 1965) found Torrence wandering over to a Beach Boys session. He was promptly drafted to not only pick an oldie to record, but to sing lead on it. The song was "Barbara Ann," which became a worldwide hit. Because of label politics, Dean's name was not credited as the lead; but he and Jan were incorrectly credited by *Billboard*'s reviewer as the original hit's act when it was actually The Regents.

By late 1965, creative friction was growing. Jan Berry consequently released his first solo single, a strange response record to a popular folk-protest song.

The Universal Coward.

Half of the duo of Jan and Dean has a hot entry in this solo performance of hard-driving and timely material describing the opposite side of "The Universal Soldier." (11/27/65)

In March 1966, the pair was scheduled to do a weekly ABC-TV show and readied themselves for the Elvis Presley film *Easy Come, Easy Go*, but it was not to be. Burdened by his draft notice and pressing for his medical school final, Jan took off in his Corvette. As if he had to bring the prophecy of "Dead Man's Curve" to fruition, on April 12 he and three friends took a 65-mph drive into a parked truck on L.A.'s Whittier Boulevard. Jan was the only survivor and he was paralyzed for many years. Their next release, "Popsicle," released a month after the crash, was their last Top-30 hit.

Popsicle.

Cute summer novelty from the duo aims right at the teen market with swinging dance beat production. (5/14/66) (#21 Pop)

A previously unissued cut, "Fiddle Around," became their last chart single.

Rhythm novelty with clever teen lyric. Left fielder should prove one of their biggest sales entries. Flip: "A Surfer's Dream." (8/20/66) (#93 Pop)

Dean started his own label to keep the name alive and helped pay Jan's medical bills, but his J&D label was not a success. In 1967, Dean signed with Columbia as Jan and Dean. By midyear he had formed his own graphic company,

and began creating award-winning album cover art for many of the era's top acts.

By 1975, Berry recovered sufficiently for Jan and Dean to perform again. In February 1978, ABC TV's bio film, "Dead Man's Curve" revived interest in the duo, and they continued showcasing on and off into the 1990s.

JAY AND THE AMERICANS

John Traynor: Lead vocals (1959–1962)
Born: 11/2/41, Brooklyn, NY
David Blatt (aka Jay Black): Lead vocals (1962–1970)
Born: 11/2/38, Brooklyn, NY
Kenny Rosenberg
Born: 12/9/43, Brooklyn, NY
Sandy Yaguda
Born: 1/30/43, Brooklyn, NY
Howie Kirshenbaum
Born: 6/6/42, Brooklyn, NY
Marty Sanders
Born: 2/28/41, Brooklyn, NY
Influences: Al Jolson, Mario Lanza, Roy Orbison, Four Lads, Four Aces, (Black's influences), Ben E. King's Drifters, Roy Orbison (group's influences)
Influenced: Walker Brothers

More than any act of the 1960s, Jay and The Americans paid tribute to the vocal groups of the 1950s with new versions of songs by The Drifters, Passions, Harptones, Cleftones, and Impressions, among others.

The Brooklyn-bred buddies formed as The Harbor Lights, with Traynor (formerly of The Mystics), Rosenberg, Kirshenbaum, and Yaguda in 1959. They made a couple of small-label singles under this name in 1960.

Is That Too Much to Ask.

★ ★ ★ *The Harbor Lites [sic] sell the rocker in interesting style. They all have high voices and they turn in a most attractive reading of the tune. Good wax here. (4/11/60)*

Tick-a-Tick-a-Tock.

★ ★   *A ballad, with the refrain . . . worked into the arrangement in fugue fashion by various voices. (10/10/60).*

A 1961 meeting with Drifters producers Jerry Leiber and Mike Stoller led to a United Artists contract, but not before the brain trusts at UA decided to rename them, Binky Jones and the Americans! The label settled on the group's antiphon as Jay (John Traynor's nickname) and The Americans, and soon after, the quartet debuted with a New York success, "Tonight." It failed nationally but their sophomore single scored.

Tonight.

★ ★ ★ ★ *The fine Leonard Bernstein tune from "West Side Story;" is given an interesting cha cha rhythm reading from the group. Strong and well arranged side could really step out. (9/18/61)*

She Cried.

A haunting tune soulfully sung by Jay over good support from the group and fine backing by the combo. It could turn this ballad into a good seller. (1/20/62) (#5 Pop)

This Is It/It's Your Turn to Cry.

Two solid sides by the group, just coming off a big hit with "She Cried." On top is a wailing ballad performance in moderate tempo while the flip, another ballad, in the weeper groove, is a bit slower. Both have fine arrangements with good thrush choruses, and both can move out. (6/23/62)

When "This Is It" languished on the radio, Traynor left for what would become a short, undistinguished solo career. Guitarist Marty Sanders moved into the vocal background and brought in his friend, David Blatt (who sang with the Empires, "A Time and a Place") from Tilden High School as lead singer. Rather than change the group's name, Blatt became Jay Black. The name game continued as Rosenberg became Kenny Vance, and Kirshenbaum (a mortician when he wasn't harmonizing) became Howie Kane. The reviewer of "Yes" was on the mark regarding the "Drifters style" as producers Leiber

and Stoller simultaneously had a hit by The Drifters ("When My Little Girl Is Smiling") with the same feel.

Yes.

★ ★ ★ ★ *An interesting piece of material, which employs a Latinish rhythm in the Drifters style. Good lead is ably backed by the group. (9/8/62)*

What's the Use/Stranger Tomorrow.

Two sides that could garner teen attention. Side I is a warm ballad sold by an emotional lead and aided by a classy arrangement. Side II is also a ballad, with a bit of a Latin-styled beat, also with a good and moving job by the lead singer. Both build well, too. (2/16/63)

In 1963, Leiber and Stoller produced a single for The Drifters, "Only in America," but Atlantic Records felt issuing that song with a black group in those racially troubled times was inflammatory. So the producers replaced The Drifters' vocals with Jay and company. It became their first hit with Jay Black as lead.

Only in America.

The strongest effort in a spell for the group. It's got a patriotic flavor to it, in which it extols the opportunities that exist in the U.S.A. and the fact that the gal could go for the guy in this great country. Fine reading and a slick arrangement. Watch it. (7/20/63) (#25 Pop)

The quintet's biggest winner came in late 1963 with "Come a Little Bit Closer" (#3 Pop), which opened the door for their participation in The Beatles' first American tour during early 1964. Two Wes Farrell penned charters followed.

Let's Lock the Door (and Throw Away the Key).

Group tops their current hit with a rouser that moves from start to finish. Fast chart climber. (12/19/64) (#11 Pop)

Think of the Good Times.

Change of pace material as the group tackles a ballad with a slight tempo backing. (3/20/65) (#57 Pop)

By the middle of 1965, the group began recording standards with great success, beginning with "Cara Mia" (#4 Pop) issued as a B-side (and unreviewed by *Billboard*). Another standard followed.

Some Enchanted Evening.
> *Hot on the heels of their smash "Cara Mia," the group puts this "South Pacific" standard in the same vein and it comes up with a smash hit sound. (8/28/65) (#13 Pop)*

Neil Diamond's first hit as a songwriter, "Sunday and Me" was next.

Sunday and Me.
> *As "Some Enchanted Evening" slips down the chart, this rhythm production ballad will hit with impact, hard and fast. (11/6/65) (#18 Pop)*

Why Can't You Bring Me Home.
> *Right up the teen market alley is this hot, pulsating rocker aimed at the top of the chart. (2/12/66) (#63 Pop)*

Crying.
> *The boys revivie Roy Orbison's goldie with a strong rhythm backing and exceptional vocal work in the Orbison style. Could repeat at the top. (5/14/66) (#25 Pop)*

In early 1967, Jay tried his hand at a solo recording, while still fronting the Americans.

Jay Black:
What Will My Mary Say?
> *His solo debut on a fine updating of the Johnny Mathis hit of a few years back. First-rate Gerry Granahan production and Arnold Goland arrangement. (1/14/67)*

French Provincial.
> *One of the group's most unusual and commercial entries in a long time should hit hard and fast. Combining folk, baroque and rock, group is in top form with clever material. (10/28/67)*

No Other Love.
> *The group have a sure-fire hit in this updating of the Rodgers and Hammerstein classic from "Victory at Sea" and "Me and Juliet." Powerful production. (3/9/68)*

Jay and The Americans' 1968 version of "This Magic Moment" even surpassed The Drifters' hit chartwise. More outstanding group remakes, including "Hushabye" and "When You Dance," were forthcoming.

This Magic Moment.
> *The past hit of The Drifters is brought up to date in what could easily prove a hot chart item for this group. One of their most commerical contenders in some time. (11/30/68) (#6 Pop)*

A new decade brought changing musical times that The Americans couldn't keep up with, so they tried to "Capture the Moment." It was their last hit. They followed with a few more cover tunes, and made their last recording in 1971.

Capture the Moment.
> *Change of pace for the group is this top folk flavored ballad that will not only put them up the Hot 100 rapidly, but move them right up the easy listening chart as well. Will pick up additional audience for the top group. (3/7/70) (#57 Pop)*

There Goes My Baby.
> *Group updates the Drifters smash . . . and offers much for top 40. (12/11/71)*

The oldies revival of the 1970s and 1980s kept the group active. Although members come and go, Jay Black still fronts an exciting show in the 1990s. One of only a handful of hit acts to reside with the same label throughout their career, Jay and The Americans' 18 charters in 32 tries certainly qualify them as a team with a Hall of Fame average.

CAROLE KING

Real Name: Carol Klein
Birthdate: 2/9/42
Birthplace: Brooklyn, NY
Influences: Acts that appeared at the Brooklyn
    Paramount, such as Jerry Lee Lewis, Chuck Berry,
    Little Richard, Everly Brothers
Influenced: Little Eva, James Taylor

One of America's premier songwriters of the 1960s, Carole helped initiate the singer/songwriter trend of the 1970s.

Carol learned piano at age five, and by the time she was in high school Carol Klein had her first band, The Co-signs. Although it was Carol who added the "e" to her first name, it was her father, Sid Klein, who named her King to avoid confusion with Patsy Cline. In 1957, Carole met ABC-Paramount's Don Costa, who guided her first recordings.

The Right Girl (A-side) 76
Ballad gets solid reading from rich-voiced chick. Good wax. Some coin possible.

Goin' Wild (B-side) .71
Chick's own rocker gets so-so job, with author submerged in girl group. (5/5/58)

Baby Sittin'.

Miss King has an exciting debut disk that should create quite a name for her. She tells all about her boy-friend on the swingin' side with fine support from a male group and the ork. Teens could easily take to this, if the side is exposed. (3/16/59)

In 1958, while a Queens College student, she met lyricist Gerry Goffin and the two began writing together. Her friendship with neighbor Neil Sedaka led to King and Goffin joining the staff writers at Don Kirshner's and Al Nevins' Al Don Music in 1959. That, in turn, led to her next

recordings, like "Short Mort," which were mostly novelties. When Sedaka hit with "Oh! Carol," which he wrote for King, she tried unsuccessfully to reciprocate.

Oh, Neil.
The thrush has a cute parody of Neil Sedaka's hit, "Oh! Carol." The take-off is clever and amusing, and it's read in multi track style. This should easily catch on. (1/25/60)

The 18-year-old had her first writing hit and #1 with then-husband Goffin on "Will You Love Me Tomorrow" by The Shirelles in 1960. King's writing successes mounted so fast ("Every Breath I Take" for Gene Pitney, "Half Way To Paradise" for Tony Orlando, and "Take Good Care of My Baby" for Bobby Vee), that she didn't get around to recording again until Kirshner formed Dimension Records in 1962. The first Dimension hit was a Goffin/King-penned #1 worldwide smash titled, "The Loco-Motion" performed by the songwriter's babysitter, Little Eva (see Little Eva). The second hit for the label was King's.

It Might as Well Rain Until September.

The lass makes her debut here singing a song penned by husband Gerry Goffin and herself, one of the hottest writing teams in the business. The tune is a first-class rockaballad that's handled in wide style by the songstress against smart arrangement that builds in excitement. (8/11/62) (#22 Pop)

School Bells Are Ringing.

Carole King might have her second hit in a row with this calypso-ish ditty about returning to school and having trouble with her boy. Good teen wax. (11/10/62)

We Grew Up Together/He's a Bad Boy.

These are Carole King's best sides to date. First up is a soft, warm ballad in the country style, and sung in compelling fashion. Flip is a ditty that's bound to have strong impact on teen-dom. (4/6/63) (#94 Pop)

Carole's initial solo career quickly came to an end, but her cowriting career was booming, with hits like "Don't Bring Me Down" (Animals), "Up on the Roof" (Drifters), "One Fine Day" (Chiffons), and "Just Once in My Life" (Righteous Brothers). By 1964, Dimension had folded and King recorded for Atco.

The Road to Nowhere.

A fine Cher-style vocal . . . on own cleverly written off-beat rhythm tune. (3/12/66)

The mighty writing team that was hot on the charts went cold relationship-wise, and by 1967 King and Goffin separated. It put a crimp in her writing until 1968 when she and journalist Al Aronowitz formed Tomorrow Records and released King's "Some of Your Lovin'," which went unnoticed.

King then formed The City with Charles Larkey (bass) and Danny Kortchmer (guitar). King's stagefright hindered the success of their single and album, because she wouldn't tour. The City:

Why Are You Leaving.

Driving, soul-flavored ballad material serves as an impressive and commercial debut for the new group. Producer Lou Adler has a winner here. (6/21/69)

Kortchmer had previously been in The Flying Machine with the then-unknown James Taylor. Taylor's subsequent association with her encouraged Carole to write both lyrics and music and to record again.

In 1970, now living in Los Angeles, King signed as a solo artist with Adler's Ode label and issued a modest-selling debut album. Her next LP, *Tapestry,* became a legend. "It's Too Late" was #1 for five weeks and the album stayed in the top spot for nearly four months! The album sold an amazing thirteen and a half million copies, the most any one LP had ever sold to that date, remaining on the charts almost six years! 1970's creative output earned King four Grammys: Album of the Year, Song of the Year ("You've Got a Friend"), Record of the Year ("It's Too Late") and Best Pop Female Vocalist.

I Feel the Earth Move/It's Too Late.

From her current Top 20 LP, "Tapestry," come two strong sides and

both or either should put her high on the Hot 100. First is a funky beat folk rock ballad, while flip is an equally strong ballad performance. (5/1/71)

So Far Away.

Followup to the million seller "It's Too Late," is also a cut from the "Tapestry" LP and another super ballad performance! (8/21/71) (#14 Pop)

Meanwhile, Taylor's recording of "You've Got a Friend" was #1 in 1971. Records like "Sweet Seasons" (#9) proved King's staying power. She overcame her stagefright to the delight of millions, although her hits slowed up.

Believe in Humanity.

This song has an infectious drive and lilt to it, which is a marked contrast to the other side of the single, "You Light Up My Life". . . . Both songs are gaining fast airplay. "Humanity" is the uptempoed of the two. "Life" is a beautiful ballad offering programmers and listeners two contrasting qualities of this fine songwriter/singer. (6/30/73) (A-side, #28 Pop; B-side, #67 Pop)

Jazzman.

One of the most commercial items this superstar has yet turned out. Slightly more uptempo than other hits, backed by strong saxophone and powerful backup vocals. Watch for this one on pop, easy listening and FM stations. (8/24/74) (#2 Pop)

Nightingale.

Taken from her "Jazzman" LP, and following her number two single of the same name, Ms. King moves back to the style more closely associated with her—the fine soft melodies set off by her distinctive vocalizing. Strong, almost soul backup chorus helps here on this in-between sound of her more recent material and the great things she was writing a decade ago. (12/21/74) (#9 Pop)

In 1975, King created the music for the off-Broadway children's musical "Really Rosie," with the album featuring backups from daughters

Louise and Sherry. 1976 hailed the return of the writing duo of King and Goffin.

Only Love Is Real.

> *Cut already on the Hot 100 at 77 is from new "Thoroughbred" LP. Sounds a bit like "It's Too Late" and is probably the most commercial and most listenable King single since the "Tapestry" days. Return to general simplicity with usual superb lyrics and distinctive vocals. Fine Lou Adler production. (2/14/76) (#28 Pop)*

A move to Capitol produced a gold LP (*Simple Thing*) first time out and a minor hit single, "Hard Rock Cafe."

> *A juicy latin-flavored rocker. The writer-singer's pulsating piano intro punches out beneath a cute lyric about the funky goodtime bar to be found in any worthy neighborhood. Powerful horns add to the cheery funk. This is a blazing mid-tempo drive song, no laid-back mannerisms to slow the intensity. (7/23/77) (#30 Pop)*

During 1980, King finally recorded some of the hits she'd written for others such as "The Loco-Motion," "Chains," "Hi De Ho," and had a hit herself with "One Fine Day" (#12) from the *Pearls* LP. Throughout the 1980s and 1990s, King's desire for a low profile took her to a new home in Stanley, Idaho. In 1987, Carole King was inducted into the Songwriters Hall of Fame.

THE KINGSMEN

Jack Ely: Guitar
Born: 1940s, Portland, OR
Mike Mitchell: Guitar
Born: 1940s, Portland, OR
Don Gallucci: Keyboards
Born: 1940s, Portland, OR
Bob Nordby: Bass
Born: 1940s, Portland, OR

Lynn Easton: Drums
Born: 1940s, Portland, OR
Influences: Wailers, Paul Revere and The Raiders
Influenced: Kinks, Zombies, Searchers

The 1960s' premier garage band, The Kingsmen churned out one of rock's raunchiest classics.

The Pacific Northwest was the setting for the emergence of a group that started as The Journal Juniors in 1957. When a local band, The Kingsmen, broke up, The Juniors confiscated their name and developed a wide following in Oregon. During 1961, a Tacoma, Washington band, The Wailers, heard an old blues rocker recorded in 1956 by Richard Berry and The Pharaohs called "Louie, Louie," which had just been reissued. The Wailers' locally successful version was in turn added to the repertoire of The Kingsmen in 1962, with Jack Ely singing lead.

When The Kingsmen performed "Louie" at deejay Ken Chase's (KISN) "Club Chase," he suggested they record it. They did, but decided to use the recording as an example of their style for a summer stint on a cruise line. (They never did get the job.) The session in May 1963 cost The Kingsmen $38 and was reportedly made in a drunken stupor. The original lyric concerned a customer in a bar talking with the bartender about how he had to go to Jamaica to find his love. When Ely and company were through with it, you could barely interpret more than "Louie, Louie."

The day after The Kingsmen recorded it, Paul Revere and The Raiders cut "Louie" in the same studio. Columbia picked up The Raiders and the local Jerden label signed The Kingsmen, thanks to Chase who sent them a copy. Both singles surfaced, with the initial edge going to Revere. Marvin Schlacter at Scepter/Wand in New York heard about "Louie" from Jerden, but upon hearing it, shelved it. Only after powerful Boston deejay Arnie "Woo Woo" Ginsburg (WMEX) called Marvin, telling him that he'd play it to death if Wand would promote it, did Schlacter issue it in earnest. The record reached into the 30s on the Top 100, then rigor mortis set in. The *Billboard* reviewer seemed to think that the side was recorded by a solo artist.

Louie Louie.

> *Powerful shouting from the lad here on a side that could be his biggest in some time. Roaring sound and exciting back-*

ing make the side go. (10/26/63) (#2 Pop)

Indiana College students hearing "Louie" defined it as a "dirty record." The state's governor, along with many radio stations, then banned it. Naturally, "Louie" took off! Before it became a hit, however, a dispute arose between Easton and Ely. Jack, along with Nordby, left, replaced on drums by Dick Peterson, who became the new "Louie" lead.

The federal government went so far as to hold hearings on the song, subpoenaing Ely and Easton to testify, and wound up redfaced when an FCC investigation determined, "the record to be unintelligible at any speed we played it"!

Because they were literally banned in Boston, the group could only perform at unconventional masquerades, such as fashion shows. They were so hot that acts such as Dionne Warwick were opening for them! The band continued to chart with remakes of Barrett Strong's "Money" (#16, 1964) and The Righteous Brothers' "Little Latin Lupe Lu" (#46, 1964). Meanwhile, Jack formed his own Kingsmen, and the whole situation was thrown into court. As if they didn't have enough trouble, their next major hit, "Jolly Green Giant" was the same melody as The Olympics' "Big Boy Pete."

The Jolly Green Giant.
Dedicated to the vegetable folks, this novelty with riotous lyrics should hit hard and fast! (12/19/64) (#4 Pop, #25 R&B)

The court decision allowed Ely to perform only as "Jack Ely, formerly of The Kingsmen." In 1965, the group cut "Annie Fannie," a comical tribute to a cartoon character in *Playboy;* the melody was the same as "Alley Oop" by The Hollywood Argyles.

The Clime.
New dance gets a rousing beat and wailing vocal from the "Jolly Green Giant" group. (4/24/65) (#65 Pop)

If I Need[ed] Someone.
The George Harrison ballad serves as a powerful hit material and points up the versatility of the group in a smooth new blend of voices. (10/15/66)

Bo Diddley Bach.
This is the infectious item that should bring the "Louie Louie" group back to a high spot on the Hot 100. Loaded with dance appeal and strong production work of Snuff Garrett. (10/28/67)

Their first chart 45 was also their last, as "Louie" re-entered the charts at #97 in 1966.

By 1967, Easton had quit and the band became inactive. They reformed with Peterson and Mitchell in the 1970s. "Louie Louie" became so much a part of 1960s culture that the Washington state legislature considered making it the state song! In 1996, The Kingsmen (Peterson, Mitchell, Barry Curtis, Todd McPhearson, and Steve Peterson) were still at it on the revival circuit, as was "Louie, Louie."

GLADYS KNIGHT AND THE PIPS

Gladys Knight: Lead vocals
Born: 5/28/44, Atlanta, GA
Merald "Bubba" Knight
Born: 9/4/42, Atlanta, GA
Brenda Knight
Born: 3/27/41, Atlanta, GA
William Guest
Born: 6/2/41, Atlanta, GA
Eleanor Guest
Born: 6/26/40, Atlanta, GA
Influences: Jackie Wilson, Flamingos, Frankie Lymon and The Teenagers, Hi-Lo's, Four Freshmen, Hank Ballard and The Midnighters, Platters, Five Royales, McGuire Sisters, Elizabeth Knight
Influenced: Temptations, Sister Sledge

This is one of the greatest and longest-lived of the 1960s African-American vocal groups.

When Merald Knight celebrated his tenth birthday, he had no idea it would be the start of a lifelong career. Nor did his sisters, Gladys and Brenda, or their cousins, William and Eleanor

Guest, but when the five gave an improvised vocal performance for the party guests, a singing group was born.

Gladys had been singing with the Mount Mariah Baptist Church since she was four. At age seven, she won $2,000 on The Ted Mack Amateur Hour performing Nat Cole's "Too Young." The group's name came from an encouraging cousin, James "Pip" Woods, who became the teens' manager. By 1957, he had the quintet working the tour circuit with notables such as Jackie Wilson and Sam Cooke. Wilson brought them to his label, Brunswick, for their debut disc.

Whistle My Love 68
Blues group does a good vocal with a touch of spiritual quality in the reading.

Ching Chong 67
A rock and roller with an Oriental flavor. Sung in a blues, chanted wail. (1/27/58)

In 1959, Brenda and Eleanor heard wedding bells and were replaced by two more cousins, Edward Patten and Langston George.

The group recorded again in 1961 for the local Hunton label, releasing their first hit, "Every Beat of My Heart." When their single erupted, Hunton licensed it through Vee-Jay. Bobby Robinson, head of Fury Records, heard the record and, finding that the family was unsigned, whisked them to New York to record "Every Beat of My Heart" again. This was one of the few times an act had the same song on two separate labels, with two different recordings, on the charts at the same time!

Every Beat of My Heart (Vee-Jay).
★ ★ ★ ★ *Feelingful warbling by the lead singer and group on a beautiful rockaballad. Dual market appeal. (5/1/61) (#6 Pop, #1 R&B)*

Every Beat of My Heart (Fury).
★ ★ ★ ★ *Heartfelt warbling by canary and group on gospel flavored rockaballad. Lass can really sell a tune. (5/8/61) (#45 Pop, #15 R&B)*

Gladys Knight and The Pips continued turning out fine singles until Gladys married in 1962; George also left that year.

Guess Who.

The gal and the group should have another hit with this attractive ballad which is sold with heart and feeling. (7/17/61)

Letter Full of Tears.

The thrush sings with feeling and heart on a moving rockaballad with bluesy flavor. Another dual market item. Cute backing by the Pips. (11/13/61) (#19 Pop, #3 R&B)

After the birth of her first child, Gladys returned and the group (now a quartet) recorded several superior singles, including the Van McCoy-penned "Giving Up" in 1964 for Maxx Records. By 1966, they joined a Motown package tour as special guests and were soon linked with Motown's Soul affiliate. Gladys and company recorded "I Heard It Through the Grapevine" a year before Marvin Gaye's #1 version. His recording overshadowed their original, even though The Pips' original sold well over a million copies.

I Heard It Through the Grapevine.
Pulsating pile driver . . . Loaded with electricity and soul, it should ride straight to the top. (10/14/67) (#2 Pop, #1 R&B)

The End of Our Road.
With all the pulsating rhythm of "I Heard It Through the Grapevine," group has a sure-fire, wailing winner in this mover. Headed right for the top. (2/3/68) (#15 Pop, #5 R&B)

If I Were Your Woman.
Driving blues ballad . . . Loaded with potential for the charts . . . Hot 100 and Soul. Flip: "The Tracks of My Tears." (11/14/70) (#9 Pop, #1 R&B)

Neither One of Us (Wants to Be the First to Say Goodbye).
Ms. Knight is right back in the middle of the hitmaker groove with a hard-driving yet powerfully-worded record that simply does everything right. Sure-fire pop crossover potential. . . . (1/13/73) (#2 Pop, #1 R&B)

In 1973, feeling neglected at Soul, Gladys and the boys bonded with Buddah. The label change finally brought the group consistent success on the charts.

Where Peaceful Waters Flow.

There's lots of care going into this first production on Buddah, with a rich, willowy background sound incorporating gentle guitar and harp and a slow tempo which allows Gladys to show off her powerfully soulful voice as she offers a helping hand pointing to happiness. (6/2/73) (#28 Pop, #6 R&B)

The million-selling "Midnight Train to Georgia" was first called "Midnight Plane to Houston" before producer Sonny Limbo changed it for his original version with Cissy Houston (mother of Whitney Houston). Another gold single ensued.

Midnight Train to Georgia.

The group sings slowly and sadly about crushed dreams in the big city. Gladys cries about having to be without her man back home, and that he's coming back to find what's left of their world together. (8/18/73) (#1 Pop, #1 R&B)

I've Got to Use My Imagination.

Follow to "Midnight Train" is more upbeat and showcases more powerful vocals from Gladys with strong backup from the group. Strong horn breaks and repetition in chorus highlight cut. (11/17/73) (#4 Pop, #1 R&B)

In 1974, The Pips won two Grammys, for Best Vocal Performance by a Group ("Neither One of Us") and Best R&B Vocal Performance by a Group ("Midnight Train to Georgia").

They also recorded the soundtrack for the film *Claudine* that year, another gold performance, along with further top R&B hits.

Best Thing that Ever Happened to Me.

A sobbing type of love refrain, medium in tempo, with pretty strings, but all formula slickness, with the leader's powerful voice the dominant instrument. (2/9/74) (#3 Pop, #1 R&B)

On and On.

Usual excellent job from the group that rarely misses. This time they're back in the up-tempo vein, with exchanges between Gladys and the group the spotlight. Song should be strong in pop and soul. (5/14/74) (#5 Pop, #2 R&B)

I Feel a Song (in My Heart).

It's unlikely that Gladys Knight could make a bad record, and this one, with her usual superb vocal stylizing backed by the masterful harmonizing of the Pips is one of her best. This mid tempo cut features Gladys mixing soft and throaty vocals, complicated musical changes, and should add up to another across the board hit for these veteran hit makers. (10/5/74) (#21 Pop, #1 R&B)

In 1975, their popularity was so great that NBC-TV gave the quartet a summer replacement variety series. During 1976, Gladys began an acting career, starting with the film *Pipe Dreams*. Meanwhile, contractual complications led to The Pips (sans Gladys) recording two unsuccessful albums for Casablanca, while she did a solo LP for Buddah. They were back together in 1980 on Columbia with "Landlord" and their only other early 1980s' hit, "Save the Overtime."

Save the Overtime (for Me).

For all their years of experience, Knight and the Pips can come out sounding as fresh and contemporary as any group on the charts. This sleek production has all the rhythmic elements of the current crop of dance-funk hits, with the added benefit of Knight's formidable force of personality. (4/2/83) (#66 Pop, #1 R&B)

The foursome gained a new lease on life in 1986 when they united with MCA.

Love Overboard.

They're back with a potential monster, the Calloways ("Jump Start," "Casanova") provide the perfect r.&b. setting for the always-in-sync vocal outfit. (11/7/87) (#13 Pop, #1 R&B)

Lovin' on Next to Nothin'.

The "All Our Love" album is nearing the No. 1 slot, and with good reason, given its abundance of chartworthy material; this is in the same groove as "Love Overboard." (2/20/88) (#3 R&B)

Gladys Knight:
License to Kill.

Theme from the forthcoming James Bond film finds Knight's vocal reigning supreme in a lush ballad setting. (5/13/89)

Popular worldwide, Gladys and the family are in their fifth decade of recording and touring. They were inducted into the Rock and Roll Hall of Fame in 1996.

BRENDA LEE

Real Name: Brenda Mae Tarpley
Birthdate: 12/11/44
Birthplace: Lithonia, GA
Influences: Hank Williams, Mahalia Jackson, Billie
    Holliday, Bessie Smith, Edith Piaf, Carmen McRae,
    Frank Sinatra, Judy Garland, Al Jolson, Mel Tormé,
    Tony Bennett
Influenced: Elton John, Barbara Mandrell, Dolly Parton

Known consecutively as Little Miss Brenda Lee, Little Brenda Lee, and Little Miss Dynamite (because of her petite physical stature but big voice), Brenda Lee was the most successful crossover artist of the 1960s. Starting as an impassioned country vocalist in the 1950s, she switched to rock 'n' roll through the 1960s and, when the pop chart well ran dry, she captivated country listeners through the 1970s and 1980s.

In 1951, at age seven, Brenda was already a veteran of local Atlanta radio and TV. In 1956, she met manager Dub Albritton, who arranged an appearance on Red Foley's regional programs, such as Ozark Jubilee and national shows, including the Ed Sullivan Show.

Her recording career began that year for Decca, although a blues artist on Apollo put the Brenda Lee name on wax first. Amazingly, "Little Brenda" went on to have six hits on the R&B charts between 1957 and 1963.
Little Brenda Lee:

Bigelow/Jambalaya.

This nine-year-old country chick has the projection, voice and sincerity that can skyrocket her to great heights, not only in the country field but in the pop field as well. On this strong two-sided disk she also has the material for a most impressive debut on wax. "Bigelow," with her bright-eyed rendition, is a tune that could catch, while on the flip she takes the Hank Williams oldie for a real ride. (9/22/56)

Brenda, who would become known for her Christmas recordings, began the tradition in 1956. Her first chart 45, "One Step at a Time," followed.

I'm Gonna Lasso Santa Claus.

This nine year old singer currently getting attention due to her "Jambalaya" waxing, has a loud, piercing voice reminiscent of Barry Gordon. She also has a lot of style and know how for her age, and so this Hollywood opus will have to be watched.

Christy Christmas.

A cute, bouncy tune with a catchy melody, this will have strong pop and hillbilly appeal in the moppet department. (11/3/56)

One Step at a Time.

The young lady essays the hiccup approach in this rocking rendition. An exciting job that has strong potential for spins and sales. (1/26/57) (#43 Pop, #15 C&W)

With Brenda's next release, "Dynamite" (as a B-side), the Decca brass revised her nickname to "Little Miss Dynamite."

Dynamite . . . . **.79**

Personable belting job on rhythm tune . . . complete with incongruous but cute growl-sounds. (5/27/57) (#72 Pop)

Ain't That Love 86

Young thrush socks out a sensational rendition of the Ray Charles r.&b. hit. Fine styling and rocking beat could score both pop and country. One to watch. (8/19/57)

In 1958, Decca issued another Christmas single but it didn't catch on for two years, after which it became a seasonal standard.

Rockin' Around the Christmas Tree.

★ ★ ★ ★ *The youngster has a good, easy reading of a new Johnny Marks Christmas tune. This can get spins in country and pop areas. (11/17/58) (#14 Pop, 1960)*

Hummin' the Blues Over You.

★ ★ *Brenda Lee rocks over the lyrics in this listenable effort in a semi-rockabilly kick. Nice side could get some attention. (12/29/58)*

Lee's initial Pop Top-10 disk and first million seller, "Sweet Nothin's," was reviewed as "the throwaway side."

Weep No More My Baby (A-side).

★ ★ ★ *Brenda Lee sails into a nifty new novelty based on the Stephen Foster tune to good results here. Thrush has a chance for coins with this one.*

Sweet Nothin's (B-side).

★ ★ ★ *A rocker is sung with spirit by the thrush over a tricky ork backing. Cute intro features a lad saying "sweet nothin's" to the thrush. (9/28/59) (#4 Pop)*

In March 1959, the 18-year-old was scheduled to play the Olympia in Paris until the French promoters, believing they were getting an adult, learned of her age and canceled the show. Albritton then spread a rumor through the press that Lee was actually a 32-year-old midget and she wound up performing for five weeks!

Brenda hit her stride in 1960 with more gold singles; the classic "I'm Sorry" was again issued as a B-side. More of the same came in 1961.

That's All You Gotta Do/I'm Sorry.

 The little lass with a big voice comes thru with a sock reading of a rhythm tune on the top side, and then sells a ballad with wistful tenderness. (5/16/60) (A-side, #6 Pop; B-side, #1 Pop)

I Want to Be Wanted/Just a Little.

 The petite thrush has two more tremendous sides here, the top one a ballad, and the second side a rhythm tune. On each she comes thru with a heartfelt vocal. (9/5/60) (A-side, #1 Pop, B-side, #40 Pop)

Emotions/I'm Learning About Love.

 Two great sides for the tiny thrush. On top is "Emotions" which is patterned closely on the idea of "I'm Sorry" her recent smash. The flip is a wild, happy rocker. Gal really shouts it out here. Either way. (12/26/60) (A-side, #7 Pop; B-side, #33 Pop)

You Can Depend on Me/It's Never Too Late.

 Two very moving sides by the fine young thrush. The first is the old standard with exceptional warmth and heart at an unusually slow tempo. The flip is another ballad sung with great emotion by the gal, embellished effectively by a wide string background. (3/20/61) (#6 Pop)

Eventually/Dum Dum.

 The canary has another smash in "Eventually," a moving ballad. Flip is a catchy item with gospel-flavored organ backing. The young star is in top-flight vocal form on both sides. (6/12/61) (A-side, #56 Pop; B-side, #4 Pop)

Fool #1/Anybody but Me.

The best selling artist has another two-sided smash in this disc. "Fool #1" is a fine country-oriented weeper with rich ork and chorus backing. Flip is a bluesy item with an easy, swinging treatment by the thrush. Both sides are strong. (9/18/61) (A-side, #3 Pop; B-side, #31 Pop)

After the Jackie DeShannon penned "Dum Dum" smash and emotive "Fool #1," it was Christmas time again with a repeat of "Rockin'

Around the Christmas Tree." In 1962, Brenda continued pouring her heart out into hits.

Break It to Me Gently/So Deep.

The thrush is in her usually sock vocal form on both sides of this potential smash. "Break It to Me Gently" is a bluesy ballad with a moving weeper-styled lyric. The flip is a catchy rhythm item with an infectious tempo. (1/6/62) (A-side, #4 Pop; B-side, #52 Pop)

Everybody Loves Me but You/Here Comes That Feelin'.

The young thrush has two more potential winners here. On top is an unusually strong ballad, handled with great warmth. Flip is a smart rhythm styling with a solid performance and strong arrangements. Either or both here. (4/7/62) (A-side, #6 Pop; B-side, #89 Pop)

Save All Your Lovin' for Me/All Alone Am I.

Two fine, contrasting sides for Brenda here. First up is a breezy rocker which she delivers in her own telling rockin' style. Flip is an interesting Hadjidakis ballad done in the European tradition with a rich ork backing. Both can happen. (9/15/62) (A-side, #53 Pop; B-side, #3 Pop)

Although "Everybody Loves Me but You" was a stateside winner, Brenda had her biggest hit in England, with "Speak to Me Pretty" (#3), from the children's film *The Two Little Bears,* in which Lee had a small role. "Pretty" was never issued in America but at the rate she was having hits, its absence was inconspicuous.

On December 30, 1962, the world almost lost "Little Miss Dynamite" when she attempted to rescue her poodle from a fire in her Nashville home. Although the pet died, Brenda was only slightly injured. Once again, Brenda had a big hit B-side with "Too Many Rivers."

As Usual/Lonely, Lonely, Lonely Me.

The first is a lovely ballad sung in the great tradition. The flip is a middle tempo swinger in which Brenda gets a beguiling Fats Domino sound that's most appealing. (11/30/63) (#12 Pop)

No One.

By far one of her strongest ballad offerings to date which should spiral to the top of the charts. Flip: "Too Many Rivers." (5/15/65) (A-side, #98 Pop; B-side, #13 Pop)

Approaching the age of 21 in 1965, Lee had already recorded over 250 sides and was named The Most Programmed Female Vocalist in America, in 1961 through 1965. In 1966, she had her last Top-20 pop entry, "Coming on Strong." Also in 1966, Decca issued an album few artists could justify; entitled *Ten Golden Years,* it contained one of her hits for each year, 1956 to 1965.

Coming on Strong.

This strong swinger could be the one to put Miss Lee back up on the top half of the chart. Good material and dance beat. (9/10/66) (#11 Pop)

Her last of 52 pop charters was "Nobody Wins" (#70, #3 country, 1973), and by then Brenda was deeply immersed in the creatively comfortable country market. In 1980, she had a small part in the Burt Reynolds film *Smokey and the Bandit II.* Lee continues to perform on the country music circuit today.

BOBBY LEWIS

Birthdate: 2/17/33

Birthplace: Indianapolis, IN

Influences: Billy Eckstine, Paul Robeson, Big Joe Turner, LaVern Baker, Ruth Brown, Dinah Washington, Della Reese

Influenced: Cleftones

The phrase "one good turn deserves another" aptly fits the king of 1961, Bobby Lewis.

Having been born and brought up in an orphanage, the good-natured youth showed an early talent for music, and was playing piano at age five while singing in the school glee club. He was adopted in 1945 and moved to Detroit with his new family. By the time he was 16, Bobby had been an ice man, a truck driver, and a janitor, and he had also been featured regularly on a local radio show and found singing to be his calling. He became a vagabond blues artist, playing clubs (like The Chesterfield Lounge and the Twenty Grand) and theaters throughout the Midwestern states.

In the early 1950s, he struck up a friendship with Dominoes' lead singer Jackie Wilson while working in a Detroit nightclub. Jackie's manager brought Lewis to Parrot records label owner Al Benson, who gave Bobby his first recording shot with "My Love Is Solid as a Rock." He then moved to Spotlight.

Memphis Blues 76
Good version of the novelty blues in rapid tempo. Some funny lines. (3/10/56)

Later in 1956, Bobby was appearing at the Fox Theater with LaVern Baker, The Cadillacs, and a young, nervous, novice act named The Cleftones. The teens had no song charts and didn't even know what they were, so Bobby helped them out, and to this day Cleftones lead Herbie Cox still refers to Lewis as their "show business father." Bobby's career, however, was not helped out by this act of kindness. In 1958, he recorded for Mercury, recutting his first Spotlight single.

Memphis Blues 67
A snappy, fairly swinging upbeat blues by the new artist. Material is no great shakes but the artist could get attention with latter sides. He has energy and enthusiasm, anyway. (1/6/58)

Yes, Yes, I Feel So Gay 75
Vociferous vocal by Lewis and group with strong backing. Good possibilities. (3/31/58)

In 1960, Wilson (who was now a star attraction thanks to hits like "Lonely Teardrops") urged Bobby to come to New York, even sending him money for a train ticket. New York did not exactly open its arms to Bobby, as record label after record label turned him down and even Wilson couldn't help. Lewis did work at a few clubs and spent a week at The Apollo Theater where, once again, he met a nervous young group about to per-

form. The act, known as The Fireflies (who had a hit, "You Were Mine," in 1959), had good reason to be fearful because The Apollo crowd was the toughest around and thought nothing of booing a black act, let alone three white teens. Bobby went beyond the call of duty to calm and encourage them.

A month later, Lewis was making the record company rounds again when he came upon a new label, Beltone Records. He went in for an audition with the owner Les Cahan and A&R man Joe Rene while one of their artists looked on. As Bobby sang, he realized the artist was Ritchie Adams, leader of The Fireflies. When Lewis finished his song, Ritchie, obviously trying to return the Apollo favor, pulled out a song for Bobby to try. The match was made in solid-gold heaven as Bobby put histouch on "Tossin' and Turnin'."

Tossin' and Turnin'.
★ ★ ★ *Bobby Lewis tries hard on this material, but in spite of good backing by group and chorus, it's only fair wax. (2/13/61) (#1 Pop, #1 R&B)*

Billboard's reviewer wasn't thrilled with "Tossin'," but the public was, as it spent seven weeks at #1 and became the biggest record of 1961. In fact, of all the records in the rock era, "Tossin' and Turnin'" placed #23 on the all-time Top 1000 compiled by *Billboard* chart historian Joel Whitburn.

Lewis's followup was also a hit, but he soon fell to the lower ends of the charts.

One Track Mind.
 Bright rock and roll effort. It should be another hit for the chanter. (8/21/61) (#9 Pop, #8 R&B)

What a Walk.
 The "Tossin' and Turnin'" lad has a ball with this swinging, twisting styled side. A bright job with backing to match. Watch it. (11/20/61) (#77 Pop)

Mamie in the Afternoon.
 A catchy rhythm tune from the forthcoming Broadway musical "Family Affair" is wrapped up in a showmanly vocal treatment by Lewis and a femme group. A solid dual market—pop and r.&b.—entry. (1/20/62)

His chart run ended in 1962 with his own answer record to "Tossin' and Turnin'," which was backed by The Angels.

I'm Tossin' and Turnin' Again.

★ ★ ★ ★ *Bobby Lewis returns to the scene of his first hit with a sock performance of a swinging effort that could turn into a big one. It goes—watch it. (6/23/62) (#98 Pop)*

Further recordings through the 1980s failed to do much to revive his career. Bobby continues to work theaters and clubs into the 1990s, thanks to the legacy of his hit.

JERRY LEE LEWIS

Birthdate: 9/29/35
Birthplace: Ferriday, LA
Influences: Al Jolson, Jimmie Rodgers, Gene Autry
Influenced: Rolling Stones, Bruce Springsteen, Creedence Clearwater Revival, Paul Revere and The Raiders, Bobby Vee, many more

Nicknamed "The Killer" in high school, that's exactly what Jerry Lee did to audiences and record buyers for 40 years of his rockin' & rollin' life.

Elmo Lewis's son Jerry showed such an aptitude for music that dad bought him a piano and hauled it around on a flatbed truck so the boy could play local shows. His musical influences were a cross-section of pop, rockabilly, gospel, country and western, and blues, but by the time the public at large heard him, he was what many would call the epitome of 1950s rock 'n' roll.

In 1949, Lewis's first performance, at age 14, was in the parking lot of a Ford dealer in Natchez, where he earned $9 for singing songs like "Drinkin' Wine Spo-Dee O'Dee" with a country and western band. Between his 14th and 21st birthday, Lewis was more than occupied by bible school (until he was expelled), playing clubs, and getting married (first at age 16 to a 17-year-old and then in a shotgun wedding to Jane Mitchum).

In 1956, Lewis went to Memphis, auditioned for Sun Records, and met house producer Jack

Clement, who steered Lewis's piano style in a rock 'n' roll direction similar to an artist Sun had just lost to RCA named Elvis Presley. Lewis's debut 45 was a former Ray Price country hit "Crazy Arms." Surprisingly, Lewis started as a shy performer but when Carl Perkins (who was then touring with Lewis and Johnny Cash) told him, "make a fuss!" the real Lewis exploded the very next night with kicked stools, pounding piano, and all.

Crazy Arms/End of the Road.

An exceptionally strong entrant by a new artist is this flavor-packed disk. His reading of "Crazy Arms" shows a powerful feeling for country blues, and his sock warbling is accompanied by a Domino-type piano backing which brings a distinct New Orleans feeling to the rendition. Flip is another honey, right in the rhythm groove abetted by the same piano beat. Disinctly smart wax. (12/22/56)

On December 4, 1956, Cash, Presley, Perkins, and Lewis were all at Sun Studios when an extemporaneous recording session broke out. These tracks were later immortalized as "The Million Dollar Quartet" recordings. Actually, Cash was not on those recordings, as his wife insisted that they go shopping, thereby making the much-publicized quartet, in fact, a trio.

In May 1957, Jerry recorded one of rock's definitive 45s, "Whole Lot of Shakin' Goin' On." At first, the single was banned for being vulgar, but by July it had sold over 100,000 copies, mostly in the South. Then Lewis let loose on Steve Allen's TV show and the record astounded the naysayers to the tune of six million plus sales. Another rock 'n' roll classic followed.

Whole Lot of Shakin' Goin' On/It'll Be Mine.

A recent Billboard *talent nomination, Lewis comes thru with what should be a sure hit, in a driving blues shouter in the typical Sun tradition. Flip rockabilly could go too, on strength of another top performance and cute lines. (5/27/57) (#3 Pop, #1 R&B, #1 C&W)*

Great Balls of Fire/You Win Again.

Lewis pours his all into "Fire," a rockabilly tune which he performs in the

flick *"Jamboree."* Side appears a strong bet to match the success of *"Whole Lot of Shakin' Goin' On."* Flip is an appealing styling of Hank Williams's old hit that should also be a winner. Both sides figure in all markets. *(11/11/57) (#3 Pop, #1 R&B, #1 C&W)*

Lewis was a last-minute inclusion in the film *Jamboree* and the song "Great Balls of Fire" was given to him by the film's musical director, Otis Blackwell. The picture also starred Fats Domino, Connie Francis, Frankie Avalon, Carl Perkins, and 18 nationally powerful deejays such as Dick Clark and Jocko Henderson. (Not a bad way to get your record played when the movie hit theaters!) Lewis's "Great Balls" sold over five million copies but was kept from #1 by Danny and The Juniors' "At the Hop."

Before his next single, "Breathless," could reach radio, Jerry's career was nearly crippled. While on tour in England with his third bride, second-cousin Myra Gale Brown, the press and public were shocked to learn that Myra was only 13! The British audience was scandalized, and Lewis was booed off the stage, his shows were canceled, and his next single, "High School Confidential," was cut down in its prime.

Breathless/Down the Line.

Two rockabilly blues . . . The artist is at his energetic best on both sides, and both appear strong bets to make it. (2/17/58) (#7 Pop, #3 R&B)

High School Confidential/Fools Like Me.

Lewis belts "Confidential," a crazy, swingin' rocker, in his usual frantic style. It's the title tune from a forthcoming flick in which he does a guest stint. Flip, "Fools," is in more of a traditional country vein, and the artist is backed by a chorus. Strong stuff for all markets. (5/19/58) (A-side, #21 Pop, #5 R&B; B-side, #11 R&B)

Lewis continued turning out driving, spirited singles but radio turned off to him and he would never again have a Top-20 pop chart hit.

Break-Up/I'll Make It All Up to You.

"Break-Up" is a rocker, and Lewis sells the tune with great drive and spirit. His pounding style of piano is promi-

nent in support. Flip, "I'll Make It" is a country and western ballad read along traditional lines. Chorus and ork support help sell the side. It's a strong contender and a likely tri-market click. *(9/1/58) (A-side, #52 Pop; B-side, #85 Pop)*

I'll Sail My Ship Alone.

★ ★ ★ ★ *Lewis's first disk in a spell is set in medium rhythm framework with a boogie woogie piano by Lewis against his good vocal. (12/1/58) (#93 Pop)*

Far from discouraged, "The Killer" was still a "mind-blowing" performer. On one occasion he was denied the prestigious position of closing an Alan Freed show by Chuck Berry. Forced to be the opening act, he did three minutes of electrifying rock 'n' roll, poured lighter fluid on his piano, set it afire, and left the stage with the immortal message, "I'd like to see any son of a bitch follow that!"

Big Blon' Baby/Lovin' Up a Storm.

The pumpin' piano cat has two frantic sides. His energetic vocals on each have the hit sound. "Big Blon' Baby" is a rockabilly song that's given a driving vocal. "Lovin'" is performed at a slower clip, but is rendered with equal excitement. Strong c.&w. appeal also. (3/2/59)

In February 1958, Myra gave birth to a son who Jerry named after the man who helped his first hit, Steve Allen Lewis. Never seemingly humbled and sometimes menacing, Jerry was prone to tell an unenthusiastic audience, "If you don't like what I'm doing you can kiss my ass!!"

I Could Never Be Ashamed of You/Little Queenie.

Lewis has two powerful outings that with exposure could easily coast in. "I Could Never" is a fine revival of the Hank Williams side. "Little Queenie" is a rhythmatic belt of Chuck Berry's hit of a season or so ago. Both rate spins. (9/28/59)

What'd I Say.

It's been a long dry spell for Lewis but this outstanding rendition of the Ray Charles song . . . can bring him back,

with proper push. Lewis's pumping piano work is tops and the vocal matches it. This can go. (3/6/61) (#30 Pop, #26 R&B)

Save the Last Dance for Me.

★ ★ ★ ★ *A showmanly reading . . . on the infectious recent hit for the Drifters and Damita Jo. Could break out again, especially with this solid, rocking performance. (9/11/61)*

Money.

★ ★ ★ ★ *Heavy blues styling from Lewis here with punching beat and big bands sounds in the background. The boy also plays some mean piano. Good wax. (12/4/61)*

How's My Ex Treating You.

This moving treatment . . . of a country weeper, which features his exciting piano work, could turn into his best record in over a year. It spots a mighty good vocal performance by the singer on a strong lyric and the wild pianoing is there too. Flip "Sweet Little Sixteen." (7/21/62)

Good Golly Miss Molly.

★ ★ ★ ★ *This was once a smash for Little Richard and Jerry and his pumping piano hand it a rousing reading. A lot going on here. This side pulsates. (11/17/62)*

By 1963, Jerry left sun for Smash. In 1968, Lewis switched to country music and, although the change was a minor adaptation for him, it did wonders for his career. He had more than 40 country hits between 1968 and the 1990s, including "To Make Love Sweeter for You" (1968), "Would You Take Another Chance on Me" (1971), and "Chantilly Lace" (1971), all #1s.

Once More with Feeling.

Lewis rode right up to the top of the country charts with his "She Even Woke Me Up to Say Goodbye" hit and now he has even more potential with a smooth, rhythm ballad that should fare even better. Top material, performance and production. (1/13/70) (#2 C&W)

His last pop charter was his 1949 favorite, "Drinking Wine, Spo-Dee O'Dee" (#41, 1973). On April 23, 1981, Lewis, Cash, and Perkins, the three survivors of the 1956 Sun session, did a concert for German television that later became a 1982 LP, *The Survivors.* That time, Cash did not go shopping! Two months later, "The Killer" was hospitalized with a stomach ulcer and was given a 50/50 chance of recovery. Damning the odds, he was on the road by year's end. In 1986, Jerry Lee was one of the first inductees to the Rock and Roll Hall of Fame. A movie biopic starring Dennis Quaid (whom Jerry taught piano for the part) in 1989 brought renewed attention to the aging rocker.

Crazy Arms.

Rock'n'raucous Lewis remains in spirited voice and his piano bashing continues as rambunctious as ever in this soundtrack release that should benefit from the "Great Balls of Fire" movie hoopla. (9/12/89)

By the time Jerry Lee Lewis saw the movie he had been married six times, had four books written about him, and was one of America's most colorful rock 'n' roll legends.

LITTLE ANTHONY AND THE IMPERIALS

Anthony Gourdine: Lead vocals
Born: 1/8/40, Brooklyn, NY
Tracy Lord: First tenor
Born: 1940s, Brooklyn, NY
Ernest Wright, Jr.: Second tenor
Born: 8/24/41, Brooklyn, NY
Clarence Collins: Bass
Born: 3/17/41, Brooklyn, NY
Glouster Rogers: Baritone
Born: 1940s, Brooklyn, NY
Influences: Flamingos, Ella Fitzgerald, Nat "King" Cole
Influenced: Delphonics, Ronettes, Shangri-Las, Shirelles, Capris, Marcels

One of rock's great vocal groups, Little Anthony and The Imperials were one of the few acts of the 1950s to competitively survive in the changeable 1960s.

Starting with pop songs as a preteen on New York's Startime Studio TV show, Gourdine became a Boys High School student with singing-group aspirations. In 1954, he and friends William "Doc" Dockery, William Delk, and Bill Bracey created The Duponts, named after a Dupont paint sign. One of their "battle of the groups" appearances pitted the quartet against a young Harlem aggregation known as Frankie Lymon and The Teenagers.

The Duponts met songwriter Paul Winley in 1956. He was so impressed that he recorded them and then started his own Winley label with "Must Be Falling in Love."

Must Be Falling in Love **68**
> *Tone and treatment are close to several of the disks by the Teen-Agers. Slim chance here, unless the disk can get extra heavy pushing. (8/25/56)*

Without promotion, the record was doomed from inception, as was their 1957 Royal Roost effort, "Prove It Tonight." The gang then broke up after performing on Alan Freed's Easter show with The Cleftones, The Cadillacs, and Frankie Lymon, among others.

In 1957, Gourdine joined a neighborhood group needing a lead singer, and The Chesters were spawned. During 1958, a member of The Cellos introduced The Chesters to Apollo records' Charles Merenstein. A colorful *Billboard* review did not help the record achieve chart success.

The Fire Burns No More **73**
> *Group has the wild, and somewhat desperate quality that can click with exposure. Fervant, high lead gets a cacophonic backing by the group. Interesting hunk of wax.*

Lift Up Your Head **70**
> *On this side, the group has a bouncier tune, with the lead again showing an interesting meshuga quality. Flip would be the choice here. (2/10/58)*

By mid-1958, The Chesters cajoled End Records' Richard Barrett into signing them. Label executive George Goldner bumped Ernest Wright from lead-singing duties, pulling Gourdine out front; he also insisted they record a song, "Tears on My Pillow," that no one in the group liked. The 45 was issued under a new group name picked by promo man Lou Galley without their knowledge, and so The Chesters became, simply but eloquently, The Imperials. One night shortly after its release, Anthony sat on a park bench listening to Alan Freed announce, "here's a new record that's making a lot of noise, Little Anthony and The Imperials and 'Tears on My Pillow'." Goldner took the hint and Little Anthony was born, along with a million seller.

The Imperials:
Tears on My Pillow (A-side) **79**
> *Lead voice is given strong group backing on this pretty rockaballad. Side has a chance.*

Two People in the World (B-side) **74**
> *Salable sound by the mixed group on a rockaballad against a falsetto voice in counterpoint. It can cop both pop and r&b loot. (7/21/58) (#4 Pop, #2 R&B)*

The Imperials could have made it two in a row but Barrett issued a single he wrote against Goldner's instructions. Although a beautiful ballad, "So Much" couldn't match the chart potential of George's choice, a Neil Sedaka-penned tune Goldner recorded with The Imperials called "The Diary." When it wasn't released, Sedaka had his own hit with it. End belatedly issued "The Diary" but it couldn't catch Neil's version. Several strong but underpromoted sides followed through 1959.

So Much.

> *Somewhat along the lines of "Tears on My Pillow." Anthony's fine vocal is given listenable group support. Tune is a rockaballad. (10/27/58) (#87 Pop, #24 R&B)*

Wishful Thinking/When You Wish Upon a Star.

> *Little Anthony and crew appear to be in chart form again on these two fine efforts. "Wishful Thinking" is similar in sound to "Tears on My Pillow," the group's first click. "When You Wish," the oldie, is also wrapped up in saleable rockaballad style. Two potent sides. (1/19/59) (#79 Pop)*

A Prayer and a Juke Box.

Anthony gives out with a meaningful chant on "Prayer," a slow organ backed side. He appears to have developed a new style. (5/18/59) (#81 Pop)

I'm Alright.

★ ★ ★ ★ *Spiritual derived rocker is given a lusty belt by Anthony with a vigorous group assist. Side bears watching. (7/20/59)*

Gourdine always felt his next 45 was just plain "stupid" but it became their second biggest hit of the 1950s.

Shimmy Shimmy Ko Ko Bop.

A clever, nonsense song with novelty lyrics. It's done with an attractive, Latinish flavor. (11/2/59) (#24 Pop, #14 R&B)

"Shimmy" was the last song Alan Freed played before he went off the air in 1960, resigning as the scapegoat for record label payola activities. Despite its success, the group didn't come up with a followup hit for a while.

Bayou, Bayou, Baby/My Empty Room.

"Bayou" is a spiritual-type rocker that is sold with verve. "My Empty Room" is a warmly delivered rockaballad based on a Tchaikovsky theme. (3/14/60) (B-side, #86 Pop)

Limbo (Parts I and II).

The group sells this wild limbo effort with much enthusiasm over wild, rhythmic backing. The second side is a particularly frantic and potent offering. The Caribbean stunt-dance (sliding under a bar, which is lowered each time) could catch on among agile teeners. Watch it. (10/24/60)

In 1961, Gourdine went solo on Roulette and The Imperials (with Lord and Rogers replaced by Sammy Strain of The Fantastics and new lead George Kerr of The Serenaders) moved to Carlton.

During 1963, Anthony and The Imperials reunited after developing a modern harmony blend. Their manager, Ernie Martinelli, matched them with writer Teddy Randazzo and a dynamic musical merger was formed with the debut of "I'm

On the Outside Looking In." The group wasn't sure about recording "Outside" until they performed at a Murray The K show and Jay and The Americans' enthusiastic response convinced them they had a hit.

The Imperials (Gourdine, Wright, Collins, and Strain) were now in the midst of the 1960s side of their successes.

Goin' Out of My Head.

The boys are coming off a hit. This entry should prove to be a tremendous seller as well. Big sound arrangement and group sings with dramatic impact. (10/31/64) (#6 Pop, #22 R&B)

Anthony's favorite song, "Hurt So Bad," followed.

Hurt So Bad.

Strong follow-up to current hit. Production ballad in same vein as "Goin' Out of My Head." Written and produced by singer Teddy Randazzo. (1/30/65) (#10 Pop, #3 R&B)

Take Me Back.

This well-written Teddy Randazzo ballad will put them back on top of the chart again. (6/19/65) (#16 Pop, #15 R&B)

I Miss You [So].

Powerful lush 101 string production revival of the evergreen has a smash hit sound throughout. . . . Dramatic vocal performance. (9/25/65) (#34 Pop, #23 R&B)

Hurt.

This big production revival of the Timi Yuro oldie should prove to be one of the first hit ballads of the new year! Fine vocal performance and top string arrangement by Teddy Randazzo. (12/25/65) (#51 Pop)

As DCP (Don Costa Productions) folded, Anthony et al. moved to Veep, another UA distributed label, but promotion of their singles was not a priority. "It's Not the Same" became the first single to be credited to "Anthony and The Imperials." However, the hits stopped coming.

It's Not the Same.

With the feel and sound of another "Goin' Out of My Head," this wailing

blues performance should skyrocket the group rapidly up the chart. (10/22/66) (#92 Pop)

You Only Live Twice.

The much recorded James Bond film theme is a compelling new adult bag for the stylist. Loaded with sales potential and all types of programming. (7/22/67)

In 1969, they resurrected themselves with remade oldies and returned to using their old name.

Ten Commandments of Love.

Will prove more potent chart material for them. (10/18/69) (#82 Pop)

By 1970, The Imperials were trying to push into the soul market. Their last charter was "Hold On" (#106 Pop, #79 R&B, 1972) on Avco.

Gourdine went solo again in 1975 and Strain joined The O'Jays. Always popular and always performing, Dick Clark helped put Gourdine, Strain, Wright, and Collins back together in the 1990s. The Imperials are still a most enjoyable act to see and hear.

Real Name: Eva Narcissus Boyd Harris
Birthdate: 6/29/43
Birthplace: Bellhaven, NC
Influences: Mahalia Jackson, LaVern Baker, Carole King
Influenced: Linda Ronstadt, Kyle Minogue

Little Eva became an overnight star as the vocalist on one of America's biggest dance hits, even though there was no such dance at the time.

The tenth of 13 singing children, Eva originally sang gospel with The Boyd Five (her sisters and brothers). The North Carolina native visited New York in 1960 to see her brother Jimmy and met Cookies' lead singer Earl Jean McCrea. On a second trip a few months later, she auditioned for writer/producer Carole King to fill a fourth spot

with The Cookies. King needed a babysitter and someone to do demos for her songs, so Eva earned the slot with The Cookies, and also picked up extra cash babysitting for Carole and husband Gerry Goffin's daughter Lulu (Louise Goffin). Ironically, Eva was only 16 months younger than Carole.

In early 1962, Dee Dee Sharp had a hit with "Mashed Potato Time," so Goffin and King set about writing a follow-up for her. They had Eva do the demo and when Sharp nixed the song, King's publisher, Don Kirshner, picked it as the debut disc for his new Dimension label. Although all concerned agreed to call the tiny (4'11", 96 lbs.) singer Little Eva, no one knew that another artist had preceded her recording under that name ("Ain't Got No Home," King, 1957). The song, of course, was "The Loco-Motion" and charted on June 30, five days after Eva's 19th birthday.

The Loco-Motion.

 A new thrush and a new label (owned by the successful Nevins and Kirschner combine) and it all adds up to a hot side. It's a new dance, with a rhythm close to the Twist and the gal belts it in fine style over a solid arrangement. (6/9/62) (#1 Pop, #1 R&B)

Within 77 days of its release, Eva went from a $35 a week live-in babysitter to an artist with an international, million-selling, #1 platter. The record was so huge that a Long Island group tried cashing in on its success by calling themselves The Loco-Motions and issuing "Little Eva" (Gone).

Two weeks after the release of "Loco-Motion," Eva was to appear on American Bandstand when all concerned realized they didn't have a dance to go with the record, so "The Loco-Motion" was quickly created. Eva had two more hits before her train slowed down: "Keep Your Hands Off My Baby" (issued as a B-side) and "Let's Turkey Trot," an unadulterated "rip-off" of The Cleftones' 1956 hit, "Little Girl of Mine."

Where Do I Go?/Keep Your Hands Off My Baby.

On top, she sings a listenable ballad stylishly, aided by smart ork arrangement with a catchy beat and some neat double-tracking. Flip is a bright ditty which she sells with lots of spirit over sock support. (10/27/62) (B-side, #12 Pop, #6 R&B)

Let's Turkey Trot.

A snappy, swinging upbeater by the gal, much in the blues framework, featuring a solid vocal and an insistent beat. Strong wax for the teen set. (1/26/63) (#20 Pop, #16 R&B)

The upswing her career needed almost happened in early 1963. King had recorded a new song with Eva but at the last minute decided to eliminate her vocal, replacing it with The Chiffons'; the song was "One Fine Day."

The babysitting singer's singles started losing ground at that point. She didn't receive credit for her duet with Big Dee Irwin on "Swingin' on a Star," a minor hit, while her own "Old Smokey Locomotion" peaked at #48.

A few more Dimension disasters never even climbed the Top 100 and by 1965 the diminutive Dimension doll connected with Amy. After a short stint on Verve, Eva began doing oldies in the Spring of 1968. She quit performing in 1971 and returned to Bellhaven, but times were hard. In 1972, when "The Loco-Motion" was reissued in Britain and hit #11, she was working as a custodian at City Hall, totally unaware of its success. In 1987, a *People* magazine "Where are they now" piece regarding the 25th anniversary of "The Loco-Motion" brought overdue attention to Eva, who then cut her first recordings in 15 years. In 1989, her album *Back on Track* (Malibu) was released.

LITTLE RICHARD

Real Name: Richard Wayne Penniman
Birthdate: 12/5/32
Birthplace: Macon, GA
Influences: Billy Wright, Esquerita, Louis Jordan, Fats Domino
Influenced: Elvis Presley, Bob Dylan, Buddy Holly, Bobby Darin, Paul Anka, Righteous Brothers, Beatles, David Bowie, Mick Jagger, Tom Jones, Ritchie Valens, Lovin' Spoonful, Paul Revere and The Raiders, Mitch Ryder, Steppenwolf, Elton John, many more

"I am the architect of rock and roll! I am the originator!" screamed Little Richard at a 1988 Grammy Awards audience while he was presenting another artist with an award he'd never received . . . and he had a good argument for it.

One of 12 children, Richard sang in church, learning gospel music and piano in his teens. He also sang with The Penniman Singers and The Tiny Tots Quartet but was forced out of his home when his homosexuality surfaced at age 13. He was then adopted by a white couple, the Johnsons, who owned the Tick Tock club in Macon where Richard first performed. Touring with Dr. Hudson's Medicine Show (selling snake oil at carnivals) and Sugarfoot Sam's Minstrel Show, he began experimenting with blues and boogie woogie music, while throwing in a gospel scream he would soon perfect for records.

His early flamboyance, pompadour, heavy makeup, and mascara were attributable to blues artist Billy Wright's influence. It was also Wright who introduced Little Richard to white deejay Zenas Sears, which led to Penniman winning a radio contest and an RCA record deal. His first single, "Every Hour," recorded October 16, 1951, was only of local note, as were his next few releases.

Get Rich Quick 83–84–80–84
Ork and chanter cut this raucous, carefree number solidly. Backing is in ragtime style. Good juke wax. (4/5/52)

Please Have Mercy on Me 72
> *The warbler turns in a good vocal on this blues-weeper, as he asks his girl to show him a little mercy. Ork backs him in bluesy style. (11/22/52)*

After four RCA 45s, Penniman moved to Houston, paired with the vocal group, The Tempo Toppers, and the band, The Deuces of Rhythm, recording for Peacock.

Dukes of Rhythm-Tempo Toppers/Ain't That Good News 73
> *Interesting arrangement lifts this blues out of the routine category. Little Richard, as lead singer, shouts his part convincingly. (6/13/53)*

In 1954, Penniman met Specialty artist Lloyd Price, who recommended he send a demo to label head Art Rupe. As Richard's rock 'n' roll originals, such as "Tutti-Frutti," weren't going over well with black audiences, he decided to send Rupe a blues demo. It took a year for Specialty to show interest, and when he first recorded for them on September 14, 1955, his song "Tutti-Frutti" was a "throw-in." The original lyric was so bawdy that producer Otis Blackwell had New Orleans writer Dorothy La Bostrie clean it up. After Penniman sold the publishing rights to Specialty for only $50, the record sold three million copies. The era of pounding piano, overt sexuality, and falsetto wailing had begun.

Tutti-Frutti.
> *A cleverly styled novelty with nonsense words delivered rapid-fire. The singer shows a compelling personality and an attractive vocal style. (10/29/55) (#17 Pop, #2 R&B)*

Little Richard's Boogie.
> *After "Tutti-Frutti" anything released by the artist might seem an anti-climax. But here Little Richard rides the Johnny Otis band in a fast and furious rhythm opus that could easily be a repeater. It certainly is an outstanding juke box offering. (3/10/56)*

Little Richard's first film appearance was in *Don't Knock the Rock*, featuring another standard-to-be, "Long Tall Sally." He continued with hit after two-sided hit.

Slippin' and Slidin'/Long Tall Sally.
> *Little Richard has a sock follow-up to "Tutti-Frutti" in this two-sided hit, which should grab off plenty of play in both the r&b and pop markets. "Slippin' and Slidin'" is a swingy, rhythm-novelty with a rockin' beat, spicy lyrics and a showmanly vocal performance. "Long Tall Sally" is an equally effective rhythm-novelty team with humorous lyrics and another great warbling job by the artist. (3/17/56) (A-side, #33 Pop, #2 R&B; B-side, #6 Pop, #1 R&B)*

Rip It Up/Ready Teddy.
> *Here's a tremendous two-sided follow-up to "Long Tall Sally." Little Richard grooves it up on both sides with wild, rip-roaring abandon that's sure to excite the fans. The exceptional band backing keeps up the frantic swinging pace thru both sides. Both have big potential in the pop field as well. (6/16/56) (A-side, #17 Pop, #1 R&B; B-side, #44 Pop, #8 R&B)*

Heeby-Jeebies.
> *Next to Fats Domino, Little Richard seems like r.&b.'s most consistent hit maker. He also has a huge pop following that is buying this in large enough quantities to guarantee early representation on both pop and r.&b. charts. (10/13/56) (A-side, #7 R&B; B-side, #9 R&B)*

All Around the World/The Girl Can't Help It.
> *"All Around," is frisky, fast moving rhythm item. The flip—another great rhythm tune with amusing lyrics—is the title tune from the forthcoming Jayne Mansfield movie about the juke box industry. Little Richard also appears in the film. (11/14/56) (A-side, #13 R&B; B-side, #9 Pop, #7 R&B)*

Penniman's recording, "The Girl Can't Help It," featured The Coasters and was his eighth Top-10 R&B smash in a row. "Lucille" gave him his third film appearance in a year as he performed in Alan Freed's film, *Mr. Rock and Roll*. The singer went on to work in more than ten pictures.

Lucille/Send Me Lovin'.

> *The first disk by the dynamic stylist in some weeks looks like an easy double smash. The top side is a wild, wailing tribute to Lucille. The flip is a switch to a slow-paced blues which strongly resembles the melody of the old blues, "Birmingham Jail." Both these have power aplenty. (3/2/57) (A-side, #21 Pop, #1 R&B; B-side, #54 Pop, #3 R&B)*

Jenny, Jenny.

> *In the frantic, dedicated, hootin' and howlin' mood of "Lucille." (5/27/57) (#10 Pop, #2 R&B)*

On top of the world, Little Richard abruptly stopped performing. While touring Australia, his plane caught fire; Richard swore if the plane landed safely, he would dedicate his life to God. On October 13, 1957, he recorded what was to become a final session for Specialty, who were trying to keep his conversion a secret. Their next single, "Keep a-Knockin'," had to be patched together from that unfinished session.

Keep a-Knockin'.

> *Little Richard fairly explodes with energy in his selling of "Knockin'," a fast rocker. (8/9/57) (#8 Pop, #2 R&B)*

In 1958, Little Richard became ordained a Seventh-Day Adventist minister but that didn't stop Specialty. They pulled a number of hits from out of the can, including "Kansas City" from a September 14, 1955, session.

Good Golly, Miss Molly.

> *The frantic cat at his vigorous best on this rocker. Ork backing is good and helps give side potential. It can click in both pop and r.&b. marts. (1/20/58) (#10 Pop, #4 R&B)*

Baby Face/I'll Never Let You Go.

> *Little Richard's at his shoutin' best on his rockin' revival of "Baby Face." "I'll Never" is also in the rocker vein, and the artist uses lots of vocal gimmicks in presenting the tune. Both sides appear naturals for pop and r.&b. loot. (9/1/58) (#41 Pop, #12 R&B)*

Kansas City.

> *Little Richard's pitch in the "Kansas City" sweepstakes will offer strong competition. He knows how to shout the blues, and this version should figure. (4/6/59) (#95 Pop)*

Shake a Hand.

> ★ ★ ★ ★ *Richard really shouts this one out. It's the oldie, and he does a great performance with support from a fem vocal group. Fine side can go. (6/15/59)*

Whole Lotta Shakin'.

> *The frantic chanter wails this rocker at a high pitch and maintains the excitement all the way. It could prove a winner this time. (10/12/59)*

In 1961, Reverend Richard signed with Mercury for gospel releases.

He's Not Just a Soldier/Joy, Joy, Joy.

> *Little Richard should come back strongly in the pop market with these two powerful sides. He sings them with his old-time enthusiasm as he tells on the first side about a soldier who is somebody's son. Flip is a potent jubilee gospel disking. (10/16/61)*

By 1962, Little Richard had returned to rock 'n' roll with a U.K. tour, including the then-little-known bands The Beatles and The Rolling Stones. One of the young members was so enamored with him that he asked Little Richard to teach him his singing style. The moptop was Paul McCartney! Little Richard even performed at the legendary Cavern Club in Liverpool, where The Beatles started.

In 1964, with Specialty still issuing 45s, Richard signed with Vee-Jay and then Modern; these sides reportedly included the guitar work of Maurice James, better known as Jimi Hendrix.

Annie Is Back.

> *And so's Little Richard (who hasn't had a big one since "Long Tall Sally"). The side really moves along with his wailing. Traditional rock 'n' roll. (6/6/64) (#82 Pop)*

Holy Mackeral.

> *This is the one that could put Little Richard back in the hit class. A swinging rocker with a James Brown backing should prove a sales monster. (1/22/66)*

On September 13, 1969, Little Richard performed at the Rock 'n' Revival concert in Toronto with legends John Lennon, Jerry Lee Lewis, Bo Diddley, and Gene Vincent. During 1970, after a quiet half decade, record wise, he coupled with Reprise for his first Top-50 single in 12 years, "Freedom Blues."

Freedom Blues.

> *This rock outing should bring him straight to the charts. (4/25/70) (#47 Pop, #28 R&B)*

With the death of his brother Tony, Reverend Richard once again became "born again" to his faith in 1975. In 1985, his fast moving sports car totaled a Santa Monica Boulevard (Los Angeles) telephone pole and he was hospitalized for six months. The next year, Little Richard was inducted into the Rock and Roll Hall of Fame, and had his first Top-50 charter in 16 years with the theme song from the comedy film *Down and Out in Beverly Hills*, in which he was featured in a flamboyant cameo role. Although it was his last Top-100 single, the artist who is the self-proclaimed "King of Rock & Roll" has sold 18 million records and the evangelist rocker shows no signs of letting up.

Great Gosh A'Mighty.

> *Theme song from "Down and Out in Beverly Hills" frames a spiritual message in the riproaring style of his 1950s classics. (3/1/86) (#42 Pop)*

In December 1994, Little Richard was honored by President Clinton on a national television show for his contribution to American music after he performed "Keep a-Knockin'."

THE LOVIN' SPOONFUL

John Sebastian: Lead guitar
Born: 3/17/44, New York, NY
Zal Yanovsky: Guitar
Born: 12/19/44, Toronto, Canada
Steve Boone: Bass
Born: 9/23/43, Camp Lejeune, NC
Joe Butler: Drums
Born: 1/19/43, Long Island, NY
Influences: Mississippi John Hurt, Elvis Presley, Chuck Berry, Little Richard, Fats Domino, Jim Kweskin Jug Band, Peter, Paul and Mary, Lightnin' Hopkins, Huey Smith, Jimmy Reed
Influenced: Buffalo Springfield, Eagles, Tom Petty

Before the innocence of the 1960s was laid to rest by protest songs, psychedelia, and the new wave of insightful message music, The Lovin' Spoonful got in several good licks with their "good time" sound.

In 1963, Zal Yanovsky and Denny Doherty, former members of the Canadian folk group The Halifax Three, along with friends Cass Elliott and her then-husband James Hendricks, formed the group Cass Elliott and The Big Three. By 1964, with the addition of John Sebastian (who had played guitar on Tom Rush and Fred Neil sessions and was a member of the Even Dozen Jug Band), the group became The Mugwumps. After one single, "I'll Remember Tonight," and a Warner Brothers album that remained unreleased until all were stars, the group went in separate but historic directions. Elliott and Doherty joined The Mamas and The Papas, Hendricks joined The Lamp of Childhood, and Zal and John formed The Lovin' Spoonful.

The group's name came about after John took a trip through the South and met blues great, Mississippi John Hurt, whose song "Coffee Blues" mentioned "lovin' his baby by the lovin' spoonful." In 1965, with the addition of Joe Butler and Steve Boone, The Lovin' Spoonful set out to create what they called "good time music." They met producer Erik Jacobson, who brought them to the fledgling Kama Sutra label and the good times began with their first single.

Do You Believe in Magic.
> *Pulsating folk-flavored rhythm number serves as a strong and exciting debut for a new group in The Byrds vein. (8/7/65) (#9 Pop)*

You Didn't Have to Be So Nice.
> *Good lyric and strong dance beat serves us a follow-up to their "Do You Believe in Magic." This one can't help but equal the initial hit. (11/13/65) (#10 Pop)*

Daydream.
> *An off-beat shuffle-blues rhythm that will quickly equal their "You Didn't Have to Be So Nice" success. (2/19/66) (#2 Pop)*

The fun-loving band was known for their performing antics as well as their recording style. With their first million seller ("Daydream") in tow, Sebastian wrote their next hit, "Did You Ever Have to Make Up Your Mind," in a taxi on the way to the studio.

Did You Ever Have to Make Up Your Mind?
> *Another off-beat winner for the hot group. Easy rockin' ballad should quickly equal "Daydream." (4/30/66) (#2 Pop)*

Their hottest sizzler, "Summer in the City" (#1) was another gold 45, followed by the soundtrack for Woody Allen's film *What's Up, Tiger Lily?* The band did another film soundtrack, this time for Francis Ford Coppola's *You're a Big Boy Now*, featuring "Darling Be Home Soon."

Rain on the Roof.
> *Continuing their string of unpredictable, fresh, original material, the Spoonful have another blockbuster in this clever rhythm ballad with baroque feel. (10/15/66) (#10 Pop)*

Darlin' [Be] Home Soon.
> *Medium-paced rock ballad given that "extra special" Lovin' Spoonful treatment should quickly surpass their*

"Nashville Cats" smash on the Hot 100. (2/4/67) (#15 Pop)

Six O'Clock.
> *More creative top 10 material from the pen of John Sebastian treated to a groovy rhythm dance beat and arrangement that builds into a production frenzy. (4/22/67) (#18 Pop)*

In late 1967, Yanovsky left after a drug arrest and was replaced by former Modern Folk Quartet member and Association producer, Jerry Yester.

She Is Still a Mystery.
> *Another unique offering by the group to follow-up their "Six O'Clock" hit. Easy beat ballad material is delivered in their fine style, which spells hit. (10/21/67) (#27 Pop)*

After nine Top-20 hits in nine releases, the group's mounting pressures, lost enthusiasm, and Sebastian's solo sojourn caused their demise in 1968. Sebastian's first solo single came in late 1968, and The Spoonful's last chart single, "Me About You," came only three months later. However, neither were as successful on their own.

John Sebastian:
She's a Lady.
> *This initial entry is a strong one. The original folk-flavored ballad is an exceptional one and should fast establish Sebastian as a top solo disk seller. Top, lush arrangement by Paul Harris. (11/30/68) (#84 Pop)*

The Lovin' Spoonful:
Me About You.
> *With new lead singer Joe Butler turning in a strong performance, and equally strong Bonner-Gordon ballad material, this should prove a top sales item for the group. Good sound and compelling lyric and rhythm. (2/1/69) (#91 Pop)*

In 1969, Sebastian performed at Woodstock. Butler appeared in the Broadway production of *Hair* in 1970, and Boone moved to Baltimore, continuing his bass playing.

In mid-decade, Sebastian's label was about to drop him after five stiffs until he clicked with a self-penned TV theme, "Welcome Back," written for "Welcome Back, Kotter."

Welcome Back.
> *This is definitely a season for series themes to come across big on charts. And Steve Barri, who co-produced this with Sebastian, is the current champ at making it happen. "S.W.A.T." did it and "Happy Days" is coming. In essence, this is . . . exactly what Sebastian sings on the weekly show. (3/27/76) (#1 Pop)*

Twelve years after their breakup, the four original Spoonfuls temporarily regrouped for an appearance in Paul Simon's Warner Brothers film, *One Trick Pony*. In the mid-1990s, Butler, Boone, Yester, and his daughter Lena have a new Spoonful on the oldies circuit, whereas Sebastian tours separately and writes music for TV and films such as *The Care Bears* series.

FRANKIE *LYMON* AND THE TEENAGERS

Frankie Lymon: Lead vocals
Born: 9/30/42, New York City (died 2/28/68)
Jimmy Merchant: Tenor
Born: 2/10/40, New York City
Herman Santiago: Tenor
Born: 2/18/41, New York City
Joe Negroni: Baritone
Born: 9/9/40, New York City (died 9/5/78)
Sherman Garnes: Bass
Born: 6/8/40, New York City (died 2/26/77)
Influences: Spaniels, Penguins, Dominoes, Cadillacs
Influenced: Danny and The Juniors, Ronettes, Supremes, Temptations, Manhattan Transfer, Gladys Knight and The Pips, Happenings, Elegants, Mellokings, Delphonics, Dovells, Chantels, Millie Jackson, Desires, many more

Rock 'n' roll did not become a complete music style until R&B acts, performing their own music, could outsell their white cover-record counter-parts. The first act of the rock era to do so was Frankie Lymon and The Teenagers.

The group was the contrivance of Harlem natives Jimmy Merchant and Sherman Garnes, who formed The Earth Angels (named after The Penguins' standard) in 1954 while still in junior high. When The Angels dispersed, Merchant and Garnes joined forces with two Puerto Ricans, Joe Negroni and Herman Santiago, and crafted The Coupe DeVilles and then The Premiers.

A talent show rehearsal in a school auditorium led to their meeting a 12-year-old singer and bongo player from a Latin band, Frankie Lymon. The youngster began hanging out with The Premiers and eventually became their first tenor. His background was mainly gospel; he sang in the group The Harlemaires Juniors along with his brothers Louis and Howie (his truck driver father sang with The Harlemaires). In 1955, The Premiers (sometimes called The Ermines) were known in the neighborhood as The Hallway singers, since that's where they'd usually be seen and heard. One neighbor, fed up hearing the same songs, gave them some poems from his girlfriend and told them to create something original. Out of that now-historic encounter came a song originally called, "Why Do Birds Sing So Gay."

By the Spring, The Premiers met Valentine's vocalist Richard Barrett, who was also the A&R director of George Goldner's label. The group auditioned in Goldner's office, singing "Why Do Birds" with Santiago leading. Goldner heard Lymon sing and moved him into the lead spot and changed the title to "Why Do Fools Fall in Love." At the same session, musical director Jimmy Wright renamed the group The Teenagers. The single sold over two million records despite heavily promoted, pasteurized white cover versions by Gale Storm (#9), The Diamonds (#12), and Gloria Mann (#59). "Why" became the first rock 'n' roll, black vocal group single to reach #1 in England.

Why Do Fools Fall in Love.
> *Here's a hot new disk, which has already sparked a couple of covers in the pop market. The appealing ditty has a frantic arrangement, a solid beat and a sock lead vocal by 13-year-old Frankie Lymon. Jockeys and jukes should hand it plenty of spin and they could easily break pop. (2/4/56) (#6 Pop, #1 R&B)*

Their next 45, "I Want You to Be My Girl," was another huge hit. A cover of friend Jimmy Castor and The Juniors' new single, "I Promise to Remember," followed.

I Want You to Be My Girl.

Thirteen-year-old Lymon and the Teenagers are riding high right now on both the pop and the r.&b. charts, and this platter has all the makings of a repeat smash for them in both markets. Lymon belts across the solid jump material in his now familiar style, with plenty of excitement and a frantic, infectious beat. (4/14/56) (#13 Pop, #3 R&B)

Who Can Explain?

Lymon sets off a real storm with those crazy soprano notes. This can move just as fast as its predecessors and is likely pop entry as well. Flip is "I Promise to Remember." (7/7/56) (A-side, #7 R&B; B-side, #57 Pop, #10 R&B)

While on a Canadian tour, The Teenagers met a young songwriter backstage in Toronto who was pitching his new tune. They promptly rejected it, so he recorded it himself. The song was "Diana" and the 15-year-old writer was Paul Anka. Next, it was on to films for the quintet. Surprisingly, the single, "Baby, Baby," was a huge hit in England but did nothing in America.

The ABCs of Love.

In his now familiar style, [Lymon] belts across this solid piece of jump material with strong backing by the group and band. (9/22/56) (#77 Pop, #8 R&B)

The Harlem harmonizers then toured Europe, performing at the London Paladium and a private concert for Princess Margaret.

Baby, Baby/I'm Not a Juvenile Delinquent.

Both sides are warbled by Lymon in deejay Alan Freed's new movie, "Rock, Rock, Rock," and as such should grab off plenty of jockey and juke attention. "Baby, Baby" is a bouncy rhythm ditty, while the flip has a strong beat and a sock lyric with a timely slant for both the pop and r.&b. markets. (11/24/56)

(A-side, #4 Pop [U.K.]; B-side, #12 Pop [U.K.])

Teen-Age Love/Paper Castles.

Spotlights a typical frantic Lymon vocal, backed by the big beat, on a sock rhythm item, with lyrics that should appeal to the teen set. Flip, a pleasant ballad, features an interesting change of pace for the group. (2/16/57)

Out in the Cold Again.

Off-beat version of the nostalgic oldie. Lymon sells the plaintive ballad with intensity and feeling and the group backs him. Should move out in both pop and r.&b. markets. (4/27/57) (#10 R&B)

By early 1957, Goldner made the greatest mistake of his career by persuading Lymon to go solo on "Goody, Goody." Even though the label and reviews included the group, it was actually Lymon and The Ray Charles Singers performing on the recording. The Teenagers wound up paired with inappropriate lead, Bill Labram. Although "Goody Goody" was a minor hit, Lymon's follow-up solo platters and The Teenagers' future recordings did not fare well.

Goody Goody.

Johnny Mercer's bright and bouncy standard gets a powerful reading by the group with a stronger than ever spotlight on Lymon's vocalizing. Band backing is smoother and bigger than before which adds solid class to the disk. A strong contender. (7/8/57) (#20 Pop, #24 R&B)

Flip-Flop 73

This is the first entry by the crew without the services of Frankie Lymon. The new lead is backed on this medium-paced rocker by good group work and ork support. However, distinctive Lymon sound may be missed too much. (12/2/57)

Lymon's brother Louis jumped in to fill the high tenor void with his own group, but they also failed. Frankie finally hit the lower levels of the charts in 1960 once more with the Thurston Harris rocker, "Little Bitty Pretty One."

Frankie Lymon:
Little Bitty Pretty One.

★ ★ ★ *This starts with an interesting harmonic treatment to a happy beat then Lymon moves up in a shouted vocal style with a chorus. A lot of beat here. (6/27/60) (#58 Pop)*

Frankie Lymon:
Waitin' in School/Buzz, Buzz, Buzz.

Lymon's last single "Itty [sic] Bitty Pretty One," made the charts, and his new waxing should enjoy similar success. The lad exhibits spirited vocal form on both sides, "Waitin' in School" is a snappy teen-appeal ditty with country-oriented backing. Flip is a verveful rocker. (9/12/60)

The Teenagers stayed relatively intact, adding lead singer Pearl McKinnon (Kodaks), who sounded amazingly like Lymon. In 1977 Garnes died of a heart attack and Negroni passed on the next year. Jimmy and Herman have kept a Teenagers group going right through the 1990s. Frankie, meanwhile, battled both a changing and maturing voice and a drug problem, only to succumb from an overdose at age 26 in his grandmother's apartment.

The star, who helped usher in a new era in popular music and who earned hundreds of thousands of dollars, today lies in an unmarked grave at St. Raymond's Cemetery in the Bronx while his estate and substantial royalties are being fought over in the courts.

THE **M**AMAS AND THE PAPAS

Denny Doherty: Vocalist
Born: 11/29/41, Halifax, Nova Scotia
John Phillips: Guitar, vocalist
Born: 8/30/35, Parris Island, SC
Holly Michelle Gilliam: Vocalist
Born: 6/4/45, Long Beach, CA
Cass Elliot (Ellen Naomi Cohen): Vocalist
Born: 9/19/43, Baltimore, MD
Influences: Four Freshmen, Hi-Lo's, Jordonaires, Modernaires, Sons of The Pioneers
Influenced: 5th Dimension, Fleetwood Mac, Abba, Cowsills

As flower power, protest power, Beatles power, and soul power took over the American airwaves in the mid-1960s, folk and pop power hung on in the form of a few acts, the best of which was The Mamas and The Papas.

The group assembled from members of four other unsuccessful acts that started early in the decade. John Phillips, Dick Weissman, and Scott McKenzie (Phillip Blondheim) created The Journeymen, a folk group with several albums on Capitol. Meanwhile, Doherty had his own group, The Halifax Three. In 1963, he teamed with Zal Yanovsky, James Hendricks, and Hendricks's then-wife, Ellen Cohen, soon to be known as Cass Elliot, forming The Big Three in New York. After one unreleased Warner Brothers LP as The Mugwumps, John Sebastian came aboard. Across the nation in San Francisco, Michelle Gilliam, a 17-year-old aspiring model, met The Journeymen at The Hungry i club and became a member of the new group after marrying Phillips.

By late 1964, The Journeymen and The Mugwumps were both in New York. When the sorting out finalized, Sebastian and Yanovsky had molded The Lovin' Spoonful, whereas John, Michelle, Denny, and Cass fashioned their new Journeymen group, first in the Virgin Islands, then in Los Angeles. They soon met former New

Christy Minstrel Barry McGuire, who was recording for Dunhill. He arranged for the foursome to sing backup on his album, including a song producer Lou Adler liked titled, "California Dreamin'," written by Phillips.

In 1965, The Journeymen were signed by Adler and started recording. They also started the search for a new name, considering The Magic Circle before selecting The Mamas and The Papas after hearing Hell's Angels members on a talk show refer to their women as "Mamas." Their debut single, "Go Where You Wanna Go" was retracted at the last minute in favor of the group's own recording of "California Dreamin'" (with the same instrumental track as was used on McGuire's *This Precious Time* album).

California Dreamin'.

New West Coast quartet display a fascinating new sound with well written commercial material that should prove a giant in sales. Fine production work by Lou Adler. (12/25/65) (#4 Pop)

Their first gold record led almost immediately to their second, "Monday, Monday" (#1). 1966 continued with a solid showcase of their sensational sound.

I Saw Her Again.

Hot follow-up to their "Monday Monday" smash is this lyric rhythm rocker, sure to hit the chart with impact. (6/25/66) (#5 Pop)

Words of Love/Dancing in the Streets.

First side is a blockbuster change of pace with a wild blues shouting solo by Cass Elliott. Flip is an equally potent winner . . . An exciting revival of the Martha and the Vandellas hit. (11/26/66) (A-side, #5 Pop; B-side, #73 Pop)

Michelle left the group owing to personal problems with John and was replaced on tour, but not recordings, by Jill Gibson (girlfriend of Jan and Dean's Jan Berry). 1967 started with the return of Michelle and the group's fourth million seller, "Dedicated to the One I Love." The quartet also won a Grammy for Best Contemporary Group Performance of 1966 on a song all but John held in disfavor, "Monday, Monday."

Dedicated to the One I Love.

Hot on the heels of their "Words of Love" hit comes this classy revival of the Shirelles' hit, which should keep the unique quartet at the top of the Hot 100. (2/18/67) (#2 Pop)

Warner Brothers then decided to release The Mugwumps' album.

The Mugwumps:
Searchin'.

The Leiber-Stoller hit of the past by The Coasters has strong possibilities for a smash again via this Mamas and Papas-sounding group treatment. The Cass Elliott sound is there. ('67)

The quartet's autobiographical "Creeque Alley" (#5) peaked about the time the group appeared at the now-legendary Monterey Pop Festival on June 16, 1967 (which Adler and John Phillips helped organize), with Simon and Garfunkel, The Who, and Jimi Hendrix. Meanwhile, Scott McKenzie's "San Francisco, Wear Some Flowers in Your Hair" (#4) maintained Phillips's elite writing status.

Hey Girl/Glad to Be Unhappy.

Chalk up a two-sided winner for the groovy group. Top is an easy rock ballad in the teen selling bag, while the flip is a smart revival of the Rodgers and Hart classic. (10/21/67) (B-side, #26 Pop)

Although they were on top of the musical world in 1967, John and Michelle's relationship could no longer hold together and, by the middle of 1968, the group was no more. Cass then became a solo sensation, even though her initial single, "Dream a Little Dream of Me," had the group behind her. Her follow-up singles were less successful, however.

Mama Cass:
Dream a Little Dream of Me.

Mama Cass makes her solo debut with an easy rhythm revival of the old standard that should quickly ride right into the No. 1 spot on the Hot 100. Lou Adler's production work is perfect. (6/29/68) (#12 Pop)

Cleaning out its stock of unreleased sides, Dunhill still managed to reach the lower level of the charts by the defunct group with such numbers as "Do You Wanna Dance" (#76 Pop). In February 1972 the quartet, having reunited, did one LP and a single for Dunhill, "People Like Us"/"Step Out" before again disbanding. Doherty signed with Columbia and Elliott joined RCA. Her last 45, "Listen to the World" was issued in 1973; in 1974, she tragically died in London of a heart attack at age 32. Michelle became an actress, appearing in *Dillinger* and *Brewster McCloud* and in 1977 recorded an album (*Victim of Romance*) for A&M; she continues to act on television through the 1990s.

In 1982, John and Denny put a new The Mamas and The Papas together along with John's actress daughter Mackenzie ("One Day at a Time" and *American Graffiti*) and the next-best powerhouse to Cass Elliott, Spanky and Our Gang's Elaine "Spanky" McFarlane. Surprisingly, they never recorded, but toured the nostalgia circuit through the 1980s with ex-Journeyman Scott McKenzie coming full circle to replace Doherty in 1987. In the 1990s, John Phillips, McKenzie, McFarlane, and Melanie Doane were keeping the phenomenal sound of The Mamas and The Papas alive. Meanwhile, John and Michelle's daughter Chynna had some success in the late 1980s with Wilson Phillips (in conjunction with Beach Boy Brian Wilson's daughters Carnie and Wendy), and has since embarked on a solo recording career.

THE MARCELS

Cornelius Harp: Lead vocals
Born: 1940, Pittsburgh, PA
Ronald Mundy: Tenor
Born: 4/20/40, Pittsburgh, PA
Gene Bricker: Tenor
Born: 1939, Pittsburgh, PA (died 1982)
Richard Knauss: Baritone
Born: 1938, Pittsburgh, PA
Fred Johnson: Bass
Born: 3/11/42, Pittsburgh, PA

Influences: Little Anthony and The Imperials, Dell-Vikings, Harptones, Spaniels, Cadillacs, Five Keys, Moonglows, Drifters, Dominoes

A vocal group without peer, The Marcels were the last great mixed-race doo wop quintet to succeed before the British invasion banished their type of harmony from 1960s' charts.

The membership was culled from several unnamed Pittsburgh-area groups in 1959, including the best vocalists of each. Bricker and Knauss were white, whereas Mundy, Johnson, and distinctive lead Cornelius Harp were black. They named themselves after an in-vogue hairstyle that Harp wore called a marcel. As the quintet did not write, they polished up other R&B groups' past hits, adding their own imaginative vocal arrangements to songs like The Cadillacs' "Zoom."

In 1960, a tape of those recreations was sent to Colpix Records' Stu Phillips, who brought The Marcels to New York. Although under orders to work with another Colpix act, Phillips smuggled The Marcels into RCA studios on February 15, 1961, to record the oldie, "Heart and Soul." The problem was no one knew the words, so they tried the standard "Blue Moon." Then Phillips had a brainstorm: Why not do "Blue Moon" up tempo and have bass Fred Johnson employ the "Bomp Ba Ba Bomp" intro they had used on "Zoom" for "Blue Moon"? Two takes later it was a record, which was lucky since there were only eight minutes of studio time left.

Before "Blue Moon" could be pressed, it was featured on New York radio when an overly anxious promotion man hustled the tape to WINS deejay Murray The K. The fifth Beatle (as Murray would later be known) was so excited, he played the record 26 times during his four-hour show. In the four weeks after release, it was a million seller and became the biggest international doo wop hit of all time. They followed with more standards, but had less success on the charts.

Blue Moon.

Here's a wild and woolly old time rock and roll treatment of the well-known standard. There's a great deal happening on this arrangement and the side figures to have a strong chance. (2/20/61) (#1 Pop, #1 R&B)

Summertime.

The "Blue Moon" boys should have another hit with this frenetic platter. "Summertime" features the group's saleable vocal gimmicks, on a "Blue Moon" type treatment of the great Gershwin standard. (5/8/61) (#78 Pop)

You Are My Sunshine.

★ ★ ★ ★ *The Marcels, who clicked with an r.&r. version of "Blue Moon," give the same hit-potential treatment to the c&w oldie with startling results. Watch it. (7/17/61)*

Infighting with manager Jules Kruspir caused Knauss and Bricker to exit, replaced by Fred Johnson's brother Alan and Walt Maddox, who had recorded solo in 1960.

In late 1961, the now all-black group hit the Top 10 again with the outrageous reworking of the evergreen "Heartaches." The quintet next appeared in the rock 'n' roll film *Twist Around the Clock* with Chubby Checker and Dion, singing "Blue Moon" and premiering the novelty song "Merry Twist-mas."

Merry Twist-mas.

A doubly timely item for the hot group, now swinging with "Heartaches." This rockin' Twist item has a lot of sound and beat with the boys' familiar gimmick touches. Watch it. (11/20/61)

Mundy left in late 1961 and the group became a first-time quartet for their last Top-100 entry.

My Melancholy Baby.

The "Blue Moon" boys could have another sock contender here. The great standard is wrapped up in their amusing bomp-de-bomp-styled delivery and a rocking beat. Watch it. (1/20/62) (#58 Pop)

Allright Okay You Win.

★ ★ ★ ★ *The Count Basie-Joe Williams hit of some years back gets a wild going over. . . . The side is a swinger with the low-voice ba-bed-de-dah-bah figures that have become the boys' trade-mark. It's a swinger that teens should dig. (11/10/62)*

The soul of The Marcels, Cornelius Harp, left in late 1962, and the once-mighty music makers moved from Colpix to minor-league labels like Kyra and 888, creating solid but unsupported singles such as "Comes Love." Harp made one appearance as lead for a brilliant version of "Lucky Old Sun" (St. Claire) in 1975. For most of the 1970s, 1980s, and 1990s, the group was Johnson, Maddox, and two members of Pittsburgh's Altairs, Richard Harris and William Herndon.

As the 1990s began, Harp was still living in Pittsburgh but reportedly not singing. Mundy was a bus driver, and Knauss, a school janitor. Gene Bricker died in the 1980s.

MARTHA AND THE VANDELLAS

Martha Reeves: Lead vocals
Born: 1/18/41, Eufaulia, AL
Rosalind Ashford
Born: 9/2/43, Detroit, MI
Annette Sterling
Born: 7/4/43, Detroit, MI
Gloria Williams
Born: 1940s, Detroit, MI
Influences: Della Reese, Soul Stirrers, Five Blind Boys, Clara Ward
Influenced: Supremes, Linda Ronstadt

One of the mainstays of Motown, Martha and The Vandellas had a more soulful style than their label-mate competitors, the soft-sounding Supremes.

In 1959, 18-year-old Martha Reeves began performing at Detroit talent shows as Martha LaVelle, and soon met Motown A&R man, Mickey Stevenson. He hired her for her secretarial skills, not her singing; however, Reeves formed The Del-Phis, a group of ex-Northeastern High School friends, Rosalind Ashford, Annette Sterling, and lead singer Gloria Williams. After an unsuccessful single, "It Takes Two" (Checkmate,

1961), the girls earned another chance when Mary Wells missed a session and The Del-Phis (now The Vels) recorded "There He Is" for Motown's Melody affiliate (1961). When the record bombed, Williams quit, making Martha Reeves the leader by default. Stevenson recognized their ability and began using The Vels as backups, most notably for J. J. Barnes and Marvin Gaye's fourth 45, "Stubborn Kind of Fellow" (#46 Pop, #8 R&B). Reeves then renamed the group after a combination of Van Dyke Street (where her grandmother resided) and Della Reese, a Reeves favorite.

In September 1962, another aborted Mary Wells session led to Martha and the Vandellas' first single.

I'll Have to Let Him Go.

The group with great emoting from lead Martha scores with this initial outing. The side has the sound and the heartbreak that could go right to teen hearts. (10/13/62)

Six months later they had their first hit with Holland, Dozier, and Holland's "Come and Get These Memories" (#29 Pop) (given a four-star rating but unreviewed). With their driving dance formula established, more hits ensued.

Heat Wave.

The group has a success with "Memories" and they indicated that it won't be a one-shot with this sizzling side that features a shouting vocal and first-rate band backing. It should boil its way up the charts. (7/27/63) (#4 Pop, #1 R&B)

Quicksand.

"Heat Wave" was the last hit by the group and this is the new winner. Side has propulsive swing and the hit sound. Martha really belts it out. (11/16/63) (#8 Pop)

In late 1963, Sterling left, replaced by Betty Kelley. Their signature song, "Dancing in the Street," came in 1964.

Live Wire.

Martha and her crew have another electrifying stomper like "Quicksand." The side has swing and excitement. (2/1/64) (#42 Pop)

Dancing in the Street/There He Is (at My Door).

Both sides pack a catchy vocal with the first side featuring a repetitive, driving beat. Both will be warmly accepted by the teen set. (8/15/64) (#2 Pop)

The group took part in Motown's historic, first European package tour along with The Miracles, Stevie Wonder, The Temptations, and The Supremes while their next single rocketed up the charts.

Nowhere to Run.

A good dance beat piece of material which features a gospel piano and a wailin' vocal. (2/20/65) (#8 Pop, #5 R&B)

You've Been in Love Too Long.

The exciting and pulsating Detroit beat wins again on this well-performed follow-up. (8/7/65) (#36 Pop, #25 R&B)

Never Leave Your Baby's Side.

The soulful blues rocker that will put the group back up the charts. A winning number and vocal performance. Flip: "My Baby Loves Me." (12/15/66) (B-side, #22 Pop, #3 R&B)

In 1966, Kelley left, replaced by Lois Reeves (The Orlons and Martha's sister). The trio's first 45 to read: Martha Reeves and The Vandellas (prior to this they were billed as "Martha and The Vandellas") was their last Top-10 R&B single.

Jimmy Mack.

Solid rhythm entry by the girls. . . . Top performances is [sic] right in the Motown bag. (2/18/67) (#10 Pop, #1 R&B)

Honey Chile/Show Me the Way.

Top side has that "Love Bug" feel and should prove even bigger than that recent hit. (11/11/67) (#11 Pop, #5 R&B)

Constant competition with Motown's darlings, The Supremes, contributed to Martha's 1969 nervous breakdown. She recovered by 1971 and went on tour to Europe with Lois and Sandy Tilley. When The Vandellas returned to Detroit from Europe, they found Motown had moved to

Los Angeles, but incredibly, no one had informed them.

Bless You.

> *Been a long time between releases, but this swinger loaded up with the Motown sound has it to put the group right on top with sales impact. (10/2/71) (#53 Pop, #29 R&B)*

The group's last single and chart record was "Tear It on Down" in 1973. On December 31, 1972, they gave a farewell concert at Cobo Hall, Detroit, followed by Martha's pursuit of a solo career. She signed with MCA, charting first with "Power of Love."

Wild Night.

> *Long awaited return of Martha proves well worth waiting for with this powerful rendition of classic Van Morrison song. If anything, her vocals are stronger than ever, particlarly in front of the excellent organ-horn arrangement. (8/3/74) (#74 Pop)*

In 1978, the group reunited in Santa Cruz, California, for a benefit for actor Will Geer. Martha then hit the road through the 1970s and 1980s, often touring as part of "The Legendary Ladies of Rock and Roll" with The Crystals and Ronnie Spector, among others. In 1995, the group was inducted into the Rock and Roll Hall of Fame, and Martha published her autobiography.

THE MARVELETTES

Gladys Horton: Lead vocals
Born: 1944, Inkster, MI
Georgia Dobbins: Lead vocals
Born: 1944, Inkster, MI
Wanda Young
Born: 1944, Inkster, MI
Georgeanna Tillman
Born: 1944, Inkster, MI
Katherine Anderson
Born: 1944, Inkster, MI

Juanita Cowart
Born: 1944, Inkster, MI
Influences: Shirelles, Chantels, Bobbettes

In the early 1960s, Motown had a bevy of big city, street-smart hit acts like The Supremes, The Miracles, and Mary Wells, but it took a group of shy country girls from Inkster, Michigan, to give the label its first #1. Such was the legacy of The Marvelettes, a collection of five teens including leads Gladys Horton and Georgia Dobbins with Juanita Cowart, Katherine Anderson, and Georgeanna Tillman.

In 1961, the girls, calling themselves The Marvels, won an Inkster High School talent contest. The prize was an audition with Motown's Berry Gordy. After hearing them sing Chantels and Shirelles songs, he sent them home to create an original. Dobbins wrote "Please Mr. Postman" and promptly resigned to care for her ailing mother, thus opening a spot for Wanda Young.

Soon after, the Marvels returned to Detroit where Gordy lengthened their name to The Marvelettes and issued their debut disk. "Postman" took 14 weeks to deliver the #1 spot, at the time the longest chart trek to the top, but it still beat out Gordy's favorites, The Supremes, and led to a sometimes bitter rivalry. More hits followed.

Please Mr. Postman.

> *Here's a mighty interesting group, with much of the down-to-earth quality of The Bobbettes. They turn to a strong hunk of rock material and pound it out in rousing style. One to watch. (8/14/61) (#1 Pop, #1 R&B)*

Twistin' Postman.

> *The "Postman" girls pound out the wild rocker, "Twistin' Postman," tied in with their current hit, but with a more heavily accented blues beat. (1/20/62) (#34 Pop, #13 R&B)*

Playboy.

> *The gals have another potential hit, that follows in the footsteps of their "Postman" hit. This is done in a similar rocking tempo, with a good, gospel piano in the backing. Watch it. (4/21/62) (#7 Pop, #4 R&B)*

Some Day, Some Way/Beechwood 4–5789.

First up is a soulful strongly gospel-oriented ballad, with organ, while the flip is a bright and breezy teen-slanted ditty. . . . Strong wax either way. (7/21/62) (A-side, #8 R&B; B-side, #17 Pop, #7 R&B)

Locking Up My Heart.

The Detroit sound is on the scene again with a few ramifications. The girls swing this bright rocker which makes for top teen dance stuff. (3/2/63) (#44 Pop, #25 R&B)

In 1964, The Marvelettes passed up an opportunity to record a song by Holland, Dozier, Holland that was then handed to The Supremes; it was the #1 "Baby Love." Still the quintet managed to have a few more strong sellers.

You're My Remedy.

Hand-clappin' rocker featuring solo by lead and pronounced beat. Hit sound all the way. (6/27/64) (#48 Pop)

Too Many Fish in the Sea.

Bongos and good percussion beat up a storm as group swings neatly with the beat. Charged with electricity! (10/24/64) (#25 Pop, #15 R&B)

I'll Keep Holding On.

Has a driving dance beat and a strong soulful belting vocal. (5/22/65) (#34 Pop, #11 R&B)

By 1965, Cowart left, reportedly because of a nervous breakdown, and Tillman left soon after owing to illness, leaving the quintet a trio. Although Horton sang lead on most of their hits, Young was out front on their next big one, "Don't Mess with Bill." In 1968, Horton left to have a son and Ann Bogan joined as the new lead voice.

Don't Mess with Bill.

The strong Detroit beat backs a good lyric and vocal performance right up the teen market alley. Should prove a monster. (12/18/65) (#7 Pop, #3 R&B)

The Hunter Gets Captured by the Game.

Clever lyric and solid dance beat combine for a sure fire sales winner for the group. Easy rhythm supports excep-

tional soft-sell vocal performance. (1/7/67) (#13 Pop, #2 R&B)

The Marvelettes 23rd and last chart single came in 1969.

That's How Heartaches Are Made.

Good entry for the group is this smooth swinger with a top performance for much play and sales action. (10/11/69) (#97 Pop)

When Motown decided to move to Los Angeles in 1971, the group decided, rather than uproot their home lives, to disband. Young eventually married Miracles member Bobby Rogers and Anderson wed Temptations roadie Joe Shaffner. Tillman tied the knot with Contours vocalist Billy Gordon but died in 1980 of sickle cell anemia. Bogan went on to sing with New Birth, whereas Gladys Horton revived The Marvelettes name with new members in the 1980s.

THE MIRACLES

William "Smokey" Robinson: Lead vocals
Born: 2/19/40, Detroit, MI
Bobby Rogers: Tenor
Born: 2/19/40, Detroit, MI
Emerson Rogers: Tenor
Born: 1940s, Detroit, MI
Ronnie White: Baritone
Born: 4/5/39, Detroit, MI
Warren "Pete" Moore: Bass
Born: 11/19/39, Detroit, MI
Influences: Nolan Strong and The Diablos, Flamingos, Isley Brothers
Influenced: Stevie Wonder, Dramatics, Camelots

One of the greatest of all the Motown groups, led by singer/songwriter William "Smokey" Robinson.

When, in 1960, Robinson convinced his friend Berry Gordy, Jr. to take an $800 loan and start his own record company, he had no idea how that would help make him one of America's best-loved recording artists. In fact, when Robinson and his friends founded their group at Northern High School in Detroit during 1954, it was mostly for the joy of singing.

The quintet of Robinson, Bobby and Emerson Rogers, Moore, and White liked the name The Matadors even though their 1956 lineup included Claudette Rogers, sister of Army-bound Emerson.

A 1957 audition with Jackie Wilson's manager, Nat Tarnapol, proved fortunate, even though he vetoed the group as sounding too similar to The Platters. Instead, he introduced Robinson to his songwriting associate, Berry Gordy, Jr., who was impressed with The Matadors. Berry recorded the quintet and, in 1958, released their single, "Got a Job," an answer record to "Get a Job," to End Records under the group's new moniker, The Miracles. By 1959, they had moved to Chess, and scored a minor hit with the Gordy-Robinson composition, "Bad Girl."

Got a Job.

One of the several "answers" to "Get a Job," this appears the most likely to score. It has a crazy lyric and an outstanding vocal gimmick. (3/3/58)

Bad Girl.

★ ★ ★ ★ *An unusual ballad is sung with a lot of feeling by a lead voice who sells it strongly. It could break out quickly. (7/27/59) (#93 Pop)*

The success of "Bad Girl" convinced Robinson that Gordy should form his own label, Tamla Records (which was originally to be called Tammy after the film). Their initial single was not actually a Miracles record, because Tamla 54025 reads Ron (White) and Bill (Robinson) doing "It" in August 1959. It was almost a year later that "The Feeling Is So Fine" was released as The Miracles' debut Tamla issue, but it was immediately withdrawn and replaced by "Way Over There" (#94 R&R).

Way Over There.

★ ★ ★ *Lead singer is showcased by an exciting arrangement. The church-styled vocal is set off by a touch of Latin rhythm. Very interesting. (6/27/60)*

When this release flopped, Tamla tried again and scored big time with "Shop Around." Having become Motown's first hit act and in appreciation

for Smokey's writing and producing contributions, Gordy made him a Tamla vice president in late 1961.

Shop Around.

The lead singer warbles with fervent sincerity on an amusing item with good lyrics about the need for a young man to look over the "field." Dual market potential. (10/24/60) (#2 Pop, #1 R&B)

Ain't It Baby.

The Miracles could follow "Shop Around" with the lively r&r side. (3/13/61) (#49 Pop, #15 R&B)

What's So Good About Goodbye.

★ ★ ★ ★ *A strong lead performance on a ballad question song. Singer really gets wound up and gets solid support from the group and the band. Strong wax that could step out. (12/18/61) (#35 Pop, #16 R&B)*

I'll Try Something New.

A very pretty tune, smartly arranged and smartly played by the large ork, receives a first-rate interpretation from The Miracles with the lead coming through with a fine lead vocal. Strong teen disking. (5/5/62) (#39 Pop, #11 R&B)

You've [Really] Got a Hold on Me.

A potent item from the Detroit group. Lead sings with devastating feeling as the rest of the group fills with solid sound at a walking tempo. (11/24/62) (#8 Pop, #1 R&B)

The act then jumped on the dance-craze bandwagon.

Mickey's Monkey.

The Monkey is the latest teen dance craze and The Miracles tell all about it on this bright rocker, with powerful down-to-earth backing. It should be welcome to the dancers and it'll please everyone with its sales. (8/10/63) (#8 Pop, #3 R&B)

In 1963, Claudette Rogers married Robinson and withdrew from the act. The British invasion had little effect on The Miracles as they turned out classic after classic like "Ooo Baby Baby" (unreviewed, but awarded four stars) and "The Tracks of My Tears."

The Tracks of My Tears.

First rate teen ballad with pulsating dance beat. (7/10/65) (#16 Pop, #2 R&B)

Going to a Go-Go.

Pulsating dance beat backs a powerful vocal on clever material headed for the top of the chart. (12/18/65) (#11 Pop, #2 R&B)

I'm the One You Need.

This one is headed for Hitsville. The Detroit group does a fine job on this solid rocker, which should make its mark on the charts in short order. (10/29/66) (#17 Pop, #4 R&B)

Through it all, Robinson managed to find time to write hits for other Motown stablemates like The Temptations ("The Way You Do the Things You Do") and Mary Wells ("My Guy"). By 1967, the labels read Smokey Robinson and The Miracles.

More Love.

A groovy blues entry. (6/10/67) (#23 Pop, #5 R&B)

Baby Baby Don't Cry.

With even more sales potential than their recent "Special Occasion," this strong follow-up should put this group higher on the Hot 100. (12/28/68) (#8 Pop, #3 R&B)

Their biggest smash was, surprisingly, not issued in America until it was a hit in England. "The Tears of a Clown" sold over 900,000 copies in Britain and then a million stateside. It was taken from the three-year-old *Make It Happen* LP in England by British Motown executive John Marshall, who was looking for a follow up to "Tracks of My Tears."

The Tears of a Clown.

This powerhouse swinger topped the British chart and will hit with the same impact here. Culled from an early LP, the driving beat never lets up. (10/10/70) (#1 Pop, #1 R&B)

In 1972, Robinson retired from The Miracles and went solo. Meanwhile, Billy Griffin took over the daunting task of replacing Robinson.

Do It Baby.

Sure looks like the Miracles have their biggest grabber since Smokey quit. Lush, intensive production surrounds high tenor soaring lead vocal in a sophisticated plea for loving. Veteran group is really back in the commercial groove. (6/29/74) (#13 Pop, #4 R&B)

In 1975, the group's last pop charter was a #1 single "Love Machine." In 1977, they left Motown for Columbia. On May 16, 1983, Robinson and The Miracles reunited for Motown's televised 25th anniversary bash.

Between 1973 and 1989, Robinson had 24 pop and 38 R&B chart singles including "Cruisin'" and "Being with You."

Rick James and Friend: Ebony Eyes.

A gracious ballad less characteristic of James than "friend" Smokey Robinson. (12/10/83) (#43 Pop, #22 R&B)

In 1987, Smokey Robinson was honored as a new member of the Rock and Roll Hall of Fame, whereas the Miracles were conspicuously ignored.

Davy Jones: Lead vocals
Born: 12/30/45, Manchester, England
Mike Nesmith: Guitar
Born: 12/30/42, Houston, TX
Peter Tork: Bass
Born: 2/13/44, Washington, DC
Mickey Dolenz: Drums
Born: 3/8/45, Tarzana, CA
Influences: Chuck Berry, Beatles

American TV's answer to The Beatles were The Monkees, a zany collection of four young men, handpicked by Columbia Pictures' executives to star in a small screen musical comedy series. The concept was imagined by producers Bert Schneider and Bob Rafelson who, along with Colgems Music honcho Don Kirshner, felt that America's teens would take to a weekly show that exhibited the same irreverent humor as the Beatles' films.

A 1965 *Daily Variety* casting call that read "MADNESS!! Running Parts for Four Insane Boys, aged 17 to 21" resulted in over 400 hopefuls auditioning. The mixed bag of applicants who were rejected included Stephen Stills, Paul Williams, Danny Hutton (later of Three Dog Night), and, believe it or not, mass murderer Charles Manson. Obviously, musical ability wasn't a priority but personality and charisma were, as the producers settled on Jones, Tork, Dolenz, and Nesmith.

Jones had been a jockey and actor, appearing on Broadway in the musical, *Oliver*. He recorded for Colpix in 1965, achieving a minor pop hit with "What Are We Going to Do?," and appeared with The Beatles on their U.S. TV debut on the Ed Sullivan show. Coincidentally, Nesmith had recorded as a folk artist for Colpix at the same time ("The Journey" and "Until It's Time for You to Go") as Michael Blessing. Tork was also a folkie with the Greenwich Village group, The Phoenix Singers. Dolenz was a television child star in "Circus Boy," appearing under the pseudonym, Mickey Braddock.

With Kirshner and Screen Gems Publishing guru Lester Sill calling the musical shots, every hit writer in their stable (from Neil Sedaka and Neil Diamond to Carole King and Gerry Goffin) had a chance with the newly christened Monkees. On September 12, 1966, the show premiered. At the same time, a single, "Last Train to Clarksville," was already chugging up the charts. The sitcom was a smash and so was the recording career of the American moptops.

Last Train to Clarksville.
All the excitement generated by the promotional campaign of the new group, which debuts on a fall TV show, is justified by this debut disk loaded with exciting teen dance beat sounds. (8/27/66) (#1 Pop)

I'm a Believer/Steppin' Stone.
Two blockbuster sides that will hit with immediate impact. "Believer" side is

an easy-go dance mover penned by Neil Diamond. "Stone" composed by Boyce and Hart is a hard driving groovy rocker with a strong teen lyric. (12/3/66) (#1 Pop)*

Although all had sung before, only Nesmith and Tork were musicians at the outset and so the scramble to learn their instruments was on. Their early hits all featured top studio musicians like David Gates, Glen Campbell, and Leon Russell. Screen Gems kept the fact that the group didn't play on its records a secret until Nesmith blew the lid off at a New York press conference, causing Kirshner to resign and The Monkees to become their own musicians. Meanwhile, the hits kept coming.

A Little Bit Me, a Little Bit You/The Girl I Knew Somewhere.
Destined to become their third million seller in a row, the TV stars have another double sided smash. Neil Diamond penned the first side and Michael Nesmith the flip. Equal potential. (3/18/67) (#2 Pop)

Pleasant Valley Sunday.
Strong easy rocker, penned by the Goffin-King team, and excitingly performed by the group will make this their fourth Top 10 record in a row. Will hit with sales impact. (7/15/67) (A-side, #3 Pop; B-side, #11 Pop)

In mid-1967, they embarked on a tour to prove that they could, in fact, perform as a band. They invited a hot new act, Jimi Hendrix, to open for them! However, his wild style did not sit well with The Monkees' teenybopper audience. He was regularly booed off stage and left after two weeks.

Daydream Believer.
With a clever opening, the winning group has a No. 1 contender. With this well written easy beat rhythm ballad one of their finest sounds to date. (11/4/67) (#1 Pop)

Valleri/Tapioca Tundra.
Two blockbuster sides. First is penned by Boyce and Hart and is an easy beat rocker while the flip is a driving swinger with a clever megaphoned

vocal workout and an old-timey feel. (3/2/68) (A-side, #3 Pop; B-side, #34 Pop)

D. W. Washburn.

A catchy rhythm novelty item with an old timey feeling. (6/8/68) (A-side, #19 Pop; B-side, #51 Pop)

After 58 episodes, The Monkees' TV fad was over and the program was canceled in June 1968. Later that year, The Monkees appeared in the experimental film *Head* cocreated by Bob Rafelson and a then-unknown actor, Jack Nicholson. The film was a bomb and their 45s were starting to drop off the chart.

Porpoise Song/As We Go Along.

From the forthcoming film "Head," the group has two unusual commercial sides. A change of pace for them in tempo and material. The writing is by Goffin-King and Stern with arrangements by Jack Nitzsche. (10/5/68) (#62 Pop)

Tork then bought out his contract for $160,000 and the rest of the band gave up in 1970 after "Oh My My."

The Monkees, now a duo, have a rocking bubble gum item with this rhythmic Jeff Barry-Andy King tune. Top programming item. (4/25/70) (#98 Pop)

Tork spent some time in the early 1970s teaching French and guitar in Venice, California. Nesmith formed the country-rock First National Band (followed by the Second National Band, and various solo projects); he had a Top-25 hit in 1970 with "Joanne."

Smooth, easy beat original that has all the earmarks of bringing the former Monkee back to the charts with impact. (7/18/70) (#21 Pop)

In 1975, Dolenz and Jones, along with writer/producers Bobby Hart and Tommy Boyce regrouped for a two-year odyssey, "The Golden Great Hits of The Monkees" tour. By 1980, Nesmith hadn't had a chart single in 9 years, although its relevance became inconsequential when compared with his inheritance. In 1979 his

mother sold her patent for liquid paper to Gillette Corp. for $47 million and died the next year.

Reruns of The Monkees' TV show in 1982 started a new wave of Monkee business as Tork and Jones went back on tour. By 1986, Dolenz had joined and the trio began recording again. Also that year, seven of the act's original albums were on the *Billboard* albums chart at the same time and Monkee Mania had returned. A new "Monkees" was then formed for another TV and record go round, but they were no competition for the original.

THE MOONGLOWS

Bobby Lester: Lead vocals
Born: 1/13/30, Louisville, KY (died 10/15/80)
Harvey Fuqua: Baritone
Born: 1930, Louisville, KY
Prentiss Barnes: Bass
Born: 1921, Cleveland, OH
Alexander "Pete" Graves: Tenor
Born: 1937
Influences: Orioles, Ravens
Influenced: Dells, Spinners, Rascals, Temptations, Skyliners, Ray Stevens, Cleftones, Monotones, Marcels, Crests, Lee Andrews and The Hearts, Orlons, Dreamlovers, Dell-Vikings, many more

A highly original-sounding group, The Moonglows were one of the 1950s' legendary quartets and the developers of the singing style that would eventually be known as "blow harmony."

Cleveland was the setting for the historic union, in 1952, of Kentuckians Harvey Fuqua (nephew of Ink Spots member Charlie Fuqua) and Bobby Lester with locals Pete Graves and Prentiss Barnes. Calling themselves The Crazy Sounds, they began playing clubs like the Chesterfield Lounge. There, a friend of deejay Alan Freed was so impressed he called Freed and made him listen to the group over the phone.

In no time, the Crazy Sounds were recording at radio station WJW and their first single "I Just

Can't Tell No Lie" was issued on Freed's hastily conceived Champagne label. The quartet's new name, The Moonglows, was the deejay's tribute to his own "Moondog" radio personality. In 1953, when the 45 went unpromoted beyond the Cleveland area, The Moonglows traveled to Chicago and signed with Chance Records. Their Chance debut was a classy blues ballad (Fuqua's favorite Chance release) "Baby Please," which did well in Chicago and Cleveland. They followed with a Christmas-season novelty.

Hey Santa Claus . . . .**.69**

"Bring my baby back," these lads importune Santa. It's a driving r.&b. item with good beat but not much originality. Red Holloway's ork backs the Moonglows. (12/12/53)

Although each subsequent Chance recording was the epitome of great R&B, neither of the *Billboard* commentaries referenced blues or R&B in their critiques. "I Was Wrong" was their biggest success to date but the label couldn't spread it beyond the Midwest.

Real Gone Mama **81**

Here's a strong effort by the Moonglows on a real gone piece of material. They sell it with life and sparkle and the side has a chance for loot. Watch this one.

Secret Love **79**

A smooth version of the current pop hit, sparked by a bright lead singer and a booming bass. Side is most listenable and could get juke and jock action. (12/17/54)

Ooh Rocking Daddy (A-side) **82**

The distinctive sound, the crazy riff and the rocking beat that the group works up here ought to be a formula for success on this side. It's wild and exciting stuff that ops can certainly use. Strong wax.

I Was Wrong (B-side) **76**

In a more subdued voice, the lead singer tells his girl he's sorry and begs forgiveness. A pretty, smoothly harmonized ditty with a solid dance beat. (6/5/54)

A 1954 move up the street to the Chess label changed all that with the Fuqua conceived "Sincerely."

Sincerely.

This is a solid hunk of wax. The tune is melodic, the performance is outstanding and the arrangement is retentive. It could take off immediately and pull many coins. (11/6/54) (#20 Pop, #1 R&B)

The song's popularity encouraged Chess to take the group's up tempo "Shoo Doo-Be Doo" and issue it as by "Bobby Lester and the Moonlighters."

Shoo Doo-Be Doo **76**

Lester and the boys warble effectively on a rhythmic bouncy novelty. (11/13/54)

More fantastic plastic followed, but Chess was either preoccupied with Chuck Berry or lapsing promotionally on Moonglows masterpieces.

Most of All.

The boys are still riding high on the charts with "Sincerely," so dealers should have no trouble moving their new record. The disk has plenty of merit on its own, with "Most of All" a lovely ballad, accorded a showmanly vocal arrangement with a fine beat. (3/12/55) (#5 R&B)

Starlight/In Love.

The boys come thru with showmanly vocal performances on two fine songs. "Starlight" is dreamy ballad with a poignant warbling stint by the group's lead singer. "In Love" is a delightful rhythm-ballad, highlighted by a fascinating phrasing gimmick on the title. The platter has a bright future. (9/10/55)

In My Diary.

A fancy piece of material in the super-refined groove, with a definite story idea well carried thru by the high lead singer. (12/10/55)

We Go Together.

A . . . recent disk that is surging ahead with above-average force. A wide variety of territories reported strong activity. (4/14/56) (#9 R&B)

See Saw/When I'm with You.

This coupling gives the cats two shots at the money. "See Saw" is a light rhythm novelty with brisk pace. Flip is the ballad side, featuring tenor lead to fine effect. (7/28/56) (A-side, #25 Pop, #6 R&B; B-side, #15 Pop, #15 R&B)

During 1956, their first film, compliments of longtime fan Alan Freed, birthed both sides of their next single, which, despite *Billboard*'s prediction, again failed to chart.

Over and Over Again/I Know from the Start.

Two songs that the Moonglows perform in the pic "Rock, Rock, Rock." The first is a weeper-ballad, with a standout lead part. Its slow thrusting rhythm backing adds weight. "I Knew from the Start" is an effective ballad at a faster tempo. The group offers a tasty, prettily blended backdrop to the lead's happy outburst. Could be a strong seller on either side. (12/8/56)

The Moonglows took a pop stance for one single, "Don't Say Goodbye." One of Fuqua's few leads while Lester was still a group member, "Please Send Me Someone to Love," followed, returning them to the upper reaches of the R&B charts. Lester's last lead, "Confess It to Your Heart," was next, and then he returned to Louisville to manage a nightclub.

Don't Say Goodbye.

You'd never believe that this came out of the Chess studios; but there it is, the Moonglows with a lush string backing, and in their most sophisticated slicing to date. It's mighty pretty and should have wide pop appeal as well as r.&b. The flip—"I'm Afraid the Masquerade Is Over"—is in the group's more characteristic style. They put a good beat and kind of skittish styling to the standard. It's cute as a button and could do well. (3/9/57)

Please Send Me Someone to Love.

This appealing ballad with good lyrics and a spiritual flavor gets an expressive and artful rendition by the lead with fine support from the group. The side should click. (6/17/57) (#73 Pop, #5 R&B)

Confess It to Your Heart.

A ballad done in a swingy, relaxed fashion, to a tastefully simple guitar backing. (9/16/57)

With Bobby gone, the group became known as Harvey and The Moonglows, although label and review credit varied. The last of The magical Moonglows monuments, "Ten Commandments" was also their last pop hit. Chess then tried issuing three-year-old Lester-led singles but it didn't help.

Ten Commandments of Love.

★ *Harvey lists the ten commandments of love which are echoed by the bass of the group. Tune is a slow ballad with beat. It bears watching. (9/1/58) (#22 Pop, #9 R&B)*

I'll Never Stop Wanting You.

★ ★ ★ *Starts with pleasant vocal harmonies, followed by a devoted lead performance in slow sock tempo. The cat really puts his heart in this. Watch it. (1/19/59)*

About that time, Harvey witnessed an impromptu audition in the Howard Theater (Washington) alleyway by four youngsters known as The Marquees who were discovered by Bo Diddley. By the time they finished, Fuqua decided to disband his quartet and make those kids (Reese Palmer, James Nolan, Chester Simmons, and Marvin Gaye—yes, that Marvin Gaye!) The New Moonglows. They began recording, with the addition of The Dells' Chuck Barksdale (bass). "Mama Loocie" was Marvin's first lead.

Harvey and The Moonglows:
Mama Loocie.

★ ★ ★ *A catchy rhythm rocker is wrapped up in a fervent reading. (10/5/59)*

In 1960, the new group split up as Marvin began his solo career and Harvey went dueting and then produced and wrote. By 1964, Graves had a new Moonglows and Lester came out of retirement in 1970 to form yet another. In 1972, Lester, Fuqua, and Graves, along with Chuck Lewis, recorded *The Return of The Moonglows* LP, yielding the single "Sincerely 72" (#43 R&B), their last chart 45.

In 1983, Fuqua and the latter-day Moonglows (with Clyde McPhatter's son Billy on lead) performed at the Grammys as a tribute to the monumental harmony groups of a bygone era. No act was more deserving.

RICK NELSON

Real Name: Eric Hilliard Nelson
Birthdate: 5/8/40
Birthplace: Teaneck, NJ
Died: 12/31/85
Influences: Elvis Presley, Carl Perkins
Influenced: Buffalo Springfield

Ricky Nelson was the first teen idol to be promoted through television. The son of former bandleader Ozzie Nelson and his pretty wife and singer Harriet, Ricky (along with older brother David) appeared weekly on the family's "Ozzie and Harriet" radio show. Nelson started on the radio version at age nine in 1949 and was a veteran of 12 by the time the family frolics were moved to the visual version on ABC-TV in 1952.

Ricky had no interest in singing until 1957, when the 16-year-old decided the only way to impress a girlfriend (who was infatuated with Elvis) was to make his own record. Dad helped out, arranging a recording with the jazz label, Verve, and both Ricky's romance and recording career were off with a bang. With TV exposure aplenty, the two-sided single sold a 100,000 45s a week on its way to million-selling status.

A Teen-Ager's Romance . . . .[72]
Ozzie and Harriet's son Ricky Nelson makes his record debut on this disk, which was kicked off on the family TV show. The teen-ager sells the appealing

ballad with sock sincerity. This could be a sleeper.

I'm Walkin' . . . .[72]
The lad covers the catchy Fats Domino rhythm blues with considerable sales savvy and relaxed know-how. Hip rockabilly backing by Barney Kessel. Flip is side to watch. (4/27/57) (A-side, #8 Pop; B-side, #17 Pop, #10 R&B)

You're My One and Only.
Nelson registers strongly on a medium-tempo rhythm ballad with Domino-type backing. Sock selling here can be a smash followup. (8/12/57) (#16 Pop)

Strangely, Verve never contracted Ricky, and when they appeared to be slacking on royalties, Ozzie brought his teen idol to Imperial. His first release on the new label sported a big hit on the B-side, and was followed by a series of two-sided hits.

Have I Told You Lately That I Love You/Be-Bop Baby.
The hot young chanter has his first on the new label and figures to shake up plenty of action, even tho his last on the Verve label has also hit the charts. The top is a strong oldie sung with great heart. Has a commercial rural flavor with a solid rock and roll beat. Flip is another rock and roller with a bit more bounce. (9/16/57) (A-side, #29 Pop; B-side, #3 Pop, #5 R&B)

Waitin' in School/Stood Up.
Two strong entries by the young artist, who hasn't missed yet. "Waitin'" is a rockabilly effort that should go well with the kids. Flip, "Stood Up," is also in the rockabilly idiom. Good support on both sides helps make it a threat in all markets. (12/9/57) (A-side, #18 Pop, #12 R&B; B-side, #2 Pop, #4 R&B)

Rick's first #1 was also an international hit, "Believe What You Say."

Believe What You Say/My Bucket's Got a Hole in It.
Two fine rockabilly sides. . . . Both are loaded with teen appeal and are likely clicks in all markets. Good backing on

both tunes. Second side is a traditional blues. (3/10/58) (A-side, #14 Pop, #6 R&B; B-side, #18 Pop)

Poor Little Fool/Don't Leave Me This Way.
Nelson handles both of these rockabilly tunes nicely. "Fool" is presented with a strong vocal and good rhythm support. "Don't Leave Me" starts out like "Raunchy" and has that contagious feeling all the way thru. The side can score in all markets. (6/23/58) (#1 Pop, #3 R&B)

I Got a Feeling/Lonesome Town.

"Feeling" is a listenable rocker that is handed a solid reading over good ork support. Flip is a ballad that is also warbled to excellent effect. Both can happen. (8/29/58) (A-side, #10 Pop; B-side, #7 Pop, #6 R&B)

During 1959, Nelson, after three years of radio and seven years on TV, had his film debut with John Wayne and Dean Martin in *Rio Bravo*. His second film performance came in the Jack Lemmon comedy *The Wackiest Ship in the Army*, in 1960. Meanwhile, the hits kept coming.

Never Be Anyone Else but You/It's Late.

Nelson appears to have another two-sided click with these excellent sides. "Never Be" is a haunting ballad-type in which the chanter registers with strong appeal. Flip, "It's Late," is taken at a swifter pace. Highest potential on both. (2/9/59) (A-side, #6 Pop; B-side, #9 Pop, #1 R&B)

Just a Little Too Much/Sweeter Than You.

"Just a Little Too Much" is an upbeat rocker. "Sweeter" is a rockaballad. Warbles on each are highly saleable. (6/22/59)

Young Emotions/Right By My Side.

"Young Emotions," a pretty ballad, shows a change of pace for the singer. It's done over a listenable, string-filled arrangement. "Right By My Side" is a driving rocker that also has the sound. (4/11/60)

In the Spring of 1961, the singer had his best-known two-sided smash with "Hello Mary Lou"

backed with "Travelin' Man" (a song rejected by Sam Cooke), both of which became signature songs for him. All told, the singer had 18 two-sided hits. By his 21st birthday, Ricky had become Rick.

Hello Mary Lou/Travelin' Man.

Nelson comes thru with a powerful vocal on a bright Latin tune penned by Gene Pitney. Side II is an easy-moving ditty about a lover with many flames. Both have a chance. (4/10/61) (A-side, #9 Pop; B-side, #1 Pop)

A Wonder Like You/Everlovin'.

Rick Nelson (he's grown up now) turns in two first-rate readings of a pair of light, happy items that should keep his sales a-booming. Top side is warm ballad sold with style by Rick; flip is a bright rocker that is also handled neatly. (9/18/61) (A-side, #11 Pop; B-side, #16 Pop)

Young World.

A pleasing, relaxed styling in the "Travelin' Man" vein. Has a fine sound. (2/24/62)

Teen Age Idol.

A ballad with an intensely personal touch about the thoughts and feelings of a big record star. (8/4/62) (#5 Pop)

In 1963, Rick left Imperial for Decca and a one-million dollar, 20-year deal!

You Don't Love Me Anymore (and I Can Tell).
Rick's first for his new label is a winner. It's a weeper type of teen ballad that's got to touch the girls' hearts. Simple arrangement adds to the class of the side. (3/2/63) (A-side, #47 Pop; B-side, #49 Pop)

By April 1963, Nelson married football star Tom Harmon's daughter, Kristin, who became the newest member of the Nelsons' TV family.

Fools Rush In/Down Home.

Rick Nelson has his next smash well in hand. Two sides go all the way with a fast-stepping version of the standard that has a country twang and huge novelty appeal. Second side is a nostalgic

tune that features the vocalist against country type backing. (9/7/63) (#12 Pop)

For You.

A bright reading of the standard in reverb-ful style. (12/21/63) (#6 Pop)

During 1964, Nelson made his third film, "Love and Kisses," including Kristin as costar. In September 1966, "The Adventures of Ozzie And Harriet" finally left the airwaves after a 14-year run, and Rick Nelson found himself too old to be a teen star. He then moved into the country and country-rock field, impressing with every record. In 1969, Nelson formed The Stone Canyon Band. In its various forms, the group included future and past members of Little Feat, The Eagles, Buck Owens's Buckaroos, and Every Mother's Son.

She Belongs to Me.

Nelson takes on a fresh new sound with the Bob Dylan material that has all the earmarks of an important chart item. Top Nelson performance. (8/30/69) (#33 Pop)

Easy to Be Free.

Nelson made a strong chart comeback with his "She Belongs to Me" and this folk ballad follow-up has all the sales potential and more. (2/21/70) (#48 Pop)

I Shall Be Released.

Nelson has a sure-fire winner in this potent Dylan classic that takes on even more meaning today. The sing-a-long arrangement and top vocal workout will spiral it right to the top. (5/2/70)

On October 15, 1971, at an oldies-style concert in Madison Square Garden, Nelson defied audience expectations by playing new material. He was rudely booed. His retaliation (and revelation) half a year later was the hit he wrote about that "Garden Party." It was his first Top 10 in nine years and first million-seller since "Travelin' Man"; *Billboard* highlighted it in their "Hot Chart Action" section.

Garden Party.

Nelson's first smash in some time showing up strong in top 40 radio stations. . . . Disc riding high on the Easy

Listening chart at #11 with strong sales and MOR reports. (9/9/72) (#6 Pop, #44 C&W)

After 18 hits in England, Rick made his first British tour in November 1972. Rick recorded for Epic (1977) and Capitol (1981) but his last of 54 Top-100 singles was "Palace Guard" (#65) in 1973 on MCA (Decca). In 1983, an interesting bit of casting made Rick a school principal and his mother Harriet his secretary in an NBC-TV movie, "High School U.S.A."

Always active on the tour circuit, Nelson's career tragically ended on a chartered flight between Guntersville, Alabama, and Dallas, Texas. The plane caught fire and crashed, killing all (including his new fiancee Helen Blair and members of his band) except the pilots.

Having sold over 35 million records and charted Top-10 18 times, Rick Nelson remains well entrenched in rock 'n' roll history.

ROY ORBISON

Birthdate: 4/23/36
Birthplace: Vernon, TX
Died: 12/6/88
Influences: Lefty Frizzell, Webb Pierce
Influenced: Bruce Springsteen, Del Shannon, Beatles, Tom Petty, Jay Black, Jeff Lynne, Buffalo Springfield, Jackson Browne, Eagles, Bonnie Raitt, Elvis Costello, k. d. lang, many more

With a remarkably rich voice of uncommon range, Roy Orbison blended country and western and rock into pop stardom like few before or since.

The man who influenced scores of stars, from The Beatles to Bruce Springsteen, had his humble beginnings in Vernon, Texas, where, at age six, his father began teaching him the virtues of guitar playing. By Roy's teens, his mastery of the instrument led to the forming of The Wink Westerners, a hillbilly group. Still, Orbison planned to be a geologist, and by 1954 was attending North Texas University. A friend and fellow student, Pat Boone, encouraged him to follow his musical instincts instead.

Forming a new group, The Teen Kings, in 1955, Roy and company journeyed to Norman Petty's Clovis, New Mexico, studio and recorded his original, "Ooby Dooby." Issued on Je-Wel records of Albuquerque in April 1956, the single stiffed. The Teen Kings performances brought Orbison in contact with Johnny Cash, who suggested he send a tape to Sun Records, Cash's label at the time. Although Orbison was more desirous of recording ballads, he sent "Ooby Dooby" to Sun's Sam Phillips, believing he would be more interested in rockabilly. He was right, as Sun issued the side as recorded by Roy Orbison and The Teen Kings (#59 Pop). Other Sun releases didn't fare as well.

Oobie Doobie [sic].

Orbison is one of the few of the numerous group of country blues singers to have sprung up recently who is succeeding. It has taken several weeks for this disk to make its full impact felt, but by now it is well established in most key Southern and Northern markets. For the past two weeks it has been on the Memphis territorial charts. A previous Billboard *"Spotlight" pick. (6/9/56)*

You're My Baby/Rockhouse.

Orbison displays vocal sock showmanship on . . . a fast country blues with a strong rockabilly beat. Flip, another good rockabilly rhythm side, is wrapped up solidly by Orbison. (10/20/56)

Devil Doll 81

A swingy song, with an unusual lyric. Orbison chants this solidly. It's backed with a chorus and an instrumental combo that contributes a fine beat. Will get action. (4/20/57)

In 1957, Orbison moved to Nashville and signed with Acuff-Rose Music as a staff writer. His composition, "Claudette" (written for his wife) became a hit for The Everly Brothers as the flip of their #1 "All I Have to Do Is Dream" in 1958. That same year he signed (albeit briefly) with RCA.

Seems to Me/Sweet and Innocent.

 A strong Boudleaux Bryant tune is given a fine warble by the artist. It's a great chanting stint that's sure to catch

fire, if the side is exposed. Talented cat is just as powerful in his treatment of the flip. Tune is a rockabilly on which he has a chorus assist. (10/20/58)

Wesley Rose of Acuff-Rose took the reigns of management and shifted the singer to the new independent label, Monument. At first it looked like a mistaken move, with a couple of failed singles appearing in late 1959.

With the Bug (A-side).

★ ★ ★ ★ *A good rocker by Orbison. Material is interesting and the side has a good sound. Spinnable wax.*

Paper Boy (B-side).

★ ★ ★ ★ *A sad ballad nicely performed by Orbison. (9/28/59)*

Up Town.

 The smart rockabilly artist packs a lot of emotion and punch into a tune with strong teen appeal. (11/30/59)

Orbison then wrote "Only the Lonely," a tune that The Everly Brothers rejected, so he recorded it himself. Two million sales later, Orbison was off on one of the hottest streaks of any 1960s' act, encompassing 26 consecutive chart singles.

Only the Lonely.

 The classy artist well-known on the Nashville-Memphis scene, has a solid outing here [on] a listenable ballad with fine vocal support. (5/9/60) (#2 Pop, #14 R&B)

Blue Angel/Today's Teardrops.

Roy Orbison should continue his hit string with these two fine readings. Top side is a ballad, flip swings. Strong wax. (8/29/60) (#9 Pop, #23 R&B)

I'm Hurtin'/I Can't Stop Loving You.

 "I'm Hurtin'"—a smart rocker—is sold with sock personality and style by Orbison. The flip, a great country tune penned by Don Gibson, is accorded a solid interpretation by the singer. Both sides are strong. (12/5/60) (#27 Pop)

With his success at Monument, Sun sought to cash in by reissuing an earlier side.

Sweet and Easy to Love.

★ ★ ★   *Here's a strongly country-oriented side which highlights Orbison's high-pitched vocal chords. Good effort taken from Sun's vaults. (12/5/60)*

During 1961, Orbison had two back-to-back smashes that would forever be the epitome of his bolero ballad style.

Running Scared/Love Hurts.

Orbison is in feelingful vocal form on "Running Scared," an effectively off-beat western-styled ditty with dramatic backing. Another unusual arrangement backs "Love Hurts," an appealing ballad. Should move in both pop and country and western markets. (3/27/61) (#1 Pop)

Crying/Candy Man.

Orbison has sock sides here—a fine follow-up to his recent smash hit "Runnin' Scared." "Crying" features an expressive reading on a moving country-flavored ballad. Flip is an effective folk blues with standout delivery by Orbison. (7/31/61) (A-side, #2 Pop; B-side, #25 Pop)

His hits continued through 1962 and 1963.

Dream Baby (How Long Must I Dream).

A bright rhythm effort sparked by a lively arrangement. (2/10/62) (#4 Pop)

Workin' for the Man/Leah.

Two fine songs penned by the chanter are handed sock readings by Orbison on this potent double-sided disking. Topper is a smartly styled work song that reaches a powerful climax; flip is a Hawaiian-flavored ballad that has strong vocal plus steel guitar and ukulele backing. (9/8/62) (A-side, #33 Pop; B-side, #25 Pop)

Falling.

A moving ballad sung by Orbison with his usual feeling and vocal gimmicks. (5/25/63) (#22 Pop)

When Orbison accidentally left his glasses on a plane in May 1963, he began wearing sunglasses, which, along with his dark hair and suits, created his legendary look of foreboding. His first major appearance with that new persona was on a U.K. tour with a new act, The Beatles.

Mean Woman Blues/Blue Bayou.

Two of the best sides to come along in many months are these sock performances by Roy Orbison. Topper is a powerful rocker [which] Orbison sings with excitement over swinging backing. Side II is a tender ballad in the "Only the Lonely" tradition and it is as strong as the first side. Both are headed for chartsville. (8/31/63) (A-side, #5 Pop, #8 R&B; B-side, #29 Pop)

It's Over.

The drama-ballad king scores again with pathos and chorus and strings that build, build, build. (4/4/64) (#9 Pop)

In 1964, the vocalist hit the motherlode with a seven-million seller, "Oh, Pretty Woman," his last release on Monument. Orbison wanted a greater opportunity to do films and in 1965 joined MGM. However, the hits soon dried up, and an acting career never materialized.

Oh, Pretty Woman.

Great dance beat coupled with fine arrangement. Expected highly commercial treatment from Roy. (8/15/64) (#1 Pop)

Ride Away.

Making his debut on the MGM label, Orbison has a winner in a driving piece of material that moves from start to finish with a strong dance beat. (8/14/65) (#25 Pop)

Monument combed the vaults to get more material.

Let the Good Times Roll.

The rhythm-blues classic gets the outstanding Orbison treatment which spells hitsville all the way! Solid dance beat backing. (10/23/65) (#81 Pop)

Meanwhile, he continued to produce lesser hits at MGM.

Twinkle Toes.

Orbison employs the party-style, "live" recording technique and dual-track vocal for a top-of-the-chart contender. (4/9/66) (#39 Pop)

On June 6, 1966, Orbison's wife Claudette was killed in a motorcycle accident. The grieving singer threw himself into a heavy tour schedule. He also appeared in the MGM film *The Fastest Guitar Alive*, a musical western and his only important film role. In 1967, Orbison returned to recording but with less than hoped for results. In September 1968, another tragedy struck when his house caught fire, killing two of his three sons, Roy, Jr. and Tony, while he was performing in England. Still, the veteran showman managed to pick up the pieces and continue. By 1974, he was with Mercury Records.

Sweet Mamma Blue.

A little longer than usual but a really different sound. Excellent arrangement blending bluesy harmonica, piano riffs and strings with choral background voices, making it smooth MOR listening and soulful too. Could be a real sleeper. (8/17/74)

During 1980, Orbison's duet with Emmylou Harris on "That Lovin' You Feelin' Again" became his first chart hit (#55) in 13 years, and won a Grammy Award for Best Country Performance by a Duo or Group. By this time, Roy's songs had become hits for a whole new generation of listeners through recordings by Linda Ronstadt ("Blue Bayou"), Van Halen ("Oh, Pretty Woman"), and Don McLean ("Crying"). In 1987, signed to Virgin, he began rerecording some of his treasures. He also cut a classic duet with new country star k. d. lang.

In Dreams.

One of Orbison's most haunting and powerful creations sounds as fresh today as it did back in 1963, when he took it to the top 10 of the pop charts. (8/15/87) (#75 C&W)

Roy Orbison and k. d. lang: Crying.

Not exactly new, but definitely noteworthy; classic selection has been rerecorded and is one of the highlights of the "Hiding Out" soundtrack. Orbison's vocals can still make you shiver, while

lang's poignant delivery serves as the perfect complement; simply brilliant. (11/14/87) (#42 C&W)

Also in 1987, the Rock and Roll Hall of Fame enshrined Orbison. Bruce Springsteen introduced him saying, "I wanted to write words like Bob Dylan that sounded like Phil Spector, but with singing like Roy Orbison, but nobody sings like Roy Orbison."

By 1988, Orbison had reached another milestone when he recorded as a member of The Traveling Wilburys, a collection of superstars also including Bob Dylan, George Harrison, Jeff Lynne, and Tom Petty. Sadly, Orbison died unexpectedly on December 7, 1988, of a heart attack while visiting his mother in Nashville. Two months later, he had his biggest single in 25 years.

You Got It.

It's hard to believe he's left us, but this fine selection from the artist's forthcoming "Mystery Girl" album charms with the appeal of the singer's vintage material. With the aid of Lynne and Petty the songwriting and production on this one are first-rate. That voice will undoubtedly continue to live on. . . (1/21/89)

The song was revived in 1995 by Bonnie Raitt and was a hit all over again, a testimony to Orbison's lasting appeal as songwriter and performer.

In 1977, Elvis Presley introduced Roy during his last Las Vegas performance as "the greatest singer in the world." Many would agree.

THE ORIOLES

Erlington Tilghman (Sonny Til): Lead vocals
Born: 8/18/28, Baltimore, MD (died 12/9/81)
Alexander Sharp: Tenor
Born: 1920s (died 1970s)
George Nelson: Baritone
Born: 1920s (died 1959)
Johnny Reed: Bass
Born: 1920s
Tommy Gaither: Guitar
Born: 1920s (died 1950)
Influences: Soul Stirrers, Mills Brothers
Influenced: Flamingos, Five Keys, Clovers, Hank Ballard
and The Midnighters, Crests, Drifters, Billy Ward and
The Dominoes, Moonglows, Larks, Chantels, Lee
Andrews and The Hearts, Sha Na Na, many more

Sonny Til and The Orioles helped pioneer the rock 'n' roll ballad and inspired a generation of vocal groups to stand in a hall or under a streetlamp searching for the same sound that made The Orioles famous.

The quartet emerged when Sonny began harmonizing with a few winners of a Baltimore talent show after his Army discharge in 1946. The group dubbed themselves The Vibranairs and by 1948 had secured an appearance on *Arthur Godfrey's Talent Scouts* TV show. Seeing their performance, label head Jerry Blaine signed them, renamed them, and issued their first single, which was written by sales clerk turned songwriting manager, Deborah Chessler.

It's Too Soon to Know.
> New label kicks off with a fine quartet effort on a slow race ballad. Lead tenor shows a fine lyric quality. (9/4/48)

"Too Soon" reached #1 R&B and #13 Pop, the high water mark on the pop charts for this new breed of vocalizers, and was quickly covered by Ella Fitzgerald.

It's Too Soon to Know.
Ella Fitzgerald–Male Quartet and Ork.
The Orioles.

> The Orioles platter, first disk effort of small Natural label, serves to intro the quintet as well—a fine group of chanters with a strong tenor lead. Ditty, a pretty, slow ballad, has also been waxed by Ella Fitzgerald, on the strength of the Natural clicking which appears to be another sleeper. Ella's effort is one of her best ever on a ballad, and tune, purchased by a major pub this week, may blossom forth as a top pop. (11/4/48)

The Baltimore balladeers continued through 1948 and 1949 with memorable slow sides like "Lonely Xmas" (#8 R&B), "Tell Me So" (#1 R&B), "A Kiss and a Rose" (#12 R&B), "Forgive and Forget" (#5), and "Lonely Xmas" again, on its way to becoming a seasonal standard. Although the group was a success, playing for top dollar, some of their now-treasured collector's singles never charted.

Would You Still Be the One in My Heart 85–85–85–85
> A strong blues ballad gets an arresting, sinuously slow treatment from the group. Should be a hot side for the Orioles—and tune should get attention from other r. & b. performers. (2/11/50)

At Night .85–85–85–85
> Chalk up another hit for the high flying group. Tune is standout; group delivers one of their best jobs yet. (4/8/50)

I Wonder When 85–85–85–85
> Group does one of their top performances here on a promising torcher. Orking is rich, with full fiddle effects. (6/3/50)

I'd Rather Have You Under the Moon 81–81–81–81
> Warblers do a Mills Brothers here as they double the tempo for second chorus. Ditty is attractive. (9/23/50)

In late 1950, tragedy struck as a car accident killed guitarist Tommy Gaithers while injuring Reed and Nelson. Ralph Williams became the guitarist and sometimes baritone and Sonny Til performed his first solo single as The Orioles tried to regain their touch.

Sonny Til:
My Prayer 73–74–72–73
> *Til goes it solo with Hammond organ backing on this recent pop revival. Pleasant job. (9/8/51)*

Subsequent single releases reflected their lack of enthusiasm following the accident.

You Belong to Me 74
> *The group works over the pop hit in schmaltzy style. Not their best effort, tho their fans will probably take to it. (11/22/52)*

They returned to form in 1953, recording their take on several standards. By then, Nelson quit while Gregory Carroll (Four Buddies, Savoy) and Charlie Harris made The Orioles a quintet.

I Miss You So ....7[5]
> *The group does up the oldie in their typical style. The chanting is good and the material is strong enough. (2/14/53)*

I Cover the Waterfront 69
> *The group tackles the oldie, but results are not as strong because of a lack of highlights. It's all just a bit too even in all respects. (6/27/53)*

On June 30, 1953, Til and company recorded one of rock's enduring masterpieces, "Crying in the Chapel," and *Billboard*'s reviewer sensed its importance.

Crying in the Chapel.
> *The Orioles have here what is undoubtedly their strongest record in two years, and one of the strongest r.&b. disks released in the past few months. The tune is the serious ditty now getting action in the country and pop markets, and the boys hand it a powerful rendition, full of feeling and sparked by the fine lead singer. This could be a big, big hit. (7/25/53) (#11 Pop, #1 R&B)*

On the heels of that landmark single came their last national best seller.

In the Mission of St. Augustine.
> *The Orioles are in good form for this side. Their delivery has delicacy and precision. Tune is getting action in the pop field and is a strong follow-up to "Crying in the Chapel." Good wax from both r.&b. and pop. (10/3/53) (#7 R&B)*

Secret Love.
> *An outstanding record . . . of the nation's current top tune on disks. The boys sing it with feeling and it should be a fast breaking disk. (2/6/54)*

As the hits slowed and competition soared, the group disbanded. Til, however, was not about to quit and he found a new, ready-made Orioles in the group, The Regals, who were performing at New York's Apollo Theater in 1954. Still, there were no hits.

I Love You Mostly.
> *The ditty now getting action in the country field receives a first-rate reading here from The Orioles, over a solid backing by the ork. Side is in the boys' most commercial style, and it has a real chance. Watch this one. (2/5/55)*

Please Sing Me Blues Tonight 75
> *A tender rendition of pretty material. Here's a dreamy side that deejays could spin to good reaction on late-hour segs. Has pop potential too. (10/29/55)*

In 1956, Til and ex-Regals Gerald Holeman, Albert Russell, Billy Adams, and Jerry Rodriquez moved to Vee-Jay.

Sonny Til:
Happy 'Til the Letter 82
> *Til wraps up a folksy ballad in a powerful vocal with a strong country flavor, augmented by the familiar r.&b. beat. Interesting switch on the current rock-a-billy trend. (6/23/56)*

Orioles:
For All We Know 75
> *This pretty ballad will have a lot of potential in the pop market, as well as*

in r.&b. There are listening kicks here for everybody, regardless of taste. Deejays have a "quality" item here they'll enjoy. (12/29/56)

Sonny then had a short stint with Roulette while Jubilee continued to release past singles anew, including, "Crying in the Chapel," "Tell Me So," and "Come on Home."

Several Orioles groups (with Til leading) endured through 1978. The 1981 *Sonny Til and The Orioles visit Manhattan Circa 1950* LP was Til's last recording. By then, Reed had retired, Williams was singing with a band in St. Louis, and Nelson and Sharp had died. Legendary lead Sonny Til passed on at age 51 in 1981. The Orioles were inducted into the Rock and Roll Hall of Fame in 1995.

THE PENGUINS

Cleveland Duncan: Lead vocals
Born: 7/23/35, Los Angeles
Dexter Tisby: Tenor
Born: 3/10/35, Los Angeles
Bruce Tate: Baritone
Born: 1935, Los Angeles
Curtis Williams: Bass
Born: 1935, Los Angeles
Influences: Clyde McPhatter and The Drifters, Mills Brothers, Nat Cole, Clovers, Johnny Ray, Billy Eckstine
Influenced: Crests, Magnificents, Cleftones, Dell-Vikings, Dion and The Belmonts, Frankie Lymon and The Teenagers, Fleetwoods, Righteous Brothers, Gene Pitney, Neil Sedaka

The fabulous 1950s were not only an era of experimentation and change in music, they were a time of great opportunity for teen hopefuls, long on enthusiasm and short on experience, like The Penguins.

Eighteen-year-old Cleve Duncan met songwriter/singer Curtis Williams in 1953; soon after, Williams' friends Bruce Tate and Dexter Tisby joined the unnamed Los Angeles quartet. Searching for a "cool" moniker, the group looked

no further than Dexter's Kool cigarettes with the cute penguin on the pack. The foursome began practicing originals written by Williams, like "Ese Chiquita" and "Earth Angel" (although the latter is known to have had the creative involvement of Jesse Belvin, Gaynel Hodge, and Duncan prior to its re-cording). Former bass player for Jimmie Lunceford's band and Duncan's uncle, Ted Brinson, directed the group to Dootsie Williams' Dootone label where The Penguins' 1954 uncredited session of "Ain't No News Today" (fronted by Willie Headon) became their first record.

Their next session generated what is considered by many to be rock 'n' roll's favorite oldie, "Earth Angel." The one-track recording, made in Brinson's garage, was so primitive that the group had to sing the song eight times, as a dog barking at passing cars leaked onto the tape. Even the record's success was unexpected. Dootsie gave the demo to KGFJ deejay Dick "Huggy Boy" Hugg to play with "Ese Chiquita" (now titled "Hey, Senorita"), their pick as the future A-side. The next morning Hugg informed Williams that calls were coming in nonstop for "Earth Angel." Unconvinced, Williams pressed the 45 with "Senorita" as the top side, but radio reaction changed all that. Although the single had the first five seconds of its introduction missing (it later appeared on LPs and reissues), and cover records like The Crew-Cuts' version (#3 pop) were cutting into sales, The Penguins' hit took center stage as they became the first West Coast group to crack the Pop Top 10.

In spite of many groups that now crowd the r.&b. field, this new quartet has a chance for action. They come thru with a rhythmic performance of a new ballad, "Earth Angel" on Dootone 348. Flip is "Hey, Senorita." (10/19/54)

Earth Angel.
After a sensational take-off on the West Coast, the disk is now racking up impressive sales in New York (where it is on the territorial chart), Philadelphia, Cincinnati, Cleveland, Buffalo, Pittsburgh and Nashville as well. Flip is "Hey, Senorita" (a previous Billboard talent pick). (11/13/54) (#8 Pop, #1 R&B)

Their future looked bright, but it wasn't. Three more Dootone singles failed, including the beautiful, "Love Will Make Your Mind Go Wild." After a car accident in early 1955, Tate left and was replaced by Randolph Jones.

By the Spring of 1955, The Penguins were on Mercury courtesy of manager Buck Ram and his now famous two-for-one deal. ("If you want The Penguins you gotta take my other group, The Platters too.") Unfortunately, their quality cuts went unnoticed on the radio.

Don't Do It/Be Mine or Be a Fool.

The Penguins are still up there on the charts with "Earth Angel," and this platter should grab off plenty of play from jukes and jocks. "Don't Do It" is a bouncy novelty, sung with charm and enthusiasm. "Be Mine or Be a Fool" features fine work by the lead singer. (4/23/55)

It Only Happens with You . . . .[74]

Love ballad is sung tenderly . . . with the lead tenor projecting effectively. The steady beat behind the boys helps. (7/30/55)

Devil That I See 73

The Penguins' lead is featured in this pretty ballad, and he does a good job of embroidering the melody to an unusual piano and rhythm backing. (9/24/55)

A Christmas Prayer 75

A strong entrant for the r.&b. Christmas sweepstakes. It's a sincere reading of a good seasonal ballad. (12/10/55)

Ram, busy promoting The Platters, left The Penguins to their own devices. A one-shot on Mercury affiliate Wing and even a rerecording of the two-million selling "Earth Angel" didn't help.

My Troubles Are Not at an End 73

This pretty close-harmony reading is pleasant listening. (2/11/56)

Dealer of Dreams .77

A moving reading . . . on a serenely paced ballad with imaginative lyrics. Excellent job by the lead singer. (5/12/56)

Earth Angel 75

A new waxing of the group's first hit. The arrangement is a fresh one and the group offers a few interesting variations on the original. It's a fine job, but whether lightning can strike twice in the same place is doubtful. (9/1/56)

In 1957, the quartet recorded just one single for Atlantic before returning to Los Angeles from New York, Williams joined The Hollywood Flames and Cleve Duncan was hospitalized for a throat operation. Upon his recovery, Teddy Harper joined and the group went back to Dootone.

Pledge of Love 76

Formerly on Mercury, the group bows on [Atlantic] with a late cover of this already fast-moving tune. It's a convincing reading but competition is very strong (4/13/57) (#15 R&B)

Sweet Love.

Here's a good, wild type side with lots of noise. Lead man shouts out the message with plenty of activity by the group in the backing. This has a driving quality that could go. Worth spins.

Let Me Make Up Your Mind.

A slow, meshuga type ballad with a pounding triplet backing. A dedicated performance by the lead but the flip has more action. (1/13/58)

In 1959, Duncan tried a different mix with two girls and Tisby, forming The Radiants ("To Keep Our Love") but to no avail. Their old material was doing better than their new sides as "Earth Angel"'s Dootone reissue in 1960 hit #101 Pop. The Penguins' last 45s were in the mid-1960s but even the Frank Zappa penned "Memories of El Monte" in 1963 couldn't bring back their one-time glory.

In 1966, Jones, Harper, and Tisby joined Cornel Gunter as The Coasters. Williams and Tate died, but Duncan is still active in the 1990s with Walter Saulsberry and Glen Madison as the modern-day Penguins.

CARL PERKINS

Birthdate: 4/9/32
Birthplace: Lake County, TN
Influences: John Lee Hooker, Hank Williams
Influenced: Beatles, Eric Clapton, Dave Edmunds, Keith
Richards, Rick Nelson, Tommy Roe, Creedence
Clearwater Revival, Vince Gill

Considered by many to be the father of rockabilly, timing and circumstances kept Carl Perkins from being known as a superstar, yet his extraordinary talent has made him a legend.

Carl grew up with country, gospel, and Delta blues as one of three sons of a poor sharecropping family. By age 18, Carl, with brothers Jay and Clayton, began playing honky tonks as The Perkins Brothers Band. To make ends meet, Carl also picked cotton and worked in a bakery. In 1954, Perkins and his wife Valda moved to Jackson, Mississippi, living in a government housing project. After seeing Elvis Presley perform at a high school dance in Bethel Springs, and hearing his first single, "Blue Moon of Kentucky," on the radio, Carl and company were convinced that Elvis's label would be interested in them. Sun owner Sam Phillips signed Carl to his Flip label, and recorded him with his brothers backing on January 22, 1955. Their first single was "Movie Mary," which Carl had written at age 13.

In February, Perkins toured the South with Presley. During July, Carl recorded his second single, "Gone, Gone, Gone," this time for release on Sun. When Elvis's contract was sold to RCA that year, Phillips began grooming Perkins as his next Elvis and encouraged him to write in a more R&B style. While performing one night, Carl noticed a poor youth with new shoes, and overheard him chastising another dancer for "steppin' on" them. At 3 A.M. after the dance, Carl awoke to write "Blue Suede Shoes" on a potato sack, since he had

no notepaper. On December 19, 1955, "Shoes" was recorded and rush released.

Blue Suede Shoes.

★ *Difficult as the country field is for a newcomer to "crack" these days, Perkins has come up with some wax here that has hit the national retail chart in almost record time. New Orleans, Memphis, Nashville, Richmond, Durham and other areas report it a leading seller. Interestingly enough, the disk has a large measure of appeal for pop and r.&b. customers. Flip is "Honey, Don't." (2/18/56)*

On March 17, "Shoes" was the #14 best seller in America. Five days later, the Perkins brothers drove to New York to appear on Perry Como's TV show. They never made it, as they hit a pickup truck in Delaware and were hospitalized. "Shoes" reached #2 in *Billboard* (#1 *Cashbox*) and became the first rock 'n' roll record to be #1 Pop, R&B, and C&W. Meanwhile, Elvis Presley's version of the song reached #20 and he appeared on Ed Sullivan's show performing it. He then sent a note to Carl indicating that Perkins might have been the superstar if the accident hadn't happened.

Although Carl recuperated, his chart momentum never did. "Boppin' the Blues" anchored at #70 (despite an enthusiastic report in *Billboard*) and "Dixie Fried" didn't chart at all; further Sun singles through 1958 stalled.

Boppin' the Blues.

In 10-days time, Perkins's new release has established the fact that "Blue Suede Shoes" was no flash-in-the-pan success. The artist's new record is moving out faster than the predecessor, and is already among the top 10 lists. Action is heavy on both sides with a slight preference for "Boppin' the Blues." As before, sales are good in the pop stores as the c.&w. A previous Billboard "Spotlight" pick. (6/23/56)

Your True Love/Matchbox.

Perkins registers strongly on "Your True Love," a swingy blues with an attractive off-beat quality and interesting backing by a youthful sounding vocal chorus. Flip is a driving blues featuring Sun's familiar sound with heavy emphasis on the beat. Both sides should grab off plenty of attention in the field. "Your True Love" is also a possibility for the pop market, a la Perkins's big hit "Blue Suede Shoes." (2/16/57) (#67 Pop)

Lend Me Your Comb/Glad All Over.

Two strong sides. "Lend Me Your Comb" has other versions, but this could be tops in the market, and it also has pop appeal. "Glad" . . . is also in a rockabilly vein. Perkin does this in the film, "Jamboree." Either side can make it. (1/6/58)

Hoping to improve his chart activity, he signed with Columbia in 1958. The label pushed him in more of a teen-pop direction, at least in subject matter ("Pink Pedal Pushers" and "Levi Jacket" both addressing teen fashion concerns), but Perkins's chart allure was gone.

Pink Pedal [Pushers].

Perkins's initial offering on the label is strong wax. Top side is a cute rockabilly and it's handed a stirring go. Potential in all markets. (3/17/58) (#91 Pop)

Levi Jacket 78

Perkins warbles exuberantly on amusing rockabilly item about a gal who wears "Levi jacket with a long-tailed shirt." Considerable teen-appeal.

Papa, Let Me Have the Car 76

Bouncy rocker revolves around guy's need for car to take his gal to record hop. . . . merits spins. (7/14/58)

In 1959, Carl had his last Top-100 record, another fashion statement, "Pointed-Toe Shoes," but it only reached #93.

Pointed-Toe Shoes.

Top side reminds a bit of the artist's click "Blue Suede Shoes." It's a moving rockabilly item that he sings with spirit . . . should score in pop and c.&w. marts. (4/20/59)

Honey Cause I Love You.

The best side that Carl Perkins has turned out in years . . . a swinging rocker . . . Perkins shines. (10/31/60)

Further recordings on Columbia through 1962, and then Decca from 1963 to 1966, failed to chart. However, in 1963, Perkins toured Europe for the first time and in May 1964 did the British circuit with Chuck Berry. The Beatles, ardent admirers of Carl, recorded three of his songs after an impromptu jam session with him. When they hit with Carl's "Matchbox" (#17) his career was revived.

In 1965, what was to be a two-day gig with friend Johnny Cash turned into 10 years of performing together, including three years on Cash's weekly TV show. Carl hit the country charts with "Me Without You" (1971) and "Cotton Top" (1972), among others. By 1976, he left the Cash tour for his own band featuring sons Stan on drums and Greg on bass.

In April 1981, Perkins, Jerry Lee Lewis, and Cash recorded an album in Stuttgart, Germany, called *The Survivors*. That same month, Paul McCartney invited Carl to work on his *Tug of War* LP, which included a duet on the Perkins-penned "You Gotta Get It." During 1985, Carl had his own HBO TV special, "Carl Perkins and Friends" including George Harrison, Dave Edmunds, Ringo Starr, and Eric Clapton. In January 1987, Carl was inducted into the Rock and Roll Hall of Fame. The 1990s haven't slowed Carl down, as he continues to perform extensively with his sons.

GENE PITNEY

Birthdate: 2/17/41

Birthplace: Hartford, CT

Influences: Penguins, Crows, Flamingos, Clyde McPhatter and The Drifters, George Jones

Influenced: Elton John, John Lennon, Soft Cell, Buffalo Springfield

A successful songwriter before he became a singing star, Gene Pitney possessed a sparkling tenor voice and an identifiable sound that earned him 24 chart singles in nine years.

Studying drums, piano, and guitar, the Hartford-born teen had placed several songs with New York publishers by graduation time at Rockville High School. His first recordings, on Decca, came under the name Jamie and Jane (Gene and Ginny Arnell) with "Strolling," in the Spring of 1959, followed by the summertime release of "Classical Rock and Roll." That same year, Gene, who was heavily influenced by R&B vocal groups (he once drove from Rockville to Manchester, Connecticut, just to hear The Crows' "Gee" on a jukebox), recorded four unreleased gems with a local quartet, The Embers (finally issued on Don Fileti and Eddie Gries's Relic LP 5085 in 1990).

Jamie and Jane:
Strolling.
★ ★ ★　*Boy-girl duo render this rockaballad in hiccuppy style. Danceable item with a chance. (3/30/59)*

Classical Rock and Roll.
★ ★ ★　*The snappy blues . . . has an interesting idea and sound. Material is imaginative and the beat is strong. Persuasive wax. (7/20/59)*

In late 1959, he recorded as Billy Bryan.

Billy Bryan:
Cradle of My Arms.
★ ★ ★ ★ *An insinuating ditty with spiritual over-tones receives a strong performance from the chanter helped by a choral group and rhythmic backing. (11/23/59)*

The Gene Pitney name first appeared on wax in 1960, when Marty Kugall (early Five Satins producer) introduced him to Herb Abramson's Festival label, where he sang "Please Come Back." Also in 1960, Gene debuted as a song-writer for others with "Loneliness" by The Kalin Twins (of "When" fame). "Today's Teardrops" followed as the B-side of Roy Orbison's "Blue Angel" (#9), becoming Gene's first money maker.

By then, Pitney had attended the University of Connecticut but dropped out to study at Wards Electronic School. His understanding of

electronics helped him develop his recording techniques. He cut a four-track demo, singing seven vocal parts and playing all the instruments but bass (for which he paid $30 to a bass player). He then placed that demo, "I Wanna Love My Life Away," with Musicor Records through his publisher, Aaron Schroeder. His career was on its way.

I Wanna [Love] My Life Away.
★ ★ ★ ★ *Gene Pitney, writer of many of today's pop hits, comes thru with a sock performance here on his first outing on wax as a singer. Lad sells the tune he cleffed with excitement, and the rhythm tune has a solid chance. (11/21/60) (#39 Pop)*

Louisiana Mania.
★ ★ ★ ★ *A touch of Latin in the rhythm makes this record cook. The chanter does a strong job out front telling the story of his New Orleans girl.*

Take Me Tonight.
★ ★ ★ ★ *Soft ballad gets a warm performance from the boy. Tune is a familar melody based on a Tchaikovsky opus. Strings and soft piano color the background. (3/20/61)*

Meanwhile, on January 9, 1961, Bobby Vee's recording of Gene's "Rubber Ball" gave Pitney his first Top-10 writing success (#6). The record's songwriter credits read Anne Orlowski (Gene's mother). Schroeder wanted the song published by his ASCAP-affiliated company (Pitney was a BMI writer and a writer can't be registered by both music licensing societies) so Pitney's moth-er received the credit. 1961 continued to be Gene's "dual career" year, as Rick Nelson reached #9 on May 22 with the Pitney-penned "Hello Mary Lou."

From that point on, Gene primarily recorded the material of other writers, such as Goffin/King. The Phil Spector-produced "Every Breath I Take" included Pitney's doo wop influence, courtesy of background vocals by The Halos. Pitney's famous falsetto finale against Spector's spectacu-lar shimmering strings was the result of Gene's bad cold that day. Film flings followed. Actually, "(The Man Who Shot) Liberty Valance" (by

Bacharach and David) was written for the John Wayne film but the rush release of the picture caused the song to be omitted. Meanwhile, early Pitney sides were reissued to take advantage of his new chart success.

Every Breath I Take.
★ ★ ★ ★ *Pitney sings a ballad against a tricky rhythm backing which features a chorus. There's a Latin feeling to the beat, somewhat on the style of sides by The Drifters. Fervent performance.*

Mr. Moon, Mr. Cupid and I.
★ ★ ★ ★ *Pitney sings this medium-beater with much of the hiccup style in evidence. A good effort neatly arranged. Watch both sides. (7/3/61) (#42 Pop)*

Town without Pity.
★ ★ ★ ★ *A haunting movie title theme is sung with feeling by Pitney, who also sings it in the film. Watch it. (10/9/61) (#13 Pop)*

Please Come Back.
★ ★ ★ ★ *An early Gene Pitney record spotlights the singer in a bright reading of a swinging rocker. The backing is clever and the side has possibilities. (10/30/61)*

The Man Who Shot Liberty Valance.

This western-type saga song inspired by the forthcoming picture of the same name, is handed a powerful performance by Gene Pitney. The ork backing and choral work is very interesting too. Could be big. (3/31/62) (#4 Pop)

If I Didn't Have a Dime (to Play the Juke Box)/Only Love Can Break a Heart.

On top is a rhythmic effort that tells a fine teen story; flip is a weeper sold with much feeling by the chanter. Ork support is fresh and bright on both. (8/11/62) (A-side, #58 Pop; B-side, #2 Pop, #16 R&B)

"Only Love," although issued as the B-side, became Gene's first million seller. It was, ironically kept from #1 by The Crystals' recording of "He's a Rebel," written by Pitney and produced by Spector.

Half Heaven-Half Heartache.

Ballad material and arrangement are tops here for the singer . . . offering has the vocalist in his torchiest style . . . arrangement using strings, tympani and voices. (12/1/62) (#12 Pop)

Mecca.
A song of social significance on the "Worlds Apart" theme. (3/9/63) (#12 Pop)

Twenty-Four Hours from Tulsa.
This is a tragic story ballad that's told with authority by Pitney. Side has production billed with big orchestral effects. (10/12/63) (#17 Pop)

Gene's first trip to England helped "Twenty Four Hours from Tulsa" become his first Top-5 hit there. He then met the Rolling Stones through his publicist and Stones producer, Andrew Loog Oldham, and recorded their "That Girl Belongs to Yesterday" (#49 Pop and #7 U.K.). The first American to cut a Stones song, Gene was asked to play piano for their "Not Fade Away" session while Spector provided percussion by "playing" a Cognac bottle with a half dollar! Another B-side smash ensued.

Hawaii.
Big arrangement and usual dramatic Pitney delivery. It's a love song to a Hawaiian gal with ukes, big drums and chorus lending support. Flip: "It Hurts to Be in Love." (7/11/64) (#7 Pop)

I'm Gonna Be Strong.
Emotional impact coupled with a really big sound. Gene at his best. (10/17/64) (#9 Pop)

I Must Be Seeing Things.
One of his srongest records to date. Good material with a powerful Pitney vocal. Production ballad with a Mexican flavor. (2/13/65) (#31 Pop)

Last Chance to Turn Around.
Pulsing performance and arrangement on a well-written rouser. Exciting Pitney sound! (5/1/65) (#13 Pop)

Looking Through the Eyes of Love.

Currently topping the British charts, this dramatic, emotional production performance has all the earmarks of a No. 1 hit. (7/17/65) (#28 Pop)

Gene began his country-influenced period in 1966, singing an album of duets with George Jones in Nashville, but his single "I've Got $5.00 and It's Saturday Night" only reached #99 Pop. His appearance and second-place finish at The San Remo Song Festival in Italy gave Gene a hit there and a new single stateside. Pitney followed with more medium-sized hits.

Nessuno Mi Puo' Giudicare.

One of the top tunes in Italy is given a fine emotional Pitney vocal, with commercial production and rhythm dance beat in strong support. (2/19/66)

Backstage/Blue Color.

A twin winner from Pitney. Top side is heading for No. 1 in the British charts, while the flip is a blues rocker from the pen of Rick Shorter. (4/2/66) (#25 Pop)

Although the Randy Newman-penned "Nobody Needs Your Love" bombed in America, its hit level in England (#2) showed that Gene (like contemporary Roy Orbison) was destined to be more revered in Britain than at home. In fact, Pitney was an international star and his status, in Italy for example, was such that he recorded several albums of country songs in Italian. In England, "Billy, You're My Friend" was joined with the Goffin/King multicovered "Yours Until Tomorrow," which reached #34 but was never issued in America as a single.

She's a Heartbreaker.

New blues bag for the stylist and he moves and grooves all the way through this patent Charlie Foxx rocker in top form. Will hit hard and fast and prove one of Pitney's all-time hot sellers. (4/20/68) (#16 Pop)

Billy, You're My Friend.

Pitney comes up with a blockbuster that should prove his "MacArthur Park." The most unique disk of the week, this symphonic rock production number is one of his finest disk perfor-

mances and loaded with sales appeal. Exceptional writing, arrangement and production work. (10/5/68) (#92 Pop)

Inexplicably, his popularity waned by decade's end, and his last pop charter was "She Lets Her Hair Down" (#89) in 1969.

(Your Love Keeps Lifting Me) Higher and Higher.

Pitney back in his commercial soul sound returns with a wild revival of the Jackie Wilson hit. . . . Top performance that will bring him back to the Hot 100. (4/17/71)

Gene, Are You There?

★ *This touching ballad written by a blind fan especially for Pitney gets a warm reading . . . with likely activity coming from pop and easy listening play. (7/31/71)*

In 1974, "the Rockville Rocket" (as Gene was known in Hartford) signed to England's Bronze label. His last British charter was "Blue Angel" (#39) that same year. Gene continued to record on occasion through the 1970s and remains a popular draw on the nostalgia circuit today.

THE PLATTERS

Tony Williams: Lead vocals
Born: 4/5/28, Roselle, NJ (died 1/2/81)
David Lynch: Tenor
Born: 1929, St. Louis MO
Paul Robi: Baritone
Born: 1930s, New Orleans, LA (died 1989)
Herb Reed: Bass
Born: 8/7/31, Kansas City, MO
Zola Taylor
Born: 1939, Los Angeles, CA
Influences: Ink Spots, Golden Gate Quartet, Deep River Boys, Five Blind Boys, Soul Stirrers
Influenced: Dell-Vikings, Olympics, Righteous Brothers, Blue Jays, Dimensions, Moments

The most popular vocal group of the 1950s, The Platters might never have succeeded if it weren't for the one-hit winners, The Penguins.

Los Angeles in 1953 was the setting for the merger of voices belonging to Joe Jefferson, Alex and Gaynel Hodge, and Cornel Gunter. The quartet met car washer Tony Williams and knew his identifiable and warm tenor was just right for their lead singing spot. An introduction to manager Samuel "Buck" Ram through Tony's sister, recording artist Linda Hayes ("Yes I Know," #2, R&B, 1953), led The Platters into Ram's stable, which included The Colts and Linda. The raw recruits soon experienced Ram's intuitive changes as he tinkered with their sound. Gaynel and Joe left, and were replaced by bass Herb Reed and cab driver/tenor David Lynch. Signed by Federal Records, one of their early recordings was the Ram-penned "Only You," which was so badly produced that Federal refused to issue it, opting for the gospel-flavored "Give Thanks." Buck soon added Zola Taylor (Shirley Gunter and The Queens) to smooth out the group's R&B style. Alex left next, replaced by baritone Paul Robi.

Give Thanks 75
> *New group on label kick off with a spiritual flavored number that packs some appeal in today's market. It starts quietly and has a fine jump spot in the middle. (11/21/53)*

Tell the World 73
> *A routine ballad, vocal-pop in style . . . group sings it pleasantly. (6/26/54)*

Shake It Up Mambo 68
> *This West Coast vocal group which stirred considerable excitement on their last release has now come up with material that could put them on top. It is in the vein of Ruth Brown's current hit and has a style and a beat that is almost as fabulous as that of "Mambo Baby." (11/13/54)*

Maggie Don't Work Here Anymore 77
> *Contrary to expectations, this is not a take-off on the "Annie" series, but a bright and funny piece of material in its own right. The boys have a ball on this one, and should do well sales-wise as on any previous record. (1/15/55)*

The Platters worked often and were well paid, which impressed another L.A. group, The Penguins, who were recent hit makers with "Earth Angel." They signed with Ram and he quickly brought them to Mercury Records. Knowing how badly the label wanted The Penguins, he forced them to accept his hitless Platters as well.

When the April 1955 Penguins single came and went unnoticed, it was The Platters turn to score. Buck rerecorded the group on "Only You" and a legend was born. It was the first rock 'n' roll record to outdistance a white cover counterpart. (The Hilltoppers reached #8.)

Only You (and You Alone).
> *The group's lead does a fine job with this pretty ballad. His smooth styling stands out impressively with rhythmically solid backing of the group.*

Bark, Battle and Ball.
> *This is one of those noisy, outgoing novelties that have such great appeal for the youngsters these days, and ought to make out as well as most others. (7/9/55) (#5 Pop, #1 R&B)*

To keep the label's enthusiasm high, Ram told Mercury he had an even better follow up. Queried for the title he said, "The Great Pretender" (a good description of Buck, who hadn't yet written the song). "Pretender" was the first of 11 two-sided hits for the quintet, and it also secured their international star status.

The Great Pretender.
> *This great act, currently riding way up on the r.&b. and pop charts both with "Only You," has a hunk of great follow-up material here. It's a strong song with definite two-market potential again. (12/3/55) (#1 Pop, #1 R&B)*

The year 1956 continued with more standards. The Platters crossed over to pop like no other group since The Ink Spots and, in some cases, with the latter act's songs, such as "My Prayer."

You've Got the Magic Touch.
> *The Platters are riding high right now on both the pop and r.&b. charts and this disk should do equally well playwise and sales-wise in the two markets. . . . an appealing ballad, sung with*

evocative phrasing and rich sincerity. (3/10/56) (#4 Pop, #4 R&B)

My Prayer/Heaven on Earth.

A moving rendition of the poignant oldie, "My Prayer," with a standout performance by the lead singer. The flip spotlights another solid vocal treatment on an appealing theme with a deft beat. (6/16/56) (A-side, #1 Pop, #1 R&B; B-side, #39 Pop, #13 R&B)

It Isn't Right/You'll Never Never Know.

The smash act never stops rolling, and two powerful sides like these can just add momentum. Both sides figure to break out in both the pop and r.&b. markets, following the pattern of their previous hits. Tunes are ballad featuring a crisp back beat. (9/15/56) (A-side, #23 Pop, #10 R&B; B-side, #11 Pop, #9 R&B)

On My Word of Honor/One in a Million.

The Platters cover B. B. King's current hit in a winning version to kick off the tune in the pop market with great force. Their styling is leisurely and luxurious with the high-flying lead embroidering the melody profusely. "One in a Million" is reminiscent of the early hits of the group and could also click solidly. (12/1/56) (A-side, #20 Pop, #7 R&B; B-side, #31 R&B)

In 1957, Tony did his first solo recording, but it was The Platters' sound that the public wanted to hear. They became the first rock 'n' roll group to have a Top-10 album, and their film performance of "Twilight Time" on American Bandstand became a promotional clip for other TV shows, making it one of the first music videos. "Smoke" was the first rock 'n' roll group hit not produced in America; The Platters recorded it on tour while in Paris.

I'm Sorry.

The sales and play picture is as bright as ever for the Platters' latest release which—again as usual—should move out strongly in both pop and rhythm and blues fields. The group warbles with sock emotional appeal on the

effective ballad "I'm Sorry." The flip, "He's Mine," spotlights Zola Taylor in a pert and personable lead vocal stint on an up-tempo ballad. (3/2/57) (A-side, #11 Pop, #15 R&B; B-side, #23 Pop, #5 R&B)

Twilight Time.

Beautiful lead rendition by Tony Williams of the ballad standard originally a hit by the Three Suns. This is right in the Platters' hit groove and it should move right out. (3/17/58) (#1 Pop, #1 R&B)

Smoke Gets in Your Eyes.

Lead by a stirring vocal from Tony Williams, the group presents their strongest side since "Twilight Time." They hand the evergreen a warm reading that's sure to attract heavy loot. (11/10/58) (#1 Pop, #3 R&B)

Enchanted.

Spots the group on a hit reading of a pretty Buck Ram tune . . . excellent offering with top potential. (3/9/59) (#12 Pop, #9 R&B)

Wish It Were Me/Where.

A pretty ballad from the coming flick, "Girl's Town." "Where" is based on a motif from Tchaikovsky's sixth symphony. Both are likely clicks. (8/24/59) (A-side, #61 Pop; B-side, #44 Pop)

Although still a potent seller, their last Top-10 single came in 1960 with "Harbor Lights."

Sleepy Lagoon/Harbor Lights.

Tony Williams offers strong lead reading on both the pretty oldies, and the group comes thru with listenable harmonies in support. The disk is their strongest in a while . . . lush rockaballads. (1/17/60) (A-side, #65 Pop; B-side, #8 Pop)

Red Sails in the Sunset.

Lead warbler Tony Williams—who has since left the group to become a single—chants with expressive showmanship on the great standard. (7/4/60) (#36 Pop)

To Each His Own/Down the River of Golden Dreams.

 Two fine, smooth sides by the Platters that show off their familiar sound on two solid standards. Both sides could make the big time. (9/26/60) (#21 Pop)

In 1961, the lead spot was taken by Sonny Turner as Tony joined Reprise. Williams's solos didn't equal his Platters success, even when he rerecorded their original hits. The Platters continued to cover pop standards, with lesser chart action.

I'll Never Smile Again.

 The group, with its new lead, Sonny Turner, wrap up the tender oldie in a smooooth, expressive vocal treatment. An effective side. (7/10/61).

Tony Williams:
My Prayer.

★ ★ ★ ★ *The ex-lead of the Platters warbles expressively on the poignant oldie (a hit for the group in 1959). Could happen again. (10/16/61)*

Mercury refused to issue Platters sides that weren't led by Williams, and "It's Magic" became their last charter for the label.

It's Magic.

 The memorable Doris Day hit, handsomely up-dated by the lead and group. (1/27/62) (#91 Pop)

Robi and Taylor left in 1962 and in stepped Sandra Dawn and former Flamingo, Nate Nelson. Mercury released eight previously unissued Platters 45s through 1964; the last was "Love Me Tender." In 1966, Ram brought the group to Musicor for a brief series of chart activity.

I Love You 1000 Times.

A new bag for the veteran rock group in [this] strong dance beat number with full Detroit sound in strong support. (3/19/66) (#31 Pop, #6 R&B)

"I'll Be Home" featured Nelson on lead, the same role he took on the Flamingos' waxing of the song ten years earlier!

I'll Be Home.

An outstanding revival of Pat Boone's hit of a decade ago. Moving recitation and steady dance beat add to the potential of this strong ballad entry. (11/5/66)

With This Ring.

Top vocal workout of a good rock ballad could be the one to bring the Platters back to the Hot 100 in fine style. Outstanding Luther Jackson production has all the earmarks of a hit. (2/11/67) (#14 Pop, #12 R&B)

Sweet, Sweet Lovin'.

This blockbuster never lets up from start to finish. Swinger should prove their hottest sales item since "With This Ring" winner. (10/14/67) (#70 Pop, #32 R&B)

Through the 1970s and 1980s there were more different Platters groups than new releases. One of the groups calling themselves the Platters had Robi, Lynch, and Taylor; another employed Nelson and Reed; whereas Ram (who legally owned The Platters name and was suing everyone in sight) formed his own, with the closest thing to an original member being Craig Alexander, a cousin of Zola Taylor. Williams also succumbed, forming a quintet with his wife Helen that was still active in the late 1980s. The original Platters were inducted into the Rock and Roll Hall of Fame in 1990.

ELVIS PRESLEY

Birthdate: 1/8/35
Birthplace: Tupelo, MS
Died: 8/16/77
Influences: Dean Martin, Bill Haley and The Comets
Influenced: Practically everyone

Elvis Presley, the indisputable king of rock 'n' roll, is the standard by which all rock artists have been judged.

His upbringing combined gospel and hillbilly music with a love for crooning (amazingly, Dean Martin was his idol) and when that union merged with blues, not only was a new music born, but a new American culture. Presley was named after his father's middle name ("Helwiss") which came from 17th century Scotland. His parents, Gladys and Vernon Presley, were poor but the family was fervently religious. The youngster, an only child (twin brother Jesse was stillborn), sang in the First Assembly of God Church. The first inkling of any vocal aptitude came at age 10 when he placed second at the Mississippi-Alabama Fair and Dairy Show, singing Red Foley's "Old Shep." On his birthday in 1946, his parents chose a $12.98 guitar as a gift instead of a bicycle, reasoning that he couldn't get hurt with a guitar.

In 1948, the Presleys moved from Tupelo to Memphis. Their son attended Humes High School while gaining a separate education in the black section of town, watching blues artists like B. B. King perform. After graduation in 1953, Presley worked as a theater usher, as an employee of the Precision Tool Company, and as a truck driver for Crown Electric. It was at the latter that he began wearing his hair in a pompadour as other truckers did.

In July 1953, Presley, during his lunch hour, made a personal recording for his mother's birthday (and to hear how he sounded on record). The four-dollar session at Memphis Recording Service disappointed him, but the studio manager, Marion Keisker, who worked for Sam Phillips, owner of the service and Sun Records, liked the raw trucker's voice and kept a tape of "That's When Your Heartaches Begin" and "My Happiness."

Presley returned on January 4, 1954, to try again, but Phillips still wasn't interested in the singer's hillbilly style, although Keisker insisted that he give the boy a second chance. Phillips finally relented and, on July 5, 1954, Presley recorded a wild version of Arthur "Big Boy" Crudup's "That's All Right Mama." Two days later, it aired on radio WHBQ and the response was so overwhelming that Presley signed to Sun within the week and quit truck driving forever.

That's All Right/Blue Moon of Kentucky.

Presley is a potent new chanter who can sock over a tune for either the country or the r.&b. markets. On this new disk he comes thru with a solid performance on an r.&b.-type tune and then on the flip side does another fine job with a country ditty. A strong new talent. (8/7/54)

"That's All Right" was a local hit and Presley's first performance was on the back of a flatbed truck for a drugstore's grand opening. The first indication of his sensual style came on August 10, 1954 during his first appearance with other performers, notably Slim Whitman. The shy 19-year-old was encouraged by WHBQ deejay Dewey Phillips to "rock out," and so "Elvis the pelvis" was born amid frantic screams from the audience and total bewilderment by the following act, Webb Pierce. By contrast, his first (and only) performance on the Grand Ole Opry stage (September 25, 1954) before a sedate crowd elicited a suggestion from the Opry's booker, Jim Denny, that Presley go back to trucking!

Although his next two singles did little, Presley (then called The Hillbilly Cat) attracted the attention of a former carnival huckster and dog catcher, Tom Parker, manager of Eddy Arnold. Parker became involved in Presley's bookings and eventually his management.

I Don't Care If the Sun Don't Shine/Good Rockin' Tonight.

Elvis Presley, a Billboard talent "Spotlight" a few months ago, proves again that he is a sock new singer with his performances on these two oldies. His style is both country and r.&b. and he can appeal to pop. A solid record here that could easily break loose. (11/6/54)

Milcow Blues Boogie 80

Presley continues to impress with each release as one of the slickest talents to come up in the country field in a long, long time. Item here is based on some of the best folk blues. The guy sells all the way. Ops will particularly like it.

You're a Heartbreaker 76

Here Presley tackles the rhythmic material for a slick country-style reading. What with the good backing this one should get action, too. (1/29/55)

In July 1955, Presley had his debut chart 45, "Baby Let's Play House." It was also his first recording with drums. His first country #1, "I Forgot to Remember to Forget," followed.

Baby Let's Play House 77
A highly distinctive country effort, this is patterned after primitive Southern blues. Great rhythm effects and trick warbling. Should get played.

I'm Left, You're Right, She's Gone 71
Presley has the maracas loaded for this unusual, rhythmic country chant. But the content fails to keep pace. (5/14/55) (#10 C&W)

I Forgot to Remember to Forget/Mystery Train.
With each release, Presley has been coming more and more quickly to the forefront. His current record has wasted no time in establishing itself. Already it appears on the Memphis and Houston territorial charts. It is also reported selling well in Richmond, Atlanta, Durham, Nashville and Dallas. Both sides are moving, with "I Forgot" currently on top. A previous Billboard *"Spotlight" pick. (9/10/55) (A-side, #1 C&W; B-side, #11 C&W)*

On October 15, Presley played a club in Lubbock, Texas. The opening act was a hillbilly duo named Buddy and Bob (Buddy Holly and Bob Montgomery); hearing Presley, Holly decided to forgo country music and focus on rock 'n' roll.

Meanwhile Phillips, whose label was in debt and cash poor, created a bidding war for Presley's services and his past recordings. Adding to his bargaining power, Presley was recently named Most Promising Country and Western Artist in a deejay poll. Decca ($5,000), Dot ($7,500), Mercury ($10,000), Columbia ($15,000), and Atlantic ($25,000) all jumped on the bandwagon, but RCA, with a then-astronomical offer of $35,000 (with a $5,000 advance to Presley), won the prize.

Presley's first RCA recordings (January 10–11, 1956) featured a song whose initial inspiration came from a note left by a suicide victim in Miami that read, "I walk a lonely street." When writer Tommy Durden brought the line to Mae Axton, Parker's publicist, she and Durden developed the idea for a hotel on the street, the "Heartbreak Hotel" (#1 Pop, #1 C&W, #5 R&B). Even the B-side, a doo wop recording (with The Jordanaires), "I Got a Woman," was a hit (#23 Pop). Presley's next charter lost a cover battle with Carl Perkins's original, "Blue Suede Shoes" (Perkins #2, Elvis #20). His second million seller followed hot on the heels of "Shoes."

Heartbreak Hotel.
Another record that has demonstrated Presley's major league stature. Sales have snowballed rapidly in the past two weeks, with pop and r.&b. customers joining Presley's hillbilly fans in demanding this disk. . . . A previous Billboard *"Spotlight" pick. (2/18/56)*

My Baby Left Me/I Want You, I Need You, I Love You.
Another pair of exciting Presley sides have the big-money look. The top features a real blues with that wild r.&b. infusion so well calculated to hit the all-market pay-off. On the flip, it's a different, more gentle Presley, but he still vibrates with that husky, coin-pulling charm. Either one or both could be the big "Heartbreak Hotel" follow-up. (5/12/56) (A-side, #31 Pop; B-side, #1 Pop, #3 R&B)

While in Las Vegas, Presley heard Freddy Bell and The Bellboys' novelty rendition of Big Mama Thornton's "Hound Dog" and it was their version he copied (in 31 takes) for his own recording. Presley made a hilarious Steve Allen TV Show appearance on July 1, singing "Hound Dog" in a tuxedo to a totally indifferent basset hound.

Hound Dog/Don't Be Cruel.
Presley hyped the "Hound Dog" side on a recent Steve Allen TV airing which gave a solid, early kickoff. It's a highly charged rhythm opus in Presley's characteristic style and should enjoy heavy commercial acceptence. "Don't Be Cruel" is in a more subdued, frankly popish vein and demonstrates that the singer is a versatile artist. (7/21/56) (A-side, #1 Pop, #1 R&B; B-side, #1 Pop, #1 R&B)

In August, Presley started on his second career, acting in 20th Century-Fox's *Love Me Tender* (originally titled *The Reno Brothers* but retitled for the song).

Love Me Tender/Any Way You Want Me— That's How I Will Be.

> *Title tune from Presley's first flick has set a record for advance orders, which now exceed a million. Further comment unnecessary. (10/6/56) (A-side, #1 Pop, #3 R&B; B-side, #20 Pop, #12 R&B)*

Love Me Tender.

> *A hit before it was ever released, this disk since issued has chalked up an all-time record for first week volume. Acceptance in the pop, country and rhythm & blues fields is complete, and, as on his last record, should soon be dominating the charts of all three categories. "Love Me Tender" has gotten the lion's share of the attention so far, but there are some indications that the flip may also come in for a share of the spotlight a little later. (10/13/56)*

His legendary Ed Sullivan Show performance on September 9 was watched by one-third of the nation's population; Presley was shown only from the waist up, to avoid broadcasting his scandalous hip-shaking moves! In November, Presley was voted Most Played Male Artist of 1956 by *Billboard*'s national deejay poll.

After holding down the #1 position for 25 weeks in 1956, his torrid pace continued in 1957. In March, Elvis spent $100,000 for a new home and its 13 3/4 acres outside of Memphis. He called it Graceland.

Playing for Keeps/Too Much.

> *As heavily pre-ordered as this record is, not much description of it is necessary to sell the trade on it. For the record, "Playing for Keeps" is a ballad with an easy, loping melody akin in spirit to "Love Me Tender." Presley's moaning delivery has the usual endocrinal punch. "Too Much" is closer in style to some of his early rockabilly hits. Its lurching, groovy rhythm is spell-binding on teen-agers, as is all too well known. To spur sales the disk*

is being merchandised in a special jacket with a color photo of Presley-cum-guitar. 'Snuffsed? (1/12/57) (A-side, #21 Pop; B-side, #1 Pop, #3 R&B)

His next #1 arrived courtesy of songwriter Otis Blackwell's publisher Al Stanton, who entered his office shaking a Pepsi as was his custom, and exclaiming "Otis, why don't you write a song called 'All Shook Up.'" "Shook Up" was Presley's first of 17 #1s in England. Coincidentally, he also had 17 #1s in America, although only six were chart toppers in both countries.

All Shook Up/That's When Your Heartaches Begin.

> *Presley is at it again and this coupling is so strong it can hardly miss. The top side is a typical, hoarsely belted swinging rockabilly job while the flip is a complete change of pace into the closest the singer has come to the traditional country weeper ballad. Top may have a slight edge but both are powerful. (3/23/57) (A-side, #1 Pop, #1 R&B; B-side, #58 Pop)*

Teddy Bear/Loving You.

> *Both tunes are from Presley's forth-coming movie, "Loving You." "Teddy Bear" is a sock rockabilly item, while flip features a tender reading of the film's poignant title theme. Special sleeve, spotlight Elvis and a teddy bear, is powerful display material. (6/10/57) (A-side, #1 Pop, #1 R&B; B-side, #20 Pop)*

A false rumor about Presley collecting Teddy bears led to Cameo Record execs Kal Mann and Bernie Lowe delivering their own musical teddy bear for "The King" to record. Three weeks after "Jailhouse Rock" exited the Top 100 (December 20), Presley received his draft notice.

Jailhouse Rock/Treat Me Nice.

> *Another sock platter by the phenomenal artist. "Rock" is a vigorous rocker and is the title tune from Presley's forthcoming flick. Flip is an equally strong side somewhat like "Don't Be*

Cruel." Both should score. (9/23/57) (A-side, #1 Pop, #1 R&B; B-side, #18 Pop, #7 R&B)

By the end of 1957, Presley had equaled his unprecedented 1956 record of 25 weeks at #1, and "Don't" became his ninth pop chart topper.

Don't/I Beg of You.

"Don't" is a clever Leiber and Stoller tune and Presley sings it with winning appeal . . . both sides are good bets to score in all categories. (12/30/57) (A-side, #1 Pop, #4 R&B; B-side, #8 Pop, #5 R&B)

Wear My Ring Around Your Neck/Doncha' Think It's Time.

Top side is an uptempo item that gets the artist's usual sock delivery. Flip is a ballad with rhythm backing. Both are likely clicks in all markets. (4/7/58) (A-side, #2 Pop, #1 R&B; B-side, #15 Pop, #10 R&B)

In May 1958, Private Elvis Presley (#53310761) had been sworn in and instantly went from earning $100,000 a month to $78. He returned home on emergency leave August 12. His beloved mother Gladys died of heart failure two days later. In October, Presley was shipped to Freiberg, Germany. Few recordings were made prior to his departure, thus keeping the public hungry for Elvis.

Hard-Headed Woman/Don't Ask Me Why.

Both tunes are from the artist's coming flick, "King Creole." Top side is a driving rockabilly tune. . . . "Don't" is a rockaballad that is sung with equal appeal. It should score in all fields. (6/16/58) (A-side, #1 Pop, #2 R&B; B-side, #25 Pop, #9 R&B)

One Night/I Got Stung.

"One Night" is a rockaballad that is delivered in the artist's usual smash style. Excellent New Orleans-type backing with the emphasis on plucked strings is effective. Flip . . . is a rockabilly effort that is sung with vigor and drive. Tri-market appeal. (10/27/58) (A-side, #4, #10 R&B; B-side, #8 Pop)

A Fool Such as I/I Need Your Love Tonight.

Strong warbling on both adds up to a two-sided click. "Fool" is a ballad, while "I Need Your Love Tonight," is more on the swinging side. Both should coast in. (3/16/59) (A-side, #2 Pop, #16 R&B; B-side, #4 Pop)

Fifteen days after his army discharge in 1960, Presley was back in the studio for "Stuck on You," his first single in stereo. The King's favorite song, "A Mess of Blues," followed. "It's Now or Never" (the B-side) sold over 20 million singles worldwide and opened the adult market to Presley. Now his Dean Martin influence surfaced, adding yet another dimension to his star status. Originally recorded by Al Jolson in 1926, "Are You Lonesome Tonight?" became Presley's 14th #1.

Stuck on You/Fame and Fortune.

Presley is back and he's as hot as ever. This figures to be another strong two-sider. "Stuck on You" is in a rhythm vein. "Fame and Fortune" is a rocka-ballad. (3/21/60) (A-side, #1 Pop, #6 R&B; B-side, #17 Pop)

A Mess of Blues/It's Now or Never.

Elvis handles a fine blues and his usual feeling on the top side and comes thru with a great reading of a familiar melody on the other. Both sides are potent. (7/11/60) (A-side, #32 Pop; B-side, #1 Pop, #7 R&B)

Are You Lonesome Tonight?/I Gotta Know.

Elvis Presley turns in a warm and touching performance on the oldie, which also features a tender recitation. Flip is a swinging side that has almost as much power as the top side. (11/7/60) (A-side, #1 Pop, #3 R&B; B-side, #20 Pop)

Lonely Man/Surrender.

Top side is from his new movie, "Wild in the Country," and it is sung with warmth. Flip, just as strong, is an updated version of "Sorrento." (2/13/61) (A-side, #32 Pop; B-side, #1 Pop)

I Feel So Bad/Wild in the Country.

"I Feel So Bad" is an exciting rhumba blues penned by the late Chuck Willis. Flip is the romantic title theme from Presley's new movie. Both sides are potent with Presley turning in standout vocals on both tunes. (5/8/61) (A-side, #5 Pop; B-side, #26 Pop)

Little Sister/His Latest Flame.

Elvis is back and the kids will be back buying records of these two sock sides. "Little Sister" is a catchy rocker which Elvis sings with spirit; flip is more in the ballad vein and it's sold smoothly. (8/14/61)

Rock-a-hula Baby/Can't Help Falling in Love.

Here's a Presley Twist special taken from the track of the "Blue Hawaii" pic, opening this week. Top side is a great rhythm rocker that's ideal for the new dance craze and it should go big. Flip is a fine ballad performance that should also move out. Watch both. (11/20/61) (A-side, #23 Pop; B-side, #2 Pop)

His next chart topper would be his last for almost seven years as the British invasion, Motown mania, and the psychedelic phenomena relegated most Presley records to lower chart levels. Lightweight, mostly film source song scores didn't help either.

Good Luck Charm/Anything That's Part of You.

"Good Luck Charm" is a bright, medium-tempo rocker, featuring an enthusiastic reading by the star and the Jordanaires. The flip, a pretty ballad, is wrapped up in sock vocal with effective piano solo work by Floyd Cramer. Both sides are strong. (3/10/62) (A-side, #1 Pop; B-side, #31 Pop)

Just Tell Her I Said Hello/She's Not You.

Two pretty ballad sides . . . here, both showing off cleffing by Leiber and Stoller. The first is a weeper that showcases some fine singing in the lad's most restrained manner. The second,

written by L&S and Doc Pomus, is handled at a medium tempo with Presley singing in his best crooning style. (7/28/62) (A-side, #55 Pop; B-side, #5 Pop)

Where Do You Come From/Return to Sender.

Both of these sides are from Presley's new flick, "Girls, Girls, Girls." They are not the strongest material he has ever had but he sings them in his usual exciting fashion and the flick should help push up sales. Topper is a ballad based on a familiar melody; flip is a catchy rhythm novelty. (10/13/62) (A-side, #99 Pop; B-side, #2 Pop)

More movie-score ballads, along with some more interesting rockin' tracks, followed.

One Broken Heart for Sale.

A bright rocker with that "Return to Sender" bounce. It's also from the new flick "It Happened at the World's Fair." (2/9/63) (#11 Pop)

Bossa Nova Baby.

A swinging up-tempo, Leiber-Stoller tune that has humor and comes from the new Elvis flick, "Fun in Acapulco." (10/12/63) (#8 Pop)

Kissin' Cousins/It Hurts Me.

Two more contenders for chart honors from Elvis. First side is from a forthcoming film and features good middle tempo rock with voices and guitars in support. Flip is slow ballad with strong gospel touches. (2/15/64) (A-side, #12 Pop; B-side, #29 Pop)

Ask Me.

One of his most powerful ballad performances since "Love Me Tender." Flip: "Ain't That Loving You Baby"— Swingin' revival of the great Ivory Joe Hunter-Clyde Otis shouter. Chartbuster all the way. (10/3/64) (A-side, #12 Pop; B-side, #16 Pop)

Do the Clam.

From his forthcoming film, "Girl Happy," comes a swinging new dance. (2/20/65) (#21 Pop)

In December 1960, Presley recorded his first full gospel session, which became the album, *His Hand in Mine.* Five years later he broke a two-year drought of Top-5 singles with the issuing of "Crying in the Chapel" from that LP (a cover of The Orioles' 1953 classic).

Crying in the Chapel.
> *First time for release for this strong revival. (4/17/65) (#3 Pop)*

(Such an) Easy Question.
> *With "Crying in the Chapel" No. 3 in BB singles charts, [this tune] from the new Presley film "Tickle Me" [is] rushed into release . . . a slow easy-go ballad with slight rhythm background. (6/12/65) (#11 Pop)*

After 10 years together, Presley and Parker had earned over $150 million in record sales (on over 100 million records) and $135 million from Elvis's first 17 films. Parker pocketed 25% of Elvis's share!

I'm Yours.
> *Strong ballad material with straight, plaintive performance. (8/21/65) (#11 Pop)*

On August 27, Elvis and The Beatles gathered at his Belair, California, home to swap stories and jam all night.

Puppet on a String.
> *From his film "Girl Happy," comes a warm, smooth country ballad. . . . Top of the chart contender. (11/6/65) (#14 Pop)*

Blue Christmas.
> *From the Gold Standard Series this Presley holiday material can't miss running up the chart for the season. Flip: "Santa Claus Is Back in Town." (11/27/65)*

Please Don't Stop Loving Me.
> *An emotional ballad. (3/12/66) (#45 Pop)*

Love Letters.
> *Presley revives the beautiful standard, with Ketty Lester's hit arrangement. (6/25/66) (#19 Pop)*

In 1967, Presley's second gospel album, *How Great Thou Art,* earned him his first Grammy, for Best Religious Recording. That same month (May), he married Priscilla Beaulieu, the girl he met in 1959 while stationed in Germany when she was only 14.

In December 1968, Elvis made a spectacular comeback with an NBC-TV special. The show's finale became his first Top-15 hit in three years and encouraged him to record songs not strictly written for a film script but solely for their quality. "In the Ghetto," a fine Mac Davis song, followed, bringing Elvis back to the Top 10; "Suspicious Minds" became Presley's first #1 in seven years but turned out to be his last.

If I Can Dream.
> *From the forthcoming December 3 NBC-TV special, Elvis comes up with one of his strongest commercial entries in a while. Potent and timely lyric message with exceptional production work by Bones Howe and Steve Binder. (11/23/68) (#12 Pop)*

In the Ghetto.
> *This performance is Elvis at his best and the vital lyric line is right in today's selling bag. This one could easily prove one of his all-time biggest items. (4/26/69) (#3 Pop)*

Suspicious Minds.
> *Elvis should have no trouble getting back into his "In the Ghetto" selling bag with this easy rocker that gets an outstanding performance. A sure winner. (9/6/69) (#1 Pop)*

Don't Cry Daddy.
> *His "Suspicious Minds" brought Elvis back to the No. 1 spot! This compelling rhythm ballad with potent lyric line offers much of that play and sales power. (11/22/69) (#6 Pop)*

Kentucky Rain.
> *A driving rock-ballad penned by singer Eddie Rabbit[t] and producer Dick Heard. This one has all the sales potential of his recent string of hits. Top*

performance and material. (2/7/70) (#16 Pop)

The Wonder of You.

Presley updates the Ray Peterson ballad hit of the past and comes up with another top of the chart winner. (5/2/70) (#9 Pop)

In 1970, Elvis played his first U.S. tour since the 1950s. His last Top-10 smash was the pulsating "Burning Love" (#2) in 1972 (unreviewed by *Billboard,* although "hot chart action" was noted for the single).

On October 9, 1973, Priscilla and Elvis were divorced. In January 1975 he was hospitalized for stomach woes and his treatments caused a weight gain that dogged him for the rest of his life. The year 1976 seemed to be the one everyone wanted to crash in on Presley. Bruce Springsteen was caught climbing the Graceland wall on April 29 and was physically removed; whereas in November, a pistol packin', drunken Jerry Lee Lewis was arrested outside Presley's home when he demanded to see The King.

A series of lasts ensued in 1977. Presley's final recording session was in April in Saginaw, Michigan, and his final performance was at Indianapolis's Market Square Arena. On August 16, Elvis was found on his bathroom floor at Graceland and died at 3:30 P.M. of heart failure. His funeral included 150 invited guests and 75,000 uninvited fans mourning outside Graceland's gates. RCA rushed out "My Way," which became his 147th chart hit. His last was appropriately, "The Elvis Medley" (#71, 1982), released five years after his death.

My Way.

The natural choice for the first Presley single since his death, this is the prophetic song written by Paul Anka. This should reach the No. 1 spot that his last single "Way Down" captured on the Hot Country singles chart. It's the live version taken from his final concert swing. Though his electric moves were gone, he still had that magnificent voice that makes this song a personal and powerful final statement. (11/12/77) (#22 Pop)

The career of The King was full of contradictions. Although he was the world's greatest rock 'n' roll star, he never appeared outside of North America (partly because his manager, Colonel Tom Parker, was an illegal alien), and although he was synonymous with rock and pop, his three Grammy Awards were all for gospel recordings. His swivel hip sensuality started a musical and cultural revolution, yet he was a polite and religious person. Be that as it may, the Michelangelo of modern music and the Babe Ruth of rock 'n' roll will live, musically, forever.

LLOYD PRICE

Birthdate: 3/9/33
Birthplace: New Orleans, LA
Influence: Fats Domino

A major contributor to early rock 'n' roll, the New Orleans native was a multitalented singer, songwriter, pianist, band leader, trumpet player, and even record company entrepreneur.

Like many black youths in the post-Depression South, Price started singing in church choirs, learning piano and trumpet in high school. He formed his own five-piece combo by 1950, playing local clubs and dances. By his sophomore year, he was writing songs for his band and station break jingles for WBOK. One such jingle received so many phone requests that Price decided to cut a complete version and brought "Lawdy, Miss Clawdy" to Specialty Records, who released it as by the "Lloyd Price Ork." Price had first brought the song to Imperial records who turned it down, but along the way he met his idol, Fats Domino, who played piano on "Lawdy" and the flip (praised by *Billboard*).

Lawdy, Miss Clawdy (A-side) . .78–78–76–80

Price socks a very effective vocal on this Southern-flavored blues, while the ork supplies a solid beat. A coin catcher.

Mailman Blues (B-side) 74–75–73–74
A letter from the draft board is the theme for this fast-tempo boogie blues, sung with spirit by Price. Piano work spices the platter. (4/26/52)

"Lawdy" was #1 for seven weeks and became one of the biggest R&B hits of 1952. He followed it with two more two-sided R&B hits. "Ain't It a Shame," perhaps his best-remembered song, charted twice in 1953, both in February and December, a rare occurrence on the American charts.

OOOOH-OOOOH-OOOOH 80
Price socks this one across in top style. It's a blues type item which he shouts for all he's worth, and the band behind him pounds out a solid driving accompaniment.

Restless Heart 79
A pounding effort by the ork with the leader chipping in with an exciting vocal. (9/20/52) (A-side, #4 R&B; B-side, #5 R&B)

Tell Me Pretty Baby (A-side) 85
A great side in every way that should be another winner for Price. It's a jump item with the band introing with a provocative syncopated beat. The singer shouts his way thru a bright vocal. It rides all the way. There's a lot of potential here.

Ain't It a Shame (B-side) 82
Tempo slows on this side, but the solid driving beat remains. Blues styled vocal by Price is a powerful one. (1/17/53) (A-side, #8 R&B; B-side, #4 R&B)

In 1953, Price encouraged Little Richard to send a tape to Specialty's Art Rupe. Subsequently, Richard recorded all his classic rockers for that label thanks to Price.

By the end of 1953, Price became Private Price when the Army drafted him. (They must have heard his "Mailman Blues.") When he left Specialty, they signed his valet, Larry Williams, to sing and, owing to Lloyd's misfortune, classics by Larry Williams, such as "Bony Maronie" and

"Dizzy Miss Lizzy" (which was a takeoff of "Lawdy, Miss Clawdy") followed. Not one to miss a beat, Price formed a band in the military and played bases in Japan and Korea until his 1956 discharge.

He moved to Washington, D.C., met an old friend, Harold Logan, and formed his first label, Kent Record Company (KRC). Soon after, his first self-penned master, "Just Because," was leased to ABC. Price and Logan then dusted off an old folk song, "Stack-O-Lee," giving it an R&B, rock persona that resulted in his first million seller.

Just Because.
This disk has not been available in most areas more than a week, but it is taking off with great speed. (3/2/57) (#29 Pop, #3 R&B)

Stagger Lee.

A cheerful rendition of the old folk tune that should . . . cop lots of coin. Also a strong bet for r.&b. coin. (11/3/58) (B-side, #1 Pop, #1 R&B)

The years 1959 and 1960 produced more of the same, as Lloyd became known as "Mr. Personality."

Where Were You (on Our Wedding Day)?/Is It Really Love?

Price has two great sides to follow up his hit "Stagger Lee." Both are equally potent and it's hard to name a top side. "Where Were You" is a driving, pounding rocker that is brightly belted with great ork backing by Don Costa. Flip, "Is It Really Love?" is also in the pounding groove and the cat really pours a lot of meaning in the lyrics. (2/9/59) (#23 Pop, #4 R&B)

Personality/Have You Ever Had the Blues?

"Personality" is a bright change of pace for Price. A clever moderate-beater tells all about the troubles of love. Good chorus work helps the chanter. Flip is a fine go on a bluesy rockaballad. (4/20/59) (#2 Pop, #1 R&B)

I'm Gonna Get Married.
Song has great teen appeal and hit sound. (7/27/59) (#3 Pop, #1 R&B)

Come Into My Heart/Won'tcha Come Home.

Price sounds in chart form again with two strong items. "Come" has him backed by a crazy chorus and a powerful ork beat. "Won'tcha" is a powerful blues and this could also be a winner. (10/19/59) (A-side, #20 Pop, #2 R&B; B-side, #43 Pop, #6 R&B)

Lady Luck.

A leisurely paced rocker that has the singer in fine form. Ork and chorus work . . . is tops. (1/18/60) (#14 Pop, #3 R&B)

For Love/No If's-No And's.

Price exudes his usual sock showmanship on both sides. "For Love" is an infectious rhythm number. "No If's" is a lively rhythm-novelty. Both should figure. (4/4/60) (B-side, #40 Pop, #16 R&B)

Question/If I Look a Little Blue.

Two great sides here . . . which show the blues shouter off to good advantage. Top side is on the order of "Personality," and the flip is a most attractive blues. Solid wax. (6/13/60) (#19 Pop, #5 R&B)

After mid-1960, the hits dried up, although Price kept trying. By 1963, Price set up his second label, Double L, and had his first Hot-100 single in three years with "Misty" (#21 Pop, #11 R&B). He also signed other acts to the label, such as Pookie Hudson (of The Spaniels) and Wilson Pickett (of The Falcons). By the late 1960s, Lloyd opened a nightclub called The Turntable in New York and began a scholarship fund for black students to attend college.

In a bizarre incident, his Double L partner Logan was found murdered at their office in 1969 while a Lloyd Price record was playing on the office record player. That same year, Lloyd returned to the Top 25 of the R&B charts.

Bad Conditions.

That "Personality" man is back in the groove with this potent rocker that is sure to ride high on the Soul charts, and spill right over in the Hot 100. Exceptional performance and material. (9/20/69) (#21 R&B)

Hooked on a Feeling.

Updated and wild reading of B. J. Thomas's hit of two years ago. Could prove a smash. (3/27/71)

In 1974, Price and fight promoter Don King created the three-day Zaire Music Festival in Africa. By 1976, the duo crafted LPG records where Price had his last chart 45, "What Did You Do With Your Love" (#99 R&B, 1976). Price has continued touring into the 1990s, primarily playing the oldies and Las Vegas arena circuit.

THE RASCALS

Felix Cavaliere: Lead vocals/keyboards
Born: 11/29/44, Pelham, NY
Eddie Brigati: Vocals/tambourine
Born: 10/22/46, New York City
Dino Danelli: Drums
Born: 7/23/45, New York City
Gene Cornish: Guitar
Born: 5/14/45, Ottawa, CA
Influences: Flamingos, Moonglows, Spaniels, Heartbeats, Ray Charles, Marvin Gaye, Beatles, Olympics
Influenced: Billy Joel, Vanilla Fudge, Sly Stone

The Rascals became one of the foremost exponents of "Blue-Eyed Soul" in the 1960s after their dues-paying days as the core of a Twist band.

Cavaliere, Brigati, and Cornish became the nucleus of Joey Dee's Starliters in 1964 after Dee had run his course of Twist hits between 1961 and 1963. In fact, Brigati's brother David (The Hi Fives, Decca) had been with Dee from the beginning. Prior to the Dee days, Cavaliere was a student of classical piano. As a fan of R&B acts like the Flamingos and Ray Charles, he also sang with nonrecording doo woppers, The Stereos. A premed student at Syracuse University, he fronted Felix and the Escorts on the great obscurity, "The Syracuse" (Jag, 1962). Danelli was a jazz prodigy and began playing drums for Lionel Hampton at age 15. He later moved to New Orleans, where the Bourbon Street blues sound hooked him. Danelli returned to New York, backing Little Willie John and met Cavaliere at the Metropole Cafe. The twosome then tried their luck in Las Vegas as part of a casino band before returning to the Big Apple.

Cavaliere then joined Dee (at The Peppermint Lounge), whose backup band now included a young R&B styled vocalist/percussionist, Eddie Brigati and guitarist Gene Cornish. Cornish had previously recorded two singles with his group, The Unbeatables. It wasn't long before Cavaliere, Brigati, and Cornish, tired of the dance-band scene, left to form a white rock/R&B band with the inclusion of Danelli on drums.

Their first gig was in Brigati's home town of Garfield, New Jersey at The Choo Choo Club. The group was now called The Rascals and, by July 1964, they began playing at a fashionable floating club off Southampton, Long Island, called The Barge. Replete with a gimmick dress code of knickers and Little Lord Fauntleroy shirts, the group was an immediate smash. Manager Sid Bernstein (who brought The Beatles to America) got the band signed to Atlantic Records (for a $10,000 advance), but prior to their debut disk, the label changed their name to The Young Rascals. Their second release, the million-selling "Good Lovin'," originally recorded by The Olympics, was the last outside song the group would record. Soon-to-be writing stars Cavaliere and Brigati carried the torch from there on, producing a slew of hits.

I Ain't Gonna Eat Out My Heart Anymore.
Debut of new foursome proves a hot entry for chart action. Slow driving arrangement right up the alley of the teen market. Flip: "Slow Down." (11/27/65) (#52 Pop)

Good Lovin'.
Hot follow-up to their initial hit . . . the exciting group has a definite winner in this driving, wailing rock number. Flip: "Mustang Sally." (2/26/66) (#1 Pop)

You Better Run/Love Is a Beautiful Thing.
Big-beat wailer is backed by an off-beat rocker and both could go all the way. (6/4/66) (#1 Pop)

Come On Up.
Solid dance beat number from the pen of organist Felix Cavaliere. (9/17/66) (#43 Pop)

I've Been Lonely Too Long.
The "Good Lovin'" boys have a winner in this easy rocker featuring a good vocal performance that should bring them back to the Hot 100 in a hurry. Solid dance beat keeps moving. (1/21/67) (#16 Pop, #33 R&B)

With the release of "Groovin'," the band entered a more sophisticated Latin- and jazz-inspired period. "Groovin'," a two million seller, reached #1 for two weeks, dropped out for two, and came back for two more, a rare occurrence on the American charts.

Groovin'.
A smooth summertime blockbuster and well titled is this groovy easy-go ballad which should top their successful "I've Been Lonely Too Long." (4/15/67) (#1 Pop, #3 R&B)

A Girl Like You.
As "Groovin'" starts its slow chart decline, this well done rocking mover has the sales potential to take the group right back up to the top of the Hot 100. (7/8/67) (#10 Pop)

Their next single was inspired by Cavaliere's pending wedding plans.

How Can I Be Sure.
Hot on the heels of "A Girl Like You," the group comes up with a topper in this exceptional ballad material enhanced by the compelling Arif Mardin arrangement. (9/2/67) (#4 Pop)

In Spring 1968, the group convinced Atlantic to drop the "Young" from their name. Their first "Rascals" single was a classic.

It's a Beautiful Morning.
Right in the hot selling bag and sound of "Groovin'," group can't miss going right to the top with this easy-beat rhythm rocker. (4/6/68) (#3 Pop, #36 R&B)

Greatly distressed by the deaths of Robert Kennedy and Martin Luther King, Cavaliere and Brigati wrote a political song that Atlantic was averse to release. But Cavaliere persevered and "People Got to Be Free" (#1 Pop, 5 weeks, #14 R&B) became their greatest success. The sequel, "A Ray of Hope," was dedicated to Senator Edward Kennedy, who wrote the group a note of thanks. "Ray" became the last Cavaliere/Brigati A-side single as dissension among the members arose.

[A] Ray of Hope.

With all the blockbuster sales power of their "People Got to Be Free" smash, group can't miss the top with this potent lyric and driving beat entry. (11/23/68) (#24 Pop, #36 R&B)

Heaven.

One of their best swingers to date, this one can't miss going right to the top of the charts. The Arif Mardin arrangement provides drive all the way thru for the solid vocal workout. (2/1/69) (#39 Pop)

In 1970, Brigati left the group. No Rascals record had ever missed the Top 60 until their December 1970 release, "Right On." Changes were inevitable, Cornish left, and the group added guitarist Buzzy Feiten (Butterfield Blues Band), bass Robert Popwell (who had played with Bob Dylan and Aretha Franklin), and backup singer Ann Sutton (an opera-trained vocalist who sang with soul and jazz groups). Lured by a million-dollar signing offer, they joined Columbia, but their decline continued as the magic foursome was no longer intact. Their first Columbia release, "Love Me," was their 18th and last chart 45.

Love Me.

The Rascals' first for the label, culled from their "Peaceful World" LP, is a wild gospel rock swinger, with much of the flavor of a Sly and the Family Stone sound. Should go all the way! (6/12/71) (#95 Pop)

By the summer of 1972, The Rascals were no more. Danelli and Cornish formed Bulldog (Decca), which evolved into Fotomaker by 1978. Eddie and brother David formed Brigati with a discoized remake of "Groovin'" (Elektra), and

Cavaliere went on to produce (Laura Nyro) and record. His high water mark was "Only the Lonely Heart Sees" (#36 Pop, 1980, Epic). The group, minus Brigati (who retired to his New Jersey chicken farm), got together again for the 1988 "Good Lovin'" U.S. tour. As recently as 1995, Cavaliere was working on a new album with producer Don Was. Without a doubt, The Rascals were one of the 1960s' best and most innovative bands.

OTIS REDDING

Birthdate: 9/9/41
Bithplace: Dawson, GA
Died: 12/10/67
Influences: Little Richard, Sam Cooke
Influenced: Carla Thomas, Arthur Conley, Buffalo Springfield

If James Brown was the king of 1960s' soul music, the crown prince was surely Otis Redding. When the shy country boy sang, his electrifying, gravel-voiced performance belied his quiet demeanor.

The son of a Baptist minister, Redding grew up singing in choirs. He left school at age 16. His Little Richard imitations led him to many a talent show and club performance. By 1959, the 18-year-old was a sometimes singer with Johnny Jenkins and The Pine Toppers, but more often he was their chauffeur. He recorded a few Little Richard-styled sides, including "Shout Bama Lama" (Confederate, 1960) and "Gettin' Hip" (Alshire, 1961), as well as one single with The Pine Toppers, "Love Twist" (Gerald, 1962) that received little recognition.

In October 1962, thanks to Atlantic's Joe Galkin (Atlantic distributed the Gerald single), The Pine Toppers and their "chauffeur," Redding, drove to Memphis, auditioning for Stax label owner, Jim Stewart. The Pine Toppers flopped but, with 20 minutes of session time left, someone suggested Redding try something. Once again he tested his Little Richard style on "Hey, Hey Baby" but Stewart felt one Little Richard was enough.

Then Redding belted a ballad, "These Arms of Mine." Although Stewart wasn't completely sold, he apparently heard something in Redding's rendition and "These Arms" became the singer's first single for Stax's new Volt subsidiary label, reaching #85 Pop and #20 R&B. Not considered very seriously, his first *Billboard* review (for "That's What My Heart Needs," his second 45, listed on 7/6/63) was given four stars but without comment.

Redding began writing with Steve Cropper of Booker T and The MGs, who performed on most of Redding's records and a series of strong R&B disks ensued.

Come to Me.

This is another "Pain in My Heart," Otis's last chart entry. It's a soft, low blues ballad sung with feeling. Otis sings with much raw feeling against a simple backing. (2/29/64) (#69 Pop)

I've Been Loving You Too Long.

Another winning tender and soulful piece of material and performance by "Mr. Pitiful" himself. A strong follow up to his recent hit. (5/8/65) (#21 Pop, #2 R&B)

His following, growing along with widespread touring, was almost strictly black. After one such stint, Redding lamented to MGs' drummer Al Jackson about the disappointments of road life, to which Jackson responded, "What are you griping about, you're on the road all the time. All you can look for is a little respect when you come home!" Voila! A hit was hatched. The Redding/Cropper composition became a signature song for Aretha Franklin two years later and a soulful anthem for decades to come.

Respect.

A wailing blues belter that can't miss hitting the top of the chart. (8/21/65) (#35 Pop, #4 R&B)

Satisfaction.

By request, this hard-driving and wailing blues version of the Rolling Stones hit is pulled from the current Redding LP. Song could repeat its successes all over again in the pop field and prove a giant on the r.&b. chart. (2/26/66) (#31 Pop, #4 R&B)

Try a Little Tenderness.

Culled from his "Dictionary of Soul" LP, this powerful new conception of the standard will work its way onto the charts in rapid fire. (11/26/66) (#25 Pop, #4 R&B)

In August 1967, Redding formed Jotis records; among the recordings he wrote and produced, one ("Sweet Soul Music," #2 Pop and R&B) started the career of Arthur Conley. The song was actually a revision of "Yeah Man" by Redding's other idol, Sam Cooke. Meanwhile, Otis continued to record for Volt, recutting Cooke's "Shake" and the standard "The Glory of Love"; sadly, though, pop chart success continued to elude him.

Shake.

Culled from his "in-person" London concert LP, Redding generates excitement from start to finish with this driving revival of the Sam Cooke hit of the past. Should quickly catch fire and skyrocket to the top. (5/13/67) (#47 Pop, #16 R&B)

The Glory of Love.

This standard is given a solid soul reading by blues wailer Redding, and is sure to be a top sales item in both pop and r.&b. markets. Much in the vein of his "Try a Little Tenderness" smash revival. (7/15/67) (#60 Pop, #19 R&B)

Redding's popularity in Europe earned him top honors in France, and England's Melody Maker weekly named him "The World's Best Male Vocalist" in 1967, ending the eight-year streak of Elvis Presley. Still, he had not significantly crossed to white popularity. His performance on June 16, 1967 at the Monterey Pop Festival (which featured such rock stars as Janis Joplin and Jimi Hendrix), however, began to change that, as his midnight showcase of seething soul music captured the hearts of what Redding called, "the love crowd."

Soon after Monterey, Redding was resting on a rented houseboat in Sausalito, California, when he wrote the lines, "sittin' in the mornin' sun," which would lead to his lasting legacy. On December 7, the resulting ballad, the Cropper/

Redding penned "Sitting on the Dock of the Bay," was recorded. Unfortunately, Redding never saw its release or even heard the final recording. Three days later, Redding died with his road band, The Bar-Kays, in a plane crash by a lake near Madison, Wisconsin, on the way to a performance. Only one 20-year-old Bar-Kay, Ben Cauley, survived; Otis was 26 years old.

Cropper finished the recording soon after and it became the first posthumous #1 Pop hit in history (and Redding's only #1), selling over four million singles.

(Sittin' on) the [Dock] of the Bay.

The late Redding has a solid, bluesy rhythm ballad here penned by Steve Cropper and himself. Should prove one of his strongest sales items for both Pop and r.&b. markets. (1/20/68) (#1 Pop, #1 R&B)

Following its success, Atco (the Atlantic subsidiary label that distributed Volt/Stax) released many more posthumous singles to cash in on Redding's popularity.

Amen.

A highly potent revival of the classic gospel number. Should prove a hot sales item in pop and r&b markets. Flip: "Hard to Handle." (6/29/68) (A-side, #36 Pop, #15 R&B; B-side, #51 Pop, #38 R&B)

I've Got Dreams to Remember.

Powerful and soulful reading of a solid blues ballad. (9/14/68) (#41 Pop, #6 R&B)

Papa's Got a Brand New Bag.

Redding comes on strong with a revival of the James Brown smash. This "live performance" cut was taken from his LP "At the Whiskey a Go Go" and it's a wild discotheque winner. (11/23/68) (#21 Pop, #10 R&B)

A Lover's Question.

The Clyde McPhatter oldie is given a driving updating by Redding which comes on strong following up his "Papa's Got a Brand New Bag." Wild performance and arrangement. (2/15/69) (#48 Pop, #20 R&B)

Free Me.

More potent soul ballad material from Redding. By far one of his best in recent times. (7/26/69)

"Free Me" was Redding's last charter, nine months after his death. Fourteen years later, his sons and nephew, known as The Reddings, unveiled "Dock of the Bay" for a new generation of record buyers; white popster Michael Bolton revived the song in 1988 for a Top-20 pop hit.

PAUL REVERE AND THE RAIDERS

Mark Lindsay: Lead vocals/saxophone
Born: 3/9/42, Cambridge, ID
Paul Revere: Keyboards
Born: 1/7/42, Boise, ID
Bill Hibbard
Born: 1940s
Richard White
Born: 1940s
Robert White
Born: 1940s
Michael Smith: Drums
Born: 1940s
Jerry Labrum
Born: 1940s
Influences: Jerry Lee Lewis, Ray Charles, Elvis Presley, Gene Vincent, Chuck Berry, Little Richard, B. B. King, Bobby Bland, Etta James, Jessie Hill
Influenced: David Bowie, Roger Daltrey, Pete Townshend, Brownsville Station

From an instrumental band to rock 'n' rollers to teenybopper idols, Paul Revere and The Raiders were regular visitors of the pop charts throughout the 1960s and early 1970s.

Paul Revere (his real name) was an enterprising teen who started as a barber and soon became a drive-in restaurant owner in Caldwell, Idaho. Having learned piano and organ, the 17-year-old formed The Downbeats in 1959. In 1960, delivery boy Mark Lindsay brought some baked goods to Revere's drive-in and left with the knowledge that, if he could play saxophone, he could join Revere's group. Lindsay then bought a copy of an album by The Champs and was soon knocking on Revere's door, sax in hand.

During the summer of 1960, they became Paul Revere and the Nightriders but changed to the Raiders upon recording for the tiny California-based Gardena label with their first instrumental, credited by *Billboard* to Revere alone.

Beatnik Sticks.

★ ★ ★ ★ *This is a wild, rocking version of the Chopsticks theme. An instrumental, it never lets up for an instant. Watch it. (8/1/60)*

Their second release, arranged by Gary "Alley Oop" Paxton, surprised everyone by charging up the Top 100. The flip, "Sharon," was the first of many Mark Lindsay-led vocals to come.

Like, Long Hair.

★ ★ ★ *After a gag concerto-ish opening this side swings into a hard stomping piano instrumental. Rhythm is strong and could give disk a chance.*

Sharon.

★ ★ *Mark Lindsay sings this side with a vocal chorus of what sounds like electronic pipers. Side is a hard bumping blues in a middle rocking tempo. (12/26/60) (#38 Pop)*

Like Charleston.

The boys follow up their last chart item with a brightly swinging instrumental here that sports hard-driving piano in the boogie-woogie style, and solid tenor sax work. (6/12/61)

Shortly after "Long Hair" charted, Revere was drafted. By 1962, the group split up. Still, five more singles followed under their name, led by eccentric rock legend-to-be, Kim Fowley.

In 1963, Revere and Lindsay, now living in Portland, Oregon, formed a new combo with Mike Smith, Steve West, and Dick Walker. The band did one single for Jerden ("So Fine") that went unnoticed. One night they performed at a dance with The Kingsmen. During a break both acts noticed the kids rollicking to a song on the juke-

box by yet another Northwestern band, The Wailers. The song was called "Louie, Louie." Both groups then recorded "Louie" at the same studio, a day apart. The Raiders' version came out on the local Sande label. Meanwhile, a tape was sent to Columbia, and The Raiders became the first rock 'n' roll band signed by the record giant; "Louie" was also their first single. Obviously, Columbia was not yet prepared to promote rock and, although the Raiders never charted in America, the Kingsmen garnered legendary status.

Changes started with West and Walker walking, whereas Drake Levin and Philip Volk joined the band. They also took on the image of Revolutionary War Minutemen with outrageous costumes, including three-cornered hats, frilled shirts, and tunics. The idea came when Paul and Mark walked past a Portland costume shop where mannequins were dressed in full regalia.

In 1965, after four failures, the group charted with "Steppin' Out." The record impressed impresario Dick Clark and he hired The Raiders as the house band for his daily afternoon TV show, "Where the Action Is." The constant exposure ensured their records' success with teenyboppers, but their hard rock fans abandoned them.

Steppin' Out.

With their album currently riding the hit charts, this pulsating rocker is a definite winner for the Hot 100 chart. Exciting, raucous vocal. (8/28/65) (#46 Pop)

Just Like Me.

Strong follow-up to their "Steppin' Out" is this raucous and driving rocker loaded with excitement and wild sounds. (11/20/65) (#11 Pop)

Kicks.

Emotional rhythm rocker. (3/12/66) (#4 Pop)

In April 1966, Jim Valley replaced Levin and a revolving door of some 30 musicians came and went during the group's life, with Revere and Lindsay remaining at its core.

Good Thing.

Penned by Mark Lindsay and Terry Melcher, this raucous swinger should hit hard and fast aimed right at the top of the charts. (11/26/66) (#4 Pop)

Him or Me—What's It Gonna Be?

Wild rocker with strong dance beat and infectious arrangement. Has No. 1 possibilities. Flip: "Legend of Paul Revere." (4/15/67) (#5 Pop)

I Had a Dream.

Driving rock ballad given a powerful vocal workout is a change of pace for the group and should quickly work its way to a high position on the Hot 100. (8/12/67) (#17 Pop)

In 1967, Volk, Smith, and Levin formed an ill-fated group, Brotherhood, signing with RCA. Freddy Weller (later to be a country star) among others joined The Raiders and the group rolled on. For most of 1968, the band had its own TV show, "Happening '68."

Too Much Talk.

This pile-driving mover is just the solid number to put them back in the Top 20 once again. . . . Disk rocks from start to finish. (2/3/68) (#19 Pop)

Mr. Sun, Mr. Moon.

Hard-driving, strong Mark Lindsay rhythm material. It's a mover all the way through. (1/25/69) (#18 Pop)

In May 1969, Lindsay began a solo career while remaining as producer of The Raiders with Revere running the business end. The group's records were now credited "Paul Revere and The Raiders Featuring Mark Lindsay."

Let Me.

Group rode to the top of the Hot 100 with their "Mr. Sun, Mr. Moon," and as it slowly slips down they come up with this solid rocker that's sure to repeat that success. (5/3/69) (#20 Pop)

Mark Lindsay:
First Hymn from Grand Terrace.

Sensitive treatment of the Jim Webb beauty. . . . Much middle of the road programming here as well. (5/31/69) (#81 Pop)

Arizona.

Hard driving rock ballad has all the ingredients to take him way up the chart with solid sales. Top performance. (11/15/69) (#10 Pop)

And the Grass Won't Pay No Mind.

Neil Diamond wrote this powerhouse rhythm ballad and Lindsay turns in a strong delivery, certain to put him up the Hot 100 with sales impact. (9/12/70) (#44 Pop)

In 1971, Columbia staffer Jack Gold recommended a three-year-old song to Lindsay for the band. With Weller's lead vocal, The Raiders had their only #1 and last Top-20 hit.

Raiders:
Indian Reservation (The Lament of the Cherokee Reservation Indian).

The Raiders turn in a top revival of Don Fardon's hit of a few years back and the good John D. Loudermilk material should prove a top programmer with sales to follow. (2/27/71)

However, they were unable to capitalize on their sucess; their chart finale was "Love Music" (#97, 1973). That same year they appeared on Clark's 20th Anniversary American Bandstand TV special.

THE RIGHTEOUS BROTHERS

Bill Medley: Bass
Born: 9/19/40, Santa Ana, CA
Bobby Hatfield: Tenor
Born: 8/10/40, Beaver Dam, WI
Influences: Don and Dewey, Ray Charles, Little Richard, Penguins, Platters, Fats Domino, B. B. King
Influenced: Bruce Springsteen, Billy Joel, Michael Bolton

The originators of "blue-eyed soul," bass Bill Medley and tenor Bobby Hatfield sang some of the most awesome and powerful recordings of any duo in rock history.

William Thomas Medley began singing with his high school band in Santa Ana, California, which evolved into The Paramours. Bobby Hatfield, whose family moved to Anaheim, California, when he was a child, formed his own school group, The Variations. Medley's group had two singles in 1961, their debut disk, "That's the Way We Love" followed by "Cutie Cutie"; neither saw chart action.

The Paramours:
That's the Way We Love.
★ ★ ★ ★ *Happy jumping tune gets a vigorous reading from the group. Tune takes in all the wonders of love. Fine combo romps in the background. (3/27/61)*

In 1962, Medley and Hatfield met at a club. A mutual friend, John Wimber, wanted to start a working group and asked Medley and his Paramours' guitarist along with Hatfield and his Variations' drummer to join him, forming a new Paramours. In 1962, they debuted their first recording, "There She Goes," for the small Moonglow label. About that time, The Paramours performed at Santa Ana's Black Derby; black marines in the audience, drawn to Medley and Hatfield's soul/gospel and blues style, dubbed them The Righteous Brothers.

Their next Moonglow single was the first to bear the new name. "Little Latin Lupe Lu," a Medley composition, took off after it was used in a KRLA radio commercial for a record hop; it was rated with three stars by *Billboard,* but went unreviewed. A few singles followed, until *Billboard* finally "picked" their late 1963 release, "Koko Joe," although it failed to chart.

Koko Joe.
 This is a hand-clappin', stompin', screamer with a beat that's right on top of their last one, "Right Now." The disk really goes for the kids. (11/16/63)

In 1964, the duo became the opening act for The Beatles' U.S. tour, but quit halfway, because it was a thankless task to precede an act that thousands of screaming teen girls were waiting to hear. On September 16, the Righteous Brothers became regulars on the new rock 'n' roll TV show, "Shindig." The debut episode included Sam Cooke and The Everly Brothers. A month earlier they appeared at San Francisco's cavernous Cow Palace with numerous acts, including The Ronettes, produced by legendary rock recluse Phil Spector.

Spector quickly bought the boys out of their remaining 2½-year contract with Moonglow, and signed them to his Philles label. He brought Barry Mann and Cynthia Weil to L.A. and, inspired by their current favorite, "Baby, I Need Your Loving" (The Four Tops), they wrote with Spector "You've Lost That Lovin' Feeling," a worldwide hit (#1 Pop, #3 R&B). Hatfield, however, wasn't so sure. Upon hearing the song for the first time he asked, "What do I do while he (Bill) is singing the whole first verse?" Spector's blunt retort was, "You can go directly to the bank!"

Meanwhile, Moonglow had several albums worth of material in the can and continued issuing singles through 1965, including the powerful "Bring Your Love to Me."

Bring Your Love to Me.
Currently hot on the Philles label, boys give their wailing all on rouser with production backing. (1/23/65) (#83 Pop)

Spector's Philles label countered with the brilliant Carole King/Gerry Goffin penned "Just Once in My Life."

Just Once in My Life.
More exciting, dramatic, emotion filled production performances by the "Lovin' Feeling" boys. Can't miss! (4/3/65) (#9 Pop, #26 R&B)

When Spector released his next, expected smash "Hung on You," deejays flipped it, preferring the standard "Unchained Melody," which became the hit.

Hung on You/Unchained Melody.
Two powerhouse sides. Top deck is a dramatic, emotional performance of a strong new ballad from the winning pen of Carole King, Gerry Goffin and Phil Spector. The dynamic revival of "Unchained Melody" is released by popular demand. (7/10/65) (A-side, #47 Pop; B-side, #4 Pop, #6 R&B)

Spector's reaction was to record more oldies like "Ebb Tide" with the duo. However, he took it too far with the act's noncharting "White Cliffs of Dover." Surprising everyone after only five singles, Spector sold their contract to MGM's Verve subsidiary for $1 million. Their first 45 was a song previously written (but unfinished) by Mann and Weil as the aborted follow up to "Lovin' Feeling." Medley asked them to finish it, and the dynamic duo's second #1 was the result.

(You're My) Soul and Inspiration.

With the sound of their early hits this builds into an emotional production. A No. 1 contender. (2/26/66) (#1 Pop, #13 R&B)

Go Ahead and Cry/Things Didn't Go Your Way.

Top is a dramatic ballad with full chorus and lush string backing while the flip is a strong r.&b. wailer with comedy overtones. Either could go all the way. (7/30/66) (#30 Pop)

Lacking strong songs, Righteous Brothers records started peaking at midchart.

On This Side of Goodbye.

The Goffin-King ballad serves as strong material for the soulful duo as they wail with emotion. Fine production work of Bill Medley. (10/22/66) (#47 Pop)

Along Came Jones.

A new bag with this strong commercial revival of The Coasters' hit. Should bring them back to winner's circle. (2/4/67)

Melancholy Music Man.

Has the feel and electricity of the early Righteous hits and should fast meet with that kind of smash success. Powerhouse ballad and performance. (4/15/67) (#43 Pop)

Their last MGM/Verve Top-100 disk was the appropriately titled "Stranded in the Middle of No Place" (#72, 1967).

Medley decided to go solo as did Hatfield, although for performances Hatfield recruited Jimmy Walker (of the Knickerbockers) to continue as The Brothers. Neither had much chart success.

In 1974, Medley and Hatfield reteamed on Sonny and Cher's Comedy Hour and on record; "Dream On" was their last newly recorded chart single, whereas their disk finale was "Hold On" in 1975.

Rock and Roll Heaven.

The original Righteous Brothers are back with an extremely powerful song reminiscent of their best material in days gone by with this tribute to some of the biggest rock stars who have passed away. Should click immediately with new fans and those who remember them. (5/18/74) (#3 Pop)

Give It to the People.

Top notch vocals from Bill Medley and Bobby Hatfield and the superb production of Lambert and Potter make this another certain bet for Top 40, easy listening and possibly soul airplay. (8/31/74) (#20 Pop)

Dream On.

A powerful ballad entry highlighted by the individual singing of Bill Medley and Bobby Hatfield and the unique harmonizing that the pair has always used. Reminiscent in parts of some of their earlier Phil Spector material, particularly when they trade off lead slots. Certain to catch the AM crowd instantly. (11/9/74) (#32 Pop)

They continued to reunite on and off, including American Bandstand's 30th Anniversary Show in 1982. Meanwhile, their recordings continued to reach fans via films like *Top Gun* ("Lovin' Feeling") in 1986 and *Ghost* ("Unchained Melody") in 1990. Medley finally had the solo hit he longed for, also from a film, when his duet with Jennifer Warnes on "The Time of My Life" reached #1 thanks to the *Dirty Dancing* flick.

JOHNNY RIVERS

Real Name: John Ramistella
Birthdate: 11/7/42
Birthplace: New York City
Influences: Fats Domino, Ray Charles, B. B. King

The king of covers in the 1960s and early 1970s, Johnny Rivers biggest hit was a song of his own, 1966's "Poor Side of Town."

Although born in New York, from the age of three Rivers was raised in Baton Rouge, Louisiana. He received an old guitar at eight and later learned the mandolin. By high school, the youngster had played with several bands and, in 1958, ventured to New York City. He had resolved to meet premier deejay Alan Freed and camped out in front of radio station WINS until Freed arrived for work. When they met, Alan suggested the 15-year-old return the following day. Freed was moved by his music but not his last name, so, in tribute to the boy's childhood by the Mississippi, Freed dubbed him Johnny Rivers. He then brought Rivers to George Goldner's Gone Records, where he recorded in a rockabilly style.

Baby, Come Back .71
A swinging rockabilly job with Rivers lending it a frantic sound. Has a real aching, pleader. Spins possible. (3/24/58)

During 1959, the 17-year-old moved to Nashville, eventually making demonstration recordings for Elvis Presley and Johnny Cash (along with another singer/songwriter hopeful, Roger Miller). He returned to New York as a staff writer for Hill and Range Music Publishing. Between 1958 and 1964, Johnny recorded 16 singles for 10 labels, including "A Hole in the Ground," "Your First and Last Love," "The Customary Thing," "Call Me," "I Get So Doggone

Lonesome," and "Blue Skies"; all went down for the count.

The White Cliffs of Dover.
★ ★ ★ *River selects one of the saccharine World War II ballads for the up-dated jumping, rocking, triplet-backed treatment. A good rollicking sound . . . could create some noise. River has a Domino touch on this side. (3/23/59)*

Knock Three Times.
★ ★ ★ *Bluesy effort is handled in warm style . . .over basic blues support. (3/13/61)*

In late 1962, Rivers moved to Los Angeles after a job playing with Louis Prima's band led him to Las Vegas.

His live set of rockified R&B oldies drew a legion of Los Angeles fans to Gazzari's in 1963 and the newly established Whiskey a Go Go in 1964. When word reached Imperial Records, they decided to not only sign him but record him live, an unheard-of prospect for a new teen-style act. His first single, "Memphis," was from the Chuck Berry bag of tricks. The "overnight sensation" (that only took six years) continued clicking with retreads of soul, blues, and folk.

Memphis.
The Chuck Berry hit is re-done in grand style. With driving beat and great lyric message, it should happen all over again. (5/16/64) (#2 Pop)

Oh, What a Kiss.
One of the most exciting performers on pop records today. Genuine rockaboogie side. Guitar, simmering strings and groove beat. There's still a career for American artists. (7/4/64)

Maybellene.
Look out! Johnny's done it again! Powerful "Memphis" rockin' sound. A hand-clappin', wailing harmonica, and tom tom beat. A smasheroo! (8/8/64) (#12 Pop)

Mountain of Love.
This tune's been there before and Johnny gives it plenty of punch that should drive it right back on the charts. Zapo beat and groovy instrumental and chorus backing. (10/24/64) (#9 Pop)

Seventh Son.

> *Pulsating rhythm number with a strong vocal and guitar performance. (5/29/65) (#7 Pop)*

Where Have All the Flowers Gone.

> *Change of pace . . . is this rhythm version of the Pete Seeger folk classic. Excitement and solid dance beat should spiral this one up the charts rapidly. (9/25/65) (#26 Pop)*

Rivers got a boost when he was invited to record a theme for a British-imported TV spy drama, "Secret Agent Man."

> *The TV theme by Rivers was recorded and released by popular demand. Swinger should hit hard and fast in the teen market. (3/12/66) (#3 Pop)*

After nine cover (and nonoriginal) hits in a row, Rivers wrote his own ticket to success, the million-selling "Poor Side of Town." Even with a #1 original, Johnny shied away from his own songs, preferring the safety of well-chosen oldies.

Poor Side of Town.

> *Easy rhythm ballad and a change-of-pace for Rivers should hit hard and fast. Well-thought-out lyric penned by Rivers and producer Lou Adler. (9/10/66) (#1 Pop)*

By the end of 1966, Rivers had formed a publishing company and record label (Soul City distributed by Imperial), signing talent such as Jimmy Webb and The 5th Dimension. No one could fault his choice of "Baby, I Need Your Lovin'" for his next single but in doing so, he turned down Webb's "By the Time I Get to Phoenix."

Baby, I Need Your Lovin'.

> *Rivers brings the Four Tops smash up to date with a smooth vocal interpretation. (1/28/67) (#3 Pop)*

The Tracks of My Tears.

> *Exciting revival of the Marvelettes [sic] former hit. . . . Exceptional Lou Adler production should hit hard and fast and soar straight to the top. (5/27/67) (#10 Pop)*

Summer Rain.

> *A powerhouse entry from Rivers is this easy-beat folk rocker with well-written lyric. Another top vocal outing that's headed straight for the top of the charts. (11/11/67) (#14 Pop)*

By late 1969, his Soul City label produced 11 5th Dimension hits. He then sold the label to Imperial for $2.5 million and went into performance retirement, preferring to travel through Japan and India; he even charted with "The Guru Ram Das Ashram Singers" in 1971! By that time, he was on UA (the Imperial parent) and had sold his publishing company, including the Jimmy Webb catalog, for another million.

Johnny Rivers and Friends:
Fire and Rain.

> *Easy-beat ballad has all the earmarks of a winner. Production and arrangement are top notch. (8/22/70) (#94 Pop)*

Sea Cruise.

> *The Frankie Ford smash of the fifties is brought up to date by Rivers and it's his most commercial entry in some time. Wild vocal workout and beat for discotheques. (4/24/71) (#84 Pop)*

Johnny Rivers and The Guru Ram Das Ashram Singers:
Think His Name.

> *Rivers comes up with an infectious Jesus-rock rhythm number loaded with top chart possibilities. (8/7/71) (#65 Pop)*

Still a hit threat, he stormed the charts again in 1973 with Huey "Piano" Smith's "Rockin' Pneumonia and Boogie Woogie Flu." In 1975, he coaxed Beach Boy Brian Wilson into singing background on his version of "Help Me Rhonda," and by 1977 had reacquired the Soul City name, although nothing of chart significance emerged. After a remake of the Funky Kings' "Slow Dancin'," Johnny had his last hit, "Curious Mind."

Curious Mind (Um, Um, Um, Um, Um).

> *A remake of the song which went top 5 for Major Lance in 1964. It opens soft*

and mellow, but builds in intensity with a good soulish Stax-styled sax break towards the end. (12/17/77) (#41 Pop)

Through the 1980s and 1990s, Rivers returned to touring, having built a base on 30 million record sales.

TOMMY ROE

Birthdate: 5/9/42
Birthplace: Atlanta, GA
Influences: Buddy Holly, Carl Perkins, Chuck Berry

Thomas David Roe was a pop/rock/bubblegum star with an affinity for Buddy Holly, coupled with an ultracommercial songwriting style.

As a student at Brown High School, Tommy formed a rock band, The Satins, playing Georgia Tech fraternity parties and school hops in 1958. By 1960, Roe and company hooked up successively with Trumpet Records, Mark 1V, and Florence, Alabama's Judd Records (owned by Judd Phillips, brother of Sun Records Sam Phillips) as each label passed their recording of "Cave Man" on in hopes of greater distribution. Tommy Roe and The Satins:

Caveman.
★ ★ ★   *Story is about a cool caveman who goes a-wooing. It's a rocker sort and Roe handles it nicely over twangy guitar support. (3/28/60)*

Judd then issued a song Tommy wrote at 15 titled "Sheila." *Billboard* reviewed the record twice, first as an A-side and then a week later oddly as a B-side, while the rating dropped from three to two stars.

Sheila.
★ ★ ★   *Roe has a good rockabilly quality, somewhat reminiscent of Buddy Holly. He handles this dedication to a chick*

well and he has the support of a girl vocal group. Good sound. (10/10/60)

Sheila.
★ ★   *Lad sells this rocker with some feeling over good support. (10/17/60)*

Neither "Caveman" nor "Sheila" caused much commotion, and the band played on.

In 1961, Paul Drew, an Atlanta deejay who had booked the band for many shows, introduced them to ABC-Paramount producer, Felton Jarvis. Felton would later have his hands full producing Elvis Presley, but for now he was looking for talent and Roe had it. The first ABC single was a rerecording of "Sheila" with Jerry Reed on guitar. At the time, Roe was earning a living at General Electric soldering wires for $70 a week.

Sheila.
★ ★ ★ ★   *This tune has a novel rhythmic bass. Rolling drum effects with guitar and vocal chorus form the background for the singer. Side could catch some attention. (6/2/62) (#1 Pop, #6 R&B)*

"Sheila" hit No. 1 in *Billboard* and ABC asked Tommy to stop soldering and start singing cross country. He responded that leaving would jeopardize his promotion chances and his salary. When they advanced him $5,000 (71 weeks' pay!), he hit the road.

Susie Darlin'.
 The young chanter has had a fine smash with ["Sheilah"], and here he's back with another fine girl's name tune. It's a ballad and it's handled with much style. (9/22/62) (#35 Pop)

Everybody.
 A shouting rocker that swings with viable chorus shouting and an incessant beat. (9/14/63) (#3 Pop)

With "Everybody" (his second million seller) and "Sheila" enjoying U.K. success, Tommy toured Britain in March 1963 accompanied by a young opening act, The Beatles.

By 1964, 22-year-old Roe was Army-bound but returned in 1966 with a vengeance. "Sweet Pea," unreviewed, was his third gold single. It was followed by more hits.

Hooray for Hazel.

Hot on the heels of "Sweet Pea," Roe has another sure-fire winner here with some of the flavor of his hit "Sheila." Well-written mover penned by the performer. (9/10/66) (#6 Pop)

It's Now Winter's Day.

An exceptional ballad. The well-written lyric, penned by Roe, is right in the teen alley. (12/17/66) (#23 Pop)

Owing to Tommy's overwhelming popularity in England, he moved there in the mid-1960s. By decade's end, he and producer Steve Barri were turning out a bounty of bubblegum hits. "Dizzy" became his biggest million seller and second #1. He wrote it with Raiders' lead Freddy Weller while the two were on a Dick Clark "Caravan of Stars" tour in 1968.

Dizzy.

Here's one of Roe's most infectious and commercial outings in some time. Rhythmic rocker is loaded with teen dance and sales appeal and features a top Steve Barri production. (12/7/68) (#1 Pop)

Heather Honey.

Roe comes on strong with an equally potent sales item in this rhythm number. He's headed right for the top again. (4/19/69) (#29 Pop)

Jam Up Jelly Tight.

Bubblegum item that is certain to take [Roe] far higher on the Hot 100. (11/8/69) (#8 Pop)

"Jam Up" was Roe's fifth and last million seller.

Pearl.

Roe is in a strong commercial bag in this easy beat blues ballad, an original he wrote with Freddy Weller. A sure-fire sales and chart topper. (6/13/70) (#50 Pop)

Stagger Lee.

Roe updates Lloyd Price's rhythm classic and it has all the ingredients to re-establish him on the Hot 100 with solid Top 40 and sales impact. (8/7/71) (#25 Pop)

By the 1970s, his sales were declining and he returned to Atlanta about the time "Working Class Hero" became his last chart single in 1973 (#97, MGM). In 1979, he moved to Los Angeles, recording for Monument, Warner/Curb, Warner Brothers, BGO, and Awesome through 1984, but with less than hoped for results. During the mid-1980s "oldies" revival, Tommy's performing career took an upturn and he began recording again in a country mode.

Back When It Really Mattered.

Ear-pleasing, upbeat tempo throughout . . . simple tension-and-release country formula. (5/2/87)

Still touring regularly, Roe's recording plans as of 1995 included a new album with Danny and The Juniors' Joe Terry.

THE RONETTES

Veronica "Ronnie" Bennett Spector: Lead vocals
Born: 8/10/45, New York City
Estelle Bennett
Born: 7/22/44, New York City
Nedra Talley
Born: 1/27/46, New York City
Influences: Frankie Lymon and The Teenagers, Little Anthony and The Imperials, Chantels
Influenced: Billy Joel, Bruce Springsteen

It's hard to believe that a trio with only eight chart records and one Top-20 hit could have had such a profound effect on the history of 1960s' music, not to mention the libido of millions of teen males, but The Ronettes were no ordinary girl group. In fact, they were the first of the sensual singing groups in rock 'n' roll. With piled-high bouffants and tighter-than-tight short skirts, the trio of two sisters (Ronnie and Estelle) and a cousin (Nedra) only had to wiggle on stage to set hearts-a-pounding.

As early as 1959, the three teens found a positive way to pass the time when they were grounded by their grandma: harmonize. With confidence building, they challenged the Apollo Amateur

Night contest and won, encouraging grandma to spring for singing lessons. In 1961, the girls (who were playing Bar Mitzvahs and sock hops until then) waited on line at New York's in spot, The Peppermint Lounge, when they were mistaken for the overdue talent, pulled inside, and pushed onstage. Their impromptu performance with house band Joey Dee and The Starliters earned them a regular spot at the club for $10 a night each. Calling themselves The Darling Sisters, they were soon drafted as deejay Murray the K's dancing girls after he saw them perform at the Miami Peppermint Lounge.

By summertime 1961, the Harlem teens were contracted to Colpix Records and the label renamed them Ronnie and The Relatives for one uptempo release, "I Want a Boy." By their second single, the girls' aunts and uncles started making name suggestions, noting there were numerous "ettes" groups around, i.e., Marvelettes, Bobbettes, etc. Ronnie's mom then volunteered, The Rondettes. Soon after they were renamed The Ronettes, and alternated between Colpix and its May affiliate.

You Bet I Would.
★ ★ ★ ★ *The gals sell a catchy rocker with verve and cute performance by lead canary. Teen-appeal side. (3/17/62)*

I'm on the Wagon.
★ ★ ★ ★ *The girls have a wild one here. The lead singer's on the wagon until the boy returns. The side has a similar sound to "Playboy" and features some sharp trumpet work about halfway through. This one could go. (7/21/62)*

A full album's worth of material was recorded but not released until the group's later success. While recording in 1962 and 1963, they sang backup on records for Joey Dee, Del Shannon, and Bobby Rydell.

Memory.

This three-girl group has been known in the past for the fine twist act it puts on. Now the gals have a disk winner, too, with a bright teen item with a forceful lead and solid help from the others. Good recitation spot too. Watch it. (3/23/63)

In 1963, after five failing singles with Colpix, the trio of 17- to 19-year-old girls picked the producer they wanted, Phil Spector, but didn't know how to reach him. All they knew was that his record company was on 62nd Street. Estelle simply phoned Philles Records and asked for him. Astounded that the secretary actually put him on, the shocked Estelle mustered her most adult voice and told Spector she was one of The Ronettes. The conversation led to an audition the next night at Mira Sound. That night, Svengali Spector found his Trilby in Veronica Bennett. Soon after, Spector's "wall of sound" ushered in the era of powerhouse girl groups with a song Beach Boy Brian Wilson would later call "the most perfect pop record of all time"—"Be My Baby," their first Philles release. Backing vocals on "Baby" included Cher, Darlene Love, The Blossoms, and Ronnie herself.

Be My Baby.

This is the best record The Ronettes ever made and more than that it's one of the strongest records of the week. It was made by Phil Spector and he has transformed the gals into a sock singing group who handle this dramatic piece of material with flair. Backing has a stunning, rolling rock sound that's bound to make the disk score with the kids. (8/17/63) (#2 Pop, #4 R&B)

Their follow up, "Baby, I Love You," was equally strong. Oddly, the *Billboard* reviewer identified them as a "Philadelphia" group.

Baby, I Love You.

The strong Philadelphia vocal group has another swinging, glandular side that should soar. It features that big Philadelphia sound. (12/14/63) (#24 Pop)

At Christmas 1963, Spector's awesome Christmas album was released, including The Ronettes singing "Sleigh Ride," "Frosty the Snowman," and "I Saw Mommy Kissing Santa Claus." The record's hit journey was stopped in the wake of President Kennedy's death.

In February 1964, the bad girls in bouffants toured England with The Rolling Stones and met the kings of the continent, The Beatles. The head-lines read, "Girls Scream at Stones, Boys at Ronettes" and with that the first female group to induce mass hysteria was born.

The Best Part of Breakin' Up.

The gals swing in with a stompin' rock-aballad that has that famous Spector sound. Side brings full effect of strings, horns etc. to bear. (3/21/64) (#39 Pop)

Do I Love You?

Phil Spector and Jack Nitzsche bring the group in for another chart landing. (6/13/64) (#34 Pop)

Also in 1964, Spector recorded two singles featuring "Veronica" alone (although The Ronettes were singing backup) but both were only meant to test the waters for Ronnie as a solo and were quickly recalled. The first was The Students' 1958 hit "So Young," followed by another teen wailer, "Why Don't They Let Us Fall in Love" released on the "Phil Spector" label.

Veronica/Why Don't They Let Us Fall in Love.

Teen-grooved with that moaning-wailing delivery featuring a high-pitched femme voice. An expected Spector. (7/25/64)

Meanwhile, the Ronettes' "Walking in the Rain" won a Grammy in 1964 for best sound effects. The same year's "Home of the Brave," released on the "Phi-Dan" label and credited to Bonnie and the Treasures, is believed to be by The Ronettes.

Walking in the Rain.

A smash sound! Bluesy rendition featuring fine lead solo. Phil backs them with his new world symphony orchestra and a terrific arrangement. (10/17/64) (#23 Pop, #28 R&B)

Born to Be Together.

Big production rocker. (1/30/65) (#52 Pop)

Is This What I Get for Loving You?

Teen-oriented ballad from the pens of Phil Spector, Carol [sic] King and Gerry Goffin. (5/22/65) (#75 Pop)

Bonnie and The Treasures:
Home of the Brave.

Teen sound interpretation of the hot teen message piece of material. Driving beat from start to finish and vocal reading to match. (8/14/65)

Their last Philles 45 was the only one not produced by Spector.

I Can Hear Music.

Their first production ballad by Jeff Barry, combined with strong material, should be just the one to send the girls to the top of the chart again. (10/15/66) (#100 Pop)

The group's chart decline and Estelle and Nedra's friction with Spector hastened their split. Ronnie began a relationship with Spector that led to a 1968 marriage and, eventually, a 1974 breakup. Although the label read The Ronettes, 1969's "You Came, You Saw, You Conquered" was actually Ronnie and studio singers, as the trio never recorded together again. Although forced into seclusion by Spector, Ronnie still managed an occasional single, including 1971's George Harrison-penned "Try Some, Buy Some," coproduced by Spector and released on the Beatles' Apple label.

You Came, You Saw, You Conquered.

Featuring the voice of Veronica, backed by an enormous production, group returns to the disk scene via A&M and with all the current hits with the sound of the '50s this one has much sales appeal. In the bag of their original "Be My Baby." (3/15/69)

Ronnie Spector:
Try Some, Buy Some.

Former lead singer of the Ronettes, now Mrs. Phil Spector, debuts on Apple with a powerful production ballad . . . With a little help from Ringo, George and Clapton, this one has all the ingredients to break through big. Flip: "Tandori Chicken." (4/24/71) (#77 Pop)

In 1973, she appeared at Richard Nader's Rock and Roll Revival Show in New York with a new Ronettes, Denise Edwards and Chip Fields. During 1976, The Ronettes' most spectacular unreleased recording of the 1960s, "Paradise," was finally issued but was not promoted; *Billboard* inexplicably listed it in the August 7 issue with no comment.

The gutsy girl charged back in 1986, powering a duet with Eddie Money. "Take Me Home Tonight" reached #4, and Ronnie signed to Columbia. During the 1980s and 1990s, Ronnie continues to captivate her generation with performances as one of the legendary ladies of rock 'n' roll.

BOBBY RYDELL

Real Name: Robert Ridarelli
Birthdate: 4/26/42
Birthplace: Philadelphia, PA
Influences: Bobby Darin, Frank Sinatra

Clean-cut, good looking teen idol types of the 1960s were a dime a dozen, but few had any real musical talent. One who did was Bobby Rydell.

At age six, Bobby was playing drums and, with the encouragement of his parents, became a nightclub attraction at seven. (So much for child labor laws in 1949!) His audition for Paul Whiteman's "Teen Club" TV show in 1951 led to three years of singing and playing drums for the bandleader. In fact, it was Whiteman who changed his last name from Ridarelli to Rydell.

By 1957, the 15-year-old had joined a hot Philly band, Rocco and The Saints, which included an 18-year-old trumpet player named Francis Avallone, later known as Frankie Avalon. The group's high point was an appearance in the film *Disc Jockey Jamboree*, singing "Teacher's Pet." While Avalon's solo pursuits bore fruit in early 1958 on Chancellor Records, Rydell's career hit a series of roadblocks when Decca, RCA, and Capitol all rejected him. In 1959, his manager,

Frank Day, issued Rydell's first single on his own Los Angeles-based Veko label but with no results.

Dream Age.

★ ★   *This is a feelingful reading of a tender rockaballad. (1/19/59)*

Day then signed Rydell with Cameo Records where owner Kal Mann directed Rydell through singing and dancing lessons. The first Cameo release came early in 1959.

Please Don't Be Mad/Makin' Time.

 Rydell has a handsome wax item to mark his initial recording efforts. He has a pleasant voice, and handles the material in capable style. "Please" is a pounding ballad that is emotionally belted. "Makin' Time" is in the rocker groove. Both have sales potential. (2/16/59)

One more single, "All I Want Is You," also failed to chart, but then he hit his stride with "Kissin' Time."

Kissin' Time.

 Rydell, who has come close before, seems a likely chart prospect with this driving side. It's a good tune with a strong message for teens, delivered in the Avalon-Fabian tradition. (6/22/59) (#11 Pop, #29 R&B)

His next, "We Got Love" broke the Top 10, and was the first of seven two-sided hits. It was followed by Rydell's biggest record, "Wild One." "Swingin' School" was from the movie *Because They're Young* starring Dick Clark in his first dramatic role.

Wild One/Little Bitty Girl.

 The chanter should keep his string going. Both sides have the hit sound, and this could be a two-sider. "Wild One" is on the rockin' side. "Little Bitty Girl" has Latinish overtones. (1/18/60) (A-side, #2 Pop, #10 R&B; B-side, #19 Pop)

Swingin' School/Ding-a-ling.

"Swingin' School" is a bright rocker, and he delivers it with verve. "Ding-a-

ling" is also in the rhythm vein, and it's handled equally well. (4/18/60) (A-side, #5 Pop; B-side, #18 Pop)

Although "Nel Blu, Di Pinto Di Blu" was translated from its Italian hit format by Mitchell Parish in 1958, and over a dozen artists covered it in English, it wasn't until Rydell's B-side version two years later that it became a hit as "Volare." The follow up was another unexpected B-side hit, "Sway."

I'll Do It Again/Volare.

Rydell has another potent coupling, lead off by a solid, rocker abetted by wide-eyed chicks. It's in the "Wild One"-"Swinging School" vein. Flip is a smartly handled reprise of the Modugno hit. Either can happen. (7/11/60) (#4 Pop, #9 R&B)

Groovy Tonight/Sway.

A couple of solid rockers by Rydell. Top side is faster, in the "Wild One" groove with solid fem vocal support. Flip is the tune recently done by Dean Martin and this also moves. Either way with a possible nod to "Groovy." (10/24/60) (A-side, #70 Pop; B-side, #14 Pop)

Goodtime Baby/Cheerie.

Rydell brings his usual sock delivery to the catchy r&r ditty "Goodtime Baby," with cute femme chorus on backing. Flip is a strong follow-up to his current smash single—a dramatic reading of an attractive theme. Both sides are potent. (1/9/61) (A-side, #11 Pop; B-side, #54 Pop)

On January 24, 1961, the first International Rock and Roll Festival was held in Paris with Rydell representing America.

That Old Black Magic.

The oldie [is] done up in a smart updating with a gingerly rockin' beat. (4/17/61) (#21 Pop)

In late 1961, Cameo paired Rydell with Chubby Checker for a Christmas single, "Jingle Bell Rock," and the surprise hit spawned a best selling album. Meanwhile, Rydell's solo hits kept coming.

Lose Her.

A happy, rousing tune in fine rocking fashion. Backing by chorus and ork has solid, showmanly beat. Flip is "I've Got Bonnie." (1/27/62) (A-side, #69 Pop; B-side, #18 Pop)

Bobby Rydell-Chubby Checker: Swinging Together/Teach Me to Twist.

Two bright rockers. They both get a chance to show off their vocal styles on "Swinging Together" and Chubby tells Bobby how to twist on the flip. Solid teen wax, and strong programming material. (4/14/62)

Gee It's Wonderful.

The boy sings a bright, breezy swinger backed by ork, strings and chorus that's bound to climb up the charts. Flip: "I'll Never Dance Again" (5/19/62) (B-side, #14 Pop)

The Cha-Cha-Cha.

A bright dance side sporting a good vocal and warm support from a chorus. (9/29/62) (#10 Pop)

In May 1963, the singer starred with Dick Van Dyke in the film *Bye Bye Birdie*.

Wildwood Days.

This is a real rocker, a great piece of material that should be a natural for the summer since it's about the New Jersey summer resort area. (5/4/63) (#17 Pop)

Forget Him.

A strong teen item. Side has certain pathos. The singer is spotlighted in a big rockaballad production that involves female chorus and big string and guitar sound. (10/26/63) (#4 Pop)

Although both Rydell's and Peter and Gordon's version of "World Without Love" charted the same day (May 9, 1964), the latter's #1 status served notice of things to come. The British rockers were replacing American pop teen idols in the hearts of stateside fans and Rydell was being swept away like most of the others.

A World Without Love.

> *This is the first U.S. version of the Peter and Gordon British hit. It's an outstanding arrangement that's done in the medium tempo and builds and builds against femme voices and strings. (5/2/64) (#80 Pop)*

By late 1964, Rydell coupled with Capitol hoping for better results but singing well didn't mean radio was listening, and his 1965 releases scraped the bottom of the Top 100.

I Just Can't Say Goodbye.

> *Medium-tempo dramatic dual-tracked vocal with good beat. (11/14/64) (#94 Pop)*

Diana.

> *Intriguing new approach to the Paul Anka hit. Good new sound for Rydell. (1/23/65) (#98 Pop)*

Paul Anka's first hit, "Diana," turned out to be Rydell's last. His last original single, "It Must Be Love," was a one-shot for RCA issued in 1970. In 1976, a remake of "Sway" was done disco style; the 1978 film *Grease* honored him by naming the setting Rydell High School. Through the 1970s and 1980s, Rydell toured the oldies circuit and occasionally hooked up with Philadelphia friends Fabian and Avalon for a teen idol's tour. The singer is well remembered on oldies radio, having had 14 Top-20 hits.

SAM & DAVE

Sam Moore
Born: 10/12/35, Miami, FL
David Prater
Born: 5/8/37, Ocilla, GA (died 4/9/88)
Influences: Sam Cooke, Jackie Wilson, Soul Stirrers, Dixie Hummingbirds, Mahalia Jackson, Bullmoose Jackson
Influenced: Blues Brothers, Paul McCartney, Don Henley, Stevie Winwood, Bonnie Raitt, Eurythmics, Z. Z. Top, Bruce Springsteen

Known as "Double Dynamite," the duo of Sam & Dave created some of the most energetic soul sounds of the 1960s.

Both were brought up on large doses of gospel music. Sam was the son of a Baptist minister and sang with the gospel group The Melionaires, whereas Dave was heavily entrenched in his family's church choir. By the early 1960s, both also found that it was more profitable to sing secular songs than gospel, and each began performing in local clubs. Before that, however, Sam auditioned and won a spot with the legendary Soul Stirrers. Set to leave that night for a tour, Sam was faced with a momentous decision, go see his favorite artist, Jackie Wilson, perform or leave with the group. He went to see Wilson.

In 1958, while performing at the King of Hearts club in Miami, Sam was spontaneously joined on stage by Dave, who had been working as the club's cook. Their impromptu performance encouraged them to go out as a team. In early 1962, the twosome recorded one single for Alston ("Lotta Lovin'"), then signed with Roulette for their May 1962 debut, "No More Pain." When it and five more gospel-flavored disks fell on deaf ears, the pair joined Atlantic. Producer Jerry Wexler sent Sam & Dave to Atlantic's Stax label in Memphis. The writing team of Isaac Hayes and David Porter took the duo under their wings and began turning out soundsational soul for the masses.

I Take What I Want.

> *Hard-driving wailer that just won't quit. Rocking dance beat will appeal to pop market as well. (9/11/65)*

Having breached the charts with "You Don't Know Like I Know" (#90 Pop, #7 R&B), Hayes and Porter sequestered the singers in the studio to create a follow up when Porter suddenly disappeared. Hayes found him in the men's room and impatiently told him to hurry up. Porter's irritated reply was "Hold On! I'm Comin'," and the road to a hit was paved. "Hold On" would have been even bigger except many stations refused to play it concluding the title was overtly suggestive.

Hold On! I'm Comin'.

> *Soulful wailin'-blues shouter with exceptional vocal performance . . . will fast replace their "You Don't Know*

Like I Know." (3/26/66) (#21 Pop, #1 R&B)

Said I Wasn't Gonna Tell Nobody.

Hot on the heels of "Hold On! I'm Comin'," the wailing duo have an equally solid entry in this easy-rocker. (9/3/66) (#64 Pop, #8 R&B)

When the term "soul" took on a new meaning in teen language, Hayes and Porter came up with Sam & Dave's biggest single: "Soul Man." Due to their constant in-motion performances, the duo were dubbed the "Sultans of Sweat."

Soul Man.

Solid wailer is this rocking rhythm entry that should spiral the duo right up the Hot 100 in short order. Exciting performance backed by a pulsating dance beat. (9/2/67) (#2 Pop, #1 R&B)

I Thank You.

Those wailing soul men come up with another blockbuster blues item . . . sure-fire winner for the Hot 100 as well as an r&b chart topper. (1/20/68) (#9 Pop, #4 R&B)

On February 29, 1968, Sam & Dave won a Grammy for "Soul Man" as Best R&B Performance of 1967, however, their career was soon headed downhill. In May, a domestic argument led Prater to shoot his wife, although he managed to avoid prison. By late 1968, they were on the parent Atlantic label.

You Don't Know What You Mean to Me.

Chalk up another smash for the dynamic duo as they move and groove right over to the Atlantic label. This blockbuster swinger will fast top the sales of "I Thank You." (5/18/68) (#48 Pop, #2 R&B)

Soul Sister, Brown Sugar.

This is the wild blockbuster that will put the dynamic duo back on the top of the Hot 100 and the r&b charts once again. They really move and groove with this rhythm item. (12/14/68) (#41 Pop, #18 R&B)

As personality conflicts deepened, Sam & Dave separated in 1970. Sam remained with Atlantic, whereas Dave moved to Alston but, without chart success, they found themselves back together in 1971 on Atlantic, and then in 1974 on United Artists.

Don't Pull Your Love.

The recent pop hit is given a heavy soul reading by the duo, their first together in some time. Loaded with soul chart potential, it offers much for pop as well. (10/16/71) (#102 Pop, #36 R&B)

A Little Bit of Good (Cures a Whole Lot of Bad).

One of the more dynamic and original duos in soul history is back with the kind of funky song that has always been their trademark. Working their vocals together and off one another they've come up with a song that should hit pop as well as soul. (5/18/74) (#89 R&B)

Their off-again, on-again reunions got a boost in 1979 when filmdom's Blues Brothers (John Belushi and Dan Aykroyd) hit with a remake of "Soul Man." Sam & Dave then toured with The Clash and appeared in Paul Simon's film *One Trick Pony*, in 1980. By 1981, however, they had separated for good. Their last charter, "The Sam & Dave Medley," came in 1985, with a "stars on 45" treatment. In March 1988, while driving to see his mother in Georgia, Dave hit a tree and was killed. Two months later, Sam paired with Dan Aykroyd to perform for Atlantic's 40th Anniversary Party at New York's Madison Square Garden. As of 1996, Sam still maintains an active performance schedule.

NEIL SEDAKA

Birthdate: 3/13/39
Birthplace: Brooklyn, NY
Influences: Penguins, Rosemary Clooney, Guy Mitchell

One of the few writer/artists to have Top-20 hits in each of four decades, Neil Sedaka was equally at home churning out winners for others.

In 1952, the 13-year-old Sedaka began composing when he met 16-year-old Howie Greenfield, a fledgling poet who happened to be his next door neighbor. Although classically trained, Sedaka's ear was tuned to rock, especially when he and his neighborhood friend Carol Klein (later famous as Carole King) heard a pizza parlor jukebox playing The Penguins' "Earth Angel." By 1956, Sedaka had joined with schoolmates Hank Medress, Cynthia Zoliton, and Eddie Rabkin to form The Linctones of Lincoln High School. Two Sedaka/Greenfield songs graced The Linc Tones' first recording. By the time it was issued on Morty Craft's Melba label, they had become The Tokens. The Tokens:

I Love My Baby 73
A novelty blues, chanted with ecstatic sighs and vocal gimmicks. The lads make a bright side of it, swingy and lively.

While I Dream 70
This group chants a ballad of the refined type. Fair job. (5/26/56)

The record did little beyond New York. Medress left, eventually joining a new Tokens (of "Lion Sleeps Tonight" fame).

In 1957, Sedaka earned a piano scholarship at the prestigious Juilliard School of Music, by winning a competition judged by conductor Arthur Rubinstein. That same year he was signed by Decca as an artist. Rejected by publisher Hill and Range, a recommendation from fellow scribes Doc Pomus and Mort Shuman put Sedaka and Greenfield on the writing staff of Aldon Music run by Don Kirshner and Al Nevins. Sedaka continued to pursue a solo career, without much success, meanwhile Aldon hawked their songs. Their first placement was "Passin' Time" by The Cookies (Atlantic). The pair's debut chart 45 came via a song they promised to The Sheppard Sisters (of "Alone" fame) that was instead issued by Connie Francis ("Stupid Cupid," #14). At the same time, Sedaka again tried for a solo single, "Ring a Rockin'," but again came up dry.

Laura Lou 73
Bright, cheerful sound by the chorus on this rock-a-blues gives it good potential in both pop and c.&w. markets. It could catch on. (12/9/57)

Ring a Rockin' 76
A driving rocker with a novelty lyric. Sound is unusual, and pace is maintained. (9/15/58)

In late 1958, Sedaka's "The Diary" was recorded by Little Anthony and The Imperials. When another single ("So Much") was issued instead, Nevins went to RCA's Steve Sholes (who also signed Elvis Presley) offering Sedaka as the artist. Anthony's version then came out, but it was too late. Sedaka had his first of 30 hits during a 22-year span. Note that *Billboard* reviewed it as if it were his first release.

The Diary.

Sedaka has a fresh, new sound that could catch on. "Diary" is a cute topical theme about a lad who wonders how he rates in his chick's diary. The tune is a rockaballad. . . . Impressive first try. (11/17/58) (#14 Pop, #25 R&B)

I Go Ape.

A peppy rocker with the teen phrase figuring prominently in the lyrics. (2/16/59) (#42 Pop)

In between his own recordings, Sedaka found time to play piano on Bobby Darin's "Dream Lover" in March 1959.

"Oh! Carol" was written for Carole King, who reciprocated in 1960 with "Oh! Neil."

Oh! Carol.
A dual-track treatment of a Latin-tinged rocker. (9/7/59) (#9 Pop, #27 R&B)

Its success ushered in a slew of teeny-bop ballads and mild rockers that defined the Sedaka style.

Stairway to Heaven.

A rocker sort. (3/7/60) (#9 Pop, #16 R&B)

Run Samson Run/You Mean Everything to Me.

Sedaka contributes a strong vocal on "Run Samson Run," an amusing novelty based on Biblical theme. Flip spotlights a feelingful reading on a moving rockaballad. (7/18/60) (A-side, #28 Pop; B-side, #17 Pop)

Calendar Girl.

Sedaka registers with solid impact on "Calendar Girl," a swinging teen-appeal ditty. (12/5/60) (#4 Pop, #22 R&B)

Little Devil.

A rhythmic effort styled much along the lines of "Calendar Girl," his recent click. (4/17/61) (#11 Pop)

Happy Birthday, Sweet Sixteen.

Sedaka has one of his strongest records in a long time and the disk could easily hit the top of the charts. . . a bright rocker with teen-slanted lyrics. (10/30/61) (#6 Pop)

Inspired by The Showmen's "It Will Stand" (#61, 1961), the songwriting team penned Sedaka's first million-seller, "Breaking Up Is Hard to Do."

Breaking Up Is Hard to Do/As Long As I Live.

Neil Sedaka has two of his strongest sides here and both could land way up on the charts. Top side is a bright novelty that spots a stylish vocal and smart arrangement. Flip is a strong ballad outing for the lad with neat triplet and vocal chorus support. (6/16/62) (#1 Pop, #12 R&B)

Next Door to an Angel.

The bright novelty is an excellent follow-up to the singer's current smash. It's got a beat and carries on the "Breaking Up Is Hard to Do" tradition. (7/29/62) (#5 Pop, #19 R&B)

Alice in Wonderland.

A mighty smart ditty penned by the chanter and Howard Greenfield could turn out to be one of Sedaka's biggest hits. Solid vocal gimmicks and a smart backing make this novelty go. (1/26/63) (#17 Pop)

As the British invasion overwhelmed U.S. radio in 1964, the Sedakas of the music world found themselves lucky to reach the bottom of the charts. Sedaka's hit-making days ended abruptly. In 1968, the writing duo of Sedaka and Greenfield

signed to Screen Gems Music as staff writers, where Kirshner was in charge. Their songs, such as "Puppet Man" (5th Dimension, #24), charted but Neil's records did not.

In 1972, the lack of activity convinced Sedaka to move his family to London where he began writing with Phil Cody. Sedaka managed several U.K. hits, including "That's Where the Music Takes Me" (#18), but his records were not being circulated stateside. His British singles were backed by a group called Hotlegs, later known as 10CC. When Sedaka's song, "Laughter in the Rain" became a Brit-hit, he threw a party and among the guests were Elton John, a long-time fan who Sedaka met in New York at a Bee Gees concert. John had just started his MCA-distributed Rocket Records and Sedaka mentioned he had no U.S. affiliation. Before you could say comeback, Sedaka's third decade of U.S. hits was under way, including "Laughter in the Rain" (#1 Pop) (reviewed without comment in *Billboard*) and "The Immigrant."

The Immigrant.

Sedaka follows his number one "Laughter in the Rain" with a different type of song supposedly dedicated to John Lennon. In a more serious vein than his last hit, the words and melody are just as infectious and should firmly establish Sedaka as an artist for today, not simply a one shot comeback. (3/15/75) (#22 Pop)

During 1975, Sedaka had one of his hottest streaks, three #1s in eight months including "Laughter," "Love Will Keep Us Together" (recorded by Captain and Tennille), and "Bad Blood" (with Elton John on call-and-response vocals). Sedaka then did what no artist had ever done before, taken a previous #1 recording of his own, rerecorded it (making it a ballad), and reaching the Top 10, with the same song: "Breaking Up Is Hard to Do." His subsequent recordings fared less well on the chart.

Love in the Shadows.

Sedaka moves into disco this time out, with an easy disco rocker with interesting lyrics. Quite different from past hits, but loyal Sedaka fans should accept it with little difficulty. Disco not overdone, so whole thing works quite well. (4/10/76) (#16 Pop)

You Gotta Make Your Own Sunshine.

A single just as sunny and warm as might be expected from Sedaka's recent hits. The lyrics are clever and direct. The over-all sound, with a chugging base line, is not unlike "Love Will Keep Us Together," which Sedaka also wrote although it was the Captain and Tennille who had the monster hit. Sedaka here makes a welcome return from his "Love in the Shadows" semi-grimness into the thoroughly upbeat style he seems most at home in. (9/4/76) (#53 Pop)

Then in 1980 he entered his fourth decade of hits by dueting with his daughter Dara on "Should've Never Let You Go" (#19), his last chart single. Although he's yet to chart in the 1990s, with a few years left, don't count the hit-master of the decades out!

THE SHANGRI-LAS

Mary Weiss: Lead vocals
Born: 1948, Queens, NY
Betty Weiss
Born: 1948, Queens, NY
Mary Ann Ganser
Born: 1947, Queens, NY (died 1971)
Marguerite "Marge" Ganser
Born: 1947, Queens, NY (died 7/28/96)
Influences: Little Anthony and The Imperials, Four Seasons

The Shangri-Las were the "Queens of Musical Melodrama." Looking both hip and innocent at the same time, the two sets of sisters carved a niche of soap-opera sounds in their brief but well-remembered career.

Mary and Betty met twins Mary Ann and Marge at Andrew Jackson High School where they began harmonizing. Publisher/producer Artie

Ripp of Kama Sutra productions heard the group and in December 1963 coupled them with Smash Records for "Simon Says" and, in early 1964, "Wishing Well." It's rumored that the girls recorded at this same time under the name The Bon Bons for Coral; note the allusion to Beatlemania in the title of the B-side!

Bon Bons:
Come on Baby.

Wild, driving rocker with pulsing, exciting, penetrating sound from girl group. Flip is "What's Wrong with Ringo?" (3/21/64)

After one more with Coral (the Barry Mann/Artie Kornfeld rocker "Everybody Wants My Boyfriend"), the Queens quartet went back to their teen hop performances.

About the same time, self-styled producer/vagabond, George "Shadow" Morton, was bluffing his way through an encounter with writer Jeff Barry, claiming he could write a hit but having nothing to show at the meeting. Morton convinced some musicians (including a 15-year-old piano player named Billy Joel) to record his demo, and The Shangri-Las (whom he met at a hop) to sing his song. Trouble was, Morton had no song! Letting such a minor detail get in his way was not Shadow's style, so, on the drive to the demo session, he wrote one: "Remember (Walkin' in the Sand)." He took the demo to the astonished Barry and his wife, songwriter supreme, Ellie Greenwich. They rushed it to neighboring Leiber and Stoller's Red Bird Records.

Between "Remember" (which featured seagull sound effects) and its follow up, "Leader of the Pack" (replete with its famous revving motorcycles), The Shangri-Las established themselves as the act that integrated sound effects into rock 'n' roll. To create the motorcycle sounds on the record, engineer Joe Vineri actually brought his Harley into the studio and revved it onto the tape. "Leader" became so popular in England, it charted four times!

Remember (Walkin' in the Sand).

For those who like a different sound try this haunting delivery. Sea gulls in the background will no doubt help this side fly away. Quite a switch. (8/1/64) (#5 Pop)

Leader of the Pack.

The Red Bird label flies in with another hit. This hot group has the hot hit sound without question. (10/3/64) (#1 Pop)

Their Christmas 1964 release of The Chantels' "Maybe," charted the same day as "Give Him a Great Big Kiss" (December 26, 1964), but only reached #91. Why Red Bird issued two singles at once is anyone's guess, but by then, even pre-Red Bird singles were being issued.

Give Him a Great Big Kiss.

Smart vocalizing and hippy arrangement for "Leader of the Pack" gals. Hand-clapper has good pace and smash sound. (12/12/64) (#18 Pop)

Wishing Well.

Has the "Leader of the Pack" sound. (2/6/65)

The group's instant fame served to place them on The Beatles' tour and more tearjerkers followed. "He Cried" was actually a remake of Jay and The Americans' 1962 (#5) hit, "She Cried."

Out in the Streets.

Writers Jeff Barry and Ellie Greenwich provide powerful "Nitty Gritty" type material which fits the group like a glove. Exciting performance and arrangement by Artie Butler. (3/27/65) (#53 Pop)

Give Us Your Blessing.

★ *A slow beat ballad with teen lyric on the subject of young love and marriage with a tragic ending. A powerhouse of material, performance and production. (5/15/65) (#29 Pop)*

Right Now and Not Later.

Teen-beat rhythm number. Fine performance and production. (9/4/65) (#99 Pop)

I Can Never Go Home Any More.

Offbeat message number featuring narration and slow back beat that works into a frenzy. Watch this left fielder! (10/30/65) (#6 Pop)

He Cried.

Right in the groove of their hit "I Can Never Go Home Any More," this slow rhythm weeper should hit hard and fast in today's teen market. (4/2/66) (#65 Pop)

Past, Present and Future.

An emotional nostalgia-filled recitation ballad aimed at the teen market. (6/4/66) (#59 Pop)

Despite its achievements, the label was failing; "Past, Present and Future" was the last (and eeriest) of their Red Bird releases. The label and the group might have weathered the storm if they had pushed the brilliant Harry Nilsson B-side, "Paradise," the Shangri-Las' most Spector-like single.

In less than two years, with 11 chart disks, the Shangri-Las went from stardom to oblivion. Shadow and The Shangri-Las moved to Mercury for two ill-fated 45s, "The Sweet Sounds of Summer" and "Take the Time."

By 1968, The Shangri-Las had tendered their rock 'n' roll resignation. Betty married writer Jeremy Storch; Marge became Mrs. Marge Droste and later died of breast cancer; Mary Ann died of encephalitis in 1971; and Mary became an interior decorator, running a furniture store in the 1980s under her married name, Mary Weiss Stoker. The group (Mary, Betty, and Marge) did some oldies shows in the 1970s and 1980s but, by the 1990s, a bogus trio was performing under their name because the Weiss sisters refused to appear any longer.

DEL **S**HANNON

Real Name: Charles Westover
Birthdate: 12/30/39
Birthplace: Coopersville, MI
Died: 2/8/90
Influences: Hank Williams, Bobby Darin, Roy Orbison,
    Carl Smith, Webb Pierce, Faron Young, Ink Spots
Influenced: Bruce Springsteen, Stevie Wonder, Tom
    Petty, Jeff Lynne

The only artist to beat out The Beatles (chartwise) with one of their own songs, Del Shannon was a uniquely styled star of the 1960s as well as a hit producer in the 1970s.

Young Charles Westover's first instrument was a kazoo. In his teens, he learned guitar by watching country musicians during club performances. His school principal let him use the gym for practice after class so he could take advantage of the acoustics.

Drafted in 1958, he spent most of his time entertaining troops in the States and West Germany. Upon his discharge, he settled in Battle Creek, Michigan, playing with Charlie Johnson and the Big Little Show Band at The Hi-Lo Club. During the day, he worked as a carpet salesman. In fact, that's where he did most of his writing (and changed his name), admitting, "I didn't sell many carpets." His new name was a combination of Mark Shannon, a would-be wrestler who frequented the club, and a variation of his boss's car, a Cadillac Coupe De Ville, hence, Del.

When deejay Ollie Mclaughlin (WGRJ) saw Shannon perform, he introduced him to Embee Productions' honchos Irv Micahnik and Harry Balk of Detroit. They signed Shannon to Johnny Bienstock's New York label, Big Top. Encouraged to write, his first session produced a few unusable ballads, so Shannon was asked to come up with a rocker. While performing one night, a chord change by Max Crook (the band's organist) stopped Shannon in his tracks and the beginning of "Runaway" developed right on

stage. Shannon and Crook then drove to New York during a bitter cold spell in a car with a dead heater. Along the road Shannon thought, "If this record isn't a hit, I'm going to stay in the carpet business."

The two recorded, then turned around and headed back the same day. Shortly after, Balk called Shannon to tell him "Runaway" was selling 80,000 records a week! The writer was shocked. When he recovered, all he could say was "Does this mean I don't have to work in this carpet store anymore?"

Runaway (A-side).

★ ★ ★ ★ *A folkish air is set to an interesting Latinish rocker beat. Shannon, a new chanter, hands it an exciting go. This has a sound and it can move.*

Jody (B-side).

★ ★ ★ *A slow "girl's name," done to a rippling piano and alto sax backing. Shannon again offers a good performance. (2/27/61) (#1 Pop, #3 R&B)*

Sitting atop the *Billboard* Hot 100 for four weeks, "Runaway" was the first hit to employ a musitron (forerunner of a synthesizer), and the instrumental break had as much to do with the record's success as Shannon's falsetto vocal (which he learned by singing old Ink Spots' songs in school). The label was quick to capitalize on his success with more releases.

Hats Off to Larry.

The "Runaway" lad follows up his smash hit with another potent side. Tune is a driving rocker and Shannon sings it with spirit. Flip is "Don't Gild the Lily, Lily." (5/29/61) (#5 Pop)

So Long Baby.

Shannon has an impressive disk in this hard-charging rocker, which he sings with authority and drive to an effective backing. (9/4/61) (#28 Pop)

Hey! Little Girl.

★ ★ ★ ★ *A rocking ditty with strong touches of several of his earlier hits. He belts all the way with the high-voiced gimmick used prominently. Backing pounds away. (11/13/61) (#38 Pop)*

Shannon sang "You Never Talked About Me," the British-only B-side of "Hey Little Girl," in the U.K. film *It's Trad, Dad!* in May 1962. More hits followed through 1963.

The Swiss Maid.

Highly unusual tune by Shannon tells the story of a lass who dies pining for a lost love. It's a smartly made record with telling orchestral touches and fine singing by the lad. (8/18/62) (#64 Pop)

Little Town Flirt.

The lad's back with another solid sounding side. His voice is smartly double-tracked and the vocal is handled brightly against an effective girls' chorus. (12/8/62) (#12 Pop)

Two Kinds of Teardrops.

Del Shannon is up to his old and commercial vocal tricks on this new waxing. . . . a stylish rocker. (3/30/63) (#50 Pop)

On May 9, 1963, Shannon played London's Royal Albert Hall with the Beatles. He then decided to record their current British hit, "From Me to You" in London, and by June it was out in America, the first Beatles song to chart in the states. The moptops, still unknown in the colonies, tried to compete, as their Vee-Jay release came out at the same time. They were, however, still six months away from being discovered, while Del's B-side became a minor hit (*Billboard,* and the rest of the world, were unaware of its significance).

Two Silhouettes/From Me to You.

Top side has a familiar message about the lovers behind drawn shades and it's effectively handled. Flip, a medium tempoed ditty, also has a chance. (6/15/63) (A-side, #23 Pop; B-side, #77 Pop)

In 1963, Shannon formed his own label, Berlee. However, his two singles on the label failed to find an audience.

Sue's Gotta Be Mine.

Strong Shannon wax here. It's a high-flying swinger that features the lad singing in high-voiced style against repeating gals' chorus. (10/19/63) (#71 Pop)

That's the Way Love Is.

Singer shouts this rich ballad with powerful emotional impact backed by chorus. (2/29/64)

Realizing the need for help, he signed with Amy and began applying the Shannon style to resuscitate oldies like "Handy Man" and "Do You Want to Dance." Several original and terrific rockers ensued.

Handy Man.

Shannon sings up storm to shrill organ riffs. (6/13/64) (#22 Pop)

Do You Want to Dance.

Wild rockin' side featuring an equally wild and piercing organ. Shannon sings with calculated frenzy supported by World War II. (9/12/64) (#43 Pop)

Keep Searchin'.

This is on a somewhat different track with a wee bit of English Drivin' sound. (11/7/64) (#9 Pop)

Stranger in Town.

Del gives his all to this powerful ballad that has a lyric that packs a wallop! (2/13/65) (#30 Pop)

More than a year after Shannon bested the Beatles, a British act returned the favor, as Peter and Gordon hit with Shannon's song, "I Go to Pieces" (#9). In June 1965, Shannon turned down the theme, "Action" from Dick Clark's *Where the Action Is* TV show, thus allowing second-choice Freddy Cannon to have a #13 hit. During 1966, he moved to Los Angeles and Liberty Records, where only "The Big Hurt" charted, although his smoldering live ballad version of "Runaway" was awesome.

The Big Hurt.

Strong dance beat revival of the Toni Fisher hit. Unique sound, superb vocal performance and production will rush this one up the charts. (3/19/66) (#74 Pop)

Runaway.

Shannon has re-cut his original hit in a new easy beat arrangement right in today's teen bag. History should repeat itself. (9/2/67)

Rain Drops.
> *The Dee Clark oldie gets a smooth and commercial updating . . . and could prove a left-field winner. (10/19/68)*

Deciding to produce others in 1969, Del hit immediately with Gayle McCormick's group Smith on the Shirelles' evergreen "Baby It's You" (#5). He then contracted to Dunhill as an artist.

Comin' Back to Me.
> *A new folk-rock sound which should bring him back to the charts. (5/24/69)*

In 1970, he revived Brian Hyland's career, producing a remake of The Impressions' "Gypsy Women" (#3).

In 1981, Shannon had his first hit in 15 years, a revival of Phil Phillips's "Sea of Love" (produced by longtime fan Tom Petty), which also became his last chart single. By 1984, Shannon had changed his musical direction, recording in a country vein.

In My Arms Again.
> *A name familiar to sixties pop fans makes a thoroughly convincing turn-around to traditional country on a soulfully crafted Shannon original. (2/16/85)*

Del Shannon remained popular on the nostalgia trail in both the United States and Europe but personal, internal conflicts built to the sad day in 1990 when he died of a self-inflicted gun shot.

THE SHIRELLES

Shirley Owens Alston: Lead vocals
Born: 6/10/41, Passaic, NJ
Beverly Lee
Born: 8/3/41, Passaic, NJ
Doris Kenner
Born: 8/2/41, Passaic, NJ
Addie "Mickie" Harris
Born: 1/22/40, Passaic, NJ (died 6/10/82)

Influences: Flamingos, Chantels, Little Anthony and The Imperials, Bobbettes
Influenced: Crystals, Marvelettes, En Vogue, Chiffons, Royalettes

An institution among girl groups, The Shirelles were the first black, all-female passel to have a #1 Pop hit. Although they were raised on R&B, their smooth, commercial style earned the quartet more pop charters than R&B.

Originally called The Poquellos (birds), the four high school students began singing in the school gym. Their chanting came to the attention of Florence Greenberg and her one-woman Tierra label via her daughter, who was a Poquellos classmate.

Surprisingly, the teens were not interested in recording and turned Greenberg's audition invitation down several times before conceding to perform in Greenberg's living room with their original, "I Met Him on a Sunday." In short order, the audition turned into a career as Greenberg renamed them after a variation of Shirley's name. Within the month, Decca bought the masters and "Sunday" became a hit (#49), even though it was released as the B-side. However, subsequent releases went nowhere.

I Want You to Be My Boyfriend **76**
> *The Shirelles' debut on the label with a strong reading of a listenable ballad with a beat. The girls have a good piece of material here and the record has a chance to step out. Watch it.*

I Met Him on a Sunday **73**
★ > *Another good side by the fem group which also has a chance. It's a medium tempo effort with some cute gimmicks. Two good sides by the girls. (2/10/58)*

The 17- and 18-year-old girls were in demand for performances but their mothers would not let them go unchaperoned, so Greenberg put them into package tours. Two of the more streetwise singers (Etta James and Ruth Brown) became de facto den mothers.

Decca dropped the teens in 1959, and Greenberg started her own Scepter label with Luther Dixon producing the group's first single, "Dedicated to the One I Love" (#83, a remake of The Five Royales' 1957 disk). In 1960, they broke into the Top 40 with a Alston/Dixon-scribed B-side, "Tonight's the Night."

The Dance Is Over.

★ ★ ★ ★ *A pretty ballad is intoned with warmth by the fem group, over strong support by the ork and strings. A good side that has a chance.*

Tonight's the Night.

★ ★ ★ *The girls handle this rockaballad with feeling over a big beat by the ork. It could grab both spins and loot. (4/18/60) (#39 Pop, #14 R&B)*

In midyear, new writers Carole King and Gerry Goffin brought Dixon a song simply titled "Tomorrow." The Shirelles, feeling it was too poppish, turned it down but Dixon persisted. After its release, new pressings showed a title change. With King on drums, the million seller gave The Shirelles that historic first girl group #1. Answer records and old releases abounded. Scepter then reissued "Dedicated" to a much greater response (#3), while Decca rereleased "I Met Him on a Sunday."

Will You Love Me Tomorrow/Boys.

 The gals are hot right now with "Tonight's the Night," and they have two more sides here that can step out. A slight edge goes to the top side, a good ballad with big ork backing. Flip, a swinger with blues backing, also has a good chance. (11/14/60) (#1 Pop, #2 R&B)

I Met Him on a Sunday.

★ ★ ★ ★ *The girls' smash hit of several seasons back is being reissued. Now as then, it has a good sound and on the basis of the gals' current popularity this can pull action all over again. (2/6/61)*

Mama Said.

 A bright, swinging tune, handed a powerful performance by the lead thrush. (4/10/61) (#4 Pop, #2 R&B)

A Thing of the Past/What a Sweet Thing That Was.

 First up is a neat job which starts with harmony and works into a smooth lead performance. Second up is another good ballad. Either way with an edge to the first. (6/19/61) (A-side, #41 Pop, #26 R&B; B-side, #54 Pop)

The group scored with another flip side by still another new writing team, Hal David, Burt Bacharach, and Barney Williams, originally titled "I'll Cherish You" until it became, "Baby It's You."

The Things I Want to Hear (Pretty Words)/Baby It's You.

 Two bluesy themes with dual market appeal for r.&b. as well as pop buyers. "The Things I Want to Hear" is a catchy rhythm side. Flip features heart-rending vocal by lead thrush. (12/4/61) (B-side, #8 Pop, #3 R&B)

A last-minute addition to their early 1962 session was a country-flavored song by Dixon and Greenberg, "Soldier Boy."

Soldier Boy.

 The girls sing about their "Soldier Boy" on the medium tempo ballad, supported by a warm ork backing. (3/17/62) (#1 Pop, #13 R&B)

With all their success, the group still lost out on two songs they could have had; Greenberg turned down "The Shoop Shoop Song" (later a hit for Betty Everett) and Gene Pitney's "He's a Rebel" (which became an anthem for The Crystals). During a period when Alston and then Kenner took time off to marry, a young newcomer at Scepter subbed for the newlyweds at performances: Dionne Warwick.

Welcome Home Baby.

 A slow rockaballad with a strong vocal by the lead and fine support from the group. (6/16/62) (#22 Pop, #20 R&B)

Stop the Music.

 A catchy rockaballad with a Latin touch and a strong job by the lead. (8/25/62) (#36 Pop)

After "Everybody Loves a Lover" (#19), Dixon left to produce for Capitol and Stan Green (Greenberg's son) took over. Although he hit with "Foolish Little Girl" (#4) in 1963, later disks lacked competitive material.

Don't Say Goodnight and Mean Goodbye.

 A fine rockaballad that builds all the way, like "Foolish Little Girl"... could make it big. (6/8/63) (#26 Pop)

31 Flavors.

This is a strong item from the new "It's a Mad, Mad, Mad, Mad World" flick. Side has swing and cute novelty appeal. Flip is "It's a Mad, Mad, Mad, Mad World." (10/5/63) (#92 Pop)

The Passaic quartet's last Top-100 45 was "Last Minute Miracle" (#99, 1967), after which they hopscotched to Blue Rock, Bell, U.A., and RCA. By 1968, the quartet was reduced to a trio as Kenner left. In 1969, they performed on Richard Nader's first Rock and Roll Revival concert with Bill Haley and The Comets, Chuck Berry, The Five Satins, and The Penguins, among others. The Shirelles became a part of the nostalgia era, even though they continued trying to have a contemporary hit.

Don't Mess with Cupid.

New label, a division of Mercury, should fast re-estabilish the winning group of a few years ago as top disc sellers. Wild blues rocker is performed in top wailing performance. (6/22/68)

There Goes My Baby/Be My Baby.

A top showcase for the femme group. (3/28/70)

Dedicated to the One I Love.

Trio updates their own smash of the early sixties and a beauty it is. Much chart potential here . . . could happen all over again for them. (12/26/70)

In the mid-1970s, Kenner rejoined the group. In 1982, Harris died on stage of a heart attack in Atlanta. By 1995, Alston was still performing with her East Coast Shirelles, whereas Lee was on the West Coast leading her own contingent.

SHIRLEY AND LEE

Shirley Pixley (Goodman)
Born: 6/19/36, New Orleans, LA
Leonard Lee
Born: 6/29/36, New Orleans, LA (died 10/23/76)

Nicknamed "The Sweethearts of the Blues" as a publicity gimmick by Aladdin's Eddie Meisner, Shirley and Lee were a popular 1950s duo who were really just friends.

The teens lived in New Orleans and wanted to record so badly that they and a slew of friends went about collecting pocket change to come up with two dollars to make a demo. Their recording of "I'm Gone" in 1952 impressed studio owner Cosimo Matassa enough to inform Meisner at Aladdin of his young find. The song was then redone with Dave Bartholomew producing and their first single was a #2 R&B smash.

Meisner then came up with the idea of treating each release like a mini saga as if they were sweethearts; for a while, it worked.

Shirley, Come Back to Me 79

Shirley and Lee follow up their hit waxing of "I'm Gone" with a bright new ditty based on the same tune with strong new lyrics. They sing it with gusto, and it could be another solid one for the duo. It should pull box loot. (3/21/53)

Shirley's Back 83

The twosome has another strong follow-up to their last click. Contrast of the voices is just as startling as before. A powerful side that seems certain to attract much loot. It's also great for the boxes. (6/27/53)

Keep On 78

Shirley and Lee come thru with a sock reading of a new rocker over a solid beat by the ork. The tune jumps, and the duo sells it with spirit. If the side is exposed, it has a chance for spins and juke loot. Good wax.

Confessin' **69**

Shirley confesses that she's been untrue to Lee, and Lee confesses the same thing to Shirley. It doesn't matter too much tho as neither Shirley or Lee seem to be sincere about it, and the material and arrangement are routine. (6/26/54)

"Feel So Good" was revised in 1960 by Johnny Preston as "Feel So Fine" (#14). One of rock 'n' roll's favorite dance party records followed: "Let the Good Times Roll," which eventually sold over a million singles.

Feel So Good . . . .**[80]**

Shirley and Lee sing an amusing little song in their wonderfully unique vocal style. Lyrics follow a "feel so good to be home again" pattern. This one should grab off plenty of spins. (6/4/55) (#2 R&B)

Lee's Dream.

A soft, soothing affair that drips with emotion. Lee sings with feeling about his dream while Shirley replies with spoken words of love. A unique and winning effort . . . can stir up plenty of spin action. (10/29/55)

Let the Good Times Roll.

Shirley and Lee are favored with unusually appealing material in this new issue . . . a happy, groovy side that lifts the spirit and sets toes tapping. . . . This is the most potent commercial offering of the duo in some time. (6/23/56) (#20 Pop, #1 R&B)

I Feel Good.

After the smashing success of "Let the Good Times Roll" in both the pop and r.&b. markets, Shirley and Lee can count on a receptive audience in its follow-up. This happens to be another strong piece of material very much in the extrovert vein of its predecessor, with all of its potential for another big hit. (10/27/56) (#38 Pop, #3 R&B)

The hits, however, slowed through 1957–1958, although they managed one R&B hit with "When I Saw You," issued as a B-side in November 1957. In 1960, the duo switched to Warwick, rerecording "Let the Good Times Roll" for a Top-50 hit. They managed one minor R&B hit, "Well-a, Well-a," in the following year.

Well-a, Well-a.

★ ★ ★ ★ *Frantic duo vocalizing on rocking side with catchy beat. Has strong r.&b. appeal as well as pop. (7/24/61) (#77 Pop)*

My Last Letter.

★ ★ ★ ★ *The duo does a bang-up job on this rockaballad. Features a very slow beat with excellent combo backing. (6/23/62)*

During 1963, Shirley moved to Los Angeles, leading to the duo's demise. She sang with Jesse Hill (of "Ooh Poo Pah Doo" fame) as Shirley and Jesse for awhile. She also recorded with Brenton Wood as Shirley and Alfred. Shirley (then known as Shirley Goodman) also sang studio backups for Sonny and Cher, The Rolling Stones, and Jackie DeShannon.

Meanwhile, Lee stayed in New Orleans recording as Leonard Lee for Imperial and Broadside. They reunited only once, for one of Richard Nader's Rock and Roll Revival shows in New York during 1972.

By the mid-1970s, Shirley was a switchboard operator at Playboy Records. She kept in touch with her old friend, Sylvia Robinson of Mickey and Sylvia, after their days of performing together at various shows. During one conversation, Sylvia asked Shirley to cut a song she had called "Shame, Shame, Shame," and Shirley soon became Shirley and Company. The "Company" was supposed to be Hank Ballard but when he begged off, Sylvia drafted a young Cuban named Jesus Alvarez. "Shame" reached #1 R&B and #12 Pop, putting Goodman back on the hit map. She charted twice more with "Cry, Cry, Cry" (#36 R&B and #91 Pop, 1975) and "I Like to Dance" (#91 R&B, 1976) before retiring to New Orleans where she sang gospel music.

SIMON AND GARFUNKEL

Paul Simon: Vocals, guitar
Born: 11/5/42, Newark, NJ
Arthur Garfunkel: Vocals
Born: 10/31/42, Queens, NY
Influences: Everly Brothers, Gary U.S. Bonds, Lou
    Christie, Johnny Ace

The merger of Art Garfunkel's purest-of-pop voices and Paul Simon's poetic scribing and harmony gave the folk, rock, and pop world some of its finest musical moments.

The duo met in the sixth grade at P.S. #164, Queens, New York when they performed in a school play, "Alice in Wonderland," with Garfunkel portraying the Cheshire Cat and Simon playing the White Rabbit. Their first collaboration on a song was "The Girl for Me" in 1955. In November 1957, they demoed a song with lyrics by Garfunkel and music by Simon titled "Hey, School Girl" at Sande studios in New York. Sid Prosen overheard their session and signed the twosome to his Big label under the pseudonyms Tom (Garfunkel) and Jerry (Simon).

Tom and Jerry:
Hey, School Girl 80

> *Duo sounds like cross between Everly Brothers and DeJohn Sisters on good rockabilly styled ditty with teen-appeal lyrics. Should draw plenty of play in today's market, both pop and c&w.*

Dancin' Wild 76
> *Jaunty rockabilly item is accorded personable delivery by boys. Same comment on spin potential. (12/2/57) (#49 Pop)*

The success of "School Girl" earned them a performance on American Bandstand, but succeeding singles went nowhere, including Simon's solos as "Tru Taylor" and "Jerry Landis," and

Garfunkel's two singles on Warwick in 1959 ("Dream Alone" and "Best Love"), and Octavia as "Artie Garr" in 1961 ("Private World" and "Forgive Me").

Tru Taylor:
Teen-Age Fool 79
> *Heavily stylized rockabilly delivery on plaintive rockaballad. Might be dangerous if exposed. (3/3/58)*

Tom and Jerry:
Two Teen-Agers 78
> *The "Hey, School Girl" kids turn in a warm country styled reading that could move out. It's a cute, happy side with a listenable story. (3/10/58)*

Don't Say Goodbye .76
> *Solid duo vocal treatment of effective rockabilly side. Merits spins. (5/26/58)*

After high school graduation, the two separated, with Simon matriculating to Queens College, where he met Carole King. They began singing demos for $15 a pop, including "Just to Be with You" for The Passions in 1959. He also sang backup on The Mystics' "All Through the Night" in 1960 and The Continentals' "Tick, Tick, Tock," which was reviewed the same day as his new alter ego's, Jerry Landis's, 45. Garfunkel, meanwhile, studied at N.Y.U. (mathematics) and Columbia (architecture).

Jerry Landis:
I'd Like to Be the Lipstick on Your Lips.
★ ★ ★   *This cutie gets a delicate performance, with an unobtrusive chorus in the background. (10/10/60)*

Play Me a Sad Song.

> *Landis's wistful singing on this tune could have strong teen appeal. The pretty femme choral work in the background rounds out the fine side. (2/27/61)*

In mid-1961, Simon joined an already existing Queens group, Tico and the Triumphs, as lead singer and writer, charting for the first time in five years (albeit only reaching #99!). Contrary to the reviewer's information, Simon produced the record in New York and sold it to Larry Uttal, who licensed it to Amy.

Tico and the Triumphs:
Motorcycle.

Here's a teen-slanted disking that could be a big seller to the 14-year-old set. Amy picked up the master from the Coast. Tune starts with a motorcycle sound and then the lead swings into a wild reading of the rocker with the group backing him in Marcels' style. (11/6/61)

Tico was unable to duplicate their "triumph," and, by late 1962, Simon was back to performing as Jerry Landis.

Jerry Landis:
The Lone Teen Ranger.

Here's a goofy novelty item about a lad who has lost his love to a Western star on TV who shoots straight and talks tough. It's funny and cute. (12/8/62)

By 1963, Simon was being influenced by the folk boom. He reunited with Garfunkel in 1964 playing Greenwich Village in spots like Gerde's Folk City. Columbia's Tom Wilson showed an interest in the duo (who were now going under their real names), culminating in the all-acoustic *Wednesday Morning, 3 A.M.* album in October, 1964. When *Wednesday* went unnoticed, Simon drifted to London (January 1965), where he recorded a solo album.

Meanwhile, a Boston deejay began playing one of the LP's songs, "The Sounds of Silence." Reaction was such that Wilson set about commercializing the sparse but haunting recording by adding drums, guitar, and bass. It charted November 20, 1965, reaching #1 on January 1, 1966, without Simon even knowing he had a single, much less a smash. He returned to the States, reteamed with Garfunkel, and ran up an incredible streak of 13 straight, Top-25 hits, six of which were Top 5. Simon wrote "Homeward Bound" on the Wigan Station platform in England; more hits rapidly followed through 1967.

Homeward Bound.

Just as "The Sounds of Silence" dips on the Hot 100 chart, this interesting off-beat rhythm number written by Simon will have no trouble making the chart. (1/29/66) (#5 Pop)

I Am a Rock.

Beautiful lyric ballad culled from their new LP will fast equal the success of "Sounds of Silence" and "Homeward Bound." (4/23/66) (#3 Pop)

The Dangling Conversation.

A cleverly written folk-flavored lyric ballad penned by Paul. (7/30/66) (#25 Pop)

A Hazy Shade of Winter.

Another winning number from the pen of Paul Simon in this medium-paced folk-rock ballad. Change of tempo for the duo could make this their biggest hit to date. (10/29/66) (#13 Pop)

At the Zoo.

Folk-flavored Paul Simon number which they handle in fine style. Clever lyric and rhythm arrangement make this a hot contender for Hot 100 honors. Flip: "The 59th St. Bridge Song." (3/4/67) (#16 Pop)

Fakin' It.

Intriguing folk rocker, penned by Paul Simon. The John Simon production is exceptional. (7/22/67) (#23 Pop)

In August 1967, producer Mike Nichols employed the duo to create music for his forthcoming film, "The Graduate." The soundtrack album topped the Hot 100 for nine weeks, whereas "Mrs. Robinson" was #1 for three weeks. It won two Grammys in 1969, for Record of the Year and Best Contemporary Pop Vocal Performance by a Duo or Group.

Scarborough Fair.

Featured throughout the film hit "The Graduate," the duo can't miss with this exceptional folk ballad with compelling lyric. Has the sales potential of their "Sounds of Silence." (2/24/68) (#11 Pop)

Mrs. Robinson.

Infectious rhythm ballad . . . from the film "The Graduate." (4/20/68) (#1 Pop)

The Boxer.

> *With all the sales potential of another "Mrs. Robinson," the duo comes up with a sure fire chart topper in this infectious rhythm ballad with a compelling lyric line. (3/29/69) (#7 Pop)*

By 1970, the strain of almost 800 hours work on their new *Bridge Over Troubled Water* album was showing. Garfunkel's increasing unavailability due to his new career as an actor (debuting in *Catch-22*) and his uncompromising position about singing a 12th song for the LP, titled "Cuba Si, Nixon No" (Garfunkel was against it and it was dropped), also led to the separation. The album and single of "Bridge" each topped the U.S. and U.K. charts at the same time, a rare occurrence. The success of "Bridge" must have made it doubly difficult to part, especially upon learning they'd won six Grammys, including Record, Album, and Song of the Year, while selling 11 million copies.

Bridge Over Troubled Water.

> *The duo has not had a release since their smash "The Boxer" last summer, but they are going straight to the top with this beautiful, almost religious ballad. Performance and arrangement are perfect. (1/31/70) (#1 Pop)*

Cecilia.

> *The duo's follow-up to their No. 1 smash has been culled from their No. 1 LP, and is sure to be their next big No. 1 single. Everything about it is absolutely perfect. (4/4/70) (#4 Pop)*

Not surprisingly, each maintained a recording following with numerous solo hits. While Garfunkel's recordings were consistently pop, Simon ventured into reggae, jazz, and, later, South American and African styles and rhythms. Garfunkel maintained his acting career with roles in *Carnal Knowledge* (1971), *Bad Timing* (1979), and *Good to Go* (1986), while also recording and occasionally charting as well.

Paul Simon:
Mother and Child Reunion.

> ★   *Simon cut this infectious rhythm ballad with strong lyric line in Jamaica and it*

has the sound of a top 10 winner for top 40 and MOR. (1/29/72) (#4 Pop)

Loves Me Like a Rock.

> *The cut . . . takes us to Muscle Shoals for a quasi-sounding gospel treatment of a story about how mother loved her son, even when he became the president. The Dixie Hummingbirds have flown rather far away from true gospel in doing the background work. (7/21/73) (#2 Pop)*

Art Garfunkel:
All I Know.

> *The pure, soaring tenor of Garfunkel, absent from new recordings since his split with Paul Simon, is back with the first sample from his new album. If the rest of the material is as strong as the high-flying new Jim Webb song, Columbia has two top 10 acts instead of one. Garfunkel sings with the sensitive emotionalism he was always noted for, and Webb's hauntingly simple lines are reminiscent of the "Bridge Over Troubled Water" sound. (9/1/73) (#9 Pop)*

Second Avenue.

> *Beautiful ballad from one of the finest singers in the world of pop. Lush strings, powerful production from Garfunkel and Roy Halee and Garfunkel's soft, distinctive voice make this a sure bet to be Top 40. Best thing he's come up with since "All I Know." (8/31/74) (#34 Pop)*

During 1975, Simon and Garfunkel reunited for a *Saturday Night Live* TV appearance and a one-shot recording of "My Little Town" (#9).

> *Famous pair team up for the first time in years with this easy going rocker that is already on the Hot 100 at a starred 81. A good nostalgic Americana style song that builds throughout. (10/18/75)*

Simon continued his career with hits like "Still Crazy After All These Years" and "Slip Slidin' Away." Garfunkel made his mark with covers of "(What a) Wonderful World" (featuring harmonies by Paul Simon and James Taylor) and "Since I Don't Have You."

Paul Simon:
Still Crazy After All These Years.

A superb ballad with excellent lyrics and excellent instrumentation. Jazzy saxophone break adds more luster. Possibly Simon's best single yet. (4/24/76) (#40 Pop)

Slip Slidin' Away.

The gentle acoustic musical backup provides a subtle foundation for Simon's distinctive, appealing lead vocal. Lyrics, as usual, are sensitive, thoughtful, melancholic and evocative. A muted vocal chorus adds tasteful support to the catchy tune that will appear as the only new song on a forthcoming greatest hits LP. (10/15/77) (#5 Pop)

Art Garfunkel:
What a Wonderful World.

Garfunkel's crafty reworking of the Sam Cooke oldie results in a refreshing mid-tempo tune that is graced with vocals by James Taylor and Paul Simon. The light and breezy tune is supported by excellent guitar piano and string backing. (1/21/78) (#17 Pop)

In 1977, Simon made his acting debut in Woody Allen's *Annie Hall*. He then wrote a screenplay (1979) while paying Columbia $1.5 million to jettison his contract, thus allowing him to join Warner Brothers for records and films. The resulting film, *One Trick Pony*, bombed at the box office, although it produced one hit single, "Late in the Evening."

Paul Simon:
Late in the Evening.

This song pushes the master lyricist back in the pop foreground. The irresistible hook is comprised of a hard working percussive and bass duet. (8/9/80) (#6 Pop)

In 1981, the duo united again for a concert in New York's Central Park that drew over 400,000

fans and led to a live LP, their first in 11 years, and their last.

Simon and Garfunkel:
Wake Up Little Susie.

First single from the top 10 Concert in Central Park LP is a faithful remake of the Everly Brothers' 1957 classic. An affectionate salute from one of the top duos of the rock era to another. (4/3/82) (#27 Pop)

Showing a sense of humor about himself and his music, Simon made an appearance on Randy Newman's single "The Blues" in 1983, which parodied the typically thoughtful and slightly morose Simon lyric.

Randy Newman and Paul Simon:
The Blues.

Randy Newman doing straightforward perky pop? Well, almost. The master of the skewed perspective has toned down the irony to mere wit, and Paul Simon's contribution assures Newman more airplay than he's had since "Short People." (1/15/83) (#51 Pop)

Simon returned triumphantly to the charts with his album *Graceland* in 1986, which married his witty lyrics with African rhythms. He followed this with a similar exploration of Brazilian rhythms on 1989's *Rhythm of the Saints*. Meanwhile, Garfunkel soldiered on without much success; amid continued pressure for reunions, the duo reunited briefly in 1993 for a series of shows in New York billed as "The Concert of a Lifetime."

SONNY AND CHER

Salvatore Phillip Bono
Born: 2/16/35, Detroit, MI
Cherilyn Sakisian La Pierre
Born: 5/20/46, El Centro, CA
Influences: Phil Spector, Frankie Laine, Sam Cooke, Johnny Ray, Big Jay McNeely

During their teens, Salvatore Bono and Cherilyn La Pierre had visions of being (respectively) a successful singer/songwriter and a starring actress. Over the next 30 years, they each accomplished that, and a lot more.

The teenaged Sonny moved to Inglewood, California, from Detroit with his parents. He started writing songs while a grocery stock boy, including a tune named after a brand of cookies, "Koko Joe" (recorded 15 years later by The Righteous Brothers). He later delivered meat on the Sunset Boulevard route and would rush through his deliveries in order to play his songs for the Sunset Strip publishers.

In 1957, Bono became employed by Specialty Records in Hollywood after a stint on an assembly line at McDonnell Douglas Aircraft. He worked his way up from packing records to producing Don and Dewey as well as scribing "High School Dance," the B-side of Larry Williams's 1957 hit "Short, Fat Fanny." In 1959, he recorded "One Little Answer" for Specialty and 45s for Go and Fidelity in 1960 under the name Don Christy, but without success. By 1962, arranger Jack Nitzsche had introduced Sonny to Phil Spector and Bono became his guy Friday, singing backup, doing promotion, and schlepping coffee.

Cher, who had acting aspirations and a sympathetic mother with the same desires, was performing in plays while taking acting lessons in Hollywood from teacher-actor, Jeff Corey. In 1963, Sonny wrote "Needles and Pins" with Nitzsche and it charted for newcomer Jackie DeShannon (#84). About that time, he met Cher at a coffee shop across from radio station KFWB. Learning of her singing interest, he introduced the 17-year-old to Spector. Her first session was as a background singer on The Ronettes' classic, "Be My Baby"; her booming voice made Spector move her 10 feet behind the mike while the others sang in front of it. She and Sonny sang backup for The Ronettes, The Righteous Brothers, and most of Spector's recordings through 1964. Among the non-Spector work they did was as part of Hale and The Hushabyes on "Yes Sir, That's My Baby" along with DeShannon, Darlene Love, and Brian Wilson.

During 1964, Sonny recorded a duet with Cher as Caesar and Cleo, "The Letter"; despite being a *Billboard* "pick," it didn't chart.

The Letter.

Unrelenting is the term for this driver. Side has fat, pulsing sound and pours along on driving, highly danceable rock sound. (7/14/64)

Sonny finally convinced Phil to record Cher solo but after issuing the novelty "Ringo, I Love You" (under the name Bonnie Jo Mason), Spector lost interest. Bono then borrowed $135 to produce her on "Baby Don't Go," but what started as a solo became a duet owing to Cher's sudden studio version of stage fright. When Spector offered $500 for the publishing, Sonny thought he had something and sold the master to Reprise Records, but that first Sonny and Cher single received little attention. Unperturbed, the twosome left for Tijuana, Mexico, and were married on October 27, 1964.

In 1965, Ahmet Ertegun of Atco, finding the duo had no contract with Reprise, signed them. Their first 45, "Just You," initially went nowhere. Ertegun was about to issue "It's Gonna Rain" against Sonny's better judgment, when the planned B-side began receiving hot responses from KHJ in Los Angeles. It seems Sonny gave the unreleased recording of "I Got You Babe" to deejay Ron Jacobs, who played the record to death, well actually to life, and the song reached #1. Reprise then reissued "Baby Don't Go" (#8) and "Just You" was also reissued, reaching #20.

Just You.

Well-written teen ballad pitted against a strong, slow, solid dance beat. Good vocal work. (4/10/65)

I Got You Babe.

Using the successful combination of folk and rock, this one has the performance and production of a smash. (6/26/65) (#1 Pop, #17 R&B)

As if things weren't going well enough, Cher garnered a solo deal with Imperial and began a streak of Bono-produced (and sometimes -written) hits, including "All I Really Want to Do." Sonny tried his hand at solo records too, initially outcharting Cher.

Cher:

All I Really Want to Do.

Raucous Bob Dylan tune is well performed by the female half of folksters Sonny & Cher. Powerful driving dance beat throughout. (6/19/65) (#15 Pop)

Sonny:
Laugh at Me.

> *The husband half of the team . . . debuts solo. Powerhouse teen protest material has all the ingredients of a smash. (8/7/65)*

Meanwhile, the Sonny and Cher team continued to rack up the hits.

But You're Mine.

> *With four discs riding the Hot 100 chart, the hot duo keep up their winning streak with this exciting rhythm ballad with offbeat message lyric from the pen of Sonny. Another No. 1 contender. (10/2/65) (#15 Pop)*

What Now My Love.

> *The much recorded semistandard gets its most unusual and commercial treatment. This is the one to put the duo back at the top again. Strong teen beat backing. (1/22/66) (#14 Pop)*

Cher alone scored with a story song novelty, "Bang Bang" in early 1966, followed by another hit for the duo.

Cher:
Bang Bang.

> *An off-beat rhythm, clever lyrics and great Cher vocal combine for a top-of-the-chart winner. Produced and written by Sonny. (3/5/66) (#2 Pop)*

Sonny and Cher:
Little Man.

> *More powerful off-beat material from the pen of Sonny. Top duet performance should hit hard and fast. Far-eastern flavored rhythm adds strong support. (9/24/66) (#21 Pop)*

In late 1966, the duo debuted in the film *Good Times*, written by Sonny. In 1969, they starred in their second and last film together, *Chastity* (named after their daughter).

The Beat Goes On.

> *This frug beat production is the most commercial of the recent Sonny & Cher releases and should prove a top-of-the-chart entry. The duo's performance,*

solid arrangement and good lyric spells smash. (1/7/67) (#6 Pop)

A Beautiful Story.

> *Fine story line and off-beat arrangement of Sonny's ballad makes an interesting change-of-pace winner. (4/22/67) (#53 Pop)*

It's the Little Things.

> *Re-release of their recent entry . . . should prove a giant sales item this time around. Strong material with top duo performance. (7/29/67) (#50 Pop)*

Good Combination.

> *The song's title perfectly defines this mating—top vocal performance and groovy rhythm material should carry the duo to a high spot on the Hot 100 in short order. (12/9/67) (#56 Pop)*

Cher released some solo singles between 1968 and 1970, with little success. In 1971, with their kooky, hip image suffering along with their record sales, they joined Kapp and modified their attire while pursuing the cabaret and Las Vegas set. Their live act attracted interest from CBS-TV execs and *The Sonny and Cher Comedy Hour* was born. Their records gained a tremendous boost from the show. "All I Ever Need Is You" (#7) was a smash, while Cher had one of her own, "Gypsys, Tramps & Thieves." "Gypsys" was originally titled "Gypsys and White Trash."

Sonny and Cher:
Real People.

> *The husband-wife team make their debut for the label with a smooth reading of the Paul Anka rhythm ballad. (6/12/71)*

Cher:
Gypsys, Tramps & Thieves.

> *This offbeat rock ballad with a lyric to match serves as potent material to bring her back to the charts. (8/28/71) (#1 Pop)*

The Way of Love.

> *Cher follows her #1 winner "Gypsys, Tramps & Thieves" with a change of pace, emotion-packed ballad loaded with Top 40 and MOR potency. (1/22/72) (#7 Pop)*

Sonny and Cher:
A Cowboy's Work Is Never Done.

> *This off-beat rhythm material with a wild performance has much of the flavor of another "Gypsys, Tramps & Thieves" with all of that play and sales potency. (2/19/72) (#8 Pop)*

Cher had her second story song #1 in 1973 with "Half Breed" (recommended for Top-20 to -60 action, but unreviewed) and her third, "Dark Lady," followed soon after.

Dark Lady.

> *There's a similar feel and quality to Cher's previous singles about people with some shading in their background. The question here is who is this dark lady that she sings about. A full orchestra lends a powerful backing to her fine reading. (1/7/74) (#1 Pop)*

The husband and wife duo had their last chart single in 1974 with "Mama Was a Rock and Roll Singer" (#77). A short reunion with Spector followed.

A Woman's Story.

> *First production combining the talents of Cher and Phil Spector uses her voice perfectly wrapped around his classic wall of sound production and powerful backup vocals. A completely different sound for Cher and one that works well. (11/23/74)*

Growing in separate directions, the couple was divorced on June 26, 1974. Each then did an unsuccessful TV show and reunited in February 1976 for the short-lived Sonny and Cher show. Cher continued recording while developing a tremendous career as an actress in films such as *Silkwood*, *Mask*, and *The Witches of Eastwick*, while returning to the charts again briefly in 1979 as a disco queen and again from 1987–1989 in a more hard-rock mode.

Cher:
Take Me Home.

> *An upbeat, cleanly produced sound with a light, easy melody. It's sure to catch the ears of the disco set. (2/10/79) (#8 Pop)*

I Found Someone.

> *Back from the silver screen and into the studio . . . comes a booming rock ballad that features a welcome and unrestrained performance. (10/24/87) (#10 Pop)*

We All Sleep Alone.

> *One of the media's hottest properties at the moment handles Bon Jovi ballad territory with incredible ease. (4/2/88) (#14 Pop)*

If I Could Turn Back Time.

> *A commercially tailored and very likable gingerly paced pop/rock track. (7/1/89) (#3 Pop)*

Just Like Jesse James.

> *Ballad sweeps with powerful performance by the singer and a production that builds to an emotive climax. (10/14/89) (#8 Pop)*

In 1987, Sonny and Cher appeared on David Letterman's TV show and for the first time in 10 years sang "I Got You Babe." During 1988, Cher won an Oscar for her role in *Moonstruck*. Sonny had opened a restaurant in Los Angeles called Bono's in the mid-1980s, and then moved into politics, first as mayor of Palm Springs, California, in 1988 (one day after Cher won her Oscar) and then as a member of Congress in 1995.

THE SPANIELS

James "Pookie" Hudson: Lead vocals
Born: 6/11/34, Gary, IN
Ernest Williams: First tenor
Born: 1930s, Gary, IN
Willie Jackson: Second tenor
Born: 1930s, Gary, IN
Opal Courtney, Jr.: Baritone
Born: 1930s, Gary, IN
Gerald Gregory: Bass
Born: 6/10/34, Gary, IN
Influences: Billy Williams and The Charioteers, Ink Spots, Four Tunes, Nat "King" Cole

Influenced: Frankie Lymon and The Teenagers, Ben E. King and The Drifters, Rascals, Skyliners, Crests, Dell-Vikings, Marcels, Olympics, Monotones, Silhouettes, Orlons, Manhattan Transfer, Jive Five, Dubs, many more

One of the most influential of the early vocal groups, despite the fact that they never had a Top-20 hit.

In 1952, the Gary, Indiana, teenagers met at Roosevelt High School, and as Pookie Hudson and The Hudsonaires, made their first appearance at the school Christmas show. The Hudsonaires began hunting for a new name in 1954. They decided not to be just another "bird" group, so, when the wife of a member heard them singing in the garage and commented, "You guys sound like a bunch of dogs," The Spaniels came into being.

Their impromptu performance in a record store owned by local deejay Vivian Carter Bracken of WWCA convinced her and husband James to form the now-legendary Vee-Jay label, which opened in Chicago on May 5, 1953. Vee-Jay's first single was by The Spaniels and its initial response caused the larger Chance label to distribute while issuing copies on its own label.

Baby It's You 83
> *Here's a solid effort by . . . a new group on the label. The boys have a style all of their own, and they put a lot of feeling into the ballad. The ork backing lends a mighty hand. This one shapes up a big one and a real coin-grabber. (9/5/53) (#10 R&B)*

Vee-Jay learned quickly and was soon doing its own larger scale distribution.

House Cleaning 73
> *A slow rocker guarantees the house-wife satisfaction—according to the lyric. It's spirited with a smart hand-clap interlude and a tenor solo of merit. (11/28/53)*

Their biggest hit started, like so many in that exciting era, as a B-side, but one week after its initial (non)-review, *Billboard* reconsidered and promoted it to top status.

Goodnite Sweetheart Goodnite 84
> *An almost pop-like piece of material which swings enough to make it in both the pop and r.&b. markets. The imitation of the sounds of a sax player by the bass singer give this side a gimmick which helps greatly. Strong wax. (3/17/54) (#24 Pop, #5 R&B)*

"The imitation of a sax" the reviewer referred to was not an intended imitation at all; bass Gerald Gregory was just trying to keep the group on pitch! "Goodnite" has since become one of rock's most enduring standards and the "sign off" song for hundreds of radio shows spanning five decades. Had The McGuire Sisters not covered it (#7), "Goodnite" probably would have reached #1. The group followed with more singles, but were unable to equal "Goodnite"'s success.

Don'cha Go 77
> *A highly effective group vocal on a plaintive weeper with standout work by the lead singer, who packs consider-able emotion into his warbling. Good juke wax. (5/14/55)*

Painted Picture.
> *A moving rendition of a lovely ballad with excellent lyrics and soft, relaxed pacing. The lead singer's sensitive pip-ing and delicate phrasing are particu-larly outstanding. (9/10/55) (#13 R&B)*

Since I Fell for You 72
> *Tender careening tones from the lead with much talking by-play by the others behind the solo job. Side moves with slow expressiveness. (7/21/56)*

Defections and the draft riddled the group in 1956 and by year's end, Pookie (who had left and returned) led a contingent of Gregory, Don Porter, Carl Rainge, and James Cochrane.

You Gave Me Peace of Mind.
> *The group sounds extremely classy on this. Slow, reverent and soul-satisfying bit of soloing with the group offering a wailing response. Solid breakout strength. (12/29/56)*

Everyone's Looking 70
Complex backing pattern gets a little tiresome on a mediocre hunk of cleff-ing. Lead man does a creditable job but the group has had better stuff. (5/13/57) (#69 Pop, #13 R&B)

Doo wop folklore has it that The Spaniels had an opportunity to cut a new song called "The Twist" but turned it down. Unfortunately, the standards they chose to cut instead did little for them, although they are collectors' classics today.

Stormy Weather 75
The standard is sung with spirit by the boys with a strong lead handling the lyrics. (8/11/58)

Heart and Soul.

★ ★ ★ *The standard tune is revived with a deep Jimmy Ricks type bass taking the lead with higher warbling, emotional voices in the backing group. (12/8/58)*

By 1960, the gang from Gary's membership was in an almost constant state of flux, sales slipped, and their last Vee-Jay 45 became their last Vee-Jay charter, the B-side, "I Know."

I Know.

★ ★ ★ *Lead singer warbles with feeling on the fervent rockaballad. Another dual market side. (6/20/60) (#23 R&B)*

For Sentimental Reasons.

The Spaniels, who have had many hits over the years, are back and they have . . . a strong reading of the fine old standard, featuring the lead voice of Pookie Hudson. Could please the teen crowd. (7/31/61)

Pookie did a few 1962 solos for Jamie and had his last chart single in 1970 with The Imperials (minus Little Anthony) backing him on "Fairy Tails" (#45 R&B, Calla). Through the 1970s, 1980s, and 1990s, Hudson and various Spaniels contingents were highlights on numerous "oldies" tours. In 1993, still sounding as vibrant as ever, Pookie and company recorded a masterful 27-song, a cappella CD of their past singles.

THE SUPREMES

Diana Ross: Lead vocals
Born: 3/26/44, Detroit, MI
Florence Ballard
Born: 6/30/43, Detroit, MI (died 2/22/76)
Mary Wilson
Born: 3/6/44, Greenville, MS
Barbara Martin
Born: 1940s, Detroit, MI
Betty Travis
Born: 1940s, Detroit, MI
Influences: Flamingos, Frankie Lymon and The Teenagers, McGuire Sisters, Chantels, Temptations

The most popular female trio of all time, The Supremes actually started as a quartet initially rejected by the company that later made them famous.

Their climb to stardom started in 1959, when Detroit housing-project residents Mary Wilson and Florence Ballard met at a talent show. Milton Jenkins, manager of the male group, The Primes (who later became the nucleus of The Temptations), asked Ballard to form a sister group, The Primettes. She drafted Wilson and friend Betty McGlown, whereas Primes vocalist Paul Williams recommended a 15-year-old friend, Diane Ross. Over the next year, membership changed (except for Wilson). So McGlown, Ballard, and Ross went and came along with newcomer, Barbara Martin, although the group was never more than a quartet at any one time.

In 1960, they met Diane's former neighbor, Smokey Robinson, and auditioned in the basement of his girlfriend, Claudette Rogers (later a member of the Miracles). The tryout was a washout but later that year they auditioned for Motown Records' Berry Gordy, singing The Drifters song, "There Goes My Baby." Gordy summarily dismissed them, saying, "Come back when you finish high school." Undaunted, they returned to the talent show scene and were noticed by Richard

Morris, friend of producer Bob West. He recorded "Pretty Baby" with Wilson as lead for his Lupine label in 1960. It became an instant rarity.

In 1961, they again approached Gordy and this time he signed them. Their debut disk recorded, he asked them to change their name, and so Ballard came up with The Supremes; they didn't realize there was a current male group with the same moniker. In January Martin left the group to marry and was never replaced.

I Want a Guy.

Film [sic] lead with an unusual sound handles this medium-tempo rocker with feeling aided smartly by a strong arrangement. (3/27/61)

Their next single featured Ballard, but The Supremes were going nowhere fast. The Detroit damsels' first chart 45, "Your Heart Belongs to Me," barely reached the Top 100.

Buttered Popcorn.

The gals explain on this rhythmic novelty how their boy friend loves "Buttered Popcorn." It's bright and cute and it moves. (7/17/61)

Your Heart Belongs to Me.

★ ★ ★ ★ *The South Pacific sound shows a bit on this disking which features the debut of the girls in strong fashion. Smart arrangements might make this one to watch. (6/2/62) (#95 Pop)*

By mid-1962, the trio of Ballard, Ross, and Wilson were doing so poorly that Ross found herself working in the cafeteria of Hudson's Department Store. They managed a Top-25 hit with "When the Lovelight Starts Shining Through His Eyes" in late 1963, but the follow up barely grazed the Top 100.

When the Lovelight Starts Shining Through His Eyes.

Jockeys are riding this one right out of the stable. Side has strong lead singing from the lass that sounds some like an earlier Little Esther. Side has swing and frantic sound. (11/16/63) (#23 Pop)

Run, Run, Run.

Currently riding high. Offering has a tough beat in a middle up groove that's great for dancing. (2/22/64) (#93 Pop)

In 1964, the trio finally hit the big time thanks to The Marvelettes' lead, Gladys Horton. She spurned a new Holland, Dozier, and Holland song with the immortal words, "I wouldn't sing that junk!," and the second-choice Supremes unhappily recorded what became their first million seller.

Where Did Our Love Go.

Music to hand-clap and foot stomp to. Plenty of jump in this one. Beat is unbeatable and lead is in a true rockin'-blues groove. (7/4/64) (#1 Pop)

After eight misses, the group started an unprecedented streak of five #1s in a row on *Billboard*'s Hot 100! Ross, who by now had reverted to the name on her birth certificate, Diana, began singing all the leads, much to the consternation of Ballard. "Baby Love" made the girls the first female group to reach #1 in England. With "Come See About Me," they were the first American group to have one album spew forth three #1 singles.

Baby Love.

A smash follow-up to their "Where Did Our Love Go" click. The swinging harmony style keeps it rolling all the way through. (9/26/64) (#1 Pop)

Come See About Me.

Pronounced Detroit beat, steady and exacting. Gals weave silky and controlled vocal through beat. Pop and r&b hit potential. (11/7/64) (#1 Pop, #2 R&B)

In 1965, "Stop! In the Name of Love" and "Back in My Arms Again" extended their #1 string to five straight. The streak was broken with "Nothing but Heartaches" (#11), but not for long, as "I Hear a Symphony" also went to #1.

Back in [My] Arms Again.

A strong teen lyric and a powerful vocal performance pitted against a hard rock backing in full support. A winner all the way! (4/24/65) (#1 Pop, #1 R&B)

I Hear a Symphony.
> *No problem rushing up the chart with this well-written rhythm ballad with pulsating beat and top vocal work. Blockbuster! (10/23/65) (#1 Pop, #2 R&B)*

My World Is Empty Without You.
> *Chalk up another No. 1 contender in their long list of hits. This one is right in their pulsating rhythm groove of "I Hear a Symphony" with even more excitement in the performance. (1/8/66) (#5 Pop, #10 R&B)*

Love Is Like an Itching in My Heart.
> *More exciting sounds from the girls in this slow rhythm rocker with solid back beat. (4/23/66) (#9 Pop, #7 R&B)*

You Can't Hurry Love.
> *The group's most exciting side to date. Top vocal on this Detroit rouser, with exceptional instrumental backing. (8/6/66) (#1 Pop, #1 R&B)*

You Keep Me Hangin' On.
> *Another No. 1 contender is this pulsating rocker with the trio in top form. Interesting, driving guitar figure throughout. (10/22/66) (#1 Pop, #1 R&B)*

Love Is Here, and Now You're Gone.
> *Change of pace rocker featuring a spoken interlude. (1/21/67) (#1 Pop, #1 R&B)*

The Happening.
> *In the good-time rhythm music bag, the trio changes pace with this classy performance of the new film theme. Another sure-fire rocker headed for the top of the Hot 100. (4/1/67) (#1 Pop, #12 R&B)*

After "The Happening," Holland et al. left to form their own label, having written and produced all The Supremes' prior hits. Friction between Ballard and Ross reached a peak and Ballard was fired, replaced by Bluebelles' backup, Cindy Birdsong in mid-1967. The group's new billing reflected Ross's ascendancy to star status.

Diana Ross and The Supremes: Reflections.
> *With Diana Ross getting top billing for the first time, the Supremes will quickly carry this easy rocker right up to the No. 1 spot on the Hot 100. (8/5/67) (#2 Pop, #4 R&B)*

In and Out of Love.
> *Diana Ross leads the Supremes through a highly rhythmic side, much in the vein of "You Can't Hurry Love," that has all the ingredients for high chart honors. As usual, the group's inimitable bounce and drive are hard to match and just as hard to resist. (11/4/67) (#9 Pop, #16 R&B)*

Love Child.
> *The smooth trio generates a whole new brand of excitement with this groovy rocker that's loaded with sales appeal. Change of pace item is reminiscent of their earlier hits, and gets a top vocal treatment by the girls. (10/12/68) (#1 Pop, #2 R&B)*

I'm Livin' in Shame.
> *Another swinger with another dynamic lyric line built around false pride. (1/18/69) (#10 Pop, #8 R&B)*

The Supremes' last single with Ross, "Someday We'll Be Together," offered a series of lasts, including their last of 12 #1s, the last #1 of the 1960s (December 27, 1969), the last song they performed together on TV (their 20th appearance on Ed Sullivan's show), and the final song they sang on stage (January 14, 1970, Frontier Hotel, Las Vegas). Contrary to public assumptions, "Someday" was not written as their farewell song. It was recorded nine years earlier by Johnny and Jackie (Tri-Phi) and produced by Moonglows leader, Harvey Fuqua. Actually, it wasn't even the Supremes singing on the record. Ross fronted The Waters (Maxine and Julia) along with Johnny Bristol.

Someday We'll Be Together.
> *The girls are riding in high gear with this smooth, easy rocker that should carry them high on the charts. (11/1/69)*

Jean Terrell (sister of prize fighter, Ernie Terrell) became The Supremes' lead as Diana Ross began her hugely successful solo career. Both issued their first outings in early 1970, with the group actually beating Ross on the charts.

Supremes:
Up the Ladder to the Roof.

> *First for the girls with Jean Terrell . . . is a blockbuster. Mary Wilson and Cindy Birdsong come off strong behind the fine lead in this swinger that will spiral the chart. (2/28/70) (#10 Pop, #5 R&B)*

Diana Ross:
Reach Out and Touch (Somebody's Hand).

> *The former Supreme goes it solo . . . and it's a powerhouse. Loaded with play and sales appeal, the driving rhythm ballad and a top performance could go all the way. (4/11/70) (#20 Pop, #7 R&B)*

Ross fought back with her second release, "Ain't No Mountain High Enough," which reached #1 pop and R&B.

Diana Ross:
Ain't No Mountain High Enough.

> *This heavy updating of the past Marvin Gaye-Tammy Terrell hit will prove a sales and chart topper . . . powerful performance. (8/1/70)*

Supremes:
Stoned Love.

> *Powerhouse rock ballad loaded with more sales and chart potency. (10/31/70) (#7 Pop, #1 R&B)*

Diana Ross:
Remember Me.

> *A driving rock ballad penned by Nick Ashford and Valerie Simpson. (12/19/70) (#16 Pop, #10 R&B)*

Supremes:
Nathan Jones.

> *A cleverly arranged swinging ballad that has . . . sales and chart potential*

> *. . . pop and soul. (5/1/71) (#16 Pop, #8 R&B)*

Floy Joy.

> *An infectious rhythm item. (1/1/72) (#16 Pop, #5 R&B)*

In July 1972, Cindy retired and Wilson, the last original Supreme, left in 1977. Soon after their last pop charter, "You're My Driving Wheel," the group broke up. Florence Ballard died in 1976, after years of fighting Motown in court over her firing. Diana Ross, however, marched on with several hits through the 1970s, both as a soloist and in duet.

Last Time I Saw Him.

> *Diana sings softly about a man "who's Greyhound bound" with an arrangement which fuses banjo and a happy almost two-beat feeling. It's a jazz-razz-matazz tune in the Dawn dixieland mold. (12/15/73) (#14 Pop, #1 R&B)*

Diana Ross and Marvin Gaye:
Don't Knock My Love.

> *Diana & Marvin have an utter ball with this Wilson Pickett uptempo classic. They play [the] lyrics for teasing sauciness rather than plaintive intensity and the approach works beautifully in an elegant Motown production. You gots to love it. (6/29/74) (#46 Pop, #2 R&B)*

Diana Ross and Michael Jackson:
Ease on Down the Road.

> *The first single from "The Wiz" has Ross and her onetime discovery Jackson duetting against a shimmering instrumental backdrop that is at once funky and brassy. The song was a disco smash and mid-chart pop hit three years ago, and in this year of hit duets should finally enjoy the broader acceptance it deserves. (9/28/78) (#41 Pop, #17 R&B)*

In 1980, Ross scored some big hits with a new style of disco-influenced songs.

I'm Coming Out.

Upbeat romp, which is already climbing the charts. It's an exuberant and near-irresistible track. (9/13/80) (#5 Pop, #6 R&B)

It's My Turn.

From the film of the same name, this is a soft, anthem-like ballad that is immediately infectious. Replete with stirring strings and a perfect vocal performance, this cut epitomizes romance. (10/18/80) (#9 Pop, #14 R&B)

A year later, Diana Ross and Lionel Richie enjoyed a pop/R&B #1 smash with the movie theme, "Endless Love," written by Richie. Ross followed with more fluffy pop numbers, now on new label RCA.

The past and present Motown superstars duet on this silky, sensitive ballad. (7/4/81)

Diana Ross:
Why Do Fools Fall in Love?

A giddy, lighthearted track which is a great change-of-pace from the solemn ballad "Endless Love," now in its ninth straight week at No. 1. (10/10/81) (#7 Pop, #6 R&B)

Muscles.

Finger-popping ballad which segues from a breathy, little girl vocal to a brash, erotic chorus. Unfortunately, unlike Olivia Newton-John's "Physical," she doesn't have the musical substance to back up the sexy imagery. (10/2/82) (#10 Pop, #4 R&B)

In 1983, Diana, Mary, and Cindy regrouped for Motown's 25th Anniversary reunion and a year later, Mary Wilson published her "tell all" book, Dream Girl: My Life as a Supreme. Ross continued to record through the 1980s, with lesser chart success, while also hitting the Vegas and lounge-club circuit. The Rock and Roll Hall of Fame inducted The Supremes in 1988.

THE TEDDY BEARS

Annette Kleinbard (Carol Connors): Lead vocals
Born: 11/13/41, Los Angeles, CA
Phil Spector: Tenor
Born: 12/26/40, Bronx, NY
Marshall Leib: Tenor
Born: 1/26/39, Los Angeles, CA
Harvey Goldstein: Bass
Born: 1938, Los Angeles, CA
Influences: Everly Brothers, Ray Charles, Fats Domino, Doris Day, Four Freshmen, Tony Bennett
Influenced: Fleetwoods, Carpenters, Paris Sisters, Kathy Young, Rosie and The Originals, Chris Montez

The Teddy Bears were the launching pad for a legendary record producer (Spector), a successful songwriter (Kleinbard), and a top-notch film music supervisor (Leib).

In 1958, however, they were just another group of Los Angeles teenagers, desirous of making music. Their driving force was 17-year-old Phil Spector, who moved to L.A. with his mother and sister after his father's death. Spector began playing guitar while studying the goings on at Hollywood's Gold Star Studios. Spector also led a short-lived group, The Sleepwalkers, but his first real effort came with Leib, Goldstein, and Kleinbard in 1958. They began practicing in the garage of Spector's girlfriend, Donna Kass. It was she who introduced her best friend Annette Kleinbard to Spector, and he was instantly captivated by her soft, haunting voice.

When the issue of a name came up, Goldstein, thinking of song titles, volunteered The Teddy Bears, as in Elvis's year-old hit. On May 20, 1958, the quartet recorded a demo at Gold Star on Spector's "Don't You Worry, My Little Pet." It was played for Herb Newman of Era/Dore Records who signed the group. A second session for a B-side was scheduled but by then Goldstein was stationed at Fort Ord, serving his Army reserve time. So, the three Bears attempted to record Spector's "Wonderful, Lovable You" without him. When it didn't work, Spector reverted to a song inspired by what his mother had written on her husband's tombstone. In two takes, The Teddy Bears taped "To Know Him Is to Love Him."

The single was released on August 1, to little response. Goldstein and Leib prepared to enter Los Angeles City College and Kleinbard readied herself for her senior year at Fairfax High. Spector, who had thought of being a court reporter, began business school. Then, thanks to that marvelous era of plastic, two-sided 45s and nonautomated radio, deejays in North Dakota and Minnesota flipped the record and it broke nationally. Selling over one and a half million copies, the single became #1 for three weeks.

To Know Him Is to Love Him.

This is a strong debut side by the group. The lead fem voice gets effective support from the rest of the group on the moving rockaballad. It's already stepping out in some areas, and it figures to become even stronger. Flip is "Don't You Worry My Little Pet." (9/22/58) (#1 Pop, #10 R&B)

Problems, however, set in almost immediately. Goldstein was ousted with the justification being that he didn't sing on "To Know Him" anyway. Arguments between Spector and Dore over choosing the next single found the group on Imperial for its follow ups.

You Said Goodbye.

★ ★ ★ ★ *A slow, melancholy, minor-key ballad is thrushed attractively by the gal lead for the group. It's a soulful side that could move. (3/30/59)*

Wonderful Loveable You.

★ ★ ★ ★ *The Teddy Bears sell a rockaballad with their usual charm and warmth. This side was made before the group joined Imperial. (5/11/59)*

Don't Go Away.

★ ★ ★ ★ *The fem lead lends an appealing plea on this slow and moving ballad. Group scored with "To Know Him Is to Love Him" a few months back. Side is worth spins. (6/8/59)*

Even the release of an album (an unheard-of practice for a one-hit group in the 1950s) couldn't excite the masses beyond the first single. Friction also developed among the trio when Spector's sister became the group's manager. A near-fatal car accident in September 1959 put Annette Kleinbard in the hospital and reportedly, Spector never visited her during her recuperation. The Teddy Bears were dead but the individuals lived on.

Goldstein became an accountant. Leib produced Timi Yuro and The Everly Brothers while finding his niche as a film music coordinator for hits such as "Take This Job and Shove It" and "Ode to Billy Joe." Annette became Annette Bard and then Carol Connors, hit songwriter of "Hey Little Cobra" (#4, 1963, Rip Chords), "The Night the Lights Went Out in Georgia" (#1, 1973, Vickie Lawrence), and "Gonna Fly Now" (#1, 1977, the theme from "Rocky").

Annette Bard:
What Difference Does It Make.

★ ★ ★ *A tearful ballad of the things that should have been. Gal handles it in high-pitched, weepy fashion. Romantic message. (4/25/60)*

Carol Connors:
My Diary.

★ ★ ★ ★ *Appealing weeper-styled theme is talked and sung plaintively by gal. Watch it. This is her first side for the label. (3/27/61)*

In 1960, Phil Spector formed a long-since-forgotten trio called The Spector's Three that included young Russ Titelman (now a V.P. with Warner Brothers Records).

The Spectors Three:
My Heart Stood Still (A-side).

★ ★ ★ *The mixed trio offers a nice, slow arrangement of the familiar standard. An infectious side with a sound.*

Mr. Robin (B-side).

★ ★ ★ *Vocal is all but swallowed by the echo factor but the side has a catchy sound. Employs a prominent figure in the vocal backed by simple harmony in the chorus. Can catch spins. (5/9/60)*

Since then, however, nothing Spector's done has been forgotten by lovers of 1960s music. A summation might well be that, in 1989, he was inducted into the Rock and Roll Hall of Fame.

THE *T*EMPTATIONS

Eddie Kendricks: Lead vocals
Born: 12/17/39, Birmingham, AL
Melvin Franklin (David English): Bass
Born: 10/12/42, Montgomery, AL (died 3/95)
Otis Williams (Otis Miles): Baritone
Born: 10/31/41, Texarkana, TX
Paul Williams: Tenor
Born: 7/2/39, Birmingham, AL (died 8/17/73)
Elbridge Bryant: Tenor
Born: 1940s
Influences: Hank Ballard and The Midnighters, Moonglows, Frankie Lymon and The Teenagers, Flamingos, Cadillacs, Impressions, Gladys Knight and The Pips
Influenced: Supremes, Jackson Five, 5th Dimension, Whispers, New Edition, Dramatics, Magnificent Men, Persuasions, Brooklyn Dreams

The Temptations are like the royal family, forever active no matter who in the lineage is carrying the banner. Considered by many to be the heart and soul of the Motown machine, The Temps have charted their way to stardom through four decades.

The group's first lineup was derived from two acts, The Cavaliers (who became The Primes) and The Elegants (not the "Little Star" group) who evolved into The Questions and then The Distants. The Primes' only claim to fame was the introduction of member Paul Williams's 15-year-old neighbor, Diana Ross, to their manager who was forming a sister group for The Primes called The Primettes. As it turned out, that quartet of neighborhood girls later became The Supremes. Meanwhile, the Distants recorded a single ("Always," Northern, 1960) but were going unnoticed until the two male acts met at a Detroit house party. When the musical membership roulette was

over, Kendricks and Williams of The Primes joined with Melvin Franklin, Elbridge Bryant, and Otis Miles (who became Otis Williams, even though the lead singer for The Charms shared the name) of The Distants. Milton Jenkins, their manager, then renamed them The Elgins.

During one of their club dates in 1961, Berry Gordy, Jr. saw the quintet and signed them for his Miracle label. Looking for a new name, Otis and Motown staffer Billy Mitchell came up with The Temptations, neither being aware of an already existing white group ("Barbara" on Goldisc, 1960). The Temps first two singles did so poorly that the group moonlighted for one single as The Pirates on "Mind Over Matter."

Oh, Mother of Mine.
★ ★ ★ ★ *A wild and breathless performance by the lead man, who has a strong gospel feeling. (8/21/61)*

Check Yourself.
★ ★ ★ ★ *A slow and throbbing, triplet-backed rhythm chant by the group. Lead hands it a strong performance. Side should be watched. (2/10/62)*

Berry moved the quintet to his Gordy label in early 1962 and the first single "Dream Come True" made #22 R&B. However, the follow up did not chart.

Paradise.

This side has a distinctive high-voiced sound that should spark a good deal of teen action. The side is catchy and moves somewhat in a "Sherry" groove. (10/13/62)

Bryant then left, replaced by David Ruffin, who had previously recorded (unsuccessfuly) for Motown's Anna affiliate.

David Ruffin:
I'm in Love.
★ ★ ★ ★ *The boy does an exceedingly strong reading of the punching rockaballad. The effective backing is by a string section interwoven with a mixed vocal chorus. (2/20/61)*

With Ruffin on board along with Kendricks as the lead voices, all the pieces fell into place. The group had their first major hit in early 1964.

The Way You Do the Things You Do.

A smoothly moving rocker with emphasis on the dance beat. Groove is highly commercial with lead providing a distinctive sound. Could be another hit-making combo for the label. (2/8/64) (#11 Pop)

In late 1964, Ruffin sang his first Temps lead on a tune writer Smokey Robinson had planned to record with his own Miracles but The Temps asked for and received, "My Girl" (#1, Pop and R&B). More hits followed through 1966.

Since I Lost My Baby.

For their third straight top chart smash this year, the group offers a smooth rhythm ballad. Fine vocal performance. Flip: "You've Got To Earn It." (7/17/65) (A-side, #17 Pop, #4 R&B; B-side, #123 Pop, #22 R&B)

Get Ready.

The rocking rhythm ballad from the pen of Smokey Robinson should hit the chart with impact. (2/19/66) (#29 Pop, #1 R&B)

Ain't Too Proud to Beg.

Hot on the heels of their chart-topping disk, "Get Ready," comes this pulsating wailer with teen-aimed lyric that will quickly replace it. (5/14/66) (#13 Pop, #1 R&B)

Beauty Is Only Skin Deep.

Smooth rocker featuring bongo and brass and a well-done vocal on a strong lyric. Top-of-the-chart contender. (8/13/66) (#3 Pop, #1 R&B)

(I Know) I'm Losing You.

Hot follow up to "Beauty Is Only Skin Deep" is this blues swinger with a solid dance beat and powerful vocal workout. (11/19/66) (#8 Pop, #1 R&B)

Meanwhile, David's brother Jimmy Ruffin was cutting his own hit path, beginning with "I've Passed This Way Before." The Temptations' 1968 foray into psychedelic soul with "Cloud Nine" won them a Grammy for Best Group, R&B Performance (Motown's first).

I Wish It Would Rain.

This easy beat blues rocker will soar to the top in short order. (1/6/68) (#4 Pop, #1 R&B)

Cloud Nine.

Group turns in a powerhouse vocal performance of a solid driving rocker with strong lyric content. (11/9/68) (#6 Pop, #2 R&B)

The year 1968 continued as a high watermark for the quintet thanks to "I'm Gonna Make You Love Me" (#2 Pop and R&B, with The Supremes).

By 1969, David opted for a solo career, replaced by Dennis Edwards. He had an immediate major hit with "My Whole World Ended."

Hardriving blues rocker with an infectious rhythm and strong vocal workout by the former leader of the Temptations. Wild solo debut. (2/1/69)

Following Ruffin's lead, Kendricks then went solo. Williams left owing to illness, and both original Primes were gone. Damon Harris (Vandals, T-Neck) and Richard Street (an original Distants member) took their places, and the hits kept coming.

Run Away Child, Running Wild.

A blockbuster rhythm number with wild sounds and a powerhouse vocal workout. Driving beat will spiral it right to the top. (2/8/69) (#6 Pop, #1 R&B)

Don't Let the Joneses Get You Down.

The powerful rocker will carry the group right back to the top. (5/17/69) (#20 Pop, #2 R&B)

Just My Imagination (Running Away with Me).

The Temptations come on with a smooth rhythm ballad much in the style of their "My Girl" hit of the past. Should bring them to the top of the charts in a hurry. (1/30/71) (#1 Pop, #1 R&B)

"Papa Was a Rolling Stone" was originally recorded by the group Undisputed Truth in June 1972; their failure became a Temptations masterpiece when the 11-minute LP cut was edited to make "Papa Was a Rolling Stone" their fourth and last #1.

Papa Was a Rolling Stone.
Finally released from their "All Directions" LP. Strong entry pop and soul. (10/7/72) (#1 Pop, #5 R&B)

Masterpiece.
This is a complete story within a song of life in the ghetto. All of the members take turns handling lead vocal chores and combined with the complicated and superb instrumental arrangement makes for an overall top performance. (2/17/73) (#7 Pop, #1 R&B)

Hey Girl.
A simply-worded love proposal with a slow and touching melody. Not quite as instantly arresting as some of the more ambitious Temptation-[Norman] Whitfield singles (no exotic trumpet-echo introduction here). But definitely in the solid mainstream of romantic soul balladry. (8/14/73) (#35 Pop, #2 R&B)

Meanwhile, Eddie Kendricks scored a #1 pop and R&B single in 1973 with the disco-styled "Keep on Truckin'," followed by a second dance track.

A charming, Stevie Wonderish synthesizer keyboard track rivets attention to the lyrically vague riff song. Kendricks exhorts listeners to keep on trucking several dozen times as the locomotive rhythm section drives ahead. (8/11/73) (#1 Pop, #1 R&B)

Boogie Down.
Kendrick's [sic] soft voice is teamed with a funky instrumental feel, with soft choral voices and an outstanding percussive feel with fiddles and guitars weaving in and out. . . . The song, arrangement and vocal treatment are all a cohesive unit. (12/22/73) (#2 Pop, #1 R&B)

The mid-1970s found The Temptations also treading disco ground.

Shakey Ground.
The veteran group arrives at a fine soul/pop/disco mix, using the title well throughout. As always, fine blend of lead and backup singing works well. Group is currently turning out some of best material in their career, and the album is a big one. (3/1/75) (#26 Pop, #1 R&B)

By 1975, Glen Leonard (Unifics, Kapp) supplanted Harris. In 1977, the group moved to Atlantic with their best effort being "In a Lifetime," but within three years they were back at Motown.

In 1982, Melvin's nephew, James Johnson (aka Rick James) wrote, produced, and sang lead on their biggest hit in six years, "Standing on the Top." The group on that single was something akin to an all-star team, as the octet included James, Kendricks, Ruffin, Williams, Franklin, Edwards, Street, and Leonard.

The Temps previously sang backup vocals on Rick James's smash "Super Freak."

Standing on the Top.
James returns the favor on this hot rhythm number. The long version features a teasing reprise of the Temps' classic "Papa Was a Rolling Stone." (4/17/82) (#66 Pop, #6 R&B)

Other minor hits followed through the 1980s with various lineups.

Do You Really Love Your Baby.
Fits the classic Temps harmony sound to this snappy Vandross/Miller composition. (11/9/85) (#14 R&B)

I Wonder Who She's Seeing Now.
Thoughtful and elegant r&b/pop ballad finds the venerable outfit attempting a Smokey-like crossover. Stevie Wonder makes a guest appearance. (9/5/87) (#3 R&B)

In 1989, The Temptations were inducted into the Rock and Roll Hall of Fame and on September 14, 1994, were given a star on Hollywood's "Walk of Fame." The early 1990s Temps included Harris, Street, Ron Tyson, Ali-Ollie Woodson, and Louis Price. Otis and Melvin, although retiring from the group in 1986, still made appearances as recently as the mid-1990s.

THE TOKENS

Jay Siegel: Lead vocals
Born: 10/20/39, Brooklyn, NY
Phil Margo: Bass
Born: 4/I/42, Brooklyn
Mitch Margo: Second tenor/baritone
Born: 5/25/47, Brooklyn, NY
Hank Medress: First tenor
Born: 11/19/38, Brooklyn, NY
Influences: Skyliners, Dion and The Belmonts, Weavers, Ray Charles
Influenced: Happenings, Four Evers

The many facets of The Tokens talent helped them become superior singers while they assembled a series of musical firsts.

In 1956, the halls and bathrooms of Lincoln High in Brooklyn were the training ground for The Linc Tones. Students Hank Medress, Eddie Rabkin, Cynthia Zolitan, and 17-year-old lead singer Neil Sedaka (yes, that Sedaka!) parlayed their practicing into a record deal with Morty Craft's Melba label. The Linc Tones then renamed themselves, not after the famous New York subway token but as in the phrase, "token of affection." Shortly after, the members returned to their formal education.

In 1958, Hank Medress formed Darrell and The Oxfords with schoolmates Jay Siegel, Warren Schwartz, and Fred Kalkstein (and no one named Darrell). A local hit, "Picture in My Wallet," resulted (Roulette, 1959) but a failed follow up doomed the group.

On December 7, Hank and neighbors Phil and Mitch Margo began the "hit" Tokens story by cutting classes to sing together. By the summer of 1960, Medress had brought in Siegel and they began writing, singing, and playing instruments as a Dion-and-The-Belmonts-meets-The-Weavers type act. Finding a local, nonindustry backer, the group produced their own studio recordings, gaining valuable experience. By late 1960, the quartet's masters were picked up by Morty Craft, this time for his Warwick label. Craft then asked the group's name, and Medress suggested The Tokens.

Tonight I Fell in Love.

★ ★ ★ ★ *The lads turn in a snappy performance here on a bright rocker that is loaded with gimmicks and it could easily happen. Watch it. (2/13/61) (#15 Pop)*

When the single erupted, Phil was a Wall Street order clerk, Jay was a department-store buyer, and Mitch was still in school. Now they were performing on "American Bandstand" and watching "Tonight" sell over 700,000 45s. Because of lack of payment, the Brooklynites moved to RCA. Their follow up singles, however, failed to do much on the charts.

Dry Your Eyes/When I Got to Sleep Last Night.

The group follows up its recent hit with two fine debut sides on its new label. The wildly rocking first side shows off the group's dynamic style. The flip is another teen slanted rocker that should get the kids dancing. (6/12/61)

Sincerely.

★ ★ ★ ★ *The oldie gets a novel interpretation, with a slow, precise and bouncing rhythm pattern. Could get coins. (8/21/61)*

When rock 'n' roll failed them, the act switched directions with a tune from an old Weavers album, "Wimoweh," in reality, a Zulu chant called "Mbube," meaning "Lion." Further research proved the lyric to be about a lion hunt, so the song was rewritten in English as "The Lion Sleeps Tonight." The group doubted the song would be a hit, though they loved it; they were already focusing on a career as a production team when, five weeks after charting, it became #1 for three weeks. Selling over three million singles, "Superthroat" (as Jay was nicknamed), his stylized falsetto and The Tokens' harmony mix became world famous and suddenly, four years before it would have a name, The Tokens had become the first folk-rock group.

The Lion Sleeps Tonight.

★ ★ ★ ★ *The African saga "Wimmoway" is accorded an exciting vocal treatment by the group. A powerful side by the kids. (10/23/61) (#1 Pop)*

While RCA was issuing follow ups, The Tokens signed a 12 singles per year production deal with Capitol, the first vocal group to earn such a pact.

B'Wa Nina.

Here's a smart follow-up to the Tokens' recent smash, "The Lion Sleeps Tonight." The material again has a touch of the veldt about it and employs the same high yodeling vocal technique. Title is translated "Pretty Girl," and the performance has a winning sound. (1/27/62) (#55 Pop)

I'll Do My Crying Tomorrow.

★ ★ ★ ★ *Tight teen sounds by the lads on this one. It's a fetching tune that features the lead and the rest of the boys against strong rhythmic effects and strings. (9/22/62)*

Hear the Bells.

The Tokens are back on their "Lion Sleeps Tonight" kick and a most exciting kick it is. This is their best record in a year and it could take off quickly. Aimed at the teen set. (7/20/63) (#94 Pop)

By late 1962, The Tokens submitted their 12th single to Capitol, their production of The Chiffons singing "He's So Fine." The label rejected it, as did nine other labels until Doug Morris at Laurie Records picked it up, and The Tokens became the first vocal group in history to produce a #1 record for another singing group. They then formed their own label, B. T. Puppy Records (B. T. representing their production company, Bright Tunes, whereas the puppy was a smaller version of Nipper, the RCA dog).

He's in Town.

A haunting lament with distinctive sound. Could be a really big one for the talented group. (7/25/64) (#43 Pop)

In 1964, they appeared with The Beatles at the New York Paramount. They also hired out as a studio vocal group for everyone from Del Shannon and Mac Davis to Connie Francis and Bob Dylan. Their biggest anonymous hit was as the backup for Keith's "98.6" (#7 Pop, 1966).

Sylvie Sleepin'.

Dramatic wailin' complete with jungle drums to fairy tale theme. As unusual as their "Lion Sleeps Tonight" hit. Tremendous production. Watch this one! (3/6/65)

Greatest Moments in a Girl's Life.

Easy-go, surf-sound rocker. Top of the chart potential. (5/14/66) (#30 Pop)

Green Plant.

Far out, left-field material, as off-beat as "Yellow Submarine," has that commmercial potential via this powerful vocal workout and kooky arrangement. Must be heard thoughout. One to watch carefully. (1/7/67)

As if they didn't wear enough hats, by the mid-1960s The Tokens turned to jingle writing, singing and producing hit commercials like "Pan Am Makes The Going Great" and "Ban Won't Wear Off." In another unpredictable move, the act joined forces with The Kirby Stone Four, creating an album of octet harmonies. It's likely one of Kirby's former singles led to a Tokens hit as producers of The Happenings, "My Mammy" (#13, 1967).

In 1967, The Tokens scuttled their label and signed with Warner Brothers. 1969 ushered in their move to Buddah.

Portrait of My Love.

The group has adapted the Steve Lawrence hit of the past to their familiar style. Shuold prove a giant teen hit. Driving Jimmy Wisner arrangement is first-rate. (3/25/67) (#36 Pop)

Till.

The Roger Williams hit of the past is updated in the powerful Tokens' driving style. Beautifully and commercially arranged. (2/17/68)

End of the World.

Smart and stylish updating of the Skeeter Davis hit of the past, this smooth ballad offering is sure to bring the group back to the "Hot 100" and "Easy Listening" charts in short order.

Top production and arrangement. (8/30/69)

She Lets Her Hair Down (Early in the Morning).

The Clairol commercial now making noise via the Gene Pitney version, serves as a powerful piece of material for The Tokens in their move to the label. Loaded with Top 40 appeal. (11/22/69) (#61 Pop)

With the trend from vocal groups to bands in the early 1970s, the chameleon Tokens became Cross Country, a Crosby, Stills and Nash-styled vocal band that hit in 1973 with Wilson Pickett's "Midnight Hour" (#30 Pop). By the mid-1970s, the group concentrated on productions like the megahit "Tie a Yellow Ribbon" by Tony Orlando and Dawn.

In 1983, Phil and Mitch moved to Los Angeles and formed a West Coast Tokens; Hank stayed in production, and Jay created his own Tokens. Both contingents are still performing in the 1990s, and feeling the benefits of 1994's smash film *The Lion King* featuring (what else!) "The Lion Sleeps Tonight," which became a hit again in 1995.

IKE AND TINA TURNER

Ike Turner: Guitar/vocals
Born: 11/5/31, Clarksdale, MS
Tina Turner (Anna Mae Bullock): Lead vocals
Born: 11/26/38, Brownsville, TN
Influences: (Ike) Pine Top Perkins, Louis Jordan, Sonny Boy Williamson; (Tina) LaVern Baker

Ike and Tina Turner's Revue was a most electrifying musical experience. But, as individuals, Ike and Tina were like two ships headed in opposite directions through much of their lives. When Ike first became an established bandleader, Tina was not long removed from picking cotton in the fields of Tennessee. Thirty years later, Tina was a top

rock 'n' roll star and Ike had fallen to relative obscurity.

In 1937, six-year-old Ike chopped wood for an old lady in exchange for being allowed to play her piano. When he got his own piano, he quickly taught himself to play, and by 11 he was backing blues artists like Sonny Boy Williamson in clubs. During high school he formed The Kings of Rhythm band. In April 1951, Ike and company recorded "Rocket 88" at Sun Studios in Memphis. When Chess released the record, they renamed the act Jackie Brenston and The Delta Cats; Jackie was Ike's saxophonist and vocalist.

Rocket "88" 83–83–83–83
Brentson chanted a jumping boogie woogie paean to his convertible with band swinging excitingly in back.

Come Back Where You Belong .76–76–76–76
Leader chants a sob-voiced blues to a teasing, slow-dragging backing. Lots of feeling in chanting and playing. (5/5/51) (#1 R&B)

"Rocket 88" has since been elevated to legendary status, considered by many to have been the first rock 'n' roll record. Despite that, Turner only saw $40 for writing, performing, and producing it. Soon after, Brenston went solo and drifted into obscurity. Meanwhile, Ike became a proficient guitarist and talent scout for L.A.'s Modern Records. Among the artists he played with and recommended to Modern were B. B. King and Howlin' Wolf.

By 1956, The Kings of Rhythm were a hot band and always well received at St. Louis's Club Manhattan. It was there that Turner met two Tennessee sisters, Alline and Anna Mae Bullock. Anna asked Ike if she could sing with the band but he showed no interest. Both girls had sung in gospel groups and talent shows since childhood. One evening, Ike's drummer jokingly handed Alline the mike. When she shied away, Anna Mae, who had never performed professionally in her 18 years, grabbed it, jumped on stage, and sang. Soon after, she became a member of the band and, by 1958, Mrs. Ike Turner. Ike then suggested a first name change as well, and so Anna Mae became Tina Turner.

Their first recording as Ike and Tina was strictly a stroke of fate. In 1960, a session singer failed to show, and so Tina filled in singing "A

Fool in Love." It was a surprise R&B and pop success.

A Fool in Love.

★ ★   *A bluesy rocker. The chanter use a touch of gospel style in the screaming passages.*

The Way You Love Me.

★ ★   *Another bluesy side. Chick's vocal delivery shows promise if channelled. (8/1/69) (#27 Pop, #2 R&B)*

Their initial success inspired several follow ups through 1962.

Letter from Tina/I Idolize You.

"Letter from Tina" is a showmanly item featuring a good teen-slanted lyric and strong narration by Tina. Flip spotlights an exuberant thrushing stint by the gal on an emotion-packed tune with catchy Latin tempo. "Letter" has a slight edge. (11/14/60) (B-side, #82 Pop, #2 R&B)

It's Gonna Work Out Fine.

★ ★ ★ ★ *Ike and Tina talk about love on this attractive disk which also features a gospel-styled chorus. Pair handle this tune with gusto and it has a chance. (6/19/61) (#14 Pop, #2 R&B)*

(Actually, the "chorus" was singers Mickey and Sylvia!)

You Can't Blame Me.

The catchy rhythm-rocker is sung by the duo with sock showmanship and verve. A strong dual market side with r.&b. appeal as well as pop. Flip is "Poor Fool." (11/13/61) (#38 Pop, #4 R&B)

Tra La La La La.

★ ★ ★ ★ *Ike and Tina sell this wild side with enthusiasm over uninhibited backing by group and ork. Could get exposure especially on r.&b. stations. (3/17/62) (#50 Pop, #9 R&B)*

The duo then dropped from the charts for a while, although they continued to record and tour. In 1966, Phil Spector saw Tina perform and was so impressed with her power that he offered Ike

$20,000 to stay out of the studio while Phil produced her. The result, "River Deep-Mountain High," was one of the most awesome recordings ever made. Although a hit in England, its failure stateside so disturbed Spector that he folded his label shortly thereafter and retired from producing for three years. In effect, it became his last "wall of sound" masterpiece.

River Deep-Mountain High.

Exciting dance beat production backs a wailin' Tina vocal on a solid rock tune penned by Barry and Greenwich. (5/21/66) (#88 Pop)

After the failure of the single, the duo once again dropped off the charts. However, they made another comeback three years later, beginning with "I've Been Loving You Too Long."

I've Been Loving You Too Long.

This wild and raucous swinger with a hard driving slow beat is certain to climb high on the Hot 100 as well as a top r&b item. Watch out for this one! (4/19/69) (#68 Pop, #23 R&B)

During 1970, they moved to Liberty for their greatest pop success, "I Want to Take You Higher." The duo would be well-remembered for their covers of 1960s' rock classics, including John Fogerty's "Proud Mary," which became their signature tune.

I Want to Take You Higher.

The number causing a sensation in the film, "Woodstock" gets a powerhouse delivery by the dynamic duo with much chart appeal . . . both soul and pop. (5/16/70) (#34 Pop, #25 R&B)

Proud Mary.

The [John] Fogerty classic gets a powerhouse treatment with the Turner originality and drive to put it right back up the Hot 100 and soul charts. Dynamite entry. (1/23/71) (#4 Pop, #5 R&B)

In 1975, Tina acted in her first movie role in The Who's *Tommy* playing The Acid Queen. By the mid 1970s, the strain of their marriage had reached its peak. Their last chart 45 together was "Baby, Get It On" (#88 Pop, #31 R&B, 1975). That same year, amid rumors of drunken beatings by Ike, Tina suddenly quit a tour in Dallas. Fortified with a gasoline credit card and the clothes she was wearing, Tina called friend Ann-Margret, who sent her a one-way plane ticket to Los Angeles, where Tina hid in the actor's house for six months.

In 1976, Tina and Ike were divorced and Tina began a grueling performance pace for several years, hoping to get back in the public eye. In 1982, her new manager, former Australian promoter Roger Davies, signed Tina with Capitol and she had her first hit in nine years with a smoldering version of Al Green's "Let's Stay Together" (#26 Pop, #3 R&B, 1984). Follow ups like "What's Love Got to Do with It" (#1 Pop, #2 R&B) and "Better Be Good to Me" (#5 Pop, #6 R&B) established her new role as a 46-year-old superstar.

Tina Turner:
Private Dancer.

Relatively quiet tune conceals the sharp edges in both a grim storyline and the singer's smoldering growl; fourth release from her platinum LP. (1/12/85) (#7 Pop, #3 R&B)

Her 1985 Grammys for "What's Love Got to Do with It" (Record and Song of the Year, Best Female Vocal Performance), "Better" (Best Female Rock Vocal), and her role in the film *Mad Max: Beyond Thunderdome* made for a spectacular year. In 1988, while Tina was performing in Rio at The Marcana Arena before the largest audience ever to see a single artist (180,000 people!), Ike was being sentenced to one year in jail for possessing and transporting cocaine. Tina has continued to record and act in movies, although with less success than in her mid-1980s heyday.

THE TURTLES

Howard Kaplan: Vocals
Born: 6/22/47, New York City
Mark Volman: Vocals/saxophone/guitar
Born: 4/19/47, Los Angeles, CA
Al Nichol: Guitar
Born: 3/31/46, Winston Salem, NC
Jim Tucker: Guitar
Born: 10/17/46, Los Angeles, CA
Chuck Portz: Bass
Born: 3/28/45, Santa Monica, CA
Don Murray: Drums
Born: 1940s
Influences: Elvis Presley, Beatles, Zombies, Johnny and The Hurricanes, Bob Dylan, Chantels, Louis Prima, Broadway shows, B. Bumble and The Stingers
Influenced: Gary Lewis and The Playboys, Orpheus, Cowsills, Mojo Men, Cryan' Shames

One of the most popular folk-rock bands of the late 1960s, The Turtles rejected one hit-to-be while achieving stardom with a song nobody wanted.

Beginning in 1963 as an instrumental and surf band in L.A.'s Westchester High School, the group called themselves The Nightriders, then The Crossfires. The band was already together when Volman, who didn't play an instrument, joined. Instead, he played tambourine, helped with the equipment, and sang a little, all for $5 a night. Feeling underpaid, he learned to play alto saxophone and soon became a legitimate contributor. Their first single, "Fiberglass Jungle" (Capco, 1963), went by the wayside as did their second, "That'll Be the Day" (Lucky Charm, 1964).

In 1965, Jim Tucker came aboard and The Crossfires became the house band at KRLA deejay Reb Foster's Revalaire Club in Redondo Beach. To keep working, they traversed the trends, going from surf music to imitating British invasion groups to folk and electrified folk. After six months at The Revalaire, Foster (now managing them) received word of the group's intended breakup. He quickly invited two ex-Liberty

Records distributors (Ted Feigen and Lee Laseff) to see the act, and they signed The Crossfires for their new White Whale label. Asked by Ted and Lee to change their name, The Crossfires' affection for Brit groups led them to consider the name Six Pence. Foster, however, liked The Tyrtles (like The Byrds), which became The Turtles.

With a new name and a new musical direction (they were now folk rockers), the group began scouring Bob Dylan's songbook. They came up with "It Ain't Me Babe" (#8, 1965). The Turtles quickly picked the P. F. Sloan song "Let Me Be" (#29) for their next 45, while refusing Sloan's "Eve of Destruction," which became Barry McGuire's only hit.

You Baby.

Chalk up a third straight winner for the hot group. This rocker with a surfin' sound in the vocal is from the pen of Sloan and Barry. (1/22/66) (#20 Pop)

Grim Reaper of Love.

Unusual lyric ballad rouser . . . strong dance beat backing. (5/28/66) (#81 Pop)

In June 1966, Murray quit, replaced by John Barbata. It was the first of a series of changes that would leave only Volman, Kaplan (now Kaylan), and Nichol as constants. While playing New York's Phone Booth, the band was approached by songwriters Alan Gordon and Gary Bonner with a tape. Their song had been cashiered by everyone who listened, and the tape was so worn it was barely distinguishable. Still, The Turtles heard something and recorded "Happy Together" (after 15 tries). With the follow up winner, "She'd Rather Be with Me" (#3), The Turtles found themselves as the darlings of "good time pop rock."

Happy Together.

Group scored high with their "It Ain't Me, Babe" and this groovy folk-oriented item could repeat that success. Joe Wissert's production is tops. (1/28/67) (#1 Pop)

She's My Girl.

In their long string of consecutive hits, the group can't miss with this intriguing rock material with well written lyric. This could be their biggest to date. (11/4/67) (#14 Pop)

Elenore.

With all the powerful sales ingredients of their hits such as "Happy Together," the quintet has one of their best to date in this swinger. Headed right to the top 10. (9/7/68) (#6 Pop)

You Showed Me.

The group changes pace with a smooth, easy-beat rhythm ballad that has all of the sales power of their last smash. One of their best to date. (12/21/68) (#6 Pop)

On May 10, 1969, The Turtles played The White House courtesy of Tricia Nixon; stories of Volman and Kaylan snorting cocaine on Abraham Lincoln's desk still abound. Meanwhile, Volman and Kaylan's unusual musical tastes began to manifest themselves in more offbeat songs.

You Don't Have to Walk in the Rain.

The Turtles continue their hit making with this smooth rock ballad with much of the sales appeal of their recent "You Showed Me" smash. Exceptional Ray Davies production work. (5/24/69) (#51 Pop)

Who Would Ever Think That I Would Marry Margaret.

This is the clever rhythm item the group needed to bring them back to a high spot on the Hot 100. Watch this one—it grows on you and will prove a big one. (3/7/70)

During 1970, the group split up owing to internal conflict and strife over royalties due from White Whale. Ironically, their last chart 45 was the one they could have had a hit with if they'd picked it five years earlier.

Eve of Destruction.

The past hit of Barry McGuire is updated by the Turtles and the commercial appeal is there for chart action. (5/30/70) (#100 Pop)

Mark and Howard then linked with Frank Zappa's Mothers of Invention and became prominent backup vocalists for Bruce Springsteen, T-Rex, Blondie, Alice Cooper, and John Lennon. After several albums with Zappa and an appearance in his movie, *200 Motels*, the duo formed Phlorescent Leech and Eddie, soon abbreviated to Flo and Eddie. Their varied pursuits at that time included a column for the lovelorn in the *Los Angeles Free Press,* a column in *Phonogram* magazine for blind dates, and a radio show in L.A. called "Flo and Eddie by the Fireside." In 1975, their Columbia album featured a new version of "Elenore." Starting in 1982, partially because Rhino Records reissued their entire catalog, a new Turtles toured the country featuring Flo (Mark) and Eddie (Howard).

RITCHIE VALENS

Real Name: Richard Valenzuela
Birthdate: 5/13/41
Birthplace: Pacoima, CA
Died: 2/3/59
Influences: Chuck Berry, Bo Diddley, Little Richard, Duane Eddy
Influenced: Santana, Neil Diamond, Los Lobos, Eddie Quinteros, Chris Montez, Cannibal and The Headhunters, Sunny and The Sunglows

An artist whose recording career only lasted 135 days (from his first chart record until his death), Ritchie Valens was a major influence on, and ground breaker for, Chicano rockers from the 1950s' Eddie Quinteros to the 1970s' Santana and the 1980s' Los Lobos.

Born of Mexican and Indian parents, Valens grew up on Latin and rock rhythms in his home 14 miles west of Los Angeles. By the age of 15, he had crafted his own solid-body electric guitar and, in 1957, joined a Mexican band, The Silhouettes, featuring a Japanese sax player. Valens's big break came in May 1958 when he performed at the American Legion hall in San Fernando City. Del-Fi Records owner Bob Keene had been informed by a local printer who worked for Del-Fi that a hot new talent was appearing locally. Keene came away from the concert so impressed that he immediately signed the 17-year-old boy. For mainstream acceptability, he shortened the singer's name to Valens.

Valens's first recording session featured a tune that did not yet have a lyric, so Valens made up the words as he went along. It became, "Come On, Let's Go." Valens's first tour included a performance on American Bandstand. When he returned home in October, he wrote a song for his high school sweetheart, Donna Ludwig, called simply "Donna." It was coupled with an old Mexican party song sung in Spanish titled "La Bamba." Ritchie then quit school to go on tour.

Come On, Let's Go.

Ritchie, a new artist, has an effective approach on the rocker. Supported by good r&r backing, he delivers the catchy tune which he cleffed himself in a saleable manner. It's a fine debut disk, and the lad appears to have a winner with this first attempt. Flip is "Framed." (9/1/58) (#42 Pop, #27 R&B)

Donna/La Bamba.

The cat, who is still scoring with "Come On, Let's Dance [sic]," could have a two-sided click with his latest effort. Top side is a ballad with beat that is warbled to good effect over listenable ork support. Flip is a Latin-tinged rocker that can also come in for a fair share of coin. (11/17/58) (A-side, #2 Pop, #11 R&B; B-side, #22 Pop)

"Donna" charted on November 24 at #93. By December, Valens had appeared in Alan Freed's film *Go, Johnny, Go!* singing "Oh, Oh My Head." He also did a concert at his old school, Pacoima Junior High, on December 5 that was taped by Keene (and later issued as a posthumous album). "Donna" was now #55. "La Bamba" charted on December 29, the same time Ritchie was performing at Freed's Christmas show in New York with The Everly Brothers and Eddie Cochran ("Donna" was now #18).

In January 1959, Valens recorded numerous sides in Los Angeles and then joined the tragically memorable "Winter Dance Party" tour with Dion and The Belmonts, Buddy Holly, and The Big Bopper. "Donna" had reached #4 by now. The show took them through the harshest, coldest winter the Midwest had seen in years and the constant breakdowns and heater failure of their bus didn't help. Finally, after a performance at

The Surf Ballroom in Clear Lake, Iowa, Holly decided to charter a plane so they could reach their next show in Fargo, North Dakota. Valens, eager for his first flight in a small plane, convinced guitarist Tommy Alsup to flip Ritchie's shiny 50-cent piece for the seat. Valens called heads, and he won his ill-fated spot in history.

The plane crashed shortly after its late-night takeoff in horrendous weather and all aboard died, including The Big Bopper, Buddy Holly, and Valens. "Donna" was #3 and had been since January 26. On February 23, four weeks after being #3, it peaked at #2 behind Lloyd Price's "Stagger Lee," selling over a million copies. "Little Girl" was Ritchie's last charter, issued five months after his death. After that, the label issued a few more singles to little response.

That's My Little Suzie/In a Turkish Town.

The late artist has two powerful efforts that should appeal to his fans. "Suzie" is a rocker in the rockabilly tradition that really moves. "Turkish Town" has a slight Oriental flavor and it's given soft chant with quiet ork backing. (3/23/59) (#55 Pop)

Little Girl.

The late artist's newest platter should catch strong play. "Little Girl" is a medium-beat rocker that is done up in good style. . . . Disk is part of a series of special memorial releases on the artist. (6/1/59)

Stay Beside Me.

Ritchie Valens sells the pretty tune over simple, strummed guitar backing with a chorus filling in late on the side. It's a good side and a likely click for the late artist. (10/19/59)

Paddiwack Song/Cry, Cry, Cry.

The late artist rocks and rolls exuberantly on "Paddiwack Song," a rocking treatment of the "Children's Marching Song." "Cry" is an insistent blues that is expressively sung. (2/22/60)

In 1987, Taylor Hackford's film biography *La Bamba*, starring Lou Diamond Phillips as Valens, with music by Santana and Los Lobos, resurrected the Valens legacy. The latter's hits of "La Bamba" (#1) and "Come On, Let's Go" (#21) from the film

showed a whole new generation what it was like to be the first Chicano rock star.

BOBBY VEE

Real Name: Robert Thomas Velline
Birthdate: 4/30/43
Birthplace: Fargo, ND
Influences: Buddy Holly and The Crickets, Elvis Presley, Hank Williams, Fats Domino, Everly Brothers, Eddie Cochran, Jerry Lee Lewis, Ronnie Hawkins

One of the 1960s' most-enduring teen idols, Bobby Vee's career began the day his idol, Buddy Holly, died.

Just two weeks before the first rock 'n' roll concert in Fargo, North Dakota, Bobby Velline, his brother Bill, and friends Jim Stillmen and Bob Korum formed a band called The Shadows. Fifteen-year-old Bobby learned guitar from another brother, Sidney. Excitedly anticipating the great event of February 3, 1959, the group was shocked and saddened to hear that the plane carrying Ritchie Valens, The Big Bopper, and Bobby's favorite, Buddy Holly, had crashed, killing all aboard. KFGO radio, Fargo's Top-40 station, sent out a call for a local act to perform that night and help fill the void. The Shadows of Central High School were the second act to appear (the opening act was Terry Lee and The Poor Boys), singing "Long Tall Sally" and "Bye Bye Love" and, as luck would have it, their impressive 15-minute showing (which they performed for free) caught the eye of promoter Bing Bingstrom, who was sitting in the "Winter Dance Party" audience.

On February 14, The Shadows earned their first $60 playing a Valentine's Day dance. By June, armed with a Velline tune, "Suzy Baby," The Shadows produced their own session at Soma Studios in Minneapolis. The Soma label issued the single under Bobby's then-shortened name, Bobby Vee and The Shadows. The record became a local success, and the band decided to fatten its sound by adding a piano player who went by the name of Elston Gunn. Elston (whose real name was Bob Zimmerman) lasted through only two shows because his playing was limited, so the band paid him $30 and let him go. Don't cry for Elston, however; he changed his name again and went on to make a decent living as a folk-rocker named Bob Dylan.

Meanwhile, play from a San Diego station resulted in Liberty buying the initial single's master from Soma for national release. The Shadows' name was omitted from the *Billboard* review, which was credited to Vee alone.

Suzie Baby.

★ ★ ★   *Vee sings this Latinish rocker softly over prominent guitar support. Side might attract, if plugged.*

Flyin' High.

★ ★ ★   *Rocker spotlights tangy guitars over driving combo support. Danceable item can move. (8/10/59) (#77 Pop)*

Vee's second single was a cover of an Adam Faith U.K. hit, "What Do You Want," which was Holly-influenced. In effect, Vee was copying someone who was copying his favorite artist!

What Do You Want.

★ ★   *Vee is a rocker who has traces of Buddy Holly in his approach. Here he sings to rocking string backing. Listenable. (2/1/60) (#93 Pop)*

Snuff Garrett, Liberty's producer, then took Vee to Norman Petty's studio (where most of Buddy Holly's hits were cut) and had him record old R&B songs, much to Vee's displeasure. The B-side of his next single, however, put him on the map, a cover of an old Clovers' hit.

Since I Met You Baby.

The warbler wraps up the pretty Ivory Joe Hunter oldie in a relaxed, satisfying vocal with effective violin work on backing. Flip is a tasteful rocker, "Devil or Angel." (7/18/60) (A-side, #81 Pop; B-side, #6 Pop)

Bobby's next smash was (according to the label) written by a middle-aged lady named Anne Orlowski, but in reality, was penned by her son, Gene Pitney. His name didn't appear on the record because of the shady maneuvering of his publisher, Aaron Schroeder.

Rubber Ball/Everyday.

Vee turns in a smash reading on an attractive item with amazing lyrics. Flip is the old Buddy Holly hit, featuring a strong vocal airing. Both sides are potent. (11/21/60) (#6 Pop)

Stayin' In/More Than I Can Say.

On top is a hot rhythm item, penned by John Loudermilk and much in the teen groove. Flip features effective dual-channel chanting. Both have a chance to go. (1/30/61) (A-side, #33; B-side, #61 Pop)

In a rare West Coast show, Alan Freed presented Vee, The Shirelles, Jerry Lee Lewis, and Brenda Lee at the Hollywood Bowl on June 25, 1961. That same month, Garrett returned from New York with a new Carole King/Gerry Goffin song, "Take Good Care of My Baby," that had been recorded by Dion but not released. So Garrett cut it with Vee, giving him his biggest winner. Vee made his U.K. tour debut with Tony Orlando and Gary U.S. Bonds. He achieved one of his dreams by recording an entire album of Buddy Holly's material in tribute to the fallen star, backed by Holly's own band, The Crickets. Meanwhile, the chart hits continued through 1962.

Take Good Care of My Baby.

Vee swings on an effect duo-track vocal treatment of . . . a catchy rhythm-rocker. (7/31/61) (#1 Pop)

Walkin' with My Angel/Run to Him.

Here's another two sided hit for chart-topper Bobby Vee. "Angel" is a catchy tune with an infectious beat sold solidly by the lad; flip is an interesting ballad about self sacrifices. Strong wax. (11/6/61) (A-side, #53; B-side, #2 Pop)

Please Don't Ask About Barbara.

A plaintive ballad . . . sung with tenderness and feeling. (2/17/62) (#15 Pop)

Sharing You.

Spotlights a feelingful unison multi-track vocal on a romantic theme that builds with bolero-like intensity. (5/12/62) (#15 Pop)

Anonymous Phone Calls/The Night Has a Thousand Eyes.

Bobby Vee has an intriguing lyric and title here that could perk up teen ears, showcased in a smart arrangement. Tune tells of how the lad discovered his gal was two-timing him, and it's done with strings and chorus. Flip is a romper in the old Vee fashion with solid chorus and ork. (11/24/62) (B-side, #3 Pop)

About that time, he appeared in his first film, 20th Century Fox's *Swingin' Along*, singing "More Than I Can Say." He also appeared in the U.K. film *Play It Cool* and Columbia's *Just for Fun* (singing Ben Weisman's "The Night Has a Thousand Eyes"). Meanwhile, the disks kept coming, but the British invasion of 1963–1964 put a damper on his chart success. "Charms" was his last Top-20 hit until 1967.

Charms.

Cute piece of material which he sells in his own lively fashion, aided by solid support from chorus and ork. (3/23/63) (#13 Pop)

A Letter from Betty/Be True to Yourself.

On top is a first rate piece of material about a Dear John letter, which he sells with emotion. Side II is another fine, up-tempo ballad, which also receives a sock reading from the chanter. Both have it. (6/8/63) (A-side, #85 Pop; B-side, #34 Pop)

Stranger in Your Arms.

Vee sticks to his double-tracked off-key singing on this up-tempo ballad, supported closely by chorus and big orchestra. Side should register big with tone-deaf teeners. (1/18/64) (#83 Pop)

I'll Make You Mine.

This coupling, featuring a Beatles kind of touch, could . . . go. Either way here. (2/8/64) (#52 Pop)

Ironically, while Vee's U.S. popularity was hurt by the young British bands, he remained very popular in Britain. Vee toured the United Kingdom in 1964 with The Rolling Stones and did a British-styled album called *Bobby Vee Sings the New Sound from England,* including "She's Sorry," a clone of The Beatles' "She Loves You." Even Beatles producer George Martin became involved in Vee's career, producing the single "Keep on Trying" (#85) in 1965. In 1967, he hit with his fourth and last million seller, "Come Back When You Grow Up" (#3). Bobby's last chart 45 was "Sweet Sweetheart."

In 1972, Vee once again became Robert Thomas Velline for an LP (*Nothin' Like a Sunny Day*), featuring a slowed version of "Take Good Care of My Baby." Through the 1980s and 1990s, Bobby remained active on the nostalgia and club circuit.

GENE VINCENT

Real Name: Eugene Vincent Craddock
Birthdate: 2/11/35
Birthplace: Norfolk, VA
Died: 10/12/71
Influences: Elvis Presley
Influenced: Tommy James and The Shondells, Paul Revere and The Raiders, Ian Dury

Gene Vincent was one of several early rock 'n' roll comets whose musical fireworks were spectacular, although short-lived.

Probably one of the few rock pioneers whose mother not only encouraged his musical career but suggested he pursue it, Gene was in need of direction after returning from the Korean War in 1955 as an injured Navy man. The loss of his leg and replacement with an artificial limb put him in a Norfolk hospital where he and another patient, Donald Graves, wrote a song about a hip comic book character named Little Lulu titled, "Be-Bop-a-Lula."

By 1956, Vincent was a regular visitor to local radio station WCMS, where he sporadically jammed with the station's band, The Virginians. Deejay Tex Davis heard Vincent perform "Be-Bop" and arranged a demo session. The tape was sent to Capitol Records, who were looking for their own version of Elvis Presley. Vincent fit the bill and on May 4, 1956, "Be-Bop," a Vincent original, "Women Love," and two other tunes were recorded at famous country music producer Owen Bradley's studio in Nashville. Backing was supplied by drummer Dick Harrell, bass player Jack Neal, and guitarists Willie Williams and Cliff Gallup, who became known as The Blue Caps. (They were named after the identifying blue golf caps they wore courtesy of President Eisenhower's famous cap.)

Vincent's first single's A-side was "Women Love," but its sexual overtones caused deejays to flip the 45 for "Be-Bop-a-Lula." The "Money Honey" (Drifters, 1953)-styled rocker sounded so much like Elvis that when Gladys Presley heard it on the radio, she complimented her son on his newest hit. The label's songwriting credit read Vincent and Davis, as Graves's involvement was bought out for a paltry $25 before its release.

Woman Love (A-side) **78**
[Capitol's] entry in the general scramble to find another Presley. This side is a blues, in the extreme high-tension style popular currently.

Be-Bop-a-Lula (B-side) **77**
Another blues in the same extreme style—this one additionally gimmicked with echo. (6/2/56) (#7 Pop)

The unexpected B-side hit led Capitol to rush out a second single, "Blue Jean Bop."

"Be-Bop-a-Lula" created a big market for Vincent, and it is proving very receptive to his new release. Boston, Providence, New York, Philadelphia, Pittsburgh, St. Louis, Nashville and Milwaukee are among the cities indicating excellent sales. As before, c&w customers are as enthusiastic as pop buyers. Its chart potential in both areas is good. Flip is "Who Slapped John?" a previous Billboard *"Spotlight" pick. (10/27/56) (#49 Pop)*

By year's end, Gene and the Blue Caps had appeared in the hit film *The Girl Can't Help It* performing "Be-Bop."

In early 1957, Capitol issued a "Be-Bop" clone, with another stuttering, hyphenated title, but the song failed to chart. In mid-1957, Gene's second biggest hit was another B-side, "Lotta Lovin'."

B-I-Bickey-Bi, Bo-Bo-Go **82**
Another rock and roller a la ["Be-Bop-a-Lula"]: for Vincent, with possibilities in both pop and c.&w. markets. A loud, lively side that could click despite the sameness of the material. (4/6/57)

Wear My Ring.
Pretty rhythm ballad with excellent guitar support is rendered with feeling. Good teen stuff.

Lotta Lovin'.
This is the strongest for the artist since "Be-Bop-a-Lula." The bright rocker shows the artist in top form with a solid delivery that should attract plays. (7/8/57) (#13 Pop)

In a rare move, Capitol reissued the single a month later, inverting the A- and B-sides, and *Billboard* spotlighted "Lotta Lovin'" again.

All the top country markets report heavy sales and it's also doing well in the pop markets. (8/12/57)

In September, Eddie Cochran, Little Richard, and Vincent toured Australia. Little did the black leather-clad rocker realize that a mere year and a half after his first hit, he would have his last, at least in America.

Dance to the Bop.
Vincent, who is still riding high with "Lotta Lovin'," has another powerful side . . . The rockabilly effort features listenable guitar support to back the strong vocal. (10/28/57) (#23 Pop)

More singles followed through 1958, but Vincent's chart-making days were over.

Baby Blue **80**
Gene Vincent can regain his winning ways with this sock reading of a funky blues effort. He sells it powerfully and the backing is low down. This can happen. (4/21/58)

Rock Road Blues ....**.79**

> *Feelingful vocal by Vincent on rockabilly blues with fast, zestful beat and solid piano solo work. (7/14/58)*

Git It ....**.76**

> *This starts with a deep bass intro—similar to some of r.&b. field. It's a rocker with a rather inane lyric. It's the echoey sound here that gets the attention. Can get spins.*

Little Lover ....**.74**

> *Vincent adopts the Buddy Holly hiccup style on this snappy up-beater in the rocking groove. Moderate potential. (9/15/58)*

Over the Rainbow.

> *Vincent has his strongest side in quite a spell. . . . Feelingful rockabilly chant of the oldie. (2/23/59)*

In June 1959, Vincent, with a totally new Blue Caps, became one of the first rock acts to tour Japan. Still, his records were going nowhere, as U.S. radio was softening its output. Vincent then accepted promoter Larry Parnes's invitation to move to England where early American rockers were still idolized. He became a regular on TV producer Jack Good's "Boy Meets Girl" in December 1959.

Right Here on Earth.

★ ★ ★ ★ *Gene Vincent comes thru with a sock reading of a rocking effort helped solidly by a chorus and pounding rhythm section. His fans will enjoy. (12/7/59) (#21 Pop [U.K.])*

On April 17, 1960, Gene was injured again, this time in a car crash on the way to London's airport. Killed in the accident was his close friend, Eddie Cochran. His next single, "Pistol Packin' Mama," was recorded at EMI's Abbey Road Studio in London with backing by Georgie Fame (piano) and The Beat Boys.

Pistol Packin' Mama.

★ ★ ★ *The novelty standard gets a smart go, with the vocal abetted by a bright effort on the part of the horns and other instrumentalists. (9/12/60) (#15 Pop [U.K.])*

1961 saw Vincent's final British hits "She, She Little Sheila" (#22) and "I'm Going Home" (#36). He also appeared in the U.K. film *It's Trad, Dad!* in 1962.

In 1969, after short stays on Dandelion, Challenge, Playground, and Forever Records, Vincent became the subject of the BBC documentary, "The Rock and Roll Singer." His last singles came from Kama Sutra in a country vein. Gene's constant ill health, lack of hits, and four failed marriages, not to mention heavy drinking, contributed to the bleeding ulcer that took his life in Newhall, California, at the age of 36.

Twenty-five single releases just don't sum up this hard-luck rocker whose music is still popular today.

BILLY WARD AND THE DOMINOES

Clyde McPhatter: Lead vocals (1950–1953)
Born: 11/15/33, Durham, NC (died 6/13/72)
Jackie Wilson: Lead vocals (1953–1957)
Born: 6/9/34, Detroit, MI (died 1/21/84)
Eugene Mumford: Lead vocals (1957–1958)
Born: Durham, NC
Charlie White: Tenor
Born: 1930s
Joe Lamont: Baritone
Born: 1930s
Bill Brown: Bass
Born: 1930s
Billy Ward: Piano
Born: 1920s, Los Angeles, CA
Influences: Ink Spots, Ravens, Swan Silvertones, Mills Brothers, Five Blind Boys, Orioles, Deep River Boys, Delta Rhythm Boys, Joe Van Loon
Influenced: Dells, Diablos, Five Satins, Flamingos, Jackie Wilson, Dell-Vikings, Isley Brothers, Frankie Lymon and The Teenagers, Marcels, El Doradoes, Maurice Williams and The Gladiolas, Silhouettes

One of the legendary founding fathers among R&B groups, Billy Ward and the Dominoes boasted three of history's greatest lead singers, Clyde McPhatter, Jackie Wilson, and Eugene Mumford.

Founder Billy Ward moved to Philadelphia in his teens with his preacher father and choir-member mother. At age 14, his classical composition, "Dejection," won a citywide competition. He later enrolled at New York's prestigious Juilliard School of Music and upon graduation became an arranger and vocal coach. Ward formed a short-lived vocal group but their unreliability convinced him to create a quartet out of his best students, including Clyde Ward, Charlie White, Joe Lamont, Bill Brown, and himself on piano and occasional tenor.

Contrary to legend, the group never called themselves the Ques. According to Ward, he had seen a pop mixed-race group (The Mariners) on Arthur Godfrey's show. He thought an R&B group with two black and two white members (like The Dominoes!) would be a great idea. Booking agents dissuaded him, but when he created his all-black group, he called them The Dominoes anyway. As for the rumor that he named the young McPhatter, Clyde Ward, Billy stated, "Clyde called himself that."

In 1950, The Dominoes handily won the Apollo Theater's Amateur Night Contest singing gospel, which led to a winning night on Arthur Godfrey's "Talent Scouts." That led to their signing with King/Federal Records and their first single, "Do Something for Me." The group's unique merger of gospel and blues differentiated them from almost every other act.

Do Something for Me 76–76–74–78
A new group, sporting a wheezing, note-bending lead voice who phrases a la Ruth Brown, lends a winning performance to a rather fetching blues. (1/20/51) (#6 R&B)

One of the most definitive and enduring of R&B hits was their fourth single, "Sixty Minute Man" (#1 R&B, 14 weeks). A million seller, the Bill Brown-led rocker spent 30 weeks on the R&B charts and was the first vocal group R&B side to chart pop (#17). The midsection of one of their next singles, "That's What You're Doing to Me," appeared three years later (note for note) in The Moonglows' hit "Sincerely." By 1951's end, White and Brown left, replaced by David McNeil (Larks) and James Van Loon.

Harbor Lights 76–77–75–75
Group does the revival winningly, with a note-bending tenor lead. (2/24/51)

That's What You're Doing to Me ....
80–80–80–80
The boys pound out a rousing, hand-clapper in another effective chanting job (3/15/52)

The group scored their second #1 R&B hit with their next B-side release, "Have Mercy, Baby." It was followed by more hits, with the group now credited as "Billy Ward and the Dominoes"; *Billboard* mistakenly credited Ward as the lead singer, when in fact McPhatter held that chair.

Deep Sea Blues 81–82–80–81
This is one of the best sides turned out by the group in some time. The slow blues has a spiritual-like feel and should get action.

Have Mercy, Baby 80–80–80–80
This side is a rocking, hand-clapper which the boys deliver in fine style. Excellent, fade-out gimmick adds interest. (4/26/52) (B-side, #1 R&B)

Billy Ward and the Dominoes. "I'd Be Satisfied" 82
Sparked by the bright lead singing of Ward, the Dominoes turn in a swingy, bouncy reading of a spiritual-type item, over a mighty strong ork backing. A solid platter that could pull coin. (10/18/52) (#8 R&B)

The Bells 80
This is an unusual side, could be a big one for the group. It bears watching. Sad blues includes a crying jag as the lad tells the story of his sweetheart's funeral.

Pedal Pushin' Papa 76
Ward's group, as usual, delivers a solid reading of the material. The gimmick here is in the lyrics of the ditty. Should do well for the group. (12/20/52) (A-side, #3 R&B; B-side, #4 R&B)

These Foolish Things Remind Me of You . . 84
> *Billy Ward and his Dominoes have a potent waxing here and one that could easily break thru for the big loot. The group performs the evergreen in meaningful style with Ward turning in a solid lead vocal and the bass adding some cute vocal effects. It's a mighty strong side by the boys. (5/9/53) (#5 R&B)*

"These Foolish Things" turned out to be McPhatter's last lead for The Dominoes. Low pay and a desire for his own group convinced him to leave after a show in Providence, Rhode Island. He then formed the now-legendary Drifters. Ward found his replacement, not at Detroit's Fox Theater during an audition as numerous publications have claimed, but at a hotel near the Michigan State Fair. An elderly lady, according to Ward, was looking for him in the lobby with her son in tow. The boy was a singer and she wanted him to vocalize for Ward. The boy was Jackie Wilson.

Wilson's first single with The Dominoes, "You Can't Keep a Good Man Down," soon followed. The quartet's biggest Wilson-led hit was "Rags to Riches." By late 1953, King began issuing Dominoes sides in a pop vein while the King-subsidiary label, Federal, released the group's R&B sides.

You Can't Keep a Good Man Down 82
> *The Dominoes have a good side here, and one that should grab a lot of juke coins. It's a wild, bouncy effort and the boys sing it in exciting fashion, full of handclapping and shouting and a solid beat by the ork. The boys have had more powerful sides in the past, but this one should do well in the market. (7/18/53) (#8 R&B)*

Rags to Riches 87
> *The Dominoes come thru with a wonderful reading of the big pop hit, sparked by an outstanding performance by the mellifluous lead singer. It's truly a potent side, one that could easily be one of their biggest hits to date. Watch this one; it should break thru quickly. (11/7/53) (#2 R&B)*

Christmas in Heaven 74
> *Good seasonal item by the group should please its fans, but doesn't figure to be a smash in the market because of it's [sic] seasonal theme. (11/14/53)*

During 1954, the Dominoes' lineup was Wilson (lead), James Van Loon (tenor), Milton Merle (baritone), Cliff Givens (bass), and Ward.

Until the Real Thing Comes Along 83
> *Good choice of material. The vocal combo delivers the fine old standard for an effetively blended reading. Could move out quickly. (1/2/54)*

I'm Gonna Move to the Outskirts of Town.
> *This new slicing could be one of the Dominoes' biggest. An outstanding tenor handles the lead work on "Move," the ork hit of the 40's . . . (3/17/54)*

A Little Lie 76
> *The Dominoes, one of the country's top r.&b. groups, have a chance for pop action with this new release. The tune is a rhythmic effort and the group hands it a mighty solid reading, backing neatly by a combo. (4/3/54)*

Three Coins in the Fountain 83
> *A first-rate reading of the current pop hit, sung with warmth and much feeling . . . sparked by a strong lead singer. The boys do a mighty good job . . . and the disk could grab returns in the r.&b. field, tho it is a little late for much pop action. (6/12/54)*

Little Things Mean a Lot 79
> *The group covers the current hit tune here and comes up with a powerful offering that could pull in a lot of coins in both the r.&b. and pop fields. It is effectively harmonized and set to an easy, swingy beat. (7/10/54)*

Can't Do Sixty No More 73
> *A fair reading . . . of a solid new rocker . . . Material is weak, however, and the reference to "Sixty Minute Man" may*

stop it from getting some jockey spins. (2/19/55)

Even though the group was doing well (Ward signed a deal with the Sahara Hotel in Las Vegas for the then-astronomical sum of $5,000 a week), Billy and company bolted from King to sign a one-shot deal with Jubilee ("Sweethearts on Parade") in late 1955 and then moved to major-label Decca. King issued some back catalog material in September ("Over the Rainbow"). The group's first Decca release, "St. Therese of the Roses," showed them moving further in a popish direction.

Sweethearts on Parade 79
Here's a bright reading of the oldie. The arrangement emphasizes the march rhythm. Neat and uncommon r.&b. wax, could get good pop play. (8/22/55)

Over the Rainbow .75
A good one for deejay programming. The standard gets a dignified reading. Good sound. (9/24/55)

St. Therese of the Roses.
Ward and the boys wrap up a moving ballad with a strong spiritual flavor in a warmly, sincere reading. Ward is a particular standout on the solo. Disk should pull plenty of jockey and juke play. (6/16/56) (#13 Pop)

Rock, Plymouth Rock.
History gets drastically rewritten by Ward, all to little avail. It boils down to a routine rocker. Group has a regular following that undoubtedly will respond. (3/16/57)

September Song 73
A rhythmic, fleet-moving reading of the great standard. . . . This type of reading is unusual for the song—being heavily accented and swingy. (12/16/57)

In 1957, Wilson decided to go solo and went on to a brilliant career where he righteously earned the nickname "Mr. Excitement," singing hits like "Lonely Teardrops" and "Higher and Higher." The Dominoes then moved to Liberty and acquired the tremendous voice of Eugene Mumford, former front man for The Larks

(Apollo) and Serenaders (Whiz). He led them through their biggest hits, beginning with a reworking of the pop standard, "Stardust." However, their last charter was a radical style change as they hit with a cover of teen popsters Jan and Arnie's "Jennie Lee."

Stardust.
The Carmichael standard . . . is rendered in an interesting blend of lush strings and rock and roll beat. (5/27/57) (#12 Pop, #5 R&B)

To Each His Own 80
The standard is given a bright, medium-tempo styling . . . Similar treatment given "Stardust" was highly successful. (8/26/57)

Deep Purple.
The evergreen is given a sock approach by Ward with listenable support from the group. Similar treatment given "Stardust" was highly successful, and this attractive vocal stint against lush rhythm backing can also find favor. (9/2/57) (#20 Pop)

Jennie Lee.
Another frantic version of the Civil War ballad that is currently making the rounds by Jan and Arnie. It has the money sound, and could take off. (4/28/58) (#55 Pop)

By 1958, Mumford also opted for a solo career, but his never took off. In 1960, Ward et al. moved to ABC but the public's tastes had changed and The Dominoes were soon gone from the scene.

As of 1995, Billy Ward was still living in Los Angeles and, although their music lives on, the trendsetting Dominoes' immortal lead voices were forever stilled by 1984.

DIONNE WARWICK

Real Name: Marie Dionne Warwick
Birthdate: 12/12/40
Birthplace: East Orange, NJ
Influences: Cissy Houston, The Drinkard Singers, Alex Bradford

Among the most successful, long-term artist/writer collaborations in pop music is Dionne Warwick's hypnotic vocalizing to the words and music of songwriters supreme, Hal David and Burt Bacharach.

Dionne began her odyssey at six, singing in the choir of the New Baptist Church in Newark, New Jersey. She was surrounded by family talent, as her father (a former chef and train porter) was head of Chess Records' gospel promotion department while her mother managed the gospel act The Drinkard Singers, including Dee Dee Warwick (Dionne's sister), Emily "Cissy" Houston (her aunt and mother of Whitney Houston), and Judy Clay. Dionne sang and played piano for them and by 1960 had formed The Gospelaires with Cissy and Dee Dee. They sang backup on sessions starting with Bobby Darin and Nappy Brown.

By 1961, the trio was a quartet with the addition of Doris Troy ("Just One Look" #10, 1963). They sang on a number of Drifters records, starting with "Some Kind of Wonderful." Later that year, while working on a session for The Drifters' "Mexican Divorce," Dionne's vocal prowess came to the attention of the song's cowriter, Burt Bacharach, who asked her to make some demos for him and his new writing partner, Hal David. Singing behind The Shirelles and other Scepter acts such as Tommy Hunt and Chuck Jackson followed.

It was no surprise when she was signed by Scepter in 1962 and the incredible hit string began.

Don't Make Me Over.

★ ★ ★ ★ *Please don't try to change me, sings the lass on this side which also features an exceptional arrangement and strong support from the chorus. Thrush can sell a tune. (10/27/62) (#21 Pop, #5 R&B)*

Warwick's first big tour was in France where she became known as Paris's "Black Pearl." At her first Parisian concert, she was introduced by legendary actress, Marlene Dietrich. So great was the French ardor for her that in 1965 she devoted an entire album to *Dionne Warwick in Paris.* "Walk on By" was her first million seller.

Make the Music Play.

Dionne is back with a strong song here that's going to twist a lot of teen hearts. It's a flowing ballad that builds with strings and chorus. (7/6/63) (#81 Pop)

Walk on By.

The slow, blues ballad is the order of the day again for Miss Warwick and she sings this one with a passion that builds. (4/18/64) (#6 Pop)

In mid-1964, the pop-styled vocalizing of Warwick attracted the attention of Hollywood, and she cut her first movie song, "A House Is Not a Home." It led to more film work.

A House Is Not a Home.

Plenty of emotional impact on this tender ballad. (7/25/64) (#71 Pop)

Reach Out for Me.

Bluesy ethereal vocal from thrush accompanied by lush instrumentation. Great performance. Hit sound all the way! (10/12/64) (#20 Pop)

Here I Am.

From the forthcoming film "What's New Pussycat" comes a sensitive lyric and melody soulfully delivered by Miss Warwick. Flip: "They Long to Be Close to You." (6/19/65) (#65 Pop)

The flip of "Here I Am" (written specifically for her) became The Carpenters' trademark hit in 1971. Warwick's next two major hits—"Message to Michael" and "Alfie" (the movie theme song)— were both unreviewed B-side releases that became big hits! She ended 1967 with her biggest two-sided hit.

Here Where There Is Love.

> *Pretty rhythm ballad with strong back beat. Flip: "Message to Michael." (3/12/66) (B-side, #8 Pop, #5 R&B)*

Trains and Boats and Planes.

> *A strong revival of the Billy J. Kramer hit. (6/25/66) (#22 Pop, #49 R&B)*

The Beginning of Loneliness.

> *Miss Warwick fares well with Bacharach-David songs, and this gem is loaded with her own unique brand of excitement. Top programming and sales item. Flip: "Alfie." (3/4/67) (A-side, #79 Pop, #44 R&B; B-side, #15*

(Theme from) Valley of the Dolls/I Say a Little Prayer.

★   *Miss Warwick offers two powerful sides with equal sales potential. First is the beautiful and sensitive Previn ballad from the film, while the other side is a smooth rocker loaded with programming and sales appeal. (10/7/67) (A-side, #2, #13 R&B; B-side, #4 Pop, #8 R&B)*

The year 1968 saw Warwick continuing with a stream of soft-pop hits, including the theme song from Bacharach-David's Broadway show *Promises, Promises* and a (slight) rewrite of Herb Alpert's hit "This Guy's in Love With You."

(There's) Always Something There to Remind Me/Who Is Going to Love Me.

★   *Two powerhouse sides . . . Either or both will go right up there on top. First is the infectious rhythm ballad, while the flip is a driving production ballad. (8/17/68) (A-side, #65 Pop; B-side, #33 Pop, #45 R&B)*

Promises, Promises.

★   *Title tune of the forthcoming Broadway musical . . . is a catchy rhythmic item that grows on you fast. . . . Top vocal workout and production. (10/26/68) (#19 Pop, #47 R&B)*

This Girl's in Love With You.

★   *The recent Herb Alpert smash gets a powerful femme reading here . . . (1/25/69) (#7 Pop, #7 R&B)*

You've Lost that Lovin' Feelin'.

★   *Strong rhythmic treatment . . . first-rate production ballad. (9/13/69) (#16 Pop, #13 R&B)*

On March 12, 1969, Warwick won her first Grammy for "Do You Know the Way to San Jose" as Best Female Vocal Performance. In June, she made her acting debut in *Slaves*.

I'll Never Fall in Love Again.

> *The much recorded rhythm ballad beauty from Broadway's "Promises, Promises" gets just the right treatment to put her in the Top 10. (12/20/69) (#6 Pop, #17 R&B)*

Make It Easy on Yourself.

> *Recorded in live performance at the Garden State Arts Center, New Jersey, this past summer, the stylist updates one of her earlier Bacharach-David hits . . . (9/26/70) (#37 Pop, #26 R&B)*

In 1971, Dionne won a second Grammy for Best Female Vocal Performance for "I'll Never Fall in Love Again." Although she had 33 chart singles with Bacharach and David (1963–1971), the final two years yielded no Top-20 hits, so Dionne moved to Warner Brothers. "If We Only Have Love" (#84, 1972) proved to be her last pairing with them, as they opted for separate writing careers.

About that time, Dionne decided to change her name's spelling to Warwicke for good luck. The opposite happened as she went two years without a chart single until 1974, when producer Tommy Bell suggested she join with The Spinners. It became her (and their) first #1 Pop hit.

Dionne Warwick and The Spinners: Then Came You.

> *Combination of Dionne's excellent vocals and the distinctive sound of The Spinners make this one of the more interesting records of the year. Instrumental arrangements reminiscent*

of the major Spinner hits of the past year. But both Dionne and the group hold their own in this uptempo cut. Should hit all types of radio play. (7/13/74) (#1 Pop, #2 R&B)

There was no follow up hit, and Warwick (now without the "e" again) would wait until 1977 for another slight R&B charter, this time a reworking of two of her 1960s hits cut with Isaac Hayes.

Isaac Hayes and Dionne Warwick:
By the Time I Get to Phoenix/I Say a Little Prayer.

Stunning, high-class musicianship and a uniquely rueful impact achieved by singing these two oldies in alternate phrases and eventual unison are the most immediately apparent hallmarks of this first single from the stunning album of this pair's groundbreaking concept concert tour. Hayes also displays that without his past gimmicks he is a vocalist of mindboggling artistry and conviction. However, it may well take a more uptempo selection from the LP to make an across-the-board hit. (2/26/77) (#65 R&B)

Dionne's hitmaking drought continued until she coupled with Arista in 1979.

I'll Never Love This Way Again.

This ballad has the same build in crescendo instrumental bombast that characterizes Barry Manilow's hits, which is not surprising since Manilow produced it and it was written by the creators of "Mandy," "Looks Like We Made It" and "Somewhere in the Night." Warwick's vocal is effectively understated. (5/12/79) (#5 Pop, #18 R&B)

Deja Vu.

Warwick follows her top five Arista debut hit with a sincere, moody ballad co-written by Isaac Hayes. While "I'll Never Love This Way Again" was very much in the Barry Manilow mold, here Warwick's own cool, relaxed style is allowed to shine. (9/20/79) (#15 Pop, #25 R&B)

The Best Female Pop Vocal Performance Grammy of 1979 went to Warwick for "I'll Never Love." She also won the Best Female Vocal Performance award for "Deja Vu." By September 1980, her renewed career received another shot in the arm when she became host of the TV show, "Solid Gold." Warwick continued to record in a soft-pop style, both in duet and as a solo artist.

Dionne Warwick and Johnny Mathis:
Friends in Love.

Two of the classiest performers of our time join forces for the first time on this rhythm ballad written by the team [Jay Graydon, Bill Champlin, and David Foster] that won a Grammy for composing "After the Love Has Gone." Warwick and Mathis are the Hepburn and Fonda of black pop. (4/10/82) (#38 Pop, #22 R&B)

Dionne Warwick:
Heartbreak.

The Bee Gees make Dionne over on this rhythm ballad targeted at pop and AC formats. The sound is more Bee Gees than Warwick, but this should comfortably fill the void until Arista releases Warwick's hotly awaited collaboration with Luther Vandross. (9/16/82) (#10 Pop, #14 R&B)

Dionne Warwick and Luther Vandross:
How Many Times Can We Say Goodbye.

Although these two familiar voices have never recorded together before, they meet and blend so comfortably that the pairing seems inevitable. There's an audience for a good romantic duet, and it should be . . . receptive to this one. (10/8/83) (#27 Pop, #7 R&B)

In 1985, Dionne became one of the illustrious 45 singers to perform on the historic "We Are the World" recording. Her second #1 came that same year in what started as a remake of Rod Stewart's 1982 recording in the film Night Shift. It developed into a duet and grew from there into a quartet. Interestingly, Dionne's only two #1 Pop hits came as duets, so it's not surprising that she continued the trend, pairing up with diverse artists such as Howard Hewett and Kashif.

Dionne and Friends:
That's What Friends Are For.

> *Ms. Warwick's friends include Elton John, Gladys Knight and Stevie Wonder, who join together in a stately Bacharach-Sager ballad created to raise funds for the American Foundation for AIDS Research. (11/2/85) (#1 Pop, #1 R&B)*

Dionne Warwick and Jeffrey Osborne:
Love Power.

> *Duo collaborates with Warwick's hit songwriting/production team ("That's What Friends Are For") on a delicate, easy-paced ballad. (7/4/87) (#12 Pop, #5 R&B)*

In 1986, "That's What Friends Are For" won the Song of the Year Grammy for 1985. Following her 1980s' resurgence, Warwick spent much of the 1990s as spokesperson for the controversial Psychic Friends Network, a 900-number service. She continues to record and perform.

MARY WELLS

Real Name: Mary Esther Wells
Birthdate: 5/13/43
Birthplace: Detroit, MI
Died: 8/90
Influences: Jackie Wilson, LaVern Baker, Etta James, Jo Stafford, Mahalia Jackson
Influenced: Lesley Gore, Rod Stewart, Stevie Wonder, Bruce Springsteen

Long before Diana Ross and Martha Reeves became Motor City Hitmakers, Motown's queen was Mary Wells, the first in the legendary label's stable to have a #1 hit.

The Detroit native began singing publicly by age 10 and eventually sang in North Western High School's choir. During 1960, her friend, Robert Bateman, a member of The Satintones (the first act on Berry Gordy's Motown label), introduced

Wells to Gordy. When only 15, she had written a song called "Bye Bye Baby" for Jackie Wilson and knew Berry had produced and written for Wilson. Gordy was so impressed, he signed both the song and the singer; it was a Top-10 R&B hit and major pop hit, launching the singer's career.

Bye Bye Baby.

★ ★ ★ ★ *Strong emotional vocal performance by canary on frantic gospel-flavored theme.*

Please Forgive Me.

★ ★ ★ *Expressive thrushing stint on moving rockaballad. (9/19/60) (#45 Pop, #8 R&B)*

I Don't Want to Take a Chance.

> *Mary Wells, who hit big with "Bye, Bye, Baby" sells this heartfelt ballad with much warmth and feeling over ear-catching backing by the large ork. Should be a winner. (5/29/61) (#33 Pop, #9 R&B)*

Smokey Robinson began producing the 17-year-old singer and suddenly there was magic at Motown. Wells's following 1962 releases were all Top-10 pop and R&B hits.

The One Who Really Loves You.

★ ★ ★ ★ *Mary Wells sells the infectious tune with feeling over an intriguing arrangement. Song has a message for the teens and could grab a lot of action. (2/24/62) (#8 Pop, #2 R&B)*

You Beat Me to the Punch.

> *Infectious beat and fine singing from the lass here makes this side a natural . . . The chick is backed by a throbbing rhythm section that uses a tantalizing Latin figure, vocal group and wailing piano. (7/28/62) (#9 Pop, #1 R&B)*

Two Lovers.

> *The "You Beat Me to the Punch" girl comes through again with a strong reading of a catchy ballad with a teen-slanted lyric. Backing moves neatly and disk could take off. (11/17/62) (#7 Pop, #1 R&B)*

Wells scored lesser pop hits in 1963, although she managed a two-sider in September.

Laughing Boy.

The gal has another winner here and a fine follow-up to her recent hit, "Two Lovers." The tune and the treatment, in fact, are not unlike that of the recent entry. It can move fast. (2/23/63) (#15 Pop, #6 R&B)

You Lost the Sweetest Boy/What's Easy for Two Is Hard for One.

Two more solid sides for Miss Wells. The first is a potent rhythm tune that falls into an unusual cadence and the background is filled with sharp shouting group of gals and guys. The flip is in a softer groove cut with the beat and a fine lyric line. (9/14/63) (A-side, #22 Pop, #10 R&B; B-side, #29 Pop)

The year 1964 ushered in Mary's milestone million seller, "My Guy," although *Billboard* gave it their shortest of Wells's reviews. It became her last Robinson-penned and -produced single.

My Guy.
All's Wells with a swinging lilt. (3/28/64) (#1 Pop)

Her international hit allowed Wells to become the first Motown artist to tour England, performing with an admiring John Lennon and The Beatles.

In mid-1964, Mary had a double-sided smash ("Once Upon a Time," #19 Pop/"What's the Matter With You Baby," #17 Pop) dueting with Marvin Gaye, but it turned out to be her last hit for Motown. In late 1964, on the advice of her husband Herman Griffin, Mary, tempted by a film contract (that never materialized), signed a four-year deal with 20th-Century Fox Records for $500,000. Her first release on the label netted a minor pop hit, with the B-side doing better than the top. It was followed by a more successful tune that fared better on the R&B and pop charts.

Stop Takin' Me for Granted/Ain't It the Truth.
Side one is smoothy rendition. Lyrics carry strong messages with thrush delivering the goods in great style. Flip is powerful pop-r.&b. performance coupled with great dance beat. Mary's first waxing for the label. (10/24/64) (A-side, #88 Pop; B-side, #45 Pop)

Use Your Head.
Whispery delivery on medium-tempo rocker. Detroit beat and good boy-girl lyrics. (12/26/64) (#34 Pop, #13 R&B)

In 1965, mainly owing to "My Guy," *Billboard* named Wells the Top R&B Artist of the Year in its deejay voting. By late 1965, Mary and Fox parted by mutual consent and she moved to Atco, where she hit with her debut B-side (which went unreviewed). It was her last Top-10 hit, R&B or otherwise.

Can't You See.
Back in her original rockin' Detroit beat sound, Miss Wells has a blockbuster in this rhythm number which marks her Atco debut. A teen winner. Flip: "Dear Lover." (1/15/66) (B-side, #51 Pop, #6 R&B)

In August 1966, Mary married Cecil Womack, brother of Bobby Womack. By 1968, she was on Jubilee for her last pop chart run.

The Doctor.
Away from the disk scene much too long, this fine blues stylist makes a potent comeback on the Jubilee label with an easy beat mover which she sings for all it's worth. Strong entry. (4/13/68) (#65 Pop, #22 R&B)

In the 1970s, Wells recorded unsuccessfully for Reprise; her last charter was "Gigolo" on Epic in 1982. In 1983, Mary appeared on Motown's 25th Anniversary TV-special and finished the year on Allegiance Records, redoing some of her old hits. Through the 1980s, Mary performed at oldies shows, sometimes as part of a Motown revival. The first lady of Motown sadly was diagnosed with throat cancer in 1990 and died at age 47.

JACKIE **W**ILSON

Birthdate: 6/9/34

Birthplace: Detroit, MI

Died: 1/21/84

Influences: Clyde McPhatter, Al Jolson, Louis Jourdan, Billy Ward, Roy Brown, Little Willie John, Dixie Hummingbirds, LaVern Baker

Influenced: Five Satins, Isley Brothers, Sam & Dave, Tom Jones, Mary Wells, Gladys Knight and The Pips, Dells, Diablos, Joey Dee, Van Morrison, Elvis Presley's stage act, Bobby Freeman, Silhouettes, Blue Jays, Gary U.S. Bonds, many more

Amateur boxing's loss was rock 'n' roll's monumental gain when 16-year-old Jackie "Sonny" Wilson hung up his gloves to sing.

The Golden Gloves welterweight champ was raised in the ghetto of Detroit and earned his title shot by lying that he was 18. When his mom found out, she convinced him to finish Highland Park High School and pursue singing instead of swinging. The Ever Ready Gospel Singers became Jackie's first vehicle in 1950. Soon after, he and Levi Stubbs (later of The Four Tops) became informal members of The Royals (later, Hank Ballard and The Midnighters), although neither singer ever recorded with them.

In 1951, Wilson made his first single, the standard "Danny Boy" for Dee Gee Records owned by Dizzy Gillespie. During April 1953, his mother (with Jackie in tow) cornered Billy Ward at a hotel near the Michigan State Fair and an impromptu audition ensued. Wilson won the spot his idol, Clyde McPhatter, was vacating in the legendary Dominoes. Jackie spent the next four years leading Billy Ward and The Dominoes through 18 tremendous singles. (See Billy Ward and The Dominoes for reviews.)

Discouraged over being the lead without lead billing, Wilson signed with Brunswick. He inadvertently established two careers when the first six A-side singles he recorded were cowritten by another young talent, Berry Gordy, Jr. "Lonely Teardrops" was #1 R&B for seven weeks and his and Gordy's first million seller.

Reet Petite (Finest Girl You Ever Want to Meet).

A rock and roller, with a lively, gimmicked vocal belted out by Wilson. Dick Jacobs's arrangement moves right along. (8/9/57) (#62 Pop)

Come Back to Me/To Be Loved.

Two impressive bids by Wilson, who scored well with ["Reet Petite."] Top side is a rocker with excellent country-string-type support that shows the vocal to its best advantage. "To Be Loved," the flip, is a ballad. . . . Watch it! (1/27/58) (B-side, #22 Pop, #7 R&B)

We Have Love **77**

Rockaballad of quality. Wilson belts it in stylish fashion. Arrangement has chorus and strings, and includes a triplet figure. Jocks will give it good exposure. (8/11/58) (#93 Pop)

Lonely Teardrops **80**

Jackie Wilson pulls out all the stops on his emotion-packed reading of Latinish effort that moves all the way. He is backed by a group of chicks who wail. Watch it. (10/27/58) (#7 Pop, #1 R&B)

Alan Freed's 10-day Christmas show at New York's Loew's State Theater showcased Wilson's dynamic and energetic talent alongside such hit makers as The Everly Brothers and Bo Diddley. In April 1959, Jackie sang "You Better Know It" in Freed's film *Go, Johnny, Go!* a month after his latest release hit the Top 10 of the R&B charts, and went #13 Pop.

That's Why I Love Her So.

"That's Why" is on the gospel kick and Wilson belts the tune with a strong chorus and ork assist. Strong follow-up to "Lonely Teardrops." (3/9/59) (#13 Pop, #2 R&B)

I'll Be Satisfied.

Wilson sounds chart bound again with the pleader rockaballad. It's in gospelish style, and the strong warble is backed by organ. It should follow the path of his previous clicks. (6/1/59) (#20 Pop, #6 R&B)

You Better Know It.

 A spiritual-derived rocker on which he is given a strong fem chorus assist. (8/24/59) (#37 Pop, #1 R&B)

Talk That Talk.

 Wilson belts the rocker with verve. It's a bright, happy tune, and the chorus and ork support help give it strong potential. (11/2/59) (#34 Pop, #3 R&B)

By 1960, Nat Tarnapol became Wilson's manager. He encouraged the singer to pursue a pop, almost operatic direction with occasional forays into blues and R&B. Tarnapol knew what the masses wanted as Jackie received his second gold record for the two-sided smash "Night/Doggin' Around" (the first of several two-sided hits). In December 1960, Wilson was named Entertainer of the Year by *Cashbox* magazine.

Night/Doggin' Around.

 Wilson reads "Night," a pretty ballad adaptation of a theme from "Samson and Delilah" over a lush arrangement. "Doggin' Around" is a smart blues side that also shows a fine approach by the singer. Both can score. (2/29/60) (A-side, #4 Pop, #3 R&B; B-side, #15 Pop, #1 R&B)

All My Love/A Woman, a Lover, a Friend.

 Wilson lends his big-voiced, dramatic vocal quality to two strong sides. "All My Love" is a pretty ballad, featuring lush violins and a rocking beat. The flip has a church quality with a chorus on backing. (6/27/60) (B-side, #15 Pop, #1 R&B)

Alone at Last/Am I the Man.

 Wilson turns in his usual sock emotional treatment of "Alone at Last," a lush adaptation of Tchaikovsky's Piano Concerto for B Flat. Flip features a verveful vocal on an exciting r.&r. ditty. Watch both sides. (11/3/60) (A-side, #8 Pop, #20 R&B; B-side, #32 Pop, #10 R&B)

My Empty Arms/The Tear of the Year.

 First comes another pop-styled version of a classic-"Vesti la Guibba," from "Pagliacci." The flip is a stylish, blues-oriented ballad that can also go. (12/26/60) (A-side, #9 Pop, #25 R&B; B-side, #44 Pop, #10 R&B)

On February 15, 1961, Jackie's career almost ended when a fanatic so-called fan, Juanita Jones, gained entrance to his apartment with a gun. Vying for attention and threatening to shoot herself, a struggle for the weapon resulted in a bullet being lodged in Wilson's back. By the end of March, however, Jackie was out of the hospital, although the bullet could not be safely removed, and back on stage.

Please Tell Me Why/Your One and Only Love.

 "Please Tell Me Why" is a dramatic item, with gospel styling in the chorus. The flip is an attractive tune with a familiar melody. (3/6/61) (A-side, #20 Pop, #11 R&B; B-side, #40 Pop)

Lonely Life/I'm Comin' on Back to You.

 Jackie Wilson . . . sells "Lonely Life" in emotional style, displaying his powerful pipes, and he comes through with a strong performance on "Back to You." (6/5/61) (A-side, #80 Pop; B-side, #19 Pop, #9 R&B)

You Don't Know What It Means.

 Wilson wraps up a moving blues-flavored theme in an exciting, emotion-packed reading. Watch it in both pop and r.&b. markets. Flip is "Years from Now." (7/31/61) (A-side, #79 Pop, #19 R&B; B-side, #37 Pop, #25 R&B)

In 1962, he had his first chart album, *Jackie Wilson at the Copa* (#137 Pop). His 1963 hit "Baby Workout" (#5 Pop, #1 R&B; given four stars without further comment) marked his entrance into the soul field and was his fifth #1 R&B winner.

Jackie Wilson/Linda Hopkins: Shake a Hand.

The old hit is handed a revitalized performance . . . over swinging, driving backing by the ork. Could be big. (5/11/63) (#42 Pop, #21 R&B)

Shake, Shake, Shake.

 Here's a wild rocker that Jackie Wilson hands a sock performance on the order of his big smash "Baby Workout" . . .

Could be one of his biggest ever. (7/6/63) (#33 Pop, #21 R&B)

Jackie fell off the charts for a couple of years, but came roaring back with the classic "Higher and Higher," his last million seller, which also became his sixth and last R&B #1.

(Your Love Keeps Lifting Me) Higher and Higher.

Hard driving wailing blues item is Wilson's most potent release since "Whispers." Can't miss proving a smash both pop and r.&b. Electrifying vocal workout. (7/29/67) (#6 Pop, #1 R&B)

His last minor pop charter came in early 1972, "You Got Me Walking." Just as his first R&B charter was with a group, so was his last, as "Don't Burn No Bridges" (#91 Pop, 1975) featured Jackie Wilson and The Chi-Lites. On September 29, 1975, Jackie suffered a heart attack on stage at Cherry Hill, New Jersey's Latin Casino while powering his way through "Lonely Teardrops." He lapsed into a coma that lasted on and off for over nine years. The Spinners and Barry White were among numerous acts who performed at benefits to raise money for his medical bills. Tragically, he died on January 21, 1984, at a hospital in Mount Holly, New Jersey. In 1986, Jackie's "Reet Petite," a hit in England 29 years earlier, was reissued and incredibly reached #1. "Mr. Excitement," as he was justifiably known, was inducted into the Rock and Roll Hall of Fame in 1987.

STEVIE WONDER

Real Name: Steveland Judkins
Birthdate: 5/13/50
Birthplace: Saginaw, MI
Influences: Ray Charles, Jesse Belvin, Aretha Franklin, Ella Fitzgerald, Miracles, Coasters, Five Royales, Del Shannon, Dinah Washington, Staple Singers, Dixie Hummingbirds, Sam Cooke, Mary Wells
Influenced: Chaka Khan, Ray Parker, Jr., Deniece Williams, Wynton Marsalis, David Sanborn, Stanley Turrentine, Keith Sweat

The boy wonder of the 1960s, Stevie Wonder has matured into an eloquent musical spokesman whose work encompasses four decades.

One of six children (a sister and four brothers), the family moved to Detroit soon after his birth. Stevie sang in the Whitestone Baptist Choir and by nine was proficiently playing harmonica, drums, and piano, and had formed a duo with his friend John Glover. Ronnie White, a cousin of John's and a member of The Miracles, introduced 11-year-old Steveland Judkins to Motown A&R man, Brian Holland, who in turn took him to Berry Gordy, Jr. The Motown founder was so moved, he signed Stevie, and began thinking of a stage name for the youthful prodigy, considering Stevie, The Little Wonder, and Stevie Little Wonder, before picking Little Stevie Wonder.

In May 1962, Wonder had his first single, "I Call It Pretty Music but the Old People Call It the Blues" (with Marvin Gaye on drums), but it garnered little attention (it was given three stars by *Billboard,* but went unreviewed). The follow up, "Little Water Boy," credited to Stevie and Motown A&R man Clarence Paul (formerly Clarence Pauling, tenor for the 1950s' R&B group, The Five Royales), was another three-star, no comment listing in *Billboard.* Wonder's third single "Sunset" wasn't even rated by *Billboard.*

Despite the lack of success of these early recordings, Gordy kept his faith in the young musician. Gordy felt the exuberant youth's performance was especially effective live and recorded him at Chicago's Regal Theater including a seven-minute long song titled "Fingertips." Gordy split it into two sides of a single and it went to #1 along with the following album, *12 Year Old Genius*. It was the first time a single and its LP were #1 at the same time, and also the first time a live recording was a #1 hit. The song was given four stars without comment.

Little Stevie Wonder:
Workout Stevie, Workout/Monkey Talk.

> *Two big follow ups to Little Stevie's "Fingertips" hit. First is a fast, bright rocker that has good harmonica and shouting chorus. Flip is part instrumental with Wonder talking and some sharp piano and big band blowing. (9/28/63) (#33 Pop)*

Wonder's sixth single was the first to do away with "Little Stevie."

Hey Harmonica Man.

> *Stevie has hung his harmonica on a strong beat and a hit sound this time. It's all done in unison with a male chorus and hard hand clapping. Flip: "This Little Girl." (6/6/64) (#29 Pop)*

Meanwhile, the 14-year-old appeared in the films *Bikini Beach* and *Muscle Beach Party*, each starring Annette Funicello and Frankie Avalon. Both flicks were done within months of each other and were the only movies Wonder ever performed in. By the end of 1964, after four more singles (up to "Happy Street") failed, one Motown producer suggested they drop Wonder, but Gordy stuck by him.

The singer's "Uptight (Everything's Alright)" (#3 Pop and R&B, 1965) and Bob Dylan's "Blowin' in the Wind" (#9 Pop and R&B, 1966) demonstrated his widening musical pursuits. He even studied music theory using Braille song sheets and books. "I Was Made to Love Her" was Stevie's third million seller and was written at 17 for a girl he knew named Angie.

A Place in the Sun.

> *Wonder has a hot top 20 contender in this folk-oriented release, which is in the same bag as his highly successful "Blowin' in the Wind." Exciting treatment by the artist. (1/5/66) (#9 Pop, #3 R&B)*

I Was Made to Love Her.

> *Solid beat blues rocker loaded with discotheque appeal and first rate Wonder vocal workout can't miss hitting hard and fast. (6/3/67) (#2 Pop, #1 R&B)*

I'm Wondering.

> *More driving, pulsating material with a wailing performance that moves and grooves all the way. Chalk up another chart topper for Wonder. (10/14/67) (#12 Pop, #4 R&B)*

Wonder returned to his harmonica-playing roots on a single that was mysteriously issued under a backwards appellation. This was followed by some of his best-known hits.

Eivets Rednow:
Alfie.

★   *It must be Stevie Wonder spelt backwards and it's his instrumental harmonica showstopper from his live performance. The Bacharach-David ballad could prove a smash all over again via this exceptional workout backed by lush strings. All types of programming. (9/7/68) (#66 Pop)*

For Once in My Life.

> *An up-tempo, driving version of the much-recorded ballad. (10/26/68) (#2 Pop, #2 R&B)*

My Cherie Amour.

> *Poignant reading of this love ballad previously released as the flip side of Wonder's "I Don't Know Why." It should score in r.&b., easy listening markets as well as pop and quickly surpass sales of the original side. (5/24/69) (#4 Pop, #4 R&B)*

On May 5, 1969, Wonder met President Nixon at the White House to receive the President's Committee on Employment of Handicapped People's Distinguished Service Award. On September 14, 1970, Wonder married former Motown secretary Syreeta Wright.

Signed, Sealed, Delivered I'm Yours.

> *Wonder has all the blockbuster sales appeal of another "Yester-Me, Yester-You, Yesterday" in this funky beat*

swinger. Top Wonder vocal workout. (6/20/70) (#3 Pop, #1 R&B)

Heaven Help Us All.

Wonder follows his smash "Signed, Sealed, Delivered" with a potent piece of rhythm material with an equally potent lyric line. (10/10/70) (#9 Pop, #2 R&B)

We Can Work It Out.

Wonder follows his Top 10 winner "Heaven Help Us All" with another powerhouse in this super updating of the Beatles classic. (3/6/71) (#13 Pop, #3 R&B)

After 24 hits during eight years, Wonder was still on a salary with Motown as a minor while his actual income was supposedly put in trust. Upon reaching his 21st birthday on May 13, 1971, he only received one million of the 30 million he earned, so Stevie and his eccentrically brilliant attorney, Johanon Vigoda, pressured Motown into an unprecedented deal whereby Stevie would maintain total creative control of his recordings and have his own production and publishing companies.

In 1973, a song he wrote for Jeff Beck was not issued by the time Wonder's own version was ready and so he had his second #1 Pop (and seventh #1 R&B) with "Superstition" (unreviewed).

You Are the Sunshine of My Life.

Perhaps the most commercial Wonder single ever with a rich orchestral backing and female voice on some duetting. This is a soft, haunting ballad with outstanding electric piano runs and outstanding production work. (3/10/73) (#1 Pop, #3 R&B)

On August 6, 1973, Wonder was injured in a car accident on the way to Durham, North Carolina, when logs on a truck broke loose and slammed through the windshield of the car in which he was riding. He lapsed into a week-long coma, only coming out when his friend Ira Tucker began singing "Higher Ground" in Wonder's ear. Five days after the accident, the song was reviewed.

Higher Ground.

A "Superstition" type guitar riff opens the door for the multi-tracked vocal about people who are moving ahead in love and in all phases of life. The lyrics match the infectious flavor of the background sounds. (8/11/73) (#4 Pop, #1 R&B)

By July 1974, Stevie was back at full steam. His fourth #1, "You Haven't Done Nothin'," featured backing vocals by The Jackson Five.

You Haven't Done Nothin'.

Opening with an interesting synthesizer arrangement and moving into an immediately infectious vocal, Stevie gives us a song that may well be referring to the current state of affairs in our government. Put subtly enough to avoid the tired protest type songs we've often heard. Exceptionally powerful cut which should be instant hit. (8/3/74) (#1 Pop, #1 R&B)

The year 1974 began a string of 16 Grammy Awards, including Best Pop Vocal Performance, Male ("You Are the Sunshine of My Life," 1974; "I Wish," 1977); R&B Vocal Performance ("Superstition," 1974; "Boogie on Reggae Woman," 1975); and Album of the Year ("Innervisions," 1974; "Fulfillingness," 1975; "Songs in the Key of Life," 1977).

Boogie on Reggae Woman.

The man who never misses comes up with another uptempo, irresistible beat done in a not quite reggae but certainly Caribbean flavor. Infectious melody makes for good dancing disk while fun lyrics make for easy hook. Should be another across the board smash for one of rock's true giants. (11/9/74) (#3 Pop, #1 R&B)

In 1976, Stevie renewed his contract with Motown for the then-largest renewal pact ever negotiated in record history, $13 million!

Sir Duke.

One of the most irresistible cuts on the phenomenal Grammy-winning "Songs in the Key of Life" LP appears as a 7-incher.

With a bouncy bass line and all-star jazz hornmen fillers, this is Wonder's tribute to Duke Ellington and other pioneers of the previous generation of black jazz-pop. Wonder's cheery vocal winds through some 16 repetitions of the phrase "You Can Feel It All Over" while the rhythm and horns weave around it. (4/21/77) (#1 Pop, #1 R&B)

Send One Your Love.

Softly-swaying midtempo ballad, which features some tasty harmonica breaks. Already on the charts at a starred number 51. (11/3/79) (#4 Pop, #5 R&B)

Master Blaster.

This represents his most astonishing effort in recent years. Propelled by a reggae beat and a potent lyrical message. Wonder adds a new dimension in his illustrious career. (9/20/80) (#5 Pop, #1 R&B)

In 1982, Wonder teamed with Paul McCartney for his seventh #1, "Ebony and Ivory."

The years 1984–1985 were big for the artist, with a #1 movie theme ("I Just Called to Say I Love You") followed by "Part-Time Lover," which became the first single to top the pop, R&B, adult contemporary, and dance/disco charts.

Happy Birthday.

In honor of the newly-declared national holiday comes a single release of Wonder's loving tribute to Martin Luther King, Jr. first heard on his 1980 LP "Hotter Than July." The song has been issued in 12-inch form, with excerpts from Dr. King's most famous speeches comprising the B side. (11/19/83)

Part-Time Lover.

A playful, jazzy dance tune that swings like crazy. (8/31/85) (#1 Pop, #1 R&B)

In 1989, Stevie Wonder was inducted into the Rock and Roll Hall of Fame. He won a Grammy Lifetime Achievement Award in 1996.

Index of Song Titles

About the Author

Jay Warner was born and raised in Brooklyn, New York. He started playing piano at age seven and guitar in his late teens. His career pursuits began with a singing group, The Carolons. Their little-known collectable "Let It Please Be You" (Mellomood) set the tone for Jay's diversified future.

In the late 1960s he wrote and recorded with the rock group The Love Six and with the well-known folk trio The Travelers. Since 1970, he has held numerous positions in the music industry, before forming his own music publishing company in 1983. The six-time Grammy Award–winning publisher is the author of *How to Have Your Hit Song Published* (1977) and *The* Billboard *Book of American Singing Groups* (1993). Warner lives in Los Angeles, California, with his wife, Jackie.